Business Tax Answer Book

2008 Edition

Terence M. Myers
Dorinda D. DeScherer

Editorial Staff

Production . . . . Christopher Zwirek

Index . . . . Lynn Brown

This publication is designed to provide accurate and authoritative information in regard to the subject matter covered. It is sold with the understanding that the publisher is not engaged in rendering legal, accounting, or other professional service and that the authors are not offering such advice in this publication. If legal advice or other expert assistance is required, the services of a competent professional person should be sought.

ISBN 978-0-8080-1775-2

Printed in the United States of America

Preface

The *Business Tax Answer Book* is designed to help small business owners, attorneys, accountants, and other small business advisors to understand and comply with the myriad of ever-changing tax rules. Whether a business is just starting up or has been in existence for years, whether it is a sole proprietorship, partnership, corporation, or limited liability company, this book will provide, in simple, no-nonsense language, answers to the key questions regarding the business's income and payroll tax liabilities. Inside you will find the answers to such questions as:

- What are the tax advantages and disadvantages of operating a business as a corporation?

- When can a business use the simple, cash method of accounting to report income and claim deductions?

- When can a business owner deduct the cost of "commuting"?

- Who can claim the new, generous, first-year depreciation allowance?

- Which employee fringe benefits qualify for favorable payroll tax treatment?

- What pitfalls should business owners avoid when borrowing money from their businesses?

- What is the key tax benefit of S corporation status?

- What is a medical savings account and how does it help small businesses reduce employee health care costs?

Planning Pointers, located throughout the book, highlight practical steps to take to reduce taxes with a minimum of time and trouble. Citations to authority are provided as research aids for those who need to pursue particular items in greater detail.

The appendices contain a tax calendar for use in 2008. The calendar provides key filing and payment deadlines for income and payroll tax purposes. Also included in the appendices are key tax facts for 2007-08 (e.g., inflation-adjusted depreciation limits for business cars and contribution limits for retirement plans) and tax-saving checklists.

Highlights of the 2008 Edition

The 2008 Edition of the *Business Tax Answer Book* reflects all of the latest tax law changes, including the 2006 Tax Relief and Health Care Act, which was signed into law on Dec. 20, 2006 (P.L. 109-432) and the Small Business and Work Opportunity Tax Act of 2007, which was signed into law on May 25, 2007 (P.L. 110-28).

The *2008 Business Tax Answer Book* also brings the reader up to date on the latest court decisions and rulings and regulations from the IRS, including:

- New regulations changing the employment tax rules for limited liability companies (Chapter Two);

- An important new Tax Court ruling affecting the tax rates of incorporated tax return businesses (Chapter Three);

- Recently finalized regulations governing the calculation of a corporation estimated tax payments (Chapter Three);

- New regulations dealing with family-owned S corporations (Chapter Four);

- New IRS guidance on the computation of the Section 199 production activities deduction by S corporation owners (Chapter Four);

- A new IRS ruling explaining the timing of the deduction for payroll taxes by companies using the accrual method of accounting (Chapter Five);

- A new legal advice memorandum issued by the IRS Chief Counsel restricting the use of certain exceptions to the "economic performance" rule for deductions (Chapter Five);

- A new Tax Court ruling allowing taxpayers increased deductions when they use a personal hobby to promote their business activities (Chapter Six);

- A new IRS ruling liberalizing writeoffs for rotable spare parts (Chapter Seven);

- A new IRS ruling allowing lodging deductions in certain cases when a taxpayer is not away from home (Chapter Eight);

- Recently issued IRS guidance on deductions for company-owned airplanes (Chapter Eight);

- A new IRS crackdown on employee reimbursements of business expenses (Chapter Eight);

- Recently proposed IRS regulations dealing with cafeteria plans (Chapter Nine);

- Newly finalized regulations limiting the amount of compensation taken into account when computing retirement benefits (Chapter Eleven);

- New final regulations governing nonqualified deferred compensation arrangements (Chapter Eleven);

- A new federal appeals court decision taxing shareholders on inter-company loans (Chapter Twelve);

- A new favorable IRS ruling regarding dispositions of intangible assets (Chapter Thirteen); and

- A tough new federal appeals court decision regarding employer liabilities when the payroll tax process is outsourced (Chapter Fourteen).

The 2008 Business Tax Answer Book also provides new or expanded coverage in a number of areas, including:

- Corporate estimated tax payments;

- Consolidated returns;

- Changes in accounting methods;

- Deductions for farming expenses;

- Business tax credits;

- Roth 401(k) arrangements;

- Applications for employer identification numbers;

- IRS tip reporting compliance programs and;

- Offers in compromise.

Terence M. Myers
Dorinda D. DeScherer

December 2007

About the Authors

Terence M. Myers, J.D., is a graduate of Georgetown University and the National Law Center, George Washington University. He is former managing editor of the Tax & Professional Practice unit of Prentice Hall, Inc. He has more than 25 years of experience launching, writing, and editing tax and business publications.

Dorinda D. DeScherer, J.D., is a graduate of Barnard College of Columbia University and the University of Maryland School of Law. She was formerly associate managing editor for Prentice Hall Information Services where she had primary responsibility for special projects, including explanatory materials on new tax laws. Ms. DeScherer has more than 25 year of writing and editing experience for a wide range of tax and business publications.

The authors are the chief editors of Editorial Resource Group, Inc. (ERG). Through ERG they create, write, edit, and market successful tax, financial, business, and management-related publications. ERG's products are targeted to CPAs, tax lawyers, corporate officers and human resource professionals, tax return preparers, and small business owners. ERG's clients have included Aspen Publishers, the Institute of Management & Administration, Inc., Harcourt Professional Publishing, RIA, the American Institute of Certified Public Accountants, and Intuit. The IRS has used CPE materials prepared by ERG for in-house staff training.

Acknowledgments

We want to express our appreciation to Christopher Zwirek of CCH for his cooperation and support. Thanks to him, writing and revising this book has been an altogether pleasurable experience. This one is for you, Chris!

How to Use This Book

Business Tax Answer Book is designed for practitioners who need quick and authoritative answers to questions concerning the tax rules affecting business entities. This book uses simple, straightforward language. The question and answer format, with its breadth of coverage, effectively conveys the complex tax rules related to operating a business. In addition, the book provides an extensive index.

List of Questions. A detailed list of questions follows the table of contents in front of the book in order to help the reader locate areas of immediate interest. This list provides both the question number and the page number on which the question appears. A series of subheadings help to group and organize the questions by topic within each chapter.

Question Numbers. The questions are numbered consecutively within each chapter (e.g., Q 2:1, Q 2:2, Q 2:3).

Index. At the back of the book is an index provided as a further aid to locating specific information. All references are to question numbers rather than page numbers.

Table of Contents

List of Questions

Interest Expenses

Taxes

Insurance Premiums

Costs of Starting a Business

Research Expenses

Section 197 Intangibles

Chapter 9 Employee Health and Accident Benefits

Chapter 12 Owner-Corporation Transactions

Lending and Borrowing Money

Sale and Lease of Property

Compensation for Shareholder-Employees

Involuntary Conversions

Like-Kind Exchanges

Sales of Small Business Stock

Chapter 1

Sole Proprietorships

A sole proprietorship is the simplest form of business organization for tax purposes. An individual who starts a business is automatically treated as a sole proprietor unless he or she elects some other form of business organization. Income and losses from the business are reported on the sole proprietor's individual return; no separate tax return is required for the business.

On the other hand, nothing is truly simple when it comes to taxes. Like other businesses, a sole proprietorship must follow myriad tax rules and regulations for reporting income and expenses from business operations, keeping records, filing returns, and paying taxes. This chapter spells out the basic tax accounting, recordkeeping, filing, and payment rules that apply to sole proprietorships. In addition, because many sole proprietorships are started as home-based businesses, this chapter contains an in-depth look at the rules for claiming a home office deduction.

Setting Up Shop

Q 1:1 What is a sole proprietorship?

A sole proprietorship is an unincorporated business that is owned by one individual. The business has no existence apart from the owner. The owner must report and pay tax on all of the income derived from the business, unless the tax law provides a special exclusion. The owner also has unlimited liability for business debts, even if they exceed his or her investment in the business.

Q 1:2 Is any special tax action required to set up a sole proprietorship?

Generally no. For federal income tax purposes, a business with a single owner is automatically treated as a sole proprietorship unless the owner elects another form of business organization (for example, by incorporating the business). [Reg. § 301.7701-2(a)]Income or loss from a sole proprietorship is reported on the owner's individual tax return (see Q 1:14).

Q 1:3 What if a business is owned by a husband and wife?

A partnership for federal tax purposes can be organized as a joint venture, a syndicate, a group, a pool, or any other organization that is not a corporation, a trust or an estate. [IRC § 761(a)] Therefore, an unincorporated business jointly owned by a married couple is classified as a partnership for federal income tax purposes. As such, the business is generally subject to the income tax rules for partnerships (see Chapter 2) and is required to file a partnership income tax return.

However, under the Small Business and Work Opportunity Act of 2007 (P.L. 110-28), a qualified joint venture whose only members are a husband and wife filing a joint return can elect not to be treated as a partnership for Federal tax purposes. [IRC § 761(f)(1)] A qualified joint venture is a joint venture involving the conduct of a trade or business, if:

- The only members of the joint venture are a husband and wife;
- Both spouses materially participate in the trade or business; and
- Both spouses elect to have the partnership provisions not apply.

For this purpose, "material participation" is generally determined under the passive activity limitation rules (see Chapter 6).

If the election is made, all items of income, gain, loss, deduction and credit are divided between the spouses in accordance with their respective interests in the venture. Each spouse takes into account his or her respective share of these items as a sole proprietor. Thus, each spouse would account for his or her respective share on the appropriate form, such as Form 1040, Schedule C.

Q 1:4 Is a sole proprietor required to obtain a special tax identification number?

Income from a sole proprietorship is reported using the business owner's individual Social Security number (SSN). If the business has employees, however, it will be necessary to obtain a federal employer identification number (EIN) to report payroll taxes for the business (see Chapter 13). Also, an EIN is required if a sole proprietorship has a qualified retirement plan, even if it has no employees.

If a sole proprietor buys an existing business, he or she cannot use the former owner's EIN. The proprietor must get a new EIN for the business or use one he or she already has. [Reg. § § 49.6109-1; 301.6109-1(d)(2)]

A business owner may need to obtain a new EIN if the organization or ownership of the business changes. For example, a new EIN will be required if a sole proprietorship is incorporated or the owner takes in a partner. However, a new EIN is not required if the business owner simply changes the name or location of the business. [Reg. § 301.6109(h)(2)]

A sole proprietor may need to provide his or her SSN or EIN to customers or clients. A business must file an information return on Form 1099-Misc, *Miscellaneous Income*, to report payments of $600 or more for services performed by individuals or unincorporated businesses. [IRC § 6041(a)]The information return must show both the payee's and the payor's identification numbers (either an SSN or EIN).

> **Planning Point:** A sole proprietor should be sure to provide an identification number when asked for it. A payment may be subject to "backup withholding"—at a 28 percent rate—if no number is provided. Payments subject to backup withholding include interest, dividends, rents, royalties, commissions, nonemployee compensation (i.e., payments to independent contractors), payments to attorneys, and certain other payments made in the course of a trade or business. [IRC § 3406]

A sole proprietorship must file a Form 1099-Misc information return to report payments of $600 or more made to individuals and unincorporated businesses that provide services for the business. [IRC § 6041(a)] Therefore, a business owner must obtain the service provider's identification number. Form W-9, *Request for Taxpayer Identification Number and Certification*, may be used to obtain a service provider's number. A business owner should contact the Internal Revenue Service (IRS or the Service) if he or she is unable to obtain an identification number from a service provider. The IRS will advise the business owner on whether backup withholding is required.

Q 1:5 What is a tax year?

A business must figure taxable income and file tax returns based on an annual accounting period called a tax year. A tax year is usually 12 consecutive months. There are two types of tax years:

1. A *calendar tax year* is a period of 12 consecutive months beginning January 1 and ending December 31.
2. A *fiscal tax year* is a period of 12 consecutive months ending on the last day of a month other than December (or a 52-53 week period that always ends on the same day of the week).

Tax years are discussed in detail in Chapter 5.

Q 1:6 Can a sole proprietorship choose a tax year other than a calendar year?

Although most sole proprietorships operate on a calendar year, a sole proprietorship may elect to use a fiscal tax year. However, there are some restrictions on the ability to elect a year other than a calendar year. [Rev. Rul. 57-389, 1957-2 C.B. 298]

A sole proprietorship and its owner must use the same tax year. [Rev. Rul. 57-389, 1957-2 C.B. 298] Moreover, if the owner has already filed returns on a calendar-year basis, he or she will have to obtain IRS approval to change to a fiscal year. [Reg. § 1.442-1(b)]

> **Planning Point:** A business may want to use a fiscal year if its natural business year does not conform to the calendar year. A business has a natural business year when it has peak and nonpeak periods. The natural business year is considered to end at or soon after the end of the peak period. For example, if a business's peak period is in the summer, it may want to use a year that ends in August or September. A business whose income is steady from month to month does not have a natural business year.

> **Planning Point:** Regardless of the year a business uses for income tax purposes, employment taxes must be reported on a calendar-year basis. [IRC §§ 3101, 3111, 3301]

Q 1:7 What is an accounting method?

A business's accounting method determines when and how income must be reported for tax purposes. There are two basic accounting methods:

1. The cash method; and

2. The accrual method.

Under the cash method, income is reported in the year it is actually or constructively received, and expenses are deducted in the year they are paid. However, if expenses are paid in advance, a business must generally wait to claim the deduction in the year to which the payment applies. [Reg. § 1.461-1(a)(1)]

> **Example 1-1:** In Year 1, Amos Arnold, a calendar-year sole proprietor, paid $1,000 for a business insurance policy that is effective for one year beginning July 1 of Year 1. Arnold can deduct $500 in Year 1, but must wait until Year 2 to the claim the remaining $500 deduction.

Under the accrual method, income generally is reported in the year it is earned, even if it is not received until a later year. Deductions for expenses are generally claimed in the year that all events have occurred that determine the fact of liability and the amount of the expense and economic performance has occurred. [IRC § 461(h); Reg. § 1.461-1(a)(2)] For example, in the case of expenses for property or services, economic performance occurs when the property or services are provided.

Special rules apply to various types of income and expenses. Accounting rules are discussed in detail in Chapter 5.

Q 1:7

Q 1:8 Is a business free to use either the cash or accrual accounting method?

As a general rule, there is no required method of accounting for tax purposes. However, a business must use a method that clearly reflects income and expenses. In addition, the use of a specific method may be required in some circumstances. For example, a business that is required to maintain inventories must generally use the accrual method to account for sales and purchases of inventory items. [Reg. § 1.446-1(c)(2)]The business may, however, use the cash method to account for other business income and deduction items.

Small businesses generally prefer the cash method of accounting, and the IRS granted some leeway in this area. Businesses with less than $1 million in average annual gross receipts may use the cash method of accounting, even if they produce, purchase, or sell merchandise. Qualifying taxpayers may also choose not to keep an inventory, even if they do not change to the cash method. [Rev. Proc. 2001-10, 2001-2 I.R.B. 272]

For further details on the choice of an accounting method and the special break for small businesses, see Chapter 5.

Q 1:9 What kind of records must be maintained for tax purposes?

Taxpayers must keep records to support the income they report and the deductions they claim for tax purposes. [Reg. § 1.446-1(a)(4)]The tax law does not require a business to use any particular recordkeeping system. However, a recordkeeping system must clearly reflect income. The recordkeeping system a business uses should correspond to the tax year and the accounting method used for tax purposes (see Qs 1:5, 1:7).

A good recordkeeping system includes a summary of all business transactions. A taxpayer with more than one business should keep a complete and separate set of records for each business.

Business transactions are ordinarily summarized in books called journals and ledgers. A journal is a book used to record each business transaction. A ledger is a book that contains the totals from all business journals. It is organized into different accounts. For example, a recordkeeping system for a small business might include the following items.

- Business checkbook;
- Daily summary of cash receipts;
- Monthly summary of cash receipts;
- Business expense disbursements journal;
- Depreciation journal; and
- Payroll journal

Business books and records may be maintained using either a single-entry or double-entry bookkeeping system (see Q 1:11).

In addition, a business must keep supporting documents to back up the entries in its books and records.

Q 1:10 What kind of supporting documents should be kept for tax purposes?

Purchases, sales, payroll, and other business transactions will generate supporting documents. Supporting documents include sales slips, paid bills, invoices, receipts, deposit slips, and canceled checks. These documents contain the information needed to record transactions in a business's books and should be retained because they support the entries in the business's books and on the business's tax return.

Supporting documents should be retained to back up all of the following:

1. *Gross receipts.* Gross receipts are the income received from a business. Sole proprietors should keep supporting documents that show the amounts and sources of gross receipts. Documents that show gross receipts include the following:

   - Cash register tapes;
   - Bank deposit slips;
   - Receipt books;
   - Invoices;
   - Credit card charge slips; and
   - Forms 1099-MISC.

2. *Purchases.* Purchases are the items a business buys to resell to customers. Supporting documents should show the amount paid and that the amount was for purchases. Documents for purchases include the following:

   - Canceled checks;
   - Cash register tape receipts;
   - Credit card sales slips; and
   - Invoices.

3. *Expenses.* Expenses are the costs incurred (other than purchases) to carry on a business. Supporting documents should show the amount paid and that the amount was for a business expense. Documents for expenses include the following:

   - Canceled checks;
   - Cash register tapes;
   - Account statements;
   - Credit card sales slips;
   - Invoices; and
   - Petty cash slips for small cash payments.

Q 1:10

4. *Travel, transportation, entertainment, and gift expenses.* Special recordkeeping rules apply to these expenses (see Chapter 8).

5. *Employment taxes.* There are specific employment tax records that a business must maintain (see Chapter 14).

6. *Assets.* Assets are the property, such as machinery and furniture that are owned by a taxpayer and used in a business. Certain records are needed to determine annual depreciation and the gain or loss when an asset is sold. Business records should show the following information:

   a. When and how taxpayer acquired the asset;

   b. Purchase price;

   c. Cost of any improvements;

   d. Section 179 deduction taken;

   e. Deductions taken for depreciation;

   f. Deductions taken for casualty losses, such as losses resulting from fires or storms;

   g. How taxpayer used the asset;

   h. When and how taxpayer disposed of the asset;

   i. Selling price; and

   j. Expenses of sale.

Documents that may show this information include the following:

- Purchase and sales invoices;
- Real estate closing statements;
- Canceled checks; and
- Employee compensation records.

See Chapter 7 for information on depreciation. See Chapter 13 for information on sales of business assets.

Q 1:11 What is the difference between a single-entry and double-entry bookkeeping system?

A business owner must decide whether to use a single- or a double-entry bookkeeping system. A single-entry system of bookkeeping is the simplest to maintain. A double-entry system is more complicated, but has built-in checks and balances to assure accuracy and control.

A single-entry system is based on the income statement (profit or loss statement). The system records the flow of income and expenses through the use of:

1. A daily summary of cash receipts; and

2. Monthly summaries of cash receipts and disbursements.

A double-entry bookkeeping system uses journals and ledgers. Transactions are first entered in a journal and then posted to ledger accounts. These accounts show income, expenses, assets (property a business owns), liabilities (debts of a business), and net worth (excess of assets over liabilities). Income and expense accounts are closed at the end of each tax year. Asset, liability, and net worth accounts are maintained on a permanent basis.

In the double-entry system, each account has a left side for debits and a right side for credits. Amounts added to an account are listed as debits, while amounts taken out of an account are listed as credits. (Take this on faith. Even accounting students struggle with what appears to be a contradiction in terms.)

A double-entry system is self-balancing because every transaction is listed as a debit entry in one account and as a credit entry in another. Total debits must equal the total credits after journal entries are posted to the ledger accounts. If the amounts do not balance, there is an error that must be corrected.

> **Example 1-2:** In October, Bill's Bookkeeping Service makes a $780 payment for supplies. Here is how Bill's business enters the expenditure in its records:

Date	Description of Entry	Debit	Credit
Oct. 5	Supplies	780.00	
Oct. 5	Cash		780.00

Q 1:12 Can a business maintain its tax records on a computer?

Yes, it can, provided certain requirements are met. The records must provide sufficient information to support and verify entries made on the taxpayer's return and to determine the correct tax liability. Computer records will meet this requirement only if they reconcile with the taxpayer's books and the taxpayer's return. In addition, the computer system must be capable of generating printed records if the IRS requests them. [Rev. Proc. 98-25, 1998-1 C.B. 689]

Q 1:13 How long must a business keep tax records?

By law, tax records must be kept "as long as they are material" to the administration of any provision of the Internal Revenue Code. [IRC § 6001; Reg. § 1.6001-1(e)] The IRS generally has three years after a return is filed (or after the return due date if that is later) to assess additional tax. Therefore, records should be kept for a minimum of three years. However, once the IRS has made an additional assessment, it has six years to collect the additional tax, and the taxpayer has at least two years to claim a refund after payment. [IRC § § 6502; 6511]Therefore, records for a given tax year could potentially be "material" for up to 11 years.

Documents connected to business property or other long-term assets should be maintained throughout the entire period of ownership. If an asset is sold, records relating to the sale should be kept with other tax records relating to that year's return.

Q 1:12

If property is received in a nontaxable exchange, the basis of the property is determined by reference to the property given up in the exchange (see Chapter 13). Therefore, records on the old property, as well as on the new property, must be maintained until the period of limitations expires for the year in which the new property is disposed of in a taxable disposition.

Employment tax records must be kept for at least four years after the date the tax becomes due or is paid, whichever is later. [Reg. § 31.6001-1(e)(2)]

Tax Reporting and Payment Obligations

Q 1:14 When is a sole proprietor required to file an income tax return?

An income tax return is required if net earnings from self-employment were $400 or more for the year. [IRC § 6017] If the sole proprietor's net earnings from self-employment were less than $400, he or she may still be required to file a return if he or she had income from other sources. As a general rule, an income tax return must be filed if an individual has taxable income from any source that exceeds the sum of the standard deduction and personal exemption amount for the year. In the case of married individuals filing jointly, a return is required if taxable income exceeds the standard deduction plus two personal exemptions. [IRC § 6012]

Q 1:15 What forms are used to report the profit or loss from a sole proprietorship?

Profit or loss from a sole proprietorship is reported on the sole proprietor's Form 1040, *U.S. Individual Income Tax Return*. Profit or loss from a sole proprietorship is generally figured on Schedule C, *Profit of Loss from Business*, which is attached to Form 1040. The net profit or loss from Schedule C is carried over to the proprietor's Form 1040.

If a taxpayer operated more than one business as a sole proprietorship, a separate Schedule C must be completed for each business.

A taxpayer may qualify to use the simpler Schedule C-EZ, *Net Profit from Business*, if the business ran at a profit for the year. Schedule C-EZ may be used only if all of the following requirements are met: [Instructions to Schedule C-EZ]

- The taxpayer operated only one business as a sole proprietorship;
- The taxpayer uses the cash method of accounting for the business;
- The business had expenses of $5,000 or less for the year;
- The business did not have an inventory at any time during the year;
- The business had no employees during the year;
- The taxpayer is not required to report depreciation or amortization of business assets;
- The taxpayer does not deduct expenses for business use of a home; and

- There are no unallowed passive activity losses for prior years for the business.

Only income and expenses from normal business operations are reported on Schedule C or Schedule C-EZ. Sales and exchanges of business assets are reported elsewhere on the return (see Chapter 13). Business tax credits are computed on separate forms. If a business claims more than one credit, it must also complete Form 3800, *General Business Credit*. Once a taxpayer calculates the credits, he or she enters them on Form 1040 to offset the tax due for the year. (For a checklist of business credits, see Appendix C.)

Q 1:16 How is a profit from a sole proprietorship taxed?

If Schedule C or C-EZ shows a profit for the year, the net income is carried over to the owner's Form 1040 and combined with income from other sources. The income may be offset by the personal and dependency exemptions and the standard deduction or itemized deductions, and tax credits. In addition, a self-employed taxpayer may claim certain special deductions, including a deduction for a portion of self-employment tax due for the year (see Q 1:19) and a special deduction for health insurance costs (see Q 1:23).

Income shown on Form 1040 is generally taxed at normal income tax rates. These rates currently range from 10 percent to 35 percent. [IRC § 1] But under the sunset provisions of the Economic Growth and Tax Relief Reconciliation Act of 2001 [P.L. 107-16], these rates will revert to the pre-Act levels after 2010. The top rate will jump to 39.6% and the bottom 10% rate will disappear.

In some cases, a taxpayer may owe more tax than that computed under the normal tax rates. A taxpayer must pay an alternative minimum tax (AMT), calculated with different income inclusions, deductions and tax rates, if it is higher than his or her regular tax liability.

Q 1:17 What is the alternative minimum tax?

The alternative minimum tax (AMT) is a separate system of taxation that operates parallel to the regular income tax. The AMT has a lower top rate than the regular income tax and its own exemption amount. However, the AMT defines taxable income more broadly than the regular tax system by eliminating certain "tax preferences"—deductions and other offsets that reduce tax liability—and making other adjustments to taxable income. [IRC §§ 56, 57] A taxpayer owes the AMT to the extent it exceeds the regular income tax for the year. [IRC § 55]

The starting point for calculating the AMT is alternative minimum taxable income (AMTI). AMTI is equal to regular taxable income increased by preference items and with certain other adjustments. AMTI is reduced by an exemption amount.

Since 1993, the exemption amount has been $45,000 for married couples filing jointly, $22,500 for marrieds filing separately, and $33,750 for single filers or heads of households. However, since then, several tax laws have temporarily increased the excemption amount. For example, the Tax Increase Prevention and Reconciliation Act of 2005 (P.L. 109-222) raised the 2006 exemption to;

- $62,550 for married individuals filing a joint return and surviving spouses;
- $42,500 for unmarried individuals; and
- $31,275 for married individuals filing separate returns [IRC § 55(d)(1)(A) and (B), as amended by the Tax Increase Prevention and Reconciliation Act of 2005]

The exemption amounts are phased out by an amount equal to 25 percent of the excess of an individual's AMTI over a threshold amount. These thresholds are $150,000 for joint filers, $75,000 for marrieds filing separately, and $112,500 for other individuals.

A tentative minimum tax is calculated by applying (1) a 26 percent tax rate to the first $175,000 of AMTI in excess of the exemption amount and (2) a 28 percent rate to the amount above $175,000. The tentative minimum tax (reduced by allowable credits, if any) is compared to the regular tax liability for the year. The amount of the tentative AMT in excess of the regular tax is payable in addition to the regular tax for the year. (There is also an AMT for corporations; see Chapter 3.)

Q 1:18 What are the preferences and adjustments used to calculate AMTI?

The minimum tax preference items are:

- The excess of the deduction for percentage depletion over the adjusted basis of mineral property at the end of the tax year. This preference does not apply to percentage depletion allowed with respect to oil and gas properties.
- The amount by which excess intangible drilling costs arising in the tax year exceed 65 percent of the net income from oil, gas, and geothermal properties. This preference does not apply to independent producers to the extent the producer's AMTI is reduced by 40 percent or less by ignoring the preference.
- Tax-exempt interest income on private activity bonds (other than qualified Section 501(c)(3) bonds) issued after August 7, 1986.
- Accelerated depreciation or amortization on certain property placed in service before January 1, 1987.
- Forty-two percent of the amount excluded from income under Section 1202 (relating to gains on the sale of certain small business stock.) [IRC § 57]

In addition, losses from any tax shelter farm activity or passive activities are not taken into account in computing AMTI.

The adjustments that individuals must make to compute AMTI are:

- Depreciation on property placed in service after 1986 and before January 1, 1999, must be computed by using the generally longer class lives prescribed by the alternative depreciation system of IRC Section 168(g) and either (a) the straight-line method in the case of property subject to the straight-line method under the regular tax or (b) the 150 percent declining balance method in the case of other property. Depreciation on property placed in service after December 31, 1998, is computed by using the regular tax recovery periods and the AMT methods described in the previous sentence.

- Mining exploration and development costs must be capitalized and amortized over a 10-year period.

- Taxable income from a long-term contracts (other than a home construction contract) must be computed using the percentage of completion method of accounting.

- The amortization deduction allowed for pollution control facilities placed in service before January 1, 1999 (generally determined using 60-month amortization for a portion of the cost of the facility under the regular tax) must be calculated under the alternative depreciation system (generally, using longer class lives and the straight-line method). The amortization deduction allowed for pollution control facilities placed in service after December 31, 1998, is calculated using the regular tax recovery periods and the straight-line method.

- Miscellaneous itemized deductions are not allowed.

- Deductions for state, local, and foreign real property taxes; state and local personal property taxes; and state, local, and foreign income, war profits, and excess profits taxes are not allowed.

- Medical expenses are allowed only to the extent they exceed 10 percent of the taxpayer's adjusted gross income.

- Standard deductions and personal exemptions are not allowed.

- The amount allowable as a deduction for circulation expenditures must be capitalized and amortized over a three-year period.

- The amount allowable as a deduction for research and experimentation expenditures must be capitalized and amortized over a 10-year period.

- The special regular tax rules relating to incentive stock options do not apply. [IRC § 56]

Q 1:19 What if a sole proprietorship shows a loss for the year?

If expenses of a sole proprietorship are more than the income for the year, the difference is a net loss. A net loss from self-employment can generally be used to offset gross income from other sources shown on Form 1040.

Q 1:19

If a sole proprietor does not have enough other income to absorb a net loss from self-employment, the remaining amount is a net operating loss. A net operating loss can be carried backwards or forwards to reduce taxable income in other tax years. [IRC § 172](See Chapter 6.)

Q 1:20 What is the due date for a sole proprietor's return?

Form 1040, including Schedule C or C-EZ, is due by the 15th day of the fourth month after the close of the tax year—April 15 for calendar-year taxpayers. If a sole proprietor cannot file by the return due date, he or she may request an extension.

An individual may obtain an automatic *six-month* extension to file an income tax return by submitting a timely, completed application for extension on Form 4868. [Reg. § 1.6081-4T] An individual does not have to give any reason justifying the extension request.

> **Planning Point:** An extension of time to file will protect a taxpayer from penalties for failure to file on time. However, an extension does not extend the time for paying any tax due with the return. [Reg. § 1.6081-1(a)] If the tax is not paid on time, a taxpayer with an extension will be subject to late payment penalties and interest.

Q 1:21 How does a sole proprietor pay the tax due for the year?

The federal income tax is a pay-as-you-go system. The tax must be paid as income is earned or received during the year. For employees, this is generally taken care of through income tax withholding from each paycheck. However, sole proprietors generally must make periodic estimated tax payments to cover the tax due for the year.

Estimated tax payments are generally required if the tax due for the year, including self-employment tax (see Q 1:22), will total $1,000 or more. [IRC § 6654(e)(1)]Form 1040-ES, *Estimated Tax for Individuals*, is used to figure and pay the tax.

If there is a shortfall in estimated tax payments, a proprietor may owe an estimated tax penalty on the amount not paid. The IRS will figure the penalty and send a bill. However, taxpayer can use Form 2210, *Underpayment of Estimated Tax by Individuals, Estates, and Trusts*, to figure the penalty amount.

Q 1:22 Is a sole proprietor required to pay Social Security and Medicare tax?

A sole proprietor must pay Social Security and Medicare tax in the form of a self-employment tax on net earnings from self-employment. [IRC § 1401] The tax must be paid if net earnings from self-employment were more than $400 for the year. As a general rule, a taxpayer calculates net earnings from self-employment by multiplying the total earnings subject to self-employment tax by 92.35 percent.

[IRC § 1402(a)] The SE tax rate on net earnings is 15.3 percent (12.4 percent Social Security tax plus 2.9 percent Medicare tax). The 2.9 percent Medicare portion of the tax applies to total net earnings from self-employment as well as wages, tips, and other compensation. [IRC § 1401(b)] However, the Social Security portion of the tax is payable only up to the Social Security wage base for the year. For 2007, the wage base is $97,500. So a taxpayer with self-employment earnings of $97,500 or more in 2007 owes a self-employment tax of $12,090 (12.4 percent of $97,500). Self-employment tax is calculated on Form 1040 Schedule SE, *Self-Employment Tax.*

Self-employed taxpayers can claim an income tax deduction equal to one-half the self-employment tax for the year. [IRC §§ 164(f), 1402(a)(12)] The deduction is an "above-the-line" deduction from gross income, which means it may be claimed in addition to the standard deduction or itemized deductions.

The deduction is designed to put self-employed taxpayers on approximately the same footing as employees, who do not pay tax on the portion of Social Security and Medicare taxes paid by their employer.

Q 1:23 How do self-employed taxpayers deduct health insurance costs?

The cost of health insurance for employees is claimed as a deduction when a taxpayer calculates the profit or loss from a sole proprietorship on Schedule C. However, the costs of a proprietor's own health coverage is not included in that calculation. Instead, a proprietor can claim a deduction on Form 1040 for amounts paid for his or her own health insurance and for coverage for a spouse and dependents. [IRC § 162(l)]The deduction is an "above-the-line" deduction for adjusted gross income. Therefore, the deduction may be claimed in addition to the standard deduction or itemized deductions.

The deduction is equal to 100 percent of qualifying costs. However, the deduction is limited to the amount of earned income from the trade or business for which the health plan was established.

The deduction may not be claimed for costs incurred in any month in which a proprietor is eligible to participate in a plan maintained by his or her employer or the employer of his or her spouse.

Home-Based Businesses

Q 1:24 Can a taxpayer deduct expenses connected with business use of a home?

Home-based businesses are becoming increasingly common. In some cases, a new business owner will set up shop in a spare room at home until revenue is sufficient to rent proper office space. In other cases, a business owner may prefer to operate from home and avoid the daily hassle of commuting to a downtown office. Moreover, these days many former business executives have set up lucrative consulting practices that they run from the comfort of home.

Whether an expense associated with a home-based business is deductible depends on the nature of the expense. Ordinary and necessary business expenses that would be incurred regardless of where a business is operated are clearly deductible. [IRC § 162]So, for example, a deduction may be claimed for the cost of a business telephone line, office supplies, and repairs to business equipment.

On the other hand, the rules for deducting expenses associated with the home itself—rent or mortgage interest, utilities, insurance, and repairs—are not as clear-cut.

1. The business portion of the home must be used (a) regularly and (b) exclusively for a trade or business; *and*

2. The business portion of the home must be (a) the business owner's principal place of business, (b) a place to meet with clients and customers in the normal course of business, or (c) a separate structure (not attached to the home) that is used in connection with a trade or business.

[IRC § 280A(c)]

Q 1:25 When is a portion of a home regularly used for business?

According to regulations, whether a portion of a home is used regularly for business depends on all the facts and circumstances. [Prop. Reg. § 1.280A-2(h)] However, IRS publications make it clear that to pass the regular-use test, a home office must be used on a continuing basis. The test will not be met if business use is only occasional or incidental, even if the area is not used for any other purpose. [IRS Pub. No. 587, *Business Use of Your Home*]

Q 1:26 When is a portion of a home used exclusively for business?

The exclusive use requirement is met only if there is no other use of the business portion of the home during the tax year. [Prop. Reg. § 1.280A-2(g)]

Example 1-3: Susan Smith runs a picture-framing business out of a studio in the basement of her family home. Smith's children often use the studio after-hours to work on homework and art projects.

Result: Smith's studio does not pass the exclusive-use test.

Planning Point: This rule may seem excessively strict. After all, Smith's kids do not use the space during her working hours. Moreover, many taxpayers may wonder how the IRS would know if home office space is occasionally used for other purposes. The answer, of course, is the IRS would not know— unless it challenges the deduction. In which case, it is up to the taxpayer to prove that the space is exclusively devoted to business.

There are two exceptions to the exclusive-use requirement. One involves home-based day care businesses (see Q 1:36). The other exception covers the storage of inventory or product samples.

Storage of inventory or product samples. The exclusive-use requirement does not apply if part of a home is used for storage of inventory or product samples. However, all of the following tests must be met:

- The taxpayer's trade or business involves selling products at wholesale or retail;
- The inventory or product samples are stored in the home for use in that trade or business;
- The home is the only fixed location of the trade or business;
- The storage space is used on a regular basis; and
- The space is an identifiably separate space suitable for storage.

[Prop. Reg. § 1.280A-2(e)]

Example 1-4: Henry Thorner sells mechanics' tools. Thorner's home is the only fixed location for his business. Thorner regularly uses half of his basement for storing inventory and product samples. The basement is sometimes used for personal purposes.

Result: Expenses connected with the basement storage space are deductible even though Thorner does not use the basement storage area exclusively for business.

Q 1:27 What rules apply if a home office is used to meet with clients or customers?

A taxpayer will qualify for home office deductions if an office at home is used regularly and exclusively for business and serves as a place to meet with clients, customers, or patients in the normal course of business. The use of the home office must be substantial and integral to the conduct of the taxpayer's business. [Prop. Reg. § 1.280A-2(c)]However, the taxpayer may do business at another fixed location. Moreover, the home office does not have to be the taxpayer's principal place of business.

Example 1-5: Jane Quinn, a self-employed business consultant, works three days a week at an office in a nearby city. She spends two days a week working from a home office that is used regularly and exclusively for business. Jane regularly meets local clients in her home office.

Result: Jane may claim deductions for expenses connected with her home office because she uses the office to meet with clients in the normal course of her business.

Q 1:28 When does a home office qualify as a principal place of business?

If a home office is used for "paperwork only," office-related expenses will be deductible only if the home office qualifies as the taxpayer's principal place of business. A taxpayer may do business in more one location. However, a taxpayer may have only one *principal* place of business. [Prop. Reg. § 1. 280A-2(b)]A home office will qualify as a principal place of business if:

Q 1:27

1. The home office is used exclusively and regularly for administrative or management activities of the taxpayer's trade or business; and

2. The taxpayer has no other fixed location where substantial administrative or management activities are conducted. [IRC § 280A(c)(1)]

Administrative or management activities include billing, keeping books and records, setting up appointments, forwarding orders, and writing reports. However, the fact that some of these activities are conducted at another location will not disqualify a home office as a principal place of business. For example, a home office will not be disqualified if another company does billing at its location. Similarly, a home office will not be disqualified if the business owner occasionally does administrative or management tasks outside the home office.

Example 1-6: John Lincoln is a self-employed plumber. Most of John's work time is spent at customer's homes and offices installing and repairing plumbing. He has a small office at home that he uses exclusively and regularly for the administrative and management activities of his business, such as phoning customers, ordering supplies, and keeping records. John does not, however, do his own billing. He uses a local bookkeeping service to bill his customers.

Result: John's home qualifies as his principal place of business. He uses the home office for the administrative and managerial activities of his business and does not have another fixed location for conducting those activities. His choice to have his billing handled by another company at its location does not disqualify his home office.

Example 1-7: Pamela Smart is a self-employed sales representative for several different product lines. To make sales, Pamela regularly visits customers at various locations throughout her territory. She has a home office that she uses regularly and exclusively to set up appointments, write up orders, and prepare reports for the companies whose products she sells. She occasionally writes up orders and sets up appointments in her hotel room when she is away on business overnight.

Result: Pamela's home office qualifies as her principal place of business. The fact that she conducts some administrative or management activities in hotel rooms does not disqualify the home office.

Most significantly, a home office will not be disqualified even if the business owner conducts substantial nonadministrative or nonmanagement activities at a fixed location outside the home. [IRC § 280A(c)(1)] Moreover, a home office will not be disqualified even if a taxpayer has other suitable space available to conduct administrative or management activities.

Example 1-8: Paul Henderson is a self-employed anesthesiologist. He spends the majority of his time practicing his profession at three local hospitals. One of the hospitals provides him with a small, shared office where he could conduct administrative or management activities. However, Paul does not use that office. Instead he uses a room in his home that he has converted into an office. He uses the home office regularly and exclusively for scheduling, preparing for treatments and presentations, billing, maintaining patient records, satisfying continuing education requirements, and reading medical journals and books.

Result: Paul's home office qualifies as his principal place of business. His choice to use his home office instead of the one provided by the hospital does not disqualify his home office as his principal place of business. In addition, his performance of substantial nonadministrative and nonmangement activities at the three hospitals is not a disqualifying factor.

If a taxpayer has more than one fixed location for performing administrative and management activities, the principal place of business is generally determined based on the relative importance of the activities performed at each location. If they are equivalent, a taxpayer may consider the time spent at each location.

Q 1:29 What if a home office is located in a separate structure?

Expenses connected with a freestanding structure, such as a studio, garage, or barn, are deductible if the structure is regularly and exclusively used for business. [Prop. Reg. § 1.280A-2(d)] The structure does not have to be the taxpayer's principal place of business or a place for meeting with clients, customers, or patients.

Example 1-9: Glenda Burton operates a flower shop that is located in her town's business district. Glenda grows flowers for the shop in a greenhouse behind her home.

Result: Because she uses the greenhouse regularly and exclusively for business, Glenda can deduct expenses related to its use.

Q 1:30 What if a taxpayer operates more than one business from a home office?

Whether a home office qualifies as a principal place of business or a place for meeting with clients and customers must be determined separately for each business. One home office may be the principal place of business for more than one business. Moreover, a home office may be used for meeting with clients or customers of more than one business. However, a taxpayer will not meet the regular and exclusive use requirements unless each business conducted in the office qualifies for home-office deductions.

Q 1:31 What if a home office is used for business for only part of the year?

A taxpayer cannot deduct expenses for business use of a home that were incurred during any part of the year that the home was not used for business purposes. For example, if a home-based business begins operations on July 1, only expenses for the second half of the year can be used in calculating the home-office deduction.

Q 1:32 What types of expenses qualify for the home-office deduction?

Home-related expenses fall into three categories:

1. *Direct expenses* that relate only to the business portion of the home are deductible in full. Examples of direct expenses include painting or repairs to the area of the home used for business.

2. *Indirect expenses* for running the entire home are deductible based on the percentage of the home used for business (see Q 1:33). Examples of indirect expenses include:

   - Insurance;
   - General repairs;
   - Security systems;
   - Utilities and services;
   - Real estate taxes;
   - Rent;
   - Mortgage interest;
   - Casualty losses; and
   - Depreciation.

      Note: The nonbusiness portions of real estate taxes, mortgage interest, and casualty losses may be claimed as personal itemized deductions.

3. *Unrelated expenses* that relate only to the personal use portion of the home are not deductible. Examples include lawn care or repairs to a room not used for business.

Q 1:33 How is a home-office deduction calculated?

The first step in calculating a home-office deduction is to determine the percentage of the home that is used for business. As a general rule, the business use percentage is calculated by dividing the area used for business by the area of the entire home. If the rooms in the home are all about the same size, the business-use percentage can be calculated by dividing the number of rooms used for business by the total number of rooms.

Example 1-10: Bill Burton's home office is 240 square feet (12 feet × 20 feet). The total area of Bill's home is 1,200 square feet. Bill's office is 20 percent (240/1,200) of the total area of the home. Therefore, Bill's business-use percentage is 20 percent.

Example 1-11: Sandra Nolan uses one room in her home for business. The home has four rooms, all of about equal size. Sandra's office is 25 percent

(1/4) of the total area of her home. Therefore, Sandra's business-use percentage is 25 percent.

Q 1:34 Are there any limits on a home-office deduction?

If gross income from business use of the home equals or exceeds the total expenses of the business (including depreciation), expenses related to business use of the home are deductible in full. However, if gross income from business use of the home is less than total business expenses, the deduction for certain expenses is limited. [Prop. Reg. § 1.280A-2(i)]

The deductions for otherwise nondeductible expenses, such as insurance, utilities, and depreciation (with depreciation taken last), allocable to the business, are limited to the gross income from the business use of the home minus the sum of the following: [IRC § 280A(c)(5); Prop. Reg. § 1.280A-2(i)(5)]

1. The business portion of expenses that would be deductible even if the home were not used for business (e.g., mortgage interest, real estate taxes, and casualty and theft losses that can be claimed as itemized deductions); and

2. Business expenses that relate to the business activity in the home (e.g., business phone, supplies, and depreciation on equipment), but not to the use of the home itself.

Deductions that exceed the limit can be carried over to the following year, subject to the deduction limit for that year. [IRC § 280A(c)(5)]

Example 1-12: Patricia Keith meets the requirements for deducting expenses for the business use of her home. Patricia uses 20 percent of her home for this business. Patricia figures her deduction as follows:

Gross income from business	6,000
Less:	
Business portion of deductible mortgage interest and taxes (20 percent)	3,000
Business expenses unrelated to business use of home (100 percent)	2,000
Deduction limit:	1,000
Less other expenses allocable to business use:	
Maintenance, insurance, and utilities (20 percent)	800
Depreciation allowed (20 percent = $1,600 allowable)	200
Depreciation carryover ($1,600 – $200)	1,400

Patricia can deduct 100 percent of the business portion of deductible mortgage interest and real estate taxes ($3,000) and 100 percent of business expenses not related to the use of her home ($2,000). In addition, she can deduct the entire business portion of her expenses for maintenance, insurance, and utilities, because the total ($800) is less than the $1,000 deduction limit. On the other hand, Patricia's deduction for depreciation on the business portion of her home is limited to $200 ($1,000 minus $800) because of the deduction limit. Patricia can carry over the $1,400 balance and add it to her depreciation deduction in the following year, subject to that year's deduction limit.

Q 1:35 How does a sole proprietor claim home-office deductions?

Home office deductions are calculated on Form 8829, *Expenses for Business Use of Your Home*. The deduction is carried over to Form 1040 Schedule C of Form 1040. A sole proprietor cannot use Schedule C-EZ if deductions are claimed for business use of a home.

Q 1:36 Do special rules apply to home-based day care businesses?

Yes. The exclusive-use rule (Q 1:26) does not apply to space in a home that is used on a regular basis for providing day care if the following requirements are met:

- The taxpayer is in the trade or business of providing day care for children, persons 65 or older, or persons who are physically or mentally unable to care for themselves; and
- The taxpayer has applied for or been granted a license, certification, registration, or approval as a day-care center or as a family or group day-care home under state law (unless an exemption applies).

[Prop. Reg. § 1.280A-2(f)]

Taxpayers who do use a portion of their homes exclusively for a day care business can compute their deduction, including the business percentage, the same way that other home-based businesses do (Q 1:33). However, taxpayers who do not use a portion exclusively for business must perform an added calculation. They must not only calculate the portion of the home that is used for business but also the percentage of the time that portion is used for business. [Rev. Rul. 92-3, 1992-1 C.B. 141]

A room that is *available* for use throughout each business day and that is regularly used in the day care business is considered to be used for day care throughout each business day. The taxpayer does not have to show the specific hours the area was used for business. The taxpayer may use the area occasionally for personal reasons without disqualifying its availability for business use. However, a room that is used only occasionally for business is not considered available for business use.

Example 1-13: Mary Nolan uses the basement in her home to operate a day care facility. The basement comprises 50 percent of the space in her home. The basement is available for business use 12 hours a day, 5 days a week, 50 weeks a year. So the basement is available for business use for 3,000 hours out of the 8,760 hours during the year—or 34.25 percent. There Nolan can deduct 17.13 percent of home expenses (50 percent × 34.25 percent).

Meals. If a taxpayer provides food to the care recipients, these costs should *not* be treated as a cost of using the home for business. This should be treated as a separate expense (like the cost of advertising).

Home-based day care providers may use standard rates to deduct meals provided to children instead of deducting actual meal expenses. [Rev. Proc. 2003-22, 2003-10 I.R.B. 577]

A day care business using the standard rates is automatically deemed to meet the Internal Revenue Code's substantiation requirements insofar as the deduction for meal costs is concerned.

The standard rate can be used to compute the deductible cost of each meal and snack actually purchased and served to each eligible child. There is one set of rates for day care providers in Alaska, one set for Hawaii, and one set for everywhere else. The rates are tied into the reimbursement rates provided by the U.S. Department of Agriculture's Child and Adult Care Food Program and are adjusted annually. For July 1, 2007 through June 30, 2008, the rates are: [72 Fed. Reg. 37505, July 10, 2007]

Alaska: breakfast, $1.76; lunch/dinner, $3.34, snack, $0.99

Hawaii: breakfast, $1.29; lunch/dinner, $2.41, snack, $0.72

Other states: breakfast, $1.11; lunch/dinner, $2.06, snack, $0.61

The standard rates include beverages but do not include non-food supplies used for food preparation, service, or storage, such as containers, paper products, or utensils. The standard rates do not include other non-food items such as medication, administrative supplies, or toys. A day care provider who uses the standard rates may separately deduct the cost of these non-food items (assuming they otherwise qualify as ordinary and necessary business expenses).

To claim the standard rates, a day care provider must keep records that include the name of each eligible child, dates and hours of attendance in the day care, and the type and quantity of meals and snacks served. The IRS has provided a sample log in Revenue Procedure 2003-22 that can be used for this purpose.

Q 1:37 Do any special tax rules apply when a home with a home office is sold?

Taxpayers can generally exclude up to $250,000 of gain on the sale of a home ($500,000 for certain married persons filing a joint return). To qualify for the exclusion, the home must have been owned and used as a principal residence for two of the five years preceding the sale. [IRC § 121]

Business use of all or a portion of a property may—or may not—affect the taxpayer's ability to claim the home-sale exclusion or reduce the amount of gain that is excludable.

Nonresidential use of a separate portion of the property. The home sale exclusion does not apply to gain allocable to any portion of a property that is separate from the taxpayer's dwelling unit if the taxpayer does not meet the use requirement for that portion of the property. [Reg. § 1.121-1(e)(1)] Thus, if a portion of the taxpayer's property separate from the dwelling unit was used exclusively for business purposes, only the gain allocable to the residential portion of the property will qualify for the home sale exclusion.

For this purpose, a dwelling unit *does not* include appurtenant structures or other property. [Reg. § 1.121-1(e)(2); IRC § 280A(f)(1)]

If a taxpayer does not meet the use requirement for a separate portion of the property, the basis and amount realized for the entire property must be allocated between the residential and nonresidential portions using the same method that was used to determine depreciation deductions (if any). [Reg. § 1.121-1(e)(3)]

The gain attributable to the nonresidential portion of the property is subject to the capital gain tax rules for property used in a trade or business. [IRC § 1231]

Depreciation claimed on the nonresidential portion of the property is subject to the recapture rules for real property. [IRC § 1250] In other words, gain is taxed as ordinary income to the extent of prior accelerated depreciation. However, there is no recapture if the home was held for more than one year and only straight-line depreciation was claimed. Under the modified accelerated cost recovery system (MACRS), straight-line depreciation is required for residential rental property and nonresidential real property placed in service after 1986. Therefore, the recapture rules will generally not apply to most home sales. On the other hand, gain that represents unrecaptured depreciation (called unrecaptured Section 1250 gain) will be subject to a 25 percent maximum capital gain rate (rather than 15 percent) for taxpayers above the 15 percent bracket. [IRC § 1(h)] For taxpayers in the 15 percent bracket or below, unrecaptured Section 1250 gain is taxed at the regular capital rate (generally 15 percent).

Example 1-14: In year 1, Harold Benton purchased a property that consists of a house, a stable, and 35 acres of land. Benton sells the property in year 7, realizing a gain of $24,000. Benton used the house and 7 acres of land as his principal residence for the entire time he owned the property. However, he used the stable and 28 acres of the land as a commercial riding academy for more than three of the five years preceding the sale. Benton claimed depreciation of $9,000 for the nonresidential use of the stable.

Result: Based on the allocation method used to determine depreciation deductions, Benton determines that $10,000 of gain is allocable to the residential portion of the property and $14,000 to the portion used as a riding academy. Therefore, Benton can exclude $10,000 of gain under the home sale rules. Benton must recognize the $14,000 of gain allocable to the academy, with $9,000 treated as unrecaptured Section 1250 gain.

If the entire property is used as a residence at the time of the sale and the two-year use requirement of IRC Section 121 *is* met with respect to the entire property, a taxpayer is not required to allocate gain between the separate portions of the property. However, the home-sale exclusion does not apply to that portion of the gain that does not exceed depreciation adjustments for periods after May 6, 1997. That portion of the gain is treated as unrecaptured Section 1250 gain. [Reg. § 1.121-1(d)(1); IRC § 1(h)]

Example 1-15: Same facts as Example 1-14, except that Benton shut down the riding stable more than two years before the sale and used the stable and acreage for residential purposes until the date of the sale.

Result: The entire property was used as his principal residence for at least two of the five years preceding the sale. Therefore, no allocation of gain is required. However, only $15,000 of gain is excludable ($24,000 gain realized - $9,000 of depreciation deductions for periods after May 6, 1997). The $9,000 of gain representing depreciation on the property is treated as unrecaptured Section 1250 gain.

However, allocation of gain will be required if the entire property is not used as a residence at the time of sale—even if the taxpayer meets the two-year use requirement with respect to the entire property.

Nonresidential use within a dwelling unit. If a taxpayer uses a space within his or her home for business purposes, there is no need to allocate gain between the business and residential portions of the home. However, the home-sale exclusion does not apply to the extent of depreciation claimed for periods after May 6, 1997. The depreciation must be treated as unrecaptured Section 1250 gain. [Reg. § 121-1(d)(1); IRC § 1(h)]

Example 1-16: Joan Craig, an attorney, bought her home in year 1. The house is a single dwelling unit, but Craig uses a portion of the home as her law office. Craig sold the home in year 7, realizing a gain of $13,000. She claimed $2,000 of depreciation on the office portion while she owned the home.

Result: Craig does not have to allocate her gain between the office and residential portions of the home. However, the $2,000 of gain representing depreciation is not eligible for the exclusion and must be treated as unrecaptured Section 1250 gain. Craig can exclude $11,000 of gain on the sale.

Example 1-17: Same facts as Example 1-16, except that Craig was not entitled to claim depreciation deductions in connection with her business use of the home.

Result: Craig is not required to allocate gain between the business and residential portions of the home. Moreover, her entire $13,000 qualifies for the home-sale exclusion.

Q 1:38 How is gain reported on a tax return when a residence is used for business purposes?

If a separate portion of the property is used for business in the year of the sale, gain from that portion (including unrecaptured Section 1250 gain) must be reported on Form 4797, *Sales of Business Property*. The home-sale exclusion allocable to that portion is also claimed on Form 4797. Gain from the residential portion is not reported unless it exceeds the allocable home-sale exclusion or the taxpayer elects not to claim the home-sale exclusion. Taxable gain from the residential portion is reported on Form 1040 Schedule D, *Sales and Exchanges*. However, unrecaptured Section 1250 gain attributable to the residential portion is reported on Form 4797.

If the home is used entirely as a residence in the year of sale, taxable gain (if any) is reported on Form 1040, Schedule D. However, unrecaptured Section 1250 gain is reported on Form 4797. Conversely, if the entire home is used for business in the year of the sale, the entire transaction—including any home-sale exclusion—is reported on Form 4797.

If the business use portion is within the home, taxable gain (if any) is reported on Form 1040, Schedule D. However, unrecaptured Section 1250 gain is reported on Form 4797. [IRS Pub. 523, *Selling Your Home*]

Chapter 2

Partnerships and Limited Liability Companies

For tax purposes, a partnership is what is known as a "pass-through" entity. Instead of paying tax itself, the partnership passes income and losses through to its partners, who report their shares on their separate returns. Although a partnership is not a taxpaying entity, it must file an information return—Form 1065, *U.S. Return of Partnership Income*—with the Internal Revenue Service (IRS or the Service) and provide income and loss information to its partners. Each partner includes its share of the partnership's income or loss on his or her tax return.

Like a sole proprietor, a partner is considered self-employed and must pay self-employment (SECA) tax on income from the partnership.

Limited liability companies (LLCs) are a relatively new form of business organization, combining features of a corporation and a partnership. Depending on the situation and the wishes of the owners, an LLC may be taxed as a partnership, sole proprietorship, or corporation.

Partnership Basics

Q 2:1 What is a partnership?

A partnership is the relationship between two or more persons who join to carry on a trade or business. Each person contributes money, property, labor, or skill, and expects to share in the profits and losses of the business.

As a general rule, each partner in a partnership is considered an agent of the partnership. Thus, all partners can be bound by one partner's actions. In addition, if one partner causes damages or injury while engaged in partnership business, the other partners can be held personally liable. Partners can also be held personally liable for business debts of the partnership. Partners are also generally liable for any federal tax obligations of the partnership, such as employment taxes. [*U.S. v. Papandon*, 331 F.3d 52 (2d Cir. 2003); *Remington v. United States*, 210 F.3d 281 (5th Cir. 2000)]

Most partnerships execute formal agreements that govern the partners' actions and their rights to income from the partnership. However, a formal agreement is not necessary for a partnership to exist for tax purposes.

Q 2:2 What issues should a partnership agreement address?

A formal partnership agreement is a good idea for most partnerships. An agreement should address all of the following issues:

- How will the profits from the business be shared among the partners? Without an agreement, the partners share the profits equally, even if their contributions to the partnership are not equal.

- How will management decisions be made? Without an agreement, each partner has an equal voice in management of the business.

- What will happen if a partner dies or withdraws from the business? Without an agreement, death or withdrawal of a partner causes dissolution of the business.

- What will happen to a deceased or withdrawing partner's share of the business? A partnership agreement can specify the terms and conditions for the surviving partners to buy out a partner's interest.

- Can the partnership add a new partner—or terminate a partner's interest? A partnership agreement can spell out how a partnership can expel a partner or add a new partner without dissolving the partnership.

- How will assets be distributed if the partnership is dissolved? A partnership agreement can minimize conflicts over division of the partnership assets if the partnership ends.

Q 2:1

- How will the assets be valued when the partnership ends? Again, a partnership agreement can minimize conflicts by specifying the method for appraising the partnership assets if the partnership is dissolved.

Q 2:3 How is a partnership defined for tax purposes?

The tax code states that a partnership includes a syndicate, group, pool, joint venture, or other organization that is not a corporation, trust, or estate. [IRC §761(a)]

Most businesses that qualify as partnerships may elect out of partnership tax treatment under the IRS's "check-the-box" regulations. [Reg. §301.7701-3]The check-the-box regulations permit most noncorporate businesses to select how they are treated for tax purposes, regardless of their status under local law. A noncorporate business with two or more owners can elect to be taxed either as a partnership or an association taxed as a corporation. If no election is made, the default status is a partnership.

A partnership makes its election about its tax status by filing IRS Form 8832, *Entity Classification Election.*

Some states have enacted laws making it possible for a business entity to be treated as organized under the laws of more than one state at the same time. This, for example, allows an entity to be organized as a partnership in one jurisdiction and a corporation in another. IRS regulations provide that if an entity in one jurisdiction is treated as a corporation for federal tax purposes, then the entities organized in other jurisdictions will be treated as corporations, regardless of how they are actually organized in those other jurisdictions. [Reg. §301.7702-2T(b)(9)]

Q 2:4 What must be done to set up a partnership?

Setting up a partnership is an informal process; there are no official forms to file to obtain partnership status. Like a sole proprietorship, a partnership is presumed to operate under the names of its partners. So, if the business will use some other name, the name may have to be registered with your state's Secretary of State. In addition, depending on local requirements, a partnership may have to file a business certificate or obtain a business license before it can begin doing business.

A partnership must obtain a federal employer identification number (EIN). An EIN is required even if the partnership does not have employees.

Q 2:5 What is a limited partnership?

A partnership can be set up so that only some of its partners operate the business and bear personal liability for the partnership's obligations. Those partners are called general partners. The remaining partners—called limited partners—share in the profits of the business, but their liability for partnership obligations is limited to the amount of their contributions to the partnership.

Limited partners generally cannot participate in the management of the partnership.

Q 2:6 What must be done to set up a limited partnership?

Unlike general partnerships, limited partnerships must meet specific state law requirements. In addition, a certificate of limited partnership generally must be filed with the state. The specific legal requirements can be obtained from a state's Secretary of State.

Like a general partnership, a limited partnership must obtain a federal employer identification number (EIN).

Family Partnerships

Q 2:7 Is a partnership with family members as partners recognized for tax purposes?

It depends. If capital is a material income-producing element in the partnership, gifts of partnership interests to other family members will be recognized for tax purposes. Capital is ordinarily an income-producing factor if the operation of the business requires substantial inventories or investments in plants, machinery, or equipment.

On the other hand, if capital is not a material income-producing element, the transfer of a partnership interests to other family members may be ignored. So, for example, if the income from a business comes exclusively from the personal services of a taxpayer, he or she cannot set up a partnership with another family member. The income from the business will be taxed solely to the taxpayer and the partnership will be disregarded. [Reg. § 1.704(1(e)]

Even when capital is a material income-producing factor, the donor of a partnership interest must receive reasonable compensation for services he or she provides to the partnership. The donee's share of partnership income must be reduced to reflect the donor's compensation. [IRC § 704(e); Reg. § 1.704(e)]

Planning Point: Family limited partnerships have become popular as an estate-planning tool. For example, parents can transfer a business to a family limited partnership set up with themselves as the general partners and their children as limited partners. Because of the child's minority ownership and lack of control, the value of the gifts to the children can be discounted for gift tax purposes. Family limited partnerships also offer income-splitting benefits. A portion of the parents' former income from the business is now passed through and taxed to the children in their lower tax brackets.

The use of a family limited partnership as a vehicle for avoiding estate taxes should be approached cautiously. Using IRC § 2036, the IRS has managed to win a series of cases that resulted in transferred limited partnership interests being included in the estate of the transferor. IRC § 2036 mandates inclusion in the transferor's gross estate of lifetime transfers in which the transferor retains for life (or for a period which does not, in fact, end before his or her death):

- the possession or enjoyment of, or the right to the income from, the property, or
- the right to designate the persons who shall possess or enjoy the property or the income from the property.

IRC § 2036 will also apply if there is an express or implied understanding at the time of transfer that the transferor will retain the economic benefits of the partnership property.

If a transfer with retained interest occurs pursuant to a bona fide sale for full and adequate consideration, then no amount of the value of the interest transferred is includible in the gross estate. In cases where the decedent received partial, but insufficient, consideration, only the excess of the property's fair market value over the consideration received is includible.

A couple of court cases illustrate the IRC § 2036 issue in the context of family limited partnerships. In one case, a federal appeals court ruled that the assets transferred by a decedent to two family limited partnerships were includible in the decedent's gross estate because there was an implied agreement between the decedent and his family that the decedent would retain the enjoyment and economic benefit of the property transferred to the partnership. The existence of the implied agreement was inferred from the decedent's failure to retain sufficient assets to support himself for the remainder of his life and the testamentary characteristics of the partnership arrangements. [T. Thompson Est., 382 F3d 367 (3rd Cir., 2004)]

In another appeals court case, the assets transferred to a family limited partnership were not includible in a decedent's gross estate under § 2036 because the court held that the transfer qualified as a bona fide sale for adequate and full consideration. The decedent's transfer to the partnership was deemed made for adequate and full consideration because: (1) the decedent received a partnership interest that was proportionate to the assets that she contributed; (2) the decedent's capital account was properly credited with the assets that she contributed; and (3) the decedent was entitled to a distribution equal to her capital account balance upon termination or dissolution of the partnership. [D. Kimbell, Sr., Exr., 371 F3d 257 (5th Cir., 2004)]

Q 2:8 Is a "mom-and-pop" business treated as a partnership for tax purposes?

If spouses carry on a business together and share in the profits and losses, they may be partners whether or not they have a formal partnership agreement. If so, they should report income or loss from the business on Form 1065. However, under the Small Business and Work Opportunity Act of 2007 (P.L. 110-28), a couple may elect to have their business not treated as a partnership. If they make election, each spouse would report his share of income and expenses on a separate Schedule C, Form 1040 (see Chapter 1).

Tax Year

Q 2:9 Are there any restrictions on a partnership's choice of which tax year to use?

Yes, most partnerships must use their "required tax year." For a partnership, a required tax year is generally the same as the tax year of its partners. [IRC §706(e)] If one or more partners having the same tax year own an interest in partnership profits and capital of more than 50 percent (a majority interest), the partnership must use the tax year of those partners. [IRC §706(b)(1)(B)(i)]

The partnership determines if there is a majority interest tax year on the testing day, which is usually the first day of the partnership's current tax year. [IRC §706(b)(4)]

If there is no majority interest tax year, the partnership must use the tax year of all its principal partners. A principal partner is one who has a 5 percent or more interest in the profits or capital of the partnership. [IRC §706(b)(1)(B)(ii)]

If there is no majority interest tax year and the principal partners do not have the same tax year, the partnership generally must use a tax year that results in the least aggregate deferral of income to the partners. [Temp. Reg. §1.706-1T]The tax year that results in the least aggregate deferral of income is determined as follows.

1. Figure the number of months of deferral for each partner using one partner's tax year. Count the months from the end of that tax year forward to the end of each other partner's tax year.

2. Multiply each partner's months of deferral figured in step (1) by that partner's interest in the partnership profits for the year used in step (1).

3. Add the results in step (2) to get the total deferral for the tax year used in step (1).

4. Repeat steps (1) through (3) for each partner's tax year that is different from the other partners' years.

The partner's tax year that results in the lowest number in step (3) is the tax year that must be used by the partnership.

Example 2-1: Bill Black and John Lacy each have a 50 percent interest in a partnership that uses a fiscal year ending June 30. Bill uses a calendar year while John has a fiscal year ending November 30. The partnership must change its tax year to a fiscal year ending November 30 because this results in the least aggregate deferral of income to the partners. This was determined as shown in the following table.

Year-End Dec. 31	Year-End	Profits Interest	Months of Deferral	Interest Deferral
Bill	Dec. 31	0.5	-0-	-0-
John	Nov. 30	0.5	11	5.5
				5.5

Year-End Nov. 30	Year-End	Profits Interest	Months of Deferral	Interest Deferral
Bill	Dec. 31	0.5	1	0.5
John	Nov. 30	0.5	-0-	-0-
				0.5

If more than one year qualifies as the tax year that has the least aggregate deferral of income, the partnership can choose any year that qualifies. However, if one of the years that qualify is the partnership's existing tax year, the partnership must retain that tax year.

Q 2:10 Are there exceptions to the "required tax year" rule?

There are two exceptions to the required tax year rule:

1. *Business purpose tax year.* If a partnership establishes an acceptable business purpose for having a tax year different from its required tax year, the different tax year can be used. The deferral of income to the partners is not considered a business purpose. [IRC § 706(b)(1)(C)]

2. *Section 444 election.* Partnerships can elect under Section 444 of the Internal Revenue Code (IRC or Code) to use a tax year different from both the required tax year and any business purpose tax year. Certain restrictions apply to this election; basically, the deferral period cannot be longer than three months. [IRC § 444(a)]. In addition, the electing partnership may be required to make a payment representing the value of the extra tax deferral to the partners.

Q 2:11 How does a partnership establish an acceptable business purpose for having a tax year other than a required tax year?

A partnership can establish a business purpose for a tax year based on all the relevant facts and circumstances. Administrative and convenience business reasons such as the following are *not* sufficient to establish a business purpose for a particular tax year:

- Using a particular year for regulatory or financial accounting purposes.
- Using a hiring pattern, such as typically hiring staff during certain times of the year.
- Using a particular year for administrative purposes, such as admission or retirement of partners or shareholders, or promotion of staff.
- Using a price list, model year, or other item that changes on an annual basis.
- Deferring income to partners or shareholders.
- Using a particular year used by related entities and competitors.

[Rev. Proc. 2002-39; 2002-22 I.R.B. 1046]

Q 2:11

Natural business year. A partnership can establish a business purpose for a tax year using a *natural business year.* [Rev. Proc. 87-32, 1987-2 C.B. 396]A natural business year is the annual accounting period encompassing all related income and expenses.

A partnership that changes its tax year so that it coincides with its natural business year has established a business purpose. The natural business year of an entity can be determined under any of the following tests.

- Annual business cycle test.

- Seasonal business test.

- 25-percent gross receipts test.

Annual business cycle test. Apply this test if the partnership's gross receipts from sales and services for the short period and the three immediately preceding tax years indicate that the entity has a peak and a non-peak period of business. (When a partnership changes its tax year, a "short period" return must be filed, covering the months between the end of the partnership's old tax year and the beginning of its new tax year. See Chapter 5.) The natural business year is considered to end one month after the end of the highest peak period. A business whose income is steady from month to month throughout the year will not meet this test.

Seasonal business test. Apply this test if the partnership's gross receipts from sales and services for the short period and the three immediately preceding tax years indicate that the partnership's business is operational for only part of the year (due to weather conditions, for example). As a result, during the period the business is not operational, it has gross receipts equal to or less than 10 percent of its total gross receipts for the year. The natural business year is considered to end one month after the end of operations for the season.

25-percent gross receipts test. To apply this test, take the following steps:

1. Total the gross receipts from sales and services for the most recent 12-month period that ends with the last month of the requested tax year. Figure this for the 12-month period that ends before the filing of the request. Also, total the gross receipts from sales and services for the last 2 months of that 12-month period.

2. Determine the percentage of the receipts for the 2-month period by dividing the total of the last 2-month period by the total for the entire 12-month period. Carry the percentage to two decimal places.

3. Figure the percentage following steps (1) and (2) for the two 12-month periods just preceding the 12-month period used in (1).

If the percentage determined for each of the three years equals or exceeds 25 percent, the requested tax year is the natural business year.

If one or more tax years (other than the requested tax year) produce higher averages of the 3 percentages than the requested tax year, then the requested tax year will not qualify as the natural business year under the 25-percent gross receipts test.

Q 2:11

If the partnership does not have at least 47 months of gross receipts (36-month period for requested tax year plus additional 11-month period for comparing the requested tax year with other potential tax years), it cannot establish a natural business year using the 25-percent gross receipts test.

A partnership can obtain automatic IRS approval to retain or change to a natural business year that meets the 25-percent gross receipts test. [Rev. Proc. 2002-38, 2002-22 I.R.B. 1037] To get automatic approval, a partnership must file a tax return for the short period. The short period tax return must be filed by the due date of the taxpayer's federal income tax return (including extensions) for the first effective tax year.

A Form 1128, *Application to Adopt, Change, or Retain a Tax Year*, must be filed no earlier than the day following the end of the first tax year for which the adoption, change, or retention is effective (first effective year) and no later than the due date (including extensions) for filing the tax return for the first effective year. In the case of a change, the first effective year is the short period required to effect the change.

If a partnership wants to change to or retain a natural business year other than under the 25-percent gross receipts test, the approval of the IRS is required (see Rev. Proc. 2002-39, 2002-22 I.R.B. 1046, for rules relating to nonautomatic changes).

Q 2:12 Which partnerships are eligible for the Section 444 election, and how does it work?

A partnership can make a Section 444 election if it meets all the following requirements:

- It is not a member of a tiered structure (defined in Regulations Section 1.444-2T).
- It has not previously had a Section 444 election in effect.
- It elects a year that meets the deferral period requirement.

If the partnership is adopting or changing to a tax year other than its required year, the deferral period is the number of months from the end of the new tax year to the end of the required tax year. The IRS will allow a Section 444 election only if the deferral period of the new tax year is less than the shorter of:

1. Three months or
2. The deferral period of the tax year being changed. This is the tax year immediately preceding the year for which the partnership wishes to make the Section 444 election. [Reg. § 1.444-1T(b)(2)]

Example 2-2: XYZ, a newly formed partnership, begins operations on December 1, 2005. XYZ is owned by calendar year partners. XYZ wants to make a Section 444 election to adopt a September 30 tax year. XYZ's deferral period for the tax year beginning December 1, 2008, is three months, the number of months between September 30 and December 31.

Q 2:12

The Section 444 election is made by filing Form 8716, *Election To Have a Tax Year Other Than a Required Tax Year,* with the Internal Revenue Service Center where the partnership will file its tax return. Form 8716 must be filed by the earlier of:

- The due date (not including extensions) of the income tax return for the tax year resulting from the Section 444 election, or
- The 15th day of the 6th month of the tax year for which the election will be effective. For this purpose, count the month in which the tax year begins, even if it begins after the first day of that month. [Reg. § 1.444-3T(b)]

Attach a copy of Form 8716 to the partnership's tax return for the first tax year for which the election is made.

Required payment for partnership. A partnership must make a required payment for any tax year if the required payment for an applicable election year (or any preceding tax year) is more than $500. [Temp. Reg. § 1.7519-1T(a)] This payment represents the value of the tax deferral the owners receive by using a tax year different from the required tax year.

Form 8752, Required Payment or Refund Under Section 7519, must be filed each year the Section 444 election is in effect, even if no payment is due. If the required payment is more than $500 (or the required payment for any prior year was more than $500), the payment must be made when Form 8752 is filed. If the required payment is $500 or less and no payment was required in a prior year, Form 8752 must be filed showing a zero amount.

Computing Partnership's Income

Q 2:13 How is partnership income taxed?

A partnership does not pay tax on its income; its partners do. However, the partnership must compute its "taxable income" to determine the amount that is passed through and reported on each partner's tax return. [IRC § § 701, 703]

Q 2:14 How does a partnership compute its taxable income that is passed through to partners?

The partnership generally computes its income in the same way that an individual does. Certain deductions, however, are not allowed, and certain items must be separately stated on the partnership return and claimed as separate items on the partners' returns.

After the separately stated items are segregated, the partnership computes its taxable income or loss based on the items that do not have to be separately stated.

Items not deductible. In computing its taxable income, a partnership cannot claim a deduction for:

- Personal exemptions;
- Foreign taxes;
- Net operating losses;
- Charitable contributions;
- Other itemized expenses allowed individuals; and
- Depletion for oil and gas wells.

[IRC § 703(a)]

Separately stated items. These include:

- Ordinary income or loss from trade or business activities;
- Net income or loss from rental real estate activities;
- Net income or loss from other rental activities;
- Gains and losses from sales or exchanges of capital assets;
- Gains and losses from sales or exchanges of property described in IRC Section 1231 (relating to certain property used in a trade or business and involuntary conversions);
- Charitable contributions;
- Dividends (passed through to corporate partners) that qualify for the dividends-received deduction;
- Taxes paid or accrued to foreign countries and U.S. possessions;
- Other items of income, gain, loss, deduction, or credit, as provided by regulations. Examples include nonbusiness expenses, intangible drilling and development costs, and soil and water conservation expenses.

[IRC § § 703(a)(1), 702(a)]

Tax elections. In computing taxable income, the Code sometimes gives tax-payers a choice about how a particular item is to be handled. In the case of a partnership, it is the partnership—and not the partners—that makes most of these choices. For example, the partnership can make elections regarding:

- Accounting method;
- Depreciation method;
- Method of accounting for specific items, such as depletion or installment sales;
- Nonrecognition of gain on involuntary conversions of property; and
- Amortization of certain organization fees and business start-up costs of the partnership.

[Reg. § 1.703-1(b)]

Each partner, however, can choose how to treat the partner's share of foreign and U.S. possessions taxes, certain mining exploration expenses, and income from cancellation of debt. [IRC § 703(b)]

Q 2:15 Can a partnership deduct organization expenses and syndication fees?

Generally speaking, neither the partnership nor any partner can deduct, as a current expense, amounts paid or incurred to organize a partnership or expenses connected with promoting and selling a partnership interest. [IRC § 709(a)] However, a partnership may affirmatively elect to deduct/amortize certain organizational expenses.[IRC § 709(b)]

A partnership can claim a current deduction for the lesser of:

1. The amount of the qualifying organization expenses, or

2. $5,000, reduced by the amount of organization expenses in excess of $50,000. [IRC § 709(b)(1)(A)]

For example, If a partnership incurs $4,000 of qualifying organizational expenses, it can elect to deduct $4,000. If it incurs $40,000 of organization expenses, it can elect to deduct $5,000. If it incurs $54,000 of organization expenses, it can elect to deduct $1,000.

If the election is made and the organization expenses exceed the allowable deduction, the excess is amortizable ratably over the 180-month period beginning with the month in which the partnership begins business. [IRC § 709(b)(1)(B)]

If the partnership elects to deduct/amortize these expenses and the partnership is liquidated before the end of the amortization period, the remaining balance in this account is deductible as a loss under IRC Section 165. [IRC § 709(b)(2)]

The partnership makes the election to deduct/amortize organization expenses by attaching a statement to the partnership's return for the tax year in which the partnership begins its business. The statement must include the following information:

- A description of each organization expense incurred (whether or not paid);
- The amount of each expense;
- The date each expense was incurred; and
- The month in which the partnership began its business.

[Reg. § 1.709-1]

Expenses of less than $10 need not be separately listed, provided the total amount is listed with the dates on which the first and last of the expenses were incurred. A cash basis partnership must also indicate the amount paid before the end of the year for each expense.

The up-to-$5,000 deduction and 180-month amortization applies to expenses that are:

1. Incident to the creation of the partnership;

2. Chargeable to a capital account; and

3. The type that would be amortized if they were incurred in the creation of a partnership having a fixed life.

[IRC § 709(b)(2)]

To satisfy (1), an expense must be incurred during the period beginning at a point that is a reasonable time before the partnership begins business and ending with the date for filing the partnership return (not including extensions) for the tax year in which the partnership begins business. In addition, the expense must be for creating the partnership and not for starting or operating the partnership trade or business. To satisfy (3), the expense must be for a type of item normally expected to benefit the partnership throughout its entire life. [Reg. § 1.709-2]

Organization expenses that can be amortized include the following:

- Legal fees for services incident to the organization of the partnership, such as negotiation and preparation of a partnership agreement;
- Accounting fees for services incident to the organization of the partnership; and
- Filing fees.

[Reg. § 1.709-2(a)]

Expenses that cannot be amortized (regardless of how the partnership characterizes them) include expenses connected with the following actions:

- Acquiring assets for the partnership or transferring assets to the partnership;
- Admitting or removing partners other than at the time the partnership is first organized;
- Making a contract relating to the operation of the partnership trade or business (even if the contract is between the partnership and one of its members); and
- Syndicating the partnership. Syndication expenses, such as commissions, professional fees, and printing costs connected with the issuing and marketing of interests in the partnership, are capitalized. They can never be deducted by the partnership, even if the syndication is unsuccessful.

[Reg. § 1.709-2(b)]

Computing Partner's Income

Q 2:16 How is each partner's share of the partnership income or loss figured?

A partner's income or loss from a partnership equals the partner's "distributive share" of partnership items (both the partnership's separately stated items and its non-separately stated income or loss) for the partnership tax year that ends with or within the partner's tax year. These items are reported to the partner on Schedule K-1 (Form 1065).

Q 2:17 How is each partner's distributive share of partnership items computed?

Generally, the partnership agreement states how each item of income, gain, loss, deduction, or credit will be allocated among the partners. However, the IRS will disregard stated allocations if they do not have "substantial economic effect." If the partnership agreement does not provide for an allocation—or an allocation does not have substantial economic effect—partnership items generally will be allocated according to each partner's interest in the partnership. [IRC § 704; Reg. § 1.704-(1)(b)]

Q 2:18 When is an allocation of partnership items considered to have a "substantial economic effect"?

An allocation will be treated as having a substantial economic effect if it meets both of the following tests:

- There is a reasonable possibility that the allocation will substantially affect the dollar amount of the partners' shares of partnership income or loss independently of tax consequences.

- The partner to whom the allocation is made actually receives the economic benefit or bears the economic burden corresponding to that allocation.

[Reg. § 1.704-1(b)(2)]

Q 2:19 When an allocation has to be based on a partner's "interest" in the partnership, how is that interest determined?

The partner's interest is determined by taking into account all of the following items:

- The partners' relative contributions to the partnership;

- The interests of all partners in economic profits and losses (if different from interests in taxable income or loss) and in cash flow and other nonliquidating distributions; and

- The rights of the partners to distributions of capital upon liquidation.

[Reg § 1.704-1(b)(3)]

> **Example 2-3:** Bill and Bob contribute $75,000 and $25,000, respectively, in forming a general partnership. The partnership agreement provides that all income, gain, loss, and deduction will be allocated 50-50 between Bill and Bob, but that all partnership distributions will, regardless of capital account balances, be made 75 percent to Bill and 25 percent to Bob. Following the liquidation of the partnership, neither partner is required to restore the deficit balance in his capital account to the partnership for distribution to partners with positive capital account balances. The allocations in the partnership agreement do not have economic effect. Since contributions were made in a 75/25 ratio and the partnership agreement indicates that all

economic profits and losses of the partnership are to be shared in a 75/25 ratio, partnership income, gain, loss, and deduction will be reallocated 75 percent to Bill and 25 percent to Bob.

A change in a partner's interest during the partnership's tax year requires the partner's distributive share of partnership items to be determined by taking into account his or her varying interests in the partnership during the tax year. Partnership items are allocated to the partner only for the portion of the year in which he or she is a member of the partnership. [IRC § 706(d)]

This rule applies to a partner who sells or exchanges part of an interest in a partnership, or whose interest is reduced or increased (whether by entry of a new partner, partial liquidation of a partner's interest, gift, additional contributions, or otherwise).

Q 2:20 How does a partner report his or her distributive share of partnership items?

A partner must report his or her distributive share of partnership items on his or her tax return, whether or not the items are actually distributed. These items are reported to the partner on Schedule K-1 (Form 1065).

The character of each item of income, gain, loss, deduction, or credit included in a partner's distributive share is determined as if the partner realized the item directly from the same source as the partnership or incurred the item in the same manner as the partnership. [IRC § 702(a)] For example, a partner's distributive share of gain from the sale of partnership depreciable property used in the trade or business of the partnership is treated as gain from the sale of depreciable property the partner used in a trade or business.

Generally, partners must treat partnership items the same way on their individual tax returns as they are treated on the partnership return. If a partner treats an item differently on his or her individual return, the IRS can immediately assess and collect any tax and penalties that result from adjusting the item to make it consistent with the partnership return. [IRC § 6222(c)]

Q 2:21 When a deduction or exclusion is subject to a limit, where is the limit applied—at the partnership level or at the partner level?

It may apply at both levels. The general rule is that, when an exclusion or deduction is subject to a limit, a partner must combine any separate exclusions or deductions on his or her income tax return with the distributive share of partnership exclusions or deductions before applying the limit. [Reg. § 1.702-1(a)(8)] However, depending on the situation, a limit on an exclusion or deduction may be applied at the partnership level before the partner's distributive share is computed. For example, consider the case of the Section 179 (expensing) deduction. A partnership can elect to deduct all or part of the cost of certain depreciable assets under IRC Section 179. The deduction is passed through to the partners as a separately stated item.

The Section 179 deduction is subject to certain limits. The deduction (1) cannot exceed a dollar limit ($125,000 for 2007, $128,000 for 2008), (2) is phased out if the amount invested in eligible assets placed in service during the year exceeds a threshold ($500,000 for 2007, $510,000 for 2008), and (3) cannot exceed taxable income for the year. These limits apply to the partnership and to each partner. [IRC § 179(d)(8)] The partnership determines its Section 179 deduction subject to the limits. It then allocates the deduction among its partners.

Each partner adds the amount allocated from the partnership (shown on Schedule K-1) to his or her other non-partnership Section 179 costs and then applies the maximum dollar limit to this total. To determine if a partner has exceeded the investment limit, the partner does not include any of the cost of Section 179 property placed in service by the partnership. After the maximum dollar limit and the investment limit are applied, the remaining cost of the partnership and non-partnership Section 179 property is subject to the taxable income limit.

> **Example 2-4:** In 2007, ABC Partnership placed in service Section 179 property with a total cost of $511,000. The partnership must reduce its dollar limit by $11,000 ($511,000 - $500,000). Its maximum Section 179 deduction is $114,000 for 2007 ($125,000 - $11,000), and it elects to expense that amount. Because the partnership's taxable income from the active conduct of all its trades or businesses for the year was $150,000, it can deduct the full $114,000. It allocates $38,000 of its Section 179 deduction and $50,000 of its taxable income to Bill Dean, one of its partners.

In addition to being a partner in ABC Partnership, Dean is also a partner in the XYZ Partnership, which allocated to him a $24,000 Section 179 deduction and $36,000 taxable income from the active conduct of its business. Dean also conducts a business as a sole proprietor and, in 2007, placed in service in that business Section 179 property costing $30,000. He had a net loss of $6,000 from that business for the year.

Because Dean does not have to include partnership costs to figure any reduction in his dollar limit, his total Section 179 costs for the year are not more than $500,000, and his dollar limit is not reduced. His maximum expensing deduction is $125,000. He elects to expense all of the $62,000 in Section 179 deductions allocated from the partnerships, plus $30,000 of his sole proprietorship's Section 179 costs. However, his deduction is limited to his business taxable income of $80,000 ($50,000 from ABC Partnership, plus $36,000 from XYZ Partnership, minus $6,000 loss from his sole proprietorship).

Dean carries over $12,000 ($92,000 - $80,000) of the elected Section 179 costs to 2008.

Q 2:22 Is partnership income subject to the self-employment tax?

Yes. Partners must generally include their distributive share of partnership income or loss in their net earnings from self-employment. [IRC § 1402(a); Reg. § 1.1402(a)-1(a)2] "Guaranteed payments" (see below) should also be included.

Q 2:22

In the case of limited partners, net earnings from self-employment include guaranteed payments, such as salary and professional fees received for services performed during the year. They do not include the distributive share of partnership income (or loss). [IRC § 1402(a)(13)]

In the case of a retired partner, retirement income received from the partnership under a written plan is not subject to self-employment tax if all the following apply:

- The partner receives lifelong periodic payments;
- The partner's share of the partnership capital was fully paid to him or her;
- The partner did not perform any services for the partnership during the year; and
- The partner is owed nothing but the retirement payments by the partnership.

[IRC § 1402(a)(10)]

Partnership Losses

Q 2:23 Is there any limitation on a partner's distributive share of a partnership's loss?

Yes. A partner's distributive share of partnership loss is allowed only to the extent of the adjusted basis of the partner's partnership interest. [IRC § 704(d)]

The adjusted basis of the partner's interest in the partnership is figured at the end of the partnership's tax year in which the loss occurred, before taking the loss into account. [IRC § 704(d)](To learn how to determine a partner's basis, see Q 2:32, below.) Any loss that exceeds the partner's adjusted basis is not deductible for that year. However, any loss not allowed for this reason will be allowed as a deduction (up to the partner's basis) at the end of any succeeding year in which the partner increases his or her basis to more than zero. [Reg. § 1.704-1(d)(4)]

> **Example 2-5:** Mike and Joe are equal partners in a partnership. Mike files his individual return on a calendar year basis. The partnership return is also filed on a calendar year basis. The partnership incurred a $10,000 loss last year, and Mike's distributive share of the loss is $5,000. The adjusted basis of his partnership interest before considering his share of last year's loss was $2,000. Joe could claim only $2,000 of the loss on last year's individual return. The adjusted basis of his interest at the end of last year was then reduced to zero.

The partnership showed an $8,000 profit for this year. Mike's $4,000 share of the profit increases the adjusted basis of his interest by $4,000 (not taking into account the $3,000 excess loss he could not deduct last year). His return for this year will show his $4,000 distributive share of this year's profits and the $3,000 loss not allowable last year. The adjusted basis of his partnership interest at the end of this year is $1,000.

Q 2:24 Are there any other limits on partnership losses?

Yes. For example, losses from an activity "not engaged in for profit" are limited (see Chapter 1). Other restrictions on losses involve the "at risk" rules and the "passive activity" rules.

At-risk rules. These rules apply to most trade or business activities, including activities conducted through a partnership. The at-risk rules limit a partner's deductible loss to the amounts for which that partner is considered at risk in the activity. [IRC § 465]

A partner is considered at risk for all of the following amounts:

- The money and adjusted basis of any property he or she contributed to the activity.

- The partner's share of net income retained by the partnership.

- Certain amounts borrowed by the partnership for use in the activity if the partner is personally liable for repayment or the amounts borrowed are secured by the partner's property (other than property used in the activity).

A partner is not considered at risk for amounts protected against loss through guarantees, stop-loss agreements, or similar arrangements. Nor is the partner at risk for amounts borrowed if the lender has an interest in the activity (other than as a creditor) or is related to a person (other than the partner) having such an interest.

Passive activity rules. Generally, the Code limits the amount a partner can deduct for passive activity losses and credits. [IRC § 469]The passive activity limits do not apply to the partnership. Instead, they apply to each partner's share of income, loss, or credit from passive activities. Because the treatment of each partner's share of partnership income, loss, or credit depends on the nature of the activity that generated it, the partnership must report income, loss, and credits separately for each activity.

Generally, passive activities include a trade or business activity in which the partner does not materially participate. Passive activities also include rental activities, regardless of the partner's participation. However, a rental real estate activity in which the partner materially participates is not considered a passive activity. The partner must also meet both of the following conditions for the tax year:

- More than half of the personal services the partner performs in any trade or business are in a real property trade or business in which the partner materially participates.

- The partner performs more than 750 hours of services in real property trades or businesses in which the partner materially participates.

[IRC § 469(c)(7)]

Limited partners are generally not considered to materially participate in trade or business activities conducted through partnerships.

Partnership Return

Q 2:25 Which partnerships are required to file a tax return?

Every partnership that engages in a trade or business or has gross income must file an information return on Form 1065 showing its income, deductions, and other required information. [IRC §6031]The partnership return must show the names and addresses of each partner and each partner's distributive share of taxable income. The return must be signed by a general partner. [IRC §6063; Instructions to Form 1065]

A partnership is not considered to engage in a trade or business, and is not required to file a Form 1065, for any tax year in which it neither receives income nor pays or incurs any expenses treated as deductions or credits for federal income tax purposes.

Q 2:26 When is Form 1065 due?

Form 1065 generally must be filed by April 15 following the close of the partnership's tax year if its accounting period is the calendar year. A fiscal year partnership generally must file its return by the 15th day of the 4th month following the close of its fiscal year. [IRC §6072]

If a partnership needs more time to file its return, it should file Form 7004, *Application for Automatic 6-Month Extension of Time to File Certain Business Income Tax, Information, and Other Returns,* by the regular due date of its Form 1065. The automatic extension is six months. The partnership must furnish copies of Schedule K-1 (Form 1065) to the partners by the date Form 1065 is required to be filed.

Contributions and Sales to Partnership

Q 2:27 Does a partner owe tax when he or she contributes property to a partnership?

Usually, neither the partner nor the partnership recognizes a gain or loss when property is contributed to the partnership in exchange for a partnership interest. [IRC §721; Reg. §1.721-1] This applies whether a partnership is being formed or is already operating. For purposes of the long-term capital gain holding period, the partnership's holding period for the property includes the partner's holding period. [IRC §1223]

Q 2:28 Does a partner owe tax when he or she contributes services to a partnership in exchange for a partnership interest?

The answer depends on the type of partnership interest the partner acquires in the exchange—is it a capital interest or a profits interest?

Capital interest. A capital interest is an interest that would give the partner a share of the proceeds if the partnership's assets were sold at fair market value and the proceeds were distributed in a complete liquidation of the partnership. This determination generally is made at the time of receipt of the partnership interest.

If a partner receives a capital interest in exchange for services, the fair market value of the interest must generally be included in the partner's gross income as compensation. This inclusion takes place in the first tax year in which the partner can transfer the interest or the interest is not subject to a substantial risk of forfeiture. [Reg. § 1.721-1(b)]

Profits interest. A profits interest is a partnership interest other than a capital interest. If a person receives a profits interest for providing services to a partnership, the receipt of such an interest is not a taxable event for the partner or the partnership. [Rev. Proc. 93-27, 1993-2 C.B. 343, *clarified by* Rev. Proc. 2001-43, 2001-34 I.R.B. 191] However, this does not apply in the following situations:

- The profits interest relates to a substantially certain and predictable stream of income from partnership assets, such as income from high-quality debt securities or a high-quality net lease.

- Within two years of receipt, the partner disposes of the profits interest.

- The profits interest is a limited partnership interest in a publicly traded partnership.

The determination under Revenue Procedure 93-27 of whether an interest granted to a service provider is a profits interest is tested at the time the interest is granted, even if, at that time, the interest is substantially nonvested. [Rev. Proc. 2001-43, 2001-34 I.R.B. 191]

Q 2:29 What are the tax consequences if a taxpayer acquires an interest in a partnership through the exercise of an option?

In a variety of situations, partnerships may issue options or convertible instruments that allow the holder to acquire by purchase or conversion an equity interest in the partnership. The IRS recently proposed tax regulations governing the issuance and exercise of partnership "noncompensatory" call options, warrants, convertible debt, and convertible preferred equity. [Prop. Reg. §§ 1.7041(b))(2)(iv)(h); 1.704(b)(2)(iv)(s); 1.704-1(b)(4)(ix), (x)] Compensatory options—those issued in connection with the performance of services—will be the subject of a separate set of forthcoming regulations.

The proposed regulations generally provide that the exercise of a noncompensatory option does not cause recognition of gain or loss to either the issuing partnership or the option holder. The issuance of a noncompensatory call option or warrant (stand-alone option) is generally an open transaction for the issuing partnership. The partnership's income or loss from the option does not become fixed and determinable until the lapse, exercise, repurchase, or other termination of the option.

Q 2:29

For the holder of the option, the purchase of the option is merely an investment in the option—a capital expenditure that is neither taxable to nor deductible by the holder. However, if the holder uses appreciated or depreciated property (property with a value greater or less than the holder's basis in the property) to acquire the stand-alone option, then the holder recognizes gain or loss under the general tax rules that apply to the purchase of other types of property.

Under IRC Section 704(b), a partner's distributive share of income, gain, loss, and so forth is determined under the partnership agreement if the allocation under the agreement has "substantial economic effect." If the allocation does not have substantial economic effect (or there is no mention of an allocation), the allocation must be made in accordance with the partner's interest in the partnership, taking into account all facts and circumstances (see Q 2:17).

The proposed regulations provide that noncompensatory options generally should not be treated as entitling the holder to a fixed right to share in partnership income until the option is exercised. However, if a noncompensatory option provides the holder with rights that are substantially similar to the rights afforded to a partner, the holder should be treated as a partner and the option should be taken into account in allocating partnership income.

Q 2:30 Is a sale of property by a partner to a partnership a taxable event?

Generally speaking, yes. When a partner sells property to a partnership, it's as if he or she were selling to a stranger. [IRC § 707(a)] Gain on the sale is treated as ordinary income (and not capital gain) if both of the following tests are met:

- More than 50 percent of the capital or profits interest in the partnership is owned by the partner, either directly or indirectly (*e.g.*, owned by spouse or child).

- The property in the hands of the partnership is not a capital asset. Property that is not a capital asset includes accounts receivable, inventory, stock-in-trade, and depreciable or real property used in a trade or business.

[IRC § 707(b)(2)]

Q 2:31 If a partner sells property to his or her partnership at a loss, is the loss deductible?

A loss cannot be deducted on the sale if the partner has a direct or indirect interest in the capital or profits of the partnership that is more than 50 percent. [IRC § 707(b)(1)]

Basis of Partner's Interest and Partnership Property

Q 2:32 How is a partner's initial basis for his or her partnership interest determined?

The initial basis of a partnership interest is the money plus the adjusted basis of any property the partner contributed. [IRC § 722] If the partner must recognize gain as a result of the contribution, this gain is included in the basis of his or her interest.

Any increase in a partner's individual liabilities because of an assumption of partnership liabilities is considered a contribution of money to the partnership by the partner.

If contributed property is subject to a debt or if a partner's liabilities are assumed by the partnership, the basis of that partner's interest is reduced (but not below zero) by the liability assumed by the other partners. This partner must reduce his or her basis because the assumption of the liability is treated as a distribution of money to that partner. [Reg. § 1.722-1]

> **Example 2-6:** John acquired a 20 percent interest in a partnership by contributing property that had an adjusted basis to him of $80,000 and a $40,000 mortgage. The partnership assumed payment of the mortgage.
>
> The basis of John's interest is:

Adjusted basis of contributed property	$80,000
Minus mortgage assumed by other partners (80% × $40,000)	$32,000
Basis of John's partnership interest	$48,000

Q 2:33 What subsequent adjustments must be made to the basis of a partner's interest?

The basis of an interest in a partnership is increased or decreased by certain items.

Increases. A partner's basis is increased by the following items:

- The partner's additional contributions to the partnership, including an increased share of or assumption of partnership liabilities.
- The partner's distributive share of taxable and nontaxable partnership income.

[IRC § 705(a)(1)]

Decreases. The partner's basis is decreased (but never below zero) by the following items:

- The money (including a decreased share of partnership liabilities or an assumption of the partner's individual liabilities by the partnership) and adjusted basis of property distributed to the partner by the partnership. [IRC § 705(a)(2)]

- The partner's distributive share of the partnership losses (including capital losses). [Reg. § 1.705-1(a)]

- The partner's distributive share of nondeductible partnership expenses that are not capital expenditures. This includes the partner's share of any Section 179 expenses, even if the partner cannot deduct the entire amount on his or her individual income tax return. [IRC § 705(a)(2)]

Q 2:34 What is the partnership's basis for property contributed to it by a partner?

The partnership's basis is generally the same as the partner's basis for the property before he or she contributed it to the partnership. [IRC § 723]

Partnership Distributions and Guaranteed Payments

Q 2:35 Is a partner taxed on a distribution from a partnership?

A distribution generally has no current tax consequences to a partner. A partnership distribution is not taken into account in determining the partner's distributive share of partnership income or loss. A partner's adjusted basis in his or her partnership interest is decreased (but not below zero) by the money and adjusted basis of property distributed to the partner.

A partner generally recognizes gain on a partnership distribution only to the extent any money (and marketable securities) included in the distribution exceeds the adjusted basis of the partner's interest in the partnership. [IRC § 731(a)] Any gain recognized is generally treated as capital gain from the sale of the partnership interest on the date of the distribution. If partnership property (other than marketable securities) is distributed to a partner, he or she generally does not recognize any gain until the sale or other disposition of the property. [Reg. § 1.731-1(a)]

> **Example 2-7:** The adjusted basis of Joan's partnership interest is $140,000. She receives a distribution of $80,000 cash and land that has an adjusted basis of $20,000 and a fair market value of $30,000. Because the cash received does not exceed the basis of her partnership interest, Joan does not recognize any gain on the distribution. Any gain on the land will be recognized when she sells or otherwise disposes of it. The distribution decreases the adjusted basis of Joan's partnership interest to $40,000 [$140,000 - ($80,000 + $20,000)].

> **Planning Point:** Losses passed through from a partnership are deductible only to the extent of a partner's adjusted basis for his or her partnership interest (see Q 2:23). So partnership distributions can limit loss deductions by reducing a partner's basis. If a partnership is expecting a loss for the current year, it may want to defer distributions when practical if the distributions would reduce the partners' loss write-offs for the year.

Q 2:35

Q 2:36 What is the partner's basis for property distributed by the partnership?

Unless there is a complete liquidation of a partner's interest, the basis of property distributed to the partner by a partnership is its adjusted basis to the partnership immediately before the distribution. However, the basis of the property to the partner cannot be more than the adjusted basis of his or her interest in the partnership reduced by any money received in the same transaction. [IRC §732(a)]

> **Example 2-8:** The adjusted basis of Beth's partnership interest is $30,000. She receives a distribution of $4,000 in cash and property that has an adjusted basis of $20,000 to the partnership. Beth's basis for the property is $20,000.

> **Example 2-9:** The adjusted basis of Mike's partnership interest is $10,000. He receives a distribution of $4,000 in cash and property that has an adjusted basis to the partnership of $8,000. His basis for the distributed property is limited to $6,000 ($10,000 - $4,000, the cash Mike receives).

Q 2:37 What are "guaranteed payments" to a partner, and what are the tax consequences when a partnership makes guaranteed payments?

Guaranteed payments are those made by a partnership to a partner that are determined without regard to the partnership's income. A partnership treats guaranteed payments for services, or for the use of capital, as if they were made to someone who is not a partner. [IRC §707(c)] Guaranteed payments are not subject to income tax withholding.

The partnership generally deducts guaranteed payments as a business expense. The individual partner reports guaranteed payments on Schedule E (Form 1040) as ordinary income, along with his or her distributive share of the partnership's other ordinary income.

> **Example 2-10:** Under the ABC partnership agreement, Claire is entitled to a fixed annual payment of $100,000 for services, without regard to the income of the partnership. Her distributive share is 10 percent. After deducting the guaranteed payment, the partnership has $500,000 ordinary income. Claire must include $150,000 as ordinary income ($100,000 guaranteed payment plus $50,000 distributive share).

Guaranteed payments made to partners for organizing the partnership or syndicating interests in the partnership are capital expenses and are not deductible by the partnership. [IRC §709(a)]However, these payments must be included in the partners' individual income tax returns.

Sale of a Partnership Interest

Q 2:38 If a partner sells his or her partnership interest, how is gain or loss computed?

Gain or loss is the difference between the amount realized on the sale and the adjusted basis of the partner's interest in the partnership. [IRC §741; Reg. §1.741-1(a)]If the selling partner is relieved of any partnership liabilities, that partner must include the liability relief as part of the amount realized for his or her interest.

> **Example 2-11:** Fred became a limited partner in the ABC Partnership by contributing $10,000 in cash upon the formation of the partnership. The adjusted basis of his partnership interest at the end of the current year is $20,000, which includes his $15,000 share of partnership liabilities. Fred sells his interest in the partnership for $10,000 in cash. He had been paid his share of the partnership income for the tax year. Fred realizes $25,000 from the sale of his partnership interest ($10,000 cash payment + $15,000 liability relief). He reports $5,000 gain ($25,000 realized less $20,000 basis).

> **Example 2-12:** The facts are the same as in Example 2-11, except that Fred withdraws from the partnership when the adjusted basis of his interest in the partnership is zero. He is considered to have received a distribution of $15,000, his relief from liability. He reports a gain of $15,000.

Q 2:39 Is the gain or loss on the sale of a partnership interest capital gain (loss) or ordinary income (loss)?

The sale or exchange of a partner's interest in a partnership usually results in capital gain or loss. [IRC §741]However, there is an important exception. The gain or loss on the sale is ordinary to the extent that the amount realized represents the selling partner's share of the partnership's unrealized receivables or inventory items. [IRC §751]

Q 2:40 What are "unrealized receivables"?

Unrealized receivables include any rights to payment not already included in income for the following items:

- Goods delivered or to be delivered to the extent the payment would be treated as received for property other than a capital asset.

- Services rendered or to be rendered.

[IRC §751; Reg. §1.751-1(c)]

These rights must have arisen under a contract or agreement that existed at the time of sale or distribution, even though the partnership may not be able to enforce payment until a later date. For example, unrealized receivables include accounts receivable of a cash method partnership and rights to payment for work or goods begun but incomplete at the time of the sale or distribution of the partner's share.

Q 2:41 Does the sale of a partnership interest affect the partnership's basis for its assets?

Under IRC § 743, t the transfer of a partnership interest will generally not affect the basis of partnership assets. However, provision is made in IRC § 754 whereby the partnership may elect to adjust the basis of partnership assets to reflect the difference between the transferee's basis for the partnership interest and his proportionate share of the adjusted basis of all partnership property. This applies to a "transfer of an interest in a partnership by sale or exchange or on the death of a partner." Thus, it would appear to apply where a partner sells his interest to the remaining partners as well as where he sells it to an outsider.

The amount of the increase or decrease is an adjustment affecting the transferee partner only.

A partner's proportionate share of the adjusted basis of partnership property must be determined in accordance with his or her interest in partnership capital. Thus, if a partner's interest in such capital is one-third, the proportionate share of the adjusted basis of partnership property will, in general, be one-third of such basis.

The regulations make it clear that a transferee's share of the adjusted basis to the partnership of partnership property is equal to the sum of the transferee's interest as a partner in the partnership's previously taxed capital, plus the transferee's share of partnership liabilities. [Reg. § 1.743-1(d)(1)]A transferee's interest in the partnership's previously taxed capital is determined by assuming that the partnership sells all of its assets for fair market value in a hypothetical, fully taxable transaction which follows the transfer of the partnership interest. The transferee's share is then equal to the amount of cash the transferee would receive upon a liquidation of the partnership following the hypothetical sale increased by the amount of tax loss allocable to the transferee upon the hypothetical sale and decreased by the tax gain allocable to the transferee upon the hypothetical sale. [Reg. § 1.743-1(d))]

The adjustment is an increase in basis by the excess of a transferee's basis in the partnership interest over his or her share of the adjusted basis of the property to the partnership, or a decrease in basis of the assets by the excess of the transferee partner's proportionate share of the partnership's basis of its assets over the transferee's basis in the partnership interest.

Termination of a Partnership

Q 2:42 When is a partnership treated as terminated for tax purposes?

A partnership terminates when one of the following events takes place:

1. All its operations are discontinued and no part of any business, financial operation, or venture is continued by any of its partners in a partnership.

2. At least 50 percent of the total interest in partnership capital and profits is sold or exchanged within a 12-month period, including a sale or exchange to another partner.

[IRC § 708(b)]

In the case of (1), the date of termination is the date the partnership completes the winding up of its affairs. In the case of (2), the date of termination is the date of the sale or exchange of a partnership interest that, by itself or together with other sales or exchanges in the preceding 12 months, transfers an interest of 50 percent or more.

Limited Liability Company

Q 2:43 What's a limited liability company?

Limited liability companies (LLCs) are a hybrid of partnerships and corporations. The major advantage of LLCs over partnerships is that, like corporations, LLCs limit their owners' liability. Limited partnerships provide liability protection to their limited partners but not to their general partners. LLCs also differ from limited partnerships in that, unlike limited partners, LLC owners may fully participate in governing and managing the entity.

The major advantage of LLCs over corporations is that LLCs need not be subject to an entity level tax but may elect pass-through tax treatment like partnerships (see below).

The laws governing LLCs vary from state to state. Like corporations, LLCs are created by filing articles of organization with the appropriate state agency. Some states allow an LLC to have a single owner, while others require an LLC to have two or more owners, like partnerships.

Ownership interests need not be equal. Each owner has the same limited liability afforded to shareholders of a corporation—no personal liability for corporate debts beyond the owner's investment in the enterprise.

Q 2:44 How are LLCs taxed?

Under the IRS's "check-the-box" regulations, an LLC can choose how it wants to be treated for tax purposes. The regulations provide that LLCs and other unincorporated business organizations are generally considered "eligible entities." [Reg. § 301.7701-2(c)]

An eligible entity with two or more owners may elect treatment either as an association (which is treated as a corporation) or as a partnership. An eligible entity with a single owner may elect to be treated as an association or as a "disregarded entity." Disregarded entities are ignored for tax purposes separate and apart from their owners. [Reg. § 301.7701-3(a)]

Default rules apply if an election is not made. In general, by default, a domestic LLC with two or more owners is treated as a partnership and a domestic LLC with one owner is disregarded as a separate entity. [Reg. § 301.7701-3(b)(1)] Businesses that want to elect a classification other than the default must file IRS Form 8832, *Entity Classification*.

Q 2:45 Are owners of an LLC that is taxed as a partnership personally liable for the LLC's federal tax obligations?

An LLC member is generally not liable under state law for the LLC's debts. Thus, the IRS cannot collect federal tax liabilities, such as employment taxes, from the LLC members. [Rev. Rul. 2004-41, 2004-18 I.R.B. 845]

However, there may be special circumstances such as a fraudulent transfer of assets from the LLC to its members which might expose the members to liability [*Scott v. Comm'r*, 236 F 3d 1239 (10th Cir. 2001)]. Also, depending on the facts of a particular case, an LLC may be liable for the 100-percent "responsible person" penalty under IRC Sec. 6672 (see Chapter 14).

Q 2:46 How does a "disregarded" LLC handle its employment taxes?

Currently, the IRS will accept report and payment of employment taxes in one of two ways:

1. The owner can calculate, report, and pay all employment tax obligations as if he or she employed the employees directly; or
2. The owner can calculate, report, and pay the employment tax obligations of each disregarded entity separately under its own name and taxpayer identification number.

However, the owner will still retain ultimate liability for the employment taxes. [Notice 99-6, 1999-1 C.B. 321] However, starting in 2009, disregarded LLCs will not longer have a choice. Under regulations recently finalized by the IRS, a disregarded entity must be treated as a separate entity responsible for employment tax liabilities beginning January 1, 2009. [Reg. 301.7701-2(c)(2)(iv)]

Chapter 3

C Corporations

For tax purposes, there are two types of corporations: C and S. This chapter will discuss the C variety; S corporations are covered in Chapter 4. However, in all legal aspects other than taxes, a C corporation is identical with an S corporation.

C corporations are taxable entities separate and apart from their owners. A corporation must report its income on its own tax return, Form 1120, and pay its own tax on its earnings. When the earnings are distributed to the owners, the earnings are taxed again at the individual level. There are special tax rules that apply only to corporations, and corporations may be subject to additional taxes, such as the accumulated earnings tax, over and above its regular income tax.

C Corporation Basics

Q 3:1 What is a corporation?

A corporation, chartered by the state in which it is headquartered, is an organization considered by law to be a unique entity, separate and apart from those who own it. A corporation can be taxed; it can be sued; it can enter into contractual agreements. The owners of a corporation are its shareholders. To form a corporation, prospective shareholders transfer money, property, or both, for the corporation's capital stock. The shareholders elect a board of directors to oversee the major policies and decisions. The corporation has a life of its own and does not dissolve when ownership changes.

Q 3:2 What are the advantages and drawbacks of using a corporation to conduct business?

The advantages of adopting the corporate form of business include:

- Shareholders have limited liability for the corporation's debts or judgments against the corporation.

- Generally, shareholders can only be held accountable for their investment in stock of the company. (Note, however, that officers can be held personally liable for their actions, such as the failure to withhold and pay employment taxes.)

- Corporations can raise additional funds through the sale of stock.

- Unlike a proprietorship or a partnership, a corporation has a perpetual life. Death or withdrawal of a shareholder does not terminate the corporation. Stock in the corporation can be sold or passed on to the owner's heirs.

Disadvantages of the corporate form include:

- The process of incorporation requires more time and money than other forms of organization.

- Corporations are monitored by federal, state, and some local agencies, and as a result may have more paperwork to comply with regulations.

- Incorporating may result in higher overall taxes. Dividends paid to shareholders by a C corporation are not deductible from business income; thus this income can be taxed twice. However, the Jobs and Growth Tax Relief Reconciliation Act of 2003 [P.L. 108-27 (May 28, 2003)] has reduced the impact of this double tax by reducing the tax paid on the dividends at the shareholder level (see Q 3.22).

Q 3:3 What businesses are taxed as corporations?

The following businesses are taxed as corporations:

- A business formed under a federal or state law that refers to it as a corporation, body corporate, or body politic;

- An association;

- A business formed under a state law that refers to it as a joint stock company or joint stock association;

- An insurance company;

- Certain banks;

- A business wholly owned by a state or local government;

- A business specifically required to be taxed as a corporation by the Internal Revenue Code (for example, certain publicly traded partnerships);

- Certain foreign businesses; and

- Any other business that elects to be taxed as a corporation by filing Form 8832.

Setting Up a Corporation

Q 3:4 Does a C corporation owe tax when it receives capital contributions from shareholders in exchange for stock?

No. A C corporation recognizes no gain or loss when it exchanges its stock for cash or property. [IRC § 1032(a)]The no-recognition rule applies regardless of whether the issue or subscription price is above or below the stock's par value. Likewise, it makes no difference whether the stock is original issue or treasury stock.

Q 3:5 If a C corporation receives property as a capital contribution, what is the corporation's basis for the property?

The basis of property contributed to capital by a shareholder is generally the same as the basis the shareholder had in the property before the contribution. [IRC § 362(a)(1)]However, the corporation's basis is increased by any gain recognized by the shareholder on the contribution (see below).

The basis of property contributed to capital by a person other than a shareholder is zero. [IRC § 362(c)(1)]If a corporation receives a cash contribution from a person other than a shareholder, the corporation must reduce the basis of any property acquired with the contribution during the 12-month period beginning on the day it received the contribution by the amount of the contribution. [IRC § 362(c)(2)] If the amount contributed is more than the cost of the property acquired, then the basis of other property held by the corporation must be reduced. The basis reduction for the other properties is performed in the following order:

1. Depreciable property;

2. Amortizable property;

3. Property subject to cost depletion but not to percentage depletion; and

4. All other remaining properties.

The basis of property in each category is reduced to zero before going to the next category. [Reg. § 1.362-2(b)]

Q 3:6 Are shareholders subject to tax when they make capital contributions to a C corporation?

There is no tax if only cash is contributed. Also there is usually no tax if shareholders transfer property (or money and property) to a corporation solely in exchange for stock in that corporation and immediately thereafter they are in control of the corporation. [IRC § 351(a)] This latter rule applies both to individuals and to groups who transfer property to a corporation. It also applies whether the corporation is being formed or is already operating.

Q 3:7 What does "in control" mean for purposes of avoiding tax on contributions of property?

It means that the individual or group transferring the property must own, immediately after the exchange, at least 80 percent of the total combined voting power of all classes of stock entitled to vote and at least 80 percent of the outstanding shares of each class of nonvoting stock of the corporation. [IRC § 368(c)]

> **Example 3-1:** Karen Brown and Bill Jones buy property for $100,000. They both organize a corporation when the property has a fair market value of $300,000. Brown and Jones transfer the property to the corporation for all its authorized capital stock, which has a par value of $300,000. No gain is recognized by Brown, Jones, or the corporation.

> **Example 3-2:** Same facts as before, except that the stock Brown and Jones receive represents only 75 percent of each class of stock of the corporation. The other 25 percent was already issued to someone else. In this situation, Brown and Jones must recognize a taxable gain of $200,000 on the transaction.

Q 3:8 What happens if a shareholder receives something other than stock in exchange for a capital contribution?

If a shareholder receives money or property other than stock—"boot"—in an otherwise tax-free exchange, the shareholder may have to recognize gain. [IRC § 351(b)] The shareholder's gain on the exchange is recognized to the extent of the money plus the fair market value of the other property received. No loss to the shareholder is recognized, even if boot is received.

Nonqualified preferred stock. For this purpose, nonqualified preferred stock received by the shareholder is treated as boot. [IRC § 351(g)]Generally, this is preferred stock with any of the following features:

- The holder has the right to require the issuer to redeem or buy the stock;
- The issuer is required to redeem or buy the stock;
- The issuer has the right to redeem the stock and, on the issue date, it is more likely than not the right will be exercised; or

- The dividend rate on the stock varies with reference to interest rates, commodity prices, or similar indices.

Liabilities. If the corporation assumes a shareholder's liabilities on property transferred to the corporation, the relief from the liability is generally not treated as boot. There are two exceptions to this treatment.

- If the liabilities the corporation assumes exceed the shareholder's adjusted basis in the property transferred, gain is recognized to the extent of the excess. However, if the liabilities assumed give rise to a deduction when paid, such as a trade accounts payable or interest, no gain is recognized.

- If there is no good business reason for the corporation to assume the liabilities, or if the main purpose of the exchange is tax avoidance, the assumption is treated as if the shareholder received cash in the amount of the liabilities.

[IRC § 357(d)]

Example 3-3: Jane Blair transfers property to a corporation for stock. Immediately after the transfer she controls the corporation. She also receives $10,000 cash in the exchange. Blair's adjusted basis in the transferred property is $20,000. The stock she receives has a fair market value of $16,000. The corporation also assumes a $5,000 mortgage on the transferred property for which Blair was personally liable. Gain is realized as follows:

Fair market value of the stock received:	$16,000
Cash received	$10,000
Liability assumed by corporation	$ 5,000
Total received	$31,000
Minus: Adjusted basis of property	$20,000
Realized gain	$11,000

The liability assumed is not treated as money or other property. The recognized gain is limited to $10,000, the amount of cash received.

Q 3:9 What is the shareholder's basis for stock received in exchange for a capital contribution?

The basis of the stock a shareholder receives generally equals the sum of the cash and the adjusted basis of the property he or she transferred to the corporation. [IRC § 358(a)(1)]This amount is increased by any gain recognized on the exchange and decreased by any cash and the fair market value of any other property received by the shareholder. Also, the basis is decreased by the amount of any liability the corporation assumed from the shareholder, unless payment of the liability gives rise to a deduction when paid. The basis of any property other than stock received is its fair market value on the date of the exchange.

Q 3:10 Are there any special restrictions on the choice of a tax year for a C corporation?

No, the choice of tax years is generally the same as that for other taxable entities (see Chapter 5). However, there are special rules that apply to "personal service" corporations.

A personal service corporation must use a calendar tax year unless it can establish a business purpose for a different period or it makes an election under Internal Revenue Code (IRC or the Code) Section 444. [IRC § 441(i)(1)]

A corporation is a personal service corporation if all the following conditions are met:

- The corporation is a C corporation;
- The corporation's principal activity is the performance of personal services;
- Employee-owners of the corporation perform a substantial part of the services; and
- Employee-owners own more than 10 percent of the corporation's stock.

[IRC § 269A]

The principal activity of a corporation is considered to be the performance of personal services if the corporation's compensation costs for personal service activities are more than 50 percent of its total compensation costs. [Reg. § 1.441-4T(f)]

Any activity that involves the performance of services in the fields of health, veterinary services, law, engineering, architecture, accounting, actuarial science, performing arts, or certain consulting services is considered the performance of personal services. [IRC § 448(d)(2)]

According to a recent decision of the Tax Court, a corporation providing tax preparation and bookkeeping services should be treated as a personal service corporation. The court said that a corporation may be in the "field of accounting" even though its employees are not certified public accountants. "Historically, tax return preparation and bookkeeping services are regarded as within the field of accounting" The court also pointed to the fact that tax return preparation meets a legal dictionary definition of accounting since it is an extraction of information relating to financial transactions, analysis of that information, and finally summarizing/reporting of the data. [*Rainbow Tax Service Inc.*, 128 T.C. No. 5]

Section 444 election. A personal service corporation can elect under IRC Section 444 to use a tax year other than its required tax year. Certain restrictions apply to the election.

To make the election, the corporation files Form 8716 with the Internal Revenue Service Center where the corporation will file its tax return. A personal service corporation with a Section 444 election in effect must distribute certain amounts to employee-owners by December 31 each year. If it fails to make these distributions, it may be required to defer certain deductions for amounts paid to owner-employees. The amount deferred is treated as paid or incurred in the following tax year. [IRC §280H] For information on the minimum distribution, see the instructions for Part I of Schedule H (Form 1120), *Section 280H Limitations for a Personal Service Corporation (PSC)*.

Figuring the Corporate Tax

Q 3:11 How is a C corporation taxed?

Corporations must pay tax on their taxable income. [IRC §11] The tax is computed under a graduated tax rate system as follows:

If taxable income is over—	But not over—	The tax is—	Of the amount over—
$0	$50,000	15%	$0
$50,000	$75,000	$7,500 + 25%	$50,000
$75,000	$100,000	$13,750 + 34%	$75,000
$100,000	$335,000	$22,250 +39%	$100,000
$335,000	$10,000,000	$113,800 + 34%	$335,000
$10,000,000	$15,000,000	$3,400,000 + 35%	$10,000,000
$15,000,000	$18,333,333	$5,150,000 + 38%	$15,000,000
$18,333,333		35%	$0

A "qualified personal service corporation" is taxed at a flat rate of 35 percent on taxable income. [IRC §11(b)(2)] A corporation is a qualified personal service corporation if it meets *both* of the following tests.

1. Substantially all of the corporation's activities involve the performance of personal services (as defined earlier in Q 3:10).

2. At least 95 percent of the corporation's stock, by value, is owned, directly or indirectly, by any of the following:

   a. Employees performing the personal services;

   b. Retired employees who had performed the personal services;

   c. Any estate of the employee or retiree described above; or

   d. Any person who acquired the stock of the corporation as a result of the death of an employee or retiree (but only for the two-year period beginning on the date of the employee's or retiree's death).

In addition to its regular income tax, a corporation may be subject to special taxes, such as the corporate alternative minimum tax, [IRC §55(e)] the accumulated earnings tax, [IRC §532] and the personal holding company tax [IRC §541](see below).

Q 3:12 How is a C corporation's taxable income computed?

In computing its taxable income, a corporation may generally deduct ordinary and necessary expenses paid or incurred in carrying on its trade or business. In addition, a corporation is entitled to special deductions for dividends received from other corporations and for organizational and start-up expenditures. [IRC § § 243(a)(1) and 248]

Q 3:13 What is the dividends-received deduction?

A corporation can deduct a percentage of certain dividends received during its tax year. [IRC § 243]The deduction generally equals 70 percent of the dividends received from domestic corporations if the corporation receiving the dividend owns less than 20 percent of the corporation paying the dividend. If the receiving corporation owns 20 percent or more of the paying domestic corporation, the receiving corporation can deduct 80 percent of the dividends received or accrued.

Corporations cannot take a deduction for dividends received from the following entities:

- A real estate investment trust;

- A corporation exempt from tax under IRC Section or 501 or 521 either for the tax year of the distribution or the preceding tax year;

- A corporation whose stock was held less than 46 days during the 90-day period beginning 45 days before the stock became ex-dividend with respect to the dividend; or

- A corporation whose preferred stock was held less than 91 days during the 180-day period beginning 90 days before the stock became ex-dividend with respect to the dividend if the dividends received on it are for a period or periods totaling more than 366 days.

Dividends on deposits in domestic building and loan associations, mutual savings banks, cooperative banks, and similar organizations are interest. They do not qualify for this deduction.

Q 3:14 What is the deduction for organizational and start-up expenditures?

A corporation may elect to deduct currently certain business start-up costs and organization costs. [IRC § § 195, 248] There is a $5,000 ceiling on the deduction for business start-up costs and a separate $5,000 ceiling on the deduction for organizational costs. Each $5,000 limit is phased out to the extent that the start-up or organization costs exceed $50,000. So, for example, if start-up costs are $53,000 and organizational costs are $56,000, then a $2,000 current deduction is allowed for start-up costs, but no deduction is allowed for organizational costs.

Costs in excess of the deductible limit must be amortized over a 180-month period. In the case of start-up costs, the period begins in the month the business starts; in the case of organization costs the period begins in the month the corporation begins business.

Business start-up costs. Start-up costs are costs incurred for creating an active trade or business or investigating the creation or acquisition of an active trade or business. Start-up costs include amounts paid or incurred before the trade or business begins in anticipation of the activity becoming an active trade or business. A start-up cost is amortizable if it meets both of the following tests:

1. It is a cost that could be deducted if it were paid or incurred by an existing active business in the same field; and

2. It is a cost paid or incurred before the day the active business begins.

Start-up costs include costs for the following items:

- A survey of potential markets;
- An analysis of available facilities, labor, supplies, etc;
- Advertisements for the opening of the business;
- Salaries and wages for employees who are being trained, and their instructors;
- Travel and other necessary costs for securing prospective distributors, suppliers, or customers; and
- Salaries and fees for executives and consultants, or for other professional services.

Start-up costs do *not* include costs for the following items:

- Deductible interest;
- Taxes; and
- Research and experimental costs.

[IRC § 195]

Amortizable start-up costs for purchasing an active trade or business include only costs incurred in the course of a general search for, or preliminary investigation of, the business. Investigative costs are costs that help the buyer decide whether to purchase a business and which business to purchase. Costs incurred in the attempt to purchase a specific business cannot be amortized.

Organizational costs. The costs of organizing a corporation are the direct costs of creating the corporation. An amortizable cost must meet all of the following tests:

1. It is for the creation of the corporation;

2. It is chargeable to a capital account;

3. It could be amortized over the life of the corporation, if the corporation had a fixed life; and

4. It is incurred before the end of the first tax year in which the corporation is in business. A corporation using the cash method of accounting can amortize organizational costs incurred within the first tax year, even if the corporation does not pay them in that year.

The following are examples of organizational costs:

- The costs of temporary directors;

- The cost of organizational meetings;

- State incorporation fees;

- The cost of accounting services for setting up the corporation; and

- The cost of legal services for items such as drafting the charter, bylaws, terms of the original stock certificates, and minutes of organizational meetings.

[Reg. § 1.248-1(b)(2)]

The following costs are *not* organizational costs. They are capital expenses that cannot be amortized:

- Costs for issuing and selling stock or securities, such as commissions, professional fees, and printing costs; and

- Costs associated with the transfer of assets to the corporation.

Only the corporation can choose to deduct its start-up or organizational costs. Shareholders cannot deduct any costs they incur in setting up a corporation. The corporation, however, can deduct these costs.

Q 3:15 Can a C corporation deduct charitable contributions?

Yes, up to a limit. A C corporation can deduct donations to qualifying organizations to the extent that they do not exceed 10 percent of its taxable income for the tax year. [IRC § 170(b)] For this purpose, taxable income is determined without the following:

- The deduction for charitable contributions;

- The deduction for dividends received;

- Any net operating loss carryback to the tax year; and

- Any capital loss carryback to the tax year.

A corporation can carry over to each of the subsequent five years any charitable contributions made during the current year that are more than the 10 percent limit. Any excess not used within that period is lost. For example, if a corporation has a carryover of excess contributions paid in 2008 and it does not use all the excess on its return for 2009, it can carry the remainder over to 2010, 2011, 2012 and 2013. Deductions for a carryover of excess contributions in the carryover year cannot be claimed until after the corporation deducts current contributions made in that year (subject to the 10 percent limit).

Q 3:15

Deducting Losses

Q 3:16 Can a C corporation deduct capital losses?

A C corporation can deduct capital losses only up to the amount of its capital gains. [IRC § 1211(a)] In other words, if a corporation has an excess capital loss, it cannot deduct the loss in the current tax year. Instead, it carries the loss to other tax years and deducts it from capital gains that occur in those years.

First, a corporation carries a net capital loss back three years and deducts it from any total net capital gain that occurred in that year. If the full loss is not deductible, it can be carried forward one year (two years back from the current year) and then one more year (one year back). If any loss remains, the corporation can carry it over to future tax years, one year at a time, for up to five years. When a net capital loss is carried to another tax year, it is treated as a short-term loss. It does not retain its original identity as long-term or short-term. [IRC § 1212]

> **Example 3-4:** In 2008, a calendar year corporation has a net short-term capital gain of $3,000 and a net long-term capital loss of $9,000. The short-term gain offsets some of the long-term loss, leaving a net capital loss of $6,000. The corporation treats this $6,000 as a short-term loss when carried back or forward. The corporation carries the $6,000 short-term loss back three years to 2005. In 2005, the corporation had a net short-term capital gain of $8,000 and a net long-term capital gain of $5,000. It subtracts the $6,000 short-term loss first from the net short-term gain. This results in a net capital gain for 2005 of $7,000. This consists of a net short-term capital gain of $2,000 ($8,000 - $6,000) and a net long-term capital gain of $5,000.

When carrying a capital loss from one year to another, the following rules apply:

- When figuring a current year's net capital loss, it cannot be combined with a capital loss carried from another year. In other words, capital losses can be carried only to years that would otherwise have a total net capital gain.

- If capital losses from two or more years are carried to the same year, the loss from the earliest year is deducted first. When that loss is fully deducted, then the loss from the next earliest year is deducted.

Q 3:17 Can a C corporation claim a net operating loss (NOL) carryback or carryforward?

Yes. A C corporation generally computes and deducts a net operating loss (NOL) the same way as other taxpayers do (see Chapter 6). The same carryback (two years) and carryforward (20 years) periods apply, and the same sequence applies when the corporation carries two or more NOLs to the same year. [IRC § 172(d)]

A corporation's NOL generally differs from other entities' NOLs in the following ways:

1. A corporation can take different deductions when figuring an NOL.

2. A corporation must make different modifications to its taxable income in the carryback or carryforward year when figuring how much of the NOL is used and how much is carried forward to the next year.

A corporation computes an NOL in the same way it figures taxable income. It starts with its gross income and subtracts its deductions. If its deductions are more than its gross income, the corporation has an NOL. However, in computing its current year's NOL, a corporation cannot deduct any NOL carrybacks or carryovers from other years.

> **Example 3-5:** In 2008 XYZ, Inc. has gross income of $500,000 from business operations and $625,000 of deductible business expenses. XYZ also has a $50,000 NOL carryover from 2007. Its NOL for 2008 is $125,000 ($500,000 less $625,000).

If a corporation carries back the NOL, it can use either Form 1120X or Form 1139. A corporation can get a refund faster by using Form 1139. It cannot file Form 1139 before filing the return for the corporation's NOL year, but it must file Form 1139 no later than one year after the NOL year. If the corporation does not file Form 1139, it must file Form 1120X within three years of the due date, plus extensions, for filing the return for the year in which it sustains the NOL. If a corporation carries forward its NOL, it enters the carryforward on Schedule K (Form 1120).

If a corporation expects to have an NOL in its current year, it can automatically extend the time for paying all or part of its income tax for the immediately preceding year. It does this by filing Form 1138. It must explain on the form why it expects the loss. The extension amount cannot exceed the tax overpayment in the carryback years due to the NOL carryback.

> **Planning Point:** Net operating loss deductions are more valuable in high-income years when a corporation's top tax rate is high. Thus, carrying back a net operating loss can be a good choice for corporations with high-income carryback years. The corporation may even want to increase its NOL. For example, a corporation could accelerate future expenses into the current year, which will produce a bigger NOL to be carried back to the higher income year. On the other hand, a corporation that paid tax at a low rate in the carryback year but anticipates higher income in future years may want to conserve its NOL. In this case, the corporation can elect to forgo the NOL carryback and use the NOL as a carryforward only.

Q 3:18 Is a C corporation subject to the loss limit for passive activities?

The passive activity rules apply to personal service corporations and closely held C corporations. [IRC § 469(a)(2)] (For more information on the passive activity rules, see Chapter 6.)

Q 3:18

Personal service corporations. For purposes of the passive activity rules, a corporation is a personal service corporation if it meets all of the following requirements:

1. It is not an S corporation.

2. Its principal activity during the "testing period" is performing personal services. The testing period for any tax year is the previous tax year. If the corporation has just been formed, the testing period begins on the first day of its tax year and ends on the earlier of: (a) the last day of its tax year or (b) the last day of the calendar year in which its tax year begins.

3. Its employee-owners substantially perform the services in (2). This requirement is met if more than 20 percent of the corporation's compensation cost for its activities of performing personal services during the testing period is for personal services performed by employee-owners.

4. Its employee-owners own more than 10 percent of the fair market value of its outstanding stock on the last day of the testing period.

[IRC § 269A]

Personal services are those performed in the fields of accounting, actuarial science, architecture, consulting, engineering, health (including veterinary services), law, and performing arts. [IRC § 448(d)(2)]

A person is an "employee-owner" of a personal service corporation if both of the following apply:

1. He or she is an employee of the corporation or performs personal services for, or on behalf of, the corporation (even if he or she is an independent contractor for other purposes) on any day of the testing period.

2. He or she owns any stock in the corporation at any time during the testing period.

Closely held corporation. A corporation is considered to be closely held if all of the following apply:

1. It is not an S corporation;

2. It is not a personal service corporation; and

3. At any time during the last half of the tax year, more than 50 percent of the value of its outstanding stock is, directly or indirectly, owned by five or fewer individuals. [IRC § 465(a)(1)(B)]

[IRC § 469(j)(1)]

Q 3:18

Dividends and Other Distributions to Shareholders

Q 3:19 How are distributions from a C corporation treated for tax purposes?

A corporate distribution to a shareholder is treated as a dividend to the extent of the corporation's current and accumulated earnings and profit. [IRC § 301(c)]Traditionally, dividends were taxable to the shareholder as ordinary income. However, under the Jobs and Growth Tax Relief Reconciliation Act of 2003 [P.L. 108-27 (May 28, 2003)] (JGTRRA), and the Tax Increase Prevention and Reconciliation Act of 2005 [P.L. 109-222 (May 17, 2006)] (TIPRA) dividends are temporarily taxed like net capital gain, at rates no higher than 15 percent (see Q 3:22).

If a corporation's earnings and profits for the year (figured as of the close of the year without reduction for any distributions made during the year) are more than the total amount of distributions made during the year, all distributions made during the year are treated as dividend distributions of current year earnings and profits.

Example 3-6: Carol Blake is the only shareholder of a corporation that uses the calendar year as its tax year. During the year, the corporation made four $1,000 distributions to Blake. At the end of the year (before subtracting distributions made during the year), the corporation had $10,000 of current year earnings and profits. Since the corporation's current year earnings and profits ($10,000) were more than the amount of the distributions it made during the year ($4,000), all of the distributions are treated as distributions of current year earnings and profits. The corporation does not deduct these dividends on the income tax return it files.

If a corporation's current year earnings and profits are less than the total distributions made during the year, part or all of each distribution is treated as a distribution of accumulated earnings and profits. Accumulated earnings and profits are earnings and profits the corporation accumulated before the current year.

If the corporation has current year earnings and profits, the corporation figures the use of accumulated and current earnings and profits as follows:

1. The current year earnings and profits are divided by the total distributions made during the year.

2. Each distribution is multiplied by the percentage figured in (1) to get the amount treated as a distribution of current year earnings and profits.

3. Starting at the beginning of the year, the remaining part of each distribution is treated as a distribution of accumulated earnings and profits.

Example 3-7: Tom Crane is the only shareholder of a corporation that uses the calendar year as its tax year. At the beginning of the year, the corporation's accumulated earnings and profits balance was $20,000. During the year, the corporation made four $3,750 distributions to Crane. At the end of the year (before subtracting distributions made during the year), the corporation had $9,000 of current year earnings and profits.

Since the corporation's current year earnings and profits ($9,000) were less than the amount of the distributions it made during the year ($15,000), part of each distribution is treated as a distribution of accumulated earnings and profits. The corporation treats the distributions as follows:

1. The current year earnings and profits ($9,000) is divided by the total amount of distributions made during the year ($15,000). The result is 0.6.

2. Each $3,750 distribution is multiplied by 0.6 to get the amount ($2,250) of each distribution that is treated as a distribution of current year earnings and profits to Crane.

3. The remaining $1,500 of each distribution is treated as a distribution from accumulated earnings and profits to Crane. The corporation distributed $6,000 ($1,500 × 4) of accumulated earnings and profits.

The remaining $14,000 ($20,000 - $6,000) of accumulated earnings and profits is available for use in the following year.

Q 3:20 What happens if distributions for a year exceed current and accumulated earnings and profits?

Any part of a distribution that is not from earnings and profits is applied against and reduces the adjusted basis of the stock in the hands of the shareholder. To the extent the balance is more than the adjusted basis of the stock, the shareholder has a gain (usually a capital gain) from the sale or exchange of property. [IRC § § 301(c)(2), (3)]

Q 3:21 How is the amount of a distribution figured?

The amount of a distribution is generally the amount of any money paid to the shareholder plus the fair market value of any property transferred to the shareholder. [IRC § 301(b)(1)]However, this amount is reduced (but not below zero) by the following liabilities:

- Any liability of the corporation the shareholder assumes in connection with the distribution.

- Any liability to which the property is subject immediately before, and immediately after, the distribution.

The fair market value of any property distributed to a shareholder becomes the shareholder's basis in that property.

Q 3:22 How are dividends taxed?

The Jobs and Growth Tax Relief Reconciliation Act of 2003 [P.L. 108-27 (May 28, 2003)] (JGTRRA), provides that for tax years beginning after 2002 and before 2009, qualified dividend income is taxed at the same rates that apply to net capital gains. [IRC § 1(h)(11)] In addition, under JGTRRA, the tax rate on net capital gain is generally 15 percent for taxpayers in the higher brackets. The tax rate is 5 percent for dividends and other net capital gain that would otherwise be taxed at a 10 percent or 15 percent regular tax rate. However, the 5 percent rate drops to zero for one year in 2008. The Tax Increase Prevention and Reconciliation Act of 2005 [P.L. 109-222 (May 17, 2006)](TIPRA) extends the favorable tax treatment of qualified dividend income and the reduced capital gain tax rates (including the zero rate for net capital gain that would otherwise be taxed at a 10 percent or 15 percent rate) through 2010. [IRC § 1(h)(1)]

To accomplish this tax reduction, JGTRRA (as extended by TIPRA) includes dividend income in the Internal Revenue Code's definition of "net capital gain" and "adjusted net capital gain." [IRC § § 1(h)(11); 1(h)(3)]

Long-term capital gains and losses and short-term capital gains and losses are netted separately. Long-term and short-term gains or losses are then netted against each other. If the result is a net long-term capital gain in excess of a net short-term loss, the difference is the "net capital gain". This net capital gain is than reduced by subtracting gain that is taxed at a 25 percent rate (unrecaptured Section 1250 gain from depreciable real estate) and gain that is taxed at a 28 percent rate (gain from collectibles and Section 1202 gain from certain small business stock). The result is a taxpayer's "adjusted net capital gain," which is subject to tax at the most favorable 15 percent or 5 percent rates. Thus, the inclusion of dividend income in net capital gain and adjusted net capital gain results in a tax at the most favorable capital gain rates.

Note, however, that dividend income is not treated as capital gain for all purposes. A taxpayer's dividend income is treated as net capital gain, not as long-term capital gain. Therefore, dividends cannot be offset by capital losses to arrive at net capital gain. Consequently, a taxpayer may wind up with a net capital loss and a net capital gain from dividend income in the same year.

> **Example 3-8:** Bob Blake has $4,000 of dividend income and two capital transactions—a $4,000 long-term capital gain and an $8,000 short-term capital loss. Bob has a net capital gain of $4,000 (representing his dividend income) taxed no higher than 15 percent and a net $4,000 short-term capital loss. The loss can offset up to $3,000 of ordinary income and the remainder is carried over to future years.

Q 3:23 For purposes of the temporary reduction in the capital gain tax rates, what are "qualified" dividends?

Qualified dividend income includes dividends received during the year from a domestic corporation or from a "qualified foreign corporation." [IRC § 1(h)(11)(B)(1)]

Domestic corporations. The reduced rates generally apply to dividends paid by all domestic corporations that are subject to corporate income tax.

The reduced rates do not apply to dividends received from a domestic corporation that was exempt from tax under Section 501 or that was a tax-exempt farmer's cooperative under Section 521 in either the tax year of the dividend distribution or the prior tax year. In addition, the reduced rates do not apply to dividends on deposits from a mutual savings bank, cooperative bank, domestic building and loan association, or similar savings institution that received a deduction for the dividends under Section 591. Finally, the reduced rates do not apply to deductible dividends paid on employer securities held by an employee stock ownership plan. [IRC § 404(k)]

Foreign corporations. A foreign corporation is qualified if it (1) is incorporated in a U.S. possession or (2) is eligible for the benefits of a comprehensive income tax treaty with the United States that the Treasury Department determines to be satisfactory and that includes an exchange of information program. [IRC § 1(h)(11)(C)(i)]

A corporation that does not meet either of the above requirements will nonetheless be treated as a qualified foreign corporation with respect to any dividend paid by the corporation on stock that is readily tradable on an established U.S. securities market. [IRC § 1(h)(11)(C)(ii)]On the other hand, certain foreign investment corporations do not qualify. Dividends paid by a corporation that was a foreign investment company [IRC § 1246(b)], a passive foreign investment company [IRC § 1297], or a foreign personal holding company [IRC § 552] in either the tax year of the dividend or the prior tax year are not eligible for the reduced rates.

Q 3:24 Are there any otherwise qualified dividends that are ineligible for capital gain treatment?

The temporarily reduced rates for capital gain do not apply to qualified dividends if the taxpayer does not meet certain holding period requirements or is under an obligation to make payments to another party in connection with the dividend.

Holding period requirement. Dividends received are not eligible for the reduced rates if a taxpayer does not hold a share of stock for more than 60 days during the 120-day period beginning 60 days before the ex-dividend date. [IRC § 1(h)(11)(B)(iii)] In the case of preferred stock, the periods are doubled. That is, the taxpayer must hold preferred stock for more than 120 days during the 240-day period beginning 120 days before the ex-dividend date. The ex-dividend date is the date the taxpayer becomes entitled to payment of a dividend, even if the dividend is not payable until a later date.

For purposes of this rule, a taxpayer's holding period includes the day the stock is disposed of but not the day it was acquired. In addition, a taxpayer's holding period does not include any period during which the taxpayer's risk of loss on the stock is diminished. A taxpayer's risk of loss is diminished if:

- The taxpayer has an option to sell the stock, is under a contractual obligation to sell the stock, or has made (and not closed) a short sale of substantially identical stock;
- The taxpayer granted an option to buy substantially identical stock; or

- The taxpayer holds one or more positions (including an option or a futures or forward contract) in substantially similar or related property that reduce risk because the fair market values of the stock and positions are expected to vary inversely. [IRC § 246(c); Reg. § 1.246-5(b)(2)]

Property is considered substantially similar or related to a taxpayer's stock if the fair market values of the stock and property primarily reflect the performance of a single firm or enterprise, the same industry or industries, or the same economic factor or factors (e.g., interest rates, commodity prices, or foreign currency exchange rates). In addition, changes in the fair market value of the stock must be reasonably expected to approximate, either directly or inversely, changes in the value of the property, a fraction of the value of the property, or a multiple of the value of the property. [Reg. § 1.246-5(b)(1)]

Related payments. The reduced rates also do not apply to the extent a shareholder is obligated to make payments with respect to positions in substantially similar or related property. [IRC § 1(h)(11)(B)(iii)] For example, the reduced rates would not apply if the shareholder is obligated to make dividend-like payments on stock that was borrowed to cover a short sale.

Q 3:25 What are "constructive" dividends?

Generally, dividends are in the form of cash or property distributed to shareholders. However, certain indirect benefits provided by a corporation to its shareholders may be treated as constructive dividends by the IRS and taxed like actual dividends. Examples of constructive dividends include the following:

- *Below-market loans.* If a corporation gives a shareholder a loan on which no interest is charged or on which interest is charged at a rate below the applicable federal rate, the interest not charged may be treated as a distribution to the shareholder.

- *Corporation cancels shareholder's debt.* If a corporation cancels a shareholder's debt without repayment by the shareholder, the amount canceled is treated as a distribution to the shareholder.

- *Transfers of property to shareholders for less than fair market value.* A sale or exchange of property by a corporation to a shareholder may be treated as a distribution to the shareholder. If the fair market value of the property on the date of the sale or exchange exceeds the price paid by the shareholder, the excess may be treated as a distribution to the shareholder.

- *Unreasonable rents.* If a corporation rents property from a shareholder and the rent is unreasonably more than the shareholder would charge to a stranger for use of the same property, the excessive part of the rent may be treated as a distribution to the shareholder.

- *Unreasonable salaries.* If a corporation pays an employee who is also a shareholder a salary that is unreasonably high considering the services actually performed by the shareholder-employee, the excessive part of the salary may be treated as a distribution to the shareholder-employee. [Reg. § 1.162-7]

Q 3:26 How are dividend distributions reported?

The corporation files Form 1099-DIV with the IRS for each shareholder to whom it has paid dividends and other distributions of $10 or more during a calendar year. The Forms 1099-DIV are sent to the IRS with Form 1096 by February 28 (March 31 if filing electronically) of the year following the year of the distribution. The corporation generally must furnish Forms 1099-DIV to shareholders by January 31 of the year following the close of the calendar year during which the corporation made the distributions. [IRC § 6042(c)]

Q 3:27 What are the tax consequences for the C corporation when distributions are made to shareholders?

Generally, there are no tax consequences for the corporation. A corporation, however, will recognize a gain on the distribution of property to a shareholder if the fair market value of the property exceeds the corporation's adjusted basis. [IRC § 311(b)(1)]This is generally the same treatment the corporation would receive if the property were sold. For this purpose, however, the fair market value is the greater of: (1) the actual fair market value or (2) the amount of any liabilities the shareholder assumed in connection with the distribution of the property.

Q 3:28 How is a shareholder taxed if his or her stock is redeemed by a corporation and the shareholder receives a distribution from the corporation in exchange for the stock?

IRC Section 302 governs the tax treatment of corporate distributions in redemption of stock. The rules attempt to distinguish between stock redemptions that have characteristics of a sale (and therefore should be entitled to capital gain treatment) and those that involve a distribution of corporate earnings and should be treated as a dividend. Section 302 provides that a corporation's redemption of its stock is treated as a sale if the redemption satisfies any one of the following criteria:

- *Not essentially equivalent to a dividend.* This test is designed to determine whether, based on the particular facts and circumstances, the redemption proceeds are, in reality, a dividend. Various factors are taken into account, such as the change in the proportionate ownership interests following the redemption, the corporation's pattern of dividend payments, and whether or not there has been a contraction in the corporation's business.

- *Substantially disproportionate.* This is a mechanical test. To qualify as a sale, the redemption of an owner's stock generally must result in (1) the owner's interest in the corporation dropping to less than 50 percent, and (2) the owner's ownership percentage after the redemption dropping to less than 80 percent of what it was before the redemption (e.g., from a 40 percent ownership interest to less than 32 percent interest).

- *Complete termination.* This test is met if the owner has no ownership interest in the corporation after the redemption.

- *Partial liquidation.* The redemption qualifies as a sale if it is made pursuant to a partial liquidation of the corporation's business (e.g., the sale of a business or business assets). [IRC § 302(b)]

If a redemption is treated as a sale, the redemption proceeds are nontaxable to the extent of the owner's basis for the redeemed shares; the excess is capital gain. If the redemption does not satisfy the above criteria, the redemption is treated as a dividend to the extent of the corporation's earnings and profits.

Q 3:29 Are there special rules that apply when a shareholder's stock is redeemed in a family-owned corporation?

Yes. For purposes of applying the criteria outlined in the previous question, the attribution rules of IRC Section 318(a) apply. Thus, an owner whose shares are being redeemed is treated as constructively owning stock owned directly or indirectly by or for his or her spouse, children, grandchildren, and parents.

Example 3-9: Janice Bridge and her three children each own 25 shares of XYZ Inc. XYZ redeems 10 of the shares owned by Bridge. Therefore, her percentage interest in the corporation drops from 25 percent to 16.67 percent (15 shares out of 90)—enough to meet the substantially-disproportionate test. However, under the attribution rules, Bridge is considered to own 100 percent of XYZ's shares before the redemption and 100 percent after, so she cannot qualify under the substantially-disproportionate test and the redemption will be treated as a dividend.

Example 3-10: Same facts as above except that XYZ redeems all 25 of the shares owned by Bridge. Again, although Bridge has completely terminated her interest in XYZ, the attribution rules treat her as owning 100 percent of the corporation after the redemption. So there has been no "complete termination."

However, insofar as the complete-termination test is concerned, the Internal Revenue Code does provide a method for having the attribution rules waived. If certain requirements are met, shares owned by family members will not be attributed to the owner whose interest is being completely terminated. [IRC § 302(c)(2)(A)]

To qualify for the waiver of the attribution rules in a complete termination, a taxpayer must meet the following requirements:

- Immediately after the redemption the taxpayer must have no interest in the corporation other than as a creditor. The taxpayer cannot be an officer, director, or employee of the corporation.

- The taxpayer must not acquire within 10 years after the redemption an interest other than that of a creditor except by bequest or inheritance.

- The taxpayer must not, within 10 years before the redemption, have acquired stock from or transferred stock to a person covered by the attribution rules.

Q 3:30 How does the temporary favorable treatment for qualified dividends affect the sale-vs.-dividend issue for stock redemptions?

Because dividends are taxed like capital gain under JGTRRA and TIPRA, the question of whether a stock redemption is treated as a sale or a dividend has largely been rendered moot. At least, that is the case until the qualified dividend treatment expires at the end of 2010.

Example 3-11: Jim and Betty Simpson, a married couple, are officers of Acme Corp. and each owns 50 of Acme's 100 total outstanding shares. Both Jim and Betty have a basis of $20,000 for their shares and each has owned the shares for more than 10 years. On March 1, 2008, the corporation redeems all of Betty's 50 shares in exchange for a payment of $500,000.

If Betty wants to qualify for a waiver of the attribution rules, she will have to cease all connection with Acme (other than that of a creditor) for 10 years. In that case, she will be treated as selling her shares to Acme for $500,000 and will recognize a $480,000 capital gain—taxed no higher than 15 percent under JGTRRA.

If Betty wants to continue as an officer of Acme, she cannot qualify for the attribution waiver and the $500,000 payment will be treated as a dividend (assuming XYZ has sufficient earnings and profits)—again, taxed no higher than 15 percent under the qualified dividend provision.

Q 3:31 What happens to a shareholder's basis if a stock redemption is treated like a dividend and not a sale?

In 1955, the IRS issued regulations under Section 302 that provide guidance on the basis question. [Reg. § 1.302-2(c)]The regulations state that "[i]n any case in which an amount received in redemption of stock is treated as a distribution of a dividend, proper adjustment of the basis of the remaining stock will be made with respect to the stock redeemed."

The regulations contain examples illustrating what constitutes a proper adjustment. In two of the examples, the shareholder whose stock was redeemed (redeemed shareholder) still owns stock of the corporation after a redemption that is treated as a dividend. In those cases, the basis of the shareholder's remaining shares is increased by the basis of the redeemed shares. In another example in the regulations (very much like the example with Jim and Betty above), the shareholder actually owns no stock of the corporation immediately after a redemption treated as a dividend. Since the shareholder's spouse still owns stock and that stock is attributed to the redeemed shareholder under the attribution rules, the basis in the redeemed shares shifts to the spouse's basis in the shares still owned by him or her.

However, in 2002 the IRS issued proposed regulations that took a different tack. [Prop. Reg. § 1.302-5]Under the proposed regulations, when a redemption of stock was treated as a dividend, an amount equal to the adjusted basis of the redeemed stock was treated as a loss. The loss could be claimed by the redeemed shareholder when the conditions that caused the redemption to be treated as a dividend no longer exist (i.e., when the redeemed shareholder has sufficiently reduced its actual and constructive ownership interest in the corporation).

In response to criticism of the proposed regulations, the IRS withdrew them in 2006 for further study. [Notice of Withdrawal of NPRM REG-150313-01, 4/19/06]

Q 3:32 What are the tax consequences to the C corporation if it issues stock dividends or options on its own stock to shareholders?

Distributions of stock dividends and stock options are generally tax-free to shareholders. [IRC § 305]However, stock and stock options are treated as property under the rules discussed in the prior question if any of the following apply to their distribution:

1. Any shareholder has the choice to receive cash or other property instead of stock or stock rights.

2. The distribution gives cash or other property to some shareholders and an increase in the percentage interest in the corporation's assets or earnings and profits to other shareholders.

3. The distribution is in convertible preferred stock and has the same result as in (2).

4. The distribution gives preferred stock to some common stock shareholders and gives common stock to other common stock shareholders.

5. The distribution is on preferred stock.

Q 3:33 What are the tax consequences if a C corporation distributes stock in a subsidiary to its shareholders?

It is not uncommon for a parent corporation to "spin off" a subsidiary by distributing stock in the subsidiary to the parent's shareholders. Generally, under IRC Section 355, no gain is recognized by shareholders if their corporation distributes to them stock in a controlled corporation. The shareholders will not recognize gain or loss on the distribution if:

- The spin off has an independent business purpose and is not merely a device for distributing corporate earnings;

- Immediately after the spin off, the corporation and the subsidiary are each engaged in the active conduct of a trade or business;

- Each business has been actively conducted throughout the five-year period ending on the date of the spin off; and

- Neither business was acquired in a transaction in which gain or loss was recognized, in whole or in part, within the five-year period. [IRC § 355(b)]

In determining whether an active business has been conducted for five years, the fact that a business underwent change during the period (e.g., the addition of new products, changes in production capacity) will not make the distribution taxable as long as the changes are not significant enough to constitute the acquisition of a new or different business. [Reg. § 1.355-3(b)(3)(ii)]

For example, suppose a corporation has been actively engaged in one business for at least five years and creates or buys another business that is in the same line of business. The acquisition of the new business will generally be treated as an expansion of the existing business and both parts will be treated as having been actively conducted for the five-year period. On the other hand, if the corporation creates or buys a business in a different line of business, the new business will have to be conducted for another five years before the corporation can spin it off tax-free.

In two rulings issued in 2003 [Rev. Ruls. 2003-18, 2003-7 I.R.B. 467, 2003-38, 2003-17 I.R.B. 811], the IRS examined two fact patterns where stock in controlled corporations was distributed to shareholders. In both cases, the IRS determined that the businesses conducted by the controlled corporations were expansions of existing businesses and not new businesses.

With respect to Revenue Ruling 2003-18, Acme Corp. has been engaged under a dealer franchise in the sale and service of the X brand of automobiles since 1990. Between 1995 and 2001, Acme's operations have been carried on in two buildings (A and B) within the same city. In 2001, Acme acquired a franchise for the sale and service of the Y brand of automobiles and purchased the inventories, equipment, and leasehold of a former Y dealer. Shortly thereafter, Acme relocated the inventory of X automobiles from building A to building B. Thereafter, Acme used building B exclusively for the sales and service of X automobiles and used building A exclusively for the sales and service of Y automobiles.

In 2003, Acme transferred all of the assets, including building B, and liabilities of the Y dealership to a new corporation, Newco, in exchange for the stock of Newco, and distributed the Newco stock pro rata to its shareholders.

The IRS ruled that, immediately after the distribution, both Acme and Newco are engaged in the active conduct of a business that meets the five-year-active-business requirement. The IRS said that Acme's acquisition of the Y automobile dealership constitutes an expansion of the X business and is not treated as the acquisition of a new or different business. The IRS gave three reasons for its conclusion:

1. The product of the X dealership is similar to the product of the Y dealership;
2. The business activities associated with the operation of the X dealership (i.e., sales and service) are the same as the business activities associated with the operation of the Y dealership; and

3. The operation of the Y dealership involves the use of the experience and know-how that Acme developed in the operation of the X dealership.

With respect to Revenue Ruling 2003-38, XYZ Inc. has operated a retail shoe store business under the name "FeelsRight" for many years. Until two years ago, XYZ's sales were made exclusively to customers who frequented its retail stores in shopping malls and other locations. The FeelsRight line of shoes enjoys favorable name recognition, customer loyalty, and other elements of goodwill in the retail shoe market.

Two years ago, XYZ created an Internet website and began selling FeelsRight shoes at retail on the website. To a significant extent, the operation of the website draws upon XYZ's experience and know-how. The website is named "FeelsRight.com" to take advantage of the name recognition and customer loyalty associated with FeelsRight and to enhance the website's chances for success in its initial stages. This year, XYZ transfers all of the website's assets and liabilities to PARENT Inc., a newly formed, wholly owned subsidiary of XYZ, and distributes the stock of PARENT pro rata to XYZ's shareholders.

The IRS ruled that the creation of the website was an expansion of XYZ's existing business. The IRS noted that the product of the retail shoe store business and the product of the website are the same (shoes), and the principal business activities of the retail shoe store business are the same as those of the website (purchasing shoes at wholesale and reselling them at retail).

The IRS acknowledged that selling shoes on a website requires some know-how not associated with operating a retail store, such as familiarity with different marketing approaches, distribution chains, and technical operations issues. Nevertheless, the web site's operation does draw to a significant extent on XYZ's existing experience and know-how, and the web site's success will depend in large measure on the goodwill associated with the FeelsRight name. Therefore, the IRS concluded that PARENT picks up XYZ's business history and will be treated as having been in the active conduct of a business for the required five years.

Q 3:34 What is considered a "business purpose" that would qualify a spin off for tax-free treatment under Section 355?

A spin off is tax-free only if there is a real and substantial nonfederal tax purpose germane to the business of the parent corporation or the subsidiary. [Reg. § 1.355-2(b)(2)]

In two rulings issued in 2003 [Rev. Ruls. 2003-75, 2003-29 I.R.B. 79, 2003-74, 2003-29 I.R.B. 77], the IRS looked at different fact patterns and determined that, in both cases, the business-purpose test was met.

In the first ruling, Parent Inc. is a publicly traded corporation that conducts a pharmaceuticals business. Sub Inc., a wholly owned subsidiary of Parent, conducts a cosmetics business. Both businesses require substantial capital for reinvestment and research and development.

Q 3:34

Parent does all of the borrowing for both Parent and Sub and makes all decisions regarding the allocation of capital spending between the pharmaceuticals and cosmetics businesses. In recent years, Parent has had to limit total expenditures to maintain its credit ratings. The decisions reached by Parent's senior management regarding the allocation of capital spending usually favor the pharmaceuticals business. The competition for capital prevents both businesses from consistently pursuing development strategies that the management of each business believes are appropriate.

To eliminate this competition for capital, Parent wants to distribute the Sub stock to Parent's shareholders, pro rata.

The IRS ruled that the distribution will meet the business-purpose test. The operation of the pharmaceuticals business and the cosmetics business within the same corporate group causes capital allocation problems that prevent each business from pursuing the development strategies most appropriate to its operation. The separation of the two businesses is the only nontaxable transaction that will resolve these problems. It is expected that both businesses will benefit from the separation, and that the separation will enhance the success of the cosmetics business in a real and substantial way.

In ruling two, ABC Corp. is a publicly traded corporation that conducts a software technology business. XYZ Corp., a wholly owned subsidiary of ABC, conducts a paper products business.

ABC's management devotes more of its time to the software business because it believes that business presents better opportunities for growth. Indeed, it would like to concentrate solely on the software business but is prevented from doing so by the need to service the paper products business. The management of the paper products business, on the other hand, believes that the disproportionate attention paid the software business deprives the paper products business of the management resources needed for its full development.

To enable each corporation's management to concentrate on its own operation, ABC wants to distribute XYZ's stock to ABC's shareholders, pro rata.

The IRS says that the distribution will meet the business-purpose test. The distribution will enable ABC's management to concentrate its efforts on the software business, which it believes presents better opportunities for growth, and allow the management of the paper products business to secure for that business the management resources needed for its full development. There is no other nontaxable transaction that would accomplish these goals, and it is expected that the separation of the two businesses will enhance the success of each business in a real and substantial way.

The IRS noted that two directors on ABC's board would also serve on XYZ's board. Although this appears inconsistent with the assertion that the software business and the paper products business require independent management teams, this connection does not conflict with the business purpose for the separation. One director will serve for only a short period and will further that purpose by aiding in the creation of two independently administered operations.

Q 3:34

The other director will assist the separation by calming market concerns that might otherwise adversely affect one or both businesses. Further, the two directors together constitute only a minority of each board.

Q 3:35 Does a spin-off meet the "business purpose" test if it is designed to benefit the shareholders and not the corporation itself?

Generally speaking, no. The principal reason for the business purpose requirement is to provide tax-free treatment only to distributions that are incident to readjustments of corporate structures required by business exigencies. [Reg. § 1.355-2(b)(1)]If a corporate business purpose can be achieved through a nontaxable transaction that does not involve the distribution of stock of a controlled corporation and that is neither impractical nor unduly expensive, then the separation of the corporations is not carried out for a corporate business purpose. [Reg. § 1.355-2(b)(3)].

A shareholder purpose (for example, the personal planning purposes of a shareholder) is not a corporate business purpose. [Reg. § 1.355-2(b)(2)] Depending upon the facts of a particular case, however, a shareholder purpose for a transaction may be so nearly coextensive with a corporate business purpose as to preclude any distinction between them. A transaction motivated in substantial part by a corporate business purpose does not fail the business purpose requirement merely because it is motivated in part by nonfederal tax shareholder purposes. [Reg. § 1.355-2(b)(5)].

For example, in a recent ruling, the IRS addressed a situation where both corporation and shareholders benefited from a spin-off. [Rev. Rul. 2004-23; 2004-11 IRB 1] In the ruling, XYZ corporation operated two distinct businesses through its subsidiaries. Because the two businesses attract different investors, XYZ's investment banker advised it that if each business were conducted in a separate and independent corporation, the stock of the two corporations likely would trade publicly for a higher price, in the aggregate, than the XYZ stock was currently trading for.

XYZ uses equity-based incentives as part of its program to compensate a significant number of its employees. XYZ's directors wish to enhance the value of employee compensation and have considered either granting additional equity-based incentives or making cash payments. However, granting additional equity-based incentives would unacceptably dilute XYZ's existing shareholders' interests, and making cash payments would be unduly expensive. On the other hand, the increase in the aggregate stock value that would result from the separation of the two businesses in independent corporation will enhance the value of XYZ's equity-based compensation, providing it with a real and substantial benefit.

The IRS ruled that a spin-off of one of XYZ's businesses into a separate corporation would meet the business requirement test. Because XYZ believes that the increased value of its stock expected to result from the separation will enhance the value of its employee compensation, the distribution is motivated by a real and substantial nonfederal tax purpose germane to the business of XYZ. Further, because this purpose cannot be achieved through another nontaxable transaction that is neither impractical nor unduly expensive, the distribution is carried out for a corporate business purpose.

Corporate Liquidations

Q 3:36 Do shareholders owe tax when a C corporation is liquidated and its assets are distributed?

For tax purposes, a complete corporate liquidation is treated as an exchange of the shareholders' stock for the corporation's assets. [IRC § 331] If the assets received by a shareholder (including the fair market value of property received) exceed the shareholder's basis for the stock, the shareholder recognizes gain; if the assets are less than the basis, the shareholder recognizes a loss. The gain or loss is capital.

The distribution of assets does not have to occur simultaneously to qualify for this treatment. A distribution that is one of a series of distributions in complete redemption of a corporation's stock is treated as an exchange of the assets for the stock. [IRC § 346(a)]In this situation, the shareholder first recovers his or her basis for the stock; only when the cumulative distributions exceed basis does the shareholder recognize gain. [Rev. Rul. 85-48, 1985-1 C.B. 126]

Q 3:37 Does a C corporation recognize income on the distribution of assets in a complete liquidation?

If the distribution includes property, the corporation will be treated as if it sold the property for its fair market value, and gain or loss is generally recognized by the liquidating corporation. [IRC § 336] If the property distributed is subject to a debt, or the shareholders assume a debt upon the distribution, the fair market value for this purpose is deemed to be at least equal to the amount of debt.

The liquidating corporation recognizes no loss on a distribution of property to a shareholder who owns directly or indirectly more than 50 percent in value of the corporation's outstanding stock. This rule, however, does not apply when there is a pro rata distribution to all shareholders or the property is not disqualified property, *i.e.,* the property had not been contributed to the corporation within the prior five years. [IRC § 336(d)]

Paying Taxes and Filing Returns

Q 3:38 Does a C corporation have to make estimated income tax payments?

Yes, a C corporation must make installment payments unless it expects its estimated tax for the year to be less than $500. [IRC § 6655]

Q 3:39 When are estimated tax payments due?

Estimated taxes are due in installments on the 15th day of the 4th, 6th, 9th, and 12th months of the corporation's tax year.

Example 3-12: A corporation's tax year ends June 30. Installment payments are due on October 15, December 15, March 15, and June 15. If any due date falls on a Saturday, Sunday, or legal holiday, the installment is due on the next business day.

Q 3:40 How much is a corporation required to pay with each installment?

A corporation can generally use one of the following two methods to figure each required installment. [IRC § 6655(d)] The corporation can use the method that yields the smallest installment payments.

Method 1. Each required installment is 25 percent of the income tax the corporation will show on its return for the current year.

Method 2. Each required installment is 25 percent of the income tax shown on the corporation's return for the previous year.

To use Method 2, the corporation (1) must have filed a return for the previous year, (2) the return must have been for a full 12 months, and (3) the return must have shown a positive tax liability (not zero).

A "large corporation" may use Method 2 to determine the first installment only. A large corporation is one with at least $1 million of modified taxable income in any of the last three years. Modified taxable income is taxable income calculated without net operating loss or capital loss carrybacks or carryovers. [IRC § 6655(g)(2)]

The IRS recently issued final regulations explaining how to compute corporate estimated tax payments (the regulations apply to tax years beginning after September 6, 2007). [Reg. 1.6655-1 through 1.6655-7] The final regulations provide that recaptured tax credits are not usually treated as a tax for estimated tax purposes. Also, a rule contained in the IRS's proposed regulations, which required a taxpayer to compute its prior year's tax liability using the current year's tax rates if those rates differed from the prior year's rates was eliminated since it was inconsistent with statutory language. In addition, the final regulations clarify that, for purposes of the preceding tax year safe harbor, the tax shown on an amended return is only taken into account in computing installments that are due after an amended return is filed.

Form 1120-W can be used as a worksheet to figure each required installment of estimated tax.

Other methods. If a corporation's income is expected to vary during the year because, for example, its business is seasonal, it may be able to lower the amount of one or more required installments by using one or both of the following methods. [IRC § 6655(e)]

1. The annualized income installment method.

2. The adjusted seasonal installment method.

Schedule A of Form 1120-W can be used to see if using one or both of these methods will lower the amount of any required installments.

Annualized income installment method. A corporation can also avoid the estimated tax penalty if it pays 100 percent of the tax that would be due (after subtracting allowable credits) on the basis of current income, up to a specified cut-off date, annualized for the year. [IRC § 6655(e)(1)] Under this method actual taxable income is annualized for a given number of months of the tax year. A corporation must use one standard set of monthly periods unless it elects to use one of two optional sets of monthly periods to determine the annualized income installments. The standard monthly periods are:

1. First quarterly installment—first three months of the tax year;

2. Second quarterly installment—first three months of the tax year;

3. Third quarterly installment—first six months of the tax year; and

4. Fourth quarterly installment—first nine months of the tax year.

Alternatively, a corporation may elect to determine annualized income and quarterly installments based on its income determined under either of the following sets of monthly periods:

First Set:

1. First quarterly installment—first two months of the tax year;

2. Second quarterly installment--first four months of the tax year;

3. Third quarterly installment—first seven months of the tax year; and

4. Fourth quarterly installment—first 10 months of the tax year.

Second Set:

1. First quarterly installment—first three months of the tax year;

2. Second quarterly installment—first five months of the tax year;

3. Third quarterly installment—first eight months of the tax year; and

4. Fourth quarterly installment—first 11 months of the tax year.

Once income is placed on an annualized basis, the corporation computes the tax on its annualized income at current rates and applies to that amount the percentage of estimated tax due. The percentage of estimated tax due is determined as follows: [IRC § 6655(e)(2)(B)]

Required Installment	Applicable Percentage
1st	25
2nd	50
3rd	75
4th	100

Adjusted seasonal income method. Corporations that have seasonal income are permitted to annualize their income assuming that income is earned in the current year in the same pattern as in preceding years; and estimated tax may be paid in the seasonal pattern in which income is earned. A corporation is considered to have seasonal income if, in each of the three preceding tax years, it had taxable income for any period of six successive months that averaged at least 70 percent of total income for the tax year (i.e., its "base percentage" must equal at least 70 percent). [IRC § 6655(e)(3)(B)]

The amount of any installment is determined as follows:

1. Take the taxable income for all months during the tax year preceding the month in which the installment is required to be paid (the "filing month");

2. Divide this amount by the base percentage for such months;

3. Determine the tax on the result; and

4. Multiply the tax by the base percentage for the filing month and all preceding months during the tax year. [IRC § 6655(e)(3)(C)]

Q 3:41 Is there a penalty for underpaying the corporate estimated tax?

If the corporation does not pay a required installment of estimated tax by its due date, it may be subject to a penalty. The penalty is figured separately for each installment due date. The corporation may owe a penalty for an earlier due date, even if it paid enough tax later to make up the underpayment. This is true even if the corporation is due a refund when its return is filed.

Form 2220 can be used to determine if a corporation is subject to the penalty for underpayment of estimated tax and, if so, the amount of the penalty.

If the corporation is charged a penalty, the amount of the penalty depends on the following factors:

- The amount of the underpayment;

- The period during which the underpayment was due and unpaid; and

- An interest rate for underpayments that is published quarterly by the IRS in the Internal Revenue Bulletin.

A corporation generally does not have to file Form 2220 with its income tax return, because the IRS will figure any penalty and bill the corporation. However, even if the corporation does not owe a penalty, it should complete and attach the form to its corporate tax return if any of the following apply:

- The annualized income installment method was used to figure any required installment.

- The adjusted seasonal installment method was used to figure any required installment.

- The corporation is a large corporation, and Method 2 was used to figure its first required installment.

Refiguring required installments. If after the corporation figures and deposits estimated tax it finds that its tax liability for the year will be more or less than originally estimated, it may have to refigure its required installments. If earlier installments were underpaid, the corporation may owe an underpayment penalty. In this situation, the corporation should make an immediate catch-up payment to reduce any penalty resulting from the underpayment of any earlier installments, whether caused by a change in an estimate, not making a deposit, or a mistake.

Quick refund of overpayments. A corporation that has overpaid its estimated tax for the tax year may be able to apply for a quick refund. Form 4466 is used to apply for a quick refund of an overpayment of estimated tax. A corporation can apply for a quick refund if the overpayment is

- At least 10 percent of its expected tax liability; and

- At least $500.

Form 4466 must be filed before the corporation files its income tax return. An extension of time to file the corporation's income tax return will not extend the time for filing Form 4466. The IRS will act on the form within 45 days from the date it is filed. [IRC § § 6425, 6655(h)]

Q 3:42 How are estimated taxes paid?

Payments can be mailed or delivered with a completed *Form 8109* to an authorized financial institution. However, a corporation can volunteer to use—or may be required to use—the government's Electronic Federal Tax Payment System (EFTPS). [IRC § 6302(h)] A corporation must make deposits of all depository tax liabilities (including Social Security, Medicare, withheld income, excise, and corporate income taxes) incurred in 2008, if it deposited more than $200,000 in federal depository taxes in 2006 or it had to make electronic deposits in 2007. If a corporation initially meets the $200,000 threshold in 2007, it must begin deposits using EFTPS in 2009. Once a corporation meets the $200,000 threshold, it must continue to make deposits using EFTPS in later years.

If a corporation must use EFTPS but fails to do so, it may be subject to a 10 percent penalty. If a corporation is not required to use EFTPS, then it may voluntarily make its deposits using EFTPS. However, if a corporation is using EFTPS voluntarily, it will not be subject to the 10 percent penalty if it makes a deposit using a paper coupon.

Q 3:43 Which C corporations must file a tax return?

All domestic corporations (including corporations in bankruptcy) generally must file an income tax return whether or not they have taxable income. [IRC § 6012(a)(2)] Form 1120 is filed by a corporation to report its income, gains, losses, deductions, credits, and to figure its income tax liability. However, a corporation may file the shorter Form 1120-A if its gross receipts, total income, and total assets are each less than $500,000 and the corporation meets certain other requirements.

The IRS has issued regulations that require certain large corporations to electronically file their income tax returns. The electronic filing requirement applies to corporations (1) with $10 million or more in total assets (2) that file at least 250 returns, including income tax, excise tax, information and employment tax returns, during a calendar year. [Reg. § 301.6011-5T]

Q 3:44 When must the corporate income tax return be filed?

Generally, a corporation must file its income tax return by the 15th day of the 3rd month after the end of its tax year. A new corporation filing a short-period return must generally file by the 15th day of the 3rd month after the short period ends. A corporation that has dissolved must generally file by the 15th day of the 3rd month after the date of dissolution.

Extension of time to file. Form 7004 can be filed to request a six-month extension of time to file a corporation income tax return. The IRS will grant the extension if the form is completed properly and any balance due is paid by the due date for the return.

Form 7004 does not extend the time for paying the tax due on the return. Interest will be charged on any part of the final tax due not shown as a balance due on Form 7004. The interest is figured from the original due date of the return to the date of payment.

> **Example 3-13:** XYZ, Inc.'s return is due on March 15. On March 15, XYZ files Form 7004 and makes a $2,000 payment. On July 15, XYZ files its return. The return shows an unpaid balance of $1,000, which XYZ pays. XYZ will owe interest on the $1,000 unpaid balance from March 15 to July 15.

Q 3:45 What is a consolidated return?

An affiliated group of corporations may consent to have their common parent file one consolidated income tax return in lieu of the filing of separate returns by each corporation. Consolidated returns are based on the principle of levying the tax on the true income of a single enterprise, even though the business is operated through more than one corporation.

An affiliated group of corporations is a group of includable corporations that consists of one or more chains of corporations that are connected with a common parent corporation by stock ownership of 80 percent or more. [IRC § 1504(a)]Includable corporations are domestic corporations other than tax-ex-

Q 3:43

empt corporations, pass-through corporations such as S corporations, and life insurance companies. Mexican and Canadian corporations also can be includable corporations if they meet certain requirements.

A consolidated return may be filed only if all corporations that were members of the affiliated group at any time during the tax year consent to all the consolidated return regulations prior to the last day for filing the return. The making of a consolidated return is such consent. The common parent corporation, when filing a consolidated return, must attach Form 851 (Affiliations Schedule). In addition, for the first year a consolidated return is filed, each subsidiary must attach a Form 1122 (consent to be included in the consolidated return).

The advantages in filing consolidated returns include: (1) offsetting operating losses of one company against the profits of another; (2) offsetting capital losses of one company against the capital gains of another; (3) avoidance of tax on intercompany distributions; (4) deferral of income on intercompany transactions; (5) use by the corporate group of the excess of one member's foreign tax credit over its limitation; and (6) designation of the parent company as agent of the group for all tax purposes.

The disadvantages include: (1) the effect on later years' returns; (2) deferral of losses on intercompany transactions; (3) additional bookkeeping required to keep track of deferred intercompany transactions; (4) intercompany profit in inventories still within the group must be reflected in annual inventory adjustments; and (5) possible accumulated earnings tax liability (see Q. 3:52) when the consolidated accumulated earnings and profits of the group exceed the minimum credit amount.

Alternative Minimum Tax

Q 3:46 What is the purpose of the alternative minimum tax?

The Code permits special treatment for some types of income and allows special deductions and credits for some types of expenses. These favorable provisions enable some corporations with substantial economic income to significantly reduce their regular corporate income tax. The purpose of the corporate alternative minimum tax (AMT) is to ensure C corporations pay a minimum amount of tax on their economic income. A corporation owes AMT if its "tentative minimum tax" is more than its regular tax. [IRC § 55]

Q 3:47 Are small C corporations subject to the AMT?

No. For tax years beginning after 1997, the tentative minimum tax of a small corporation is zero. This means that a small corporation will not owe AMT. [IRC § 55(e)]

For this purpose, a corporation is treated as a "small corporation" if the current tax year is its first year in existence, *or*:

1. It was treated as a small corporation exempt from the AMT for all prior tax years beginning after 1997, *and*

2. Its average annual gross receipts for the three tax-year periods ending before its current tax year did not exceed $7.5 million ($5 million if the corporation had only one prior tax year).

Q 3:48 How is the corporate AMT computed?

The AMT is imposed on corporations at the rate of 20 percent on the alternative minimum taxable income (AMTI) in excess of a $40,000 exemption amount. [IRC §§ 55(b)(1), (d)(2)] The exemption amount is phased out by an amount equal to 25 percent of the amount that the corporation's AMTI exceeds $150,000. So corporations with AMTI of $310,000 or more receive no exemption amount.

AMTI is the corporation's taxable income increased by certain preference items and adjusted in the case of other items to reduce or eliminate the tax deferral permitted by the regular corporate tax (see below). The various nonrefundable business credits allowed under the regular tax generally are not allowed against the AMT.

> **Example 3-14:** XYZ, Inc. has taxable income of $180,000 for the year. It also has $50,000 of preference items. So its AMTI is $230,000. Because XYZ's AMTI is $80,000 more than the $150,000 exemption phaseout threshold, its exemption is reduced by $20,000 (25 percent of $80,000). So its AMT is $42,000 (20 percent × ($230,000-$20,000)). Since the AMT is less than the regular tax, XYZ, Inc. is not subject to the AMT and pays the regular tax.

If a corporation is subject to AMT in any year, the amount of tax exceeding the taxpayer's regular tax liability is allowed as a credit (the "AMT credit") in any subsequent taxable year to the extent the taxpayer's regular tax liability exceeds its tentative minimum tax in such subsequent year. [IRC § 53]

Form 4626 is used to figure the tentative minimum tax of a corporation.

Q 3:49 What are the corporate AMT preference items?

Items of tax preference are:

- For percentage depletion over the adjusted basis of the property at the end of the taxable year. This preference does not apply to percentage depletion allowed with respect to oil and gas properties.

- The amount by which excess intangible drilling costs arising in the taxable year exceed 65 percent of the net income from oil, gas, and geothermal properties. This preference does not apply to an independent producer to the extent the preference would not reduce the producer's AMTI by more than 40 percent.

- Tax-exempt interest income on most private activity bonds.

- Accelerated depreciation or amortization on certain property placed in service before January 1, 1987.

[IRC § 57]

Q 3:50 What are the adjustments that must be made in computing AMTI?

The adjustments that corporations must make in computing AMTI include:

- Depreciation on property placed in service after 1986 and before January 1, 1999, must be computed by using (1) the generally longer class lives prescribed by the alternative depreciation system [IRC § 168(g)] and (2) either (a) the straight-line method in the case of property subject to the straight-line method under the regular tax or (b) the 150 percent declining balance method in the case of other property. Depreciation on property placed in service after December 31, 1998, is computed by using the regular tax recovery periods and the AMT methods described in the previous sentence.

- Mining exploration and development costs must be capitalized and amortized over a 10-year period.

- Taxable income from a long-term contract (other than a home construction contract) must be computed using the percentage-of-completion method of accounting.

- The adjusted current earnings (ACE) adjustment.

[IRC § 56(a)]

Q 3:51 What is the ACE adjustment?

The ACE adjustment is the amount equal to 75 percent of the amount by which the adjusted current earnings of a corporation exceeds its AMTI (determined without the ACE adjustment). [IRC § 56(g)] In determining ACE the following rules apply:

- For property placed in service before 1994, depreciation generally is determined using the straight-line method and the class life determined under the alternative depreciation system.

- Any amount that is excluded from gross income under the regular tax but is included for purposes of determining earnings and profits is included in determining ACE.

- The inside build-up of a life insurance contract is included in ACE (and the related premiums are deductible).

- Intangible drilling costs of integrated oil companies must be capitalized and amortized over a 60-month period.

- The regular tax rules allowing circulation expenses and organization expenses to be amortized do not apply.

- Inventory must be calculated using the FIFO, rather than LIFO, method.

- The installment sales method generally may not be used.
- Depletion (other than for oil and gas) must be calculated using the cost, rather than the percentage, method.

Accumulated Earnings Tax

Q 3:52 What is the accumulated earnings tax?

A C corporation can accumulate its earnings for a possible expansion or other bona fide business reasons. However, if a C corporation allows earnings to accumulate beyond the reasonable needs of the business, it may be subject to an accumulated earnings tax, on top of the regular corporate tax. [IRC § 532] If the accumulated earnings tax applies, interest is also added to the tax from the date the corporate return was originally due, without extensions.

The accumulated earnings tax is designed to force corporations to distribute earnings as dividends if the earnings are not needed in the business. Without the penalty tax, owners of corporations would be tempted to stockpile earnings and forgo dividend payments in order to avoid the double tax on dividends.

Q 3:53 How is the accumulated earnings tax computed?

A corporation can accumulate $250,000 of its earnings without any problem (the figure is $150,000 for corporations that have as their principal function the performance of services in the fields of accounting, actuarial science, architecture, consulting, engineering, health, law, and performing arts). Accumulations in excess of $250,000 must be for the "reasonably anticipated needs" of the business. To the extent accumulated company earnings for the year are considered excessive—that is, over $250,000 and not for reasonably anticipated business needs—they are taxed at the flat accumulated earnings tax rate. [IRC § 535]

Q 3:54 What is the accumulated earnings tax rate?

The accumulated earnings tax rate is tied into the highest tax rate on dividends for individual taxpayers. [IRC § 531] Therefore, since the top individual tax rate for qualified dividends has been temporarily reduced to 15 percent through 2010 (see Q 3:22) the accumulated earnings tax rate is also 15 percent through 2010. [IRC § 531]

Q 3:55 How are the "reasonably anticipated needs" of a corporation determined?

There is no cut-and-dried answer; it is decided on a case-by-case basis. Courts are reluctant to second-guess a company's management in this area, so there is considerable leeway. Some of the grounds for accumulation that the courts have found to be reasonable are as follows:

- The expansion of a business or the replacement of a plant;
- The acquisition of another business by buying stock or assets;
- The retirement of a business's bona fide debt; and
- The accumulation of the necessary working capital for the business, such as that needed to purchase inventories. [Reg. § 1.537-2(b)]

Q 3:56 If a C corporation will soon, say, be building a new facility, can it accumulate earnings instead of financing the project with debt?

Yes. The Tax Court has said that a corporation is free to choose how it pays for expansions or renovations. If a company wants to accumulate earnings instead of incurring debt, the court will not second-guess it. [*Starks Building Co.,* T.C. Memo 1973-256]

Q 3:57 Does a corporation have to be able to prove its future expansion plans in order to justify an accumulation of earnings?

Yes. A corporation must prove to the IRS's satisfaction that it has some specific, definite, and feasible plans in mind. Vague plans "down the road" are not sufficient.

An example of this issue is the Tax Court case of Northwestern Indiana Telephone Company (NITCO). NITCO, a closely held corporation, was an independent telephone company that provided local wire-based telephone services in rural areas of northwestern Indiana. Throughout the 1950s, NITCO's earnings were fairly moderate. But, due to economic growth in NITCO's service area in the 1960s and the breakup of the Bell system in the 1980s, NITCO's annual revenue exceeded $5 million by 1987.

From 1980 through 1989, NITCO maintained no written records documenting its specific future business needs and plans. From 1954 through 1994, NITCO did not declare any dividends to its shareholders. On audit, the IRS determined that NITCO had retained excessive earnings in the years 1987, 1988, and 1989—to the tune of $1.4 million, $1.15 million, and $700,000, respectively.

When the case came before the Tax Court, NITCO contended that the accumulations were justified by a number of reasonably anticipated business needs, such as the installation of fiber optic cable to connect its exchanges, the replacement of switching equipment, the purchase of a billing and collections computer, expansion of the headquarters' building, and the acquisition of other telephone companies.

The Tax Court generally upheld the Service's position. The court noted that NITCO produced practically nothing in terms of documents prepared during 1987-89 to reflect the alleged plans and future needs. Indeed, the court found that "these claimed future needs to be largely afterthoughts to avoid the imposition of accumulated earnings tax liability." [*Northwestern Indiana Telephone Co.,* T.C. Memo 1996-168]

Q 3:57

Personal Holding Company Tax

Q 3:58 What is the personal holding company tax?

The personal holding company (PHC) tax is a tax imposed on the "undistributed personal holding company income" of a personal holding company. [IRC § 541] In the days when personal tax rates were much higher than they are today, individuals set up PHCs as "incorporated pocketbooks" or "incorporated talent" to receive the individuals' investment and compensation income. The PHC tax was designed to eliminate these arrangements. However, with the reduction in the personal tax rates over the years, there is now much less incentive to set up PHCs.

Q 3:59 For tax purposes, what is a PHC?

A C corporation is classified as a PHC if it meets the following two conditions:

1. During any time in the last half of the tax year, five or fewer persons own, directly or indirectly, more than 50 percent of the value of its stock. (Stock owned by a taxpayer's spouse, children, parents, brothers, and sisters is considered as owned by the taxpayer. Also, stock options and securities convertible to stock are considered stock ownership for this purpose.)

2. At least 60 percent of adjusted ordinary gross income for the tax year is personal holding company income.

[IRC § 542]

Q 3:60 What is personal holding company income?

PHC income includes:

- Dividends, interest, and royalties (PHC income is based on gross income; the dividends-received deduction does not apply).

- Adjusted income from rents, mineral, oil, or gas royalties, copyright royalties, produced film rents.

- Use of corporate property by a shareholder (For example, a corporation owns an apartment building, and a shareholder rents an apartment and lives in it. If the shareholder directly or indirectly owns 25 percent of the corporation's stock, payments he or she makes to the corporation are generally considered PHC income.)

- Personal service contracts if the corporation is required to furnish personal services performed by a particular person who owns 25 percent or more of the corporation's shares (Note: Income a personal service corporation receives generally is not PHC income as long as the corporation or its owner is not required to provide the services personally.)

- Income from an estate or trust.

[IRC § 543]

Q 3:61 How is the PHC tax computed?

The PHC tax is figured by applying the PHC tax rate to the corporation's undistributed personal holding company income. Typically this equals the corporation's taxable income less the dividends it has paid out. However, in computing undistributed personal holding company income, certain adjustments must be made. These include:

- A deduction for federal taxes the corporation paid;
- Charitable contributions up to the limits allowed for individuals rather than corporations;
- No deduction for net operating loss, but deduction allowed for loss carryovers;
- The amount of net capital gains minus the corporate tax attributable to it is deducted from the corporation's taxable income; and
- No deduction for dividends received.

[IRC § 545]

Additional adjustments may have to be made, depending on the facts of the corporation's particular situation. Furthermore, the PHC tax rate is the same as the highest individual income tax rate on dividends. Therefore, like the accumulated earnings tax (see above), the PHC tax rate has been reduced to 15 percent through 2010.

Chapter 4

S Corporations

The key feature of an S corporation is the pass-through factor: Income passes through to the shareholders and is taxed to the shareholders at their personal rates. Equally important, losses also pass through to the shareholders, who can use them to offset other income. By contrast, C corporation income is taxed twice—first when it is earned by the corporation and again when it is paid out to the shareholders as dividends. Moreover, C corporations cannot pass losses through to shareholders.

For many years, the pass-through feature was touted as a prime advantage of S corporations for small businesses. Company owners paid tax on the corporation's income at individual rates that were lower than the corporate rate. However, when the top personal income tax rate rose to 39.6 percent, exceeding the top rate for small corporations of 34 percent, S corporation owners were advised to reconsider whether the pass-through was still a good deal. Now, the tax picture is changing again. Thanks to the 2001 and 2003 Tax Laws, the top personal tax rate is now closer to the corporate rate. The top personal rate is currently just 35 percent. Therefore, there may be a renewed interest in S corporation status for small and mid-sized businesses.

Basic Rules

Q 4:1 What is an S corporation?

An S corporation is solely a creature of the federal tax law. From a legal standpoint, an S corporation is just like any other corporation (but see Q 4:4). Like a regular C corporation, an S corporation protects its owners from personal liability for the corporation's debts or claims against the corporation. In addition, an S corporation offers continuity of life. Death or withdrawal of an owner does not terminate the corporation; stock in the corporation can be sold or passed on to the owner's heirs.

On the other hand, S corporation status eliminates the double taxation of corporate profits that applies to regular C corporations. A C corporation's profits are taxed to the corporation when earned and again to the shareholders when the profits are distributed as dividends (see Chapter 3). An S corporation is generally exempt from federal income tax. The corporation's income or losses pass through to the shareholders and are reported on their personal tax returns.

The S corporation designation stems from the fact that Subchapter S of the income tax portion of the Internal Revenue Code governs the tax treatment of S corporations. [IRC §§ 1361-1379]

Q 4:2 Are S corporations recognized for state tax purposes?

Many—but not all—states recognize S corporations for state tax purposes. In some states, a corporation is automatically treated as an S corporation for state tax purposes if it has elected to be treated as an S corporation for federal tax purposes. In other states, a separate election is required. And in still other states, S corporations are not recognized and are taxed as regular C corporations.

> **Planning Point:** Bear in mind that often states that do allow S corporations do not always follow the federal rules exactly. In addition, not all states that recognize S corporations have conformed their laws to recent federal tax law changes. Business owners considering an S corporation election should check the law in their states.

Q 4:3 Are all corporations eligible to be S corporations?

Not all corporations are eligible to be S corporations. To qualify for S corporation status, a corporation must meet all of the following requirements:

- It must be a qualifying domestic corporation that is not an ineligible corporation (e.g., certain financial institutions, insurance companies, and corporations that operate abroad);

- It must have no more than 100 shareholders (75 for tax years before 2005);

Q 4:1

- It must have only individuals, bankruptcy estates, decedent's estates, tax-exempt charitable organizations, or certain qualifying trusts as shareholders; and

- It must have only one class of stock.

[IRC § 1361(b)]

Q 4:4 Can a business other than a corporation elect to be treated as an S corporation?

A partnership or a limited liability company (LLC) can elect to be treated as an S corporation if it has elected to be taxed as an association.

IRS's "check-the-box" regulations provide that a partnership or multiple member LLC may elect to be classified as an association (taxed like a corporation) or as a partnership for tax purposes. A single-member LLC may elect to be classified as an association or to be disregarded as an entity separate from its owner. [Reg. § 301.7701-3(a)] Unless an election is made to the contrary, a partnership or multi-member LLC will be treated as a partnership by default and a single-member LLC will be treated as a disregarded entity. [Reg. § 301.7701-3(b)]

A partnership or LLC (single or multi-member) that elects to be classified as an association can elect S corporation status by filing Form 2553 (see Q 4:18). Normally, this process would actually require filing two election forms—a Form 8823, *Entity Classification,* to elect association classification and a Form 2553 to elect S status. However, the IRS says that a partnership or LLC that elects S status by filing Form 2553 will automatically be deemed to have elected to be classified as an association, and the filing of Form 8823 will not be required. [Reg. § 301.7701-3T]

Q 4:5 What is a qualifying domestic corporation?

Only a domestic corporation (other than an ineligible corporation) may be an S corporation. A domestic corporation is a corporation created under the laws of the United States or under the laws of a state or territory of the United States. In addition, unincorporated organizations (called "associations") that are taxable as corporations may qualify. [Reg. § 1.1361-1(c)]

Under the Internal Revenue Service's (IRS or the Service) "check-the-box" regulations, limited liability companies (LLCs) and certain other business entities may choose to be treated either as partnerships or corporations for tax purposes (see Chapter 2). LLCs are generally thought of as an alternative to S corporations. However, the IRS has ruled that an LLC that is classified as a corporation may make an S corporation election (assuming it is otherwise eligible). [Ltr. Rul. 9636007]

S Corporation Shareholders

Q 4:6 Which individuals are eligible to be S corporation shareholders?

Only individuals who are U.S. citizens or residents are eligible to hold S corporation stock. A nonresident alien is ineligible to be an S corporation shareholder. [IRC § 1361(b)(1)(C)]

Note, however, that a nonresident alien individual may elect to report his or her worldwide income on a joint return with a spouse who is a U.S. citizen or resident. A nonresident alien who makes this election is treated as a U.S. resident for tax purposes and is, therefore, eligible to own S corporation stock. [IRC § 6013 (h)]

Q 4:7 When are estates and trusts eligible S corporation shareholders?

Stock in an S corporation may be held by estates or trusts—but only under specified conditions.

Estates. The estate of a deceased shareholder who was a U.S. citizen or resident is an eligible S corporation shareholder. [IRC § 1361(b)(1)(B)]However, if the administration of an estate is unreasonably prolonged, the IRS will disregard the estate and treat the estate's beneficiary or beneficiaries as the holders of the S corporation stock. [*Old Virginia Brick Co, Inc. v. Comm'r,* 367 F.2d 276 (4th Cir. 1966)]If the beneficiaries do not qualify as S corporation shareholders (or push the corporation over the 100-shareholder limit), the corporation's S election will terminate.

A shareholder's bankruptcy estate is also a qualifying S corporation shareholder. [IRC § 1361(c)(3)]Again, however, if the stock is distributed by the bankruptcy estate to an ineligible shareholder, the corporation's S election will terminate.

Trusts. The following trusts may hold S corporation stock:

- Grantor trusts (Q 4:8);
- Testamentary trusts (Q 4:9);
- Voting trusts (Q 4:10);
- Qualified Subchapter S trusts (Q 4:11); and
- Electing small business trusts (Q 4:13).

In addition, S corporation stock may be held by a qualified retirement plan. [IRC § 1361(c)(6)]However, neither a charitable remainder trust nor a trust that qualifies as an individual retirement account (IRA) can generally hold S corporation stock. [Rev. Ruls. 92-48, 1992-1 C.B. 301; 92-73, 1992-2 C.B. 224]

However, the IRS has said that an IRA may temporarily hold S corporation stock in a very limited situation. [Rev. Proc. 2003-23, 2003-11 I.R.B. 599] The situation involved a participant in an employee stock ownership plan (ESOP) who received a plan distribution in the form of S corporation stock (the employer was an S corporation). Under IRC Section 401(a)(3), the ESOP was required to place the distribution in an IRA if the participant requested it. Under the terms of the plan, the participant must sell the stock back to the ESOP immediately upon distribution.

The IRS ruled that placing the stock distribution in an IRA would not affect the employer's S election if the stock is immediately purchased by the employer corporation. Specifically, the IRS says that it will permit an ESOP-to-IRA rollover of S corporation stock if the following conditions are met:

- The terms of the ESOP require the S corporation to repurchase its stock immediately upon the ESOP's distribution of the stock to an IRA;

- The S corporation actually repurchases the S corporation stock contemporaneously with, and effective on the same day as, the distribution; and

- No income (including tax-exempt income), loss, deduction, or credit attributable to the S corporation stock is allocated to the participant's IRA.

Q 4:8 When is a grantor trust an eligible S corporation shareholder?

A grantor trust exists when an individual transfers property to a trust but retains control over the trust property or reserves the right to revoke the trust. A deemed grantor trust exists when property is contributed to a trust for a beneficiary who is given broad powers to control the trust property. In both cases, the trust is ignored for tax purposes. The grantor or beneficiary is treated as the owner of the trust property. All of the income, deductions, and other tax items of the trust pass through to the owner and are reported on his or her return. [IRC § 671 *et seq.*]

A grantor trust is an eligible S corporation shareholder during the life of the owner. [IRC § 1361(c)(2)(A)(i)]A grantor trust may continue as an eligible shareholder following the death of the owner—but only for two years beginning on the day of the owner's death. [IRC § 1361(c)(2)(A)(ii)]

Q 4:9 When can a testamentary trust hold S corporation stock?

A testamentary trust is a trust created by will. As a general rule, a testamentary trust that receives S corporation stock on the death of an S corporation shareholder qualifies as an eligible shareholder for a two-year period beginning on the date the stock is transferred to the trust. [IRC § 1361(c)(2)(A)(iii)]

Planning Point: If the trust has a single beneficiary who has broad powers to control the trust assets, the trust may qualify as a grantor trust (see Q 4:8). Alternatively, a testamentary trust may meet the requirements for a qualified subchapter S trust (see Q 4:11). In either case, the trust will be an eligible S corporation shareholder without regard to the two-year time limit.

Q 4:9

Q 4:10 What is a voting trust?

A voting trust is a trust created primarily to exercise the voting power of S corporation stock that is transferred to it. [IRC § 1361(c)(2)(A)(iv)] A voting trust is not treated as an S corporation shareholder. Instead, under the grantor trust rules, the transferors of the S corporation stock are treated as the owners of their respective portions of the trust (see Q 4:8).

A written trust agreement must delegate the right to vote the stock to one or more trustees. In addition, the trust must provide that all distributions with respect to the stock must be paid to the beneficial owners. A voting trust cannot be permanent. The trust agreement must provide for termination of the trust on or before a specific date or event and require the stock to be delivered to the beneficial owners on termination of the trust. [Reg. § 1.1361-1(h)(1)(v)]

Q 4:11 What is a qualified subchapter S trust?

A qualified subchapter S trust (QSST) qualifies as an S corporation shareholder if the trust beneficiary makes a special election to be treated as the owner of that portion of the trust consisting of S corporation stock. [IRC § 1361(d)] In other words, that portion of the trust will be treated as a grantor trust (see Q 4:8), and income, deductions, and other tax items from that portion of the trust will be reported directly on the beneficiary's income tax return.

A QSST must meet all of the following requirements:

- The trust must have only one current income beneficiary (or husband and wife income beneficiaries, provided they file a joint return);
- Any distributions of trust property must be made only to the income beneficiary;
- The income beneficiary's interest in the trust will terminate on the earlier of the income beneficiary's death or the termination of the trust;
- All trust property must be distributed to the income beneficiary if the trust terminates during his or her lifetime; and
- The trust must require that all trust income be distributed annually or the trustee must make annual distributions if the trust does not require them.

[Reg. § 1.1361-1(j)(7)]

Although a QSST may have only one beneficiary, a single trust with multiple beneficiaries may be treated as separate trust if the beneficiaries have separate and independent shares of the trust. [Reg. § 1.1361-1(j)(3)] In that case, each beneficiary must file a separate QSST election.

Q 4:12 Who must file an election to qualify the trust as a QSST?

The beneficiary of a QSST must file an election to qualify the trust to hold S corporation shares. A separate election must be filed for each corporation whose shares are held by the trust. If S corporation shares are transferred to a trust, the election must be made within the 16-day-and-two-month period beginning on the date of the transfer. If a trust holds stock in a corporation that subsequently elects to be treated as an S corporation, the QSST election must be filed within the 16-day-and-two-month period beginning on the date the corporation's S election is effective. [Reg. § 1.1361-1(j)(6)(iii)] In the case of a newly elected S corporation, the QSST election may be attached to the corporation's S election (Form 2553, *Election by Small Business Corporation*).

Q 4:13 What is an electing small business trust?

An electing small business trust (ESBT) is a trust with multiple beneficiaries that is authorized to hold S corporation stock. [IRC § 1361(e)] All of the beneficiaries of an ESBT must be individuals or estates that are eligible to hold S corporation stock directly (although charities may hold contingent remainder interests in the trust). The trust beneficiaries must acquire their interests in the trust by gift or bequest, not by purchase. [IRC § 1361(e)]

IRS regulations clarify that the prohibition on purchases applies to purchases of a beneficiary's interest in the trust, not to purchases of property by the trust. For example, a net gift of a beneficial interest in a trust (where the donee pays the gift tax) would be treated as a prohibited purchase of a beneficial interest. On the other hand, a net gift to the trust itself (where the trustee of the trust pays the gift tax) would not be treated as a purchase. [Reg. § 1.1361-1(m)(4)]

Each potential current income beneficiary of an ESBT is treated as a shareholder for purposes of the 100-shareholder limit on S corporations. A potential current income beneficiary is a beneficiary who is eligible to receive current distributions of income or principal from the trust, whether or not the income or principal is actually received. However, for tax years beginning after 2004, the term "current income beneficiary" does not include any person who may be the beneficiary of a power of appointment if the power has not been exercised [IRC § 1361(e)(2)].

An ESBT election comes at a tax cost. The portion of the trust holding S corporation stock is treated as a separate trust for tax purposes, and the S corporation income passed through to the trust is taxed to the trust at the highest individual tax rate. [IRC § 641(c)]

IRS regulations allow a grantor trust to elect to be an ESBT for tax years ending after December 28, 2000. If the election is made, the trust consists of a grantor portion, an S portion, and a non-S portion. The items of income, deduction, and credit attributable to the grantor portion are taxed to the deemed owner of that portion. The S portion is taxed under Section 641(c) outlined above. The non-S portion is taxed under the regular trust rules. [Reg. § 1.641(c)-1]

ESBT election. The trustee of the trust must elect ESBT status by filing an election statement with the IRS. The election must be made within the same time limits that apply to QSST elections. Those rules require the election to be made within two months and 16 days of the date the S corporation stock is transferred to the trust. If the trust holds stock in a corporation that makes an S election, the ESBT election must be made within two months and 16 days of the date the corporation's S election is effective. In the case of a newly electing S corporation, the ESBT election may be attached to the corporation's S election form (Form 2553, *Election by Small Business Corporation*). [Prop. Reg. §§1.1361-1(m)(2); 1.1361-1(j)(6)(iii)]

Q 4:14 How are shareholders counted for purposes of the 100-shareholder limit?

As a general rule, if S corporation stock is owned jointly, each owner is counted as a shareholder. So, for example, if a father and son own shares of S corporation stock jointly, they count as two shareholders.

However, a husband and wife are always treated as one shareholder, whether they own their stock jointly or individually. [IRC § 1361(c)(1)(A)(i)]

In addition, for tax years beginning after 2004, all members of a family as one shareholder for purposes of the 100-shareholder limit. A "family" is defined as the common ancestor and all lineal descendants of the common ancestor, as well as the spouses, or former spouses, of these individuals. An individual shall not be a common ancestor if the individual is more than six generations removed from the youngest generation of shareholders who would (but for this rule) be members of the family. For purposes of this rule, a spouse or former spouse is treated as in the same generation as the person to whom the individual is (or was) married. The election can be made by any member of the family and remains in effect until terminated. [IRC § 1361(c)(1)(B)]

The IRS recently issued proposed regulations dealing with the six-generation test. [Prop. Reg. 1.1361-1] The regulations state that the test is only applied at the statutory date for determining if an individual meets the definition of common ancestor. The test has no continuing significance in limiting the number of generations of a family that may hold stock and be treated as a single shareholder.

Capital Structure

Q 4:15 Can an S corporation have more than one class of stock?

No. One requirement for qualification for S corporation tax treatment is that the corporation may have only one class of stock. [IRC § 1361(b)(1)(D)] For example, unlike a regular C corporation, an S corporation may not issue both common and preferred stock.

Q 4:16 Can S corporation shares have different rights?

Yes—within limits. A corporation is not treated as having more than one class of stock solely because there are differences in voting rights among the shares. [IRC § 1361(c)(4); Reg. § 1.1361-1(l)(1)] Therefore, an S corporation can issue both voting and nonvoting common stock.

Planning Point: The ability to issue both voting and nonvoting stock may be particularly appealing to family-owned corporations. It permits the corporation to limit decision-making authority to those family members who hold voting stock, while spreading the corporate wealth among the family.

In addition, buy-sell agreements and transferability restrictions do not generally create a separate class of stock. However, other differences—most particularly, differences in rights to distributions and liquidation proceeds—will be treated as creating a second class of stock. [Reg. § 1.1361-1(l)(2)(i)]

Q 4:17 Can an S corporation borrow money instead of issuing additional stock?

Yes. However, debt must be carefully structured to avoid equity-like characteristics that would cause it to be treated as a second class of stock, which would terminate the corporation's S election (see Q 4:16).

Under a special safe-harbor rule, so-called "straight debt" will not be treated as a second class of stock. [IRC § 1361(c)(5)]To qualify as straight debt, an obligation must meet all of the following requirements:

- There is a written, unconditional promise to pay a sum certain in money on demand or on a specified date;
- The interest rate and payment dates are not contingent on the corporation's profits, discretion, or other similar factors;
- The debt cannot be converted either directly or indirectly into stock; and
- The lender is an individual, estate, or trust that would qualify as an S corporation shareholder, or is a creditor that is actively and regularly engaged in the business of lending money.

Regulations also provide that debt obligations that might otherwise be classified as equity will not be treated as a second class of stock if they are owned solely by the corporation's shareholders in the same proportion as the outstanding stock. [Reg. § 1.1361-1(l)(4)(ii)(B)(ii)]

In some cases, an S corporation may need a quick infusion of cash. The regulations also create safe-harbor rules for short-term loans from a shareholder. A short-term advance from a shareholder that is not evidenced by a written debt instrument will not be treated as a second class of stock if:

- The total does not exceed $10,000 at any time during a tax year;
- Both the corporation and the shareholder treat the amounts as debt; and
- Repayment is expected in a reasonable period of time.

[Reg. § 1.1361-1(l)(4)(ii)(B)]

Planning Point: A debt that does not fall within any of the safe-harbor rules is not automatically classified as a second class of stock. A debt will not be reclassified unless it gives the holder stock-like rights, such as a right to a share of corporate profits or a right to a share of the proceeds on liquidation of the corporation. However, the only way to be certain that a debt will not cause tax trouble is to stay within the safe-harbor rules.

Electing S Corporation Status

Q 4:18 How does a corporation elect S corporation status?

A corporation makes an S election by filing Form 2553, *Election by Small Business Corporation*, with the Internal Revenue Service Center designated in the form's instructions. An officer of the corporation who is authorized to sign the corporation's federal income tax return must sign the form.

Planning Point: Filing an election form is the only way to elect S corporation status. Filing of an S corporation income tax return on Form 1120S, *U.S. Income Tax Return for an S Corporation*, will not satisfy the requirement unless the corporation has an S corporation election on record.

Q 4:19 When must the election be filed?

An election for a given year must be filed during the preceding tax year or within two months and 15 days of the current year. [IRC § 1362(b)(1)] So, for example, an election that is to take effect on January 1, 2008 must be filed during 2007 or by March 17, 2008 (March 15 falls on a Saturday).

Q 4:20 What happens if an election is late?

An election that is filed after the first two-and-one-half months of any year will take effect for the following year. [IRC § 1362(b)(1)] The IRS, however, can treat late elections as timely, provided there was reasonable cause for the failure to file on time. [IRC 1362(b)(5); Rev. Procs. 97-48, 1997-2 C.B. 521; 98-55, 1998-2 C.B. 643]

The IRS has set up a simplified method for taxpayers seeking relief when an S corporation election has been filed late. [Rev. Proc. 2003-43, 2003-23 I.R.B. 998] The simplified relief procedures are generally available to corporations that fail to qualify for their intended S corporation status solely because of the failure to make a timely election. (The IRS also provides procedures for obtaining similar relief when certain other S corporation elections are made late, such as the election to treat a trust-shareholder as a QSST; see Q 4:11).

Requirements for relief. If the corporation seeking to make the election has not filed its tax return for the first year, for the election to apply:

- The relief application must be filed no later than six months after the tax return due date (excluding extensions) and

- No taxpayer whose tax liability or tax return would be affected by the election has reported inconsistently with the S corporation election.

Q 4:18

If the corporation has filed its return for the first year, for the election to apply:

- The return must have been filed within six months of the due date (including extensions) and

- No taxpayer whose tax liability or tax return would be affected by the election has reported inconsistently with the S corporation election.

Procedural requirement. If no S corporation return has yet been filed, the corporation may request relief by filing a completed Form 2553, signed by an officer of the corporation authorized to sign and all persons who were shareholders at any time during the period that began on the first day of the taxable year for which the election is to be effective and ends on the day the election is made.

The completed election form must include the following material:

- Statements from all shareholders during the period between the date the S corporation election was to have become effective and the date the completed election was filed that they have reported their income (on all affected returns) consistent with the S corporation election; and

- A dated declaration signed by an officer of the corporation authorized to sign which states: "Under penalties of perjury, I declare that, to the best of my knowledge and belief, the facts presented in support of this election are true, correct, and complete."

Form 2553 must be filed within 18 months of the original due date of the intended election, but in no event later than six months after the due date of the tax return (excluding extensions) of the corporation's return first year in which the election was intended. The form must state at the top "FILED PURSUANT TO REV. PROC. 2003-43."

Attached to the form must be a statement establishing reasonable cause for the failure to file a timely election.

If a tax return for the first S corporation election year has already been filed, the relief procedures are the same, except that Form 2553 must be filed within 24 months of the original due date of the election.

Q 4:21 Can a corporation's officers elect S corporation tax treatment without the consent of the shareholders?

No. The election must have the consent of all of the shareholders who own stock in the corporation on the date of the election. [IRC § 1362(a)(2)] If an election is to apply retroactively, the corporation must also obtain the consent of any shareholders who owned stock in the corporation during the portion of the year before the election date. [Reg. § 1362(b)(2)(B)(ii)]For example, if an S election is made on March 1, 2008, effective for the 2008 calendar year, consent must be obtained from any shareholders who owned stock between January 1 and February 29, 2008, even if they did not own stock on March 1.

On the other hand, if an election is made during one year to be effective at the beginning of the following year, the corporation is not required to obtain the consent of new shareholders who acquire stock in the corporation after the date of the election. [Reg. §1.1362-6(a)(2)(i)]Presumably, the consent of these shareholders is not required because they will be aware of the upcoming switch to S corporation status.

S Corporation Taxation

Q 4:22 Can an S corporation operate on a year other than a calendar year?

An S corporation must generally use a calendar year as its tax year. [IRC §1378(b)(1)] The reason for this rule stems from the tax deferral that can result if the corporation uses a non-calendar fiscal year and its shareholders use a calendar year. For example, if an S corporation's year ended in June 2007, only income earned by the corporation in the first half of 2007 would be included on the shareholder's 2007 returns. The income for the second half of 2007 would not be taxed to the shareholders until 2008—and would not be reported to the IRS until the shareholders file their returns in 2009.

There are, however, two important exceptions to the calendar-year requirement:

1. *Business year.* An S corporation can use a non-calendar fiscal year if it establishes to the satisfaction of the IRS that it has a business purpose for the use of such year. [IRC §1378(b)(2)]

2. *Elected fiscal year.* An S corporation may make an election to use a fiscal year that does not defer income to the shareholders for more than three months. [IRC §444] The three-month deferral limit means that an S corporation can elect a September, October, or November fiscal year, but not an earlier year. If an S corporation makes this election, it must make special required payments to offset the tax deferral.

(These exceptions also apply in the partnership context. For more details, see Chapter 2.)

Q 4:23 How is an S corporation treated for tax purposes?

Because an S corporation is a pass-through entity, there is generally no tax at the corporate level. [IRC §1363(a)]Instead, the corporation reports its income, deductions, and other tax items to its shareholders for reporting on their returns. [IRC §1363(b)]

However, a C corporation that converts to S corporation status may owe corporate-level taxes. The most significant of these taxes is the tax on built-in gains (Q 4:24) and the LIFO recapture tax (Q 4:25).

Q 4:22

Q 4:24 What is the tax on built-in gains?

A C corporation that converts to S corporations status may have "built-in" gains on assets acquired during C corporation years. That is, the assets may have appreciated since the corporation acquired them.

Under the Internal Revenue Code (IRC or the Code), a corporate-level tax is imposed on any built-in gain that is recognized during the first ten years following the corporation's S election. [IRC § 1374] The tax is computed by applying the highest corporate income tax rate (currently 35 percent) to the corporation's net recognized built-in gain for the tax year.

In computing an S corporation's net recognized built-in gain for a year, built-in gain may be offset by recognized built-in losses on assets acquired in C corporation years. In addition, built-in gains may be offset by unused net operating losses, capital losses, and business tax credits carried forward from C corporation years. [IRC § 1374]

The amount of any built-in gain passed through to shareholders is reduced by the built-in gain tax paid by the corporation. [IRC § 1366(f)(2)]

Planning Point: The tax on built-gains is intended to prevent a C corporation from converting to S status in order to pass-through gains from assets without paying a corporate-level tax.

Q 4:25 When does an S corporation owe LIFO recapture tax?

When a C corporation that uses the last-in, first-out (LIFO) inventory method converts to S corporation status, it must pay tax on a LIFO recapture amount. [IRC § 1363(d)]The recapture amount is the excess of the value of the corporation's inventory using the first-in, first-out (FIFO) inventory method over the LIFO value of the inventory. The recapture amount is included in income for the corporation's last year as a C corporation, and the tax is calculated at the corporation's tax rate for that year. The tax, however, is payable by the corporation over four years. The first installment must be paid by the due date of the return for the last C corporation year. The three subsequent installments must be paid by the due dates of the S corporation's returns for the three succeeding years.

Observation: Calculation of the LIFO recapture tax is complicated, but the concept is relatively simple. It stems from the interplay of the built-in gains tax on sales of assets acquired during C corporation years (Q 4:24) and the inventory accounting rules.

Under the FIFO inventory rules, a corporation is treated as having sold its oldest inventory first. The LIFO rules are just the reverse; a corporation is treated as having sold its most recently acquired inventory first.

The built-in gains tax applies to gains from assets that represent appreciation during C corporation years. The tax is imposed on gains recognized during the first ten years following an S corporation election. However, a corporation using the LIFO inventory method will escape the tax on inventory items if it does not reduce its inventory level for at least ten years. In other words, as long as the corporation continues to sell newly acquired inventory and does not dip into C corporation inventory for at least ten years, the built-in gains tax will not apply to the appreciation on that inventory. Whereas, a corporation using the FIFO method will owe the built-in gains tax on inventory sales until it depletes the inventory acquired during C corporation years. The LIFO recapture tax is intended to plug that "loophole."

Under regulations finalized by the IRS, a C corporation that holds an interest in a partnership owning LIFO inventory is required to include the "lookthrough LIFO recapture" amount in its gross income where it either elects to be an S corporation or transfers its interest in the partnership to an S corporation in a nonrecognition transaction. [Reg. § 1.1363-2(b)]The lookthrough LIFO recapture amount is the amount of income that would be allocated to the corporation if the partnership sold all of its LIFO inventory for the FIFO value. [Reg. § 1.1363-2(c)] The regulations apply to S elections and transfers after Aug. 12, 2004.

Tax Treatment of S Corporation Shareholders

Q 4:26 How are S corporation shareholders taxed?

Each S corporation shareholder must report passed-though items from the S corporation on his or her own return. [IRC § 1366]

As a general rule, an S corporation computes its taxable income or loss in the same manner as an individual. [IRC § 1363 (b)] Shareholder's must report their pro rata shares of this "non-separately computed income or loss." [IRC § 1366(a)(2)]

However, an S corporation must separately report to shareholders any items that could affect the tax liability of a shareholder. [IRC § 1363((b)(1)] Each shareholder must also report his or her share of these "separately stated items." [IRC § 1366(a)(1)(A)] For example, capital gains and losses must be separately stated because they may be offset by a shareholder's gains and losses from other sources.

Items that must be separately stated include:

- Long-term capital gain or loss;
- Short-term capital gain or loss;
- Casualty or theft gains or losses;
- Section 179 expensing deductions for depreciable property;
- Investment interest expense;
- Charitable contributions; and
- Tax credits, including jobs and research credits.

[Reg. § 1.1361-1(a)(2)]

Q 4:26

The character of any income item passed through to a shareholder is determined as if it was received directly from the source from which the corporation received it. Similarly, any passed-through deduction or loss is treated as incurred in the same manner as the corporation incurred it. For example, if an S corporation has capital gain from the sale of a capital asset, a shareholder's pro rata share is characterized as capital gain. [IRC § 1366(b)]

Q 4:27 If S corporation stock changes hands during the year, how are passed-through items allocated to the shareholders?

A shareholder's pro rata share of pass-through items is generally determined on a per-share, per-day basis. [IRC § 1377(a)(1)] The process is relatively simple if ownership of the corporation remains the same throughout the year. Each item is simply multiplied by the shareholder's percentage of the outstanding shares. So, for example, two equal shareholders will each be allocated 50 percent of each pass-through item.

The allocation process becomes more complicated if shares in the corporation change hands during the year. The first step is to determine the daily portion of an item by dividing the total amount of the item by the number of days in the tax year. Then divide the daily portion by the number of shares outstanding on each day to determine the amount allocable to each share. Thus, a shareholder's pro rata share of a pass-through item is equal to the daily amount allocable to each share multiplied by the number of shares he or she owns and then by the number of days he or she held the shares.

Example 4-1: Ess Corporation is a calendar-year corporation. On January 1, Able and Baker each own 50 shares of Ess stock. On July 1, Baker sells his 50 shares to Carol. Ess has $365,000 of taxable income for the year.

Result: Ess Corporation's per-day income is $1,000 per day ($365,000/365 days) and its per-share income for each day is $10 per share ($1,000/100 shares). Therefore, Able's share of the passed-through income is $182,500 ($10 per share × 50 shares × 365 days). Since Baker held his shares for 181 days, his share of the passed-through income is $90,500 ($10 per share × 50 shares × 181 days). Carol, who held her shares for 184 days, is allocated $92,000 of the passed-through income ($10 per share × 50 shares × 184 days).

Planning Point: If a corporation has passed-though items that must be separately stated, separate calculations must be made for those items.

If one or more shareholders terminate his or her entire interest in the S corporation during the year, the corporation may elect to allocate items to shareholders based on when they were actually realized during the year. [IRC § 1377(a)(2)]

This is done by splitting the year into two accounting periods, with one period running from the beginning of the year to the termination and the other period running from the day after the termination to the end of the year. Items shown on the corporation's books and records for a period are allocated to shareholders who held stock during that period. The election requires the consent of all shareholders who owned stock in the corporation during the year.

> **Example 4-2:** Same facts as Example 4-1, except Ess Corporation elects to allocate based on separate accounting periods. The corporation's books and records show that it realized $275,000 of taxable income from January 1 through July 1 and $90,000 during the remainder of the year.
>
> *Result:* As equal shareholders, Able and Baker are each allocated one-half of the total income for the first accounting period—$137,500. Similarly, Able and Carol are each allocated $45,000, one-half of the income for the second period. (Note: In the case of unequal shareholders, the allocation is made on a per-share basis.)
>
> *Outcome:* The separate accounting period election does not affect the amount allocable to Able. However, because the corporation earned the bulk of its income in the first part of the year, the election increases the amount allocable to Baker and correspondingly decreases the amount allocable to Carol.

Q 4:28 Are there any limits on a shareholder's ability to deduct passed-through losses or deductions?

Yes. Deductions for passed-through losses and deduction items cannot exceed a shareholder's adjusted basis in his or her S corporation stock plus the basis of any loans made by the shareholder to the corporation. [IRC § 1366(d)]

> **Planning Point:** Surprisingly, S shareholders who will be affected by this basis limitation rule have a golden planning opportunity. They can readily control the timing of their write-offs for the passed-through losses. Shareholders who want to use passed-through S corporation losses or deductions to shelter current year income can act by year end to increase their basis in the S corporation either by making a capital contribution to the corporation or by making a loan to the corporation. Whereas, shareholders with little or no income for the current year or those who anticipate higher income in the future may prefer to defer their write-offs. That can easily be accomplished by holding off on any capital contributions or loans to the corporation until a later year. If passed-through losses exceed the shareholder's basis, the losses can be carried forward indefinitely and used in later years when the shareholder has sufficient basis. [IRC § 1366(d)(2)]

Spouses and ex-spouses are permitted to transfer losses and deductions that have been suspended because of the basis limitation. If a shareholder's stock in an S corporation is transferred to a spouse, or to a former spouse incident to a divorce, any suspended loss or deduction attributable to that stock is treated as incurred by the corporation with respect to the transferee shareholder in the subsequent tax year. [IRC § 1366(d)(2)]

Q 4:28

Q 4:29 How is the Section 199 deduction for qualified production activities computed in an S corporation?

An S corporation cannot claim the Section 199 deduction for qualified production activities (see Chapter 6). Instead, the deduction is determined at the shareholder level. [IRC § 199(d)(1); Temporary Reg. 1.199-5T(b)] Generally, each shareholder computes its deduction separately on Form 8903 by aggregating its pro rata share of qualified production activity (QPA) items of the S corporation (i.e., income, expenses) with its share of QPA items from other sources. The shareholder does not have to be directly engaged in the S corporation's trade or business to claim the deduction on the basis of its share of QPA items.

Q 4:30 How is the basis of S corporation stock determined?

The starting point for determining a shareholder's basis in his or her S corporation stock is the amount paid for the stock or, in the case of a newly formed corporation, the amount contributed to the corporation in return for the stock (see Chapter 3). However, an S shareholder's basis is constantly changing. A shareholder's basis is increased and/or decreased annually to reflect items passed through and distributed by the corporation.

Basis increases. The basis of an S shareholder's stock is increased by any income passed through by the corporation. [IRC § 1367(a)]

A shareholder's stock basis is also increased by a shareholder's pro rata share of items of income that were separately treated by the corporation, such as capital gains or tax-exempt income, and by the shareholder's pro rata share of the deduction for depletion in excess of the basis of the property subject to depletion.

Basis decreases. A shareholder's basis is decreased (but not below zero) by any losses passed through to the shareholder by the corporation and by any distributions to the shareholder that are not taxable to the shareholder as dividends (see Q 4:32 *et seq.*). [IRC § 1367(a)]

Basis is decreased by any deduction items that were separately treated by the corporation, such as capital losses; any expense of the corporation that was not deductible in computing taxable income (other than capital expenses); and the amount of the shareholder's pro rata share of the deduction for depletion for oil and gas wells. Under the Pension Protection Act of 2006, when an S corporation makes a donation of property to charity, a shareholder reduces his or her basis by a pro rata share of the property's basis, not a pro rata share of the property's fair market value.

If a shareholder's basis in his or her stock is reduced to zero, any excess loss reduces the shareholder's basis (but not below zero) of any debt owed by the corporation to the shareholder.

A shareholder's stock basis is adjusted first by corporate income and loss for the year and then by corporate distributions. However, if a shareholder's basis in corporate debt has been reduced, the shareholder must increase the debt basis to (but not above) its original amount before increasing stock basis. [IRC §§1367(b)(1), (2)(B)]

> **Example 4-3:** George Finn is a 50 percent shareholder in a calendar-year S corporation. Finn's stock basis is $4,000. Finn also has a $2,000 basis in a loan he made to the corporation. In 2007, the corporation loses $10,000. Finn's $5,000 share of the 2007 loss reduces his stock basis to zero and reduces his debt basis to $1,000. Finn can deduct the full $5,000 loss as an ordinary loss in 2007.
>
> In 2008, the corporation has $20,000 profit and distributes $6,000 to Finn. Finn's $10,000 share of the 2008 income first increases his reduced debt basis to its original $2,000 level, and then increases his stock basis to $9,000. Finally, Finn's stock basis is reduced to $3,000 by the $6,000 distribution.

Ordering rules. Adjustments to basis are made in the following order:

1. Increases for income items;

2. Decreases for distributions;

3. Decreases for nondeductible expenses and depletion deductions; and

4. Decreases for other loss and deduction items.

[Reg. §1.1368-1(e)(2)]

Timing rules. Stock basis adjustments are determined at the end of the corporation's tax year and are generally effective as of that date. [Reg. §1.1367-1(d)(1)]

Basis adjustments for distributions made by an S corporation during the tax year are taken into account before applying the loss limitation for the year. Therefore, distributions reduce the shareholder's basis for determining the amount of deductible losses.

> **Example 4-4:** Lucy Smith is the sole shareholder of an S corporation. Smith has a $1,000 basis in her stock. The corporation makes a nontaxable distribution of $1,000 to Smith during the year. At year-end, the corporation has a $1,000 loss, which passes through to Smith. Smith's basis is reduced to zero as a result of the distribution. Therefore, Smith cannot deduct any portion of the passed-through loss for the year.

Q 4:31 What is a shareholder's basis in debt?

When a shareholder lends money to a corporation, the shareholder has a basis in the debt equal to the face amount of the loan. If passed-through losses from the corporation exceed the shareholder's basis in his or her stock, the losses will be deductible to the extent of the shareholder's debt basis. [IRC §1366(d)] The passed-through losses will reduce the shareholder's basis in the debt (but not below zero). In subsequent years, items that increase basis must first be applied to increase the debt basis to (but not above) its original level before increasing stock basis. [IRC §1367(b)(1), (2)(B)]

Q 4:31

Q 4:32 What happens if a shareholder cannot deduct passed-through losses or deductions because of the basis limitation?

Any passed-through losses or deductions that exceed a shareholder's basis in both stock and debt can be carried forward and used in later years when the shareholder has sufficient basis to absorb them. [IRC § 1367(b)(2)(A)]

Distributions to S Corporation Shareholders

Q 4:33 How are distributions to S corporation shareholders treated for tax purposes?

Distributions to S corporation shareholders generally represent income that has already been passed through and taxed to the shareholders. Therefore, in most cases, distributions are not taxable to the shareholders. [IRC § 1368(b)] However, there are two situations in which an S corporation shareholder may owe tax on all or a portion of an S corporation distribution.

1. An S corporation that formerly operated as a C corporation may have accumulated earnings and profits (E&P) from its C corporation years that were not distributed to shareholders. A distribution of accumulated E&P is taxed as a dividend to an S corporation shareholder (see Q 4:35).

2. A distribution that exceeds an S corporation shareholder's basis in his or her stock is treated as a payment in exchange for stock. Therefore, the amount of the distribution in excess of basis is taxed to the shareholder as capital gain (see Q 4:34).

The amount of a distribution to a shareholder equals the amount of cash distributed plus the fair market value of any property distributed. [IRC §§ 301(c); 1368(a)]

Distributions (other than distributions that are taxable as dividends) reduce a shareholder's basis in his or her S corporation stock (see Q 4:34).

Q 4:34 When does an S corporation have accumulated E&P?

A C corporation's earnings and profits (E&P) represent its current year income and retained profits from prior years that have not been distributed to its shareholders. When distributions are made to C corporation shareholders, they are treated as dividends to the extent of the corporation's E&P. Distributions in excess of a C corporation's E&P reduce a C corporation shareholder's basis in his or her stock. Distributions in excess of basis are generally taxed as capital gains. [IRC § 301(c); Reg. § 1.301-1]

By contrast, an S corporation's income is passed through and taxed to shareholders whether or not it is actually distributed. Therefore, an S corporation will not have current E&P for any year. However, an S corporation that has converted from C corporation status may have accumulated E&P from its C corporation years.

Q 4:35 How are S corporation distributions treated if the corporation has not accumulated E&P?

If an S corporation has no accumulated E&P, any distributions reduce a shareholder's basis in his or her S corporation stock. The amount of a distribution in excess of basis is treated as payment in exchange for the shareholder's stock. The excess amount is taxed at capital gain rates. [IRC § 1368(b)(2)]

Q 4:36 How are S corporation distributions treated if the corporation has accumulated E&P?

If an S corporation has accumulated E&P from C corporation years, distributions are treated as coming first from the corporation's accumulated adjustment account (AAA), which represents net income from S corporation years that has already been taxed to the shareholders but has not been distributed (see Q 4:36). A distribution that does not exceed the corporation's AAA is taxed the same as a distribution from an S corporation with no accumulated E&P. That is, the distribution is tax-free to the extent of the shareholder's basis in his or her stock, while any amount in excess of basis is taxed as capital gain. [IRC § 1368(c)(1)]

If more than one distribution is made in a tax year and the total exceeds the amount in the corporation's AAA, the amount in the AAA is allocated among the distributions in proportion to the size of the distributions.

Distributions in excess of the corporation's AAA are treated as dividends to the extent of the corporation's accumulated E&P. [IRC § 1368 (c)(2)] Finally, any remaining portion of a distribution is taxed as capital gain. [IRC § 1368(c)(3)]

> **Example 4-5:** Allen and Baker are equal shareholders in an S corporation. The corporation's AAA is $10,000, and the corporation has $4,000 of accumulated E&P from years when it operated as a C corporation. The corporation distributes $15,000 ($7,500 to each shareholder). The first $5,000 of each shareholder's distribution is treated as a tax-free distribution from the corporation's AAA. The next $2,000 of each distribution is treated as a taxable dividend from the corporation's accumulated E&P. The remaining $500 of each shareholder's distribution is taxable capital gain.

Q 4:37 How is a corporation's AAA calculated?

1. An S corporation's AAA is increased each year by:

   a. Non-separately stated income;

   b. Separately stated income items (other than tax-exempt interest income); and

   c. Excess deductions for depletion over the basis of property subject to depletion.

   [IRC § 1368(e)(1)]

2. The corporation's AAA is decreased by:

   a. Non-separately stated losses;

   b. Separately stated losses and deductions;

c. Nondeductible expenses that are not treated as capital expenses (other than expenses related to tax-exempt income);

d. The depletion deduction for oil and gas wells; and

e. Distributions made from the AAA.

[IRC § 1368(e)(1)]

Q 4:38 Are distributions from an S corporation subject to FICA and FUTA taxes?

No. However, keep in mind, that salaries, wages, and other compensation paid to an owner-employee of an S corporation are subject to FICA and FUTA taxes.

This distinction provides an incentive for owner-employees to take compensation for services in the form of "dividends", which are exempt from FICA and FUTA tax.

The IRS ruled many years ago that this practice is prohibited. [Rev. Rul. 74-44, 1974-2 C.B. 287] The Service's position has been upheld by the courts. For example, Robin Dunn and Stephen Clark were the sole shareholders of Dunn and Clark, P.C., a law firm organized as an S corporation. Dunn and Clark did all of the legal work for the firm's clients. However, the firm did not pay them salaries for their legal work. Instead, the corporation paid them substantial dividends on their stock.

The IRS argued that the dividends were really salary on which the corporation, Dunn, and Clark owed FICA taxes. The court agreed that the payments had to represent compensation for the legal services the lawyers provided to the firm. According to the court, any other conclusion would require the court to accept that Dunn and Clark provided legal services "out of the goodness of their hearts." [*Dunn & Clark, P.C.*, 73 A.F.T.R.2d 94-1860]

S Corporation Subsidiaries

Q 4:39 Can an S corporation have a subsidiary?

At one time, S corporations were barred from having controlled subsidiaries. The Internal Revenue Code said that S corporations could not own 80 percent or more of the stock of another corporation. In addition, an S corporation could not have a corporate shareholder. So one S corporation could not own any stock in another S corporation. However, a law change that took effect a number of years ago, permits an S corporation to have an 80 percent or more owned C corporation subsidiary and a wholly-owned qualified Subchapter S subsidiary (QSub). [IRC § 1361(b)]

A C corporation subsidiary is treated as a separate taxpayer. If a C corporation subsidiary operates profitably, it pays tax on its income. If it operates at a loss, it cannot pass the loss through to the S corporation. A QSub is not treated as a separate corporation for federal tax purposes. Instead, its assets; liabilities; and items of income, deduction, and credit are deemed to belong to the parent S corporation. [IRC § 1361(b)(3)(A); Reg. § 1.1361-4]

Q 4:40 What are the qualification requirements for a QSub?

A domestic corporation qualifies as a QSub if (1) the parent corporation holds 100 percent of the stock of the subsidiary corporation, and (2) the parent elects to treat the subsidiary as a QSub.

For purposes of the 100 percent ownership requirement, stock of a subsidiary is treated as held by the parent S corporation if the parent is treated as the owner for federal income tax purposes. Outstanding instruments, obligations, or arrangements are not counted as stock if they would not count for purposes of the rule requiring S corporations to have a single class of stock. [IRC § 1361(b)(1)(d); Reg. § 1.1361-2]

Q 4:41 Is QSub treatment automatic?

No. The parent corporation must elect to have the subsidiary treated as a QSub. The election is made by filing Form 8869, *Qualified Subchapter S Subsidiary Election,* with the IRS. [IRS Notice 2000-58, 2000-47 I.R.B. 491]

A person authorized to sign the parent corporation's federal return must sign the election form. The election form must be submitted to the Internal Revenue Service Center where the subsidiary filed its most recent return. In the case of a newly formed subsidiary, the election form should be submitted to the Internal Revenue Service Center where the parent S corporation filed its most recent return.

The S corporation parent may make a QSub election at any time during the tax year. An election takes effect on the date specified in the election form or, if no date is specified, on the date the election form is filed. However, the effective date specified on the form cannot be more than two months and 15 days before the date of the filing or more than 12 months after the date of the filing. If an election form specifies a date that is more than 12 months after the filing date, the election will take effect 12 months after the date it is filed. [IRC § 1361(d); Reg. § 1.1361-3]

The IRS is authorized to waive inadvertently invalid QSub elections. [IRC § 1362(f)(1)(A)] To benefit from this relief provision, the QSub and its shareholder (the S corporation parent) must:

• Within a reasonable period after discovering the circumstances causing the invalidity take steps so that the corporation qualifies as a QSub; and

• Accept any adjustments required by the IRS that are consistent with the treatment of the corporation as a QSub during the relevant period.

Q 4:42 How is a QSub election treated for tax purposes?

When a parent corporation makes a QSub election with respect to a subsidiary, the subsidiary is deemed to have liquidated into the parent. The regulations provide that the tax treatment of the liquidation generally will be determined under all relevant tax law rules, including the step-transaction doctrine. Under the step-transaction doctrine, only the end result of a series of related transactions is taken into account in determining the tax consequences; earlier steps are ignored. So, for example, if a corporation forms a new subsidiary and immediately makes a QSub election, the deemed liquidation will be ignored under the step-transaction doctrine, and the subsidiary will be treated as a QSub from its inception. [Reg. § 1.1361-4(a)(2)]

Q 4:43 Is a QSub election irrevocable?

No, it is not. Although the tax law says that a QSub election may be revoked only with the consent of the Secretary of the Treasury, the regulations are more lenient. Regulations Section 1.1361-3(b) provides that a parent S corporation can revoke a QSub election by filing a statement with the Internal Revenue Service Center where the parent's most recent return was filed. [IRC § 1.1361]

The revocation statement must include the names, addresses, and employer identification numbers (EINs) of both the parent S corporation and the QSub, if any. A person authorized to sign the parent's return must sign the statement.

Revocation of a QSub election is effective on the date specified in the revocation statement or, if no date is specified, on the date the statement is filed. Again, the specified effective date cannot be more than two months and 15 days prior to or more than 12 months after the filing date. A statement that specifies a date more than 12 months after the filing date will take effect on the filing date.

A QSub election may also be terminated involuntarily—for example, if the parent corporation ceases to be an S corporation or the subsidiary ceases to be an eligible corporation. [Reg. § 1. 1361-5]

Q 4:44 What is the effect of a QSub termination?

A QSub election may be terminated voluntarily by filing a statement with the IRS. A QSub election may also be terminated involuntarily—for example, if the parent corporation ceases to be an S corporation or the subsidiary ceases to be an eligible corporation. [Reg. § 1.1361-5]

When a QSub election is terminated, the subsidiary is treated as a new corporation acquiring all of its assets (and assuming all of its liabilities) from the parent S corporation in exchange for stock. As with QSub elections, the regulations provide that the tax consequences of a QSub termination will be determined under generally applicable tax rules—including the step-transaction doctrine. This can be bad news in some situations.

Example 4-6: Parent Corp. owns 100 percent of the stock of Sub Corp., which Parent has elected to treat as a QSub. Parent Corp. sells 21 percent of the stock of Sub Corp. to an unrelated corporation for cash. Because a parent must own 100 percent of the stock of a QSub, the QSub election terminates on the date of the sale.

Result: Sub Corp. is treated as a new corporation acquiring its assets (and assuming its liabilities) in exchange for its stock immediately before the termination of the QSub election. However, the exchange does not qualify as a tax-free transfer to a controlled corporation because Parent Corp. no longer controls at least 80 percent of Sub Corp. [IRC §§ 351, 368(c)] Therefore, Parent Corp. will recognize gain on the assets transferred to Sub Corp. However, losses will be limited by the related party rules. [IRC § 267]Those rules disallow losses on sales or exchanges between certain related parties, including a parent corporation and a subsidiary.

Terminating an S Election

Q 4:45 How is an S election terminated?

An S election may be revoked voluntarily (see Q 4:45). In addition, a corporation's S election will be terminated if it ceases to qualify as an S corporation (see Q 4:46) or violates certain restrictions on passive investment income see Q 4:49). [IRC § 1362(d); Reg. § 1.1362-2]

If a corporation's status as an S corporation is terminated, it generally must wait five tax years before it can again become an S corporation. [IRC § 1362(g)]However, the IRS may consent to an earlier reelection.

As a general rule, the IRS will not consent to an early reelection unless the termination of S status was not reasonably within the control of the corporation and was not planned. Therefore, a corporation that loses its S status because of a mistake is likely to receive IRS consent to an early reelection. In addition, the regulations state that a more than 50 percent change in stock ownership following a termination is likely to justify an early reelection. [Reg. § 1.1362-5(a)]

Q 4:46 How is an S election revoked?

To revoke an S election, shareholders owning more than 50 percent of the outstanding shares of the corporation (including nonvoting shares) must consent to the revocation. [IRC § 1362(d)(1)] The consenting shareholders must own their stock in the S corporation at the beginning of the day the revocation is filed.

A revocation made on or before the 15th day of the third month of the corporation's tax year will relate back to the beginning of the year unless the corporation specifies another prospective effective date. So, for example, a calendar-year S corporation has until March 15 to file a revocation for any given year. Revocations filed after the 15th day of the third month of a tax year will be effective on the first day of the following tax year unless, again, the revocation provides for some other prospective effective date. [IRC § 1362(d)(1); Reg. § 1.1362-2(a)]

Q 4:45

If a revocation specifies an effective date other than the first day of a tax year, the revocation will create two short tax years—an S corporation short tax year ending on the day before the effective date and a C corporation year beginning on the effective date and ending on the last day of the corporation's regular tax year.

There is no official form for revoking an S election. A statement revoking the election should be filed with the Internal Revenue Service Center where the corporation's S election was filed. The statement must indicate the effective date of the revocation and be signed by a person authorized to sign the corporation's return. Consents signed by shareholders holding more than 50 percent of the corporation's stock on the day on which the revocation is made must be attached to the statement. [Reg. § § 1.1362-6(a)(3), (b)]

A corporation can rescind a revocation at any time before the effective date. A rescission must have the consent of all persons who consented to the revocation as well as all persons who became shareholders between the dates of the revocation and the rescission. A rescission statement must be filed with the Internal Revenue Service Center where the revocation was filed along with shareholder consents. [Reg. § § 1.1362-2(a)(4); 1.1362-6(a)(4)]

Q 4:47 How does failure to meet the S corporation requirements affect a corporation's S election?

A corporation's S election will terminate if it fails to meet any of the eligibility requirements and no longer qualifies for S status. [IRC § 1362(d)(2)] Therefore, a corporation's S election will terminate if:

- The number of shareholders exceeds the 100-shareholder limit,
- Stock in the corporation is transferred to an ineligible shareholder; or
- The corporation issues a second class of stock.

The IRS may, however, grant relief from certain inadvertent terminations and restore the corporation's S election retroactively.

If a corporation fails to meet the S corporation eligibility requirement, termination of the corporation's S status is effective as of the date the disqualifying event occurs. The corporation must attach a notification to its return for the tax year indicating that a termination has occurred and the date of the termination. [Reg. § 1.1362-2(b)]

Example 4-7: A calendar-year corporation with 75 shareholders properly elected S status, beginning January 1, 2001. On June 3, 2007, the corporation acquires a 101st shareholder. The corporation's S election terminates on and after June 3, 2007. The corporation has two tax years for 2007—a short S corporation tax year, beginning January 1, 2007 and ending June 2, 2007, and a short C corporation tax year beginning, June 3, 2007 and ending December 31, 2007.

In a case before the First Circuit Court of Appeals, an S corporation shareholder argued that the corporation's filing of a Chapter 11 bankruptcy petition terminated the corporation's S status. The shareholder pointed out that when the petition was filed, control of the corporation was transferred to a trustee for the benefit of the creditors. Some of these creditors were corporations and therefore not eligible shareholders. In addition, the transfer of control resulted in the creation of more than one class of stock because the creditors had different rights and preferences.

The Court of Appeals rejected the shareholder's argument. The court said that the bankruptcy trustee stepped into the shoes of the debtor—the corporation—and the shareholder's status as a shareholder was not affected (although his shares were rendered less valuable). As a result, the shareholder had to include the corporation's post-petition income on his individual return. [*Mourad*, 94 AFTR 2d 2004-5390 (1st Cir., 2004)]

Q 4:48 If a corporation's S election terminates in mid year, how does the corporation compute its income for the short tax years?

There are two ways to the corporation can handle this.

1. *Pro rata allocation.* As a general rule, the corporation's books are not closed as of the termination date. [IRC § 1362(e)(2); Reg. § 1.1362-3(a)] Instead, the corporation allocates on a daily basis its income, loss, deduction, or credit items for the entire year between the two short tax years. The shareholders report the amounts apportioned to the S corporation tax year on their returns under the S corporation rules. The corporation reports the amounts apportioned to the C corporation tax year under the C corporation rules.

2. *Closing the books.* As an alternative to the general pro rata allocation rule, a the corporation can elect to close the books at the end of the short S corporation year and report taxable income or loss for each short taxable year under the normal tax accounting rules. [IRC § 1362(e)(3); Reg. § 1.1362-3(b)] Under this method, income, loss, deduction or credit items are attributed to the short taxable years according to the time they were incurred or realized as shown in the corporation's books.

A corporation can make this election only if all shareholders owning stock during the short S corporation year and all shareholders owning stock on the first day of the short C corporation year consent to the election. The election is made by filing a statement with the return for the short C corporation year indicating that the corporation elects not to have the pro rata allocation rules apply. The statement must be accompanied by shareholder consents and must indicate the date the corporation's election terminated and the date of termination. An officer authorized to sign the corporation's income tax returns must sign the statement.

Q 4:48

Q 4:49 What if an S corporation makes a faulty S election or mistakenly terminates its S election?

The IRS will waive a mistaken termination or approve an S election that is invalid because of failure to obtain shareholder consents if:

- The IRS determines that the invalidity of the election or the termination was inadvertent;

- The corporation acts within a reasonable period after discovering the problem to requalify the corporation or to obtain the necessary shareholder consents; and

- The corporation and each person who was a shareholder during the relevant period agree to tax adjustments consistent with the treatment of the corporation as an S corporation during the relevant period.

[IRC § 1362(f)]

The IRS will grant automatic inadvertent termination relief in situations where stock is transferred to a qualified subchapter S trust (QSST) and the income beneficiary inadvertently failed to file a timely QSST election. [Rev. Proc. 98-23, 1998-1 C.B. 662]

When the IRS grants relief from an inadvertent termination, the corporation will be treated as continuing as an S corporation for the period specified by the IRS. Relief may be granted retroactively for all affected years or it may be limited to the period after the corporation requalified for S corporation status, in which case the corporation will be treated as a C corporation for the period of its ineligibility as an S corporation. A request for relief from an inadvertent termination must be made in the form of a ruling request. [Rev. Proc. 98-55, 1998-2 C.B. 645]

Q 4:50 When will an S corporation be disqualified because of too much passive investment income?

An S corporation's election will terminate if it has accumulated earnings and profits from C corporation years at the end of each of three consecutive years, and more than 25 percent of its gross receipts for each of those years is from passive investment income. [IRC § 1362(d)(3); Reg. § 1.1362(d)(3)]

A termination under the passive investment income rule is effective for the first day of the tax year beginning after the third consecutive tax year in which the corporation had excess passive investment income.

> **Planning Point:** A corporation that has always been an S corporation or one that does not have accumulated earnings and profits from a C corporation does not have to worry about passive investment income. The corporation may hold as many passive investments as it pleases—even if income from those investments makes up 100 percent of its gross receipts for the year.

Fringe Benefits for S Corporation Owners

Q 4:51 What special rules apply to fringe benefits for S corporation owners?

For purposes of the tax law's fringe benefit rules, an S corporation is treated as a partnership and more-than-2 percent shareholders of the corporation are treated as partners. [IRC § 1372] As a result of that treatment, fringe benefits provided to more-than-2 percent shareholder-employees are deductible by the corporation—but the shareholder-employees must include the value of the benefits in income, even if the same benefits are excludible from income by other employees. The benefits are subject to income tax withholding, but are not income for Social Security and Medicare (FICA) tax purposes.

Planning Point: Amounts included in a shareholder-employee's income on account of health benefits provided by the corporation are eligible for the self-employed health insurance deduction. [IRC § 162(l)]

There is a note of caution here. Some states do not allow a corporation to purchase a group health plan with only one participant. This may prevent an S corporation with only one shareholder-employee from acquiring a health plan. Instead, the shareholder-employee may purchase the health insurance in his or her own name with the premiums paid by the corporation. The IRS has informally pointed out that, in this type of situation, the shareholder-employee is not eligible for the self-employed health insurance deduction.

According to the IRS, the health insurance deduction is available to S corporation shareholder-employees only when the corporation provides health insurance under a group plan and the coverage is subject to the S corporation fringe benefit rule. When a shareholder-employee purchases the insurance directly, the corporation's premium payments are deductible by the corporation as compensation, not as a fringe benefit. Thus, the shareholder-employee is ineligible for the health insurance deduction [IRS e-News, Headliner Volume 163, May 15, 2006]

S Corporation Filing Requirements

Q 4:52 Is an S corporation required to file an annual income tax return?

Yes. An S corporation must file an annual return on Form 1120S, *U.S. Income Tax Return for an S Corporation*, even if it is not subject to tax. It reports gross income and allowable deductions, as well as information concerning the shareholders, including their stock holdings, distributions made to them, and their pro rata shares of corporate items. [IRC § 6037; Reg. § 1.6037-1]

If an S corporation uses a calendar tax year, the return must be filed by March 15 following the close of the tax year. If an S corporation is permitted to use a fiscal year, the return must be filed by the 15th day of the third month following the close of its fiscal year. An S corporation can receive an automatic six-month extension to file a return by submitting an application for extension on Form 7004, *Application for Automatic 6-Month Extension of Time to File Certain Business Income Tax, Information, and Other Returns.*

An S corporation files Form 1120S with the Internal Revenue Service Center serving the area where the principal office for keeping the corporation's books and records is located.

An S corporation must furnish each shareholder with a copy of its return on or before the day the return is filed. [IRC § 6037(b)]

Q 4:53 How do shareholders know how much passed-through income or other items to report on their returns?

Each year, the corporation must provide each shareholder with Form 1120S Schedule K-1, *Shareholder's Share of Income, Credits, Deductions, Etc.* The form shows the shareholder's passed-through share of the corporation's income or loss for the year as well as separately stated items that could affect the tax liability of a shareholder (see Q 4:26).

Schedule K-1 is used in preparing the shareholder's personal return and should be retained with the shareholder's tax records. A shareholder does not file Schedule K-1 with the IRS. The corporation is required to file a copy of each shareholder Schedule K-1 with Form 1120S.

Chapter 5

Tax Accounting

Tax accounting basically is a matter of timing—when is income reported for tax purposes and when are deductions claimed for expenses. This chapter covers basic issues in tax accounting such as selecting a tax year and accounting method, accounting for inventories, and reporting income from installment sales.

Tax accounting, however, also deals with the timing of deductions for specific types of expenses. For example, Chapter 6 discusses when business expenses must be capitalized and when they can be deducted currently, and Chapter 7 examines how and when the cost of equipment and machinery can be recovered through depreciation.

Tax Years

Q 5:1 What is a tax year?

A tax year is an annual accounting period for keeping records and reporting income and expenses. Taxpayers must figure taxable income on the basis of a tax year.

Taxpayers adopt a tax year when they file their first income tax return. The tax year must be adopted by the due date (not including extensions) for filing a return for that year. A taxpayer may be on a calendar year or a fiscal year. [IRC § 441]

A calendar year is 12 consecutive months beginning January 1 and ending December 31. If a calendar year is adopted, a taxpayer must maintain books and records and report income and expenses from January 1 through December 31 of each year. If an individual, who has been reporting income and deductions on a calendar-year basis, starts a sole proprietorship, the sole proprietorship must use the calendar year unless the Internal Revenue Service (IRS or the Service) gives approval for a change (see below).

A fiscal year is 12 consecutive months ending on the last day of any month except December. (Special rules apply to the choice of a tax year by a partnership, personal service corporation, and S corporation; see Chapters 2, 3, and 4, respectively.)

Q 5:2 Can a business adopt a tax year that ends on the same day of the week each year?

Yes. This is known as a "52-53 week": fiscal year for some tax years will be 52 weeks long and others will be 53 weeks long. A business choosing a 52-53 week year must maintain books and records and report income and expenses using the same tax year. The tax year must end on the same day of the week that: (1) last occurs in a particular month or (2) occurs nearest to the last day of a particular calendar month. [IRC § 441 (f)] For example, if a business elects a tax year that always ends on the last Friday in March, its 2008 tax year will end on March 27, 2009. If a business elects a tax year ending on the Friday nearest to the end of April, its 2008 tax year will end on May 1, 2009.

To make the election, a statement with the following information must be attached to the tax return for the 52-53 week tax year:

- The month in which the new 52-53 week tax year ends;

- The day of the week on which the tax year always ends; and

- The date the tax year ends.

When depreciation or amortization deductions are claimed, a 52-53 week tax year is generally considered a year of 12 calendar months.

Many tax law changes take effect in tax years beginning or ending after a particular date. To determine when a change applies to a business, a 52-53 week tax year is considered to:

- Begin on the first day of the calendar month beginning nearest to the first day of the 52-53 week tax year; and

- End on the last day of the calendar month ending nearest to the last day of the 52-53 week tax year.

[IRC § 441(f)(2)(A)]

Q 5:2

Example 5-1: If a new tax provision applies to tax years beginning on or after July 1, 2008, a 52-53 week tax year beginning on June 24, 2008, is treated as beginning on July 1, 2008.

Q 5:3 Can a business change to or from a 52-53 week tax year?

A business may change to a 52-53 week tax year without IRS approval as long as the day chosen for the end of the 52-53 week tax year occurs in the same calendar month in which its current tax year ends. IRS approval, however, must be obtained to change a tax year to a 52-53 week tax year that ends in a calendar month different from the month in which its current tax year ends. For example, if a business currently has a calendar tax year, it must obtain IRS approval to change to a 52-53 week tax year ending on the Saturday nearest the end of November. [Reg. § 1.441-2(b)]

Q 5:4 Is a tax year always 12 months long?

No, a "short" tax year may be required when a business is not in existence for an entire tax year or there is a change in its tax year. [IRC § 443(a)]

Example 5-2: A corporation X is organized on July 1, 2008. It elects the calendar year as its tax year, and its first tax return is due March 16, 2009 (March 15 is a Sunday). The short-period return will cover the period from July 1, 2008, through December 31, 2008.

Example 5-3: A calendar-year corporation dissolves on July 23, 2008. Its final return is due by October 15, 2008, and it will cover the short period from January 1, 2008, to July 23, 2008.

Example 5-4: Partnership YZ is formed on September 8, 2008, and elects to use a fiscal year ending November 30. Partnership YZ must file its first tax return by March 16, 2009. It will cover the short period from September 8, 2008, to November 30, 2008.

Q 5:5 How is the tax figured for a short tax year?

If the short tax year results from a change in the business's tax year, the tax is generally a pro rata portion of what it would be on an annualized basis. [IRC § 443(b)]

Example 5-5: Because a calendar-year corporation changed its tax year, it must file a short-period tax return for the six-month period ending June 30, 2008. For the short tax year, it had income of $40,000 and no deductions. The corporation's annualized income is $80,000 ($40,000 × 12/6). The tax on $80,000 is $15,450. [IRC § 11] The tax for the short tax year is $7,725 ($15,450 × 6/12).

If a business changes the month in which its 52-53 tax year ends, it must file a return for the short tax year if it covers more than 6 but fewer than 359 days. If the short period created by the change is 359 days or more, the business can treat it as a full tax year. If the short period created is 6 days or fewer, it is not a separate tax year. The business includes it as part of the following year. The tax for short tax year is figured as shown above, except that the income is prorated on a daily basis, rather than monthly. [IRC § 441(f)(2)(B)]

If the short tax year results from the fact that the business has not been in existence for a year, the tax does not have to be annualized. The tax is simply computed as if the short tax year were a full year.

Q 5:6 Are there any other methods that can be used to figure the tax for a short tax year?

Yes, there is an optional method that may be beneficial when income during the short year is disproportionately large when compared to what it would be for a 12-month period. Under the optional method, the tax is computed for the 12-month period beginning at the start of the short tax year and is then prorated to the short year in proportion to the income earned in the year. [IRC § 443(b)(2)]

Q 5:7 How does a taxpayer change its tax year?

A business that wants to change its tax year must generally obtain the approval of the IRS. [Reg. § 1.442-1(a)(1)]In certain cases, a partnership, an S corporation, or a personal service corporation will be required to change its tax year unless it establishes a business purpose and obtains the approval of the IRS or makes an election under IRC Section 444 to retain its current taxable year (see Chapter 2).

To secure IRS approval to change or retain a tax year, a taxpayer must file an application, generally on Form 1128, *Application to Adopt, Change, or Retain a Tax Year.* [Reg. § 1.442-1(b)]. In general, a change or retention of a tax year will be approved where the taxpayer establishes a business purpose for the requested tax year and agrees to the Service's prescribed terms, conditions, and adjustments for making the change or retention.

The IRS has issued revenue procedures that enable certain taxpayers to obtain automatic approval to change or retain their annual accounting periods (Rev. Proc. 2002-37, 2003-21 I.R.B. 950, for corporations, Rev. Proc. 2002-38, 2003-24 I.R.B. 1017, for partnerships, S corporations, and personal service corporations, and Rev. Proc. 2003-62, 2003-32 I.R.B. 299, for individuals).

Q 5:8 What is required to establish a "business purpose" when requesting a change of tax years?

Basically, there are two ways to establish a business purpose when changing tax years. Under Method 1, a taxpayer is subject to only "general terms and conditions." Under Method 2, the IRS imposes "additional terms, conditions, and adjustments" designed to neutralize the tax effects of a substantial distortion of income that otherwise would result from the change. [Rev. Proc. 2003-39, 2003-22 I.R.B. 971]

Q 5:6

Method 1. A taxpayer can establish a business purpose under Method 1 by either changing its tax year to its "natural business year" (see Q 5:9) or by meeting a facts and circumstances test. The facts and circumstances test means that the IRS will grant permission for a taxpayer to change tax years based on all of the relevant facts and circumstances. Nevertheless, the IRS says that this permission will be granted only in "rare and unusual circumstances." The following will *not* be considered sufficient business purposes for the change:

- The use of a particular year for regulatory or financial accounting purposes;

- The hiring patterns of a particular business, e.g., the fact that a firm typically hires staff during certain times of the year;

- The use of a particular year for administrative purposes, such as the admission or retirement of partners or shareholders, promotion of staff, and compensation or retirement arrangements with staff, partners, or shareholders;

- The fact that a particular business involves the use of price lists, model years, or other items that change on an annual basis;

- The use of a particular year by related entities; and

- The use of a particular year by competitors.

Under Method 1, the following "general terms and conditions" must be met:

- The taxpayer must file a federal income tax return for the short period (see Qs 5:4 through 5:6).

- Returns for subsequent tax years generally must be made on the basis of a full 12 months ending on the last day of the requested tax year.

- The books of the taxpayer must be closed as of the last day of the first effective year. Thereafter, the taxpayer must generally compute its income and keep its books and records (including financial statements and reports to creditors) on the basis of the requested tax year. (There are exceptions. For example, this does not apply to books and records maintained solely for foreign tax reporting purposes.)

- A taxpayer may not carry back a net operating loss (see Chapter 6) from the short year unless the loss is (1) $50,000 or less or (2) is less than the loss for the 12-month period beginning with the first day of the short period. [Rev. Proc. 2003-34, 2003-18 I.R.B. 856]

- If there is an unused general business credit or any other unused credit generated in the short period, the taxpayer must carry that unused credit forward. An unused credit from the short period may not be carried back.

Method 2. A taxpayer (other than a partnership, S corporation, or personal service corporation) that cannot qualify for Method 1 can establish a business purpose for a tax year change by merely providing a non-tax reason for the change. Any of the reasons outlined above that were not sufficient for Method 1 (e.g., the use of a particular year for regulatory or financial accounting purposes) will qualify as a sufficient business purpose under Method 2. [Rev. Proc. 2003-39, 2003-22 I.R.B. 971]

As noted above, the use of Method 2 may subject the taxpayer to "additional terms, conditions, and adjustments." Following is an example of the type of adjustments that may be required.

> **Example 5-6:** In 2008, XYZ Inc., a foreign corporation, which has a fiscal year ending on May 31, acquires all of the stock of ABC Inc., a domestic corporation that operates on a calendar tax year. ABC has a minority interest in a partnership that also uses the calendar year. In order to facilitate the filing of consolidated financial statements, ABC applies for approval to change its tax year to a tax year ending on May 31, beginning on May 31, 2009.

The change will create a substantial distortion of income as a result of increasing the deferral of ABC's share of income from its partnership interest. Consequently, the IRS will require ABC to report the partnership income that accrues between January 1 and May 31, 2009, as an ordinary income adjustment on its short period tax return.

Thereafter, on subsequent tax returns filed for its tax year ending on May 31, ABC must report the partnership income for the partnership's tax year ending December 31. To take into account ABC's double inclusion of the five months of partnership income from January 1 to May 31, 2009, ABC may claim an ordinary deduction adjustment in each of the four tax years following the first effective year.

The IRS says that no additional adjustments will be required under Method 2 if the income distortion is not "substantial." Distortion of income will not be considered substantial if the amount of the distortion is less than both:

1. Five percent of the taxpayer's estimated gross receipts for its current taxable year (computed as if the taxpayer remained on its existing taxable year); *and*

2. $500,000.

[Rev. Proc. 2003-39, 2003-22 I.R.B. 971]

Q 5:9 For purposes of establishing a business purpose for a tax year change, what is a taxpayer's natural business year?

A natural business year is the annual accounting period encompassing all related income and expenses. The natural business year of a taxpayer may be determined under any of the following tests. [Rev. Proc. 2002-39, 2003-22 I.R.B. 971]

1. *Annual business cycle test.* If a taxpayer's gross receipts from sales and services for the short period and the three immediately preceding taxable years indicate that the taxpayer has a peak and a non-peak period of business, the taxpayer's natural business year is deemed to end at, or soon after, the close of the highest peak period of business. A business whose income is steady from month to month throughout the year will not satisfy this test. A taxpayer that has

not been in existence for a sufficient period to provide gross receipts information for the three immediately preceding taxable years may provide information other than gross receipts to demonstrate a peak and non-peak period of business, such as a description of its business and/or reasonable estimates of future gross receipts.

One month will be deemed to be "soon after" the close of the highest peak period of business.

Example 5-7: ABC Inc., a corporation, operates a retail business. The highest peak of ABC's annual business cycle occurs in December each year. In January, a significant amount of the merchandise that was purchased by ABC's customers in December is either returned or exchanged. ABC's natural business year is deemed to end at (December 31), or soon after (January 31), the close of the highest peak period of business in December. Accordingly, a request by ABC for a tax year ending either December 31 or January 31 would be granted by the IRS.

2. *Seasonal business test.* If a taxpayer's gross receipts from sales and services for the short period and the three immediately preceding taxable years indicate that the taxpayer's business is operational for only part of the year (e.g., due to weather conditions) and, as a result, the taxpayer has insignificant gross receipts during the period the business is not operational, the taxpayer's natural business year is deemed to end at, or soon after, the operations end for the season. Again, a taxpayer that has not been in existence for a sufficient period to provide gross receipts information for the three immediately preceding taxable years may provide information other than gross receipts to demonstrate that it satisfies the requirements of a seasonal business, such as a description of its business and/or reasonable estimates of future gross receipts.

For purposes of the seasonable business test, an amount equal to less than 10 percent of the taxpayer's total gross receipts for the year will be deemed to be "insignificant," and one month will be deemed to be "soon after" the close of operations.

Example 5-8: XYZ, a partnership, operates a ski resort from November through March of each year. During September and October employees prepare the resort for the ski season, and during April they close the resort down for the season. The resort earns less than 10 percent of its annual gross receipts during the period of April through October, when it is closed to guests. XYZ's natural business year is deemed to end at (March 31), or soon after (April 30), the close of the resort operations. The IRS should grant a request by XYZ for a tax year ending either March 31 or April 30.

3. *25-percent gross receipts test.* A natural business year may be established using the 25-percent gross receipts test. The 25-percent gross receipts test is determined as follows:

a. Gross receipts from sales and services for the most recent 12-month period that ends with the last month of the requested tax year are totaled and then divided into the amount of gross receipts from sales and services for the last 2 months of this 12-month period.

b. The same computation as in (a) above is made for the two preceding 12-month periods ending with the last month of the requested tax year.

c. If each of the three results described in (a) and (b) equals or exceeds 25 percent, the requested tax year is generally deemed to be the taxpayer's natural business year.

However, there is an important caveat. The IRS says that the taxpayer must determine whether any tax year other than the requested tax year also meets the 25-percent gross receipts test. If one or more other tax years produce higher averages of the three percentages described in (a) and (b) than the requested tax year, the requested annual accounting period will not qualify as the taxpayer's natural business year under the 25-percent gross receipts test.

Example 5-9: Widget Inc. is a widget wholesaler. In terms of sales, August, September, and October are the biggest months for widgets. In its most recent 12-month period ending on October 31, out of a total of $2 million gross receipts for the 12-month period, Widget had gross receipts of $400,000 in August, $300,000 in September, and $300,000 in October. Widget's gross receipts for September and October ($600,000) total 30 percent of the gross receipts for the entire 12-month period. However, a tax year ending on October 31 cannot qualify as Widget's natural business year under the 25-percent gross receipts test. That is because the gross receipts for the two-month period ending on September 30 constitute a higher percentage, 35 percent ($700,000/$2 million) of Widget's gross receipts for the 12-month period.

If a taxpayer does not have a 47-month period of gross receipts (36-month period for requested tax year plus additional 11-month period for comparing requested tax year with other potential tax years), then the 25-percent gross receipts test is not available.

Q 5:10 When can a sole proprietor get automatic approval for a tax year change?

The IRS has provided procedures whereby individuals switching from a fiscal tax year to a calendar year can obtain automatic IRS approval for the switch. [Rev. Proc. 2003-62, 2003-32 I.R.B. 299]

To qualify under the automatic approval procedures, an individual must file an income tax return for the short period between the old tax year and the new calendar tax year (see Qs 5:4 through 5:6). A Form 1128 must be filed (Attention: ENTITY CONTROL) where the individual files the individual's federal income tax return. The individual also must attach a copy of the Form 1128 to the tax return filed for the short period.

If the individual generates a net operating loss (NOL) in the short period, the NOL cannot generally be carried back. However, there is an exception. A carryback is allowed if the NOL is either: (1) $50,000 or less, or (2) less than the NOL generated for the full 12-month period beginning with the first day of the short period. (The individual must wait until this 12-month period has expired to determine whether the individual qualifies for the exception in (2).)

The automatic approval is generally not available to owners of interests in pass-through entities (e.g., partnerships) unless the owners meet certain requirements. For these individuals, automatic approval will be granted only if one of the following conditions is met:

- The pass-through entity would be required by the Internal Revenue Code or the regulations to change its tax year to the individual's new calendar tax year;

- The pass-through entity is a fiscal-year partnership that is owned equally (50 percent) by two partners, one or both of whom are individuals, and the individual and the partnership both want to change to the calendar tax year of the other 50 percent partner.

- The new calendar taxable year of the individual would result in no change in, or less deferral of income from the pass-through entity than the present tax year of the individual; or

- The pass-through entity in which the individual has an interest has been in existence for at least three tax years and the interest is *de minimis*.

For purposes of the last requirement, an interest in a pass-through entity is *de minimis* only if, for each of the prior three tax years of the individual, the amount of income from all such pass-through entities is less than or equal to the lesser of (1) 5 percent of the individual's gross income for those tax years or (b) $500,000.

Q 5:11 Can an individual change his or her tax year when the individual marries someone with a different tax year?

A newly married husband and wife with different tax years who wish to file a joint return can change the tax year of one spouse without first obtaining IRS approval. [Reg. § 1.442-1(e)] They may file a joint return for the first tax year ending after the date of marriage if both of the following conditions are met:

1. The due date for filing the required separate short-period tax return of the spouse changing his or her tax year falls on or after the date of the marriage. The due date for the short-period tax return is the 15th day of the fourth month following the end of the short tax year.

2. The spouse changing his or her tax year files a timely short-period tax return. It must include a statement that the tax year is being changed pursuant to Regulations Section 1.442-1(e).

If the due date for filing the required short-period tax return passes before the couple marries, they cannot file a joint return until the end of the second tax year after the date of marriage. They can file a joint return for the second tax year only if the spouse changing his or her tax year files a timely short-period tax return.

Example 5-10: John and Jane were married on July 30, 2008. John, a sole proprietor, filed his return for the fiscal year ending June 30, 2008. Jane uses the calendar year but wants to change to John's fiscal year so they can file a joint return. If Jane files a separate return by October 15, 2008, for the short period January 1, 2008, through June 30, 2008, she will have changed her accounting period to a fiscal year ending June 30. She and John can then file a joint return for their tax year ending June 30, 2009.

A spouse who does not meet the earlier conditions must get IRS approval to change to the other spouse's tax year in order to file a joint return. Even though there is no substantial business purpose for requesting the change, approval may be granted in certain cases.

Q 5:12 When can a C corporation obtain automatic IRS approval for a tax year change?

Subject to certain conditions, the IRS will grant automatic approval to corporations changing:

- To or from a 52-53-week tax year; or

- To a natural business year that satisfies the 25-percent gross receipts test (see Q 5:10). [Rev. Proc. 2002-37, 2003-21 I.R.B. 950]

This automatic approval is generally not available to a corporation that has changed its tax year at any time within the most recent 48-month period ending with the last month of the requested tax year.

How to get automatic approval. Any corporation that wants to receive automatic approval for a tax year change must file a Form 1128 with the IRS (Attention: ENTITY CONTROL) where the corporation files its federal income tax return. The corporation also must attach a copy of the Form 1128 to the income tax return filed for the short period.

A Form 1128 will be considered timely filed only if it is filed on or before the due date (including extensions) for filing the tax return for the short period. The following statement should appear at the top of page 1 of the Form 1128: "FILED UNDER REV. PROC. 2002-37."

Q 5:13 When can a partnership or an S corporation obtain automatic approval for a tax year change?

A partnership or an S corporation can get automatic approval to change to:

- A "required tax year" (see Chapter 2 for partnerships or Chapter 4 for S corporations), or

- A 52-53-week tax year ending with reference to such required tax year. [Rev. Proc. 2002-38, 2003-24 I.R.B. 1017]

A partnership or S corporation can also get automatic approval to retain or change to a natural business year that meets the 25-percent gross receipts test (see Q 5:10) or to a 52-53-week tax year ending with reference to such natural tax year.

To get automatic approval to change its tax year, a partnership or S corporation must file Form 1128. The form must be filed no later than the due date (including extensions) for filing the tax return for the short period required to effect the change.

A corporation that elects to be an S corporation and requests to change its tax year must file Form 2553. The form must be filed when the election to be an S corporation is filed.

Form 1128 and Form 2553 must be filed with the IRS (Attention: ENTITY CONTROL), where the partnership or S corporation files its tax return. At the top of page 1 of the Form 1128 or Form 2553, the statement "FILED UNDER REV PROC. 2003-38" should appear. A copy must be attached to the tax return for the short year.

Accounting Methods

Q 5:14 What is an accounting method?

An accounting method is a set of rules used to determine when and how income and expenses are reported. A business chooses an accounting method when its first tax return is filed. If a change to a different method is later desired, the business must get IRS approval (see below).

No single accounting method is required of all taxpayers. A business must use a system that clearly shows its income and expenses, and it must maintain records that will enable it to file a correct return. [IRC § 446(a)] If a business does not regularly use an accounting method that clearly shows its income, the income will be figured under the method that, in the opinion of the IRS, does. [IRC § 446(b)]

Q 5:15 What accounting methods can be used?

The following accounting methods are available to businesses, subject to various restrictions:

- Cash receipts and disbursements method (cash method);
- Accrual method;
- Special methods of accounting for certain items of income and expenses (e.g., amortization of startup costs and intangibles. See Chapter 6); and
- Combination (hybrid) method using elements from the methods above.

[IRC § 446(c)]

Combination method. Generally, a business can use any combination of cash, accrual, and special methods of accounting provided the combination clearly shows income, and the business uses it consistently. However, the following restrictions apply:

- If inventory is necessary to account for income, a business must generally use the accrual method for purchases and sales. The cash method may be used for all other items of income and expenses.
- If a business uses the cash method for figuring income, it must use the cash method for reporting expenses.
- If a business uses an accrual method for reporting its expenses, it must use an accrual method for figuring income.

[Reg. § 1.446-1(c)(2)]

Q 5:16 If an individual operates two businesses, can he or she use different accounting methods for each?

Yes, if an individual operates two or more separate and distinct businesses, a different accounting method may be used for each. No business is separate and distinct, however, unless a complete and separate set of books and records is maintained for such business.

If an individual uses different accounting methods to create or shift profits or losses between businesses (for example, through inventory adjustments, sales, purchases, or expenses) so that income is not clearly reflected, the businesses will not be considered separate and distinct. [Reg. § 1.446-1(d)]

Cash Method of Accounting

Q 5:17 What is the cash method of accounting?

Under the cash method, a business includes in income all items actually or constructively received during the tax year. If a business receives property or services, their fair market value must be included in income. Expenses are generally deducted in the tax year in which they are actually paid. [Reg. § 1.446-1(c)(1)(i)]

If a business pays an expense in advance, the expense can be deducted only in the year to which it applies. [Reg. § 1.461-1]

Example 5-11: Joan Nelson is a calendar-year taxpayer and pays $1,800 in January of Year 1 for a business insurance policy that is effective for two years. She can deduct $900 in Year 1 and $900 in Year 2.

Q 5:18 When is income "constructively" received?

Income is constructively received when an amount is credited to the taxpayer's account or made available without restriction. A taxpayer need not have possession of the income for it to be taxable. If a taxpayer authorizes someone to act as an agent and receive income on the taxpayer's behalf, the taxpayer is considered to have received it when the agent receives it. Income is not constructively received if the taxpayer's control of its receipt is subject to substantial restrictions or limitations. [Reg. § 1.451-2]

Q 5:16

Example 5-12: Interest is credited to a company's bank account in December of Year 1, but the company does not withdraw it until Year 2. The company must include the amount in gross income for Year 1, not Year 2.

A business cannot hold checks or postpone taking possession of similar property from one tax year to another to avoid paying tax on the income. The income must be reported in the year the property is received or made available without restriction.

Q 5:19 Can any business use the cash method of accounting?

No. The cash method generally cannot be used for purchases and sales where inventories must be used. [Reg. § 1.446-1(c)]However, there is an exception for certain small businesses (see below).

The following entities are specifically prohibited from using the cash method, including any combination of methods that includes the cash method:

- A corporation (other than an S corporation) with average annual gross receipts exceeding $5 million;

- A partnership with a corporation (other than an S corporation) as a partner, and with the partnership having average annual gross receipts exceeding $5 million; and

- A tax shelter.

[IRC § 448(a)]

Exceptions. The following entities can use the cash method of accounting:

- A family farming corporation with gross receipts of $25 million or less for each prior tax year beginning after 1985; and

- A qualified personal service corporation.

[IRC § 448(b)]

Q 5:20 How is the gross receipts threshold for a corporation or partnership figured?

A corporation or a partnership meets the test if its average annual gross receipts are $5 million or less for the three tax years ending with the prior tax year (or the period of existence, if shorter). Generally, a partnership applies the test at the partnership level. Gross receipts for a short tax year are annualized.

Organizations that are members of an affiliated service group or a controlled group of corporations treated as a single employer for tax purposes are required to aggregate their gross receipts to determine whether the gross receipts test is met. [IRC § 448(c)]

Q 5:21 What is a qualified personal service corporation?

A personal service corporation that meets the function test and the owner-ship test of Temporary Regulations Section 1.448-1T(e) can use the cash method. [IRC § 448(d)(2); Temp. Reg. § 1.448-1T(e)]

Function test. A corporation meets the function test if at least 95 percent of its activities are in the performance of services in the fields of health, veterinary services, law, engineering (including surveying and mapping), architecture, ac-counting, actuarial science, performing arts, or consulting.

Ownership test. A corporation meets the ownership test if at least 95 percent of its stock is owned, directly or indirectly, at all times during the year by one of the following:

1. Employees performing services for the corporation in a field qualifying under the function test;

2. Retired employees who had performed services in those fields;

3. The estate of an employee described in (1) or (2); or

4. Any other person who acquired the stock by reason of the death of an employee referred to in (1) or (2), but only for the two-year period beginning on the date of death.

Indirect ownership is generally taken into account if the stock is owned indirectly through one or more partnerships, S corporations, or qualified per-sonal service corporations. Stock owned by one of these entities is considered owned by the entity's owners in proportion to their ownership interest in that entity. Other forms of indirect stock ownership, such as stock owned by family members, are generally not considered when determining if the ownership test is met.

For purposes of the ownership test, a person is not considered an employee of a corporation unless that person performs more than minimal services for the corporation.

Change to accrual method. A corporation that fails to meet the function test for any tax year or fails to meet the ownership test at any time during any tax year must change to an accrual method of accounting, effective for the year in which the corporation fails to meet either test. A corporation that fails to meet the function test or the ownership test is not treated as a qualified personal service corporation for any part of that tax year. [Temp. Reg. § 1.448-1T(e)]

Q 5:22 What are the inventory exceptions for small businesses?

There are two—one for the smallest businesses—those with annual receipts below $1 million—and a second, more limited exception for larger businesses (see next question).

One million dollar exception. Generally, if a business produces, purchases, or sells merchandise, it must keep an inventory and use the accrual method for purchases and sales of merchandise. However, for tax years ending on or after December 17, 1999, qualifying taxpayers may use the cash method of accounting, even if they produce, purchase, or sell merchandise. Qualifying taxpayers may also choose not to keep an inventory, even if they do not change to the cash method. [Rev. Proc. 2001-10, 2001-2 I.R.B. 272]

Qualifying taxpayers. A business is a qualifying taxpayer only if it meets the gross receipts test for each tax year ending after December 16, 1998. To qualify, the average annual gross receipts must be $1 million or less for the three tax years ending with the prior tax year.

If a business has not been in existence for three tax years, it bases its average on the period it has existed including any short tax years, annualizing the short tax year's gross receipts.

Not keeping an inventory. If a business takes advantage of the exception and does not keep an inventory, it deducts the cost of the items it would otherwise include in inventory in the year it sells the items, or the year it pays for them, whichever is later.

Q 5:23 What is the inventory exception for larger businesses?

This is available primarily to businesses, such as plumbing contractors, that sell related products along with the services they provide. [Notice 2001-76, 2001-52 I.R.B. 613; Rev. Proc. 2002-28, 2002-18 I.R.B. 815]

Under this exception a business will be able to use the cash method of accounting and will not be required to maintain an inventory if it:

- Has average annual gross receipts of more than $1 million but no more than $10 million;
- Has as its principal activity an "eligible trade or business"; and
- Is not disqualified by the rules for larger C corporations (i.e., does not have more than $5 million in average annual receipts).

Average annual gross receipts. To qualify for the current year, a business must have average annual gross receipts of $10 million or less for each prior tax year ending on or after December 31, 2000. A business has average annual gross receipts of $10 million or less for each prior year if its average annual receipts for the three-year period ending with each prior year do not exceed $10 million.

Example 5-13: XYZ, Inc. is an S corporation that installs plumbing fixtures in customers' homes and businesses. XYZ started business in 2004 and operates on the calendar tax year. XYZ's gross receipts were $2 million in 2004, $5 million in 2005, and $8 million in 2006. As a result, XYZ's average annual gross receipts for the three-year period ending with 2006 are $5 million. Therefore, if it otherwise qualifies, XYZ can use the cash method of accounting in 2007. In 2007, XYZ's gross receipts are $11 million; therefore, its average for the three-year period ending in 2007 are $8 million and it is still eligible for the cash method in 2008. In 2008, XYZ's gross receipts are $14 million. Thus, its average for the three-year period ending in 2008 is $11 million it has become ineligible for the cash method of accounting for 2009. If a business has not been in existence for three tax years, the average annual gross receipts are figured by using the number of years (including any short tax year) that it has been in existence.

For this purpose, gross receipts include total sales (net of returns and allowances), all amounts received from services, interest, dividends, and rents. Gross receipts, however, do not include amounts received as sales taxes if, under local law, the tax is imposed on the purchasers of goods and services and the business is merely collecting the tax.

Eligible trade or business. A business does not qualify under the new rules if its principal activity for the prior tax year is mining, manufacturing, wholesale or retail trade, or the information industry (e.g., publishing). However, a business can use the cash method if any of these nonqualifying activities is not its principal activity. For example, a publisher may qualify for the cash method if its principal business activity is not the sale of its publications but the sale of advertising space in those publications.

If a business has two or more separate and distinct activities, the business can treat them as separate businesses for purposes of the principal activity test as long as separate books and records are maintained. If two activities are treated as one business, then the "principal" activity will be determined on the basis of total receipts.

Example 5-14: Acme Inc. is an electrical contractor that installs electrical fixtures in customers' homes and businesses. Acme also has a store, which sells electrical supplies to homeowners and other electricians who visit the store. Acme derives 60 percent of its total receipts from electrical installations (including amounts charged for parts and fixtures used in installation) and 40 percent of its total receipts from the sale of electrical supplies through its store.

Result: Acme's principal activity is electrical installation, and it may use the cash method of accounting for both the installation business and the store business.

Example 5-15: Same as in Example 5-14, except that Acme derives 40 percent of its total receipts from the installation activity and 60 percent from its store sales. Acme cannot use the cash method for its store operations because that is its principal activity, and it is an ineligible one. However, Acme can still use the cash method for its installation activities if it keeps separate books and records. If there is only one set of books for both businesses, Acme must use the accrual method for both.

The IRS says that a company will not fall into a nonqualifying business category if its principal activity is the "fabrication or modification of tangible personal property upon demand in accordance with customer design or specifications." [Rev. Proc. 2002-28, 2002-18 I.R.B. 815] For this purpose, an item is not fabricated if a customer merely chooses among pre-selected options or if the business only makes minor modifications to meet customer's specifications.

Example 5-16: Custom Corp. makes tools based entirely on specific designs and specifications provided to it by customers in their orders. Even though

Custom is a manufacturer, it can use the cash method because its principal business activity is the fabrication of tangible personal property.

The IRS also says that a company will not fall into a nonqualifying business class if its principal activity "is the provision of services, including the provision of property incident to those services." [Rev. Proc. 2002-28, 2002-18 I.R.B. 815]

Accrual Method of Accounting

Q 5:24 What is the accrual method of accounting?

Under an accrual method of accounting, a business generally reports income in the year earned and deducts or capitalizes expenses in the year incurred. The purpose of an accrual method of accounting is to match income and expenses in the correct year.

Q 5:25 When is income "earned" for purposes of accruing income?

Income is earned in the tax year in which all events that fix the right to receive the income have occurred and the amount of the income can be determined with reasonable accuracy. [Reg. § 1.451(1)(a)]

> **Example 5-17:** XYZ, Inc. is a calendar-year accrual-basis taxpayer. It sells a computer on December 28 of Year 1, and bills the customer in the first week of January, Year 2 but does not receive payment until February of year 2. The amount received in February for the computer is included in XYZ's income for Year 1.

If a business includes a reasonably estimated amount in gross income and it is later determined that the exact amount is different, the business takes the difference into account in the tax year the determination is made.

If services are performed for a basic rate that is specified in a contract, a business must accrue the income at the basic rate, even if it agrees to payments at a reduced rate. The business should continue this procedure until the services are completed; the business can then account for the difference.

Q 5:26 How are advance payments for services treated under the accrual method?

If a business receives an advance payment for services performed in a later tax year, the payment is generally reported in the year received. However, if the advance payment is for services to be performed by the end of the following tax year, a business may elect to postpone reporting the advance payment until the following year. [Rev. Proc. 71-21, 1971-2 C.B. 549]

Postponement is not permitted if either of the following applies:

- The business is to perform any part of the service after the end of the tax year immediately following the year the advance payment is received.

- The business is to perform any part of the service at any unspecified future date that may be after the end of the tax year immediately following the year the advance payment is received.

Example 5-18: ABC, Inc. is a calendar-year accrual-method taxpayer that manufactures, sells, and services computers. ABC receives payment in Year 1 for a one-year contingent service contract on a computer it sold. ABC can postpone including in income the part of the payment it did not earn in Year 1.

Example 5-19: Jim Wilson owns a dance studio. On November 2, Year 1, he receives payment for a one-year contract for 48 one-hour lessons beginning on that date. He gives eight lessons in Year 1. Under this method of including advance payments, Wilson must include one-sixth (8/48) of the payment in income for Year 1, and five-sixths (40/48) of the payment in Year 2, even if he cannot give all the lessons by the end of Year 2.

Example 5-20: Assume the same facts as Example 5-19, except the payment is for a two-year contract for 96 lessons. Wilson must include the entire payment in income in Year 1 since part of the services may be performed *after* the following year.

The one-year deferral is available for advance payments for:

1. Services (other than for service warranty contracts for which the taxpayer uses the accounting method provided in Rev. Proc. 97-38, 1997-2 C.B. 479);

2. The sale of goods (other than for sales of goods for which the taxpayer uses a deferral method provided in Regulations Section 1.451-5(b)(1)(ii));

3. The use of intellectual property;

4. The occupancy of space or the use of property if the occupancy or use is ancillary to the provision of services (for example, advance payments for the use of rooms or other quarters in a hotel, booth space at a trade show, campsite space at a mobile home park, and recreational or banquet facilities, or other uses of property, so long as the use is ancillary to the provision of services to the property user);

5. The sale, lease, or license of computer software;

6. Guaranty or warranty contracts ancillary to the items described in subsections (1) through (5);

7. Subscriptions (other than for subscriptions for which an election under IRC Section 455 is in effect);

8. Membership in an organization (other than for memberships for which an election under IRC Section 456 is in effect); or

9. Any combination of (1) through (8). [Rev. Proc. 2004-34, 2004-22 I.R.B. 99]

Q 5:26

Q 5:27 How are advance payments for sales treated under the accrual method?

Special rules apply to including income from advance payments on agreements for future sales or other dispositions of goods held primarily for sale to customers. An agreement includes a gift certificate that can be redeemed for goods. Amounts due and payable are considered received.

How to report payments. Instead of reporting advance payment in the year received, a business can use an alternative method. Under the alternative method, a business generally includes an advance payment in income in the *earlier* tax year in which:

- The business includes advance payments in gross receipts under the method of accounting it uses for tax purposes, or

- The business includes any part of advance payments in income for financial reports under the method of accounting used for those reports. Financial reports include reports to shareholders, partners, beneficiaries, and other proprietors for credit purposes and consolidated financial statements.

[Reg. § 1.451-5(b)]

Example 5-21: Carol King is a retailer. She uses an accrual method of accounting and she accounts for the sale of goods when she ships them. She uses this method for both tax and financial reporting purposes. King can include advance payments in gross receipts for tax purposes either in the tax year she receives the payments or in the tax year she ships the goods. However, see *Exception for inventory goods,* below.

If a business uses the alternative method of reporting advance payments, it must attach a statement with the following information to its tax return each year:

- Total advance payments received in the current tax year;

- Total advance payments received in earlier tax years and not included in income before the current tax year; and

- Total payments received in earlier tax years included in income for the current tax year.

Exception for inventory goods. If a business has an agreement to sell goods properly included in inventory, it can postpone including the advance payment in income until the end of the second tax year following the year an advance payment is received. To qualify the following requirements must be met as of the last day of the tax year:

- The business accounts for the advance payment under the alternative method.

- The business has received a substantial advance payment on the agreement. A business is treated has receiving a "substantial" advance payment when, by the end of the tax year, the total advance payments received during that year and preceding tax years are equal to or more than the total costs reasonably estimated to be includible in inventory because of the agreement.

If these conditions are met, all advance payments received by the end of the second tax year, including payments received the prior years but not reported, must be included in income by end of the second tax year. Any advance payments received *after* the second year must be reported in the year received. No further deferral is allowed. [Reg. § 1.451-(5)(c)]

Example 5-22: Acme Corp. is a calendar-year accrual-method taxpayer that accounts for advance payments under the alternative method. In 2005, it entered into a contract for the sale of goods properly includible in inventory. The total contract price is $50,000 and Acme estimated that the total costs (for inventory) for the goods would be $25,000. Acme receives the following advance payments under the contract.

2005	$17,500
2006	$10,000
2007	$ 7,500
2008	$ 5,000
2009	$ 5,000
2010	$ 5,000
Total price	$50,000

Acme's customer asked it to deliver the goods in 2011. Since the advance payments Acme had received by the end of 2006 were more than the costs it estimated, the payments are substantial advance payments.

Therefore, Acme includes all payments received by the end of 2008, the second tax year following the tax year in which it received substantial advance payments, in income for 2008. Acme must include $40,000 in sales for 2008.

No further deferral is allowed. Acme must include in gross income the advance payments received in 2009 and 2010 in the years they are received.

Q 5:28 How do accrual method taxpayers handle shipping and billing errors that are discovered after goods are shipped and income accrued?

When goods are sold, income is generally reported in the year the taxpayer ships the goods and bills the customer, even if payment is not actually received until a later year. [Reg. §§ 1.446-1(c)(1)(ii)(A), 1.451-1(a)] The regulations state that if an amount of income is properly accrued on the basis of a reasonable estimate and the exact amount is subsequently determined, the difference, if any, shall be taken into account for the tax year in which such determination is made. [Reg. § 1.451-1(a)]Additionally, if a taxpayer ascertains that an item was improperly included in gross income in a prior tax year, the taxpayer should, if within the statute of limitation, file a claim for credit or refund of any overpayment of tax arising by mistake. If the right to an amount of income is substantially in controversy, the income may not be accrued until the controversy is resolved.

Q 5:28

In one ruling, the IRS reviewed three situations involving shipping and billing errors. [Rev. Rul. 2003-10, 2003-3 I.R.B 288]

Situation 1. XYZ Co. manufactures widgets, which it sells to retailers. XYZ Co. uses the accrual method of accounting and a calendar tax year. For income tax purposes, XYZ recognizes gross income from the sale of widgets when they are shipped to a retailer.

In October Year 1, a retailer orders 1,000 cases of widgets from XYZ at a price of $15 per case. In November Year 1, XYZ ships 1,000 cases of widgets to the retailer along with an invoice. However, as a result of a data entry mistake, the invoice improperly states the amount due as $16,000 rather than $15,000. In Year 2, the retailer notifies XYZ of the mistake, which XYZ acknowledges. The retailer subsequently pays XYZ $15,000.

The IRS says that XYZ should not accrue $16,000 as gross income for Year 1, because it does not have a fixed right to the amount. Instead, XYZ should report $15,000 (less the corresponding cost of goods sold) for Year 1. If XYZ had already filed its Year 1 return by the time the mistake was discovered, it should file a claim for refund of any overpayment of tax resulting from the extra income.

However, many companies have made it a routine practice to take any discrepancies into account in the year they are discovered. The IRS says that a company that has regularly and consistently followed such a practice for two or more tax years should apply for a change of accounting method if it wishes to begin taking any differences into account in the year of sale.

Situation 2. ABC Co. is a retailer that purchases products from XYZ Co. In September Year 1, ABC orders 600 cases of widgets from XYZ at a price of $15 per case. In Year 1, XYZ ships 600 cases to ABC and sends ABC an invoice for $9,000. In November, ABC discovers that the cases contain items that are not widgets and informs XYZ that it will not pay the invoice. In Year 2, the dispute is settled with ABC agreeing to pay $4,500 for the items it received.

The IRS says that, because the dispute arose in the year of sale, XYZ should not report any amount from the transaction (including the cost of goods sold) for Year 1. Instead, XYZ should include $4,500 (less the cost of goods sold) in income for Year 2 when the companies settled their dispute.

Situation 3. Acme Co. regularly purchases both large and small size widgets from XYZ. Each month, XYZ Co. ships 300 cases of small widgets at a price of $10 per case and 700 cases of large widgets at a price of $15 per case. However, in December Year 1, XYZ mistakenly ships 400 cases of small widgets and 600 cases of large widgets along with an invoice for $13,000 (the correct amount for the shipment). Early in Year 2, Acme discovers the shipping error and notifies XYZ. Acme asks XYZ to correct the error by adjusting the amounts of the two sizes in the January shipment. XYZ does so by shipping 200 cases of small widgets and 800 cases of large widgets and invoices Acme for $14,000. In February Year 2, Acme pays both the December and January invoices in full.

Although XYZ shipped the wrong amounts in December Year 1, Acme did not dispute the shipment. Therefore, XYZ has a fixed right to the income relating to that shipment in Year 1. XYZ should accrue $13,000 of gross income for the December shipment in Year 1.

Q 5:29 What is the nonaccrual experience method?

Taxpayers using an accrual method of accounting and performing certain services are not required to accrue any portion of their service-related income that, on the basis of their experience, would not be collected. [IRC § 448(d)(5) This is known as the nonaccrual experience method (NAE).

The NAE method is available only for taxpayers who provide certain professional services (i.e., health, law, engineering, architecture, accounting, actuarial science, performing arts, or consulting) or who meet a $5 million annual gross receipts test. The IRS has issued proposed and temporary regulations on how to compute the NAE exclusion [Reg § 1.448-2T]. Under the regulations, an eligible taxpayer can generally use any method to compute its exclusion as long as it clearly reflected the taxpayer's NAE. However, the regulations provide four safe harbors that are automatically be treated as clearly reflecting NAE.

1. *Six-year moving average.* Under this method, for any taxable year the NAE amount is equal to that portion of the receivables outstanding at the end of the year that is equal to the following ratio:

   - The total bad debts (with respect to accounts receivable) sustained in the current and the five preceding tax years, adjusted for recoveries of bad debts during the period, divided by

   - The sum of the accounts receivable earned throughout the entire six year period (i.e., the total amount of sales resulting in accounts receivable).

     Example 5-23: ABC Inc., a calendar-year taxpayer, earned $330,000 in total accounts receivable for the period 2002 through the end of 2007. ABC's bad debts (adjusted for recoveries) during the six-year period is $64,900. ABC has $49,300 of receivables outstanding at the end of 2007.

   ABC's NAE ratio is 19.67 percent ($64,900/$330,000). So, for 2007, ABC will not accrue as income $9,697 of its $49,300 of outstanding accounts receivable.

   Special rules apply to taxpayers who have not been in business for six years or who have had a substantial increase in their risk of loss during the six-year period.

2. *Three-year moving average.* The IRS also permits taxpayers to use a three-year moving average to compute NAE instead of a six-year moving average. The IRS provides two options in the three-year moving average method.

   Under the first option, the uncollectible portion of year-end receivables equals the actual bad debt percentage for the current year and the preceding two years. A taxpayer is allowed to increase its actual NAE amount by five percent.

Under the second option, a taxpayer may use its current year bad debt percentage for the first year this method is used; a two-year moving average percentage for the second year this method is used; and a three-year moving average percentage for the third and subsequent years.

3. *Modified Black Motor method.* The third safe harbor method is a variation of the formula addressed in the Black Motor case [41 B.T.A. 300 (1940)]. The nonaccrual-experience amount is computed by first determining the ratio of total bad debts charged off (adjusted for recoveries) for the current taxable year and the five preceding taxable years to the total accounts receivable at the end of the current taxable year and the five preceding taxable years. This ratio is applied against the accounts receivable balance at the end of the current taxable year. The resulting amount is then reduced by the credit charges (accounts receivable) generated and written off during the current taxable year, thus producing the NAE amount for the current taxable year.

Example 5-24: XYZ's bad debts (adjusted for recoveries) for the six-year period 2003 through 2008 are $75,700. XYZ's year-end accounts receivable for the six years totals $920,000. Thus, the Black Motor moving average percentage is 8.228 percent ($75,700/$920,000). XYZ's credit charges (accounts receivable) generated and written off during 2007 were $3,600 and its accounts receivable on December 31, 2008 is $180,000. XYZ's modified Black Motor amount for 2008 is $11,210. This is computed by multiplying its accounts receivable on December 31, 2008 ($180,000) by the Black Motor moving average percentage of .08228 and reducing the resulting amount by $3,600 (XYZ's credit charges generated and written off during 2008). Thus, XYZ may exclude $11,210 from gross income for 2008.

4. *Modified six-year moving average.* The fourth safe harbor method is computed by first determining the ratio of total bad debts charged off (adjusted for recoveries) for the current taxable year and the five preceding taxable years other than the credit charges (accounts receivable) that were charged off in the same taxable year they were generated to the total accounts receivable at the end of the current taxable year and the five preceding taxable years. This ratio is then applied against the accounts receivable balance at the end of the current taxable year, which results in the NAE amount for the current taxable year.

Example 5-25: Same facts as in the prior example, except that XYZ uses the modified six-year moving average method. Assume that during the six-year period 2003-2008 the credit charges that were written off in the same taxable year they were generated (adjusted for recoveries) totals $25,233. Thus, XYZ modified six-year moving average percentage is 5.486 percent (($75,700 minus $25,233)/$920,000). XYZ modified six-year moving average amount is $9,875. This is computed by multiplying the accounts receivable on December 31, 2008 ($180,000) by the modified six-year moving average percentage of .05486. Thus, XYZ may exclude $9,875 from gross income for 2008.

Alternative methods. Instead of using one of the safe harbors, the IRS regulations allow a taxpayer to use any alternative NAE method provided the taxpayer's method meets a "self-test" requirement. The taxpayer must self-test its alternative method for the first year it is used and every third year thereafter. This self-test involves comparing the NAE amount under the taxpayer's alternative method with the amount that would have been obtained using the three-year moving average safe harbor.

If the total of the alternative NAE amounts for each year of the test period is less than or equal to the NAE amount computed under the safe harbor, the alternative method will get the IRS's approval. However, the alternative method will not be allowed if the NAE amount exceeds the safe harbor NAE.

Q 5:30 When are expenses "incurred," and therefore deductible, under the accrual method of accounting?

A business using the accrual method can generally deduct a business expense when both of the following take place:

- The all events test has been met. The test is met when: (1) all events have occurred that fix the fact of liability, and (2) the liability can be determined with reasonable accuracy. [Reg. § 1.461-1(a)(2)]

- Economic performance has occurred. [IRC § 461(h)]

If a business cannot determine the precise amount of an expense before the end of a year, a reasonable estimate can be made. If the estimate later turns out to be high or low, an adjustment can be made at the time of the final determination.

If the expense creates an asset that will benefit the business substantially beyond the close of the tax year, the expense is not currently deductible in full. Instead, the expense will have to be written off over a period of time through depreciation, amortization, or similar deduction (see Chapter 6).

Special rules apply to payables to related taxpayers and contested liabilities (see below).

Q 5:31 What is "economic performance"?

If an accrual method business incurs an expense in connection with goods or services provided to it or for its use of property, economic performance occurs as the goods or services are provided or as the property is used. If the expense is for goods or property the business provides to others, economic performance occurs as the business provides the goods or services. [IRC § 461(h)(2)(A)] (There is an exception for recurring items; see Q 5:32.)

> **Example 5-26:** Magna Corp is a calendar-year accrual-method taxpayer. Magna has repairs made on its office in December Year 1. It receives the bill for the work in December, but it pays the bill in January Year 2. Magna can deduct the expense in Year 1 because all events have occurred to fix the fact of liability, the liability can be determined, and economic performance occurred in Year 1.

Workers' compensation and tort liability. If a business is required to make payments under workers' compensation laws or in satisfaction of any tort liability, economic performance occurs as it makes the payments. [IRC § 461(h)(2)(C)]

Taxes. Economic performance generally occurs as estimated income tax, property taxes, employment taxes, etc. are paid. However, a business may elect to treat taxes as a recurring item (see Q 5:32).

The IRS recently ruled that an employer on the accrual basis may be able to deduct payroll taxes in the year they arise, even though the taxes are owed on deferred compensation that will not be deductible until a later year. This treatment applies if the taxes qualify as a recurring item. The Internal Revenue Code generally postpones deductions for deferred compensation until it's includible in an employee's income (see Chapter 11). However, the IRS determined that an employer's liability for payroll taxes did not represent compensation paid or accrued on account of any employee and therefore was not subject to the deduction rules for deferred compensation. [Rev. Rul. 2007-12 , I.R.B. 2007-11]

Interest. Economic performance occurs with the passage of time. In other words, the interest is deductible as the business uses, and the lender forgoes the use of, the lender's money—not when payments are made.

Compensation for services. Generally, economic performance occurs as an employee renders service to the business. However, deductions for compensation or other benefits paid to an employee in a year subsequent to economic performance are subject to the rules governing deferred compensation (see Chapter 11).

> **Planning Point:** Payments made within two and one-half months after the close of the company's tax year are not considered deferred compensation. [Reg. § 1.404(b)-1T] For example, if a company uses the accrual method of accounting and operates on a calendar-year basis, it has until March 15, 2009 to pay a bonus that was accrued in 2008. As long as payment is made by March 15, the bonus is not considered deferred compensation and the company gets a 2008 deduction.

Vacation pay. A business can take a current deduction for vacation pay earned by its employees if it is paid during the year or, within two and one-half months after the end of the year. If it is paid later than this, it must be deducted in the year actually paid.

Q 5:32 What is the economic performance exception for recurring items?

An exception to the economic performance rule allows certain recurring items to be treated as incurred during the tax year even though economic performance has not occurred. The exception applies if all the following requirements are met:

1. The all-events test is met (see above);
2. Economic performance occurs by the *earlier* of the following dates:

    a. Eight and one-half months after the close of the year; or

    b. The date the business files its return for the year (including extensions);

3. The item is recurring in nature and the business consistently treats similar items as incurred in the tax year in which the all-events test is met;

4. Either:

    a. The item is not material; or

    b. Accruing the item in the year in which the all-events test is met results in a better match against income than accruing the item in the year of economic performance.

[Reg. § 1.461-5(b)]

This exception does not apply to workers' compensation or tort liabilities. A new expense or an expense not incurred every year can be treated as recurring if it is reasonable to expect that it will be incurred regularly in the future.

Material. Factors to consider in determining whether an item is "material" include the size of the item (both in absolute terms and in relation to the business's income and other expenses) and the treatment of the item on the business's financial statements.

An item considered material for financial statement purposes is also considered material for tax purposes.

Matching expenses with income. Generally accepted accounting principles are an important factor in determining whether the accrual of an expense in a particular year results in a better match with the income to which it relates. Costs directly associated with the revenue of a period are properly allocable to that period. For example, a sales commission agreement can require certain payments be made in a year subsequent to the year sales income is reported. In this situation, economic performance for part of the commission expense may not occur until the following year. Nevertheless, deducting the commission expense in the year the sales income is reported will result in a better match of the commission expense with the sales income. Also, if sales income is recognized in the year of sale, but the goods are not shipped until the following year, the shipping costs are more properly matched to income in the year of sale than the year the goods are shipped.

Expenses such as insurance or rent are generally allocable to a period of time. Expenses that cannot practically be associated with income of a particular period, such as advertising costs, should be assigned to the period when the costs are incurred. The matching requirement is satisfied if the period to which the expenses are assigned is the same for tax and financial reporting purposes.

In a general legal advice memorandum, the IRS Chief Counsel recently determined that services cannot be prepaid and then partially deducted by an accrual-basis taxpayer in the year of prepayment to the extent that some of the services are performed within the recurring item exceptions to the economic

Q 5:32

performance rule. The exceptions are "all or nothing" and the deduction cannot be prorated to allow a deduction for those services actually performed within the exception periods. The recurring item exception does not allow a taxpayer to split up the liability into a portion that's deductible in the earlier year and a portion that's deductible when the services are performed. [IRS Advice Memorandum AM 2007-009]

Q 5:33 Are payables to related taxpayers deductible when they are accrued?

Not if the tax relatives used the cash method of accounting. Business expenses and interest owed to a related taxpayer who uses the cash method are not deductible until the business makes payment and the amount is included in the related taxpayer's income. [IRC § 267(a)(2)] For example, suppose a calendar-year corporation awards a bonus to its president and sole shareholder in December 2007. Actual payment is made in January 2008. The payment is not deductible until the corporation's 2008 tax year because the shareholder is considered a related taxpayer, and the bonus is not included in his or her income until then.

Q 5:34 For purposes of the related taxpayer rule who is considered related?

The following persons and entities are considered tax relatives: [IRC § 267(b), (e)]

- Members of a family, but limited to brothers and sisters (either whole or half), husband and wife, ancestors, and lineal descendants.
- Two corporations that are members of the same controlled group. [IRC § 267 (f)]
- The fiduciaries of two different trusts, and the fiduciary and beneficiary of two different trusts, if the same person is the grantor of both trusts.
- A tax-exempt educational or charitable organization and a person (if an individual, including the members of the individual's family) who directly or indirectly controls such an organization.
- An individual and a corporation when the individual owns, directly or indirectly, more than 50 percent of the value of the outstanding stock of the corporation.
- A fiduciary of a trust and a corporation when the trust or the grantor of the trust owns, directly or indirectly, more than 50 percent in value of the outstanding stock of the corporation.
- The grantor and fiduciary, and the fiduciary and beneficiary, of any trust.
- Any two S corporations if the same persons own more than 50 percent in value of the outstanding stock of each corporation.
- An S corporation and a corporation that is not an S corporation if the same persons own more than 50 percent in value of the outstanding stock of each corporation.

- A corporation and a partnership if the same persons own more than 50 percent in value of the outstanding stock of the corporation and more than 50 percent of the capital or profits interest in the partnership.

- A personal service corporation and any employee-owner, regardless of the amount of stock owned by the employee-owner.

For purposes of determining if an individual directly or indirectly owns stock of a corporation, stock owned directly or indirectly by or for a corporation, partnership, estate, or trust is treated as being owned proportionately by or for its shareholders, partners, or beneficiaries. An individual is treated as owning the stock owned directly or indirectly by or for the individual's family. [IRC § 267(c)]

Q 5:35 What is the special rule for deducting contested liabilities?

If a business uses the accrual method of accounting and contests a liability, it can deduct the liability in either: (1) the year it pays it (or transfers money or other property in satisfaction of it), or (2) the year the business finally settles the contest. [IRC § 461(f)]

To claim a deduction in the year of payment, the following conditions must be met in that year:

1. *Liability must be contested.* A business does not need to bring a lawsuit to contest a liability. However, it must deny its validity or accuracy by a positive act. A written protest included with payment of a liability is enough to start a contest. In the case of taxes, lodging a protest in accordance with local law is also enough to contest a liability.

2. *Contest must exist.* The liability must continue to be contested after the payment or transfer. If no payment is made until the dispute is settled, the liability is deductible in the year in which the contest is settled.

   Example 5-27: Zeno, Inc., a calendar-year corporation, uses an accrual method of accounting. It had a $500 liability asserted against it in Year 1 for repair work completed that year. Zeno contested the asserted liability and settled in Year 2 for the full $500. It pays the $500 in January Year 3. Since Zeno did not make the payment until after the contest was settled, the liability accrues in Year 2, and it can be deducted only in Year 2.

3. *Transfer to creditor.* The business must transfer to the creditor or other person enough money or other property to cover the payment of the contested liability. The money or other property transferred must be beyond the business's control. The business satisfies this requirement if it transfers the money or other property to an escrow agent. However, if the business buys a bond, makes an entry on its books, or transfers funds to an account within its control, it will not meet this requirement.

4. *Liability deductible.* The liability must have been deductible in the year of payment or in an earlier year when it would have accrued had there been no contest.

Q 5:36 Is an adjustment necessary if the business recovers a contested liability?

Yes. An adjustment is usually necessary when a business recovers any part of a contested liability. This occurs when the business deducted the liability in the year of payment and recovers any part of it in a later tax year when the contest is settled. The business must include in gross income in the year of final settlement the part of the recovered amount that, when deducted, decreased the tax for the tax year.

Inventories

Q 5:37 What items must be included in inventory?

To reflect taxable income correctly, inventories at the beginning and end of each taxable year are necessary in every case in which the production, purchase, or sale of merchandise is an income-producing factor. [Reg. § 1.471-1]

A business's inventory should include all of the following:

- Merchandise or stock in trade:
  - Purchased merchandise if title has passed to the business, even if the merchandise is in transit or the business does not have physical possession for another reason;
  - Goods under contract for sale that have not yet been segregated and applied to the contract;
  - Goods out on consignment; and
  - Goods held for sale in display rooms, merchandise mart rooms, or booths located away from the place of business.
- Raw materials;
- Work in process;
- Finished products; and
- Supplies that physically become a part of the item intended for sale.

The following should not be included in inventory:

- Goods sold, but only if title has passed to the buyer;
- Goods consigned to the business;
- Goods ordered for future delivery if the business does not yet have title;
- Land, buildings, and equipment used in the business;
- Notes, accounts receivable, and similar assets;
- Real estate held for sale by a real estate dealer in the ordinary course of business; or
- Supplies that do not physically become part of the item intended for sale.

Q 5:38 How is inventory valued?

The two most common methods for valuing inventory are: (1) cost or (2) the lower of cost or market. [Reg. § 1.471-2(c)]

Cost. To value inventory at cost, a business must include all direct and indirect costs associated with it. For merchandise on hand at the beginning of the tax year, cost means the ending inventory price of the goods. For merchandise purchased during the year, cost means the invoice price minus appropriate discounts plus transportation or other charges incurred in acquiring the goods. It can also include other costs that have to be capitalized under the uniform capitalization (UNICAP) rules. (See Q 5:40 below.) For merchandise produced during the year, cost means all direct and indirect costs that have to be capitalized under UNICAP.

Cost or market. Under the lower of cost or market method, the market value of each item on hand on the inventory date is compared with its cost; the lower of the two is its inventory value.

This method applies to: (1) goods purchased and on hand; and (2) the basic elements of cost (direct materials, direct labor, and certain indirect costs) of goods being manufactured and finished goods on hand. This method does *not* apply to: (1) goods on hand or being manufactured for delivery at a fixed price on a firm sales contract; and (2) goods accounted for under the last-in, first-out (LIFO) method. (See Q 5:39 below.) The latter goods must be valued at cost.

Under ordinary circumstances, "market" value means the usual bid price on the date of inventory. This price is based on the volume of merchandise a business usually buys. For example, if a business buys items in small lots at $10 per item and a competitor buys identical items in larger lots at $8.50 per item, the business's usual market price will be higher than its competitor's.

When a business offers merchandise for sale at a price lower than market in the normal course of business, it can value the inventory at the lower price, minus the direct cost of disposition.

Q 5:39 How is the cost of items in inventory identified?

A business can use the specific identification method when it can identify and match the actual cost to the items in inventory. If the cost of items cannot be identified specifically, then a business can use the first-in, first-out (FIFO) or last-in, first-out (LIFO) method. [Reg. § 1.471-2(d)]

The FIFO method assumes the items purchased or produced first are the first items sold, consumed, or otherwise disposed of. The items in inventory at the end of the tax year are matched with the costs of similar items that were most recently purchased or produced.

The LIFO method assumes the items of inventory purchased or produced last are the first items sold, consumed, or otherwise disposed of. Items included in closing inventory are considered to be from the opening inventory in the order of acquisition and from those acquired during the tax year. [IRC § 472]

Q 5:38

Under the "dollar-value" method of pricing LIFO inventories, goods and products must be grouped into one or more pools (classes of items), depending on the kinds of goods or products in the inventories. [Reg. § 1.472-8]Under a simplified method, eligible small businesses can establish multiple inventory pools in general categories from appropriate government price indexes. Changes in the price index can be used to estimate the annual change in price for inventory items in the pools. A small business is eligible to use the simplified method if its average annual gross receipts are $5 million or less for the three preceding tax years. [IRC § 474]

Q 5:40 What are the uniform capitalization (UNICAP) rules?

Taxpayers are required to capitalize their direct costs and a properly allocable portion of indirect costs attributable to property produced or property acquired for resale. In order to determine these capitalizable costs, taxpayers must allocate or apportion costs to various activities, including production or resale activities. After the costs are allocated to the appropriate production or resale activities, these costs are generally allocated to the items of property produced or property acquired for resale during the tax year and capitalized to the items that remain on hand at the end of the tax year. [IRC § 263A(a); Reg. § 1.263A-1(c)(1))]

Costs that are capitalized are recovered through depreciation, amortization, cost of goods sold, or by an adjustment to basis at the time the property is used, sold, placed in service, or otherwise disposed of by the taxpayer. Cost recovery is determined by the applicable Internal Revenue Code provisions, including regulations, relating to the use, sale, or disposition of property. "Capitalize" means to include in inventory costs for property that is inventory in the hands of a taxpayer and, in the case of other property, to charge to a capital account or basis. [Reg. § 1.263A-1(c)(2)(ii), Reg. § 1.263A-1(c)(3) and Reg. § 1.263A-1(c)(4)]

A simplified production method is provided for taxpayers who produce property and a simplified resale method is provided for taxpayers who acquire property for resale.

Q 5:41 Which businesses are subject to the UNICAP rules?

A business generally must comply with the UNICAP rules if it: (1) produces real or tangible personal property; or (2) acquires property for resale. [IRC § 263A(b)]However, this rule does not apply to resellers of personal property if their average annual gross receipts are $10 million or less. [IRC § 262A(b)(2)(B)]

Producing property. A business is considered to "produce" property if it constructs, builds, installs, manufactures, develops, improves, creates, raises, or grows the property. Property produced under a contract is treated as produced by the business to the extent it makes payments or otherwise incur costs in connection with the property. [IRC § 263A(g)]

Exceptions. The UNICAP rules do not apply to:

- Property produced to use as personal or nonbusiness property or for uses not connected with a business;

- Research and experimental expenditures deductible under Section 174 of the Code;

- Intangible drilling and development costs of oil and gas or geothermal wells;

- Timber and certain ornamental trees raised, harvested, or grown, and the underlying land;

- Qualifying creative expenses incurred as a freelance writer, photographer, or artist that are otherwise deductible on the freelancer's tax return. (These expenses do not include expenses related to printing, photographic plates, motion picture films, videotapes, or similar items.);

- Property provided to customers in connection with providing services. (It must be *de minimis* in amount and not be inventory in the hands of the service provider.);

- The costs of certain producers who use a simplified production method and whose total indirect costs are $200,000 or less. [Reg. § 1.263A-2(b)(3)(iv)]

Q 5:42 What is the simplified production method?

Producers may elect to use the "simplified production method" to account for the additional costs, required to be capitalized under the uniform capitalization rules ("additional Sec. 263A costs"), that are allocable to ending inventories of property produced. Producers may elect to use the simplified production method utilizing an actual absorption ratio or an historic absorption ratio. A producer engaged in both production and resale activities may elect the simplified production method but generally may not elect the simplified resale method. If elected, the simplified production method must be applied to all eligible property produced and all eligible property acquired for resale by the taxpayer. [Reg. § 1.263A-2(a)(5) and Reg. § 1.263A-2(b)(1)]

Eligible property. A producer that elects to use the simplified production method for any trade or business is required to use it for all production and resale activities associated with four categories of property:

1. Inventory property. Stock in trade or other property properly includible in the inventory of the producer.

2. Non-inventory property held for sale. Non-inventory property held by a taxpayer primarily for sale to customers in the ordinary course of its trade or business.

3. Self-constructed assets. Self-constructed assets substantially identical in nature to, and produced in the same manner as, inventory property produced by the taxpayer and held primarily for sale to customers in the ordinary course of the taxpayer's trade or business.

Q 5:42

4. Self-constructed assets produced by the taxpayer on a routine and repetitive basis in the ordinary course of the taxpayer's trade or business. [Reg. § 1.263A-2(b)(2)(i)]

The IRS has issued temporary regulations providing guidance on the routine and repetitive basis standard (item (4), above) for qualifying for the simplified production method. [Temp. Reg. § 1.263A-2T] The IRS says that a taxpayer's production of property will be considered "routine and repetitive" only if the property is—

- mass-produced (i.e., numerous identical goods are manufactured using standardized designs and assembly line techniques) *or*
- the produced property has a high degree of turnover (i.e., the costs of production are recovered over a relatively short period of time). [Rev. Rul. 2005-53, IRB 2005-35]

Q 5:43 What is the simplified resale method?

Resellers may elect to use the simplified resale method to determine the additional Sec. 263A costs properly allocable to property acquired for resale. [Reg. § 1.263A-3(d)(1)]Taxpayers can elect to use a historic absorption ratio in lieu of an actual absorption ratio to determine allocable additional Sec. 263A costs.

The simplified resale method is generally available only to a trade or business exclusively engaged in resale activities. [Reg. § 1.263A-3(d)(2)] However, if a reseller is engaged in both production and resale activities with respect to four categories of eligible property (see below), then the reseller may only elect the simplified production method (see Q 5:42) and is not allowed to elect the simplified resale method. Two exceptions apply which allow resellers engaged in both production and resale activities to elect the simplified resale method: (1) resellers with *de minimis* production activities, and (2) resellers with property produced under a contract. A taxpayer that uses the simplified resale method and has *de minimis* production activities incident to its resale activities or property produced under contract must capitalize all costs allocable to eligible property produced using the simplified resale method. [Reg. § 1.263A-3(a)(4)]

The four categories of eligible property are as follows:

1. Inventory property. Stock in trade or other property includible in the inventory of the reseller;

2. Non-inventory property held for sale. Non-inventory property held by a taxpayer primarily for sale to customers in the ordinary course of its trade or business;

3. Self-constructed assets. Self-constructed assets substantially identical in nature to, and produced in the same manner as, inventory property produced by the taxpayer and held primarily for sale to customers in the ordinary course of the taxpayer's trade or business; and

4. Self-constructed assets produced on a repetitive basis. Self-constructed assets produced by the taxpayer on a routine and repetitive basis in the ordinary course of the taxpayer's trade or business.

Installment Sales

Q 5:44 What is an installment sale?

For tax purposes, an installment sale is a disposition of property where the seller receives at least one payment after the close of the tax year in which the sale occurs. Eligible taxpayers can use the installment method to report gain (but not loss) from an installment sale. Under the installment method, gain is prorated and recognized over the period the payments are received. [IRC § 453]

Stock or securities. The installment method cannot be used to report gain from the sale of stock or securities traded on an established securities market. The entire gain on the sale must be recognized in the year in which the trade date falls. [IRC § 453(k)(2)(A)]

Dealer sales. Sales of personal property by a business that regularly sells or otherwise disposes of property of the same type on the installment plan cannot be reported under the installment method. This rule also applies to real property held for sale to customers in the ordinary course of a trade or business. [IRC § 453(b)(2)(A)]

Q 5:45 How is the recognized gain on each payment determined?

Each payment of principal is treated as if it comprised two parts. One part is a tax-free return of the seller's adjusted basis in the property. The other part is the recognized gain.

To figure what part of any principal payment is gain, the payment is multiplied by the gross profit percentage. [IRC § 453(c)] The gross profit percentage is the expected gross profit divided by the contract price.

> **Example 5-28:** Bob Blaine sells his van in December 2008 for $5,000. His adjusted basis for the van is $2,000. Under the terms of the sale, Blaine receives a $1,000 down payment at the time of the sale and 16 monthly payments of $250 (plus interest) starting in January 2009. Blaine's gross profit percentage is 60 percent ($3,000/$5,000). So, using the installment method, 60 percent of each payment is recognized gain. Blaine reports $600 of gain in 2008, $1,800 in 2009, and $600 in 2010.

If the selling price is reduced at a later date, the gross profit on the sale will also change. The gross profit percentage must then be refigured for the remaining payments. Taxpayer subtracts the gain already reported from the reduced gross profit. The remaining gain is spread over the future installments.

> **Example 5-29:** In 2008, a business sells land with a basis of $40,000 for $100,000. The gross profit is $60,000. The business receives a $20,000 down payment and the buyer's note for $80,000. The note provides for four annual installment payments of $20,000 each, plus interest, beginning in 2009. The gross profit percentage is 60 percent. The business reports a gain of $12,000 on each payment received in 2008 and 2009.

In 2010, the business and buyer agree to reduce the purchase price to $85,000 and payments during 2010, 2011, and 2012 are reduced to $15,000 for each year.

Under the revised agreement, the gross profit is $45,000 ($85,000 less $40,000). Of that amount, $24,000 has already been reported and 21,000 remains to be reported. The new gross profit percentage is 46.67 percent ($21,000/$45,000). So the business will recognize $7,000 of each of the remaining payments.

Q 5:46 If a business makes an installment sale of property eligible for the installment method, must it use the installment method?

No, it can elect out of the installment method. [IRC § 453(d)] In this case, the business generally reports the entire gain in the year of sale, even though it does not receive all the sale proceeds in that year.

To figure the gain to report, the buyer's installment obligation is valued at its fair market value (whether or not it could be actually sold). If a business uses the cash method of accounting, the fair market value must at least equal the fair market value of the property (minus any other consideration received). [Reg. § 15A.453-1(d)(3)]

Once an election out of the installment method is made, the election can only be revoked with IRS approval. Approval will not be granted if: (1) one of the purposes is to avoid federal income tax; or (2) the tax year in which any payment was received has closed. [IRC § 453(d)]

Change of Accounting Methods

Q 5:47 What is a change of accounting method?

For tax purposes, a change of accounting method is not limited to a change in the overall system of accounting (e.g., switching from cash method to accrual). A business is also considered to have changed accounting methods when it changes the treatment of any material item. A material item is one that affects the proper time for inclusion of income or allowance of a deduction. [Reg. § 1.446-1(e)(2)(ii). *See* Rev. Proc. 2002-9, 2002-3 I.R.B. 327, Rev. Proc. 91-31, 1991-1 C.B. 566]

Q 5:48 How does a business change its accounting method?

Section 446(e) of the Internal Revenue Code requires taxpayers to obtain the consent of the IRS before changing a method of accounting for federal income tax purposes. Taxpayers can request the IRS's consent to change a method of accounting by filing a Form 3115, Application for Change in Accounting Method, that describes the current and new methods of accounting, identifies items that will be treated differently under the new method of accounting, and includes a computation of any adjustment required by Section 481(a) (see Q. 5:50).

The IRS has issued administrative procedures instructing taxpayers how and when to file Form 3115, and prescribing the terms and conditions necessary to obtain consent to change an accounting method. These procedures are contained principally in Rev. Proc. 2002-9, 2002-1 C.B. 327 (as modified and clarified by Announcement 2002-17, 2002-1 C.B. 561, modified and amplified by Rev. Proc. 2002-19, 2002-1 C.B. 696, and amplified, clarified and modified by Rev. Proc. 2002-54, 2002-2 C.B. 432) and Rev. Proc. 97-27, 1997-1 C.B. 680 (as modified and amplified by Rev. Proc. 2002-19, as amplified and clarified by Rev. Proc. 2002-54).

Rev. Proc. 2002-9 deals with the "automatic consent process" while Rev. Proc. 97-27 concerns the nonautomatic consent process.

1. The automatic consent process. The IRS grants eligible taxpayers automatic consent to change to certain methods of accounting, most of which are described in the Appendix to Rev. Proc. 2002-9. A taxpayer that seeks to change to one of these methods must attach Form 3115 to its timely filed (including extensions) original income tax return for the requested year of change and send a copy of the Form 3115 to the IRS national office no later than the date that the original Form 3115 is filed with the federal income tax return for the year of change.

In general, a taxpayer, not under audit, complying with all the applicable provisions of Rev. Proc. 2002-9 will be considered to have the IRS's consent to change its method of accounting and ordinarily receives both "audit protection" and "ruling protection." That is, the IRS will not require the taxpayer to change its method of accounting for the same item for a taxable year prior to the year of change ("audit protection"). The IRS also will not require the taxpayer to change or modify the new method of accounting except in certain circumstances specifically enumerated in Rev. Proc. 2002-9 and, if the IRS does require the taxpayer to change or modify the new method of accounting, the required change or modification to the new method of accounting generally will not be applied retroactively ("ruling protection"). In other words, the taxpayer receives protection with respect to the use of the new method of accounting in future years.

Rev. Proc. 2002-9 is the *exclusive* procedure for a taxpayer within the scope of Rev. Proc. 2002-9 to obtain the IRS's consent for an accounting method change. Accordingly, a taxpayer that qualifies to make a change through the automatic consent process may not opt to make the change under the nonautomatic consent process.

The IRS national office reviews Forms 3115 filed through the automatic consent process to determine whether the form is properly completed and whether the taxpayer qualifies for automatic consent. If the IRS national office reviews a Form 3115 and determines that the form is not properly completed, or if supplemental information is needed, the IRS national office notifies the taxpayer, specifies the information that is needed, and permits the taxpayer 30 days to furnish the necessary information. If the IRS national office tentatively determines that the taxpayer has changed its method of accounting without complying with all the applicable provisions of Rev. Proc. 2002-9, the IRS national office notifies the taxpayer of its tentative adverse determination and offers the taxpayer a conference if the taxpayer has requested such a conference. In cases where the IRS national office remains adverse after the conference, it notifies the taxpayer that consent to make the change in method of accounting is not granted.

2. The nonautomatic consent process. Changes that do not qualify for automatic consent must be requested under the nonautomatic consent process described in Rev. Proc. 97-27. A taxpayer that seeks the IRS's consent to change a method of accounting through the nonautomatic consent process must file Form 3115 with the IRS national office during the taxable year in which the taxpayer desires to make the proposed change. There is a user fee for a nonautomatic consent request (in general, the current fee is $2,500 per request).

In processing a request for a change in method of accounting made through the nonautomatic consent process, the IRS national office considers, among other factors, whether the requested method of accounting is legally permissible for the taxpayer, whether the requested method clearly reflects the taxpayer's income, and whether the taxpayer has appropriately computed any adjustment required by Section 481(a). The processing of a taxpayer's request for an accounting method change may involve requests for supplemental information from the taxpayer, including requests for additional facts and clarification of how the taxpayer intends to apply the requested method to particular types of transactions. If supplemental information is needed, the IRS national office notifies the taxpayer and the taxpayer generally is permitted 21 days to furnish the necessary information.

If the taxpayer's requested accounting method change is approved by the IRS national office, the taxpayer receives a letter ruling granting the taxpayer consent to make the change subject to certain terms and conditions. The taxpayer also generally receives audit protection and ruling protection. In cases where the IRS national office is tentatively adverse to the taxpayer's requested change in method of accounting, the IRS national office notifies the taxpayer of its tentative adverse determination and offers the taxpayer a conference if the taxpayer has requested such a conference. If the IRS national office remains adverse after the conference, it notifies the taxpayer that consent to make the change in method of accounting is denied.

Changes in the works. The IRS recently announced that it is considering revising the consent process for accounting method changes. [Notice 2007-88, 2007-46 IRB] The IRS announcement contained one possible approach and invited taxpayers to comment and submit other suggestions. Changes to the process, including any pilot program, would not become effective until the IRS considers taxpayers' comments and suggestions.

Q 5:49 What changes has the IRS proposed in the consent process for accounting method changes?

In Notice 2007-88, the IRS announced that it is considering modifying the consent process so that the existing "automatic consent" process and "nonautomatic consent" process are replaced with a system under which a taxpayer requests "standard consent," or "specific consent."

Standard consent process. The IRS anticipates that, under this proposal, the majority of accounting method change requests would be made through the standard consent process in a manner similar to the existing automatic consent process. The proposal contemplates that taxpayers would file Form 3115, Application for Change in Accounting Method, with their returns for the requested year of change. However, the IRS is considering an alternative approach, under which taxpayers would be required to file Form 3115 for changes to methods of accounting not specifically identified in Rev. Proc. 2002-9 or other automatic guidance, by the last day of the ninth month of the requested tax year of change.

Under the proposal, the IRS would screen accounting method change requests for completeness and for compliance with the procedures governing the standard consent process. Requests that are not substantially complete would be denied and the taxpayer would be notified that consent to change accounting method is not granted.

Specific consent process. The specific consent process is proposed for only two categories of accounting method changes: (1) accounting method changes specifically identified in published guidance as required to be made under the specific consent process, and (2) changes that otherwise qualify under the standard consent process, but for which the taxpayer seeks different terms and conditions or a waiver of certain scope limitations that apply to the standard consent process. Under the proposal, a taxpayer that seeks a change in accounting method other than a change that is specifically identified in Rev. Proc. 2002-9 or other automatic consent guidance, may request a letter ruling under Rev. Proc. 2007-1, I.R.B. 2007-1, 1, (or its successor).

Q 5:50 Are adjustments required in the year an accounting method is changed?

Yes. Businesses that voluntarily change their method of accounting with the IRS's permission, or who are compelled by the IRS to make a change because the method used does not clearly reflect income, must make certain adjustments to income in the year of the change. [IRC § 481(a); Reg. § 1.481-1] The adjustments are those determined to be necessary to prevent duplication or omission of items.

Since the adjustments for the year of change might result in the bunching of income, two statutory methods of limiting the tax in the changeover year may be applied if the adjustments for the changeover year increase taxable income by more than $3,000. [Reg. § 1.481-2] If both limitations apply, the one resulting in the lower tax should be used. In order for the first of these methods to be used, the old method of accounting must have been used in the two preceding years; if so, the tax increase in the changeover year is limited to the tax increases that would result if the adjustments were spread ratably over that year and the two preceding years.

Under the second method, a business must be able to reconstruct its income under the new method of accounting for one or more consecutive years immediately preceding the changeover year. The increase in the changeover year's tax because of the adjustments may not be more than the net tax increases that would result if the adjustments were allocated back to those preceding years under the new method. Any amounts that cannot be allocated back must be included in the changeover year's income for purposes of computing the limitation.

Recordkeeping

Q 5:51 Under the tax law, what kind of records is a business required to keep?

Except in a few cases (e.g., travel and entertainment expenses; see Chapter 8), the tax law does not require taxpayers to maintain special kind of records. A business may choose any record-keeping system that clearly shows its income. [Reg. § 1.446-1(a)]

A record-keeping system should include a summary of business transactions. This summary is ordinarily made in the business's books (for example, accounting journals and ledgers). The books must show gross income, as well as deductions and credits. For most small businesses, the business checkbook is the main source for entries in the business books. In addition, a business must retain supporting documents; purchases, sales, payroll, and other transactions that will generate supporting documents. Supporting documents include sales slips, paid bills, invoices, receipts, deposit slips, and canceled checks. These documents contain the information that needs to be recorded in the business's books. [IRS Pub. 583, *Starting a Business and Keeping Records*]

Gross receipts. A business should keep supporting documents that show the amounts and sources of gross receipts. Documents that show gross receipts include the following:

- Cash register tapes;
- Bank deposit slips;
- Receipt books;
- Invoices;
- Credit card charge slips; and
- Forms 1099-MISC.

Purchases. Supporting documents should show the amount paid and that the amount was for purchases. Documents for purchases include the following:

- Canceled checks;
- Cash register tape receipts;
- Credit card sales slips; and
- Invoices.

Expenses. Supporting documents for expenses other than purchases should show the amount paid and that the amount was for a business expense. Documents for expenses include the following:

- Canceled checks;
- Cash register tapes;
- Account statements;
- Credit card sales slips;
- Invoices; and
- Petty cash slips for *small* cash payments.

Assets. A business must keep records to verify certain information about its business assets. Records are needed to figure the annual depreciation and the gain or loss upon disposition of the asset. Records should show the following information:

- When and how the business acquired the asset;
- Purchase price;
- Cost of any improvements;
- IRC Section 179 deduction taken;
- Deductions taken for depreciation;
- Deductions taken for casualty losses, such as losses resulting from fires or storms;
- How the business uses the asset;
- When and how the business disposed of the asset;
- Selling price; and
- Expenses of sale.

Documents that may show this information include the following:

- Purchase and sales invoices;
- Real estate closing statements; and
- Canceled checks.

Q 5:52 Will the IRS accept a computerized record-keeping system?

If a business uses a computerized system, it must be able to produce sufficiently legible records to support and verify entries made on its tax return. To meet this qualification, the computerized records must reconcile with the business's books and tax return. These records must provide enough detail to identify the underlying source documents. [IRS Pub. 583, *Starting a Business and Keeping Records*]

Q 5:53 How long must records be kept?

Records must be kept for as long as they may be needed for the administration of any provision of the Internal Revenue Code. [IRS Pub. 583, *Starting a Business and Keeping Records*] Generally, this means a business must keep records that support an item of income or deduction on a return until the period of limitations for that return expires.

The period of limitations is the period of time in which a taxpayer can amend a return to claim a credit or refund, or in which the IRS can assess additional tax. Generally the period of limitations for income taxes is three years from the due date of the return. [IRC § 6501(a)] This period, however, is extended to six years if more than 25 percent of the gross income has been omitted from the return. [IRC § 6501(e)] There is no limitations period if the taxpayer files a fraudulent return or does not file a required return. [IRC § 6501(c)]

Employment tax returns should be retained for at least four years after the date the tax becomes due or is paid, whichever is later. [IRS Pub. 583, *Starting a Business and Keeping Records*]

Assets. A business should keep records relating to property until the period of limitations expires for the year in which the business disposes of the property. A business needs these records to figure any depreciation, amortization, or depletion deduction and to determine basis for computing gain or loss when the business disposes of the property.

Generally, if a business receives property in a nontaxable exchange, its basis in that property is the same as the basis of the property given up, increased by any money it paid. [IRC § 1031(d)]The business must keep the records on the old property, as well as on the new property, until the period of limitations expires for the year in which the business disposes of the new property. [IRS Pub. 583, *Starting a Business and Keeping Records*]

Chapter 6

Business Income, Deductions, and Credits

A business's taxable income is basically the difference between its gross income and its deductible businesses expenses; and the tax code defines each term broadly: Gross income is "all income from whatever source derived," [IRC § 61(a)] and deductible expenses include "all the ordinary and necessary expenses paid or incurred during the taxable year in carrying on any trade or business." [IRC § 162(a)] But then the Internal Revenue Code (IRC or the Code) proceeds to carve out a host of exceptions and special rules that may reduce both a business's income and deductions. This chapter will take a closer look at these exceptions and special rules. In addition, we will examine the various tax credits that can reduce the amount of tax a business owes on its taxable income.

Certain income and deduction topics are covered elsewhere in this book because of their importance and/or complexity. For example, income from the sale of property is discussed in Chapter 13, while deductions for depreciation and travel and entertainment expenses are covered in Chapters 7 and 8, respectively.

Also keep in mind that, just as important as *what* is taxable and deductible is the question of *when* it is taxable or deductible. The timing issue depends on the choice of accounting methods and other factors and is discussed in Chapter 5.

Business Income

Q 6:1 What business income is subject to tax?

In general. All income is subject to tax unless specifically excluded by the Code. Thus, taxable business income includes such items as fees, commissions, and other compensation for services, profits from the sale of goods, rents, and royalties. [IRC § 61(a)]

In a manufacturing, merchandising, or mining business, "gross income" means the total sales, less the cost of goods sold, plus any income from investments and from incidental or outside operations or sources. [Reg. § 1.61-3(a)] The cost of goods sold should be determined in accordance with the method of accounting consistently used by the taxpayer. Thus, for example, an amount cannot be taken into account in the computation of cost of goods sold any earlier than the taxable year in which economic performance occurs with respect to the amount. [Reg. § 1.446-1(c)(1)(ii)]

In most cases, business income will be in the form of cash, checks, and credit card charges. But business income can be in the form of property or services, commonly referred to as bartering (see below).

Cancellation of debt. If a debt incurred in a business is canceled or forgiven, the canceled amount must generally be included in the business's gross income. [IRC § 61(a)(12)] For example, if a business's creditor accepts partial payment in full discharge of the business's debt, the business has cancellation of debt (COD) income to the extent of the difference. If the borrower's payment of the debt would have been a deductible expense, no COD income is recognized. [IRC § 108(e)(2)]

> **Example 6-1:** A business receives accounting services on credit. Later, the business has trouble paying its debts, and the accountant forgives part of the amount the business owes. If the business uses the cash method of accounting, it does not include the debt cancellation in income because payment of the debt would have given rise to a deduction. On the other hand, if the business uses the accrual method, it may have already deducted the expense when it incurred the debt. In that case, the business would have COD income.

No COD income is recognized from a discharge of indebtedness in a bankruptcy proceeding. [IRC § 108(a)(2)]There is also an exemption when the debt of an insolvent taxpayer is forgiven; there is no COD income to the extent of the insolvency. [IRC § 108(a)(3)]In both cases, the taxpayer must reduce certain "tax attributes" (e.g., basis of property) by the amount excluded from COD income. [IRC § 108(b)]

A solvent business (other than a C corporation) may also elect to exclude the cancellation of "qualified real property business indebtedness." [IRC § 108(a)(1)(D)] To qualify, the debt must be (1) incurred or assumed in connection with real estate used in a trade or business, (2) secured by the real estate, and (3) incurred or assumed to acquire, construct, or substantially improve the real estate. [IRC § 108(c)(3)]

The exclusion for cancellation of real estate debt is limited to the excess of the debt over the fair market value of the property (reduced by any other qualifying debt secured by the property). The exclusion also cannot exceed the total adjusted bases of depreciable real estate held by the taxpayer immediately before the cancellation. [IRC § 108(c)(2)]

Insurance recoveries and damages. What a business receives in the form of insurance reimbursements and damage awards and settlements may be taxable income. For example, if a business receives a damage award or settlement for lost profits, it is taxable income, because the lost profits would have been taxable. [E.g., *Sporck v. Comm'r*, T.C. Memo 1978-79]However, insurance proceeds received for property damage are not taxable to the extent they do not exceed the basis for the property. Even if the proceeds exceed the basis, the excess is not taxable if the business reinvests the proceeds in similar property. [IRC § 1033]

Rental income. Rental income is taxable, whether paid in cash or property. [IRC § 61(a)(5)] Advance rentals have to be included in income for the year of receipt regardless of the period covered or the method of accounting employed by the taxpayer. [Reg. § 1.161-8(b)]

Certain advance rent payments received by accrual method taxpayers are eligible for a one-year tax deferral. The IRS say that this deferral is available for payments for the occupancy of space or the use of property when the occupancy or use is ancillary to the provision of services (see Chapter 5). [Rev. Proc. 2004-34, 2004-22 I.R.B. 99]

Q 6:2 If a business provides goods or services in exchange for other goods or services, is the value of the goods or services taxable to the business?

Yes. The fair market value of the property or services taken in payment must be included in income. If the services were rendered at a stipulated price, such price will be presumed to be the fair market value of the compensation received in the absence of evidence to the contrary. [Reg. § 1.61-2(d)(1)]

Example 6-2: In return for personal legal services performed by a lawyer for a housepainter, the housepainter painted the lawyer's personal residence. Both the lawyer and the housepainter are members of a barter club, an organization that annually furnishes its members a directory of members and the services they provide. All the members of the club are professional or tradespersons. Members contact other members directly and negotiate the value of the services to be performed. The fair market value of the services received by the lawyer and the housepainter is includible in their gross incomes.

Example 6-3: An individual who owned an apartment building received a work of art created by a professional artist in return for the rent-free use of an apartment for six months by the artist. The fair market value of the work of art and the six months' fair rental value of the apartment are includible in the gross incomes of the apartment-owner and the artist.

[Rev. Rul. 79-24, 1979-1 C.B. 60]

Business Expenses: The Basics

Q 6:3 What business expenses are deductible?

Business expenses are generally deductible if they are the ordinary and necessary expenditures directly connected with the taxpayer's trade or business. Among the items included in business expenses are management expenses; commissions; labor; supplies; incidental repairs; operating expenses of automobiles used in the trade or business; traveling expenses while away from home solely in the pursuit of a trade or business; advertising and other selling expenses, together with insurance premiums against fire, storm, theft, accident, or other similar losses in the case of a business; and rental payments for the use of business property. [Reg. § 1.162-1(a)]

An ordinary expense is one that is commonly incurred in a trade or business. It may vary, depending on the time, place, and circumstances under which it is incurred. [*Welch v. Helvering,* 290 U.S. 111 (1933)] A necessary expense need not be "essential." It may be necessary if it is "appropriate and helpful" to a business or occupation. [*Commissioner v. Heininger,* 320 U.S. 467 (1943)]

Q 6:4 What are capital expenses, and when can they be deducted?

A capital expense is an outlay to acquire property or make a permanent improvement that extends beyond the tax year. Such expenditure generally, is not fully deductible in the year incurred. [IRC § 263(a); Reg. § 1.263(a)-1]

Although taxpayers generally cannot take a current deduction for a capital expense, they may be able to take deductions for the amount spent through depreciation (see Chapter 7) or amortization. For example, the cost of certain intangible assets can be written off through amortization deductions (see "Section 197 Intangibles" below).

Q 6:5 What is the difference between a capital improvement and a repair?

The costs of making improvements to a business asset are capital expenses, while repair expenses are currently deductible. [Reg. § 1.162-4] One statement on the difference between repairs and improvements was given more than 75 years ago by the Board of Tax Appeals (the predecessor to the Tax Court) and has often been cited since then.

In determining whether an expenditure is a capital one, or is chargeable against operating income, it is necessary to bear in mind the purpose for which the expenditure was made. To repair is to restore to a sound state or to mend, while a replacement connotes a substitution. A repair is an expenditure for the purpose of keeping the property in an ordinarily efficient operating condition. It does not add to the value of the property, nor does it appreciably prolong its life. It merely keeps the property in an operating condition over its probable useful life for the uses for which it was acquired. Expenditures for that purpose are distinguishable from those for replacements, alterations, improvement or additions which prolong the life of the property, increase its value, or make it adaptable to a different use. The one is a maintenance charge, while the others are additions to capital investment which should not be applied against current earnings. [*Illinois Merchants Trust Co.*, 4 B.T.A. 103 (1926)]

Some examples from the Internal Revenue Service (IRS or the Service) of the distinction between improvements and currently deductible expenses are as follows:

- *Business vehicles*. While the cost of a business vehicle is a capital expense, repairs are generally currently deductible. However, amounts paid to recondition and overhaul a business vehicle are capital expenses.

- *Roads and driveways*. The costs of building a private road on business property and the cost of replacing a gravel driveway with a concrete one are capital expenses. The cost of maintaining a private road on business property is a deductible expense.

- *Tools*. Amounts spent for tools used in a business are deductible expenses if the tools have a life expectancy of less than one year.

- *Machinery parts*. The cost of replacing short-lived parts of a machine to keep it in good working condition and not add to its life is a deductible expense.

- *Heating equipment*. The cost of changing from one heating system to another is a capital expense.

[IRS Pub. No. 535, *Business Expenses*]

The IRS recently proposed comprehensive regulations on the capitalization of tangible assets. [Prop. Reg. § 1.263(a)-1 through 1.263(a)-2] The regulations introduce "exclusive-factors" tests, rules on economic useful life, safe harbors and simplified assumptions. They do so within the context of recent cases—some which the IRS has won and others which the IRS has lost—to provide an overall framework that expands the standards for capitalization or expensing found in the current regulations. To add to the drive toward even further simplification, the IRS also is throwing open to discussion a *de minimis* rule under which small cost items would be exempt from capitalization.

The IRS predicts that, "If adopted as proposed, the regulations should reduce the amount of controversy between taxpayers and the IRS in this area." As proposed, the regulations would not officially apply until tax years beginning on or after final regulations are issued. The IRS emphasized that taxpayers may not change a method of accounting in reliance upon the rules contained in the proposed regulations until the rules are finalized.

The proposed regulations provide a straightforward 12-month "bright-line" rule—a taxpayer cannot capitalize amounts paid to acquire or produce a unit of property that has a useful life less than 12 months. A similar rule was adopted in the intangible regulations (see next question).

Taxpayers will be required to capitalize expenses of repairing or restoring property with a useful life longer than one year. Taxpayers will also be required to capitalize inventory costs, including amounts paid to acquire real property for resale or produce personal property for sale.

Taxpayers can elect not to apply the 12-month rule. This election is irrevocable. The election can be made for each unit of property acquired or produced by the taxpayer. The rule cannot be used for property that is part of other property produced for sale or resale, for improvements to a unit, and for components of a unit.

The proposed regulations provide an elective safe harbor for repairs. There is a separate allowance for each class of property under the MACRS system. Amounts up to the safe harbor are deductible; excess amounts must be capitalized.

The proposed regulations do not include a *de minimis* rule allowing a taxpayer to deduct an amount paid below a certain dollar threshold for the acquisition of tangible personal property. The IRS is considering including such a rule in the final regulations and specifically requests practitioner comments on this issue.

The preamble to the proposed regulations acknowledges that taxpayers often have an established policy of deducting amounts paid below a certain dollar threshold and that IRS examining agents usually do not challenge such an expensing practice so long as it does not have a material effect on tax liability. The preamble indicates that the absence of a *de minimis* rule in the proposals is not intended to change this practice.

Under the proposed regulations, amounts paid to improve tangible property must generally be capitalized. Amounts (including repairs) must be capitalized if they materially increase the value of property or restore a unit of property.

Q 6:5

There are five tests for determining if an amount materially increases value:

1. amounts paid prior to the initial date of service to put property into operating condition;
2. improvements in the condition of the property;
3. amounts that fix a defect;
4. adding a new or different use; and
5. an increase in capacity.

There is an exception for the 12-month rule.

The proposed regulations retain current principles for the concepts of value, useful life and new or different use. The government rejected a recurring expense approach or an obligation to regularly carry out repair or maintenance. The economic useful life can be determined by looking at a company's financial statements.

There are four rules for determining when an amount substantially prolongs useful life:

1. if it extends useful life more than one year;
2. replaces a major component,
3. restores to a like-new condition, or
4. represents a casualty loss deduction.

Q 6:6 When do intangible costs have to be capitalized?

More than 10 years ago, the U.S. Supreme Court ruled that business expenses that create a significant long-term benefit must be capitalized even though they do not produce a separate asset. [*INDOPCO, Inc. v. Comm'r*, 503 U.S. 79 (1992)] As a result, uncertainty arose about when the cost of intangible assets must be capitalized. For example, courts have ruled that costs incurred by a company to facilitate a "friendly" takeover must be capitalized—but the costs of an unsuccessful attempt to ward off a hostile takeover are currently deductible.

In response to this uncertainty, the IRS has finalized new regulations governing the capitalization of intangible costs. [Reg. § 1.263(a)-4 and 1.263(a)-5]The regulations contain specific categories of intangible expenditures for which capitalization is required under the significant-long-term-benefit test. If an expenditure is not covered in the regulations, capitalization is generally not required.

The IRS recognized that there might be expenditures that are not listed in the specified categories but for which capitalization is nonetheless appropriate. The IRS regulations require capitalization of non-listed expenditures if they are identified in future published guidance issued by the IRS. A determination in published guidance that a particular category of expenditure produces a benefit for which capitalization is appropriate will apply prospectively and will not apply to expenditures incurred before the publication of such guidance.

12-month rule. The IRS regulations provide for a "12-month" rule. This permits a current deduction for many expenditures that provide future benefits that extend beyond the close of the current year. Capitalization is not required if an expense does not provide a benefit that lasts beyond the earlier of (1) 12 months or (2) the end of the tax year following the tax year in which the expense is incurred.

For example, if a business with a calendar tax year pays an insurance premium payment on December 1, for a 12-month policy with a term beginning on December 15, capitalization would not be required. On the other hand, if the business pays the premium on December 1 for a 12-month policy beginning the following February, capitalization would be required. The 12-month rule would not apply because the benefits from the payment would extend beyond the end of the tax year following the tax year in which the payment was made.

Transactional costs. Under the IRS regulations, businesses must capitalize transactional costs (e.g., legal fees), if the costs facilitate the acquisition, or creation, of an intangible asset. The regulations provide that amounts facilitate a transaction if they are paid in the process of "investigating or otherwise pursuing the transaction." However, the regulations create an exception—transactional costs of $5,000 or less do not have to be capitalized. In addition, employee compensation and overhead costs do not have to be capitalized. For example, compensation paid to an employee is fully deductible, even if he or she works full time on a corporate acquisition.

"Market entry" payments. Payments made to obtain or renew membership or privileges from an organization have to be capitalized (unless they qualify for the 12-month rule). For example, a business is required to capitalize costs to obtain stock trading privileges, admission to practice medicine at a hospital, or access to a real estate multiple listing service.

Licenses and similar payments. Capitalization is required for any amount paid to a government agency for a trade name, trademark, copyright, license, permit, or other right, unless the payment is excepted under the 12-month rule. This applies to the initial fee paid to a government agency. Under the 12-month rule, businesses are not required to capitalize annual renewal fees paid to a governmental agency. However, capitalization is required if a business renegotiates or upgrades its rights. For example, a holder of a business license that pays an amount to upgrade its license, enabling it to sell additional types of products or services, must capitalize that amount.

Payments to obtain or modify contract rights. The IRS regulations require taxpayers to capitalize amounts paid to another party to induce that party to enter into, renew, or renegotiate an agreement that produces certain rights for the taxpayer. (Payments under $5,000 are exempt from the capitalization requirement.) This rule recognizes that some agreements provide contract rights that are reasonably certain to produce future benefits for the taxpayer. For example, the rule requires capitalization of amounts paid to enter into or renegotiate a lease contract or a contract providing the taxpayer the right to acquire or provide services.

On the other hand, the rule recognizes that many agreements do not provide contract rights for which capitalization is appropriate. Thus, the rule does not require a taxpayer to capitalize an amount that merely creates an expectation that a customer or supplier will maintain its business relationship with the taxpayer.

Payments to terminate contracts. The IRS regulations require taxpayers to capitalize amounts paid to terminate three types of contracts. The purpose of the rule is to require capitalization of termination payments that enable the taxpayer to reacquire some valuable right it did not possess immediately prior to the termination. Thus, capitalization is required for payments

- By a lessor to terminate a lease agreement with a lessee;

- By a taxpayer to terminate an agreement that provides another party the exclusive right to acquire or use the taxpayer's property or services or to conduct the taxpayer's business;

- To terminate an agreement that prohibits the taxpayer from competing with another or from acquiring property or services from a competitor of another.

On the other hand, the regulations do not require capitalization in cases where the taxpayer, as a result of the termination, does not reacquire a right for which capitalization is appropriate. For example, a taxpayer is not required to capitalize a payment to terminate a supply contract with a supplier, and a lessee does not have to capitalize a payment to terminate a lease agreement with a lessor.

Acquisitions and reorganizations of businesses. IRS regulations require capitalization of amounts paid to facilitate an acquisition of a business. This applies regardless of whether the transaction is structured as an acquisition of the entity or as an acquisition of assets constituting a business.

Amortization of capitalized costs. If intangible costs must be capitalized, what then? The IRS regulations provide a 15-year amortization period for certain created or enhanced intangibles that do not have a specific useful life. For example, amounts paid to obtain certain memberships or privileges of indefinite duration would be eligible for the 15-year amortization. On the other hand, if a business makes a lump sum prepayment of three years' rent, the 15-year amortization period would not apply; the payment would simply be deducted over a three-year period.

Q 6:7 Are business start-up expenses considered capital expenditures?

Yes. However, a limited current deduction is allowed for start-up expenses. Expenses that are not currently deductible can be amortized over a 180-month period. [IRC § 195(b)](See "Costs of Starting a Business" below.)

Employee Compensation

Q 6:8 Is compensation paid to employees deductible?

Yes, compensation paid for services rendered is generally deductible as long as it is reasonable in amount. [IRC § 162(a)(1)]If a corporation pays an employee who is also a shareholder a salary that is unreasonably high considering the services actually performed, the excessive part of the salary may be treated as a nondeductible distribution of earnings to the employee-shareholder (see Chapter 12). [Reg. § 1.162-7(b)]

Q 6:9 Can a business deduct achievement awards given to employees?

Employee achievement awards, whether paid in cash or property, are deductible. However, there are limits imposed on deductions for certain achievement awards that are tax-free to employees. To qualify, the awards must be:

1. Items of tangible personal property;

2. Given to an employee for length-of-service or safety achievement;

3. Given to employees as part of a meaningful presentation; and

4. Awarded under conditions and circumstances that do not create a significant likelihood of disguised pay.

[IRC § 274(j)]

An award will not qualify as a length-of-service award if the employee receives the award during his or her first five years of employment or the employee received another length-of-service award during the same year or in any of the prior four years. [IRC § 274(j)(4)(B)]

An award will not qualify as a safety achievement award if (1) it is given to a manager, administrator, clerical employee, or other professional employee or (2) during the tax year, more than 10 percent of the employees (excluding those listed in (1)) have already received a safety achievement award (other than one of very small value). [IRC § 274(j)(4)(C)]

An employer's deduction for the cost of employee achievement awards given to any one employee during the tax year is limited to the following amounts.

- $400 for awards that are not qualified plan awards.

- $1,600 for all awards, whether or not qualified plan awards.

A qualified plan award is an achievement award given as part of an established written plan or program that does not favor highly compensated employees as to eligibility or benefits. [Reg. § 1.274-3(d)]

Q 6:10 Can an employer deduct property transferred to employees as a form of compensation?

Yes. If an employer transfers property (including stock in the employer's company) to an employee as payment for services, the payment can generally be deducted as wages. The amount that can be deducted is the property's fair market value on the date of the transfer minus any amount the employee paid for the property. [IRC § 83(a)]

An employer can claim the deduction only for the tax year in which the employee includes the property's value in income. The employee is deemed to have included the value in income if it is reported it on Form W-2 in a timely manner. [Reg. § 1.83-6(a)]

The employer treats the deductible amount as received in exchange for the property and must recognize any gain or loss realized on the transfer. The gain or loss is the difference between the fair market value of the property and its adjusted basis on the date of transfer. [Reg. § 1.83-6(a)] A corporation recognizes no gain or loss when it pays for services with its own stock. [IRC § 1032]

If the property transferred for services is subject to restrictions that affect its value, the employer generally cannot deduct it until it is substantially vested in the employee. "Substantially vested" means the property is not subject to a substantial risk of forfeiture. [IRC § 83(h)]The rights of an employee are subject to a substantial risk of forfeiture if the employee's full enjoyment of the property is conditioned upon the performance of substantial future services. [IRC § 83(c)(1)]

Q 6:11 Is vacation pay deductible?

Yes. Amounts paid to employees while on vacation and amounts paid for unused vacations are deductible by employers. Employers using the cash method of accounting can deduct vacation pay in the year it is paid. Accrual method employers can deduct vacation pay in the tax year in which the employee earns it if it is vested by the end of that year and the employee actually receives it within two and one-half months after the end of that year. [IRC § 404(a)(5)] Generally, vacation pay is vested if it is payable under an oral or written vacation pay plan that the employee was informed of before the tax year, and its amount and the employer's liability for it is fixed.

Rental Expenses

Q 6:12 Are rental payments for property used in a business deductible?

In general, a taxpayer can deduct rent as a business expense if the rent is for property used in a trade or business and the taxpayer does not have, and will not have, any equity in or title to the property. [IRC § 162(a)(3)]

The question sometimes arises as to whether a taxpayer is paying bona fide rent for the use of the property or whether the "rent" is, in effect, payments toward the purchase of the property. Payments made under a conditional sales contract are not deductible as rent expense.

Whether an agreement is a conditional sales contract depends on the intent of the parties. Intent is determined based on the provisions of the agreement and the facts and circumstances that exist when the lessor and lessee make the agreement. No single test, or special combination of tests, always applies. However, in general, an agreement may be considered a conditional sales contract rather than a lease if any of the following is true:

- The agreement applies part of each payment toward an equity interest the lessee will receive;
- The lessee gets title to the property after a stated amount of required payments;
- The amount the lessee must pay to use the property for a short time is a large part of the amount that would be paid to get title to the property;
- The lessee pays much more than the current fair rental value of the property;
- The lessee has an option to buy the property at a nominal price compared to the value of the property when the option may be exercised;
- The lessee has an option to buy the property at a nominal price compared to the total amount paid under the agreement; or
- The agreement designates part of the payments as interest, or that part is easy to recognize as interest.

[Rev. Rul. 55-540, 1955-2 CB 39]

Taxpayers cannot take a rental deduction for "unreasonable" rent. Ordinarily, the issue of reasonableness arises only if the taxpayer and the lessor are related. [e.g., *Ray's Clothes, Inc. v. Comm'r*, 22 T.C. 1332 (1954)] Rent paid to a related person is reasonable if it is the same amount the taxpayer would pay to a stranger for use of the same property. Rent is not unreasonable just because it is figured as a percentage of gross sales.

Q 6:13 Can a lessee deduct rents paid in advance?

Generally, rents paid by business are deductible in the year paid or accrued. If a taxpayer pays rent in advance, the taxpayer can deduct only the amount that applies to the use of the rented property during the tax year. The taxpayer can deduct the rest of the payment only over the period to which it applies. [Reg. § 1.162-11]

> **Example 6-4:** Carol Knowland leased a building for five years beginning July 1. The building will be used in her business. Knowland's rent is $12,000 per year. She paid the first year's rent ($12,000) on June 30. She can deduct only $6,000 (6/12 × $12,000) for the rent that applies to the first year.

> **Example 6-5:** In January, XYZ Inc. leased property for three years for $6,000 a year. XYZ paid the full $18,000 (3 × $6,000) during the first year of the

lease. Each year XYZ can deduct only $6,000, the part of the rent that applies to that year.

Q 6:14 Can a taxpayer deduct a lump sum payment made to cancel a business lease?

It depends on who is making the payment. If the taxpayer is the lessee, the taxpayer can currently deduct as rent any amount paid to cancel a business lease. [Rev. Rul. 69-511, 1969-2 C.B. 24]

Whereas, when a lessor makes a payment to cancel a lease, the lessor is acquiring a valuable property right (i.e., the right to use the property for the remaining period of the lease). Therefore, the general rule is that a lump sum lease cancellation payment is not deductible by the lessor as a current business expense. Instead, the lessor must write off the payment ratably over the unexpired term of the canceled lease. [*Trustee Corp. v. Comm'r*, 42 T.C. 482 (1964)]

Q 6:15 How are lease acquisition costs treated for tax purposes?

Lease acquisition costs are generally treated as capital expenses. For example, if a taxpayer acquires a lease for real estate or equipment from an existing lessee and pays the lessee a sum of money to obtain the lease, the taxpayer must deduct the payment ratably over the remaining term of the lease. [Reg. § 1.162-11]For example, if the taxpayer pays $10,000 to get a lease and there are 10 years remaining on the lease with no option to renew, the taxpayer can deduct $1,000 each year.

The term of the lease for amortization includes all renewal options plus any other period for which the taxpayer and the lessor reasonably expect the lease to be renewed. However, this applies only if less than 75 percent of the acquisition cost for the lease is for the term of the lease remaining on the purchase date (not including any period for which the taxpayer may choose to renew, extend, or continue the lease). [IRC § 178]

> **Example 6-6:** Acme Corp. paid $10,000 to acquire a lease with 20 years remaining on it and two options to renew for 5 years each. Of this cost, Acme paid $7,000 for the original lease and $3,000 for the renewal options. Because $7,000 is less than 75 percent of the total $10,000 cost of the lease (or $7,500), Acme must amortize the $10,000 over 30 years. That is the remaining life of the present lease plus the periods for renewal.

> **Example 6-7:** The facts are the same as in Example 6-6, except that Acme paid $8,000 for the original lease and $2,000 for the renewal options. Acme can amortize the entire $10,000 over the 20-year remaining life of the original lease. The $8,000 cost of getting the original lease was not less than 75 percent of the total cost of the lease (or $7,500).

Interest Expenses

Q 6:16 Is interest deductible if paid on a debt incurred in connection with a business?

Yes, taxpayers can generally deduct all interest they pay or accrue during the tax year on debts related to their trade or business. Interest, however, is deductible only if taxpayers meet the following requirements:

- The taxpayers are legally liable for the debts;
- The taxpayers and the lenders intend that the debts be repaid;
- The taxpayers and the lenders have a true debtor-creditor relationship.

[Reg. §. 1.163-1]

Most nonbusiness interest is either subject to deduction limits (e.g., investment-related interest) or completely disallowed as a business deduction (e.g., personal interest). So taxpayers must allocate their interest payments between business-related interest and the various other types of interest.

Q 6:17 How is interest allocated between business and nonbusiness interest?

In general, taxpayers allocate interest on a loan the same way they allocate the loan proceeds. Loan proceeds are allocated by tracing disbursements to specific uses. [Reg. § 1.163-8T]

The allocation of loan proceeds and the related interest is not generally affected by the use of property that secures the loan. [Reg. § 1.163-8T(c)]

Example 6-8: Paul Kraft secures a loan with property used in his business. Kraft uses the loan proceeds to buy an automobile for personal use. Kraft must allocate interest expense on the loan to personal use (purchase of the automobile) even though the loan is secured by business property.

The period for which a loan is allocated to a particular use begins on the date the proceeds are used and ends on the earlier of the following dates:

- The date the loan is repaid; or
- The date the loan is reallocated to another use.

[Reg. § 1.163-8T(c)]

Even if the lender disburses the loan proceeds to a third party, the allocation of the loan is still based on the use of the funds. This applies whether the taxpayer pays for property, services, or anything else by incurring a loan, or the taxpayer takes property subject to a debt.

Loan proceeds deposited in an account are treated as property held for investment, not business use. It does not matter whether the account pays interest. Any interest paid on the loan is investment interest expense. If a taxpayer withdraws the proceeds of the loan, the loan must be reallocated based on the use of the funds. [Reg. § 1.163-8T(c)(4)]

> **Example 6-9:** Connie Grace, a calendar-year taxpayer, borrows $100,000 on January 4 and immediately uses the proceeds to open a checking account. No other amounts are deposited in the account during the year, and no part of the loan principal is repaid during the year. On April 1, Grace uses $20,000 from the checking account for personal purposes. On September 1, Grace uses an additional $40,000 from the account for business purposes.
>
> Under the interest allocation rules, the entire $100,000 loan is treated as property held for investment for the period from January 4 through March 31. From April 1 through August 31, Grace must treat $20,000 of the loan as used for personal purposes and $80,000 of the loan as property held for investment. From September 1 through December 31, she must treat $40,000 of the loan as used for business purposes, $20,000 as used for personal purposes, and $40,000 as property held for investment.

Generally, taxpayers must treat loan proceeds deposited in an account as used (spent) before either of the following amounts:

- Any unborrowed amounts held in the same account; or

- Any amounts deposited after these loan proceeds.

[Reg. § 1.163-8T(c)(4)]

> **Example 6-10:** On January 9, Edith Hopper opened a checking account, depositing $500 of the proceeds of Loan A and $1,000 of unborrowed funds. The following table shows the transactions in her account during the tax year.
>
> | Date | Transaction |
> | --- | --- |
> | Jan. 9 | $500 proceeds of Loan A and $1,000 of unborrowed funds deposited |
> | Jan. 12 | $500 proceeds of Loan B deposited |
> | Jan. 18 | $800 used for personal purposes |
> | Feb. 27 | $700 used for business purposes |
> | Jun. 18 | $1,000 proceeds from Loan C deposited |
> | Nov. 20 | $800 used for an investment |
> | Dec. 18 | $600 used for business purposes |
>
> Hopper treats the $800 used for personal purposes as made from the $500 proceeds of Loan A and $300 of the proceeds of Loan B. She treats the $700 used for business purposes as made from the remaining $200 proceeds of Loan B and $500 of unborrowed funds. She treats the $800 used for an investment as made entirely from the proceeds of Loan C. She treats the $600 used for business purposes as made from the remaining $200 proceeds of Loan C and $400 of unborrowed funds.

For the periods during which loan proceeds are held in the account, Hopper treats them as property held for investment.

Planning Point: To facilitate the allocation of interest among the various categories, a taxpayer should (1) maintain separate loans or loan accounts for separate expenditures, (2) avoid commingling borrowed funds and unborrowed funds, and (3) avoid financing several different expenditures with one loan.

Q 6:18 Does business-related interest ever have to be capitalized instead of deducted currently?

Yes. Under the uniform capitalization rules (see Chapter 5), taxpayers generally must capitalize interest on debt equal to their expenditures to produce real property or certain tangible personal property. [Reg. § 1.263A-8] The property must be produced by the taxpayers for use in their business or for sale to customers.

Interest paid or incurred during the production period must be capitalized if the property produced is "designated property." Designated property is any of the following:

- Real property;
- Tangible personal property with a class life of 20 years or more;
- Tangible personal property with an estimated production period of more than two years; or
- Tangible personal property with an estimated production period of more than one year if the estimated cost of production is more than $1 million.

[Reg. § 1.263A-8(b)]

Taxpayers are treated as producing property if they construct, build, install, manufacture, develop, improve, create, raise, or grow it. [IRC § 263A(g); Reg. § 1.263A-2(a)(1)]Taxpayers must treat property produced for them under a contract as produced by them directly up to the amount they pay or incur for the property. [Reg. § 1.263A-8(d)]

Capitalized interest is treated as a cost of the property produced. Taxpayers recover their interest when they sell or use the property. If the property is inventory, capitalized interest is recovered through the cost of goods sold. If the property is used in a trade or business, capitalized interest is recovered through an adjustment to basis, depreciation, amortization, or other method. [Reg. § 1.263A-8(a)(2)]

Taxes

Q 6:19 Which taxes are deductible by businesses?

Tax payments fall into three categories for federal income tax purposes: (1) those that are deductible by all taxpayers, whether or not business-connected, (2) those that are deductible only if business-connected, and (3) those that are not deductible, even if business-connected.

Q 6:18

Taxes deductible by all taxpayers include:

- State, local, and foreign real property taxes;
- State and local personal property taxes; and
- State, local, and foreign income, war profits, and excess profits taxes for 2004 and 2005, taxpayers may deduct state and local sales taxes in lieu of a deduction for state and local income taxes).

[IRC § 164(b); Reg. § 1.164-1]

Taxes deductible if paid in connection with a trade or business include:

- *Excise taxes.* Taxpayers can deduct as a business expense all excise taxes that are ordinary and necessary expenses of carrying on a trade or business.
- *Franchise taxes.* Corporations can deduct corporate franchise taxes as a business expense.
- *Fuel taxes.* Taxes on gasoline, diesel fuel, and other motor fuels that are used in a business are usually included as part of the cost of the fuel. They should not be deducted as a separate item.
- *Occupational taxes.* Taxpayers can deduct as a business expense an occupational tax charged at a flat rate by a locality for the privilege of working or conducting a business in the locality.
- *Sales tax.* Businesses can treat any sales tax they pay on a service or on the purchase or use of property as part of the cost of the service or property. If the service or the cost or use of the property is a deductible business expense, they can deduct the tax as part of that service or cost. If the property is merchandise bought for resale, the sales tax is part of the cost of the merchandise. If the property is depreciable, the sales tax should be added to the basis for depreciation. Note: Businesses cannot deduct state and local sales taxes imposed on the buyer that businesses must collect and pay over to the state or local government. These taxes should not be included in gross receipts or sales.

[IRS Pub. No. 535, *Business Expenses*, (Rev. 2005)]

Taxes that are nondeductible, whether or not business- connected, include:

- Federal income taxes;
- Social security or railroad retirement taxes withheld from an employee's pay (see Q 6:20);
- Federal war profits and excess profits taxes;
- State or federal estate, inheritance, legacy, succession, and gift taxes; and
- Income, war profits, and excess profits taxes imposed by a U.S. possession or a foreign country, if the taxpayer elects to take a credit for such taxes.

[IRC § 275]

Q 6:20 Can a business deduct employment taxes?

Yes. Employers should include the taxes withheld from their employees' pay as part of their deduction for employees' wages. However, employment taxes imposed directly on the employer should be deducted as taxes. [IRS Pub. No. 535, *Business Expenses* (Rev. 2004)]

> **Example 6-11:** Acme Corp. pays an employee $18,000 a year. However, after withholding for various taxes, the employee receives $14,500. Acme also pays an additional $1,500 in employment taxes. Acme should deduct the full $18,000 as wages. Acme can deduct the $1,500 paid from its own funds as taxes.

The IRS makes a distinction in the timing of deductions for employment taxes in the case of businesses operating on the cash method of accounting. Employment taxes withheld from an employee's pay can be deducted as wages in the year that they are withheld. The employer's share of employment taxes, however, is not deductible until the year it is paid over to the IRS. [Rev. Rul. 80-164, 1980-1 C.B. 109]

Insurance Premiums

Q 6:21 Are insurance premiums paid by a business deductible?

Yes, taxpayers can generally deduct the ordinary and necessary cost of insurance as a business expense if it is for a trade, business, or profession. Examples of deductible insurance include:

- Insurance against fire, storm, theft, accident, or other similar losses in the case of a business; [Reg. § 1.162-1(a)]

- Professional overhead insurance policies that reimburse taxpayer for overhead expenses incurred during prolonged period of disability due to injury or sickness; [Rev, Rul. 55-264, 1955-1 C.B. 11]

- Malpractice insurance that covers a taxpayer for personal liability for professional negligence resulting in injury or damage to patients or clients; [IRS Pub. No. 334, *Tax Guide for Small Businesses* (Rev. 2005)]

- Workers compensation insurance; and [*Reese Drilling Co.,* 18 BTA 816 (1930)]

- Contributions to a state unemployment insurance fund, if they are considered taxes under state law. [IRS Pub. No. 334, *Tax Guide for Small Businesses* (Rev. 2005)

Q 6:22 Is health insurance deductible as a business expense?

Yes. Premiums paid for health insurance coverage for employees are deductible as a business expenses (see Chapter 9).

Self-employed taxpayers can also deduct premiums for medical insurance and qualified long-term care insurance for themselves, their spouses, and their dependents. For 2003 and thereafter, the deduction is 100 percent of the premium cost. [IRC § 162(l)(1)(B)]

The deduction is also available to partners with net earnings from self-employment reported on Schedule K-1 (Form 1065) and to employees of S corporations who own more than 2 percent of the outstanding stock of the corporation. [IRC § § 162(l)(1)(A), (5)]

Q 6:23 Are life insurance premiums deductible as a business expense?

Taxpayers generally cannot deduct the premiums on any life insurance policy, endowment contract, or annuity contract if the taxpayer is directly or indirectly a beneficiary. [IRC § 264(a)(1)]When one partner whose continued services were essential to the success of a business took out insurance on his own life, naming the other partners as beneficiaries to induce them to retain investments in firm, the partner paying premiums was considered a beneficiary, and payments were not deductible. [Rev. Rul. 73, 1953-1 C.B. 63]

The premiums paid to provide group term life insurance to employees is a deductible expense (see Chapter 10).

Costs of Starting a Business

Q 6:24 How are the costs of starting a business treated for tax purposes?

When taxpayers go into business, they must treat all costs incurred to get the business started as capital expenses. [IRC § 195(a)] Capital expenses are part of the basis in the business. Generally, taxpayers recover costs for particular assets through depreciation deductions. However, other costs generally cannot be recovered until the business is sold.

In the case of certain qualifying costs, taxpayers may elect to (1) claim a current deduction for the costs, subject to a dollar limit, and (2) amortize costs in excess of the limit over a period of 180 months. A cost must qualify as one of the following:

- A business start-up cost; [IRC § 195(b)]
- An organizational cost for a corporation; or [IRC § 248]
- An organizational cost for a partnership. [IRC § 709(b)]

Q 6:25 What are business start-up costs?

Start-up expenditures are costs for creating an active trade or business or investigating the creation or acquisition of an active trade or business. Start-up costs include any amounts paid or incurred in connection with any activity engaged in for profit and for the production of income in anticipation of the activity becoming an active trade or business. [IRC § 195(c)(1)]

A start-up cost can be deducted/amortized if it meets both the following tests:

1. It is a cost that the taxpayers could deduct if they paid or incurred it to operate an existing active trade or business (in the same field as the one they entered into); and

2. It is a cost paid or incurred before the day the active trade or business begins.

[IRC § 195(c)(1)]

Qualifying start-up costs include expenditures for the following:

- An analysis or survey of potential markets, products, labor supply, transportation facilities, etc.;

- Advertisements for the opening of the business;

- Salaries and wages for employees who are being trained and their instructors;

- Travel and other necessary costs for securing prospective distributors, suppliers, or customers; and

- Salaries and fees for executives and consultants, or for similar professional services.

[IRS Pub. No. 535, *Business Expenses*, (Rev. 2006)]

Qualifying start-up costs do not include deductible interest, taxes, or research and experimental costs. [IRC § 195(c)(1)]

Qualifying start-up costs for purchasing an active trade or business include only investigative costs incurred in the course of a general search for or preliminary investigation of the business. These are the costs that help the taxpayer decide whether to purchase a new business and which active business to purchase. Costs incurred in an attempt to purchase a specific business are capital expenses that cannot be amortized. [Rev. Rul. 99-23, 1999-1 CB 998]

> **Example 6-12:** In June, Jane Johnson hired an accounting firm and a law firm to assist her in the potential purchase of XYZ. They researched XYZ's industry and analyzed the financial projections of XYZ. In September, the law firm prepared and submitted a letter of intent to XYZ. The letter stated that a binding commitment would result only after a purchase agreement was signed. The law firm and accounting firm continued to provide services including a review of XYZ's books and records and the preparation of a purchase agreement. In October, Johnson signed a purchase agreement with XYZ.

The costs to investigate the business before submitting the letter of intent to XYZ are amortizable investigative costs. The costs for services after that time relate to the attempt to purchase the business and must be capitalized.

Q 6:25

If a taxpayer completely disposes of a business before the end of the amortization period, any remaining deferred start-up costs can be deducted at that time. However, these deferred start-up costs are deductible only to the extent they qualify as a loss from a business.

Q 6:26 How does a taxpayer deduct/amortize start-up costs?

A taxpayer can choose to deduct up to $5,000 of the costs as a current business expense. The $5,000 deduction is reduced by the amount the taxpayer's total start-up costs exceed $50,000. So, for example, if a taxpayer incurs $53,000 of start-up costs, a current deduction of $2,000 is allowed. If the total start-up costs exceed $55,000, no current deduction is allowed. [IRC § 195(b)(1)(A)]

A taxpayer elects the current business expense deduction for qualifying costs by claiming the deduction on the income tax return (filed by the due date including extensions) for the tax year in which the active trade or business begins.

If a taxpayer elects the current business expense deduction and total start-up costs exceed the allowable deduction limit, the excess must be amortized over a period of 180 months. [IRC § 195(b)(1)(B)]The amortization period starts with the month business operations begin. Once an amortization period is chosen, it cannot be changed. [Reg. § 1.195-1(a)]

To figure the amortization deduction, simply divide amortizable start-up costs (total qualifying costs less the amount deducted as a business expense) by the months in the amortization period. The result is the amount that can be deducted for each month.

If a taxpayer amortizes start-up costs, he or she must file Form 4562 with an informational statement attached in the first year of active business. The statement must contain the following information:

- A description of the business to which the start-up costs relate;
- A description of each start-up cost incurred;
- The month the active business began (or was acquired).

[Reg. § 1.195(b)]

Q 6:27 Which costs of organizing a corporation are deductible or amortizable?

As with business start-up costs, the first $5,000 of qualifying corporate organization costs are deductible at the corporation's election, subject to a phase-out when total costs exceed $50,000 (see above). Qualifying costs in excess of the allowable deduction are amortizable over 180 months. [IRC § 248]

For purposes of the deduction/amortization, the costs of organizing a corporation are the direct costs of creating the corporation. A taxpayer may elect to deduct/amortize an organizational expenditure only if it meets all the following tests:

- It is for the creation of the corporation;
- It is chargeable to a capital account;
- It could be amortized over the life of the corporation if the corporation had a fixed life; and
- It is incurred before the end of the first tax year in which the corporation is in business.

[IRC § 248(b)]

A corporation using the cash method of accounting can deduct/amortize organizational costs incurred within the first tax year, even if it does not pay them in that year.

Examples of organizational costs are as follows:

- The cost of temporary directors,
- The cost of organizational meetings,
- State incorporation fees,
- The cost of accounting services for setting up the corporation, and
- The cost of legal services (such as drafting the charter, bylaws, terms of the original stock certificates, and minutes of organizational meetings).

[Reg. § 1.248-1(b)(2)]

The following items are not organizational costs; they are capital expenses, which cannot be deducted or amortized:

- Costs for issuing and selling stock or securities, such as commissions, professional fees, and printing costs; and
- Costs associated with the transfer of assets to the corporation.

[Reg. § 1.248-1(b)(3)]

Q 6:28 Which costs of organizing a partnership are deductible or amortizable?

As with business start-up costs, the first $5,000 of qualifying partnership organization costs are deductible at the partnership's election, subject to a phase-out when total costs exceed $50,000 (see above). Qualifying costs in excess of the allowable deduction are amortizable over 180 months. [IRC § 709(b)(1)]

For purposes of the deduction/amortization, the costs of organizing a partnership are the direct expenses incurred in creating the partnership. A qualifying expenditure must meet the following tests:

- It is for the creation of the partnership and not for starting or operating the partnership trade or business;
- It is chargeable to a capital account;
- It could be amortized over the life of the partnership if the partnership had a fixed life;

- It is incurred by the due date of the partnership return (excluding extensions) for the first tax year in which the partnership is in business; and
- It is for a type of item normally expected to benefit the partnership throughout its entire life.

[IRC § 709(b)(3)]

Organizational costs include the following fees:

- Legal fees for services incident to the organization of the partnership, such as negotiation and preparation of the partnership agreement;
- Accounting fees for services incident to the organization of the partnership; and
- Filing fees.

The following costs cannot be deducted or amortized:

- The cost of acquiring assets for the partnership or transferring assets to the partnership;
- The cost of admitting or removing partners, other than at the time the partnership is first organized;
- The cost of making a contract concerning the operation of the partnership trade or business (including a contract between a partner and the partnership); and
- The costs for issuing and marketing interests in the partnership (such as brokerage, registration, and legal fees and printing costs).

Q 6:29 How does a corporation or partnership amortize organizational costs?

If a corporation or partnership elects to deduct organizational costs, organizational costs in excess of the allowable deduction are amortized in much the same manner as start-up costs (see above, e.g., in equal amounts over 180 months, by filing Form 4562, etc.). The separate statement attached to Form 4562 must contain the following information:

- A description of each cost;
- The amount of each cost;
- The date each cost was incurred; and
- The month the corporation or partnership began active business (or acquired the business).

Research Expenses

Q 6:30 Are research expenses deductible?

Expenditures for research and experimentation are generally capital expenses. However, taxpayers can deduct these costs as a current business expense.

[IRC § 174(a)]Alternatively, for expenses not chargeable to depreciable property, taxpayers may elect to capitalize the expenses and amortize them. [IRC § 174(b)(1)]

Q 6:31 What are research and experimental costs for tax purposes?

Research and experimental expenditures are reasonable costs incurred in a trade or business for activities intended to provide information that would eliminate uncertainty about the development or improvement of a product. Uncertainty exists if the information available to a taxpayer does not establish how to develop or improve a product or the appropriate design of a product. Whether costs qualify as research and experimental expenditures depends on the nature of the activity to which the costs relate rather than on the nature of the product or improvement being developed or the level of technological advancement. [Reg. § 1.174-2(a)]

The term "product" includes any of the following items:
- Formula;
- Invention;
- Patent;
- Pilot model;
- Process;
- Technique; and
- Property similar to the items listed above.

[Reg. § 1.174-2(a)(2)]

Research and experimental costs do not include expenses for any of the following activities:
- Advertising or promotions;
- Consumer surveys;
- Efficiency surveys;
- Management studies;
- Quality control testing;
- Research in connection with literary, historical, or similar projects; and
- The acquisition of someone else's patent, model, production, or process.

[Reg. § 1.174-2(a)(3)]

Taxpayers elect to deduct research and experimental costs, rather than capitalizing them, by deducting the costs on their tax return for the year in which such costs are first incurred.

Q 6:32 What is the amortization deduction for research expenses?

If taxpayers elect to amortize research and experimental costs, they deduct them in equal amounts over 60 months or more. The amortization period begins

Q 6:31

the month the taxpayers first receive an economic benefit from the expenditures. [IRC § 174(b)].

Rather than amortizing research and experimental expenses over 60 months or more, taxpayers have the option to deduct the costs ratably over a 10-year period beginning with the tax year in which the costs are incurred. [IRC § 59(e)]

The amortization election applies only to those expenditures that are chargeable to the capital account but that are not chargeable to property of a character subject to an allowance for depreciation or depletion. Thus, the election is available only if the property resulting from the research or experimental expenditures has no determinable useful life. [Reg. § 1.174-4(a)(2)]

Section 197 Intangibles

Q 6:33 What are Section 197 intangibles?

Section 197 intangibles are certain intangibles acquired after August 10, 1993, in connection with a business or income-producing activity. Under Code Section 197, the cost of the intangibles must be capitalized and amortized over a period of 15 years.

The amortization deduction each year is the proportionate part of the property's adjusted basis using a 180-month amortization period. The period begins with the later of: (1) the month the property is acquired, or (2) the month the business or income-producing activity starts. [Reg. § 1.197-2(f)(1)] No other depreciation or amortization deduction is allowed for a Section 197 intangible. [IRC § 197(b)]

Q 6:34 What property qualifies as a Section 197 intangible?

Section 197 intangibles include the following:

- Goodwill;
- Going concern value;
- Workforce in place;
- Business books and records, operating systems, or any other information base, including lists or other information concerning current or prospective customers;
- A patent, copyright, formula, process, design, pattern, know-how, format, or similar item;
- A customer-based intangible;
- A supplier-based intangible;
- A license, permit, or other right granted by a governmental unit or agency (including issuances and renewals);
- A covenant not to compete entered into in connection with the acquisition of an interest in a trade or business;

- A franchise, trademark, or trade name (including renewals); and
- A contract for the use of, or a term interest in, any item in listed above.

[IRC § 197(d)]

Taxpayers generally cannot amortize intangibles that are created (rather than acquired) by the taxpayers unless they create them in connection with the acquisition of assets constituting a trade or business or a substantial part of a trade or business. [IRC § 197(c)(2)]

A Section 197 intangible is "created" by the taxpayer to the extent the taxpayer makes payments or otherwise incurs costs for its creation, production, development, or improvement, whether the actual work is performed by the taxpayer or by another person under a contract with the taxpayer. For example, when a technological process is developed specifically for a taxpayer under an arrangement with another person and the taxpayer retains all rights to the process, the process is "created" by the taxpayer. [Reg. § 1.197-2(d)(2)]

Goodwill. This is the value of a trade or business based on expected continued customer patronage due to its name, reputation, or any other factor. [Reg. § 1.197-2(b)(1)]

Going concern value. This is the additional value of a trade or business that attaches to property because the property is an integral part of an ongoing business activity. It includes value based on the ability of a business to continue to function and generate income even though there is a change in ownership. It also includes value that is attributable to the immediate use or availability of an acquired trade or business, such as the use of earnings that otherwise would not be received during any period if the acquired trade or business were not available or operational. [Reg. § 197-2(b)(2)]

Workforce in place. This includes the composition of a workforce (for example, its experience, education, or training). It also includes the terms and conditions of employment, whether contractual or otherwise, and any other value placed on employees or any of their attributes. [Reg. § 197-2(b)(3)]

For example, a taxpayer must amortize the part of the purchase price of a business that is for the existence of a highly skilled workforce. Also, the cost of acquiring an existing employment contract or relationship with employees or consultants must be amortized.

Business books and records, etc. This includes the intangible value of technical manuals, training manuals or programs, data files, and accounting or inventory control systems. It also includes the cost of customer lists, subscription lists, insurance expirations, patient or client files, and lists of newspaper, magazine, radio, and television advertisers. [Reg. § 197-2(b)(4)]

Patents, copyrights, etc. This includes package design, computer software, and any interest in a film, sound recording, videotape, book, or other similar property. [Reg. § 197-2(b)(5)]

Customer-based intangible. This is the composition of market, market share, or any other value resulting from the future provision of goods or services because of relationships with customers in the ordinary course of business. For example, taxpayers must amortize the part of the purchase price of a business that is for the existence of the following intangibles:

- A customer base;

- A circulation base;

- An undeveloped market or market growth;

- Insurance in force;

- A mortgage servicing contract;

- An investment management contract; and

- Any other relationship with customers involving the future provision of goods or services.

Accounts receivable or other similar rights to income for goods or services provided to customers before the acquisition of a trade or business are not Section 197 intangibles. [Reg. § 197-2(b)(6)]

Supplier-based intangible. This is the value resulting from the future acquisition of goods or services used or sold by the business because of business relationships with suppliers. Supplier-based intangibles include a favorable relationship with distributors (such as favorable shelf or display space at a retail outlet), a good credit rating, and a favorable supply contract. [Reg. § 197-2(b)(7)]

Government-granted license, permit, etc. This is any right granted by a governmental unit or an agency or instrumentality of a governmental unit. For example, the capitalized costs of acquiring (including issuing or renewing) a liquor license, a taxicab medallion or license, or a television or radio broadcasting license would fall into this category. [Reg. § 197-2(b)(8)]

Franchise, trademark, or trade name. A franchise, trademark, or trade name is a Section 197 intangible. A taxpayer must amortize the purchase or renewal costs, other than certain contingent payments, that can be deducted currently. [Reg. § 197-2(b)(10)]

Covenant not to compete. Section 197 intangibles include a covenant not to compete (or similar arrangement) entered into in connection with the acquisition of an interest in a trade or business or a substantial portion of a trade or business. An interest in a trade or business includes an interest in a partnership or a corporation engaged in a trade or business.

An arrangement that requires the former owner to perform services (or to provide property or the use of property) does not count as a covenant not to compete to the extent the amount paid under the arrangement represents reasonable compensation for those services or for that property or its use. [Reg. § 197-2(b)(9)]

The Ninth Circuit Federal Court of Appeals recently ruled that a covenant not to compete can be subject to the Section 197 rules even when a business does not change hands. The case involved Roundtree Automotive Group Inc., an owner of car dealerships. In 1987, Roundtree purchased the stock of Frontier

Chevrolet Co. and named as its executive manager a longtime Roundtree employee, Dennis Menholt. Menholt purchased 25 percent of Frontier's stock, reducing Roundtree's ownership share to 75 percent. In 1994, Frontier redeemed its stock from Roundtree. After the stock sale, Menholt was Frontier's sole shareholder. Frontier entered into a five-year noncompetition agreement with Roundtree. Frontier claimed that its payments under the agreement were not subject to Section 197 and could be amortized over the agreement's five-year life.

The court said Frontier's redemption was an indirect acquisition of an interest in a business under Section 197. The court noted that although Frontier stayed in the same business, it acquired an interest in a business because it acquired possession and control of 75 percent of its stock and Menholt became the sole shareholder. The court pointed out that the legislative history makes it clear that an interest in a business includes the assets of the business and stock in a corporation engaged in a business Thus, the noncompetition agreement was a Section 197 intangible and Frontier must amortize it over 15 years. [*Frontier Chevrolet Co. v. Comm'r*, 329 F.3d 1131 (9th Cir. 2003)]

Q 6:35 Which intangibles are excluded from Section 197 amortization?

Certain properties are specifically excluded from Section 197 coverage. [IRC § 197(e)] These include:

- Any interest in a corporation, partnership, trust, or estate;
- Any interest under an existing futures contract, foreign currency contract, notional principal contract, interest rate swap, or similar financial contract;
- Any interest in land;
- Most computer software (see Q 6:36); and
- Any of the following assets *unless* they are acquired in connection with the acquisition of a trade or business: (1) an interest in a film, sound recording, video tape, book, or similar property; (2) a right to receive tangible property or services under a contract or from a governmental agency; (3) an interest in a patent or copyright; (4) an interest in an existing lease or sublease of tangible property or a debt that was in existence when the interest was acquired; and (5) a professional sports franchise or any item acquired in connection with the franchise. [Reg. § 1.197-2(c)]

Q 6:36 Which computer software is excluded from Section 197?

Section 197 intangibles do not include the following types of computer software:

1. Software that meets all the following requirements: (1) it is (or has been) readily available for purchase by the general public; (2) it is subject to a nonexclusive license, and (3) it has not been substantially modified.

Q 6:35

2. Software that is not acquired in connection with the acquisition of a trade or business or a substantial part of a trade or business.

[Reg. § 1.197-2(c)(4)]

For this purpose, "computer software" includes all programs designed to cause a computer to perform a desired function. It also includes any database or similar item that is in the public domain and is incidental to the operation of qualifying software. [Reg. § 1.197-2(c)(4)(iv)]

Farming Expenses

Q 6:37 Are farming expenses deductible?

Yes. Deductions are permitted for expenses incurred in carrying on the business of farming, including a horticultural nursery business. [Reg. 1.162-12] Among allowable deductions are the following: cost of tools, cost of feeding and raising livestock (excluding produce grown on the farm and labor of the taxpayer), and cost of gasoline, repairs, and upkeep of a car or truck used wholly in the business of farming, or a portion of the cost if used for both farming and personal use.

Expenses for the purchase of farm machinery or equipment, breeding, dairy or work animals, a car, and drilling water wells for irrigation purposes are capital items usually subject to depreciation. [Reg. § 1.162-12]

Conservation Expenses. A farmer may generally deduct soil and water conservation expenditures that do not give rise to a deduction for depreciation, that are not otherwise deductible and that would increase the basis of the property absent the election to deduct them. However, current deductions for soil and water conservation expenses are limited to those that are consistent with a conservation plan approved by the Soil Conservation Service of the U.S.D.A. or, in the absence of a federally approved plan, a soil conservation plan of a comparable state agency. Expenses related to the draining or filling of wetlands or to land preparation for the installation or operation of center pivot irrigation systems may not be deducted under this provision. [IRC § 175(c)(3)]. The deduction is limited annually to 25 percent of the taxpayer's gross income from farming. Excess expenses can be carried over to succeeding tax years, without time limitation, but in each year the total deduction is limited to 25 percent of that year's gross income from farming. [Reg. § § 1.175-1 through 1.175-6]

Deductible soil and water conservation expenses include such costs as leveling, grading, construction, control and protection of diversion channels, drainage ditches, outlets and ponds, planting of windbreaks, and other treatment or moving of earth. No current deduction is allowed for the purchase, construction, installation or improvement of depreciable masonry, tile, metal or wood structures, appliances and facilities such as tanks, reservoirs, pipes, canals and pumps. [Reg. § 1.175-2] Assessments levied by a soil or water conservation or drainage district in order to defray expenses made by the district may also be deductible.

Q 6:38 Are development costs currently deductible?

Generally, farmers have the option of deducting or capitalizing developmental expenses that are ordinary and necessary business expenses [Reg. § 1.162-12] However, plants produced by farms that have a preproductive period of more than two years must be capitalized.

Q 6:39 Are fertilizer costs currently deductible?

A farmer (other than a farm syndicate) may elect to deduct current expenses otherwise chargeable to capital account made for fertilizer, lime, ground limestone, marl, or other materials for enriching, neutralizing, or conditioning land used in farming. If no election is made, expenditures producing benefits extending over more than one year are capitalized and recovered by amortization. [Reg. § 1.180-1] The election, which is effective only for the tax year claimed, is made by claiming the deduction on the return. [Reg. § 1.180-2]

Losses

Q 6:40 Can an individual deduct a loss from a business?

Generally, yes. Individuals may deduct losses from a trade or business, a transaction entered into for profit, or from a casualty or theft. [IRC § 165(c)] If an activity is not engaged in for profit, a loss on the activity is generally disallowed. [IRC § 183] This is known as the hobby-loss rule and is aimed at "gentlemen farmers" and similar taxpayers who engage in a hobby-type activity disguised as a business. The hobby-loss rule prevents these taxpayers from using losses on their hobbies to offset their other income.

In the case of a not-for-profit activity, deductions are allowed only as follows:

1. Expenses are deductible in full to the extent they are deductible without regard to whether an activity is engaged in for profit (e.g., real estate taxes);

2. Expenses other than depreciation are deductible to the extent, if any, that gross income from the activity exceeds the amount in (1); and

3. Depreciation deductions are allowed only to the extent, if any, that gross income from the activity exceeds the expenses in (1) and (2).

[Reg. § 1.183-1(b)]

For example, assume that a taxpayer has $10,000 of gross income from an activity not carried on for profit. In connection with the activity, the taxpayer incurs $4,000 of property taxes, $5,000 of depreciation, and $7,000 of other related

Q 6:38

expenses. Absent the hobby-loss rule, the taxpayer would have a $6,000 deductible loss from the activity. Under the hobby-loss rule, however, deductions are limited to the $4,000 of property taxes and $6,000 of expenses other than depreciation ($10,000 total). The $5,000 of depreciation and the remaining $1,000 of other expenses are not deductible.

> **Note:** Individuals must claim expenses from an activity not carried on for profit as miscellaneous itemized expenses. [Temp. Reg. § 1.67-1T(a)(1)] So the expenses are deductible only to the extent that they exceed 2 percent of the taxpayer's adjusted gross income.

Q 6:41 When is an activity considered a not-for-profit activity?

An activity is presumed for profit if it shows a profit for any three or more out of five consecutive years (two out of seven years for breeding, showing, or racing of horses. [IRC § 183(d)] If this presumption is not met, then the IRS takes all facts and circumstances with respect to the activity into account to determine whether the taxpayer has a profit motive. No one factor is conclusive in making this determination. [Reg. § 1.183-2(b)]

Among the factors the IRS normally takes into account are the following:

- *Manner in which the taxpayer carries on the activity.* The fact that the taxpayer carries on the activity in a businesslike manner and maintains complete and accurate books and records may indicate that the activity is engaged in for profit. Similarly, where an activity is carried on in a manner substantially similar to other activities of the same nature that are profitable, a profit motive may be indicated.

- *The expertise of the taxpayer or his or her advisors.* If a taxpayer prepares for the activity by extensive study of accepted business, economic, and scientific practices, or consults with those who are expert in the field, this may indicate a profit motive as long as the taxpayer actually carries on the activity in accordance with these practices.

- *The time and effort expended by the taxpayer in carrying on the activity.* The fact that the taxpayer devotes much of his or her personal time and effort to carrying on an activity, particularly if the activity does not have substantial personal or recreational aspects may indicate an intention to derive a profit. The fact that the taxpayer devotes a limited amount of time to an activity does not necessarily indicate a lack of profit motive if the taxpayer employs competent and qualified persons to carry on the activity.

- *Expectation that assets used in activity may appreciate in value.* The term "profit" includes appreciation in the value of assets, such as land, used in the activity. Even if there is no profit from current operations, the taxpayer may intend to achieve an overall profit when appreciation in the value of land used in the activity is realized.

- *The success of the taxpayer in carrying on other similar or dissimilar activities.* The fact that the taxpayer has engaged in similar activities in the past and converted them from unprofitable to profitable enterprises may indicate that he or she is engaged in the present activity for profit, even though the activity is presently unprofitable.

- *The taxpayer's history of income or losses with respect to the activity.* A series of losses during the initial or start-up stage of an activity may not necessarily be an indication that the activity is not engaged in for profit. However, where losses continue to be sustained beyond the period that customarily is necessary to bring the operation to profitable status, such continued losses may be indicative that the activity is not being engaged in for profit. If losses are sustained because of unforeseen or fortuitous circumstances that are beyond the control of the taxpayer, such as drought, disease, fire, theft, weather damages, other involuntary conversions, or depressed market conditions, such losses would not be an indication that the activity is not engaged in for profit.

- *The amount of occasional profits, if any, which are earned.* The amount of profits in relation to the amount of losses incurred, and in relation to the amount of the taxpayer's investment and the value of the assets used in the activity, may provide useful criteria in determining the taxpayer's intent. An occasional small profit from an activity generating large losses, or from an activity in which the taxpayer has made a large investment, would not generally be determinative that the activity is engaged in for profit.

- *The financial status of the taxpayer.* The fact that the taxpayer does not have substantial income or capital from sources other than the activity may indicate that an activity is engaged in for profit. Substantial income from sources other than the activity (particularly if the losses from the activity generate substantial tax benefits) may indicate that the activity is not engaged in for profit especially if there are personal or recreational elements involved.

- *Elements of personal pleasure or recreation.* The presence of personal motives in carrying on an activity may indicate that the activity is not engaged in for profit, especially where there are recreational or personal elements involved. On the other hand, a profit motivation may be indicated where an activity lacks any appeal other than profit.

The case of *Tinnell v. Commissioner* [T.C. Memo. 2001-106] is illustrative of how these various factors fit together in a real-life situation. During the late 1970s, James Tinnell, a physician, invented a cream to treat herpes and since then receives substantial royalties from the sale of the cream. Tinnell has been interested in mining and prospecting since 1978. By 1979, he began locating mining claims in Nevada. He conducted his mining activities through a sole proprietorship known as Jetco Mining. Over the years, he has employed his two sons, his daughter, and an ex-brother-in-law in his mining operations.

As of early 2000, Tinnell had on file and of record more than 300 lode mining claims. On the whole, Tinnell's mining ventures have not been too successful. For example: (1) In November 1983, Tinnell engaged in discussions with Canorex

Q 6:41

International, Inc., of Colorado regarding a lease of his claims. No agreement was reached. (2) In 1983 and 1984, Tinnell pursued a gold mining venture on the U.S.-Mexico border. The operation produced an ounce to an ounce and one-half of gold per day. The price of gold had fallen significantly, however, and the operation was not profitable. Soon thereafter, the operation was shut down. (3) In September 1986, Tinnell leased his mining claims to Great Western Basin Corp. for the purposes of prospecting, exploring, drilling, mining, and operating the property for ores and minerals. However, Great Western made no payments to Tinnell and defaulted on the lease. (4) In 1988, Tinnell provided extensive equipment and knowledge to the Rattlesnake Mine in California. He was not paid for the use of his equipment or for the information he provided, but was promised a portion of the income produced from the Rattlesnake Mine. Ultimately, Tinnell received only an old grader. (5) From 1991 through March 1996, Tinnell pursued the development and exploration of the Quartette Mine near Searchlight, Nevada. After having a geologist evaluated the property, Tinnell acquired mining rights in 1994. After he recovered approximately four ounces of gold from the Quartette Mine, the project was abandoned in 1996.

Tinnell has had more success with the sale of decorative rock. In 1996, he opened a "rock yard" for the retail sale of rock and gravel from his claims. In recent years, his gross income from the sale of decorative rock has grown steadily.

Over the period 1991 through 1994, Tinnell's mining operations generated $3,000 of revenue, but cost him more than $1.5 million in expenses. He deducted these losses against his other income, including his royalties from the sale of the herpes cream. The IRS disallowed this loss write-off on the ground that Tinnell did not have a profit motive for his mining activities.

The Tax Court upheld Tinnell's loss write-offs. The court said that, while there were a few factors that indicated a lack of a profit motive, there are more factors that weighed in Tinnell's favor.

Some factors that helped Tinnell win his case are as follows:

- Tinnell had a thorough understanding of the scientific and economic aspects of mining and he regularly consulted with industry experts.

- Tinnell devoted a substantial amount of time and effort to his mining activities. In the period 1991 through 1994, he spent about 90 percent of his time on mining and only 10 percent of his time working in his medical practice.

- Tinnell had a successful entrepreneurial venture before commencing his mining activities. The herpes cream business currently has over 200 employees and a market capitalization of approximately $200 million.

- While Tinnell's operations had a long string of losses, a mining venture is by its nature often speculative and may take years to realize a profit. Tinnel's efforts to generate revenue from the production and sale of decorative rock have proven successful and he turned a profit in 1999.

Q 6:41

- Although Tinnell acknowledged that he enjoyed being outdoors and that he was "tired of dealing with sick people."

- The small element of personal pleasure that he derived did not outweigh the hardships, dangers, and expenses connected with his mining activities.

Planning Point: If taxpayers can turn a profit—even just a few dollars—in three years out of a five-year period, they will be presumed to have a profit motive and stand little risk from the IRS. Therefore, taxpayers should try to bunch their income and expenses in those years when it will do the most good for purposes of the three-out-of-five-year test. If there is at least a faint chance of making a profit in the current year, taxpayers should accelerate income where possible. For example, if a taxpayer is planning to sell something that has appreciated in value, he or she should do so before the end of the current year. On the other hand, if there is no chance of making a profit in the current year, taxpayers may want to accelerate their expenses. That will give them a better chance of making a profit in the following year.

Q 6:42 If one business activity is used to promote another business activity, can they be treated as one activity for purposes of the hobby loss rules?

Possibly. The Tax Court recently ruled that the equestrian and interior design activities of a taxpayer constituted a single activity. The court determined that the taxpayer utilized her reputation as an equestrian competitor to become an interior designer of horse barns; thus, forming an integrated equestrian-based design business. Accordingly, the equestrian activity, which operated at a loss, was no longer subject to the hobby loss limits; its expenses were submerged in the profit-making interior design business. [*Topping*, TC Memo. 2007-92]

On the other hand, in a number of prior cases, the Tax Court has ruled that a taxpayer's activities could not be aggregated. For example, prior cases in which taxpayers have not prevailed include a real estate lawyer's farming/polo activity, a plastic surgeon's horse ranch activities and a holistic dentist's organic apple orchard. But the Tax Court found that none of those cases had the same level of integration and interdependence that the taxpayer's activities had in the new equestrian case.

Q 6:43 For tax purposes, what is a net operating loss?

A net operating loss (NOL) is generally the excess of a taxpayer's business deductions (with some adjustments) over the taxpayer's gross income. When a taxpayer has an NOL for a particular year, the NOL can be carried backwards or forwards to reduce taxable income in other tax years. [IRC § 172] The starting point for computing an NOL is the deficit in the taxable income for the year. In the case of individuals, the following adjustments must be made:

Q 6:42

- Net operating losses from other years are not allowed;
- No deduction is allowed for personal exemptions;
- Nonbusiness capital losses are deductible only up to nonbusiness capital gains. Any excess cannot be deducted;
- Nonbusiness deductions may be subtracted only from nonbusiness income (including any nonbusiness capital gains that remain after deducting nonbusiness capital losses);
- Any excess of nonbusiness income over nonbusiness losses cannot be deducted;
- Business capital losses may be deducted only up to the total business capital gains (plus any nonbusiness capital gains that remain after deducting nonbusiness capital losses and other nonbusiness deductions). A net capital loss cannot be deducted; and
- Contributions by a self-employed taxpayer to a retirement plan for selfemployeds are not deductible.

[Reg. § 1.172-3]

For corporate NOLs, see Chapter 3.

Q 6:44 To what years can a taxpayer carry back or carry forward an NOL?

Unless a taxpayer elects otherwise, an NOL is carried back to the two taxable years preceding the year of loss. It is carried back first to the second preceding taxable year; then, if any loss remains after the NOL offsets income in the second preceding year, the remaining loss is carried to the immediately preceding year. The taxpayer can file amended returns and claim refunds to the extent the tax liabilities for the carryback years are reduced. If any NOL is still remaining after it offsets income in the immediately preceding year, it can be carried over to the succeeding years, up to a maximum of 20 years. [IRC § 172(b)(1)(A)]

A taxpayer may elect not to use the carryback period and instead carry an NOL over only to succeeding years. Once the election is made for any tax year, it is irrevocable for that year. [IRC § 172(b)(3)]

Q 6:45 Are there special rules that limit loss deductions from passive activities?

Yes. There are special rules limiting loss deductions from "passive" activities. [IRC § 469] These rules are designed primarily to prevent investors, silent partners, and similarly situated taxpayers from using losses from a business activity to shelter their other income.

Under the passive activity rules, a taxpayer can generally deduct a loss from a passive activity only to the extent of income from other passive activities. The taxpayer's "passive activity loss" (the excess of deductions from all passive activities over the gross income from all passive activities) cannot be deducted against "active" income (e.g., salary or self-employment earnings) or "portfolio" income (e.g., interest and dividends). [Temp. Reg. § 1.469-1T] The disallowed loss can be carried over and deducted in succeeding years to the extent of passive income. [IRC § 469(b)] If a taxpayer disposes of a passive activity, any loss from the activity for the current year and any losses carried over from prior years are treated as nonpassive losses and can be used to offset other income. [IRC § 469(g)]

Q 6:46 Who is subject to the passive activity rules?

The passive activity rules apply to individuals, estates, trusts, and personal service corporations. They also apply in a limited fashion to other closely held C corporations. A closely held C corporation cannot deduct a passive activity loss against portfolio income, but it can deduct the loss against active business income. [IRC § § 469(a)(2), (e)(2)]

Q 6:47 What is a passive activity?

There are two kinds of passive activities.

1. Trade or business activities in which the taxpayer does not "materially participate" during the year.

2. Rental activities, even if the taxpayer does materially participate in them (there is an exception for real estate professionals; see below).

[IRC § 469(c)]

Q 6:48 When is a taxpayer treated as "materially participating" in a trade or business?

A taxpayer materially participates in a trade or business activity for a tax year if he or she satisfies any of the following tests: [Temp. Reg. § 1.469-5T(a)]

1. The taxpayer participated in the activity for more than 500 hours.

2. The taxpayer's participation was substantially all the participation in the activity of all individuals for the tax year, including the participation of individuals who did not own any interest in the activity.

3. The taxpayer participated in the activity for more than 100 hours during the tax year, and he or she participated at least as much as any other individual (including individuals who did not own any interest in the activity) for the year.

4. The activity is a "significant participation activity", and the taxpayer participated in all significant participation activities for more than 500 hours. A significant participation activity is any trade or business activity in which the taxpayer participated for more than 100 hours during the year and in which he or she did not materially participate under any of the other material participation tests.

5. The taxpayer materially participated in the activity for any five (whether or not consecutive) of the ten immediately preceding tax years.

Q 6:46

6. The activity is a personal service activity, and the taxpayer materially participated for any three (whether or not consecutive) preceding tax years. An activity is a personal service activity if it involves the performance of personal services in the fields of health (including veterinary services), law, engineering, architecture, accounting, actuarial science, performing arts, consulting, or any other trade or business in which capital is not a material income-producing factor.

7. Based on all the facts and circumstances, the taxpayer participated in the activity on a regular, continuous, and substantial basis during the year. A taxpayer will not be treated as materially participating under this test if he or she participated in the activity for 100 hours or less during the year.

In general, any work the taxpayer does in connection with an activity in which he or she owns an interest is treated as participation in the activity. [Reg. § 1.469-5(f)] However, a taxpayer's work does not count to the extent it is not work that is customarily done by the owner of that type of activity, and one of the main reasons for doing the work is to avoid the disallowance of any loss activity. [Temp. Reg. § 1.469-5T(f)(2)]

A taxpayer does not count work done as an investor as participation unless he or she is directly involved in the day-to-day management or operations of the activity. Work done as an investor includes:

- Studying and reviewing financial statements or reports on operations of the activity;

- Preparing or compiling summaries or analyses of the finances or operations of the activity for the taxpayer's own use; and

- Monitoring the finances or operations of the activity in a nonmanagerial capacity.

[Temp. Reg. § 1.469-5T(f)(2)]

If a taxpayer owns an activity as a limited partner, he or she is generally not treated as materially participating in the activity. However, the taxpayer is treated as materially participating if he or she meets test (1), (5), or (6) above. [Temp. Reg. § 1.469-5T(e)(2)]

A federal district court ruled that a trust's participation in an activity is measured not only by the trustee's actions but also by the actions of all of its employees and agents. [*Mattie K. Carter Trust v. U.S.*, NO. 4:02-CV-154-A. (N.D. Tex. (Apr. 11, 2003)]

The trust in question owned a 15,000-acre ranch. The ranch manager managed the ranch's day-to-day operations, subject to the trustee's approval. The trustee delegated oversight responsibility for the ranch to another individual who took a very active, hands-on role in supervising the ranch manager and general ranch operations. This individual spent well in excess of 500 hours a year engaged in ranch operations and management.

Q 6:48

The IRS took the position that the material participation of a trust in a business should be made by reference only to the trustee's activities. The trust countered that, as a legal entity, it can participate in an activity only through the actions of its fiduciaries, employees, and agents and that through such collective efforts, its ranching operations were regular, continuous, and substantial.

The federal district court sided with the trust. The court found that the material participation of the trust should be determined by reference to all the persons who conducted the business of the ranch on the trust's behalf. Moreover, the collective activities of those persons were sufficient to constitute material participation.

Q 6:49 Is there a special exception to the passive activity rules for real estate professionals?

Yes. If a taxpayer qualifies as a real estate professional, the rule that treats all rental activities as passive does not apply to him or her. [IRC § 469(c)(2)]

A taxpayer qualifies for a particular year if:

* More than one-half of the work the taxpayer performs for the year is performed in real estate businesses in which the taxpayer materially participates; and

* The taxpayer performs more than 750 hours of work during the tax year in real estate businesses in which the taxpayer materially participates.

[IRC § 469(c)(7)]

Q 6:50 Is there a special exception to the passive activity rules for "mom and pop" rental property owners?

Yes. A taxpayer can use up to $25,000 of losses from passive real estate rental activities to offset nonpassive income if: (1) the taxpayer "actively participates" in the rental activities; and (2) the taxpayer's income does not exceed certain limits. [IRC § 469(i)]

Active participation is not the same as material participation. Active participation is a less stringent standard than material participation. For example, a taxpayer may be treated as actively participating if he or she makes management decisions in a significant and bona fide sense. Management decisions that count as active participation include approving new tenants, deciding on rental terms, approving expenditures, and similar decisions. [IRS Pub. No. 925, *Passive Activity and At-Risk Rules* (Rev. 2006)]

The $25,000 allowance is available in full if the taxpayer's adjusted gross income does not exceed $100,000. The allowance is reduced by one dollar for each two dollars that adjusted gross income exceeds the $100,000 threshold. Thus, if adjusted gross income is $125,000, then up to $12,500 of active-participation losses can be deducted against nonpassive income; if adjusted gross income equals or exceeds $150,000, then no deduction is allowed. [IRC § 469(i)(3)]

Q 6:51 What are the "at risk" limitations on losses?

The Internal Revenue Code generally limits a taxpayer's loss deductions from an activity to the amount the taxpayer has "at risk" in the activity. [IRC § 465] The at-risk limits apply to individuals (including partners and S corporation shareholders), estates, trusts, and certain closely held corporations (other than S corporations). [IRC § 465(a)(1)] A corporation is considered "closely held" if at any time during the last half of the tax year, more than 50 percent in value of its outstanding stock is owned directly or indirectly by or for five or fewer individuals. [IRC § 542(a)(2)]

Activities subject to at risk rules. When the at risk rules were originally enacted by Congress, they covered only certain specified activities, now referred to as "old activities." [IRC § 465(c)(1)] The old activities are:

1. Holding, producing, or distributing motion picture films or videotapes;

2. Farming;

3. Leasing personal property and certain other tangible property that is depreciable or amortizable;

4. Exploring for, or exploiting, oil and gas; and

5. Exploring for, or exploiting, geothermal deposits (for wells started after September 1978).

Congress later expanded the at risk rules to include a catchall category: Any other activity not included in (1) through (5) that is carried on as a trade or business or for the production of income. For purposes of the at risk rules, these are referred to as "new activities." [IRC § 465(c)(3)]

Q 6:52 What is considered the amount at risk in a covered activity?

A taxpayer is considered at risk in an activity to the extent of:

- The money and adjusted basis of property contributed to the activity by the taxpayer and

- Amounts borrowed by the taxpayer for use in the activity to the extent that the taxpayer is personally liable for repayment or to the extent property (other than property used in the activity) is pledged as security for the borrowing.

[IRC § 465(b)]

A taxpayer is not considered at risk for amounts protected against loss through nonrecourse financing, guarantees, stop loss agreements, or other similar arrangements. [IRC § 465(b)(4)]

Nonrecourse financing is financing for which the taxpayer is not personally liable. If a taxpayer borrows money to contribute to an activity and the lender's only recourse is to the taxpayer's interest in the activity (or the property used in the activity), the loan is a nonrecourse loan.

A taxpayer is considered at risk for "qualified nonrecourse financing" secured by real property used in an activity of holding real property. [IRC § 465(b)(6)]

Qualified nonrecourse financing is financing for which no one is personally liable for repayment and that is:

- Borrowed by the taxpayer in connection with the activity of holding real property;
- Secured by real property used in the activity;
- Not convertible from a debt obligation to an ownership interest; and
- Loaned or guaranteed by any federal, state, or local government, or borrowed by the taxpayer from certain "qualified persons" such as a bank.

Excluded borrowings. Amounts borrowed for use in an activity will not increase the taxpayer's amount at risk in the activity if:

- The lender has an interest other than that of a creditor in the activity, or
- The lender is related to a person (other than the taxpayer) who has an interest in the activity. [IRC § 465(b)(3)]

The rule applies even if the taxpayer is personally liable for the repayment of the loan or the loan is secured by property not used in the activity.

In 1979, the IRS proposed regulations implementing the exclusion for amounts borrowed from lenders with an interest in the activity or related to someone with an interest. However, the 1979 regulations only applied to "old activities," and the Tax Court held that the excluded borrowing rules could not be applied to "new activities" until the IRS issued new regulations that specifically did so. [*Alexander v. Comm'r*, 95 T.C. 467]

In 2003, the IRS finally proposed borrowing regulations that apply to both old and new activities. [Prop. Reg. § 1.465-8]

Qualified Production Activities

Q 6:53 What is the deduction for income from qualified production activities?

This is a deduction authorized by Section 199 of the Internal Revenue Code and designed to spur domestic business. Section 199 allows taxpayers to deduct a percentage of income attributable to qualified domestic production activities. The deduction is available for tax years beginning after December 31, 2004.

Q 6:54 How is the Section 199 deduction computed?

For 2007-9, the deduction equals six percent (three percent for 2005-2006) of the lesser of: (1) taxable income derived from a qualified production activity; or (2) taxable income for the tax year. However, the deduction for a tax year is limited to 50 percent of qualifying W-2 wages paid by the taxpayer during the calendar year that ends in that tax year. In 2010, when the deduction is fully phased-in, the three percent rate will have increased to nine percent. [IRC § 199(a)(1)]

Q 6:55 Under Section 199, what constitutes a "qualified production activity"?

The following activities are qualified production activities:

- The manufacture, production, growth, or extraction in whole or significant part in the United States of tangible personal property (e.g., clothing, goods, and food), software development, or music recordings;

- Film production (with certain exclusions), provided at least 50 percent of the total compensation relating to the production of the film is compensation for specified production services performed in the United States;

- Production of electricity, natural gas, or water in the United States;

- Construction or substantial renovation of real property in the United States including residential and commercial buildings and infrastructure such as roads, power lines, water systems, and communications facilities; or

- Engineering and architectural services performed in the United States and relating to construction of real property. [IRC § 199(c)(4)(A)]

Under the 2006 Tax Relief and Health Care Act(PL 109-432), Puerto Rico is considered part of the U.S. for purposes of Section 199 if the gross receipts from sources within Puerto Rico are currently taxable for U.S. federal income tax purposes. (IRC § 199(d)(8)(A)] However, unless extended by Congress, this provision applies only to the first two tax years beginning after Dec. 31, 2005 and before Jan. 1, 2008.

Q 6:56 How is taxable income derived from the manufacture, production, growth, or extraction of tangible personal property determined under Section 199?

Gross receipts derived from a lease, rental, license, sale, exchange, or other disposition of tangible personal property manufactured, produced, grown, or extracted by the taxpayer in whole or in significant part within the United States are reduced by the cost of goods sold and by other expenses, losses, or deductions (other than the Sec. 199 deduction), which are properly allocable to such receipts. [IRC § 199(c)(1)]

Q 6:57 What constitutes "in significant part" for Section 199 purposes?

Property will be treated as manufactured by the taxpayer "in significant part" if:

- Based on all of the taxpayer's facts and circumstances, the manufacturing, production, growth, or extraction activity performed by the taxpayer in the United States is substantial in nature; or

- The labor and overhead costs incurred by the taxpayer in the United States for the manufacture, production, growth, and extraction of the property are at least twenty percent of the taxpayer's total cost for the property. [Reg. § 1.199-3(g)(3)]

For example, assume that a taxpayer purchases a small motor and various parts and materials for $75 and incurs $25 in labor costs at its factory in the United States to fabricate a plastic car body from the materials and to assemble a toy car. The taxpayer also incurs other non-overhead costs of $2 and sells the toy car in 2007 for $112. The toy car will be treated as manufactured by the taxpayer "in significant part" because the taxpayer's labor costs are more than 20 percent of the taxpayer's total cost for the toy car ($25 / ($25 + $75) = 25%). The taxpayer's domestic production activities deduction will be six percent of the taxpayer's $10 profit on the toy car or 60¢ (6% × ($112-$75- $25-$2). If the sale occurred in 2010, when the deduction is fully phased in, the deduction would be nine percent of the taxpayer's $10 profit on the car or 90¢ (9% × ($112-$75-$25-$2).

The domestic production activities deduction provides a tax savings on profits from production activities in the United States. If a taxpayer has satisfied the "significant part" test and the other requirements for the deduction, the deduction is a portion of the taxpayer's profits from domestic production and increases as those profits increase.

Q 6:58 Are packaging, design, and development activities taken into account in applying the "significant part" test for tangible personal property?

Packaging, repackaging, labeling, and minor assembly operations are not taken into account for purposes of the "significant part" test. Thus, a taxpayer cannot qualify for the domestic production activities deduction if the taxpayer's only activities in the United States are packaging and labeling property produced outside the United States. [Reg. § 1.199-3(e)(2)] Design and development activities also generally do not constitute manufacturing activities for purposes of the "significant part" test for tangible personal property. However, these activities are taken into account in the case of computer software and sound recordings because these activities produce an intangible asset (the design) rather than tangible personal property. [Reg. § 1.199-3(g)(2)]

Q 6:59 Is a contract manufacturer eligible for the deduction?

If one taxpayer performs manufacturing activities for another taxpayer, only the taxpayer with the benefits and burdens of ownership of the tangible personal property during the manufacturing process will be treated as the manufacturer. As a result, only one taxpayer will be entitled to the deduction with respect to a manufacturing activity performed with respect to an item of tangible personal property. [Reg. § 1.199-3(f)(1)]

Q 6:60 Are there any Section 199 safe harbor or *de minimis* rules?

Several safe harbor and *de minimis* rules reduce Section 199 computational and recordkeeping burdens, including:

- Simplified formulas to assist small businesses in determining taxable income from qualifying activities; [Reg. § 1.199-4(e)]

- *De minimis* rules to avoid the difficulty of making revenue and expense allocations as a result of small amounts of income from either qualifying or nonqualifying activities; [Reg. § 1.199-3(i)(4)] and

- Simplified formulas for determining a taxpayer's W-2 wages. [Rev. Proc. 2006-22, 2006-23 IRB 1033]

Q 6:61 Which construction activities qualify for the Section 199 deduction?

Qualifying activities include construction and substantial renovation of real property, including residential and commercial buildings and infrastructure such as roads, power lines, water systems, and communications facilities. "Real property" covers buildings, inherently permanent structures, and their structural components, including walls, partitions, doors, wiring, plumbing, central air conditioning and heating systems, pipes and ducts, elevators and escalators, and other similar property. [Reg. § 1.99-3(m)(3)]

Proceeds from the sale of land generally cannot be counted as gross receipts for construction activities under Section 199. So a taxpayer selling a qualifying structure together with land must allocate gross receipts between the structure and the land. The IRS permits a taxpayer to calculate the gross receipts attributable to the sale of land by adding a "deemed profit markup percentage" to the costs of the land and any other costs capitalized to the land. [Reg. § 1.99-3(m)(6)]

Section 199 does not provide that qualifying gross receipts for construction activities must be derived from a lease, rental, license, sale, exchange, or other disposition of the property. As a result, a taxpayer engaged in construction activities may qualify for the deduction even if the taxpayer does not have the benefits and burdens of ownership of the property being constructed. Therefore, more than one taxpayer may be regarded as constructing real property with respect to the same activity and the same construction project.

For example, a general contractor and a subcontractor may both be engaged in construction activities with respect to the installation of a roof on a new building. Each taxpayer's benefit will be a percentage of its profit on its work with respect to the installation of the roof.

Gross receipts derived from the rental of real property that the taxpayer constructs are not derived from construction, but rather are income for the use or forbearance of the property. As a result, rental income for real property is not eligible for the qualified production activities deduction. Gain on the later sale of the property may qualify for the deduction if all other requirements are satisfied. [Reg. § 1.99-3(m)(6)]

Q 6:62 Does the preparation of food and beverages qualify for the Section 199 deduction?

Food and beverages prepared at a retail establishment do not qualify for the deduction. A retail establishment is property used in the trade or business of selling food or beverages to the public if retail sales occur at the facility. For example, a restaurant at which food and beverages are prepared, sold, and served to customers would be a retail establishment. However, the IRS recognizes that some establishments prepare food and beverages for both wholesale and retail sale. Such an establishment will not be treated as a retail establishment if less than five percent of the gross receipts for a tax year are from retail sales. Moreover, even if a taxpayer's facility is a retail establishment, food or beverages prepared at the facility and sold at wholesale are not considered prepared at a retail establishment and the taxable income related to the wholesale transactions is therefore eligible for the deduction. [Reg. § 1.99-3(o)]

Q 6:63 How does a taxpayer compute W-2 wages for purposes of the Section 199 wage limitation?

For tax years beginning after May 17, 2006, W-2 wages for Section 199 purposes include only amounts that are properly allocable to domestic production gross receipts. [IRC § 199(b)(2)(B) as amended by the Tax Increase Prevention and Reconciliation Act (P.L. 109-222, 5/17/2006)]

There are three alternative methods for computing W-2 wages. The first method permits a taxpayer to use the lesser of the W-2 wages reported in Box 1 or Box 5 of Form W-2.

Alternatively, there are two methods that, although more complex, provide a more precise determination of W-2 wages. The IRS provides that the W-2 wages are those wages of common law employees of the taxpayer. [Rev. Proc. 2006-22, 2006-23 IRB 1033]

Q 6:64 What income derived from computer software is eligible for the deduction?

In general, income from a lease, rental, license, sale, exchange, or other disposition of software developed in the United States qualifies for the deduction, regardless of whether the customer purchases the software off the shelf or takes delivery of the software by downloading the software from the Internet. Computer software is not limited to software for computers and includes, for example, video game software.

Q 6:62

Gross receipts from providing software for customers' direct use while connected to the Internet is treated as derived from a qualifying "disposition" if either of the following conditions is satisfied:

1. The taxpayer also derives gross receipts from the qualifying disposition to customers of computer software that is provided to them (a) affixed to a tangible medium (e.g., a disk) or (2) via download from the Internet. This computer software must have only minor or immaterial differences from the software provided online.

2. An unrelated person derives on a regular and ongoing basis in its business gross receipts from the qualifying disposition of substantially identical software (as compared to the taxpayer's online software) to its customers affixed to a tangible medium or downloaded from the Internet. [Reg. § 1.199-3(i)(6)(iii)]

For purposes of (2), above, software is "substantially identical" if from a customer's viewpoint it has the same functional result as the taxpayer's online software and has a significant overlap of features or purpose with that software.)

Q 6:65 How does a partnership or S corporation compute the Section 199 deduction?

The deduction attributable to the qualifying production activities of a partnership or S corporation (pass-through entity) is determined at the partner or shareholder (partner) level. As a result, each partner must compute his or her deduction separately.

In general, each partner is allocated a share of items (including items of income, gain, loss, and deduction) attributable to qualifying production activities of the pass-through entity, along with any other items of income, gain, loss, deduction, or credit of the passthrough entity. The partner must aggregate his or her share of the items attributable to the pass-through entity's qualified production activities, any expenses incurred by the partner directly that are allocable to the pass-through entity's qualified production activities, and items attributable to the partner's other qualified production activities to determine the qualified production activities deduction for the tax year. Simplifying rules are provided for certain small partnerships. [Notice 2005-14, 2005-7 IRB 1, Sec. 4.06]

Q 6:66 How does a taxpayer allocate cost of goods sold and other deductions to qualifying production activities?

If a taxpayer cannot specifically identify the cost of goods sold, the taxpayer may use a reasonable method to determine the cost of goods sold related to the taxpayer's qualifying production activities.

Two methods are provided for allocating deductions (other than cost of goods sold) to qualified production activities:

- Method 1, which is available to all taxpayers and generally follows existing rules applicable to taxpayers required to determine taxable income from within and outside the United States; and

- Method 2, which is available to taxpayers with average annual gross receipts (over the three prior years) of $100,000,000 or less or total assets of $10,000,000 or less, provides a simplified formula that allocates deductions based on the ratio of the taxpayer's receipts derived from qualifying production activities as compared to the taxpayer's receipts from all sources. [Reg. § 1.199-4(e)]

Lastly, the IRS has provided a third method for small taxpayers that allocates both cost of goods sold and all other deductions based on the same ratio applicable to Method 2. This third method is generally available to taxpayers with average annual gross receipts of $5,000,000 or less and certain other small taxpayers permitted to use the cash method of accounting. [Reg. § 1.199-4(f)]

Tax Credits

Q 6:67 What is the general business credit?

The Internal Revenue Code provides for certain business incentive tax credits as direct offsets to a taxpayer's tax liability. These credits are combined into one "general business credit" that limits the amount of each credit that can be claimed for the tax year. [IRC § 38]

Q 6:68 What is the limitation on the general business credit for a tax year?

The business credit allowed for any tax year is generally limited to the excess of taxpayer's "net income tax" over the greater of: (1) the tentative minimum tax for the tax year (see Chapter 3), or (2) 25 percent of the amount of the taxpayer's "net regular tax" that exceeds $25,000. [IRC § 38(c)(1)]

"Net income tax" is the sum of the regular tax liability and the alternative minimum tax, reduced by certain (mainly personal) credits claimed by the taxpayer (e.g., dependent care credit). [IRC § 38(c)(1)]

There's a one-year carryback and 20-year carryforward for the unused business credit on an earliest-year-first (FIFO) basis. [IRC § 39(a)]If any portion of a business credit hasn't been allowed after the carryover period expires, the taxpayer is generally allowed to deduct the unused portion in the first tax year after the last tax year of the carryover period (or in the tax year of cessation if earlier). [IRC § 196(a), IRC § 196(b)]

Q 6:69 What business incentive credits make up the general business credit?

Among the components of the general business credit are the following:

Alternative fuel vehicle refueling property credit.. This credit applies to the cost of any qualified fuel vehicle refueling property placed in service. For more information, see Form 8911.

Alternative motor vehicle credit. This credit consists of the following four credits for new vehicles placed in service. For more information, see Form 8910.

- Qualified fuel cell motor vehicle credit.
- Advanced lean burn technology motor vehicle credit.
- Qualified hybrid motor vehicle credit.
- Qualified alternative fuel motor vehicle credit.

Biodiesel and renewable diesel fuels credit. This credit applies to certain fuel sold or used in business. For more information, see Form 8864.

Credit for alcohol used as fuel. his credit consists of the alcohol mixture credit, alcohol credit, and small ethanol producer credit. For more information, see Form 6478.

Credit for employee social security and Medicare taxes paid on certain employee tips. This credit is generally equal to an employer's portion of social security and Medicare taxes paid on tips received by employees of a food and beverage establishment where tipping is customary. The credit applies regardless of whether the food is consumed on or off your business premises. However, an employer cannot get a credit on those tips that are used to meet the federal minimum wage rate that applies to the employee under the Fair Labor Standards Act. For more information, see Form 8846.

Credit for employer-provided childcare facilities and services. This credit applies to the qualified expenses paid by an employer for employee childcare and qualified expenses paid for childcare resource and referral services. For more information, see Form 8882.

Credit for increasing research activities. This credit is designed to encourage businesses to increase the amounts they spend on research and experimental activities, including energy research. For more information, see Form 6765.

Credit for small employer pension plan startup costs. This credit applies to pension plan startup costs of a new qualified defined benefit or defined contribution plan (including a 401(k) plan), SIMPLE plan, or simplified employee pension. For more information, see IRS Publication 560, Retirement Plans for Small Business (SEP, Simple, and Qualified Plans).

Disabled access credit. This credit is a nonrefundable tax credit for an eligible small business that pays or incurs expenses to provide access to persons who have disabilities. The expenses must be paid or incurred to enable the business to comply with the Americans with Disabilities Act of 1990. For more information, see Form 8826.

Energy efficient appliance credit. This credit is available for each type of qualified energy efficient appliance produced by the taxpayer in a tax year ending on or after December 31, 2006. For more information, see Form 8909.

Energy efficient home credit. This credit is available for eligible contractors of certain homes sold for use as a residence. For more information, see Form 8908.

Investment credit. The investment credit is the total of the following credits. For more information, see Form 3468.

- Rehabilitation credit.
- Energy credit.
- Qualifying advanced coal project credit.
- Qualifying gasification project credit.

New markets credit (Form 8874). This credit is for qualified equity investments made in qualified community development entities. For more information, see Form 8874.

Nonconventional source fuel credit (Form 8907). This credit is for gas produced from biomass; liquid, gaseous, or solid synthetic fuels produced from coal; and coke or coke gas. For more information, see Form 8907.

Orphan drug credit (Form 8820). This credit applies to qualified expenses incurred in testing certain drugs, known as "orphan drugs for rare diseases and conditions." For more information, see Form 8820.

Qualified railroad track maintenance credit (Form 8900). Certain regional and switching railroads may be able to claim a credit for expenses made to upgrade their railroad tracks (including roadbed, bridges, and related track structures). For more information, see Form 8900.

Renewable electricity, refined coal, and Indian coal production credit (Form 8835). This credit is for the sale of electricity, refined coal, or Indian coal produced in the United States or U. S. possessions from qualified energy resources at a qualified facility. For more information, see Form 8835.

Work opportunity credit. This credit provides businesses with an incentive to hire individuals from targeted groups that have a particularly high unemployment rate or other special employment needs. For more information, see next question.

Q 6:70 What is the work opportunity credit?

The work opportunity tax credit is available on an elective basis for employers hiring individuals from one or more of nine targeted groups. [IRC § 51] The amount of the credit available to an employer is determined by the amount of qualified wages paid by the employer. Generally, qualified wages consist of wages attributable to service rendered by a member of a targeted group during the one-year period beginning with the day the individual begins work for the employer (two years in the case of an individual in the long-term family assistance recipient category).

The targeted groups include: [IRC § 51(d)]

1. *Families receiving TANF.* An eligible recipient is an individual certified by a designated local employment agency (e.g., a State employment

agency) as being a member of a family eligible to receive benefits under the Temporary Assistance for Needy Families Program (TANF) for a period of at least nine months part of which is during the 18-month period ending on the hiring date.

2. *Qualified veteran.* A qualified veteran is a veteran who is certified by the designated local agency as a member of a family certified as receiving assistance under a food stamp program under the Food Stamp Act of 1977 for a period of at least three months part of which is during the 12-month period ending on the hiring date. For these purposes, members of a family are defined to include only those individuals taken into account for purposes of determining eligibility for a food stamp program under the Food Stamp Act of 1977. A veteran is an individual who has served on active duty (other than for training) in the Armed Forces for more than 180 days or who has been discharged or released from active duty in the Armed Forces for a service-connected disability. However, any individual who has served for a period of more than 90 days during which the individual was on active duty (other than for training) is not a qualified veteran if any of this active duty occurred during the 60-day period ending on the date the individual was hired by the employer. Under the Small Business and Work Opportunity Tax Act of 2007 (P.L. 110-28), the targeted veterans group has been expanded to include veterans with service-connected disabilities. [IRC § 51(d)(3)(A)]

3. *Qualified ex-felon.* A qualified ex-felon is an individual certified as: (1) having been convicted of a felony under any State or Federal law, and (2) having a hiring date within one year of release from prison or date of conviction.

4. *Designated community residents.* A designated community resident is an individual certified as being at least age 18 but not yet age 40 on the hiring date and as having a principal place of abode within an empowerment zone, enterprise community, renewal community or rural renewal county (as defined under Subchapter U of Subtitle A, Chapter 1 of the Internal Revenue Code). Qualified wages do not include wages paid or incurred for services performed after the individual moves outside an empowerment zone, enterprise community, or renewal community.

5. *Vocational rehabilitation referral.* A vocational rehabilitation referral is an individual who is certified by a designated local agency as an individual who has a physical or mental disability that constitutes a substantial handicap to employment and who has been referred to the employer while receiving, or after completing: (a) vocational rehabilitation services under an individualized, written plan for employment under a State plan approved under the Rehabilitation Act of 1973; or (b) under a rehabilitation plan for veterans carried out under Chapter 31 of Title 38, U.S. Code.

Under the Small Business and Work Opportunity Tax Act of 2007 (P.L. 110-28,the vocational rehabilitation referral category has been expanded to include any individual who is referred to the employer while receiving, or after completing, an individual work plan that was developed and implemented by an employment network under the Social Security Administration's Ticket to Work and Self Sufficiency program. [IRC § 51(d)(6)(B)(iii)]

6. *Qualified summer youth employee.* A qualified summer youth employee is an individual: (1) who performs services during any 90-day period between May 1 and September 15, (2) who is certified by the designated local agency as being 16 or 17 years of age on the hiring date, (3) who has not been an employee of that employer before, and (4) who is certified by the designated local agency as having a principal place of abode within an empowerment zone, enterprise community, or renewal community (as defined under Subchapter U of Subtitle A, Chapter 1 of the Internal Revenue Code). As with high-risk youths, no credit is available on wages paid or incurred for service performed after the qualified summer youth moves outside of an empowerment zone, enterprise community, or renewal community. If, after the end of the 90-day period, the employer continues to employ a youth who was certified during the 90-day period as a member of another targeted group, the limit on qualified first year wages will take into account wages paid to the youth while a qualified summer youth employee.

7. *Qualified food stamp recipient.* A qualified food stamp recipient is an individual aged 18 but not yet 40 certified by a designated local employment agency as being a member of a family receiving assistance under a food stamp program under the Food Stamp Act of 1977 for a period of at least six months ending on the hiring date. In the case of families that cease to be eligible for food stamps under section 6(o) of the Food Stamp Act of 1977, the six-month requirement is replaced with a requirement that the family has been receiving food stamps for at least three of the five months ending on the date of hire.

8. *Qualified SSI recipient.* A qualified SSI recipient is an individual designated by a local agency as receiving supplemental security income (SSI) benefits under Title XVI of the Social Security Act for any month ending within the 60-day period ending on the hiring date.

9. *Long-term family assistance recipients.* A qualified long-term family assistance recipient is an individual certified by a designated local agency as being: (1) a member of a family that has received family assistance for at least 18 consecutive months ending on the hiring date; (2) a member of a family that has received such family assistance for a total of at least 18 months (whether or not consecutive) after August 5, 1997 if the individual is hired within two years after the date that the 18-month total is reached; or (3) a member of a family who is no longer eligible for family assistance because of either Federal or State time limits, if the individual is hired within two years after the Federal or State time limits made the family ineligible for family assistance.

Q 6:70

The Small Business and Work Opportunity Tax Act of 2007 (P.L. 110-28) makes the work opportunity credit available for employees hired through August 31, 2011.

Q 6:71 How is the work opportunity tax credit calculated?

The credit available to an employer for qualified wages paid to members of all targeted groups except for long-term family assistance recipients equals 40 percent (25 percent for employment of 400 hours or less) of qualified first-year wages. [IRC 51(a)] Generally, qualified first-year wages equal the first $6,000 of wages attributable to service rendered by a member of a targeted group during the one-year period beginning with the day the individual began work for the employer. [IRC §51(b)] Therefore, the maximum credit per employee is $2,400 (40 percent of the first $6,000). With respect to qualified summer youth employees, the maximum credit is $1,200 (40 percent of the first $3,000 of qualified first-year wages). Except for long-term family assistance recipients, no credit is allowed for second-year wages.

In the case of long-term family assistance recipients, the credit equals 40 percent (25 percent for employment of 400 hours or less) of $10,000 for qualified first-year wages and 50 percent of the first $10,000 of qualified second-year wages. Generally, qualified second-year wages are qualified wages (not in excess of $10,000) attributable to service rendered by a member of the long-term family assistance category during the one-year period beginning on the day after the one-year period beginning with the day the individual began work for the employer. Therefore, the maximum credit per employee is $9,000 (40 percent of the first $10,000 of qualified first-year wages plus 50 percent of the first $10,000 of qualified second-year wages). [IRC §51(e)]

Q 6:72 What is the certification process for the work opportunity credit?

An individual is not treated as a member of a targeted group unless: (1) on or before the day on which an individual begins work for an employer, the employer has received a certification from a designated local agency that such individual is a member of a targeted group; or (2) on or before the day an individual is offered employment with the employer, a pre-screening notice is completed by the employer with respect to such individual, and not later than the 28th day after the individual begins work for the employer, the employer submits such notice, signed by the employer and the individual under penalties of perjury, to the designated local agency as part of a written request for certification. [IRC §51(d)(13)] [IRC 51(a)] For these purposes, a pre-screening notice is a document (in such form as the Secretary may prescribe) which contains information provided by the individual on the basis of which the employer believes that the individual is a member of a targeted group.

Q 6:73 What is the foreign tax credit?

U.S. taxpayers who pay income taxes to foreign governments may credit these taxes dollar-for-dollar against their U.S. income tax liability. The foreign tax credit is elective and is allowed against U.S. income tax for income tax paid to a foreign country (or province, state, city, etc., thereof) or U.S. possession. [IRC § 901] In the alternative, taxpayers may choose to deduct their foreign income taxes in lieu of the credit. [IRC § 164]

If a credit is claimed for any foreign income taxes, no deductions may be claimed for other foreign income taxes, but other foreign taxes otherwise deductible (e.g., foreign real property taxes) may be deducted. [Reg § 1.901-1(c)]

Accrual basis taxpayers take the tax as a credit in the tax year it accrues, cash basis taxpayers in the tax year it's paid. However, cash basis taxpayers can make a binding election to take credit, for *all* qualified foreign taxes, in the year they accrue rather than are paid. [IRC § 905(a)]

Chapter 7

Depreciation

For many capital-intensive businesses, depreciation may be the largest single expense that they claim on their tax returns. Relatively few businesses do not deduct depreciation in some form or other.

At one time, the tax rules governing depreciation were rather loose and vague and the subject of many disputes between taxpayers and the Internal Revenue Service (IRS or the Service). Then Congress codified a very specific and rather rigid framework for depreciation known as the Accelerated Cost Recovery System, which was later superseded by the Modified Accelerated Cost Recovery System (MACRS).

These changes reduced the number of disputes with the IRS. However, it also reduced the flexibility taxpayers had previously enjoyed in the area of depreciation and put a premium on knowing the intricacies of the codified rules.

Depreciation: The Basics

Q 7:1 What is depreciation?

Depreciation is an annual income tax deduction authorized by the Internal Revenue Code (IRC or the Code) that allows taxpayers to recover their cost or other basis of certain property over a period of time. It is an allowance for the wear and tear, age, deterioration, or obsolescence of the property. [IRC §§ 167, 168]

Q 7:2 What kind of property is depreciable?

Most types of tangible property (except land) are depreciable. This includes buildings, machinery, vehicles, furniture, and equipment. Costs of certain types of intangible property (e.g., patents, copyrights, and computer software, can also be written off through amortization deductions (see Chapter 6).

To be depreciable, the property must:

- Be owned by the taxpayer;
- Be used in a business or income-producing activity; [IRC § 167(a)]
- Have a determinable useful life of more than one year; [Reg. § 1.167(a)-1(b)] and
- Be property other than inventory or stock in trade. [Reg. § 1.167(a)-2]

Taxpayers can claim depreciation deductions only if they hold the "incidents of ownership" for the property. Incidents of ownership include:

- The legal title;
- The legal obligation to pay for the property;
- The responsibility to pay its maintenance and operating expenses;
- The duty to pay any taxes; and
- The risk of loss if the property is destroyed, condemned, or diminished in value through obsolescence or exhaustion.

Leased property. If a taxpayer leases property to someone, the taxpayer can generally depreciate its cost, plus any improvements the taxpayer makes to the property. [Reg. § 1.167(a)(4)] That is true even if the lessee has agreed to preserve, replace, renew, and maintain the property. However, if the lease provides that the lessee is to maintain the property and return to the taxpayer the same property or its equivalent in value at the expiration of the lease in as good condition and value as when leased, the taxpayer cannot depreciate the cost of the property.

Personal use. Property used for personal purposes is not depreciable. [Reg. § 1.167(a)(2)] If property is used for both personal and business or income-producing purposes, depreciation is allowed only to the extent of the business use.

Inventory. A business's inventory is not depreciable. [Reg. § 1.167(a)-2] That is because inventory is held for sale and not for use in the business.

In 2003, the IRS ruled that the costs of "rotable spare parts" used by businesses to meet their obligations under service and maintenance contracts can be recovered through depreciation. The spare parts do not have to be treated as inventory held for sale. [Rev. Rul. 2003-37, 2003-15 I.R.B. 717] However, the treatment of rotable spare parts as depreciable assets continued to be the subject of controversy in situations when a business, as part of its maintenance operations, sold rotable spare parts from a pool of rotable spare parts. In 2007, for reasons of administrative convenience, and to reduce further controversy, the IRS issued a revenue procedure that created a safe harbor. If a business within the scope of the revenue procedure maintains one or more pools of rotable spare parts that it treats as depreciable assets and sells rotable spare parts from these pools, the IRS will not challenge the business's treatment of the pools as depreciable assets for a particular taxable year as long as the business uses the accounting method provided in the revenue procedure. [Rev Proc 2007-48, 2007-29 I.R.B.]

In some cases, property may be held for sale *and* held for use in the business. In that case, it is the primary purpose that controls.

> **Example 7-1:** XYZ Corp. is in the business of leasing cars. XYZ sells the cars at the end of their useful lives, when the cars are no longer profitable to lease. XYZ does not have a showroom, used car lot, or individuals to sell the cars. Instead, it sells them through wholesalers or by similar arrangements. XYZ can depreciate the leased cars because the cars are not held primarily for sale to customers in the ordinary course of business, but are leased.

If XYZ buys cars at wholesale prices, leases them for a short time, and then sells them at retail prices or in sales in which dealers intend to make a profit, the cars are treated as inventory, and they are not depreciable property. In this situation, the cars are held primarily for sale to customers in the ordinary course of business.

Q 7:3 How much can be written off through depreciation?

Annual depreciation deduction is a fraction or percentage of the taxpayer's depreciable "basis" for the property. Under the Modified Accelerated Cost Recovery System (discussed below), the depreciable basis for property is generally the same as the basis for figuring gain or loss on a sale, unadjusted for prior depreciation. [IRC § 1011]

The basis of property that is purchased is its cost plus amounts paid for such items such as sales tax, freight charges, and installation and testing fees. The cost includes the amount paid in cash, debt obligations, and other property or services.

When property is acquired in some way other than in a straight purchase, special rules may apply in determining basis. For example, when a taxpayer acquires property in a nontaxable transfer, the taxpayer's basis is generally the same as the transferor's basis. [IRC § 168(i)(7)]Similarly, if a shareholder transfers property to a controlled corporation in exchange for stock, the exchange is tax-free. [IRC § 351]So the corporation's basis is the same as the shareholder's basis before the transfer.

Property converted from personal use. A special rule applies when taxpayers convert property from personal-use property to business use or income-producing-use property. The basis for figuring depreciation is the lesser of (1) the property's fair market value at the time of conversion or (2) its adjusted basis when converted. [Reg. § 1.167(g)-1; Prop. Reg. § 1.168-2(j)(6)(ii)]The adjusted basis is the original cost or other basis for the property increased by the cost of any permanent improvements or additions and other costs that must be added to basis, and decreased by any deductions claimed for casualty and theft losses and other items that reduced basis.

Example 7-2: Several years ago Jessie Parker paid $160,000 to have her home built on a lot that cost her $10,000. Before changing the property to rental use last year, she paid $20,000 for permanent improvements to the house and claimed a $2,000 casualty loss deduction for damage to the house. Because land is not depreciable, she can only include the cost of the house when figuring the basis for depreciation.

Parker's adjusted basis in the house when she changed it to rental use was $178,000 ($160,000 + $20,000 – $2,000). On the same date, her property had a fair market value of $180,000, of which $30,000 was for the land and $150,000 was for the house. The basis for depreciation on the house is the fair market value ($150,000), because it is less than her adjusted basis ($178,000).

Q 7:4 When can depreciation be claimed on property?

Depreciation begins when an asset is "placed in service." [Reg. §1.167(a)-10(b)] Property is considered to be placed in service in the year it is ready and available to perform the function it was designed to do.

Example 7-3: XYZ, Inc. begins construction of a manufacturing plant in November 2008. The building is completed in August 2009. Equipment used in the production-line process is installed during September and October 2009. It is tested in November 2009. Equipment used in the finishing-line process is installed in December 2009 and January 2010. All of the equipment is tested during February 2010. Production actually begins in April 2010.

The building is considered placed in service in August 2009, when it becomes available for the installation of equipment. So XYZ can claim a depreciation deduction for the building in 2009. None of the equipment, however, is considered placed in service until 2010. That is when the equipment first became available to produce an acceptable product.

Taxpayers must claim a deduction for depreciation on property used in a business or income-producing activity even if it is temporarily idle. For example, if a business stops using a machine because there is a temporary lack of market for a product made with that machine, depreciation deductions must continue to be claimed for the machine.

Depreciation ceases on property when it is retired from service, even if a taxpayer has not fully recovered its cost or other basis. [IRC §§167, 169(d)] Property is considered retired from service when it is permanently withdrawn from use in a business or income-producing activity. This happens at any of the following events:

- The property is sold or exchanged;
- The taxpayer converts the property to personal use;
- The taxpayer abandons the property; and
- The property is destroyed.

Q 7:5 How is depreciation computed?

The amount of depreciation that can be deducted in any given year generally depends on (1) the basis of the property, (2) the depreciation method, and (3) the depreciation period. Traditionally, depreciation was claimed on the property's "useful life." But under MACRS, all property is assigned to one of several "cost recovery" periods.

From an accounting standpoint, the depreciation method is the rate at which property is written off. For example, if property is depreciated under the straight-line method, the basis is written off ratably over the depreciation period. If an accelerated depreciation method is used, more of the basis is written off in the first half of the depreciation period than in the latter half. Under MACRS, depreciation is generally figured under an accelerated method in the early years of the cost recovery period with a switch over to the straight-line method in later years (see below).

Modified Accelerated Cost Recovery System

Q 7:6 What is the Modified Accelerated Cost Recovery System?

The Modified Accelerated Cost Recovery System (MACRS) is the name given to the depreciation system authorized by the IRC that is used to write off the basis of most business and investment property placed in service after 1986. [IRC § 168]

Under MACRS, the depreciation allowed for any given asset depends on which depreciation system is used and on the asset's "applicable recovery period," the asset's "applicable convention," and the asset's "applicable depreciation method." [IRC § 168]"

Depreciation system. MACRS consists of two depreciation systems, the General Depreciation System (GDS) and the Alternative Depreciation System (ADS). Generally, these systems provide different methods and recovery periods to use in figuring depreciation deductions.

Applicable recovery period. Depreciable assets are divided into several classes, based on how long it takes to write off an asset. For example, the applicable recovery period for automobiles is five years. [IRC § 168(c)]

Applicable convention. Under depreciation conventions, all property placed in service during a period is treated as placed in service at a specified point in the period. Depreciation is allowed only from that point on. MACRS real estate, for example, uses the mid-month convention. For purposes of figuring depreciation, real estate placed in service any time during a month is depreciable starting at the middle of the month. Thus, the owner of a factory building actually placed in service on November 1 is entitled to a depreciation deduction for only one and one-half month's worth of depreciation on a calendar-year return for the year the property is placed in service. [IRC § 168(d)]

Applicable depreciation method. [IRC § 168(b)] Under GDS, several different methods of accelerated depreciation are used; switching to the straight-line method in the year the straight-line method produces a larger deduction. Under ADS, the straight-line method is used all the way through.

Q 7:7 For which property must MACRS be used?

MACRS must generally be used for all depreciable tangible property used in a business or income-producing activity and placed in service after 1986. There are a few exceptions.

Useful life not expressed in years. MACRS does not apply to any property that can properly be depreciated under a method not expressed in terms of years and for which a taxpayer elects to exclude it from MACRS. [IRC § 168(f)(1)] This election must be made in the year the property is placed in service. [Temp. Reg. § 5h.5(a)]

For example, some property may be depreciated under the "unit of production" method. With this method, depreciation deductions are based on the estimated number of units that the property will produce before it wears out. [Reg. § 1.167(b)-0(b)]

Example 7-4: A machine costs $100,000. The taxpayer estimates that the machine will produce 20,000 units before it is no longer useful. If it produces 4,000 units in 2008, the taxpayer can claim a depreciation deduction of $20,000 (4,000/20,000) under the unit-of-production method.

Another acceptable non-MACRS depreciation method is the "income forecast" method. Leased TV films and similar property can be depreciated under the income-forecast method (see next question).

Public utility property. MACRS is not available to public utility property unless the benefits of MACRS are "normalized." in setting rates charged customers. [IRC § 168(f)(2)] This means that the tax savings from MACRS's accelerated depreciation cannot flow to customers. Instead, they must be put in a reserve account. The reserve account is drawn upon when MACRS produces smaller deductions than a slower depreciation method. If the tax savings are not normalized, a public utility must use the same depreciation method used in its regulated books of account.

Q 7:8 What is the income forecast method of depreciation?

The income forecast method permits taxpayers to recover the depreciable basis in property over the period anticipated income is earned from the property. [IRC § 167(g). The income forecast method is available for motion picture films, videotapes, sound recordings, copyrights, books, patents and other types of property designated by the IRS. [IRC § 167(g)(6)]

Q 7:7

The IRS has issued proposed regulations governing the income forecast method. [Prop. Reg. § § 1.167(n)-1)-1.167(n)-7] These proposed regulations extend the income forecast method to theatrical productions and authorize the IRS to publish guidance designating other properties as eligible for the income forecast method.

The proposed regulations provide that a taxpayer's allowance for depreciation for a given year for eligible property is generally an amount that bears the same relationship to the depreciable basis of the property that the "current year income" for that year bears to the "forecasted total income" for the property.

Example 7-5: The cost of a TV film is $500,000, and the total estimated income to be derived from it is $800,000. If income from the film is $200,000 in 2008, then one-quarter ($200,000/$800,000) of its cost can be deducted in 2008. That is a depreciation deduction of $125,000.

Taxpayers may revise forecasted total income and use the revised computation in tax years after the property is placed in service if information becomes available that indicates that forecasted total income previously used is inaccurate. Under the revised computation, a taxpayer's allowance for depreciation for the current and all future years is an amount that bears the same relationship to the unrecovered depreciable basis of the property that the current year income for that year bears to the result obtained by subtracting from revised forecasted total income for the property the amounts of current year income for prior taxable years.

Example 7-6: Same facts as in Example 7-5. In 2009, the total estimated income from the TV film is lowered to $600,000. If income from the film is $200,000 in 2009, then one-half ($200,000/$400,000) of its unrecovered cost can be deducted in 2009. That is a depreciation deduction of $187,500 (1/2 × $375,000).

A taxpayer's adjusted basis in eligible property must be recovered by the end of the tenth tax year following the tax year in which the property is placed in service. [IRC § 167(g)(1)(C)] The proposed regulations provide that a taxpayer may generally deduct the adjusted basis in property before ten years if income from the property ceases completely and permanently.

A taxpayer using the income forecast method is required to pay, or is entitled to receive, interest for any year to which a "look-back" requirement applies. A taxpayer must pay look-back interest if deductions are accelerated due to the underestimation of total income expected to be earned with respect to the property. Conversely, a taxpayer is entitled to receive look-back interest if deductions are delayed because of overestimating total income expected to be earned with respect to the property.

Generally, the look-back method is applied in the third and tenth taxable years following the year in which the income forecast property is placed in service.

Q 7:8

Q 7:9 Under MACRS, who must use GDS, and who must use ADS?

Taxpayers generally must use GDS unless specifically required by law to use ADS or they elect to use it. Property for which the use of ADS is required includes:

- Listed property (see below);
- Any tangible property used predominantly outside the United States during the year; and
- Any imported property covered by an executive order of the President of the United States.

[IRC § 168(g)]

Although property may qualify for GDS, taxpayers may elect to use ADS. The election generally must cover all property in the same property class that is placed in service during the year. However, the election for residential rental property and nonresidential real property can be made on a property-by-property basis. Once the election is made, it cannot be revoked.

Q 7:10 What are the recovery periods for GDS?

Which GDS recovery period applies to a particular asset depends on what its class life was under the Asset Depreciation Range (ADR) system. [IRC § 168(i)] The ADR system was an optional depreciation system used before 1981. Under ADR, the IRS separated tangible property into classes and gave a range of allowable useful lives for each class. MACRS generally keys its recovery periods into the midpoint class lives under ADR.

The following is a list of the nine GDS property classes:

- 3-year property (includes tractor units for over-the-road use, race horses over two years old when placed in service, and any other horse over 12 years old when placed in service);
- 5-year property (includes automobiles, trucks, computers and peripheral equipment, office machinery, any property used in research and experimentation, breeding cattle and dairy cattle, and appliances, carpets, furniture, etc., used in a residential rental real estate operations activity);
- 7-year property (includes office furniture and fixtures and agricultural machinery and equipment;
- 10-year property (includes vessels, barges, tugs, and similar water transportation, any single-purpose agricultural or horticultural structure, and any tree or vine bearing fruits or nuts);
- 15-year property (includes certain improvements made directly to land or added to it, such as shrubbery, fences, roads, and bridges, and any retail motor fuels outlet, such as a convenience store);
- 20-year property (includes farm buildings other than single-purpose structures);
- 25-year property (water utility property);

- Residential rental property (any building or structure if 80 percent or more of its gross rental income for the tax year is from dwelling units; does not include a hotel, motel, inn, or other establishment where more than half the units are used on a transient basis);

- Nonresidential real property (includes office buildings, stores, and warehouses).

The recovery period of each of the first seven classes is identical to the name of the class. The recovery period for residential rental property is 27.5 years; for nonresidental real property, it is 38 years. [IRC § 168(c)]

Any property that does not have a class life and has not been designated by law as being in any other class is considered seven-year property. [IRC § 168(e)(3)]

Q 7:11 What are the recovery periods under ADS?

The recovery periods for property depreciated under ADS are either the same or longer than the recovery periods for GDS. Here are some of the recovery periods for ADS:

• Automobiles and light duty trucks	5 years
• Computers and peripheral equipment	5 years
• Personal property with no class life	2 years
• Single-purpose agricultural and horticultural structures	15 years
• Any tree or vine bearing fruit or nuts	20 years
• Nonresidential real property	40 years
• Residential rental property	40 years

Q 7:12 What depreciation convention is used under MACRS?

Both GDS and ADS generally use the half-year convention for personal property. [IRC § 168(d)(1)] This treats all property placed in service or disposed of during a year as placed in service or disposed of at the year's midpoint. This means that taxpayers can claim a half-year's worth of depreciation in the first year they place property in service, regardless of when during the year the property is actually placed in service. Likewise, if taxpayers dispose of property before the end of the recovery period, they can claim a half-year of depreciation for the disposition year.

As a result of the half-year convention, taxpayers must wait until the year after the end of the recovery period to fully depreciate the property. The half-year of depreciation not allowed in the first year is tacked on after the end of the recovery period.

Example 7-7: On April 1, 2008, XYZ Inc. places in service an item of five-year property. XYZ can claim only a half-year of depreciation in 2008. In 2009 through 2012, XYZ can claim a full year of depreciation. The remaining half-year is written off in 2013—the sixth year it has claimed depreciation for the item.

If a taxpayer has a short tax year, the depreciation allowed under the half-year convention is correspondingly reduced. For example, if a tax year were only four months long, any personal property placed in service during the year would be allowed two months of depreciation.

Q 7:13 Are there any exceptions to the half-year convention for personal property?

Yes. If a large portion of the depreciable personal property a taxpayer places in service during a year is placed in service in the last quarter of the year, the taxpayer may not be able to use the half-year convention. Taxpayers must use the "mid-quarter" convention if the combined bases of property placed in service during the last three months of the tax year exceed 40 percent of the combined bases of personal property put in service during the entire year. [IRC § 168(d)(3)] For this purpose, nonresidential real property, residential rental property, and property placed in service and disposed of in the same year are not counted.

If this convention applies, the depreciation that can be deducted in the first year depends on the quarter in which the property is placed in service. The first quarter in a year begins on the first day of the tax year. The second quarter begins on the first day of the fourth month of the tax year. The third quarter begins on the first day of the seventh month of the tax year. To figure the depreciation deduction for the first year under the mid-quarter convention, the depreciation for a full year is multiplied by a percentage based on the quarter the property is placed in service:

Quarter	Percentage
First	87.5%
Second	62.5
Third	37.5
Fourth	12.5

The net effect is that depreciation deductions under the mid-quarter convention are larger than with the half-year convention for property placed in service in the first half of the tax year and are smaller for property placed in service in the second half of the tax year.

If the mid-quarter convention is used and the property is disposed of before the end of the recovery period, the depreciation deduction for the disposition year is computed by multiplying a full year of depreciation by a percentage that depends on which quarter of the year the property is disposed of.

Quarter	Percentage
First	12.5%
Second	37.5

Quarter	Percentage
Third	62.5
Fourth	87.5

Planning Point: In some cases, it may be advantageous to accelerate or postpone purchases to invoke the mid-quarter convention. For example, suppose a taxpayer purchases $60,000 of MACRS personal property in the first quarter of the year. The taxpayer wants to purchase another $40,000 of MACRS personal property in the last quarter or the first quarter of the following year. The taxpayer would be better off purchasing the property in the last quarter. True, the taxpayer would be entitled only to 12.5 percent of a full-year's depreciation for the $40,000 last quarter purchase. But the first-quarter $60,000 purchase would be eligible for a deduction of 87.5 percent of a full year's depreciation. Averaged out, the taxpayer is able to deduct more with the mid-quarter convention than with the half-year convention.

Q 7:14 What is the applicable convention for real estate?

All nonresidential real property and residential rental property is depreciated using the mid-month convention. [IRC § 162(d)(2)] Under this convention, all property placed in service or disposed of during a month is placed in service or disposed of at the midpoint of the month. This means that a one-half month of depreciation is allowed for the month the property is placed in service or disposed of.

Unlike personal property, there is no special rule that applies when a substantial amount of property is placed in service during the fourth quarter.

Q 7:15 What depreciation methods are allowed under MACRS?

MACRS provides three depreciation methods under GDS and one depreciation method under ADS. [IRC § 168(b)]

1. *The 200 percent declining-balance method over a GDS recovery period.* This is allowed for nonfarm property in the 3-, 5-, 7-, and 10-year classes and switches to straight-line depreciation when that method results in an equal or bigger deduction.

2. *The 150 percent declining-balance method over a GDS recovery period.* This is used for farm property and other property in the 15- and 20-year classes and switches to straight-line depreciation when that method results in an equal or bigger deduction. A taxpayer may elect this method for property eligible for the 200 percent declining-balance method.

3. *The straight-line method over a GDS recovery period.* This method must be used for nonresidential real property and residential rental property and may be elected for property eligible for the 200 percent and 150 percent declining-balance methods.

 4. *The straight-line method over an ADS recovery period.* This method must be used for property required to be depreciated under ADS and may be elected for other property.

Q 7:16 What is the declining-balance method of depreciation?

 With the declining-balance method, the depreciation rate stays the same each year, but the amount of the deduction changes. The rate is (1) one divided by the number of years in the recovery period, multiplied by (2) either 200 percent or 150 percent, depending on which declining-balance method is allowed. For example, with five-year property, the depreciation rate is 40 percent—one-fifth multiplied by 200 percent. This same rate is applied each year to the adjusted basis for that year.

Q 7:17 How is depreciation figured under MACRS?

 To figure a depreciation deduction under MACRS, taxpayers must determine the depreciation system, property class, placed-in-service date, basis amount, recovery period, convention, and depreciation method that apply to the property. Once these are determined, they can compute the deduction manually or they can use optional tables provided by the IRS (see next question).

 Example 7-8: In February, Lois Johnson places in service depreciable property with a 5-year recovery period and a basis of $1,000. She uses GDS and the 200 percent declining-balance method to figure her depreciation. When the straight-line method results in an equal or larger deduction, she switches to the straight-line method. Because Johnson did not place any property in service in the last three months of the year, she must use the half-year convention.

 First year. Johnson figures the depreciation rate under the 200 percent declining-balance method by dividing 1 by 5 and then multiplying by 200 percent. The result is 40 percent. She multiplies the adjusted basis of the property ($1,000) by the 40 percent declining balance rate. She applies the half-year convention by dividing the result ($400) by 2. Depreciation for the first year under the 200 percent declining balance method is $200.

 Johnson figures the depreciation rate under the straight-line method by dividing 1 by 5. The result is 20 percent. Applying that rate to her adjusted basis and using the half-year convention, Johnson computes a depreciation deduction of $100 under the straight-line method.

 Because the declining balance method provides a larger deduction than the straight-line method, Johnson deducts the larger amount—$200.

 Second year. Johnson reduces the adjusted basis ($1,000) by the depreciation claimed in the first year ($200). Multiplying the result ($800) by the 40 percent declining balance rate produces a deduction of $320.

 Johnson figures the straight-line depreciation rate by dividing 1 by 4.5, the number of years remaining in the recovery period. (Because of the half-year convention, Johnson used only half a year of the recovery period in the first year.) She multiplies the reduced adjusted basis ($800) by the result (22.22 percent). Depreciation under the straight-line method for the second year is $178.

Because the declining balance method provides a larger deduction than the straight-line method, Johnson deducts the $320 figured under the declining-balance method.

Third year. Johnson reduces the adjusted basis ($800) by the depreciation claimed in the second year ($320). Multiplying the result ($480) by the 40 percent declining balance rate produces a deduction of $192.

Johnson figures the straight-line depreciation rate by dividing 1 by 3.5. She multiplies the reduced adjusted basis ($480) by the result (28.57 percent). Depreciation under the straight-line method for the third year is $137.

Because the declining-balance method provides a larger deduction than the straight-line method, Johnson deducts the $192 figured under the declining-balance method.

Fourth year. Johnson reduces the adjusted basis ($480) by the depreciation claimed in the third year ($192). She multiplies the result ($288) by the 40 percent declining-balance method rate. Depreciation for the fourth year under the 200 percent declining-balance method is $115.

Johnson figures the straight-line depreciation rate by dividing 1 by 2.5. She multiplies the reduced adjusted basis ($288) by the result (40 percent). Depreciation under the straight-line method for the fourth year is $115.

Because the straight-line method provides a deduction equal to the 200 percent declining-balance method, Johnson switches to the straight-line method and deduct the $115.

Fifth year. Johnson reduces the adjusted basis ($288) by the depreciation claimed in the fourth year ($115) to get the reduced adjusted basis of $173. She figures the straight-line depreciation rate by dividing 1 by 1.5. She multiplies the reduced adjusted basis ($173) by the result (66.67 percent). Depreciation under the straight-line method for the fifth year is $115.

Sixth year. Johnson reduces the adjusted basis ($173) by the depreciation claimed in the fifth year ($115) to get the reduced adjusted basis of $58. Because there is less than one year remaining in the recovery period, the straight-line depreciation rate for the sixth year is 100 percent. Johnson deducts the remaining $58 adjusted basis.

Example 7-9: In January, Tom Jackson bought and placed in service a building for $100,000 that is nonresidential real property. The adjusted basis of the building is its cost of $100,000. Jackson uses GDS, the straight-line method, and the mid-month convention to figure his depreciation.

First year. Jackson figures the straight-line depreciation rate for the building by dividing 1 by 39 years. The result is .02564. The depreciation for a full year is $2,564 ($100,000 × .02564). Under the mid-month convention, Jackson treats the property as placed in service in the middle of January. He gets 11.5 months of depreciation for the year. Expressed as a decimal, the fraction of 11.5 months divided by 12 months is .958. Jackson's first-year depreciation for the building is $2,456 ($2,564 .958).

Second year. Jackson subtracts $2,456 from $100,000 to get an adjusted basis of $97,544 for the second year. The straight-line rate is .02629. This is 1 divided by the remaining recovery period of 38.042 years (39 years reduced by 11.5 months or .958 year). Jackson's depreciation for the building for the second year is $2,564 ($97,544 × .02629).

Third year. The adjusted basis is $94,980 ($97,544 - $2,564). The straight-line rate is .027 (1 divided by 37.042 remaining years). Jackson's depreciation for the third year is $2,564 ($94,980 × .027).

Example 7-10: During the year, XYZ Inc., a calendar-year corporation, bought and placed in service in its business the following items in the specified months: a $4,000 safe (January), a $1,000 office chair (September), and computers worth $5,000 (October).

XYZ uses use GDS and the 200 percent declining-balance method to figure the depreciation. The total bases of all property placed in service during the year is $10,000. Because the basis of the computers ($5,000) is more than 40 percent of the total bases of all property placed in service during the year ($10,000), XYZ must use the mid-quarter convention. This convention applies to all three items of property. The safe and the chair are 7-year property, and the computers are 5-year property.

The safe. 200 percent declining-balance rate for 7-year property is .28571. This is determined by dividing 1 by 7 years and multiplying by 200 percent. The depreciation for the safe for a full year is $1,143 ($4,000 × .28571). Because XYZ placed the safe in service in the first quarter of its tax year, the full-year's depreciation ($1,143) is multiplied by 87.5 percent (the mid-quarter percentage for the first quarter). The result, $1,000, is XYZ's deduction for depreciation on the safe for the first year. For the second year, the adjusted basis of the safe is $3,000. XYZ's depreciation deduction for the second year is $857 ($3,000 × .28571).

The office chair. Because the office chair is also 7-year property, XYZ uses the same 200 percent declining-balance rate of .28571. The basis of the chair ($1,000) is multiplied by .28571 to get the depreciation of $286 for the full year. Because XYZ placed the furniture in service in the third quarter of its tax year, the full year's depreciation ($286) is multiplied by 37.5 percent (the mid-quarter percentage for the third quarter). The result, $107, is XYZ's deduction for depreciation on the chair for the first year. For the second year, the adjusted basis of the furniture is $893. XYZ's depreciation for the second year is $255 ($893 × .28571).

The computers. The 200 percent declining-balance rate for 5-year property is 40 percent. The depreciation for the computers for a full year is $2,000 ($5,000 × .40). Because XYZ placed the computers in service in the fourth quarter of its tax year, the full year's depreciation ($2,000) is multiplied by 12.5 percent (the mid-quarter percentage for the fourth quarter). The result, $250, is XYZ's deduction for depreciation on the computers for the first year. For the second year, the adjusted basis of the computer is $4,750. XYZ's depreciation deduction for the second year is $1,900 ($4,750 × .40).

Q 7:18 Does the IRS provide optional tables that can be used instead of taxpayers computing depreciation deductions themselves?

Yes. Instead of figuring the MACRS deduction as described in the previous question, a taxpayer has the option of using tables issued by the IRS. The tables provide the percentage depreciation rate to be used each year for each class of property using the different depreciation methods and conventions. The depreciation rate is applied to the unadjusted basis of the property.

Here is the GDS table for computing the depreciation deductions for 3-, 5-, 7-, 10-, 15-, and 20-year properties using the accelerated depreciation methods and the half-year convention.

General Depreciation System
Applicable Depreciation Method: 200 or 150 Percent
Declining Balance Switching to Straight Line
Applicable Recovery Periods: 3, 5, 7, 10, 15, 20 years
Applicable Convention: Half-year

and the Recovery Period is:

If the Recovery Year Is:	3-year	5-year	7-year	10-year	15-year	20-year
			the Depreciation Rate is:			
1	33.33	20.00	14.29	10.00	5.00	3.750
2	44.45	32.00	24.49	18.00	9.50	7.219
3	14.81	19.20	17.49	14.40	8.55	6.677
4	7.41	11.52	12.49	11.52	7.70	6.177
5		11.52	8.93	9.22	6.93	5.713
6		5.76	8.92	7.37	6.23	5.285
7			8.93	6.55	5.90	4.888
8			4.46	6.55	5.90	4.522
9				6.56	5.91	4.462
10				6.55	5.90	4.461
11				3.28	5.91	4.462
12					5.90	4.461
13					5.91	4.462
14					5.90	4.461
15					5.91	4.462
16					2.95	4.461
17						4.462

				and the Recovery Period is:		
					15-year	20-year
If the Recovery Year Is:	3-year	5-year	7-year	10-year		
				the Depreciation Rate is:		
18						4.461
19						4.462
20						4.461
21						2.231

Example 7-11: Acme Corp. buys an item in the five-year class for $10,000. Using the optional table above, Acme's deprecation deductions over six years are $2,000; $3,200; $1,920; $1,152; $1,152; and $576.

Q 7:19 What happens if there is a change in the use of property during the year that affects the property's allowable depreciation?

The IRS has issued regulations dealing with depreciation deductions for property when there is a change in the property's use. [Reg. § 1.168(i)-4] The changes in use include a conversion of personal use property to a business or income-producing use, or vice versa, or a change in use of depreciable property that results in a different recovery period, depreciation method, or both.

Conversion to business or income-producing use. When property is converted from personal use to business use (e.g., a taxpayer begins using a family car for business trips), the depreciation allowance for the year of change and any subsequent taxable year is determined as though the property were placed in service on the date the conversion occurs. Thus, the taxpayer may choose any applicable depreciation method, recovery period, and convention allowed by MACRS. The depreciable basis of the property for the year of change is the lesser of its fair market value or its adjusted depreciable basis at the time of the conversion.

Example 7-12: Nora Wilson purchased a house in 1985 that she occupied as her principal residence. In February 2008, Wilson ceases to occupy the house and converts it to residential rental property. At the time of the conversion to residential rental property, the house's fair market value (excluding land) is $130,000 and the adjusted depreciable basis attributable to the house (excluding land) is $150,000.

For tax purposes, Wilson is considered to have placed residential rental property in service in February 2008 with a depreciable basis of $130,000. Wilson depreciates the residential rental property by using the straight-line method, a 27.5-year recovery period, and the mid-month convention. Thus, the depreciation allowance for the house for 2008 is $4,137, after taking into account the mid-month convention ($130,000 adjusted depreciable basis multiplied by the applicable depreciation rate of 3.636 percent (1/27.5) multiplied by the mid-month convention fraction (10.5/12)).

Conversion to personal use. Under the IRS regulations, the conversion of MACRS property from business or income-producing use to personal use during a taxable year is treated as a disposition of the property in that taxable year. [Reg. § 1.168(i)-4 (c)] The depreciation allowance for MACRS property for the year of change is determined by first multiplying the adjusted depreciable basis of the property as of the first day of the year of change by the applicable depreciation rate for that taxable year. This amount is then multiplied by a fraction, the numerator of which is the number of months (including fractions of months) the property is deemed to be placed in service during the year of change (taking into account the applicable convention) and the denominator of which is 12. No depreciation deduction is allowable for MACRS property placed in service and disposed of in the same taxable year.

Upon the conversion to personal use, no gain, loss, or depreciation recapture (e.g., IRC § 1245) is recognized. However, the recapture provisions will apply to any disposition of the converted property by the taxpayer at a later date.

Change in use after placed-in-service year. A property's recovery period and depreciation method is normally determined in the year the property is placed in service. However, certain changes in use in a subsequent year may require a change in recovery period and/or depreciation method. For example, a taxpayer may begin or cease using property predominantly outside of the United States (see Q 7:8).

If a change in the use of MACRS property has occurred, the depreciation allowance for the MACRS property for the year of change is determined as though the change in the use of the MACRS property occurred on the first day of the year of change. [Reg. § 1.168(i)-4(d)] The IRS believes that this rule will help to simplify the computation of depreciation allowances in the year of change and subsequent taxable years.

If a change in the use of MACRS property results in a shorter recovery period and/or a more accelerated depreciation method (e.g., for example, MACRS property ceases to be used predominantly outside the United States), the adjusted depreciable basis of the property as of the beginning of the year of change is written off over the shorter recovery period and/or by the more accelerated depreciation method as though the MACRS property were first placed in service in the year of change.

Under certain circumstances, this rule may adversely affect taxpayers. For example, under this rule, if a change in the use of MACRS property results in a shorter recovery period, a taxpayer must depreciate that MACRS property over the new shorter recovery period even if the remaining portion of the original longer recovery period is less than the new shorter recovery period. To avoid this adverse effect, the IRS regulations allow a taxpayer to elect to continue to depreciate the MACRS property for which the new recovery period is shorter or a more accelerated method is allowed as though the change in use had not occurred.

If a change in the use of MACRS property results in a longer recovery period and/or slower depreciation method, the adjusted depreciable basis of the property is depreciated over the longer recovery period and/or by the slower depreciation method as though the taxpayer originally placed the MACRS property in service with the longer recovery period and/or slower depreciation method. Accordingly, the adjusted depreciable basis of the MACRS property as of the beginning of the year of change is depreciated over the remaining portion of the new, longer recovery period as of the beginning of the year of change.

> **Example 7-13:** In January 2007, XYZ, a calendar-year corporation, placed in service equipment at a cost of $100,000 and uses this equipment in 2007 and 2008 only within the United States. XYZ depreciates the equipment for 2007 and 2008 by using the 200-percent declining balance method, a five-year recovery period, and a half-year convention. Beginning in 2009, XYZ uses the equipment predominantly outside the United States. As a result of this change in use, the equipment is subject to MACRS's alternative depreciation system beginning in 2009. Under the alternative depreciation system, the equipment is depreciated by using the straight-line method and a nine-year recovery period. The adjusted depreciable basis of the equipment at January 1, 2009, is $48,000.

XYZ's allowable depreciation deduction for 2009 and subsequent taxable years is determined as though the equipment had been placed in service in January 2007, as property used predominantly outside the United States. In determining the applicable depreciation rate for 2009, the depreciation method is the straight-line method and the recovery period is 7.5 years. This is the number of years remaining at January 1, 2009, for property placed in service in 2007 with a nine-year recovery period (taking into account the half-year convention).

Thus, the depreciation allowance for 2009 is $6,398 ($48,000 adjusted depreciable basis at January 1, 2009, multiplied by a depreciation rate of 13.33 percent (1/7.5)). The depreciation allowance for 2010 is $6,398 ($41,602 adjusted depreciable basis at January 1, 2010, multiplied by a depreciation rate of 15.38 percent (1/6.5 years remaining at January 1, 2010)).

Listed Property

Q 7:20 What is "listed" property?

The Code imposes limits on depreciation deductions for certain types of "listed" property because the property is often used for both business and personal purposes. Listed property includes:

- Any passenger automobile;
- Any other type of vehicle unless it is of a type that is likely to have little or no personal use;

- Any property of a type generally used for entertainment, recreation, or amusement (including photographic, phonographic, communication, and video-recording equipment); and

- Any computer and related peripheral equipment, unless it is used only at a regular business establishment and is owned or leased by the owner of the establishment; and

- Any cellular telephone (or similar telecommunication equipment).

[IRC § 280F(d)]

Q 7:21 What special rules apply to listed property?

Deductions for listed property are subject to the following limitations:

- If an employee's use of the property is not for his or her employer's convenience or is not required as a condition of employment, the employee cannot deduct depreciation for the use of the property. [IRC § 280F(d)(3)]

- If the property is not used predominantly in business, the owner must figure MACRS deductions using the straight-line method over the ADS recovery period. [IRC § 280F(b)(1)](If the property is not used predominantly in business, the Section 179 expensing deduction is also not available; see below.)

- Annual dollar limits apply to depreciation deductions for passenger automobiles. [IRC § 280F(a)]

Q 7:22 When is listed property used "predominantly" in business?

For the listed property limitation, property is considered used predominantly in business if the "qualified" business use (see below) of the property exceeds 50 percent. If the qualified business use does not exceed 50 percent in the year the property is placed in service, then for that year and all subsequent years, the property must be depreciated using straight-line depreciation and the ADS recovery period. If the property's qualified business use initially exceeds 50 percent, but drops to 50 percent or less in a subsequent year, then depreciation must be computed from that point on as if the property had initially been depreciated using the straight-line method and the ADS recovery period. [Temp. Reg. § 1.280F-3T(c)]

While the depreciation rate and recovery period depends on the amount of qualified business use, the amount of the property's basis that can be depreciated depends on the "business/investment" use (see below).

Q 7:23 How is the use of listed property allocated between qualified business use and other uses?

For passenger automobiles and other means of transportation, the property's use is allocated on the basis of mileage. A taxpayer determines the percentage of qualified business use by dividing the number of miles he or she drove the vehicle for business purposes during the year by the total number of miles driven for all purposes (including business miles) during the year. [Temp. Reg. § 1.280F-6T(e)(2)]

For other items of listed property, the property's use should be allocated on the basis of the most appropriate unit of time. For example, taxpayers can determine the percentage of business use of a computer by dividing the number of hours the computer is used for qualified business purposes during the year by the total number of hours the computer is used for all purposes. [Temp. Reg. § 1.280F-6T(e)(3)]

Q 7:24 What is considered qualified business use?

Qualified business use of listed property is any use of the property in the taxpayer's trade or business. However, it does not include the following uses:

- The leasing of property to any 5 percent owner (or related person) to the extent it is used by the 5 percent owner (or related person);
- The use of property for personal reasons by a 5 percent owner (or related person), even if the use is reported as taxable compensation and income tax is withheld;
- The use of property for personal reasons by a non-5 percent owner but only if the value of the use is treated as taxable compensation and income tax is withheld.

[Temp. Reg. § 1.280F-6T(d)(2)]

Generally, a 5 percent owner is any person who owns more than 5 percent of the capital or profits interest in the business. A 5 percent owner of a corporation is any person who owns, or is considered to own, either of the following.

- More than 5 percent of the outstanding stock of the corporation; or
- Stock possessing more than 5 percent of the total combined voting power of all stock in the corporation.

Example 7-14: John Maple is the sole proprietor of a plumbing contracting business. John employs his brother, Richard, in the business. As part of Richard's compensation, he is allowed to use one of the company automobiles for personal use. The company includes the value of the personal use of the automobile in Richard's gross income and properly withholds tax on it. Because the use of the automobile is compensation by a related person, it is not a qualified business use.

Example 7-15: XYZ Inc. owns several automobiles that its employees use for business purposes. The employees are also allowed to take the automobiles home at night. The fair market value of each employee's use of an automobile for any personal purpose, such as commuting to and from work, is reported as income to the employee, and XYZ withholds tax on it. This use of company automobiles by employees, even for personal purposes, is a qualified business use for the company.

Q 7:25 What is "business/investment" use?

Once taxpayers determine their qualified business use of property, they must determine their business/investment use to figure what portion of their costs for listed property is depreciable. For this purpose, the use of property to produce income in a nonbusiness activity (investment use) is added to business use to compute the MACRS deduction in a given year. [Temp. Reg. § 1.280F-6T(d)(3)]

> **Example 7-16:** Sarah Bradley uses a home computer 50 percent of the time to manage her investments. She also uses the computer 40 percent of the time in her part-time consumer research business. Because she does not use the computer predominantly for qualified business use, she must depreciate it using the straight-line method over the ADS recovery period.

Bradley's combined rate of business/investment use for determining her depreciation deduction is 90 percent. So, for example, if her computer costs $3,000, $2,700 of the cost can be recovered through depreciation.

> **Example 7-17:** If Sarah uses her computer 30 percent of the time to manage her investments and 60 percent of the time in her consumer research business, it is used predominantly for qualified business use. She can depreciate the computer over the GDS recovery period. However, her combined business/investment use for determining her depreciation deduction remains at 90 percent.

Q 7:26 What happens if the qualified business use of listed property drops to 50 percent or less after the first year of use?

If the taxpayer meets the 50 percent requirement in the first year of use and fails to meet it in a subsequent year, the taxpayer must begin using straight-line depreciation over the ADS recovery period. In addition, the taxpayer must include in income in that year the "excess depreciation" claimed in the prior year(s). [Temp. Reg. § 1.280F-3T(d)]Excess depreciation is (1) the amount of depreciation actually claimed during the prior year(s), less the amount of depreciation that would have been allowed using straight-line depreciation under ADS.

> **Example 7-18:** Jim Pearson, a sole proprietor, bought a $10,000 computer. During the first year, he used it 60 percent of the time for business purposes and 40 percent for personal purposes. Using regular MACRS with the half-year convention, he claimed a depreciation deduction of $1,200. With ADS, his straight-line deduction would have been $600. If Pearson's business use falls to 50 percent or less the following year, he must include $600 ($1,200 less $600) in income.

Q 7:27 For purposes of the listed property rules, what is a "passenger automobile"?

A passenger automobile is any four-wheeled vehicle made primarily for use on public streets, roads, and highways and rated at 6,000 pounds or less of unloaded gross vehicle weight (6,000 pounds or less of gross vehicle weight for trucks and vans). It includes any part, component, or other item physically attached to the automobile or usually included in the purchase price of an automobile. Excluded from the definition of passenger automobiles are ambulances; hearses, or a combination ambulance-hearse used directly in a trade or business; and vehicles used directly in the trade or business of transporting persons or property for pay or hire. [Temp. Reg. § 1.280F-6T(c)]

Certain "nonpersonal use" trucks and vans are excluded from the definition of passenger automobiles. [Reg. § 1.280F-6T]These are trucks or vans that have been specially modified so that they are not likely to be used more than a *de minimis* amount for personal purposes.

For example, a van that has only a front bench for seating, in which permanent shelving filling most of the cargo area has been installed, that constantly carries merchandise or equipment, and that has been specially painted with advertising or the company's name, would qualify as a nonpersonal use vehicle.

Q 7:28 What other vehicles are subject to the listed property rules?

In addition to "passenger automobiles," the listed property rules also generally apply to other property used for transporting people or goods (e.g., trucks, buses, airplanes). However the rules do not cover "qualified non-personal-use vehicles." These are vehicles that, by reason of their nature (i.e., design), are not likely to be used more than minimally for personal purposes. [Temp. Reg. § 1.274-5T(k)] These include such vehicles as ambulances and hearses, any vehicle with a loaded gross vehicle weight of over 14,000 pounds that is designed to carry cargo, bucket trucks (cherry pickers), cement mixers, dump trucks (including garbage trucks), flatbed trucks, refrigerated trucks, combines, cranes and derricks, forklifts, qualified moving vans, specialized utility repair trucks, and tractors.

Q 7:29 Is there a special limitation on employees who claim depreciation deductions for listed property?

Yes. If a taxpayer uses listed property in his or her job, no deduction is allowed for depreciation, unless the use is for the employer's convenience and is required as a condition of employment. [Temp. Reg. § 1.280F-6T(a)] Failure to meet these requirements also bars rent deductions for listed property leased by employees.

Employer's convenience. Whether the use of listed property is for the employer's convenience must be determined from all the facts. The use is for the

Q 7:27

employer's convenience if it is for a substantial business reason of the employer. The use of listed property during regular working hours to carry on the employer's business is generally for the employer's convenience.

Condition of employment. The use of property must be required for the employee to perform his or her duties properly. The employer does not have to explicitly require the employee to use the property. However, a mere statement by the employer that the use of the property is a condition of employment is not sufficient.

> **Example 7-19:** Virginia Johnson employed as a courier with We Deliver, which provides local courier services. She owns and uses a motorcycle to deliver packages to downtown offices. We Deliver explicitly requires all delivery persons to own a car or motorcycle for use in their employment. Virginia's use of the motorcycle is for the convenience of We Deliver and is required as a condition of employment.

> **Example 7-20:** Bill Nelson is an inspector for Uplift, a construction company with many sites in the local area. He must travel to these sites on a regular basis. Uplift does not furnish an automobile or explicitly require him to use his own automobile. However, it pays him for any costs he incurs in traveling to the various sites. The use of his own automobile is for the convenience of Uplift and is required as a condition of employment.

> **Example 7-21:** Assume the same facts as in Example 7-20 except that Uplift furnishes a car to Bill, who chooses to use his own car and receive payment for using it. The use of his own car is neither for the convenience of Uplift nor required as a condition of employment.

> **Example 7-22:** Marilyn Lee is a pilot for Horizon Company, a small charter airline. Horizon requires pilots to obtain 80 hours of flight time annually in addition to flight time spent with the airline. Pilots can usually obtain these hours by flying with the Air Force Reserve or by flying part-time with another airline. Marilyn owns her own airplane. The use of her airplane to obtain the required flight hours is neither for the convenience of the employer nor required as a condition of employment.

Q 7:30 Does the Code impose dollar limits on depreciation deductions for passenger automobiles?

Yes. The depreciation deduction (including any Section 179 expensing deduction; see below) that can be claimed for a passenger automobile each year is limited. [IRC § 280F(a)] These limits are adjusted for inflation.

The limits are different for trucks and vans than for other passenger autos. That's because, beginning in 2003, the inflation adjustment for trucks and vans has been computed using a different price index component. This results in a somewhat more generous depreciation limit for trucks and vans because they are subject to a higher rate of price inflation. For this purpose, the term "trucks and vans" refers to passenger automobiles that are built on a truck chassis, including minivans and sport utility vehicles (SUVs) that are built on a truck chassis.

For "passenger automobiles" (other than trucks and vans) placed in service in calendar year 2007, the dollar amounts of the depreciation limitations are:

- $3,060 for the first tax year;
- $4,900 for the second tax year;
- $2,850 for the third tax year; and
- $1,775 for each succeeding tax year.

The depreciation caps for trucks and vans (and SUVs but only if built on a truck chassis) placed in service in 2007 are:

- $3,260 for the first year;
- $5,200 for the second year;
- $3,050 for the third year; and,
- $1,875 for the fourth year.

Because of the dollar limits, many cars cannot be fully written off by the end of their normal recovery period. Any unrecovered basis at the end of the business auto's normal recovery period is carried over and depreciated, subject to the applicable annual limitation, in the years after the normal period until the earlier of the time that the auto is fully depreciated or is disposed of. [Temp. Reg. § 1.280F-2T(c)]

Q 7:31 Do the same dollar limits for passenger automobile depreciation apply if an automobile is used partially for personal purposes?

No. The dollar limits stated above apply only if the automobile is used 100 percent for business driving. If the business use is less than 100 percent, the dollar limits are proportionally reduced. [Temp. Reg. § 280F-2T(i)]

> **Example 7-23:** Karen Taylor, a self-employed business owner, buys an automobile in July 2007 for $25,000. During the remainder of 2007, 80 percent of her automobile use is connected with her business, and 20 percent is personal. On her 2007 return, Taylor's depreciation deduction is limited to 80 percent of $2.960—or $2,368.

Q 7:32 Do the depreciation limits also apply to deductions for lease payments on leased automobiles?

No. Instead, the Code limits the lease payment deductions by requiring lessees to include in income an annual "inclusion" amount that offsets, and thus reduces, the tax savings from the deduction for lease payments. [IRC § 280F(c)] The inclusion amount is computed using a table issued annually by the IRS. Here is the table for automobiles (other than trucks and vans) and the table for trucks and vans placed in service in 2007.

Dollar Amounts for Passenger Automobiles (that Are Not Trucks, Vans) with a Lease Term Beginning in Calendar Year 2007

Fair Market Value of Passenger Automobile		Tax Year During Lease				
Over	Not Over	1st	2nd	3rd	4th	5th & Later
15,500	15,800	2	5	11	11	13
15,800	16,100	4	10	17	19	22
16,100	16,400	6	14	24	28	31
16,400	16,700	9	18	31	35	41
16,700	17,000	11	23	37	43	50
17,000	17,500	13	29	46	54	62
17,500	18,000	17	37	56	68	77
18,000	18,500	20	44	68	81	93
18,500	19,000	24	51	80	94	108
19,000	19,500	27	59	90	108	124
19,500	20,000	30	67	101	121	139
20,000	20,500	34	74	113	134	154
20,500	21,000	37	82	123	148	170
21,000	21,500	41	89	135	161	185
21,500	22,000	44	97	146	174	201
21,500	22,000	44	97	146	174	201
22,000	23,000	49	108	163	194	224
23,000	24,000	56	123	185	221	255
24,000	25,000	63	138	207	248	285
25,000	26,000	70	153	229	275	316
26,000	27,000	77	168	251	302	347
27,000	28,000	83	183	274	328	378
28,000	29,000	90	198	296	355	409
29,000	30,000	97	213	318	382	439
30,000	31,000	104	228	341	408	470
31,000	32,000	111	243	363	435	501
32,000	33,000	118	258	385	461	532
33,000	34,000	125	273	407	488	563
34,000	35,000	131	288	430	515	593
35,000	36,000	138	303	452	542	624
36,000	37,000	145	318	474	568	656
37,000	38,000	152	333	496	595	686
38,000	39,000	159	348	519	621	717
39,000	40,000	166	363	541	648	748

Fair Market Value of Passenger Automobile		Tax Year During Lease				
Over	Not Over	1st	2nd	3rd	4th	5th & Later
40,000	41,000	172	378	564	674	779
41,000	42,000	179	393	586	701	810
42,000	43,000	186	408	608	728	840
43,000	44,000	193	423	630	755	871
44,000	45,000	200	438	652	782	902
45,000	46,000	207	453	674	809	933
46,000	47,000	213	468	697	835	964
47,000	48,000	220	483	719	862	995
48,000	49,000	227	498	742	888	1,025
49,000	50,000	234	513	764	915	1,056
50,000	51,000	241	528	786	942	1,087
51,000	52,000	248	543	808	969	1,117
52,000	53,000	254	558	831	995	1,148
53,000	54,000	261	573	853	1,022	1,179
54,000	55,000	268	588	875	1,049	1,210
55,000	56,000	275	603	897	1,076	1,241
56,000	57,000	282	618	920	1,102	1,271
57,000	58,000	289	633	942	1,128	1,303
58,000	59,000	296	648	964	1,155	1,334
59,000	60,000	302	663	987	1,182	1,364
60,000	62,000	313	685	1,020	1,222	1,411
62,000	64,000	326	716	1,064	1,276	1,472
64,000	66,000	340	746	1,108	1,329	1,534
66,000	68,000	354	775	1,154	1,382	1,595
68,000	70,000	367	806	1,198	1,435	1,657
70,000	72,000	381	836	1,242	1,489	1,719
72,000	74,000	395	865	1,287	1,543	1,780
74,000	76,000	408	896	1,331	1,596	1,842
76,000	78,000	422	926	1,376	1,649	1,903
78,000	80,000	436	955	1,421	1,703	1,965
80,000	85,000	460	1,008	1,498	1,796	2,074
85,000	90,000	494	1,083	1,610	1,929	2,228
90,000	95,000	528	1,158	1,721	2,063	2,382
95,000	100,000	562	1,233	1,833	2,196	2,536
100,000	110,000	614	1,346	1,999	2,396	2,767
110,000	120,000	682	1,496	2,222	2,663	3,075

Q 7:32

Fair Market Value of Passenger Automobile		Tax Year During Lease				
Over	Not Over	1st	2nd	3rd	4th	5th & Later
120,000	130,000	750	1,646	2,444	2,931	3,383
130,000	140,000	819	1,796	2,667	3,197	3,692
140,000	150,000	887	1,946	2,890	3,464	4,000
150,000	160,000	956	2,096	3,122	3,731	4,308
160,000	170,000	1,024	2,246	3,335	3,998	4,616
170,000	180,000	1,093	2,396	3,557	4,266	4,924
180,000	190,000	1,161	2,546	3,780	4,532	5,233
190,000	200,000	1,229	2,696	4,003	4,799	5,541
200,000	2110,000	1,298	2,846	4,225	5,067	5,848
210,000	220,000	1,366	2,996	4,448	5,333	6,157
220,000	230,000	1,435	3,146	4,671	5,600	6,465
230,000	240,000	1,503	3,296	4,893	5,867	6,774
240,000	and up	1,571	3,446	5,116	6,134	7,082

Dollar Amounts for Trucks and Vans with a Lease Term Beginning in Calendar Year 2007

Fair Market Value of Truck or Van		Tax Year During Lease				
Over	Not Over	1st	2nd	3rd	4th	5th & Later
$16,400	$16,700	2	4	8	10	11
16,700	17,000	4	9	15	17	21
17,000	17,500	6	15	24	28	33
17,500	18,000	10	22	35	42	48
18,000	18,500	13	30	46	55	64
18,500	19,000	17	37	57	69	79
19,000	19,500	20	45	68	82	94
19,500	20,000	24	52	80	95	109
20,000	20,500	27	60	90	109	125
20,500	21,000	30	67	102	122	141
21,000	21,500	34	75	113	135	156
21,500	22,000	37	82	124	149	171
22,000	23,000	42	94	140	169	194
23,000	24,000	49	109	163	195	225
24,000	25,000	56	123	186	222	256
25,000	26,000	63	138	208	249	286

Fair Market Value of Truck or Van		Tax Year During Lease				
Over	Not Over	1st	2nd	3rd	4th	5th & Later
26,000	27,000	70	153	230	276	317
27,000	28,000	77	168	252	302	349
28,000	29,000	83	184	274	329	379
29,000	30,000	90	199	296	356	410
30,000	31,000	97	214	318	383	440
31,000	32,000	104	228	342	408	472
32,000	33,000	111	243	364	435	503
33,000	34,000	118	258	386	462	534
34,000	35,000	125	273	408	489	564
35,000	36,000	131	289	430	515	595
36,000	37,000	138	304	452	542	626
37,000	38,000	145	318	475	569	657
38,000	39,000	152	333	497	596	688
39,000	40,000	159	348	520	622	718
40,000	41,000	166	363	542	649	749
41,000	42,000	172	379	563	676	780
42,000	43,000	179	394	586	702	811
43,000	44,000	186	409	608	729	842
44,000	45,000	193	423	631	756	872
45,000	46,000	200	438	653	783	903
46,000	47,000	207	453	675	810	934
47,000	48,000	213	469	697	836	965
48,000	49,000	220	484	719	863	996
49,000	50,000	227	499	741	890	1,026
50,000	51,000	234	514	764	916	1,057
51,000	52,000	241	528	787	943	1,088
52,000	53,000	248	543	809	969	1,119
53,000	54,000	254	559	831	996	1,150
54,000	55,000	261	574	853	1,023	1,180
55,000	56,000	268	589	875	1,050	1,211
56,000	57,000	275	604	897	1,076	1,243
57,000	58,000	282	618	920	1,103	1,273
58,000	59,000	289	633	943	1,129	1,304
59,000	60,000	296	648	965	1,156	1,335
60,000	62,000	306	671	998	1,196	1,381
62,000	64,000	319	701	1,043	1,249	1,443

Fair Market Value of Truck or Van		Tax Year During Lease				
Over	Not Over	1st	2nd	3rd	4th	5th & Later
64,000	66,000	333	731	1,087	1,303	1,504
66,000	68,000	347	761	1,131	1,357	1,566
68,000	70,000	361	791	1,176	1,410	1,627
70,000	72,000	374	821	1,221	1,463	1,689
72,000	74,000	388	851	1,265	1,517	1,751
74,000	76,000	402	881	1,309	1,570	1,813
76,000	78,000	415	911	1,354	1,624	1,874
78,000	80,000	429	941	1,399	1,676	1,936
80,000	85,000	453	994	1,476	1,770	2,044
85,000	90,000	487	1,069	1,587	1,904	2,198
90,000	95,000	521	1,144	1,699	2,037	2,352
95,000	100,000	555	1,219	1,810	2,171	2,506
100,000	110,000	607	1,331	1,977	2,371	2,737
110,000	120,000	675	1,481	2,200	2,638	3,045
120,000	130,000	744	1,631	2,423	2,904	3,354
130,000	140,000	812	1,781	2,646	3,171	3,662
140,000	150,000	880	1,932	2,867	3,439	3,970
150,000	160,000	949	2,081	3,091	3,705	4,279
160,000	170,000	1,017	2,232	3,313	3,972	4,586
170,000	180,000	1,086	2,381	3,536	4,239	4,895
180,000	190,000	1,154	2,532	3,758	4,506	5,203
190,000	200,000	1,222	2,682	3,981	4,773	5,511
200,000	210,000	1,291	2,831	4,204	5,040	5,820
210,000	220,000	1,359	2,982	4,426	5,307	6,128
220,000	230,000	1,428	3,131	4,649	5,575	6,435
230,000	240,000	1,496	3,282	4,871	5,841	6,744
240,000	and up	1,565	3,431	5,095	6,108	7,052

How the lease table works. A taxpayer who leases a car for business driving uses a four-step process to figure the income inclusion amount for any given tax year of the lease:

Step 1—Find the fair-market value of the leased car on the first day of the lease in the first column.

Step 2—Go to the right of the appropriate column for the tax year of the lease. If a taxpayer leases a car in 2007, he or she would use the inclusion amount for the first tax year of the lease, and so on. For the fifth year and later years, the inclusion amount remains the same.

Step 3—Prorate the inclusion amount from the table by the number of days of the lease term included in the tax year. For example, if a taxpayer leases a car for 180 days in 2007, the inclusion amount will be only 49 percent (180/365) of the amount found in the column for the first tax year of the lease.

Step 4—If the leased car is not used exclusively for business (or investment) purposes, multiply the result in Step 3 by the percentage of business (and investment) use. There is no need to include any amount related to personal driving in income because the personal use portions of the lease payments are nondeductible.

The lease tables apply to cars that are leased by an employer for its employees. However, companies generally do not have to worry about Step 4. Employers can deduct 100 percent of their lease payments regardless of the mix of personal and business use. Personal use is treated as compensation to the employee. Because the company can claim a full deduction for its lease payments, it must report the entire inclusion amount as income.

Section 179 Expensing Deduction

Q 7:33 What is the Section 179 expensing deduction?

Section 179 of the Code is an elective provision that allows taxpayers to currently deduct (expense) certain property that would otherwise have to be written off over a period of years under MACRS. There is a ceiling on the amount of property that can be expensed in a tax year. In addition, the Section 179 election is not available to taxpayers who make substantial investments in depreciable property during the year, thus limiting the benefits of Section 179 mainly to small businesses.

Q 7:34 What property is eligible for the Section 179 election?

To qualify for the Section 179 deduction, the property must be eligible property acquired by purchase for use in the active conduct of a trade or business. [IRC § 179(d)(1)] Eligible property includes:

- Tangible personal property;
- Other tangible property (except buildings and their structural components) used as: (1) an integral part of manufacturing, production, or extraction or of furnishing transportation, communications, electricity, gas, water, or sewage disposal services, (2) a research facility used in connection with any of the activities in (1), or (3) a facility used in connection with any of the activities in (3) for the bulk storage of fungible commodities;
- Single-purpose agricultural (livestock) or horticultural structures; and

Q 7:33

- Storage facilities (except buildings and their structural components) used in connection with distributing petroleum or any primary product of petroleum. [IRC § 1245(a)(3)]

Tangible personal property is any tangible property that is not real property. Thus, it includes:

- Machinery and equipment;
- Property contained in or attached to a building (other than structural components), such as refrigerators, grocery store counters, office equipment, printing presses, testing equipment, and signs;
- Gasoline storage tanks and pumps at retail service stations; and
- Livestock, including horses, cattle, hogs, sheep, goats, and mink and other fur-bearing animals.

Land and land improvements, such as buildings and other permanent structures and their components, are real property, not personal property. Land improvements include swimming pools, paved parking areas, wharves, docks, bridges, and fences.

For purposes of the Section 179 election, a single-purpose agricultural (livestock) structure is any building or enclosure specifically designed, constructed, and used for both the following reasons:

- To house, raise, and feed a particular type of livestock and their produce; and
- To house the equipment, including any replacements, needed to house, raise, or feed the livestock

A single-purpose horticultural structure is either:

- A greenhouse specifically designed, constructed, and used for the commercial production of plants, or
- A structure specifically designed, constructed, and used for the commercial production of mushrooms.

[IRC § 168(i)(13)]

Property acquired for business use. To qualify for the Section 179 deduction, the property must have been acquired for use in a trade or business. Property acquired only for the production of income, such as investment property, rental property (if renting property is not the taxpayer's trade or business), and property that produces royalties, does not qualify. [Reg. § 1.179-4]

If the property is used for both business and nonbusiness purposes, a taxpayer can elect the expensing deduction only if the property is used more than 50 percent for business in the year it is placed in service. Even then, the expensing deduction is allowed only for the portion of the cost allocable to the business use. [Reg. § 1.179-1(d)]

Example 7-24: Johnny Jones bought and placed in service an item of eligible property costing $10,000. He used the property 80 percent for his business and 20 percent for personal purposes. The business part of the cost of the property is $8,000 (80 percent × $10,000). Thus, only $8,000 may be expensed. If Jones used the property, say, 40 percent for business, then no portion of the cost could be expensed.

Acquired by purchase. Eligible property can be expensed only if it has been acquired by purchase. For example, property acquired by gift or inheritance does not qualify. Property is not considered acquired by purchase if it is acquired in a tax-free exchange of like kind property or if it is purchased from a related party. [IRC § 179(d)(2)]

> **Example 7-25:** Karen Larch bought two industrial sewing machines from her father for use in her business. She placed both machines in service in the same year she bought them. They do not qualify as Section 179 property because Karen and her father are related persons. She cannot claim a Section 179 deduction for the cost of these machines. Instead, she must recover her costs through MACRS depreciation.

Excepted property. Even if all of the requirements outlined above are met, certain types of property are ineligible for the expensing deduction. These include property used predominantly to furnish lodging, air conditioning, or heating units, and property used predominately outside of the United States. [IRC § 50(b)]

Computer software. Prior to the Jobs and Growth Tax Relief Reconciliation Act of 2003 (JGTRRA), off-the-shelf software was not eligible for the Section 179 allowance. The Section 179 allowance was available for tangible property, and computer software is considered intangible property. However, JGTRRA makes computer software eligible for the Section 179 allowance if it (1) is not acquired as part of the purchase of a business (i.e., is not subject to the amortization rules of Section 197), (2) is readily available for purchase by the general public, (3) is subject to a nonexclusive license, and (4) has not been substantially modified. The JGTRRA change was originally scheduled to expire at the end of 2005, but was extended through 2007 by the American Jobs Creation Act of 2004. [P.L. 108-357 (October 22, 2004)], through 2009 by the Tax Increase Prevention and Reconciliation Act of 2005 (P.L. 109-222) and through 2010 by the Small Business and Work Opportunity Tax Act of 2007 (P.L. 110-28).

Q 7:35 How much can be expensed under Section 179?

A taxpayer's Section 179 deduction is generally the cost of the qualifying property. However, the total amount that can be expensed by any taxpayer is subject to both a dollar limit and a business income limit. These limits generally apply to each taxpayer, not to each business.

Q 7:36 What is the dollar limit for the Section 179 expensing deduction?

Prior to the enactment of the Small Business and Work Opportunity Tax Act of 2007 (P.L. 110-28), the total amount that could be expensed in any one year was limited to $100,000, adjusted annually for inflation. The Small Business and Work Opportunity Tax Act increased the expensing limitation from $100,000 to $125,000, effective for property placed in service after 2006 and before 2011. [IRC § 179(b)(1)]. The $125,000 limit will be adjusted for inflation in tax years beginning after December 31, 2007. For 2008, the adjusted limit is $128,000. [Rev. Proc. 2007-66, I.R.B. 2007-45]

> **Example 7-26:** In 2007, Acme Inc. bought and placed in service $120,000 of road-building material and $10,000 of hand tools. It elected to expense $115,000 of the road-building machinery and the entire $10,000 of the hand tools. This is the maximum amount it can deduct under Section 179. The $10,000 deduction for the hand tools completely recovered their cost. The basis for MACRS depreciation is zero. The basis for MACRS depreciation of the road-building machinery is $5,000. This is the difference between the $120,000 cost and the $115,000 expensing deduction.

> **Planning Point:** If the amount of eligible property placed in service during the year exceeds the dollar limit, the taxpayer will have to select which items will be expensed. In that case, the taxpayer will generally want to opt for the items with the longest MACRS recovery periods. The benefit of an immediate deduction is greater for those items that would otherwise be written off over long recovery periods.

Q 7:37 Is the Section 179 dollar limit the same for all taxpayers?

No. If a taxpayer invests in too much Section 179 property during the year, the maximum expensing deduction is reduced. [IRC § 179(b)(2)] Prior to the enactment of the Small Business and Work Opportunity Tax Act of 2007 (P.L. 110-28), this investment limitation was $400,000, adjusted annually for inflation. The Small Business and Work Opportunity Tax Act increased the investment limitation phase-out amount from $400,000 to $500,000 effective for property placed in service after 2006 and before 2011. The $500,000 limit will be adjusted for inflation in tax years beginning after December 31, 2007. For 2008, the adjusted investment limitation is $510,000. [Rev. Proc. 2007-66, I.R.B. 2007-45]

If the cost of eligible Section 179 property placed in service in a year is more than $500,000 (adjusted for inflation), the maximum expensing deduction is reduced by the amount of the cost in excess of $500,000. Thus, if a taxpayer put more than $625,000 of Section 179-type property into service in 2007 ($500,000 plus $125,000), the taxpayer cannot qualify for a Section 179 deduction.

Married couples. Couples filing a joint return are treated as one taxpayer in determining any reduction to the dollar limit, regardless of which spouse purchased the property or placed it in service. If a couple files separate returns, they are also treated as one taxpayer for the dollar limit, including the phaseout for annual investments over $500,000. However, separate filers must allocate the dollar limit (after any reduction) between themselves. They must allocate 50 percent to each spouse, unless they both elect a different allocation. [IRC § 179(b)(4)]

Example 7-27: Jack and Doris Elm are married. Jack and Doris file separate returns. Jack bought and placed in service $500,000 of qualified farm machinery in 2007. Doris has her own business, and she bought and placed in service $35,000 of qualified business equipment. Their combined Section 179 dollar limit is $90,000 because they must figure the limit as if they were one taxpayer. They reduce the $125,000 dollar limit for 2007 by the $35,000 excess of their costs over $500,000.

The Elms elect to allocate the $90,000 dollar limit and give two-thirds ($60,000) to Jack and one-third ($30,000) to Doris. If they did not make an election to allocate their costs in this way, they would each be limited to $45,000 ($90,000 × 50 percent).

Q 7:38 What is the business income limit for purposes of Section 179?

The total cost that can be expensed (after applying the dollar limit) cannot exceed the taxpayer's taxable income from the active conduct of any trade or business during the year. [IRC § 179(b)(3)] A taxpayer is generally considered to actively conduct a trade or business if the taxpayer meaningfully participates in the management or operations of the trade or business.

For purposes of figuring the income limit, taxable income is computed without regard to the Section 179 deduction, the self-employment tax deduction, any net operating loss carryback or carryfoward, and any unreimbursed employee business expenses.

Carryover of disallowed deduction. A taxpayer can carry over the cost of any expensed property that was not deductible because of the business income limit. [IRC § 179(b)(3)(b)] The excess expensing deduction can be claimed in the following year (assuming the taxpayer has sufficient business income).

Q 7:39 How are the Section 179 limits applied to partnerships and partners?

The Section 179 deduction limits apply both to the partnership and to each partner. [IRC § 179(d)(8)] The partnership determines its Section 179 deduction subject to the limits. It then allocates the deduction among its partners.

Each partner adds the amount allocated from partnerships to his or her nonpartnership Section 179 costs and then applies the dollar limit to this total. To determine any reduction in the dollar limit for costs over $400,000, the partner does not include any of the cost of Section 179 property placed in service by the partnership. After the dollar limit (and any reduction in the dollar limit due to nonpartnership Section 179 costs) is applied, any remaining cost of the partnership and nonpartnership Section 179 property is subject to the business income limit.

Example 7-28: In 2007, ABC Partnership placed in service Section 179 property with a total cost of $514,000. The partnership must reduce its dollar limit by $14,000 ($514,000 - $500,000). Its maximum Section 179 deduction is

$111,000 for 2007, and it elects to expense that amount. Because the partnership's taxable income from the active conduct of all its trades or businesses for the year was $150,000, it can deduct the full $111,000. It allocates $37,000 of its Section 179 deduction and $50,000 of its taxable income to Bill Dean, one of its partners.

In addition to being a partner in ABC Partnership, Dean is also a partner in the XYZ Partnership, which allocated to him a $24,000 Section 179 deduction and $36,000 taxable income from the active conduct of its business. Dean also conducts a business as a sole proprietor and, in 2007, placed in service in that business Section 179 property costing $30,000. He had a net loss of $6,000 from that business for the year.

Because Dean does not have to include partnership costs to figure any reduction in his dollar limit, his total Section 179 costs for the year are not more than $500,000, and his dollar limit is not reduced. His maximum expensing deduction is $125,000. He elects to expense $91,000—all of the $61,000 in Section 179 deductions allocated from the partnerships, plus $30,000 of his sole proprietorship's Section 179 costs. However, his deduction is limited to his business taxable income of $80,000 ($50,000 from ABC Partnership, plus $36,000 from XYZ Partnership minus $6,000 loss from his sole proprietorship).

Dean carries over $11,000 ($91,000 - $80,000) of the elected Section 179 costs to 2008.

Q 7:40 How are the Section 179 limits applied to S corporations and their shareholders?

Generally, the rules that apply to a partnership and its partners (see above) also apply to an S corporation and its shareholders. The deduction limits apply to an S corporation and to each shareholder. The S corporation allocates its deduction to the shareholders who then take their Section 179 deduction subject to the limits.

Q 7:41 What happens if business use drops to 50 percent or less in a year after the year property is expensed under Section 179?

A taxpayer may have to recapture the Section 179 deduction if, in any year during the property's recovery period, the percentage of business use drops to 50 percent or less. [IRC § 179(d)(10)] In the year the business use drops to 50 percent or less, the taxpayer includes the recapture amount as income and the basis of the property is increased by the recapture amount.

To figure the amount to recapture, take the following steps:

1. Figure the MACRS depreciation that would have been allowable on the Section 179 deduction claimed. Begin with the year the property was placed in service and include the year of the recapture.

2. Subtract the depreciation figured in (1) from the Section 179 deduction that was claimed. The result is the recapture amount.

Example 7-29: In 2005, Jean Lowell bought and placed in service Section 179 property costing $10,000. She elected a $5,000 Section 179 deduction for the property. Lowell used the property only for business in 2005 and 2006. In 2007, she used the property 40 percent for business and 60 percent for personal use.

Under MACRS, her deductions would have been $1,666.50 for 2005, $2,222.50 for 2006, and $296.20 (based on a 40 percent business use) for 2007—a total of $4,185.20. Since Lowell expensed $5,000, her recapture amount for 2007 is $814.80.

Chapter 8

Travel and Entertainment

Like other business expenses, travel and entertainment costs are deductible only if they are "ordinary and necessary." Forty years ago, however, Congress perceived a potential for abuse with travel and entertainment expenses and enacted a special set of rules governing these deductions. Over the years, these rules have been expanded and modified several times.

These rules limit the type and amount of expenses that can be deducted. They also impose special substantiation requirements on business-connected travel and entertainment that makes these expenses particularly susceptible to challenge by the Internal Revenue Service (IRS or the Service).

Travel Expenses

Q 8:1 For tax purposes, what's the difference between travel expenses and transportation expenses?

Local transportation expenses are the direct cost of going from one place to another. This typically involves an automobile, but also covers transportation by buses, taxis, and trains. A taxpayer can deduct transportation costs if they are ordinary and necessary expenses incurred in connection with a trade or business or for the production of income. [IRC § 162]

To be deductible, travel expenses must also satisfy an additional requirement—they must be incurred while a taxpayer is "away from home." [IRC § 162(a)(2)]

Travel expenses cover:

- Air, rail, and bus fares;
- The cost of operating and maintaining a car or an airplane;
- Taxi fares or other transportation costs between an airport or station and a hotel, between business meetings, and from a business meeting to a hotel or restaurant;
- Meals at restaurants;
- Hotel charges or other lodging costs;
- Cleaning and laundry services;
- Telephone and telegraph expenses;
- Public stenographers' fees; and
- Tips incidental to any of the above expenses.

In figuring the deduction for meals, a taxpayer can either deduct actual costs or the standard meal allowance (see below). However, only 50 percent of the cost of a meal is deductible. [IRC § 274(n)]

Q 8:2 When is a taxpayer considered "away from home"?

Taxpayers are considered away from home if:

- Their duties require them to be away from the general area of their "tax home" substantially longer than an ordinary day's work, and
- They need to get sleep or rest to meet the demands of their work while away from home.

[Rev. Rul. 75-432, 1975-2 C.B. 60]

A taxpayer does not have to be away from his or her tax home for a whole day or from dusk to dawn as long as relief from duty is long enough to get necessary sleep or rest. This rest requirement is not satisfied by merely napping in a car.

If a taxpayer does not satisfy the sleep-or-rest requirement, the travel expenses are not deductible. Whereas, the business-connected transportation expenses are deductible whether or not the taxpayer is away from home.

Example 8-1: Carol Baker lives and works in Los Angeles. She flies to San Francisco on business and returns the same day. Results: (1) She can deduct the cost of her airfare as a transportation expense. (2) She cannot deduct the cost of her meals in San Francisco because meals are a travel expense, and Baker was not away from home overnight. However, if Baker stays in San

Francisco overnight and returns the next day, her hotel and meal expenses in San Francisco are deductible.

Exception to away-from-home requirement. The IRS recently announced the cost of employee lodging that is located in the same town as the employer may be deductible, provided the lodging is necessary for the employee to take part in a meeting or function of the employer. The IRS provided interim guidance indicating that it expects to amend its regulations to permit the deduction. [Notice 2007-47, I.R.B. 2007-24]

Until the IRS amends the regulations, it will apply the new rule under the following conditions:

- The lodging must be on a temporary basis;
- The lodging must be necessary for the employee to participate in or be available for a business meeting or function of the employer; and
- The expenses must be otherwise deductible by the employee, or would be deductible if paid by the employee, under Internal Revenue Code Section 162.

Q 8:3 Where is a taxpayer's "tax home"?

Generally, the tax home is the taxpayer's regular place of business or post of duty, regardless of where he or she maintains a personal residence. It includes the entire city or general area in which the taxpayer's business or work is located.

If a taxpayer has more than one regular place of business, the tax home is the taxpayer's main place of business. In determining where a taxpayer's main place of business or work is located the following factors are taken into account: [Rev. Rul. 75-432, 1975-2 C.B. 60]

The total time the taxpayer ordinarily spends working in each area;

- The degree of the taxpayer's business activity in each area; and
- The relative amount of income from each area.

Example 8-2: Craig Lawson lives in Cincinnati where he has a seasonal job for eight months each year and earns $75,000. He works the other four months in Miami, also at a seasonal job, and earns $25,000. Cincinnati is the main place of Lawson's work, because he spends most of his time there and earns most of his income there.

Q 8:4 Where is the taxpayer's tax home if he or she has no main place of business or work?

If a taxpayer does not have a regular or a main place of business because of the nature of his or her work, the tax home may be the place where the taxpayer regularly lives. [Rev. Rul. 75-432, 1975-2 C.B. 60]

If a taxpayer does not have a regular place of business or post of duty and there is no place where the taxpayer regularly lives, he or she is considered a transient, and the taxpayer has his or her home wherever the taxpayer is working at any given time. A transient cannot claim a travel expense deduction because he or she is never considered "away from home." A taxpayer may have a tax home even if he or she has no regular or main place of work. The tax home may be the place where the taxpayer regularly lives. [Rev. Rul. 73-529, 1973-2 C.B. 37]

Determining whether the taxpayer has a tax home. If a taxpayer does not have a regular or main place of business or work, the following factors are used to determine whether he or she has a tax home:

1. The taxpayer performs part of his or her business in the area of the main home and uses that home for lodging while doing business in the area;

2. The taxpayer has living expenses at the main home that are duplicated because his or her business requires travel away from that home; and

3. The taxpayer has not abandoned the area in which the main home is located, the taxpayer has a family member living in the main home, or the home is used often by the taxpayer for lodging.

If the taxpayer satisfies all three factors, his or her tax home is the home where he or she regularly lives. If the taxpayer satisfies only one factor, he or she is a transient for tax purposes, and no travel expense deduction is allowed. If two factors are satisfied, whether the taxpayer has a tax home depends on his or her particular situation.

Example 8-3: Linda Nelson is single and lives in Boston in an apartment she rents. She has worked for a company for a number of years. The company enrolls Nelson in a 12-month executive training program. She does not expect to return to work in Boston after she completes her training.

During the training, Nelson does not do any work in Boston. Instead, she receives classroom and on-the-job training throughout the United States. However, she keeps her apartment in Boston and returns to it frequently. Nelson does not use the apartment to conduct any business work. She also maintains her community contacts in Boston. When she completes her training, Nelson is transferred to Los Angeles.

Nelson does not satisfy factor (1) because she did not work in Boston. She satisfies factor (2) because she had duplicate living expenses. She also satisfies factor (3) because she did not abandon her apartment in Boston as her traditional home, she kept her community contacts, and she frequently returned to live in the apartment. Therefore, Boston is considered Nelson's tax home, and her travel expenses incurred away from Boston are deductible.

Example 8-4: Mark Carey is an outside salesperson with a sales territory covering several states. His employer's main office is in Newark, New Jersey, but he does not conduct any business there. Carey's work assignments are temporary, and he has no way of knowing where his future assignments will be located. He has a room in his married sister's house in Dayton, Ohio, where he stays several weekends a year. However, he does no work in the Dayton area and does not pay his sister for the use of the room.

Q 8:4

Carey does not satisfy any of the three factors listed earlier. He is a transient and has no tax home. Because he is never away from home, he cannot deduct the cost of his meals and lodging as travel expenses.

Q 8:5 If a taxpayer and his or her family live away from the taxpayer's tax home, is the cost of travel between the two locations deductible?

Generally no. If a taxpayer lives in an area outside of his or her main place of work, no deduction is allowed for travel between the area of work and the area of residence. However, if the taxpayer is working temporarily in the same city where he or she lives, the taxpayer may be considered as traveling away from home when living in his or her residence. [Rev. Rul. 55-604, 1955-2 C.B. 49]

Example 8-5: Joe Vernon's family home is in Pittsburgh, where he works 12 weeks a year. The rest of the year he works for the same employer in Baltimore. In Baltimore, he lives in an apartment.

Because Vernon spends spend most of his working time and earns most of his salary in Baltimore, that city is his tax home. He cannot deduct any expenses there. However, when he returns to work in Pittsburgh, he is away from his tax home even though he stays at his family home. He can deduct the cost of his round trip between Baltimore and Pittsburgh. He can also deduct his part of the family's living expenses for meals and lodging while he is living and working in Pittsburgh.

Q 8:6 When taxpayers are on a job assignment away from their tax home, does the tax home change?

No, not if the assignment is "temporary." For purposes of the travel deductions, the taxpayer will be considered away from home during the entire period of the assignment. However, if an assignment is indefinite in duration, the location of the taxpayer's tax home changes. The location of the assignment or job becomes the taxpayer's new tax home, and his or her travel expenses are not deductible. [IRC § 162(a)]

Q 8:7 When is a job assignment considered temporary?

Generally, a temporary assignment in a single location is one that is realistically expected to last (and does in fact last) for one year or less. An assignment or job in a single location is considered indefinite if it is realistically expected to last for more than one year, whether or not it actually lasts for more than one year. [Rev. Rul. 93-86, 1993-2 C.B. 71]

The determination of whether a job is temporary or indefinite is generally made at the start of the job. If the taxpayer expects his or her employment to last for one year or less, it is temporary unless there are facts and circumstances that indicate otherwise. Employment that is initially temporary may become indefinite due to changed circumstances. A series of assignments to the same location, all for short periods but that together cover a long period, may be considered an indefinite assignment. [*Curtis v. Comm'r*, 28 A.F.T.R.2d 71-5693, 449 F.2d 225, 71-2 USTC 9666 (5thCir. 1971); *Brewer v. Comm'r*, T.C. Memo 1994-117 (1994)]

Example 8-6: Joan Goodman is a computer consultant. She lives and regularly works in Los Angeles. Because of a shortage of work, Goodman took a project in Fresno. The work was scheduled to end in eight months, and she planned to return to Los Angeles at that time. The job actually lasted 10 months, after which time Goodman returned to Los Angeles. Her family continued to live in her home in Los Angeles.

While in Fresno, Goodman lived in an apartment. She returned to Los Angeles most weekends and maintained business contacts to see if she could get work in Los Angeles. She realistically expected the job in Fresno to last eight months. The job actually did last less than one year. Because Goodman expected to return home when it ended, her tax home is in Los Angeles for travel expense deduction purposes.

Example 8-7: The facts are the same as in Example 8-6, except that Goodman realistically expected the work in Fresno to last 18 months. The job actually was completed in 10 months. Her job in Fresno is indefinite because she realistically expected the work to last longer than one year, even though it actually lasted less than one year. She cannot deduct any travel expenses she incurred in Fresno.

Example 8-8: The facts are the same as in Example 8-6, except that Goodman realistically expected the work in Fresno to last 9 months. After 8 months, however, she was asked to remain for 7 more months (for a total actual stay of 15 months).

Initially, Goodman realistically expected the job in Fresno to last for only 9 months. However, due to changed circumstances occurring after 8 months, it was no longer realistic for her to expect that the job in Fresno would last for one year or less. Goodman can only deduct her travel expenses for the first 8 months. She cannot deduct any travel expenses she incurred after that time.

Keep in mind that the temporary-assignment rule is designed to provide tax relief when a taxpayer is faced with duplicative living expenses for business reasons. If a taxpayer has terminated his or her connection with one location, no deduction is allowed for living expenses in a new location, no matter how temporary it turns out to be.

A recent Tax Court case illustrates that point. John Kerman was a self-employed certified public account in Austin, Texas. In March 1996, he signed a contract with Josten's Inc. in Memphis, Tennessee. Under the contract, he was to teach Josten's staff about the use of an accounting software program. The contract lasted for six months, starting April 1. Kernan moved to Memphis, but on weekends he traveled to Knoxville where his girlfriend lived. His plan was to find work in Knoxville at the end of the six-month contract. In November 1996, after the Josten's contract expired, Kerman moved in with his girlfriend in Knoxville. However, when his relationship with his girlfriend terminated, Kernan returned to Austin in March 1997.

Q 8:7

Kernan claimed a deduction for his living expenses while in Memphis, contending that his tax home during that time was Austin. The Tax Court, however, disallowed the deduction. The court pointed out that Kernan terminated his work in Austin in March 1996 and incurred no further living expenses there. The court said that it was immaterial whether Kernan's job in Memphis was temporary or indefinite because "those distinctions are relevant only when the taxpayer maintains a self-established home and is away from it." [*Kernan v. Comm'r*, T.C. Summ. Op. 2002-148]

Q 8:8 If a taxpayer is away from his or her tax home on a temporary assignment, are the costs of brief trips home deductible?

If a taxpayer returns to his or her tax home on days off, the taxpayer is not considered to be away from home while at the tax home. Therefore, the cost of meals and lodging at the tax home is not deductible. However, a taxpayer can deduct travel expenses, including airfare, meals, and lodging, while traveling from the area of the temporary place of work to the tax home and back to the place of work. The deduction for these expenses cannot exceed the amount it would have cost for meals and lodging had the taxpayer stayed at the temporary place of work.

The IRS has also ruled that expenses for an employee's additional night's lodging and an additional day's meals over the weekend at a temporary business location after business was concluded are ordinary and necessary business expenses. By having the employee stay over Saturday night, the employer saved money overall (the sum of lower airfare and additional meal and lodging expense was less than the airfare not involving a Saturday night stay). [Ltr. Rul. 9237014]

Q 8:9 If, for business reasons, the taxpayer is accompanied by his or her spouse (or other family member), are the spouse's travel expenses deductible?

Generally no. If a spouse, dependent, or other individual goes with a taxpayer on a business trip, the travel costs of the accompanying individuals are deductible only if the individual:

1. Is an employee of the taxpayer;

2. Has a bona fide business purpose for the travel; and

3. Would otherwise be allowed to deduct the travel expenses if the individual had incurred the expenses directly.

[IRC § 274(m)(3)]

If a business associate travels with the taxpayer and meets the conditions in (2) and (3) above, the taxpayer can deduct the travel expenses he or she incurs for the associate. A business associate is someone with whom the taxpayer could reasonably expect to actively conduct business. A business associate can be a current or prospective (likely to become) customer, client, supplier, employee, agent, partner, or professional advisor.

For a bona fide business purpose to exist, the taxpayer must prove a real business purpose for the individual's presence. Incidental services, such as typing notes or assisting in entertaining customers, are usually not enough to warrant a deduction.

Example 8-9: Jerry Johnson drives to Chicago on business and takes his wife, Linda, with him. Linda is not Jerry's employee. Even if her presence serves a bona fide business purpose, her expenses are not deductible.

However, Jerry can deduct the expenses to the extent that they do not exceed what it would cost him to travel alone. For example, suppose Jerry pays $215 a day for a double room while a single room would cost $190 a day. He can deduct $190 a day. In addition, because his auto expenses are the same whether or not Linda accompanies him, the expenses are fully deductible.

Q 8:10 What is the standard meal allowance?

The standard meal allowance is an alternative to deducting the actual cost of meals while traveling away from home on business. It allows a taxpayer to deduct a set amount, depending on where and when the taxpayer travels, for each full or partial travel day. [Reg. § 1.274-5(j)(1)] If a taxpayer uses the standard meal allowance, records still must be kept to prove the time, place, and business purpose of the travel. (Note: There is no optional standard lodging amount similar to the standard meal allowance. A taxpayer can deduct only the actual cost of lodging.)

Eligibility. Taxpayers may use the standard meal allowance whether they are employees or self-employed. [Rev. Proc. 2007-63 , I.R.B. 2007-42]

Amount of standard meal allowance. The standard meal allowance is the meal and incidental expenses (M&IE) rate used by the federal government to reimburse its employees for business travel. Starting October 1, 2007, the rate is $39 a day for most areas in the United States. Other locations in the United States are designated as high-cost areas, qualifying for higher rates of up to $64 a day. If a taxpayer travels to more than one location in one day, the taxpayer should use the rate for the place where he or she stops for sleep or rest. [Rev. Proc. 2007-63 , I.R.B. 2007-42; Federal Travel Regs., 41 C.F.R. Ch. 301 *et seq.* (2005)]]

Since only 50 percent of meal costs are deductible, a taxpayer can deduct only 50 percent of the standard meal allowance. [IRC § 274(n)]

Incidental expenses. Note that the standard meal allowance also covers "incidental expenses" of business travel. If a taxpayer uses the standard meal allowance, these incidental expenses may not be separately deducted.

The term "incidental expenses" has the same meaning as in the Federal Travel Regulations, 41 C.F.R. 300-3.1 (2007). Thus, based on the current definition of "incidental expenses" in the Federal Travel Regulations, "incidental expenses" means fees and tips given to porters, baggage carriers, bellhops, hotel maids, stewards or stewardesses and others on ships, and hotel servants in foreign countries; transportation between places of lodging or business and places where meals are taken, if suitable meals can be obtained at the temporary duty site; and the mailing cost associated with filing travel vouchers and payment of employer-sponsored charge card billings.

Q 8:11 What is the standard incidental expense allowance?

In lieu of using actual expenses in computing the amount allowable as a deduction for incidental expenses paid or incurred for business travel, employees and self-employed individuals who do not pay or incur meal expenses may use an amount computed at the rate of $3 per day for each calendar day (or partial day) the employee or self-employed individual is away from home. [Rev. Proc. 2007-63 , I.R.B. 2007-42]

The standard incidental expense allowance is not available to taxpayers who deduct the standard meal allowance using the M&IE rate (see previous question).

Q 8:12 Can a taxpayer deduct the full cost of a trip if he or she vacations or is engaged in other personal activities during the course of the trip?

A taxpayer who travels to a destination, and while at that destination engages in both business and personal activities, may deduct traveling expenses to and from such destination only if the trip is primarily related to his trade or business. Traveling expenses for a trip that is primarily personal in nature are not deductible, even though the taxpayer engages in some business activities while at the destination. However, expenses incurred while at the destination that are properly allocable to the taxpayer's trade or business are deductible. [Reg. § 1.162-2(b)(1)]

The primary purpose of the trip is determined on the basis of the facts and circumstances in each case. An important factor to be considered is the amount of time spent on personal activity during the period of the trip compared to the amount of time spent on activities directly relating to the taxpayer's trade or business. [Reg. § 1.162-2(b)(2)]

Example 8-10: Jennifer Parker works in Atlanta and takes a business trip to New Orleans. On her way home, she stops in Mobile to visit relatives. Parker spends $1,200 for the 9 days she is away from home for travel, meals, lodging, and other travel expenses. If she had not stopped in Mobile, she would have been gone only 6 days, and her total cost would have been $980. Parker can deduct $980 for her trip, including the cost of round-trip transportation to and from New Orleans. The cost allocable to her stay in Mobile is nondeductible, and the cost of her meals is subject to the 50-percent limit discussed below.

Q 8:12

Special Rules for Certain Trips

Q 8:13 Are the rules governing deduction for travel expenses the same for foreign travel and domestic travel?

No. If any part of a taxpayer's business travel is outside the United States, some of the deductions for the cost of going to and from the destination may be limited when there is a nonbusiness element to the trip. [IRC § 274 (c)(1)] For this purpose, the U.S. includes the 50 states and the District of Columbia.

In addition, travel from one point in the U.S. to another point is not considered foreign travel, even if the eventual destination is outside the U.S. If a taxpayer travels by airplane (or other means of public transportation), anyplace in the U.S. where the airplane makes a scheduled stop is a point in the United States. Once the airplane leaves the last scheduled stop in the U.S. on its way to a point outside the United States, the special deduction limitation for foreign travel applies. [Reg. § 1.274-4(e)]

> **Example 8-11:** Bill Tatum flies from New York to Puerto Rico with a scheduled stop in Miami. He returns to New York nonstop. The flight from New York to Miami is in the United States, so only the flight from Miami to Puerto Rico is outside the United States. Because there are no scheduled stops between Puerto Rico and New York, Tatum's entire return trip is outside the United States and subject to the deduction limit.

If a taxpayer travels by private car, travel between points in the U.S. is not considered foreign for this purpose.

> **Example 8-12:** Helen Stapleton travels by car from Denver to Mexico City and returns to Denver. Her travel from Denver to the border and from the border back to Denver is travel in the U.S. and is not subject to the deduction limit for foreign travel. The deduction limit does apply to her trip from the border to Mexico City and back to the border.

Q 8:14 Does the deduction limit apply to all business trips outside the U.S?

No. The deduction limit does not apply to trips that are exclusively for business—when the taxpayer's entire time is spent on business activities. In this situation, the travel expenses are deductible in the same way as those for domestic trips.

In addition, some trips are deemed to be exclusively business, even when the taxpayer spends some time on nonbusiness activities. [Reg. § 1.274-4(f)(5)] The deduction limit for foreign travel does not apply if the taxpayer meets at least one of the following tests.

1. *No substantial control.* A trip is considered entirely for business if the taxpayer did not have substantial control over arranging the trip. A taxpayer may be treated as lacking substantial control even when he or she does have control over the timing of the trip.

A taxpayer is considered to lack substantial control if he or she:

a. Is an employee who was reimbursed or paid a travel expense allowance;

b. Is not related to his or her employer (see above); and

c. Is not a managing executive.

   A "managing executive" is an employee who has the authority and responsibility, without being subject to the veto of someone else, to decide on the need for the business trip. A self-employed taxpayer generally has substantial control over arranging business trips.

2. *Short trips.* A trip is not subject to the deduction limit if the taxpayer is outside the U.S. for a week or less. One week means seven consecutive days. In counting the days, the day the taxpayer leaves the U.S. is not counted, but the day he or she returns is counted.

   Example 8-13: Tom Shipley travels to Brussels primarily for business. He leaves Denver on Tuesday and flies to New York. On Wednesday, he flies from New York to Brussels, arriving the next morning. On Thursday and Friday, Shipley has business discussions, and from Saturday until Tuesday, he does some sightseeing. He flies back to New York, arriving Wednesday afternoon. On Thursday, he flies back to Denver. Although Shipley is away from his home in Denver for more than a week, he was not outside the U.S. for more than a week. This is because the day he departs does not count as a day outside the U.S.

   Note: Although the special deduction limit for foreign trips does not apply to the cost of going to and from Brussels, the same rules that apply to domestic travel limit Shipley's deductions for his stay in Brussels. He can deduct his meal and lodging costs in Brussels only for the Thursday and Friday he conducts business. Shipley cannot deduct his expenses from Saturday through Tuesday, because those days are spent on nonbusiness activities.

3. *Little nonbusiness activity.* A foreign business trip will be deemed exclusively for business if the taxpayer spends less than 25 percent of the total time outside the U.S. on nonbusiness activities. For this purpose, both the departure day and the return day are counted.

   Example 8-14: Beth Powell flies from Seattle to Tokyo, where she spends 14 days on business and 5 days on personal matters. She then flies back to Seattle. She spends one day flying in each direction. (Total time outside U.S. = 21 days.) Because only 5/21 (less than 25 percent) of Powell's total time abroad is for nonbusiness activities, the special deduction limit does not apply. But, as in Example 8-13, Powell cannot deduct her expenses in Tokyo during the nonbusiness portion of her stay.

4. *Vacation not a major consideration.* A taxpayer's trip is considered entirely for business if he or she can establish that a personal vacation was not a major consideration in making the trip.

Q 8:14

Q 8:15 How is the deduction limit for foreign travel figured?

If a taxpayer's trip outside the U.S. is primarily, but not exclusively for business, the taxpayer must allocate travel time on a day-to-day basis between business days and nonbusiness days. The days of departure from and return to the U.S. are both counted as days outside the United States.

A fraction is used to calculate the deductible portion of the round-trip travel expenses to and from the foreign destination. The numerator is the total number of business days outside the United States. The denominator is the total number of travel days outside the United States. The portion of the travel expenses equal to this fraction can be deducted. [Reg. § 1.274-4(f)(1)]

For this purpose "business days" include transportation days, days the taxpayer's presence was required, days spent on business, and certain weekends and holidays.

- *Transportation days.* A taxpayer can count as a business day any day he or she spends traveling to or from a business destination. However, if because of a nonbusiness activity the taxpayer does not travel by a direct route, business days are only the days it would have taken to travel by a direct route. Extra days for side trips or nonbusiness activities cannot be counted as business days.

- *Presence required.* Business days include any day the taxpayer's presence is required at a particular place for a specific business purpose. This counts as a business day even if the taxpayer spends most of the day on nonbusiness activities.

- *Day spent on business.* If the taxpayer's principal activity during working hours is business connected, the day is considered a business day. Also included are any days the taxpayer was prevented from working because of circumstances beyond his or her control.

- *Certain weekends and holidays.* Weekends, holidays, and other necessary standby days count as business days if they fall between business days. But if the days follow the end of business activity (e.g., the taxpayer remains at a business destination for personal reasons) these days are not treated as business days.

[Reg. § 1.274-4(d)(2)]

Example 8-15: Max Hunter's tax home is New York City. He travels to Quebec where he has a business appointment on Friday. Hunter has another appointment on the following Monday. Since his presence is required on both Friday and Monday, they are business days. Because the weekend is between business days, Saturday and Sunday are counted as business days. This is true even though Hunter uses the weekend for sightseeing, visiting friends, or other nonbusiness activity.

Example 8-16: The facts are the same as in Example 8-15, except that Hunter has no business in Quebec after Friday, but stays until Monday before starting home. In this situation, Saturday and Sunday are nonbusiness days.

Q 8:15

Q 8:16 How is the deduction limit applied when a taxpayer makes a nonbusiness stop en route to or from a foreign business destination?

If a taxpayer stops for personal reasons en route to or from a foreign business destination, then the special deduction limit does not apply to the full travel costs to and from the U.S. Instead, an allocation between business days and nonbusiness days is made only for what it costs the taxpayer to travel to and from the nonbusiness stop. The nondeductible portion of these costs is the portion equal to the number of nonbusiness days divided by the total days outside the U.S. The additional expenses for traveling to the final business destination are fully deductible. [Reg. § 1.274-4(f)(3)]

> **Example 8-17:** Nancy Madison lives in Washington, D.C. On May 4, she flies to Paris to attend a business conference that begins on May 5. The conference ends at noon on May 14. That evening she flies to Dublin where she visits with friends until the afternoon of May 21, then she flies directly home to Washington. The primary purpose for Madison's trip is to attend the conference.
>
> May 4 through May 14 (11 days) are considered business days, and May 15 through May 21 (7 days) are nonbusiness days. (Total days outside U.S. = 18.) Madison can deduct the cost of her meals (subject to the 50-percent limit), lodging, and other business-related travel expenses while in Paris. She cannot deduct her expenses while in Dublin. She also cannot deduct 7/18 of what it would have cost her to travel roundtrip between New York and Dublin.
>
> Assume Madison paid $450 to fly from New York to Paris, $200 to fly from Paris to Dublin, and $500 to fly from Dublin back to New York. Roundtrip airfare from New York to Dublin would have been $850.
>
> Madison figures the deductible portion of her airfare by subtracting 7/18 of the roundtrip fare she would have paid traveling directly between New York and Dublin ($850 × 7/18 = $331) from her total expenses ($1,150). Therefore, Madison can deduct $819.

Q 8:17 How is the deduction limit applied when the nonbusiness stop is beyond the business destination?

In this situation, the allocation between business and nonbusiness days applies to the travel costs between the U.S. and the foreign business destination. The additional costs of traveling to the nonbusiness destination are completely nondeductible.

> **Example 8-18:** The facts are the same as in Example 8-17, except that after the Paris conference, Madison flies on to Venice for a vacation. In this situation, Madison cannot deduct any portion of the cost of the trip from Paris to Venice and back to Paris. In addition, she cannot deduct 7/18 of the airfare from New York to Paris and back to New York.

Q 8:18 Is the cost of travel to a business convention deductible?

Travel expenses to a business convention are generally deductible as long as: (1) the taxpayer can show that attendance at the convention benefits his or her business; and (2) the primary purpose of the trip overall is business, not pleasure. However, special rules apply to conventions held outside the "North American area" and to conventions held on cruise ships. [IRC § 274(h)]

Q 8:19 What is the "North American area"?

The North American area is defined as the United States and its possessions (including Puerto Rico), the Trust Territory of the Pacific Islands, Canada, and Mexico. It also covers Bermuda and certain beneficiary countries under the Caribbean Basin Economic Recovery Act. These countries include Antigua and Barbuda, Aruba, the Bahamas, Barbados, Costa Rica, Dominica, Dominican Republic, Grenada, Guyana, Honduras, Jamaica, the Netherlands Antilles, and Trinidad and Tobago. [Rev. Rul. 2007-28 , I.R.B. 2007-18]

> **Note:** Travel to business conventions held outside the U.S. are subject to the deduction limit for foreign travel discussed above, even if they are held inside the North American area.

Q 8:20 What are the special rules governing travel expenses to conventions outside of the North American area?

A taxpayer cannot deduct expenses for attending a convention, seminar, or similar meeting held outside the North American area unless the meeting is directly related to the taxpayer's business. In addition, no deduction is allowed unless it is as reasonable to hold the meeting outside the North American area as in it.

The following factors are taken into account to determine if it was reasonable to hold the meeting outside the North American area:

- The purpose of the meeting and the activities taking place at the meeting;
- The purposes and activities of the sponsoring organizations or groups; and
- The homes of the active members of the sponsoring organizations and the places at which other meetings of the sponsoring organizations or groups have been or will be held.

[IRC § 274(h)(1)]

Q 8:21 What are the special rules for travel expenses in connection with conventions held on cruise ships?

A special dollar cap applies to deductions for the expenses of attending conventions, seminars, or similar meetings held on cruise ships. The deduction cannot exceed $2,000. In addition, the convention must be directly related to the

taxpayer's business, and no deduction is allowed unless the following requirements are met:

- The cruise ship is a vessel registered in the United States; and

- All of the cruise ship's ports of call are in the United States or in possessions of the United States.

[IRC 274(h)(2)]

Furthermore, to obtain the deduction, the taxpayer must attach to his or her tax return:

1. A signed, written statement that includes information about: (a) the total days of the trip, excluding the days of transportation to and from the cruise ship port, (b) the number of hours each day that the taxpayer devoted to scheduled business activities, and (c) a program of the scheduled business activities of the convention; and

2. A written statement signed by an officer of the organization or group sponsoring the convention that includes: (a) a schedule of the business activities of each day of the meeting, and (b) the number of hours the taxpayer attended the scheduled business activities.

[IRC § 274(h)(5)]

Local Transportation Expenses

Q 8:22 Can a taxpayer deduct the cost of business-connected local transportation expenses?

Yes. Ordinary and necessary transportation costs directly pertaining to or connected with a trade or business are allowable as business expense deductions. [Reg. § 1.162-1(a)]

Local transportation expenses include the cost of driving and maintaining an automobile, as well as the cost of using a taxi, bus, or railroad. Deductible transportation includes the cost of:

- Getting from one workplace to another when the taxpayer is traveling within the city or general area that is his or her tax home (see above);

- Visiting clients or customers; and

- Going to a business meeting away from a regular workplace.

Deductible transportation expenses do not include meals or lodging. These expenses are deductible only when incurred by a taxpayer while away from home overnight (see above). [Reg. § 1.162-2(a)]

Q 8:23 Is commuting to work a deductible expense?

No. Regular commuting between a taxpayer's residence and his or her work location is generally considered a personal expense, even if the commute is a great distance. [Reg. § 1.162-2(e)]

A taxpayer who travels between his residence and work location during the workday cannot deduct those transportation costs, regardless of the number of trips. For instance, a waitress who travels home from a catering hall between parties is not entitled to deduct her transportation costs. [*Potenga*, T.C. Memo 1976-151] Similarly, a teacher who traveled home after school hours and back to the school for a PTA meeting was denied a deduction for the costs of transportation. [*Gudmundson*, T.C. Memo 1978-299]

However, a taxpayer may be entitled to a deduction for the cost of commuting between his or her residence and a temporary work location. [Rev. Rul. 99-7, 1999-1 C.B. 361]

Q 8:24 When can a taxpayer deduct the cost of commuting to a temporary work location?

When taxpayers have one or more regular places of business outside their residences and they commute to a temporary work location in the same trade or business, they can deduct the expenses of the daily roundtrip transportation between their residences and the temporary location. [Rev. Rul. 99-7, 1999-1 C.B. 361]

If a taxpayer's work at a location is realistically expected to last (and does in fact last) for one year or less, the location is generally considered a temporary workplace. If the work at a location is realistically expected to last for more than one year (or if there is no realistic expectation that the employment will last for one year or less), the workplace is not considered temporary, regardless of whether it actually lasts for more than one year. If the work is realistically expected to last for one year or less, but at some later date the expected duration changes to more than one year, the workplace will be treated as temporary until the point the expectation changes. [Rev. Rul. 93-86, 1993-2 C.B. 71]

Example 8-19: Gene Lacy usually works at his employer's regular office, but is assigned to a two-year project working at a client's office. This is not temporary since it is expected to last for more than a year, and Gene's commuting costs therefore are not deductible.

Example 8-20: Virginia Hargon is assigned to work at a different client's office and is expected to work there for 10 months. After 10 months, however, Hargon's assignment is extended by 8 months. Her assignment is considered temporary for the first 10 months. After that, her commuting costs become nondeductible.

Example 8-21: Joyce Street is given a 6-month assignment on a long-term assignment in another location. A year after completing the assignment, she is unexpectedly reassigned to the same project at the same location for another 7 months. Both of Street's assignments are temporary for the purposes of deducting the daily commuting costs. [Ltr. Ruls. 200027047, 200025052]

Q 8:25 Are commuting costs to a temporary work location deductible if a taxpayer has no regular place of work?

If a taxpayer has no regular place of work but ordinarily works in the metropolitan area where he or she lives, commuting to a temporary work location is deductible only if the location is outside the taxpayer's metropolitan area. Generally, a metropolitan area includes the area within the city limits and the suburbs that are considered part of that metropolitan area. Without a regular place of work, a taxpayer cannot deduct daily transportation costs between his or her residence and a temporary work site within the metropolitan area. These are nondeductible commuting costs. [Rev. Rul. 99-7, 1999-1 C.B. 361]

Occasionally, the IRS and taxpayers disagree on whether the taxpayers have an area where they "ordinarily work." Two Tax Court cases illustrate these disputes.

In 1995, Daniela Aldea resided in Yuba City, California, and worked as an apprentice ironworker. She received job assignments through a union hall located in Sacramento, California, and worked in various locations in California during 1995, including 63 days in Salinas, 49 days in Santa Cruz, 22 days in Sacramento, 16 days in Modesto, 13 days in Stockton, and 11 days in San Francisco. Between jobs, Aldea reported to the union hall in the morning, and if there were work available, she would then drive from the union hall to the job site. After obtaining work, Aldea reported directly to the job site until the job was completed.

The IRS disallowed Aldea's deductions for her auto expenses between her home in Yuba City and the job sites on the ground that Yuba City did not qualify as an area where she ordinarily worked.

The Tax Court upheld the disallowance. The court pointed out that Aldea did not establish any business reason for living in Yuba City; her decision to live there was entirely personal. Aldea did not ever work in, have the prospect of work in, or have any other business tie to Yuba City. The union hall where she received her job assignments was in Sacramento, which is south of Yuba City, and all other work sites were south of Sacramento. [*Aldea v. Comm'r*, T.C. Memo 2000-136]

In the second case, Teresita Daiz began working as a nurse and nursing consultant for Pleasant Care Corporation (PCC) in the early 1990s. During her first few years of employment by PCC, Daiz regularly worked in or near Stockton, California. From approximately March 31, 1996, until 2001, she was assigned to work at various facilities outside of Stockton. Although Daiz continued to live in Stockton, she did not work at the Stockton facility at any time during the period.

Daiz was assured by her supervisor that the assignments would only be temporary and that she would be reassigned to the facility in Stockton. The supervisor's assurances about the temporary nature of her assignments were accurate, but the assurances that she would be reassigned to the Stockton facility proved to be false. Finally in 2001, Daiz gave up her hopes for reassignment to Stockton, told her supervisor that she would not be moved about any longer, and accepted a permanent position at a PCC subsidiary's facility in Vista, California.

The IRS disallowed Daiz's deductions for trips between Stockton and the various facilities outside of Stockton. As in *Aldea*, the IRS contended that Stockton was not an area where Daiz ordinarily worked. This time, however, the Tax Court ruled against the IRS. The court noted that Daiz had established her home near her place of employment and only accepted temporary assignments outside that area on the promise of an eventual reassignment within the Stockton area. She had no reason to disbelieve her supervisor. However, in 2001, when Diaz did cease to believe the promises of her supervisor, she changed her place of employment.

The court said that, under these circumstances, Daiz properly regarded the Stockton vicinity as the metropolitan area where she normally works. The court distinguished this case from *Aldea*. In *Aldea*, the long commutes were for personal reasons and nondeductible; in contrast, the long commutes in Daiz's situation were for employment reasons and therefore deductible. [*Daiz v. Comm'r*, T.C. Memo. 2002-192]

Q 8:26 Is the cost of commuting between a residence and a business location deductible if the taxpayer has an office in his or her residence?

The cost of commuting between a home office and another business location is deductible generally only if the home office is the taxpayer's principal place of business. [Rev. Rul. 99-7, 1999-1 C.B. 361] If the home office were only a secondary business location, the commuting costs would be nondeductible unless the taxpayer was going to a temporary work location (see above).

Whether a taxpayer's residence is the principal place of business is determined under the same standards that apply to home office deductions (see Chapter 1). Under those rules, a taxpayer's home office is the principal place of business if it is used by the taxpayer to conduct administrative or management activities, and there is no other fixed location of the trade or business where the taxpayer conducts substantial administrative or management activities. [IRC § 280A(c)(1)]

Automobile Expenses

Q 8:27 Can taxpayers deduct their automobile expenses when they use a car for business?

Yes. Taxpayers, whether they are self-employed or employees, who use their cars for business can deduct their ordinary and necessary expenses to the extent of their business use. For this purpose, business use includes both local business-connected transportation and travel away from home overnight on business.

Deductible automobile expenses include parking fees, tolls, taxes, maintenance and repairs, tires, gas, oil, insurance, and registration fees. [Rev. Proc. 2005-78, 2005-51 IRB 1177]An allowance for depreciation may also be claimed if the taxpayer owns the car. (Special rules apply to automobile depreciation. See Chapter 7.) If a taxpayer leases the car, the lease payments are deductible automobile expenses.

Q 8:28 How is the deduction for business-connected auto expenses computed?

A taxpayer may use either of two methods to figure deductions for the business use of his or her automobile: (1) the actual expense method, or (2) the standard mileage rate. [Rev. Proc. 2006-49 , I.R.B. 2006-47]

A taxpayer who uses the actual expense method relies on the actual amount of costs to calculate deductible items. The taxpayer must make an allocation when the vehicle is used partly for personal purposes. For example, if the taxpayer drives 20,000 miles during the year and 15,000 miles are business-connected, he or she can deduct 75 percent of: the gas costs, the repair bills, the depreciation allowance or monthly lease payments, and so forth.

Q 8:29 What is the standard mileage rate?

In lieu of deducting actual expenses, a taxpayer may deduct so many cents for each business mile driven during the year. For 2007, the standard mileage rate is 48.5 cents. [Rev. Proc. 2006-49 , I.R.B. 2006-47] Thus, if a taxpayer drives 20,000 business miles during 2007 and chooses the standard mileage rate, the taxpayer's deduction would be $9,700.

In addition to the standard mileage rate, a taxpayer can deduct any business-related parking fees and tolls. (Parking fees, which the taxpayer pays to park a car at his or her place of work, are generally considered nondeductible commuting expenses.)

Q 8:30 Are there any restrictions on the use of the standard mileage rate?

Yes. If a taxpayer wants to choose the standard mileage rate for a car he or she owns, it must be chosen in the first year the car is available for use in the taxpayer's business. In later years, the taxpayer can choose to use either the standard mileage rate or the actual expense method. [Rev. Proc. 2006-49 , I.R.B. 2006-47]

If a taxpayer wants to use the standard mileage rate for a car that is leased, the taxpayer must use the standard mileage rate for the entire lease period.

A taxpayer is not eligible to use the standard mileage rate in certain situations. The standard mileage rate may not be used if the taxpayer: [Rev. Proc. 2006-49 , I.R.B. 2006-47]

- Uses the car for hire (such as a taxi);
- Operates no more than four cars at the same time;
- Claimed a depreciation deduction using ACRS or MACRS (see Chapter 7) in a prior year; or
- Claimed a Section 179 deduction (see Chapter 7) on the car.

Q 8:31 Can a taxpayer deduct interest paid on a car loan if the car is used in business?

If the taxpayer is self-employed, the interest is deductible to the extent of the car's business use. However, if the taxpayer is an employee, no deduction is allowed. Interest incurred as an employee is considered nondeductible personal interest. [IRC § 163(h)(2)(A)]

Entertainment Expenses

Q 8:32 Can a taxpayer deduct the cost of business-related entertainment?

A taxpayer can generally deduct 50 percent of the cost of entertaining clients or customers if the expenses are ordinary and necessary business expenses and the entertainment meets either of two tests: (1) "directly related" test, or (2) the associated test (see below). [IRC § 274(a)]Special rules apply to certain types of entertainment expenses, such as club dues, entertainment facilities, and stadium skyboxes.

For tax purposes, entertainment includes any activity generally considered to provide entertainment, amusement, or recreation. Examples include entertaining guests at nightclubs; at social, athletic, and sporting clubs; at theaters; at sporting events; on yachts; or on hunting, fishing, vacation, and similar trips. [Reg. § 1.274-2(b)(1)]

Entertainment also may include meeting personal, living, or family needs of individuals, such as providing meals, a hotel suite, or a car to customers or their families. Entertainment includes the cost of a meal a taxpayer provides to a customer or client, whether the meal is a part of other entertainment or by itself. [Reg. § 1.274-2(b)(1)]

Lavish or extravagant entertainment expenses are not deductible. However, the IRS takes the position that entertainment is not lavish or extravagant merely because it involves first class accommodations or services. The test is what is reasonable under the particular facts and circumstances. [Rev. Rul. 63-144, 1963-2 C.B. 129]

If a taxpayer entertains business and nonbusiness individuals at the same event, the entertainment expense must be allocated between business and non-business portions. Only the business portion is deductible. If the allocation cannot be made on a person-by-person basis, then a pro rata allocation can be used.

Example 8-22: Jim Hardy entertains a group of individuals that includes him, three business prospects, and seven social guests. Assuming the entertaining otherwise qualifies as a deductible expense, Hardy can deduct only 50 percent of 4/11 of the expense. No deduction is allowed for the seven social guests.

Q 8:33 For purposes of the business entertainment deduction, what is the directly related test?

To meet the directly related text for entertainment expenses (including meals), the taxpayer must be able to show that:

1. The main purpose of the combined business and entertainment was the active conduct of business;

2. The taxpayer did engage in business with the person during the entertainment period; and

3. The taxpayer had more than a general expectation of getting income or some other specific business benefit at some future time.

[Reg. § 1.274-2(c)(3)]

If the entertainment takes place in a "clear business setting" and is for the taxpayer's business, the expenses are considered directly related to business. [Reg. § 1.274-2(c)(4)]

The following situations are examples of entertainment in a clear business setting:

- Entertainment in a hospitality room at a convention where business goodwill is created through the display or discussion of business products.

- Entertainment that is mainly a price rebate on the sale of products (such as a restaurant owner providing an occasional free meal to a loyal customer).

- Entertainment of a clear business nature occurring under circumstances where there is no meaningful personal or social relationship between the taxpayer and the persons entertained. An example is entertainment of business and civic leaders at the opening of a new hotel when the purpose is to get business publicity rather than to create or maintain the goodwill of the persons entertained.

Entertainment expenses generally are not considered directly related if the taxpayer is not present or if they involve situations where there are substantial distractions that generally prevent the active conduct of business. [Reg. § 1.274-2(c)(7)]The following are examples of situations where there are substantial distractions:

- A meeting or discussion at a nightclub, theater, or sporting event;
- A meeting or discussion during what is essentially a social gathering, such as a cocktail party; or
- A meeting with a group that includes persons who are not business associates at places such as cocktail lounges, country clubs, golf clubs, athletic clubs, or vacation resorts.

Q 8:34 For purposes of business entertainment deductions, what is the associated test?

Even if a taxpayer cannot deduct entertainment expenses under the directly related test, taxpayer may still be able to deduct the expenses if the entertainment:

- Is associated with the taxpayer's business; and
- Directly precedes or follows a substantial business discussion.

[IRC § 274(a)(1)(A)]

Generally, any ordinary and necessary expense is associated with the active conduct of a business if the taxpayer can show that he or she had a clear business purpose for having the expense. The purpose may be to get new business or to encourage the continuation of an existing business relationship.

Q 8:35 What is a "substantial business discussion"?

Business discussions include meetings, negotiations, transactions, conferences, and similar business discussions. The determination of whether a business discussion is substantial and bona fide is dependent on the facts and circumstances of each case. However, the taxpayer must establish that he or she actively engaged in the business discussion (not the entertainment) for the purpose of obtaining income or other specific trade or business benefit. [Reg. § 1.274-2(d)(3)(i)]

The meeting does not have to be for any specified length of time, but the taxpayer must be able to show that the business discussion was substantial in relation to the meal or entertainment. It is not necessary that more time be devoted to business than to entertainment, and the taxpayer is not required to discuss business during the meal or entertainment.

Conventions. A taxpayer is considered to have a substantial business discussion if he or she attends meetings at a convention or similar event, or at a trade or business meeting sponsored and conducted by a business or professional organization. However, the reason for attending the convention or meeting must be to further the taxpayer's business. The organization that sponsors the convention or meeting must schedule a program of business activities that is the main activity of the convention or meeting. [Reg. § 1.274-2(d)(3)(i)(b)]

Q 8:36 When is entertainment treated as directly preceding or following a substantial business discussion?

If the entertainment is held on the same day as the business discussion, it is considered to be held directly before or after the business discussion. If the entertainment and the business discussion are not held on the same day, the facts of each case must be taken into account to see if the associated test is met. Among the facts to consider are the place, date, and duration of the business discussion. If the taxpayer or the individuals being entertained are from out of town, the IRS says the dates of arrival and departure, and the reasons for the gap between entertainment and business discussions must be considered. [Reg. § 1.274-2(d)(3)(ii)]

Example 8-23: A group of business associates comes from out of town to Jennifer Carpenter's place of business to hold a substantial business discussion. If Carpenter entertains those business guests on the evening before the business discussion, or on the evening of the day following the business discussion, the entertainment generally is considered to be held directly before or after the discussion. The expense meets the associated test, and Carpenter can deduct 50 percent of the cost.

Q 8:37 Does the deduction for entertainment expenses cover the cost of entertaining spouses?

The IRS says a taxpayer can deduct the cost of entertaining spouses if he or she can show that there was a clear business purposes to the entertainment rather than a social purpose.

Example 8-24: Same facts as in Example 8-27 above, except that Carpenter's out-of-town associates are accompanied by their spouses. The spouses join the entertainment because it would be impractical to entertain the associates without their spouses. Because the associates' spouses join the entertainment, Carpenter also invites her husband. The IRS says that the cost of entertaining the associates' spouses and Carpenter's spouse is a deductible entertainment expenses. [Rev. Rul. 63-144, 1963-2 C.B. 129]

Planning Point: There is nothing to prevent a taxpayer from including nonbusiness guests in the entertainment. For example, if a taxpayer hosts a party following a substantial business discussion and invites friends and acquaintances as well as the discussion participants, the costs of the party allocable to the discussion participants are still deductible. The costs allocable to the nonbusiness guests are, of course, nondeductible.

Q 8:38 Can a taxpayer deduct depreciation and maintenance for a boat or hunting lodge that is used to entertain customers or clients?

No. A taxpayer cannot deduct any expenses for the cost of using an "entertainment facility." [IRC § 274(a)(2)] This includes expenses for depreciation and operating costs such as rent, utilities, maintenance, and protection.

An entertainment facility is property owned, rented, or used for entertainment. Examples include a yacht, hunting lodge, fishing camp, swimming pool, tennis court, bowling alley, car, airplane, apartment, hotel suite, or home in a vacation resort. [Reg. § 1.274-2(e)(2)]

> **Note:** The disallowance of deductions for entertainment facilities does not apply to out-of-pocket expenses incurred during the entertainment. A taxpayer can deduct expenses for food and beverages, catering, gas, and fishing bait that are provided during entertainment at a facility. Of course, these expenses are subject to the directly related and associated tests discussed above.

Q 8:39 Does the Internal Revenue Code exempt any entertainment from the directly related and associated tests?

Yes, the Code provides a number of exceptions to the requirement that entertainment pass the directly related or associated tests. Three of the most important exceptions are: (1) entertainment treated as compensation; (2) entertainment for employees, and (3) reimbursed expenses for an employee. [IRC § 274(e)]

Entertainment as compensation. An expenditure for entertainment (goods, services, or use of a facility) for an employee does not have to meet either the directly related test or the associated test if the taxpayer treats the expenditure as compensation paid to the employee and wages subject to withholding. [IRC § 274(e)(2)]For example, suppose a taxpayer rewarded a star salesperson with an all-expense-paid vacation for the salesperson and his or her spouse. This is considered entertainment for tax purposes. However, the taxpayer can deduct the cost without regard to the directly related and associated test as long as the taxpayer treats the value of the trip as taxable wages.

Employee entertainment. Expenses for recreational, social, or similar activities (including expenses for facilities for such activities) primarily for the benefit of employees—other than highly compensated employees—are exempt from the directly related and associated tests. [IRC § 274(e)(4)]This exception is normally applicable to expenses of an employer incurred in holding Christmas parties, annual picnics, and summer outings for its employees or in maintaining a swimming pool, baseball diamond, bowling alley, or golf course available generally to the employees.

Employee's reimbursed expenses. When an employee is reimbursed by an employer for business expenses under an "accountable plan" (see Employee Reimbursements below), it is considered a wash for tax purposes—the reimbursement is not taxable to the employee, and the employee does not claim a deduction for the expenses. This does not change merely because the expenses do not qualify under the directly related or associated tests. Instead, the Code's disallowance of the deduction applies at the employer level—no deduction is allowed for the reimbursement. [Reg. § 1.274-2(f)(2)(iv)]This avoids both the employer and employee having to suffer a deduction disallowance for the same expense.

Q 8:40 Can a taxpayer deduct dues paid to a country club or an athletic club if he or she uses the club for business entertainment?

No deduction is allowed for dues (including initiation fees) for membership in any club organized for business, pleasure, recreation, or other social purpose. [IRC § 274(a)(3)]This rule applies to any membership organization if one of its principal purposes is to conduct entertainment activities for members or their guests or to provide members or their guests with access to entertainment facilities.

The purpose and activities of a club, not its name, will determine whether or not a deduction is allowed. The disallowance rules apply to country clubs, golf and athletic clubs, airline clubs, hotel clubs, and clubs operated to provide meals under circumstances generally considered to be conducive to business discussions. The disallowance rule does not apply to business leagues, trade associations, chambers of commerce, professional organizations, and civic or public service organizations (e.g., Lions and Rotary Clubs). [Reg. § 1.274-2(a)(2)(iii)]

Q 8:41 Can a taxpayer deduct the cost of entertaining a customer at a skybox at a sports arena?

A deduction is allowed for entertaining at a skybox (assuming the directly related or associated test is met). However, a special rule limits the amount of the deduction. If a taxpayer rents a skybox (or other private luxury box) for more than one event at the same sports arena, the deduction cannot exceed the price of a *non-luxury* box seat ticket. [IRC § 274(l)(2)]

To determine whether a skybox has been rented for more than one event, each game or other performance counts as one event. For example, renting a skybox for a series of playoff games is considered renting it for more than one event. All skyboxes rented by the taxpayer in the same arena, together with any rentals by related parties, are considered in making this determination. Related parties include: (1) members of the taxpayer's family and (2) parties who have made a reciprocal arrangement involving the sharing of skyboxes, related corporations, and a partnership and its principal partners.

> **Example 8-25:** Tom Dwyer pays $3,000 to rent a 10-seat skybox at a stadium for three baseball games. He uses the skybox for deductible business entertaining. The cost of regular non-luxury box seats at each event is $20 a seat. Dwyer can deduct (subject to the 50-percent limit) $600. That is the product of 10 seats at $20 for three events (10 × $20 × 3 = $600).

Expenses for food and beverages are not subject to the skybox rule as long as they are separately stated and reasonable in amount. (A taxpayer cannot inflate the charges for food and beverages to avoid the limited deduction for skybox rentals.)

Q 8:42 Can an employer claim a full deduction for the cost of nonbusiness entertainment provided to employees as long as the value of the entertainment is treated as taxable compensation to the employees?

Generally speaking, yes. In the *Sutherland Lumber-Southwest, Inc* case, the Eighth Circuit Court of Appeals ruled that an employer could deduct the full cost of operating an aircraft for a personal trip of an employee, even though the deduction would far exceed the amount taxable to the employee as compensation. [*Sutherland Lumber-Southwest, Inc,* U.S. Ct. App. (8th Cir., 2001)] However, for certain "specified individuals"" the American Jobs Creation Act of 2004 (P.L. 108-357 effectively reversed the *Sutherland* case. Under the Act, in the case of specified individuals, entertainment expenses for goods, services or facilities are deductible only to the extent that the expenses do not exceed the amount of the expenses which are treated by the employer as compensation paid to an employee and as wages subject to withholding. [IRC § 274(e)(2)(A)]

Specified individuals generally include officers, directors and 10-percent-or-greater owners of private and publicly held companies. An officer is defined as the president, principal financial officer, principal accounting officer, any vice-president in charge of a principal business unit, division or function, any other officer who performs a policy-making function or any other person who performs similar policy-making functions. [Conference Committee Report (H. R. Conf. Rep. No. 108-755), American Jobs Creation Act of 2004 (P.L. 108-357)]

For expenses incurred after June 30, 2005, the IRS has released interim guidance on the tax treatment of the use of business aircraft by specified individuals for entertainment travel. The IRS says the business need not own the aircraft to be subject to the deduction limitation. The use of leased or chartered aircraft for entertainment travel is also covered. The costs of maintaining and operating the aircraft, beyond the amount included in the specified individual's compensation, are not deductible. Such items include fuel costs, salaries for pilots and other flight personnel, meal and lodging expenses of flight personnel, takeoff and landing fees, costs of on-board refreshments, hangar fees, management fees, and depreciation. [Notice 2005-45, I.R.B. 2005-24]

In order to apply the limitation, the total deductible expenses attributable to the aircraft must be allocated to expenses for use of the aircraft for the entertainment of specified individuals and expenses for all other uses. The method of allocation must be based on either occupied seat hours or occupied seat miles flown by the aircraft. Occupied seat hours or miles are equal to the sum of the hours or miles flown by an aircraft, multiplied by the number of seats occupied for each hour or mile. Whatever method that is used must be applied consistently for all usage for the tax year. So-called "deadhead" flights, where an aircraft returns empty after discharging passengers or flies empty to pick up passengers, are treated as having the same number and character of occupied seat hours or miles as the legs of the trip on which passengers are aboard.

Once the occupied seat hours or occupied seat miles are determined, the cost per hour or mile must be calculated. The cost per occupied seat hour or occupied seat mile is equal to the total fixed and variable expenses for the aircraft, divided by the total occupied seat hours or occupied seat miles. Taxpayers can compute the cost per occupied seat hour or occupied seat mile for each aircraft or they can aggregate the costs of aircraft of similar cost profiles. After the cost per occupied seat hour or occupied seat mile is determined, the amount that is disallowed can be determined. The amount disallowed is equal to the sum of the cost of each occupied seat hour or occupied seat mile flown by a specified individual for entertainment purposes, less the sum of the amount treated as compensation and the amount reimbursed for each specified individual and each flight.

The IRS has also issued proposed regulations on the tax treatment of personal use of business aircraft for entertainment travel. [Prop. Reg. § 1.274-9 and § 1.274-10]Taxpayers may generally rely on the rules in the proposed regulations or those in Notice 2005-45 above for tax years beginning before final regulations are published.

The proposed regulations provide:

- An election to use straight-line depreciation in computing aircraft depreciation; [Prop. Reg. § 1.274-10(d)(3)],

- Additional rules to define similar cost profiles of aircraft; [Prop. Reg. § 1.274-10(d)(4)]

- That expenses may be allocated on a flight-by-flight basis rather than by using the occupied seat per mile or hour formula; [Prop. Reg. § 1.274-10(e)(3)]

- That disallowed depreciation amounts do not reduce aircraft basis; [Prop. Reg. § 1.274-10(f)(1)] and

- Guidance on the application of the consistency rule in valuing the entertainment use of aircraft by specified individuals and the non-entertainment use, as well as use of aircraft by non-specified individuals. [Prop. Reg. § 1.61-21(g)(14)]

Fifty-Percent Deduction Limit

Q 8:43 Which expenses are subject to the 50-percent deduction limit?

The 50-percent limit on deductible expenses generally applies to all business-related meal and entertainment expenses. [IRC § 274(n)(1)]This covers meal and entertainment expenses incurred while:

- Traveling away from home (whether the taxpayer eats alone or with others) on business;

- Entertaining customers at the taxpayer's place of business, a restaurant, or other location; or

- Attending a business convention or reception, business meeting, or business luncheon at a club.

Taxes and tips relating to a business meal or entertainment activity are included in the amount that is subject to the 50-percent limit. Expenses such as cover charges for admission to a nightclub, rent paid for a room in which the taxpayer holds a dinner or cocktail party, or the amount paid for parking at a sports arena are subject to the 50-percent limit. However, the cost of transportation to and from a business meal or a business-related entertainment activity is not subject to the 50-percent limit.

If meal and entertainment expenses are included with other expenses, a taxpayer must allocate the expenses between the portion subject to the 50-percent limit and the portion that is not. For example, a taxpayer must allocate expenses if a hotel includes one or more meals in its room charge.

Q 8:44 How is the 50-percent limit applied if an expense is already subject to some other deduction limitations?

The 50-percent limit is applied *after* determining the amount that would otherwise qualify for as a deductible expense.

> **Example 8-26:** Harry Kelly spends $300 for a business-related meal. If $150 of that amount is not deductible because it is considered "lavish," the remaining $150 is subject to the 50-percent limit. Kelly can deduct only $75.

Q 8:45 Are there any exceptions to the 50-percent deduction limit?

Yes. Generally, expenses that are exempt from the directly related or associated tests (see above) are also exempt from the 50-percent deduction limit. [IRC §274(n)(2)(A). For example, if a taxpayer gives a Christmas party for his or her employees, 100 percent of the costs are deductible. [IRC §274(e)]

Business Gifts

Q 8:46 Are gifts to customers and clients deductible business expenses?

Yes, up to a limit. A taxpayer can deduct up to $25 annually for business gifts given directly or indirectly to any one person. For this purpose, a "gift" is any item that the recipient can exclude from income under IRC Section 102. [IRC §274(b)]

Incidental costs, such as engraving on jewelry, or packaging, insuring, and mailing, are generally not included in determining the cost of a gift for purposes of the $25 limit. A related cost is incidental only if it does not add substantial value to the gift. For example, the cost of gift-wrapping is an incidental cost.

However, the purchase of an ornamental basket for packaging fruit is not an incidental cost if the value of the basket is substantial compared to the value of the fruit. [Reg. § 1.274-3(c)]

Q 8:47 What are "indirect" gifts?

A gift to a company that is intended for a particular person or a limited class of people will be considered an indirect gift to that particular person or to the individuals within the class. If a taxpayer gives a gift to a member of a customer's family, the gift is generally considered to be an indirect gift to the customer. This rule does not apply if the taxpayer has a bona fide, independent business connection with that family member and the gift is not intended for the customer's eventual use. [Reg. § 1.274-3(e)]

Q 8:48 If a couple gives a gift, is the maximum deduction doubled to $50?

No. If a taxpayer and his or her spouse both give gifts, both of them are treated as one taxpayer for this purpose. It does not matter if the couple have separate businesses, are separately employed, or whether each of them has an independent connection with the recipient. [Reg. § 1.274-3(f)(2)]

Example 8-27: Ted Benson sells products to XYZ Inc. Ted and his wife, Jan, gave XYZ three cheese packages to thank them for their business. Ted and Jan paid $80 for each package, or $240 total. Three of XYZ's executives took the packages home for their families' use. Bob and Jan have no independent business relationship with any of the executives' other family members. They can deduct a total of $75 ($25 limit × 3) for the cheese packages.

Q 8:49 Are there any exceptions to the $25 annual limit?

Yes. The following items are not considered gifts for purposes of the $25 limit:

1. An item that: (a) costs $4 or less, (b) has the taxpayer's name clearly and permanently imprinted on the gift, and (c) Is one of a number of identical items widely distributed (e.g., pens, desk sets).

2. Signs, display racks, or other promotional material to be used on the business premises of the recipient.

[Reg. § 1.274-(3)(b)]

Q 8:50 If a taxpayer gives a customer tickets to the theater or a sporting event, is that considered a business gift or business entertainment?

Any item that might be considered either a gift or an entertainment expense generally will be considered an entertainment expense. Thus, it will not be subject to the $25 limit, but will be subject to the limits on business entertainment deductions (see above). (*Note:* Packaged food or beverages given to a customer for consumption at a later time should be treated as a gift, not entertainment.)

If a taxpayer gives a customer tickets to a theater performance or sporting event and the taxpayer does not accompany the customer to the performance or event, the taxpayer has a tax choice—the cost of the tickets may be treated either as a gift expense or as an entertainment expense, whichever works better for the taxpayer. However, if the taxpayer goes to the event with the customer, the cost of the tickets must be treated as an entertainment expense. [Reg. § 1.274-2(b)(1)(iii)]

> **Planning Point:** Whether it is better to treat tickets as a gift or as business entertainment is largely a factor of costs. For example, if a ticket costs $60, then $30 would be deductible as business entertainment (50 percent of $60), while only $25 would be deductible as a business gift. On the other hand, if the ticket costs $40, then the $25 deduction for gifts is preferable to the $20 deduction as business entertainment.

Substantiation Requirements

Q 8:51 Are there special substantiation rules for travel and entertainment expenses?

Yes. A taxpayer must meet special, stringent proof requirements to deduct travel and entertainment expenses. Any deduction taken for estimated expenses will be disallowed on audit. A taxpayer should keep the necessary records to support his or her expenses in an account book, diary, statement of expense, or similar record, together with required documentary evidence (see below).

Q 8:52 What are the substantiation requirements for expenses incurred on business travel away from home?

In general, a taxpayer must be able to substantiate the following elements of each expense:

- *Amount.* The taxpayer must show the amount of each separate travel expense. At the taxpayer's option, he or she may aggregate the total daily amount of certain expenses like meals and taxi fares if the expenses are repetitious or recurrent. Tips can also be aggregated with the expense. [Temp. Reg. § 1.274-5T(b)(2)(i), (b)(3)(i), (c)(6)(i)]

- *Time and place.* The taxpayer must show the date of departure and return for each trip, the number of days away from home, and the travel destination. [Temp. Reg. § 1.274-5T(b)(3)(ii)]

- *Business purpose.* The taxpayer must show the business reason for the travel away from home. [Temp. Reg. § 1.274-5T]

The taxpayer must substantiate each element of an expense either by adequate records or by sufficient evidence corroborating his or her own statement.

However, written evidence has more value as proof than oral evidence. In addition, the value of written evidence is greater the closer in time the writing is to the time the expense is incurred. [Temp. Reg. §1.274-5T(c)(1)] No record of meal expenses is required if the taxpayer deducts the standard meal allowance (see above). A taxpayer must keep documentary evidence (e.g., receipts or paid bills) for: (1) any lodging expense, and (2) any other travel expense of $75 or more. [Notice 95-50, 1995-2 C.B. 333]

Q 8:53 What are the substantiation requirements for the business use of an automobile?

If a taxpayer is deducting actual auto expenses, he or she must be able to prove:

- The amount of each expense;
- The mileage for each business use of the car, plus the total mileage for the car during the year;
- The date each business use occurred or expense was incurred; and
- The business purpose of each use or expense.

[Temp. Reg. §1.274-5T(b)(6)]

If taxpayer claims the standard mileage rate (see above), he or she does not have to document the expenses, but proof is still required for the date and purpose for the driving as well as the amount of the mileage.

Separate uses of a car can be aggregated if part of an overall, uninterrupted business use. For example, if a taxpayer makes a sales trip out of town to see customers, a single record of the miles traveled is sufficient. [Temp. Reg. §1.274-5T(c)(6)(C)]

Sampling. A taxpayer is permitted to maintain an adequate record of business use for only part of the year if he or she can show that part is representative of the year as a whole. [Temp. Reg. §1.274-5T(c)(3)(ii)]

Example 8-28: Lisa Simpson runs a business from her home. She uses her automobile for trips around town to visit customers and suppliers. She maintains adequate records for the first three months of 2008 that indicate 75 percent of the use of the car was for her business. Her business records (e.g., invoices, billings, etc.) show that the level of her business activity was fairly uniform throughout 2008. Thus, she will be considered to have adequate records to support a 75 percent business use rate for the entire year.

Q 8:54 What are the substantiation requirements for business entertainment and gift expenses?

To claim a deduction for an entertainment expense that is directly related to business, a taxpayer must be able to prove:

- The amount of each expense for entertainment;
- The date of the entertainment;
- The name, address, or location of the site of the entertainment (including a designation of the type of entertainment if not readily apparent from the name of the place);
- The business reason for the entertainment or the nature of the business benefit to be derived and the nature of any business discussion or activity; and
- The name, title, or other designation of the person being entertained, sufficient to establish his or her business relationship to the taxpayer.

[Temp. Reg. § 1.274-5(b)(3)]

For entertainment deducted as an expense associated with business (i.e., a substantial business discussion precedes or follows it), the taxpayer must be able to prove all of the items above, plus the following:

- The date and duration of the business discussion,
- The place of the business discussion,
- The nature of the discussion, and
- The identification of the participants in the discussion.

[Temp. Reg. § 1.274-5T(b)(4)]

In the case of deductions for business gifts, the taxpayer must be able to prove the following:

- The cost of the gift;
- The date of the gift;
- A description of the gift;
- The business reason for the gift or the business benefit expected to be derived; and
- The name, title, or other designation of the recipient sufficient to establish the business relationship with the recipient.

[Temp. Reg. § 1.274-5T(b)(5)]

As with travel expenses, the taxpayer must substantiate the items above by adequate written records or by sufficient evidence corroborating his or her own statement. [Reg. § 1.2745-5T(c)(1)] In addition to the adequate records requirement, the taxpayer must keep receipts or other documentary evidence for entertainment expenses in excess of $75.

Reimbursements by Employers

Q 8:55 How does an employee claim travel and entertainment expenses if he or she is reimbursed by an employer?

The treatment of reimbursed expenses depends on whether the employee is reimbursed under an "accountable" or a "nonaccountable" plan. An employee is not taxed on an advance, reimbursement, or other expense allowance received from an employer under an accountable plan. [Reg. §1.62-2(c)(4)] On the other hand, what the employee receives under a nonaccountable plan is fully taxable and subject to employment taxes and income tax withholding. [Reg. §1.62-2(c)(5)]

If an employee reports taxable income from a nonaccountable plan, he or she can claim deductions for business travel and entertainment expenses to the extent allowed by law and properly substantiated (see above). Employees reimbursed under an accountable plan generally report no income and claim no deductions on their tax returns. However, if expenses exceed reimbursements, an employee can choose to report the reimbursements and deduct the expenses.

Q 8:56 What is an accountable plan?

To be an accountable plan, an employer's reimbursement or allowance arrangement must meet all three of the following requirements:

1. The expenses must have a "business connection";

2. The employee must "adequately account" to the employer for these expenses within a reasonable period of time; and

3. The employee must return any excess reimbursement or allowance within a reasonable period of time.

[Reg. §1.62-2(c)]

Q 8:57 When are expenses considered to have a "business connection"?

A reimbursement plan meets the business connection requirements if it provides advances, allowances, etc., only for business expenses that are deductible as itemized deductions and that are paid or incurred by the employee in connection with the performance of services as an employee of the employer. [Reg. §1.62-2(d)(1)] If both wages and reimbursements or other expense allowances are combined in a single payment, the reimbursement or other expense allowance must be identified either by a separate payment or by specific identification of the amount of the reimbursement or other expense allowance.

> **Example 8-29:** XYZ Inc., an engineering company, pays its employee $200 a day. On the days an engineer travels away from home on business for XYZ, the company designates $50 of the $200 as paid to reimburse the engineer's travel expenses.

This arrangement does not satisfy the business connection requirement because XYZ would pay the employee $200 a day whether or not the employee was traveling away from home. Therefore, payments under the arrangement are treated as paid under a nonaccountable plan.

Q 8:58 For purposes of the accountable plan rules, what is a "reasonable period of time"?

The definition of a "reasonable period of time" depends on the facts and circumstances of the particular situation. However, regardless of the facts and circumstances of the situation, actions that take place within the times specified in the following list are treated as taking place within a reasonable period of time.

- The employee receives an advance within 30 days of the time an expense is incurred;
- The employee adequately accounts for the expense within 60 days after the expense was incurred;
- The employee returns an excess reimbursement within 120 days after the expense was incurred; and
- The employee is given a periodic statement (at least quarterly) that asks him or her to either return or adequately account for outstanding advances, and the employee complies within 120 days of the statement.

Q 8:59 What is an "adequate accounting"?

An employee adequately accounts to an employer by giving the employer a statement of expense, an account book, a diary, or a similar record in which the employee enters each expense at or near the time he or she incurs it, along with documentary evidence (such as receipts) of the expenses. For travel and entertainment expenses, the employee must provide the same substantiation to the employer that would be required if there were no reimbursements and the employee was substantiating the expenses to the IRS.

Electronic accounting. The IRS recently approved a T&E recordkeeping system that eliminates most paper expense reports and receipts. Under the approved system, an employer arranges to have a credit card company issue a business credit card to each employee the employer determines is likely to incur travel and entertainment expenses for necessary business reasons. Employees who use the business credit card receive monthly billing statements from the credit card company and are personally liable to the credit card company for all charges billed to the card, including late payment fees.

The credit card company also provides the employer with an electronic receipt for all expenses billed to an employee's business credit card on a daily basis. An electronic receipt contains the date of the charge, the amount of the charge, the merchant's name, the merchant's location, and, if available, an itemization from the merchant of each expense included in the charge.

The credit card company generally issues three types of electronic receipts to the employer: (1) a receipt with sufficient information on its face to indicate the nature of the charge (such as a charge from an airline carrier for a passenger ticket); (2) a receipt with an aggregate charge itemizing each expense (such as a final bill from a hotel listing separately the costs for meals, lodging, and telephone calls); and (3) a receipt with an aggregate charge without itemizing each expense (such as a final bill from a hotel that does not list each charge separately).

Under the employer's electronic expense reimbursement arrangement, the employer transfers the electronic receipts received from the credit card company to a database. This information cannot be altered once entered. Employees access the database to create an electronic expense report to accompany the electronic receipts associated with their travel and entertainment expenses. For all expenses, the employees must indicate whether the expenses are personal or business-related travel and entertainment. For all business-related travel and entertainment expenses, the employee must provide the following information in the electronic expense reports for each travel and entertainment expense: (1) a description of the expense and the business purpose it served; and (2) for each entertainment expense, the names and business relationship of the persons entertained in addition to the date of, place of, duration of, and participants in any business discussion that occurred directly before or after the entertainment.

The employer requires employees to submit paper expense reports and receipts for: (1) any expense over $75 where the nature of the expense is not clear on the face of the electronic receipt; (2) all lodging invoices for which the credit card company does not provide the merchant's electronic itemization of each expense; and (3) any expenses paid for by the employee without using the business credit card. The employer requires that the paper receipts and expense reports contain information sufficient to substantiate the amount, date, time, place, and business purpose of each expense.

To receive reimbursements under the reimbursement arrangement, employees must submit expense reports with any necessary receipts to the employer within 30 days after returning from a business trip or incurring a travel or entertainment expense, but no later than 60 days after incurring the expense. Once the employer approves an employee's travel and entertainment expense report, the employer sends payment directly to the credit card company for the business expenses listed in the report. The employer does not reimburse any charges made to the employee's business credit card that are not listed in the expense report approved by the employer. The employer treats the reimbursement of any nondeductible business expenses as wages paid to the employee and does not reimburse personal expenses.

The IRS said that a substantiation system like this satisfies all the requirements of an accountable plan. [Rev. Rul. 2003-106, 2003-44 IRB 936]

Q 8:60 If an employer reimburses employees on a per diem or mileage basis for their travel and car expenses, does that meet the "adequate accounting" requirements?

If an employer reimburses an employee using a per diem travel allowance or a car allowance, the employee may generally use the allowance as proof for the amount of his or her expenses. [Reg. § 1.274-5(g); Temp. Reg. § 1.274-5T(g)] A per diem or car allowance satisfies the adequate accounting requirements for the amount of expenses if it meets the following requirements:

- The employer reasonably limits payments of expenses to those that are ordinary and necessary in the conduct of the trade or business;

- The allowance is similar in form to and not more than the federal rate (see below);

- The employee proves the time (dates), place, and business purpose of the expenses to the employer within a reasonable period of time; and

- The employer and employee are not "related".

For this purpose, a taxpayer is considered related to his or her employer if:

- The employer is the taxpayer's brother or sister, half brother or half sister, spouse, ancestor, or lineal descendant;

- The employer is a corporation in which the taxpayer owns, directly or indirectly, more than 10 percent in value of the outstanding stock; or

- Certain relationships (such as grantor, fiduciary, or beneficiary) exist between the taxpayer, a trust, and the employer.

If an employee is related to an employer, he or she must be able to prove the expenses to the IRS even if there has been an adequate accounting to the employer.

Q 8:61 What is the "federal rate"?

The federal rate includes the standard mileage allowance and the standard meal allowance (see above). Thus, for example, if an employee's mileage reimbursement does not exceed 48.5 cents per mile in 2007, the employee will be deemed to have made an adequate accounting at least as far as his or her expenses are concerned.

The federal rate also includes a per diem allowance for meals, lodging, and incidental expenses while away from home on business. There is a "regular" federal per diem rate and a "high-low" rate.

Regular federal per diem rate. The regular federal per diem rate is the highest amount that the federal government will pay to its employees for lodging, meals, and incidental expenses while they are traveling away from home in a particular area. The federal per diem rate is equal to the sum of the applicable federal lodging expense rate and the applicable federal meal and incidental expense (M&IE) rate for the day and locality of travel. [Rev. Proc. 2007-63 , I.R.B. 2007-42]

The rates for localities in the continental United States (CONUS rates) are issued annually by the General Services Administration. The rates for localities outside the continental United States (OCONUS rates) are established by the Secretary of Defense (in the case of non-foreign localities, including Alaska, Hawaii, and Puerto Rico) and by the Secretary of State (rates for foreign localities). These are updated on a updated on a monthly basis. The CONUS and

OCONUS rates may be found on the Internet at www.policyworks.gov/perdiem.

High-low rates. The high-low is a simplified method of computing the federal per diem rate for travel within the continental United States. It eliminates the need to keep a current list of the per diem rate for each city. Under the high-low method, the per diem amount for travel in 2008 is $237 for certain high-cost locations. All other areas have a per diem amount of $152. For employees who are reimbursed on an per diem basis for meals and incidental expenses only, the high-low system also contains an M&IE rate—$58 for high-cost locations and $45 for other locations. [Rev. Proc. 2007-63 , I.R.B. 2007-42]

No double reimbursement. If a employer pays a per diem allowance in lieu of reimbursing actual expenses for lodging, meal, and incidental expenses or for meal and incidental expenses, any additional payment for these expenses is treated as paid under a nonaccountable plan. The additional payment must be included in the employee's gross income and reported as wages or other compensation on the employee's Form W-2 and is subject to withholding and payment of employment taxes.

For example, assume an employee receives a per diem allowance from his or her employer for lodging, meal, and incidental expenses while traveling away from home on business. During that trip, the employee pays for dinner for the employee and two business associates. The employer reimburses as a business entertainment meal expense the meal expense for the employee and the two business associates. Because the employer also pays a per diem allowance to cover the cost of the employee's meals, the amount paid by the employer for the employee's portion of the business entertainment meal expense must be reported as wages or other compensation on the employee's Form W-2 and is subject to withholding and payment of employment taxes.

Partial days of travel. The M&IE rate must be prorated for partial days of travel away from home. The rate may be prorated using the method prescribed by the Federal Travel Regulations. Currently the Federal Travel Regulations allow three-fourths of the applicable M&IE rate for each partial day during which an employee or self-employed individual is traveling away from home on business.

The IRS says that the M&IE rate may also be prorated using any method that is consistently applied and is in accordance with reasonable business practice. For example, if an employee travels away from home from 9:00 AM one day to 5:00 PM the next day, a method of proration that results in an amount equal to two times the federal M&IE rate will be treated as being in accordance with reasonable business practice (even though only one and a half times the federal M&IE rate would be allowed under the Federal Travel Regulations). [Rev. Proc. 2007-63 , I.R.B. 2007-42]

The IRS has ruled that the failure to track allowances in excess of the federal rate coupled with routine payment of excess allowances that were not repaid or treated as wages evidences a pattern of abuse of the accountable plan rules. As a result, all of the reimbursements under the plan, not only those that exceeded the federal rate, must be treated as paid under a nonaccountable plan, and so were subject to withholding and employment taxes. [Rev. Rul. 2006-56, 2006-46 I.R.B]

Q 8:62 If an employer reimburses an employee for meals using the federal rate, is the employer's deduction for the reimbursement subject to the 50-percent deduction limit (Q 8:41)?

Yes. If a per diem is paid only for M&IE, an amount equal to the lesser of the per diem allowance for each calendar day or the federal M&IE rate is treated as an expense for food and beverages and thus subject to the 50-percent deduction limit. If the per diem allowance is paid for lodging as well as M&IE, the payor must treat an amount equal to the federal M&IE rate as an expense for food and beverages. For this purpose, when a per diem for lodging and M&IE is paid at a rate that is less that the federal per diem rate, the payor may treat an amount equal to 40 percent of the per diem allowance as the federal M&IE rate. [Rev. Proc. 2007-63 , I.R.B. 2007-42]

A per diem allowance is treated as paid only for M&IE if (1) the payor pays the employee for actual expenses for lodging based on receipts submitted to the payor; (2) the payor provides the lodging in kind; (3) the payor pays the actual expenses for lodging directly to the provider of the lodging; (4) the payor does not have a reasonable belief that lodging expenses were or will be incurred by the employee; or (5) the allowance is computed on a basis similar to that used in computing the employee's wages or other compensation (such as the number of hours worked, miles traveled, or pieces produced). [Rev. Proc. 2007-63 , I.R.B. 2007-42]

In one Tax Court case, an employer allocated 40 percent of its reimbursement to meals and subjected that 40 percent to the 50-percent deduction limit. The IRS, however, claimed that the 50-percent deduction disallowance applied to the entire reimbursement because the reimbursement was "computed on a basis similar to that used in computing the employee's wages."

The case involved Beech Trucking Company, Inc., which transported general commodities within the Midwest and South. On long hauls, Beech Trucking drivers were paid at a specified rate for each mile traveled. During 1995 and 1996, the drivers were paid between 24 and 26 cents per mile. Of this amount, 6.5 cents was designated as a per diem travel allowance. Short-haul drivers were paid a flat weekly salary, in addition to the 6.5 cents per mile per diem allowance. The drivers turned in their logs, receipts, bills of lading, and the like, which were used to figure their expense reimbursements. The drivers were not required to account for their expenses.

The drivers were not separately reimbursed for lodging expenses, overnight parking, or showers.

When it filed its tax returns for 1995 and 1996, Beech treated 40 percent of the per mile travel allowance as a reimbursement for meals because the reimbursements were less than the federal rate. Therefore, Beech deducted 80 percent of its total travel allowance payments—100 percent of the 60 percent allocable to lodging and 50 percent of 40 percent allocable to meals.

On audit, the IRS allowed Beech a deduction for only 50 percent of its total payments. The Service contended that, because the allowance was computed on a basis similar to the way Beech paid wages (i.e., cents per mile), the *entire allowance* should be treated as a reimbursement for meals only. As such, only 50 percent of the payments would be deductible.

When the case came before the Tax Court, Beech argued that the Service's action was "arbitrary" and "unlawful." The travel allowances were designed to cover not only the drivers' meals but also their lodging expenses and incidental expenses, such as the cost of showers, laundry, overnight parking, and local transportation.

The Tax Court ruled against Beech. The court point out that Beech's reimbursements were insufficient to cover all of its truckers' travel expenses. Because the IRS permits employers to meet the substantiation requirements through flat allowances, "the actual amounts and character of each employee's travel expenses are unknown and probably unknowable." In these circumstances, it is reasonable for the IRS to adopt accounting conventions to determine which expenses are substantiated.

The court noted that Beech was trying to have its cake and eat it too. It could have reimbursed its employees on the basis of their actual expenses, in which case only actual meal expense reimbursement would have been subject to the 50-percent limit. Instead, it opted to take advantage of the convenience of paying flat travel allowances. That being the case, Beech is subject to all of the conditions the IRS lays down for the use of such allowances.

In any case, the court said, the burden is on Beech to prove that the Service's calculations are wrong and Beech offered no independent evidence of how much its truckers spent on lodging. Therefore, Beech has failed to meet its burden of prove, and the Service's figures must stand. [*Beech Trucking Co. v. Comm'r*, 118 T.C. 428, (2002)]

Chapter 9

Employee Health and Accident Benefits

The tax law gives tax-favored status to employer-provided health and accident benefits. Federal law, however, does not require employers to provide health coverage for employees. Moreover, even when an employer does provide health coverage, the law does not mandate universal or identical coverage for all employees. For example, an employer can generally provide health coverage only for executives or can provide different levels of coverage to different groups of employees. An employer, however, cannot discriminate in providing health coverage based on an employee's health status.

Once an employer makes the decision to provide health benefits for employees, the employer must comply with certain federal laws. For example, the so-called COBRA coverage rules may require an employer to provide continued coverage to employees who terminate employment or would otherwise lose coverage under the employer's plan. In addition, in recent years, Congress has enacted several laws that mandate the type of coverage that must be provided to employees.

Basic Tax Rules

Q 9:1 How are employee health benefits treated for tax purposes?

As a general rule, an employer's payment for and employee's coverage under an accident or health plan are deductible by the employer and tax-free to the employee. [IRC § § 162, 106]In addition, amounts received by the employee under the plan as reimbursements for medical care are not included in the employee's income. [IRC § 105]This tax-favored treatment also applies to employer-provided health benefits for an employee's spouse and dependents.

Q 9:2 What is an accident or health plan?

An accident or health plan is an arrangement that provides benefits for employees, their spouses, and their dependents in the event of personal injury or sickness. [Reg. § 1.105-5(a)]

An accident or health plan may take the form of employer-provided health insurance. In addition, an arrangement to provide direct reimbursements by an employer (a so-called "self-insured" plan) also qualifies as an accident or health plan. Self-insured plans, however, are subject to some special tax rules (see Q 9:17).

Accident and health plans also include:

- Health flexible spending accounts (FSAs), which permit employees to set aside funds on a pre-tax basis to pay for out-of-pocket medical expenses,

- Employer contributions to a health savings account (HSA) or medical savings account (MSA), which can be used to pay for out-of pocket medical expenses in conjunction with high-deductible health insurance coverage, or

- Contributions to a health reimbursement arrangement (HRA) that provides funds to an employee to be used for health care costs.

Q 9:3 What is medical care?

Benefits received by an employee under a plan are tax-free only to the extent they are for medical care. For this purpose, medical care includes amounts paid for the diagnosis, cure, mitigation, treatment, or prevention of disease or for the purpose of affecting any structure or function of the body. [IRC § 213]

A drug is considered a medical care expense only if it is a prescribed drug or insulin. [IRC § 213(b)] The IRS has ruled, for example, that the cost of smoking-cessation programs and prescription drugs to alleviate nicotine withdrawal qualify as medical care. However, because medical care includes only prescription drugs, over-the-counter nicotine patches and gum to help kick the habit do not qualify as medical care. [Rev. Rul. 99-28, 1999-1 C.B. 1269] Note, however, that nonpresctiption drugs can qualify for tax-free reimbursements from health savings accounts (HSAs) and other reimbursement arrangements.

Q 9:1

Cosmetic surgery or similar procedures do not qualify as medical care unless the surgery or procedure is necessary to ameliorate a deformity due to a birth abnormality, an accident or trauma, or a disfiguring disease. For example, cosmetic breast augmentation surgery would not qualify as medical care. However, breast reconstruction following a mastectomy is part of medical care. In fact, federal legislation mandates health plan coverage for breast reconstruction in this situation. [Women's Health and Cancer Rights Act of 1998, P.L. 105-277] Moreover, the IRS has officially ruled that amounts paid for breast reconstruction surgery following a mastectomy qualify as medical care expenses. [Rev. Rul. 2003-57, 2003-22 I.R.B. 959]

In that same ruling, the IRS concluded that laser eye surgery to correct myopia constitutes medical care, but teeth-whitening procedures performed by a dentist do not qualify as medical care. According to the IRS, teeth-whitening does not treat a physical or mental disease or promote the proper function of the body. Moreover, discoloration of the teeth is not a disease and is not caused by a disfiguring disease or treatment. Instead, the procedure is directed at improving the patient's appearance.

Finally, the IRS has ruled that weight-loss programs may qualify as medical care under certain circumstances. [Rev. Rul. 2002-19, 2002-16 I.R.B. 779] In its ruling, the IRS concluded that expenses for weight-loss programs (including the cost of meetings and purchased diet plans and booklets) will qualify as medical expenses for individuals who participate in such programs to treat a diagnosed medical condition such as obesity or hypertension. [Rev. Rul. 2002-19, 2002-16 I.R.B. 779] However, the costs of a weight-loss program do not qualify as medical expenses for individuals who participate in such programs only to improve their general health or appearance. In addition, the IRS noted that although purchased diet foods may be part of a weight-loss program, those foods are substitutes for the food an individual would normally consume. Thus, the costs do not qualify as medical expenses, even for individuals with diagnosed medical conditions.

Group Health Coverage

Q 9:4 When can an employer claim a deduction for amounts paid for employee accident or health benefits?

An employer can deduct amounts paid or accrued during the year for sickness, accident, hospitalization, or medical expense benefits for employees, provided they qualify as ordinary and necessary expenses of the employer's business. [Reg. § 1.162-10(a)]

Q 9:5 Are employer contributions to an accident or health plan taxable to the employees?

Contributions to an accident or health plan are excludable from an employee's income. [IRC § 106] The exclusion covers:

- Contributions to the cost of accident or health insurance,

- Contributions to a trust or fund that provides accident or health benefits either directly or through insurance,

- Contributions to a health savings account (HSA) or medical savings account (MSA) that can be used by an employee to pay medical expenses,

- Contributions to a health reimbursement arrangement that provides funds to an employee to be used for health care costs, and

- Direct payment of an employee's medical expenses or reimbursement to an employee for his or her expenses (i.e., payments under a self-insured plan).

Q 9:6 Who is an employee for purposes of the exclusion for employer-provided accident or health benefits?

For purposes of the exclusion, an employee includes: [Rev. Rul. 82-196, 1982-2 C.B. 53; IRC § 414(n)]

- A current common law employee;

- A full-time life insurance agent who is treated as a "statutory employee" (see Q14:71);

- A retired employee;

- A widow or widower of an individual who died while employed by the employer;

- A widow or widower of a retired employee;

- A leased employee who has provided services under the employer's primary direction and control for at least a year on a substantially full-time basis.

Partners and S corporation shareholders. Partners in a partnership and 2 percent S corporation shareholders are not treated as employees for purposes of the exclusion for employer-provided health benefits. [Rev. Rul. 91-26, 1991-1 C.B. 184] A 2 percent S corporation shareholder is someone who directly or indirectly owns more than 2 percent of the corporation's stock or stock with more than 2 percent of the voting power at any time during the year. Special tax rules apply to accident or health benefits provided to partners and S corporation shareholders (see Q 9:15-9:14).

Self-employed individuals. A self-employed individual is not considered an employee of his or her unincorporated business. [IRC § 105(g)] Special tax rules apply to medical insurance coverage for self-employed individuals (see Q 9:73 *et seq.*).

Q 9:6

Q 9:7 Are an employer's contributions for health coverage for retired employees taxable to the retirees?

No. An employer's contributions for retiree health coverage are not taxable to the retirees. An individual who participated in an employer's health plan as an active employee is treated as continuing to be an employee following retirement. Therefore, contributions for the retiree's coverage are excludable from income as they would be for an active employee. [Rev. Ruls. 62-199, 1962-2 C.B. 38; 75-539, 1975-2 C.B. 45; 82-196, 1982-2 C.B. 53]

Q 9:8 Are an employer's payments for health coverage for an employee's spouse or dependents taxable to the employee?

No. The tax exclusion for employer-provided health benefits applies to coverage for an employee and his or her spouse and dependents. [Reg. § 1.106-1]

In the past, the definition of a dependent for this purpose was the same as the definition for other tax purposes (e.g., claiming dependency exemption). However, the Working Families Tax Relief Act of 2004 amended the definition of dependent. Under the new rules, an individual must either be a "qualifying child" or a "qualifying relative" to be a dependent [IRC § 152]. To be a qualifying child, a child must be under age 19 (or a student under age 24), must live with the taxpayer for more than half the year, and must not provide more than one-half of his or her own support. An individual who does not satisfy that definition may be a "qualifying relative" if he or she is related to the taxpayer (e.g., a child, parent, or sibling) or is a member of the taxpayer's household, receives more than one-half of his or her support from the taxpayer, *and* does not have gross income in excess of the exemption amount for the year ($3,400 for 2007 and $3,500 for 2008).

The addition of this gross income limit raised concerns that employer provided health coverage for certain individuals would have to be treated as taxable income to an employee. For example, if a plan covered a 19-year-old child who was not a full-time student, the coverage would be taxable if the child earned more than the gross income limit for the year.

Fortunately, the IRS allayed these concerns. An IRS notice provides that the value of employer-provided coverage for an individual who meets the definition of a qualifying relative is excludable even if the individual's gross income exceeds the gross income limit. [IRS Notice 2004-79]

Q 9:9 Is employer-provided health coverage for a deceased employee's spouse or dependents taxable?

No. Employer contributions to an accident or health plan that provides benefits for a deceased employee's surviving spouse or dependents are excludable from the income of the survivors. [Rev. Rul. 82-196, 1982-2 C.B. 53]

Q 9:10 Does an employee owe tax on amounts deducted from his or her paycheck to pay the employee's share of health coverage costs?

No, but only if the deduction is made under a plan that meets the requirements for a cafeteria plan. A cafeteria plan is an employer-provided plan that offers employees a choice between cash compensation and one or more employee benefits. Employees who choose a nontaxable benefit, such as health care coverage, do not owe tax on the forgone compensation, and the forgone compensation is not treated as wages for payroll tax purposes. [IRC § 125]

In a case where an employer did not have a cafeteria plan, the employer gave each new employee the option to receive or decline health coverage; if an employee chose the coverage, the employer reduced the compensation it would otherwise have paid to the employee. The IRS ruled that, because the employer's plan did not qualify as a cafeteria plan, an employee who chose health coverage had additional taxable income equal to the difference between the compensation paid and the compensation that the employee would have had if he or she had elected no coverage. [Ltr. Rul. 9406002]

> **Planning Point:** Both the employee and employer take a tax hit with this type of arrangement. An employee in this situation can claim a medical expense deduction for the amount of the reduced compensation contributed toward his or her health coverage. [IRC § 213]However, medical expenses are deductible only to the extent they exceed 7.5 percent of adjusted gross income. As a result, the employee may not receive any tax benefit. Moreover, both the employer and employee will owe payroll taxes on the amount of the reduced compensation.

For details about cafeteria plans, see Chapter 10.

Q 9:11 Can an employer's cafeteria plan make health coverage the default option?

Most employer-sponsored cafeteria plans require employees to make an affirmative election to receive health benefits in lieu of cash compensation. However, an IRS ruling makes it clear that a cafeteria plan may provide that health benefits are the default option and require employees to affirmatively elect to receive cash compensation. [Rev. Rul. 2002-27, 2002-20 I.R.B. 925] Proposed reliance regulations confirm that such automatic elections are permissible [Prop. Reg. Sec. 1.125-2(b)]. Moreover, the proposed regulations make it clear that contributions used to purchase health coverage through a cafeteria plan are not includible in an employee's income because the plan provides for automatic enrollment as the default option.

> **Example 9-1:** Alpha Corporation maintains a calendar-year cafeteria plan. The plan offers group health insurance with employee-only and family coverage options. The plan is in writing and is available to all employees immediately upon being hired.

Under the plan, each employee is automatically enrolled for employee-only health coverage, with the employee's salary reduced on a pre-tax basis to pay for a portion of the cost, unless the employee affirmatively elects to receive cash. Alternatively, an employee with a spouse or child can elect family coverage.

At the time an employee is hired, he or she receives a notice explaining the automatic enrollment process and the employee's right to decline coverage and have no salary reduction. The notice spells out the salary reduction amounts for employee-only and family coverage, the procedure for opting out, the time by which an election must be made, and the period for which the election will be effective. Each current employee receives the same notice before the beginning of each plan year along with a description of the employee's existing coverage, if any. An election for a prior year carries over to the next year unless it is changed.

Result: The IRS says that the cafeteria plan rules apply if an employee can choose between cash and qualified benefits. Moreover, an employee's choice can be either in the form of an affirmative election to receive qualified benefits in lieu of cash or an affirmative election to receive cash in lieu of benefits. Therefore, Alpha's automatic enrollment process, which gives employees the option of electing cash in lieu of health benefits, meets the cafeteria plan rules. Contributions used to purchase health coverage will not be taxable to employees who do not elect to receive cash.

Example 9-2: Beta Corporation's plan works much like Alpha's plan—with one key difference. Under Beta's automatic enrollment process, an employee can affirmatively elect to receive cash in lieu of health benefits only if the employee certifies that he or she has other health coverage.

Result: According to the IRS, the cafeteria plan rules apply only to those employees who can elect between health coverage and cash (i.e., those employees who have other health coverage). Thus, for those employees, contributions to purchase group health insurance can be made on a pre-tax basis. On the other hand, the cafeteria plan rules do not apply to employee-only coverage for employees who cannot certify other health coverage because those employees do not have the ability to elect cash in lieu of coverage. However, coverage provided to those employees can qualify for tax-free treatment as employer-provided health coverage [IRC § 106(a)].

Planning Point: An opt-out health plan may boost enrollment by overcoming employee inertia. Moreover, it may prove to be a time-saver for a company's employee benefits personnel. Processing the paperwork for those employees who opt out or who switch to family coverage may prove less cumbersome than processing applications from all employees who choose to be covered by the plan.

Employers should, however, check state law before establishing an opt-out plan. Such plans may violate state laws requiring specific written authorization from an employee before making deductions for benefit plan contributions from his or her paycheck. The Department of Labor has been asked for advice on whether ERISA preempts state paycheck deduction laws but has not yet ruled on the issue.

Q 9:12 Can an employer provide payments to employees to make up for amounts deducted from employees' paychecks for health care coverage?

An employer can make these kinds of payments—but they will not qualify for tax-free treatment. The IRS has ruled that amounts an employer pays to an employee as "advance reimbursements" or "loans" for future medical expenses do not qualify as medical benefits that are excludable from an employee's gross income. In addition, because the payments are not made on account of expenses incurred by the employee for medical care, the payments are subject to Social Security, Medicare, and federal unemployment tax. [Rev. Rul. 2002-80, 2002-49 I.R.B. 925]

> **Example 9-3:** Gamma Corp. provides health coverage for its employees through a group health insurance policy. The cost of the coverage is paid for through salary reductions. For employees covered by the group health plan, Gamma makes payments in amounts that cause the employee's after-tax pay to be approximately the same as it would have been if there were no salary reduction to pay the group health premiums. Gamma calls these payments "advance reimbursements" for uninsured medical expenses. During the year, employees submit claims to Gamma for uninsured medical expenses. To the extent an employee submits claims during the year, Gamma excludes the "advance reimbursement" payments from the employee's income and does not treat the amounts as wages for income tax withholding or payroll tax purposes. If an employee does not have uninsured medical expenses equal to the "advance reimbursements" made to the employee, Gamma treats the excess as additional compensation to the employee.

> *Result:* Gamma's "advance reimbursement" plan does not qualify as an accident or health plan for purposes of the Code Section 105(b) exclusion because payments are made to employees regardless of whether they incur medical expenses during the year. Therefore, none of the payments are excludable from employees' gross incomes.

> **Example 9-4:** Same facts as Example 9-3, except that Gamma calls the advance payments "loans," which only become due and payable when employees submit claims for uninsured medical expenses. When an employee submits a claim, Gamma reimburses the expenses and simultaneously offsets the amount of the reimbursement against the employee's "loan." Thus, to the extent an employee submits claims for uninsured expenses, Gamma excludes his or her "loans" from gross income and from employment taxes. If an employee does not have uninsured medical expenses equal to his or her "loans," Gamma forgives the "loans."

> *Result:* Although Gamma calls the payments "loans," it is understood that an employee will never have to repay the money. Therefore, the IRS

says the payments do not qualify as loans for tax purposes. Instead, the "loans" are essentially advance reimbursements that are not excludable from employees' gross incomes and are subject to income tax withholding and payroll taxes.

Q 9:13 Can an employer provide coverage for an employee's domestic partner on a tax-favored basis?

Perhaps. Although employer contributions for health coverage for an employee's spouse or dependents are tax-free to the employee, [Reg. § 1.106-1] the federal Defense of Marriage Act, which was enacted in 1996, provides that the word "spouse" refers only to a person of the opposite sex who is a husband or a wife. Therefore, an employee's same-sex domestic partner cannot qualify as a spouse of the employee for purposes of excluding employer-provided health benefits.

On the other hand, for health benefit purposes, a dependent can include any individual who is a member of a taxpayer's household and receives over half of his or her support from the taxpayer for the tax year, provided the relationship between the taxpayer and the individual is not in violation of local law. [IRC § § 152(a)(9), (b)(5)] Furthermore, the IRS has ruled that a domestic partner may qualify as a dependent if those conditions are met. Thus, if the domestic partner does qualify as a dependent, employer-provided coverage for the domestic partner and reimbursements for his or her medical expenses will be excludable from the employee's income. [Ltr. Rul. 9850011] *Note:* The Working Families Tax Relief Act of 2004 revised the tax definition of a dependent to include a gross income limit, effective beginning in 2005. However, an IRS notice makes it clear that the gross income limit does not apply for purposes of the exclusion for employer-provided health coverage. [IRS Notice 2004-79] See Q 9:8.

Of course, the dependency tests may not be met if the employee's domestic partner has his or her own income.

Planning Point: The IRS ruling makes it clear that the tax law does not prohibit an employer from offering health plan coverage for nondependent domestic partners. The IRS says plan coverage for nondependent domestic partners will not affect the exclusion of coverage or benefits for employees, spouses, or dependents.

An employee who opts for coverage for a nondependent domestic partner will be taxed on the fair market value of the domestic partner's coverage (over and above any amount paid by the employee). Any amounts included in an employee's gross income because of domestic partner coverage must be treated as "wages" subject to income tax withholding and payroll taxes.

However, reimbursements received by the employee for the domestic partner's medical expenses will not be taxable to either the employee or the domestic partner because the coverage for the domestic partner will be treated as having been paid for by employee's contributions. [IRC § 104(a)(3)]

Q 9:14 If health coverage for an employee's domestic partner is taxable to an employee, can the employer pay the tax?

Yes. One way to provide a taxable benefit to an employee without increasing the employee's tax bill is for the employer to pay the tax.

The Department of Labor (DOL) was asked whether a plan's payment of the tax owed by an employee on domestic partner benefits would violate the Employee Retirement Income Security Act (ERISA), which governs employee benefit plans. Under ERISA, the assets of a plan may be used only to pay benefits to plan participants and beneficiaries and to defray reasonable expenses of the plan. The DOL noted that payment of an employee's tax on domestic partner benefits could not be justified as an expense of the plan. However, the DOL said the plan could pay the tax provided the tax payments are specified as additional plan benefits in the plan document.

> **Planning Point:** Picking up the tab for an employee's taxes can get complicated. The employer's payment of the employee's tax is considered additional income to the employee for both income and payroll tax purposes. Moreover, there is a pyramid effect: The tax on the tax is treated as more compensation and so forth. An employer can, of course, keep computing and recomputing until the tax due becomes negligible. However, there is an easier way. The IRS has provided employers with a special formula for "grossing up" the amount of taxable compensation to figure the tax due. [Rev. Rul. 81-48, 1981-1 C.B. 174]

Q 9:15 What special rules apply to health coverage for S corporation shareholder-employees?

An S corporation receives the same deduction as any other employer when it pays health insurance premiums for employees, including shareholder-employees.

However, a 2 percent shareholder of an S corporation cannot be treated as an employee for health benefit purposes. [IRC § 1372; Rev. Rul. 91-26, 1991-1 C.B. 184] Therefore, the medical insurance premiums paid by the S corporation for a 2 percent shareholder must be treated as compensation to the shareholder for income tax purposes. The premiums are not, however, treated as wages for payroll tax purposes, provided the S corporation's plan covers other employees and their dependents. A 2 percent S corporation shareholder is someone who directly or indirectly owns more than 2 percent of the corporation's stock or stock with more than 2 percent of the voting power at any time during the year. [IRC § 1372]

A 2 percent S corporation shareholder can deduct the premiums as if he or she were self-employed. A self-employed individual may claim an above-the-line deduction from gross income for 100 percent of his or her premiums. [IRC § 162(l)]

Q 9:16 How is health coverage for partners in a partnership handled for tax purposes?

A partnership has a choice when it comes to handling health insurance premiums paid for its partners. [Rev. Rul. 91-26, 1991-2 C.B. 184] On the one hand, the partnership may treat the cost as guaranteed payments for the partners' services. As such, the payments are deducted by the partnership before figuring the partners' shares of partnership income or loss.

On the other hand, the partnership may treat the cost as a reduction in distributions to the partners. The benefits are deductible by the partnership and do not affect the partners' shares of income or and loss. In this case, the partners may deduct the premiums as if they were self-employed. A self-employed individual may claim an above-the-line deduction from gross income for 100 percent of his or her premiums. [IRC § 162(l)]

Benefit Payments Under Group Health Plans

Q 9:17 Are benefits provided under an employer-provided health plan taxable to employees?

Benefits received under an insured plan are not taxable to an employee. [IRC § 105(e)]This exclusion applies to benefits for an employee's own medical expenses as well as benefits for expenses of an employee's spouse and dependents. The exclusion also applies to retirees and family members of deceased employees who are covered by the plan.

Benefits received under an employer's self-insured medical expense reimbursement plan are also eligible for tax-free treatment. However, special rules apply if the plan is skewed in favor of highly compensated employees. Benefits paid to highly compensated employees under a discriminatory self-insured health plan are taxable to the extent they represent "excess reimbursements" to those employees (see Q 9:23). The tax-free treatment of benefits received by non-highly compensated employees is not affected.

Q 9:18 Can a plan reimburse medical expenses incurred by an employee before the plan is adopted?

An IRS revenue ruling makes it clear that favorable tax treatment is not available for reimbursements made by a self-insured plan for expenses incurred by an employee before the plan is adopted. [Rev. Rul. 2002-58, 2002-38 I.R.B. 541] According to the IRS ruling, reimbursements for expenses incurred prior to the establishment of a plan are not excludable from an employee's gross income because they are not paid or received under an accident or health plan.

Example 9-5: Delta Corp. established a self-insured medical expense reimbursement plan on December 1 of a given year. The plan document provided that the plan was effective as of January 1 of that year, and that reimbursements would be made for medical expenses incurred by a covered employee or the employee's spouse and dependents at any time during the plan year. Once the plan was established, Joanne Brown, a covered employee, submitted claims for medical expenses incurred early in the year, and Delta reimbursed those expenses. However, the IRS revenue ruling makes it clear that those reimbursements are taxable income to Brown.

Q 9:19 Are benefits provided for an employee's domestic partner taxable to the employee?

If an employee's domestic partner qualifies as the employee's dependent, benefits provided to the domestic partner are subject to the same tax rules that apply to other dependents. Benefits provided under an insured plan are tax-free. Benefits provided under an employer's self-insured medical reimbursement plan generally would also qualify for tax-free treatment. However, benefits paid to highly compensated employees under a discriminatory self-insured health plan are taxable to the extent they represent "excess reimbursements" to those employees (see Q 9:23).

If a domestic partner does not qualify as the employee's dependent, employer-provided coverage for the domestic partner is taxable to the employee. Letter Ruling 9850011 stated, "the excess of the fair market value of the group medical coverage over the amount paid by the employee for such coverage is includible in the gross income of the employee under section 61 of the Code." However, pursuant to IRC Section 104(a)(3), reimbursements received by the employee for the domestic partner's medical expenses will not be taxable to either the employee or the domestic partner to the extent that the coverage provided to the domestic partner was paid for by employee contributions. [Ltr. Rul. 9850011]

> **Example 9-6:** John and Jim are domestic partners. John's employer, Alpha Company, offers health insurance coverage to employees. Employees may also elect coverage for their spouses, dependents, and domestic partners. Alpha pays the full cost for an employee's coverage, but requires employees to pay half the cost of coverage for a spouse, dependent, or domestic partner. John elects coverage for himself and for Jim, who does not qualify as John's dependent. The cost of Jim's coverage is $100 per month, for which John and Alpha each contribute $50.
>
> *Result:* Because Jim does not qualify as John's dependent, Alpha's payments for Jim's coverage are treated as taxable income to John. Therefore, John's compensation from Alpha will be increased by an additional $50 each month. On the other hand, because John will be treated as having paid the entire cost of Jim's coverage, any benefits Jim receives will be entirely tax free.

Self-Insured Health Plans

Q 9:20 What special rules apply to self-insured health plans?

The tax law imposes special nondiscrimination requirements on self-insured plans. [IRC § 105(h)] Employer-provided group health plans that are fully insured may discriminate in favor of highly compensated employees without adversely affecting the favorable tax treatment of benefits received from the plan by rank-and-file employees. However, highly compensated employees in a discriminatory self-insured plan may owe tax on all or a portion of the benefits received under the plan.

> **Planning Point:** Because of the special nondiscrimination rules for self-insured plans, employers that want to provide special coverage for "execs-only" will be on safer ground with an insured plan.

Q 9:21 What is a self-insured plan?

A self-insured medical reimbursement plan is an employer plan that provides reimbursements to employees for expenses of medical care other than under a policy of accident and health insurance. [IRC § 105(h)]

A policy of accident and health insurance for this purpose is either: (1) a policy issued by a licensed insurer, or (2) a reimbursement arrangement in the nature of a prepaid health care plan (for example, an HMO) that is regulated under federal or state law in a manner similar to the regulation of insurance companies. [Reg. § 1.105-11(b)(1)(i)]

> **Caution:** A plan handled by an insurance company can be considered self-insured unless risk is shifted to the insurer. For example, an arrangement with an insurer to provide only administrative or bookkeeping services will be considered self-insured. [Reg. § 1.105-11(b)(1)(ii)]

If a plan is only partially insured, the self-insured portion is subject to the nondiscrimination rules. For example, if an employer's plan reimburses employees for benefits not covered by insurance or for insurance deductibles, the reimbursement arrangement will be treated as a self-insured plan. [IRC § 105(h); Reg. § 1.105-11(b)(2)]

Q 9:22 When is a self-insured group health plan nondiscriminatory?

To be considered nondiscriminatory, a self-insured plan must not discriminate in favor of highly compensated employees in terms of eligibility to participate in the plan or benefits provided under the plan. [IRC § 105(h)]

Q 9:23 Who is a highly compensated employee?

Highly compensated employees include:

- The five highest-paid officers of the employer;

- Shareholders owning more than 10 percent of the value of the employer's stock;
- The highest-paid 25 percent of employees.

[IRC § 105(h)(5)]

The following employees can be excluded from the highest-paid 25 percent group if they do not participate in the plan: (1) employees with less than three years of service at the start of the plan year, (2) employees under age 25 at the start of the plan year, (3) part-time or seasonal employees, (4) employees covered by a collective bargaining agreement, or (5) nonresident alien employees with no U.S.-source earned income from the employer. [IRC §§ 105(h)(3), 105(h)(5)]

Q 9:24 When is a self-insured group health plan treated as discriminating in terms of eligibility?

A self-insured plan will be treated as discriminating in terms of eligibility unless it benefits:

- 70 percent of all employees; or
- 80 percent of all eligible employees, if at least 70 percent of all employees are eligible to benefit under the plan; or
- A nondiscriminatory classification of employees.

[IRC § 105(h)(3)(A)]

The following employees can be excluded in applying eligibility tests: (1) employees with less than three years of service at the start of the plan year; (2) employees under age 25 at the start of the plan year; (3) part-time or seasonal employees; (4) employees covered by a collective bargaining agreement; and (5) nonresident alien employees with no U.S.-source earned income from the employer. [IRC § 105(h)(3)(B)]

Q 9:25 When is a self-insured group health plan treated as discriminatory when it comes to benefits?

A self-insured health plan will be treated as discriminating in favor of highly compensated employees with regard to benefits unless all of the benefits provided to highly compensated employees are provided on the same basis to all other plan participants.

Planning Point: An employer can easily avoid discrimination in benefits if all participants receive the same benefits on the same terms (e.g., premiums, co-payments, etc.).

However, being nondiscriminatory on paper is not enough. A self-insured plan is also prohibited from discriminating in operation. A plan will not be considered discriminatory in operation just because highly compensated employees use more benefits under the plan than other participants. The Internal Revenue Service, however, will also look at when and why a particular benefit is added to or dropped from a plan. If a benefit is added to a plan just when a highly compensated employee needs it and later dropped when he or she no longer needs it, the plan may be treated as discriminatory. [Reg. § 1.105-11(c)(3)(ii)]

Example 9-7: John Bowen is the sole shareholder of Bowen Corp. Bowen Corp.'s health plan has not traditionally provided maternity benefits. However, John and his wife have decided to start a family. Bowen Corp. adds maternity benefits to its plan just in time to cover the birth of the Bowens' first child. Several years later, when the Bowens' family is complete, the plan drops maternity coverage.

Result: The IRS could find the Bowen Corp. plan discriminatory in operation even though maternity benefits were available to all employees during the period they were offered under the plan.

Q 9:26 How are highly compensated employees taxed if a self-insured health plan is discriminatory?

A highly compensated employee is taxed on any "excess reimbursement" under a discriminatory self-insured plan. [IRC § 105(h)(1)]The amount of the excess reimbursement depends on whether the plan fails the eligibility test, the benefit test, or both.

Eligibility test. If a self-insured plan fails the eligibility test (see Q 9:21), highly compensated employees will be taxed on a proportionate amount of their reimbursements from the plan. The taxable amount is calculated by multiplying the total reimbursements received by each highly compensated employee for the year by a fraction. The numerator of the fraction is the total reimbursements to all highly compensated individuals for the year, and the denominator is the total reimbursements to all plan participants for the year. [IRC § 105(h)(7)(B)(i)]

Example 9-8: Alpha Corporation's self-insured health plan covers all highly compensated employees, but only a handful of non-highly compensated employees. Therefore, the plan fails the eligibility test. During the year, Ken Arnold, a highly compensated employee receives a total of $5,000 of medical reimbursements from the plan. All told, highly compensated employees receive $100,000 of reimbursements from the plan, while non-highly compensated employees receive $25,000.

Result: Arnold must pay tax on 80 percent ($100,000 reimbursements to highly compensated employees/$125,000 total reimbursements) of his reimbursements—or $4,000. The remaining $1,000 of Arnold's reimbursements is tax-free.

Benefit test. If the plan fails the benefit test, highly compensated employees will be taxed on any reimbursement that is was not available to all non-highly compensated employees. For example, if the plan provides up to $100,000 in reimbursements to highly compensated individuals each year but only $50,000 to all other employees, a highly compensated employee will be taxed on any reimbursements in excess of $50,000.

Both tests. If the self-insured group health plan fails both the eligibility and the benefit tests, the calculation under the benefit test is applied first. The amount of excess reimbursement under that test is then subtracted out from the numerator and denominator when the eligibility test calculation is applied. [Reg. § 1.105-11(e)(3)]

Archer Medical Savings Accounts

Q 9:27 What is an Archer medical savings account?

An Archer medical savings account (MSA) is a tax-exempt trust or custodial account that is set up to pay medical expenses in connection with a high deductible health plan. Contributions to the account are deductible by the account holder or excludable from income if made by an employer. Amounts in the account can be withdrawn tax-free to pay for out-of-pocket medical expenses. Only self-employed individuals and employees of small employers (generally, those with 50 or fewer employees) are eligible to establish Archer MSAs.

Archer MSAs are a pilot project, which is currently set to expire after December 31, 2007 (although the cutoff date has been repeatedly extended). After the program expires, no new Archer MSAs will be permitted; however, qualifying MSAs will remain eligible for tax benefits. [IRC § 220; HIPAA § 301]

Q 9:28 Who can set up an Archer MSA?

An individual can participate in an Archer MSA if he or she (1) works for a "small employer" that has a high deductible health plan or maintains high deductible coverage as a self-employed individual, and (2) is not covered by another health plan. [IRC § 220(c)(1)]

Certain types of health coverage are permitted in addition to a high deductible plan. An individual will not be disqualified if he or she is covered:

- For accidents, disability, dental care, vision care, or long-term care;
- By Medicare supplemental insurance;
- By other insurance if substantially all of the coverage provided under such insurance relates to liabilities incurred under worker's compensation law, tort liabilities, or liabilities relating to ownership or use of property (e.g., auto insurance);
- By insurance for a specified disease or illness; or
- By insurance that provides a fixed payment for hospitalization (e.g., so many dollars a day for each day in the hospital).

Q 9:29 What is a small employer?

A company is considered a small employer if it employed, on average, no more than 50 employees during either the preceding or the second preceding

Q 9:27

year before the Archer MSAs are set up. [IRC § 220(c)(4)] In determining whether a company is a small employer, a preceding year is not taken into account unless the company was in existence throughout the year. For new companies, the 50-employee test is determined based on the average number of employees that the company reasonably expects to employ in the current year. If two or more companies are under common ownership, they are treated as one employer.

Suppose a company meets the 50-employee test in the year it set up Archer MSAs for its employees, but grows to more than 50 employees in a succeeding year. In that case, contributions can still be made to Archer MSAs—including Archer MSAs set up for new employees—until the year following the first year in which the company has more than 200 employees. After that, contributions can still be made by or for those employees who already have Archer MSAs.

> **Example 9-9:** XYZ, Inc. had 48 employees in 1999 and 2000, and 205 employees in 2001 and 2002. XYZ is a small employer in 2001 because it had 50 or fewer employees in the preceding or the second preceding year. And XYZ is still considered a small employer for one more year through 2002. However, in years after 2002, XYZ will not be considered a small employer (even if the number of employees falls to 50 or below). In years after 2002, contributions can be made only to those Archer MSAs to which contributions were made in earlier years.

Q 9:30 What is a high deductible health plan?

A high deductible plan is a health plan with an annual deductible of at least $1,500 and no more than $2,250 in the case of individual coverage, and at least $3,000 and no more than $4,500 in the case of family coverage. In addition, the maximum out-of-pocket expenses (including deductible and co-payments) must be no more than $3,000 in the case of individual coverage and no more than $5,500 in the case of family coverage. These dollar amounts are indexed in $50 dollar increments for inflation occurring after 1998. [IRC § 220(c)(2)]

For 2008, individual coverage must have a deductible of not less than $1,950 and not more than $2,900, with a maximum annual out-of-pocket expenditure of $3,850. For family coverage the deductible must be at least $3,850 and not more than $5,800, with a cap on out-of-pocket expenditures of $7,050. [Rev. Proc. 2007-66, 2007-45 IRB 1]. For 2007, the respective figures for individual coverage were $1,900, $2,850, and $3,750. For family coverage, the respective figures were $3,750, $5,650, and $6,900. [Rev. Proc. 2006-53, 2006-48 IRB]

Q 9:31 Who makes the contributions to an Archer MSA?

An employee (or self-employed) can make contributions to his or her Archer MSA, or an employer can make contributions on an employee's behalf. An employee cannot make a contribution to an Archer MSA for any year that the employer makes an Archer MSA contribution on his or her behalf.

Planning Point: If a company plans to contribute only a small amount to each employee's Archer MSA, employees may be better off if the company skips the contributions and lets the employees make their own contributions.

Q 9:32 How much can be contributed to an Archer MSA?

The maximum annual contribution to an Archer MSA is 65 percent of the amount of the deductible in the case of individual coverage and 75 percent of the deductible in the case of family coverage. [IRC § 220(b)(2)] So, for example, if an employee has family coverage with a deductible of $4,000, the employee (or the company) can contribute up to $3,000 each year.

There are no other dollar limits on contributions.

In the case of a self-employed individual, the contribution cannot exceed the individual's earnings from the business. In the case of an employee, the contribution cannot exceed the employee's compensation received from the employer sponsoring the high deductible plan. [IRC § 220(b)(4)]

Q 9:33 Can an employer make Archer MSA contributions only for some employees?

Generally no. If a company decides to make Archer MSA contributions, it must make comparable contributions to the Archer MSAs of all employees who have high deductible coverage. Contributions are considered comparable if they are either the same amount or the same percentage of the deductible under each high deductible plan. The comparability rule is applied separately to part-time employees (i.e., employees who are customarily employed for fewer than 30 hours per week). [IRC § 4980E]

> **Example 9-10:** XYZ, Inc. maintains two high deductible plans, Plan A, with a deductible of $2,000 for individual coverage and $4,000 for family coverage, and Plan B, with a deductible of $2,400 for individual coverage and $4,800 for family coverage. For full-time employees in Plan A, XYZ makes MSA contributions of $500 for those with individual coverage and $1,000 for those with family coverage. In order to satisfy the contribution requirements, XYZ will also have to make contributions for employees covered under Plan B of either: (1) $500 for employees with individual coverage and $1,000 for employees with family coverage (i.e., the same amount as for Plan A) or (2) $600 for employees with individual coverage and $1,200 for employees with family coverage (the same percentage of the deductible as for Plan A). Different contributions (or no contributions) could be made for part-time employees covered under either high deductible plan.

If a company does not make comparable contributions, then it is subject to an excise tax equal to 35 percent of the aggregate amount contributed to Archer MSAs for the year. [IRC § 4980E(b)](*Note:* If the failure to make comparable contributions is due to reasonable cause, the IRS is authorized to waive the penalty to the extent that it would be excessive relative to the failure involved.) No penalty will be applied if the failure to make comparable contributions results from the fact that the company passed the 200-employee mark, thus becoming ineligible to make contributions to new Archer MSAs.

Planning Point: While an employer has to contribute for all employees with comparable high deductible coverage, this does not mean that a company has to give all employees the same kind of coverage. Different coverage (e.g., high deductible and low deductible) can be provided to different groups of employees.

Q 9:34 How are Archer MSA contributions treated for tax purposes?

If an employee (or self-employed individual) makes his or her own contribution to an Archer MSA, the contribution can be claimed as an above-the-line deduction for adjusted gross income (i.e., it is deductible whether or not the employee itemizes deductions). [IRC § 62(a)(16)]

If an employer makes a contribution on an employee's behalf, the contribution is not taxable to the employee. [IRC § 106(b)] Contributions for a year can be made until the original due date for that year's return. So, for example, a contribution for 2008 can be made up until April 15, 2009. However, an employer's contributions are deductible only in the year they are made. [IRC § 106(b)(3)]

Q 9:35 Are earnings on amounts in an Archer MSA taxable to the individual?

No. [IRC § 220(e)(1)]Contributions to Archer MSAs grow tax-free while they are in the account.

Q 9:36 How are Archer MSA distributions treated for tax purposes?

Withdrawals from an Archer MSA are tax-free as long as they are used to pay out-of-pocket medical expenses for the Archer MSA owner and his or her family. [IRC § 220(f)(1)]

For this purpose, medical expenses generally include any expenses for medical care that would be allowed as an itemized medical expense deduction, as well as nonprescription drugs and medical supplies. However, tax-free withdrawals cannot be made to pay the cost of medical insurance premiums other than those for long-term care insurance, health care continuation (COBRA) coverage, or health care coverage while unemployed. [IRC § 220(d)(2)]

If a withdrawal from an Archer MSA is made without corresponding medical expenses, the withdrawal is taxable. [IRC § 220(f)(2)] In addition, a 15 percent penalty tax will apply unless the withdrawal is made after the Archer MSA owner reaches age 65 or is due to death or disability of the owner. [IRC

§ 220(f)(4)] After age 65, the funds in the MSA can be withdrawn *penalty-free* for any use—medical or nonmedical.

Q 9:37 What happens to an Archer MSA at death?

If an Archer MSA owner has named his or her surviving spouse as beneficiary of the MSA, it becomes the spouse's own Archer MSA when the owner dies. The surviving spouse will be taxed on withdrawals in the same way as the owner would have been taxed (e.g., there is no tax on withdrawals used to pay medical expenses). [IRC § 220(f)(8)(A)]

If someone other than a spouse is named as beneficiary, the Archer MSA ceases to be an Archer MSA as of the owner's date of death. Any amount still in the Archer MSA is taxed immediately to the beneficiary. The beneficiary, however, will not be taxed on any amounts used, within one year, to pay medical expenses incurred by the owner prior to death. [IRC § 220(f)(8)(B)]

Upon the owner's death, any balance remaining in his or her Archer MSA will be taxable in the owner's estate unless there is a named beneficiary of the account. However, if the owner's surviving spouse is the beneficiary of the estate, the MSA will not be subject to tax, because it will qualify for the estate tax marital deduction. [IRC § 2056]

If the owner's spouse is the named beneficiary of the Archer MSA, the MSA will be treated as the spouse's own account. [IRC § 220(f)(8)(A)] If the account goes to another named beneficiary or to the owner's estate, the fair market value of the account will be included in the income of the beneficiary or estate for the tax year of the account holder's death. The recipient of the account may, however, be entitled to an offsetting deduction for any estate tax paid on the account. [IRC § § 220(f)(8)(B); 691(c)]

Q 9:38 Are there any tax reporting requirements for Archer MSAs?

Yes. Employers are required to report employer contributions to Archer MSAs on employee's W-2 forms. Self-employed individuals and employees are required to report MSA contributions and distributions on their tax returns using Form 8853, *Archer MSAs and Long-Term Care Insurance Contracts.* [IRC § § 106(b)(4), 220(d)(4); HIPAA § 301]

Health Savings Accounts

Q 9:39 What is a health savings account?

A health savings account (HSA) is a tax-exempt trust or custodial account established exclusively for the purpose of paying qualified medical expenses of the account beneficiary who is covered under a high-deductible health plan.

HSAs are established to receive tax-favored contributions by or on behalf of eligible individuals and amounts in an HSA may be accumulated over the years

Q 9:37

or distributed on a tax-free basis to pay or reimburse qualified medical expenses. Congress intended that HSAs eventually replace Archer MSAs (see above).

Q 9:40 Who is eligible to establish an HSA?

An "eligible individual" can establish an HSA. [IRC § 222(c)(1)]An "eligible individual" means, with respect to any month, any individual who:

1. Is covered under a high-deductible health plan (HDHP) on the first day of such month;

2. Is not also covered by any other health plan that is not an HDHP (with certain exceptions for plans providing certain limited types of coverage);

3. Is not entitled to benefits under Medicare (generally, has not yet reached age 65 and enrolled in Medicare); and

4. May not be claimed as a dependent on another person's tax return.

IRS guidance makes it clear than employee who has a choice between low-deductible coverage and a qualifying HDHP, is an eligible individual for HSA purposes. The fact that the employee could have chosen low-deductible coverage does not affect HSA eligibility [IRS Notice 2004-50, 2004-33 I.R.B. 196].

In the case of spouses, each spouse may have his or her own HSA if eligible. However, spouses may not have a joint HSA [IRS Notice 2004-50, 2004-33 I.R.B. 196]. A married individual who otherwise qualifies can establish an HSA even if his or her spouse has low-deductible family coverage, provided the family plan does not cover the individual [Rev. Rul. 2005-25, 2005-18 I.R.B. 971]

Q 9:41 What is a high-deductible health plan (HDHP)?

Generally, an HDHP is a health plan that satisfies certain requirements with respect to deductibles and out-of-pocket expenses.

For 2008, the minimum annual deductible for an HDHP providing self-only coverage is $1,100, and the annual limit on out-of-pocket expenses required to be paid (deductibles, co-payments, and other amounts, but not premiums) is $5,600. For 2007, the figures were $1,100 and $5,500 respectively.

For 2008, the minimum annual deductible for an HDHP providing family coverage is $2,200 and the annual out-of-pocket expense cap is $11,200. For 2007, the figures were $2,200 and $11,000 respectively. In the case of family coverage, a plan is an HDHP only if, under the terms of the plan and without regard to which family member or members incur expenses, no amounts are payable from the HDHP until the family has incurred annual covered medical expenses in excess of the minimum annual deductible. [IRC § 223(c)(2)]

The deductible and co-payment amounts will be indexed for inflation in future years.

In addition to annual deductibles, an HDHP can impose a reasonable lifetime limit on benefits provided under the plan. For example, IRS guidance provides that a $1 million lifetime limit on benefits will be considered reasonable.

A plan may also limit benefits to usual, customary, and reasonable (UCR) amounts. Moreover, amounts paid by a covered individual in excess of the UCR charges are not counted against the maximum out-of-pocket expense limit. [IRS Notice 2004-50]

A plan does not fail to qualify as an HDHP merely because it does not have a deductible (or has a small deductible) for preventive care (e.g., first dollar coverage for preventive care). However, except for preventive care, a plan may not provide benefits for any year until the deductible for that year is met. [IRC § 222(c)(2)(D)]

> **Example 9-11:** *XYZ Plan* provides coverage for A and his family. The plan provides for the payment of covered medical expenses of any member of A's family if the member has incurred covered medical expenses during the year in excess of $1,000 even if the family has not incurred covered medical expenses in excess of the minimum annual deductible. If A incurred covered medical expenses of $1,500 in 2008, the plan would pay $500. Thus, benefits are potentially available under the plan even if the family's covered medical expenses do not exceed $2,200. Because the Plan provides family coverage with an annual deductible of less than $2,200, the plan is not an HDHP.

> **Example 9-12:** Same facts as before, except that the plan has a $5,250 family deductible and provides payment for covered medical expenses if any member of A's family has incurred covered medical expenses during the year in excess of $2,200. The plan satisfies the requirements for an HDHP with respect to the deductibles.

Q 9:42 What services qualify as preventive care?

The IRS has issued a special safe harbor rule which provides that preventive care includes (but is not limited to):

- Periodic health evaluations, including tests and diagnostic procedures, in connection with routine examinations such as annual physicals;
- Routine prenatal and well-child care;
- Child and adult immunizations;
- Tobacco cessation programs;
- Obesity weight-loss programs; and
- Screening services (e.g., cancer screening). [IRS Notice 2004-23]

The IRS notice emphasizes that preventive care generally does not include any service to treat an existing illness, injury, or condition.

The IRS notice makes it clear that the characterization of a service as preventive care is not dependent on state law. State insurance laws often require health plans to provide certain services without regard to a deductible or on favorable terms. However, the determination of whether such required services are preventive care will be determined under IRS guidelines.

Q 9:43 What are the special rules for determining whether a health plan that is a network plan meets the requirements of an HDHP?

A network plan is a plan that generally provides more favorable benefits for services provided by its network of providers than for services provided outside of the network. In the case of a plan using a network of providers, the plan will not be disqualified as an HDHP solely because the out-of-pocket expense limits for services provided outside of the network exceeds the maximum annual out-of-pocket expense limits allowed for an HDHP.

Q 9:44 What kind of other health coverage makes an individual ineligible for an HSA?

Generally, an individual is ineligible for an HSA if the individual, while covered under an HDHP, is also covered under a health plan (whether as an individual, spouse, or dependent) that is not an HDHP. However, an individual remains eligible for an HSA if he or she has coverage for any benefit provided by "permitted insurance."

Permitted insurance is insurance under which substantially all of the coverage provided relates to liabilities incurred under workers' compensation laws, tort liabilities, liabilities relating to ownership or use of property (e.g., automobile insurance), insurance for a specified disease or illness, and insurance that pays a fixed amount per day (or other period) of hospitalization.

In addition to permitted insurance, an individual is still HSA-eligible if the individual has coverage (whether provided through insurance or otherwise) for accidents, disability, dental care, vision care, or long-term care.

Prescription drug plans. Insured health plans frequently do not cover the cost of prescription drugs. Therefore, many individuals are covered by separate prescription drug plans or riders. An IRS revenue ruling makes it clear that prescription drug benefits are not "permitted" insurance or coverage for HSA purposes. Therefore, an individual who is covered by both an HDHP and a prescription drug plan is not an eligible individual for HSA purposes unless the drug plan is also an HDHP (that is, the plan does not provide benefits until the required minimum annual benefit for an HDHP has been met). [Rev. Rul. 2004-38]

Health flexible spending accounts (FSAs) and health reimbursement arrangements (HRAs). As a general rule, an employee is ineligible for an HSA if he or she is covered by an employer-sponsored health FSA or HRA that pays or reimburses medical expenses incurred before the minimum annual HSA deductible has been satisfied. [Rev. Rul. 2004-45]

However, employers who sponsor FSAs or HRAs do have some options if they wish to offer HSAs to their employees. According to the IRS ruling, coverage under the following types of FSAs or HRAs will not disqualify an employee from HSA participation:

- *Limited-purpose health FSA or HRA.* A limited-purpose health FSA that pays or reimburses only benefits for "permitted coverage" (e.g., dental and vision, but not long term care) or a limited-purpose HRA that pays or reimburses benefits for "permitted insurance" (for a specific disease or illness or that provides a fixed amount per day or other period of hospitalization) or "permitted coverage" (but not for long-term care services) can be offered in tandem with an HSA. A limited-purpose health FSA or HRA may pay or reimburse preventive care benefits.

- *Suspended HRA.* An employee covered by an HRA is eligible for HSA contributions if an election is made before the beginning of the HRA coverage period to suspend all reimbursements for medical expenses other than permitted insurance and permitted coverage. Eligibility for HSA contributions is limited to the period during which the HRA reimbursements are suspended. Moreover, if the HSA is funded through salary reduction under a cafeteria plan during the suspension period, the terms of the salary reduction election must indicate that the salary reduction is used only to pay for the HSA offered in conjunction with the HRA and not to pay for the HRA itself.

- *Post-deductible health FSA or HRA.* An employee covered by a post-deductible FSA or HRA is an eligible individual for the purpose of making contributions to an HSA. A post-deductible health FSA or HRA is one that does not pay or reimburse any medical expense incurred before the minimum annual HSA deductible is satisfied. The deductible for the HRA or health FSA need not be the same as the deductible for the HDHP, but in no event may any benefits be provided before the minimum annual HSA deductible has been met. Where the HDHP and the FSA or HSA do not have identical deductibles, contributions to the HSA are limited to the lower of the deductibles.

  Overlapping coverage under an FSA and an HSA can arise if an employer's cafeteria plan allows a grace period for tapping unused benefits FSA benefits from the prior plan year (see Q 9:69). For example, suppose an employee was covered by an FSA for Year 1, but wants to set up an HSA for Year 2. If the FSA has a grace period extending until March 15 of Year 2, the employee will not be eligible to make HSA contributions until April 1 of Year 2—even if the employee is not covered by an FSA for Year 2. Moreover, the employee will be limited to 9/12 of the maximum HSA contribution for the year. Planning Point. The IRS suggests that one way to solve this problem for employees who are switching from FSA to HSA coverage is to amend the cafeteria plan document to provide for mandatory conversion of the general purpose FSA to a limited-purpose or post-deductible FSA during the grace period. [Rev. Rul. 2005-86]

- *Retirement HRA.* A retirement HRA that pays or reimburses only those medical expenses incurred after retirement (and no expenses incurred before retirement) will not cause an employee to forego eligibility for HSA contributions. However, HSA contributions are limited to the period before retirement. After retirement, when payment or reimbursements can be made from the retirement HRA, no additional HSA contributions may be made.

The IRS ruling also makes it clear that combinations of these arrangements are allowed. For example, if an employer offers a combined post-deductible health FSA and a limited-purpose health FSA, this would not disqualify an otherwise eligible employee from making or receiving HSA contributions.

An employee may not be reimbursed for the same medical expense by more than one plan or arrangement. However, if an employee has available an HSA, a health FSA, and an HRA that pay or reimburse the same medical expense, the health FSA or the HRA may pay or reimburse the medical expense so long as the employee certifies to the employer that the expense has not been reimbursed and that the employee will not seek reimbursement under any other plan or arrangement covering that expense (including the HSA). As a general rule, when an HRA and a health FSA cover the same expenses, amounts in the HRA must be exhausted before any reimbursement is made from the FSA. [IRS Notice 2002-45]

FSA and HRA rollovers. An option for an employee whose existing FSA or HRA is incompatible with the establishment of an HSA is to roll over the FSA or HRA funds to the HSA. Under a new rule enacted by the Tax Relief and Health Care Act of 2006 [Pub. L. No. 109-433, 120 Stat. 3196 (2006)], employers have a limited opportunity to allow employees to make a one-time rollover of FSA or HRA funds by means of a qualified HSA distribution. [I.R.C. § 106(e), as amended by the 2006 Tax Relief and Health Care Act] A qualified HSA distribution is treated as a contribution by the employer to an employee's HSA that is excludable from gross income and is exempt from employment taxes. A qualified HSA distribution is permitted in addition to any regular HSA contributions for the year. Only one qualified HSA distribution is allowed with respect to any health FSA or HRA. A qualified HSA distribution cannot exceed the lesser of (a) the balance of the FSA or HRA on September 21, 2006, or (b) the balance on the date of the distribution. Moreover, a qualified distribution must be made before January 1, 2012.

The qualified HSA distribution rules are intended to assist employers and employees in switching to an HSA from another type of health plan. Therefore, if, an employee is not an eligible individual for HSA purposes (e.g., is not covered by a high-deductible plan) at any time during a testing period, the amount of the qualified HSA distribution must be included in the employee's gross income for the tax year that includes the first month in which the employee is not eligible. In addition a 10% penalty tax applies to the included amount. [I.R.C. § 106(e)(3)(A)] Note, however, that if an employee ceases to be eligible because of death or disability, the addition to gross income and the penalty tax do not apply. [IRC § 106(e)(3)(B)] The testing period is the 12 month period beginning with the month in which the qualified HSA distribution is made. [I.R.C. § 106(e)(4)(A)]

Example 9-13: Jane has been covered by a traditional health plan and an HRA sponsored by her employer, Acme Co. Jane plans to switch to an

HDHP and an HSA as of January 1, 2008. The balance in her HRA on September 21, 2006, was $2,000; the balance as of January 1, 2008, is $3,000. To facilitate Jane's switch in coverage, Acme can make a tax-free qualified HSA distribution from Jane's HRA to her HSA on January 1, 2008. The amount of the distribution is limited to $2,000 (the amount in the account as of September 21, 2006).

Caution: Because the entire balance in the HRA in the example cannot be distributed to the employee's HSA, there might be a temptation to continue coverage under the HRA. However, that would be a bad move. The rule that an employee is not an eligible individual for HSA purposes if he or she has coverage under a general purpose health FSA or HRA continues to apply. Therefore, if the employee in the example remains eligible under the HRA after the qualified distribution, she would not be an eligible individual for HSA purposes, and the amount of the qualified distribution would be subject to tax and penalty.

Health discount cards. A discount card that entitles an individual to discounts for health care services or products will not disqualify an individual from HSA eligibility as long as the individual is required to meet the regular HDHP deductible. The same holds true if a plan negotiates discounted prices from health care providers. [Notice 2004-50]

Employee benefit programs. IRS guidance also makes it clear that coverage under an employee assistance program (EAP), disease management program, or wellness program will not affect HSA eligibility, provided the program does not provide significant benefits in the nature of medical care or treatment. Screening and other preventive care services are not treated as significant medical benefits. However, an employer generally cannot condition contributions to an employee's HSA on participation in such plans. [Notice 2004-50]

Q 9:45 How does an eligible individual establish an HSA?

Any eligible individual can establish an HSA with a qualified HSA trustee or custodian, in much the same way that individuals establish IRAs or Archer MSAs with qualified IRA or Archer MSA trustees or custodians. No permission or authorization from the Internal Revenue Service is necessary to establish an HSA. An eligible individual who is an employee may establish an HSA with or without involvement of the employer.

Q 9:46 Does the HSA have to be opened at the same institution that provides the HDHP?

No. The HSA can be established through a qualified trustee or custodian who is different from the HDHP provider. Where a trustee or custodian does not sponsor the HDHP, the trustee or custodian may require proof or certification that the account beneficiary is an eligible individual, including that the individual is covered by a health plan that meets all of the requirements of an HDHP.

Q 9:47 Who may contribute to an HSA?

Any eligible individual may contribute to an HSA. For an HSA established by an employee, the employee, the employee's employer or both may contribute. For an HSA established by a self-employed (or unemployed) individual, the individual may contribute to the HSA. Family members may also make contributions to an HSA on behalf of another family member as long as that other family member is an eligible individual.

Q 9:48 How much may be contributed to an HSA?

The maximum annual contribution to an HSA is the sum of the limits determined separately for each month, based on status, eligibility and health plan coverage as of the first day of the month.

For tax years beginning before 2007, the maximum monthly contribution was limited to one-twelfth of the lesser of (a) the maximum annual contribution or (b) the annual deductible under the HSA.

However, for tax years beginning after 2006, the 2006 Tax Relief and Health Care Act eliminated the plan deductible limit. Therefore, employees or their employers (or a combination) can contribute one-twelfth of the maximum annual contribution for each month of eligibility. For 2008, the maximum annual contribution for eligible individuals with self-only coverage is $2,900 and the maximum contribution for individuals with family coverage is $5,800. For 2007, the contribution limits were $2,850 for self-only coverage and $5,650 for family coverage. [Rev. Proc. 2007-36, 200-48 I.R.B.]

An individual is generally eligible for HSA contributions for a given month only if he or she is covered by a high-deductible plan as of the first day of the month. [IRS Notice 2004-50, 2004-33 I.R.B. 196] However, here again, the 2006 Tax Relief and Health Care Act, made a significant change. For tax years beginning after 2006, an individual who establishes an HSA part way through the year can contribute the full annual amount. For purposes of calculating the maximum annual contribution, an individual who is an eligible individual for the last month of the tax year is treated as (a) having been an eligible individual during each of the months in that tax year and (b) having been enrolled in the same HDHP in which he or she is enrolled for the last month of the tax year. [IRC § 223(b)(8)(A)]

However, only those part-year enrollees who begin HSA participation during the year and are covered by a high-deductible plan at year end are eligible to make the maximum annual contribution. Contributions by or for an individual who ceases to be eligible during the year continues to be limited to one-twelfth of the maximum contribution for each month of eligibility. In addition to the maximum contribution amount, catch-up contributions may be made by some individuals (see below.) [IRC § 223(b)(2)]

All HSA contributions made by or on behalf of an eligible individual are aggregated for purposes of applying the limit. The annual limit is decreased by the aggregate contributions to an Archer MSA. The same annual contribution limit applies whether the contributions are made by an employee, an employer, a self-employed person, or a family member. Unlike Archer MSAs, contributions may be made by or on behalf of eligible individuals even if the individuals have no compensation or if the contributions exceed their compensation. If an individual has more than one HSA the aggregate annual contributions to all the HSAs are subject to the limit.

Q 9:49 What are the "catch-up contributions" for individuals age 55 or older?

For individuals (and their spouses covered under the HDHP) between ages 55 and 65, the HSA contribution limit is increased by $900 in calendar year 2008. [IRC § 223(b)(3)] The catch-up amount was $800 for 2007 and will increase to $1,000 for calendar year 2009 and later years. As with the annual contribution limit, the catch-up contribution is also computed on a monthly basis. After an individual has attained age 65 (the Medicare eligibility age), contributions, including catch-up contributions, cannot be made to an individual's HSA.

> **Example 9-14:** An individual attains age 65 and becomes eligible for Medicare benefits in July, 2008. The individual had been participating in self-only coverage under an HDHP with an annual deductible of $1,000. The individual is no longer eligible to make HSA contributions (including catch-up contributions) after June, 2007. The monthly contribution limit is $175 ($1,000/12 + $900/12 for the catch-up contribution). The individual may make contributions for January through June totaling $1,050 (6 × $170), but may not make any contributions for July through December, 2008.

Q 9:50 What kinds of contributions can be made to an HSA?

Contributions to an HSA must be made in cash. Contributions may not be made in the form of stock or other property. Payments for the HDHP and contributions to the HSA can be made through an employer's cafeteria plan.

Q 9:51 What is the tax treatment of HSA contributions?

Contributions made by an eligible individual to an HSA within the allowable limits are deductible by the eligible individual in determining adjusted gross income (i.e., "above-the-line"). The contributions are deductible whether or not the eligible individual itemizes deductions. However, the individual cannot also deduct the contributions as medical expenses under IRC Section 213.

Contributions made by a family member on behalf of an eligible individual to an HSA are deductible by the eligible individual in computing adjusted gross income. The contributions are not deductible by the contributing family member.

In the case of an employee who is an eligible individual, employer contributions are treated as employer-provided coverage for medical expenses under an accident or health plan and are excludable from the employee's gross income.

Q 9:49

The employer contributions are not subject to withholding from wages for income tax or subject to the Federal Insurance Contributions Act (FICA) or the Federal Unemployment Tax Act (FUTA).

Q 9:52 When may HSA contributions be made?

Contributions for the taxable year can be made in one or more payments, at the convenience of the individual or the employer, at any time prior to the individual's tax return filing deadline for the year (without extensions), but not before the beginning of that year. For calendar year taxpayers, the deadline for contributions to an HSA is generally April 15 following the year for which the contributions are made. Although the annual contribution is determined monthly, the maximum contribution may be made on the first day of the year.

> **Planning Point:** Employers may want to exercise caution in making upfront contributions to an employee's HSA. Once a contribution is made, it is nonforfeitable. For example, an employer that makes the maximum annual contribution to an employee's HSA at the beginning of the year cannot recoup any portion of the contribution even if the employee terminates employment during the year. [IRS Notice 2004-50]

Q 9:53 Are rollover contributions to HSAs permitted?

Rollover contributions from Archer MSAs and other HSAs into an HSA are permitted. Rollover contributions need not be in cash. Rollovers are not subject to the annual contribution limits. Under special rules, a one-time rollover of FSA or HRA funds may be made by means of a qualified HSA distribution. [I.R.C. § 106(e), as amended by the 2006 Tax Relief and Health Care Act] (see Q 9:44). Rollovers from an IRA to an HSA are not permitted.

Q 9:54 Can a partnership or S corporation contribute to an HSA on behalf of a partner or S corporation shareholder-employee?

Yes, a partnership may contribute to a partner's HSA, and an S corporation may contribute to the HSA of a shareholder-employee. [IRS Notice 2005-8, 2005-4 IRB 1] However, the contributions are subject to special tax rules.

Q 9:55 What is the tax treatment of a partnership's contributions to a partner's HSA?

Contributions by a partnership to a bona fide partner's HSA are not contributions by an employer to the HSA of an employee. [See Rev. Rul. 69-184, 1969-1 C.B. 256] Instead, the partnership contributions may be treated either as distributions to the partner [IRC § 731] or as guaranteed payments for services rendered to the partnership. [IRC § 707(c)] [IRS Notice 2005-8, 2005-4 IRB 1]

Contributions by a partnership to a partner's HSA that are treated as distributions to the partner are not deductible by the partnership and do not affect the distributive shares of partnership income and deductions. The contributions are reported as distributions of money on Schedule K-1 (Form 1065). However, the distributions are not included in the partner's net earnings from self-employment, because the distributions do not affect a partner's distributive share of partnership income or loss. Assuming he or she meets the eligibility requirements, the partner can deduct the amount of the contributions made to the partner's HSA during the tax year as an adjustment to gross income on his or her federal income tax return. [IRC § § 223(a), 62(a)(19)]

Contributions to a partner's HSA that are treated as guaranteed payments are deductible by the partnership as a trade or business expense [IRC § 162] and are includible in the partner's gross income. The contributions are not excludible from the partner's gross income as employer-provided HSA contributions under section 106(d) because the contributions are treated as a distributive share of partnership income. [Reg. § 1.707-1(c)] Contributions by a partnership to a partner's HSA that are treated as guaranteed payments are reported as guaranteed payments on Schedule K-1 (Form 1065). Because the contributions are guaranteed payments that are derived from the partnership's trade or business, and are for services rendered to the partnership, the contributions are included in the partner's net earnings from self-employment. Assuming he or she meets the eligibility requirements, the partner can deduct the amount of the contributions made to the partner's HSA during the tax year as an adjustment to gross income on his or her federal income tax return. [IRC § § 223(a), 62(a)(19)]

Q 9:56 What is the tax treatment of an S corporation's contributions to the HSA of a shareholder-employee?

When it comes to fringe benefits, an S corporation is treated as a partnership, and any two-percent shareholder of the S corporation is treated as a partner of such partnership. [IRC § 1372](A shareholder-employee owning less than two percent of the corporation is treated like any other employee.) Therefore, contributions by an S corporation to an HSA of a two-percent shareholder-employee in consideration for services rendered are treated as guaranteed payments. [IRC § 707(c)]The contributions are deductible by the S corporation and are includible in the two-percent shareholder-employee's gross income. The two-percent shareholder-employee cannot exclude the contribution from gross income as employer-provided HSA contributions under IRC § 106(d). [See Rev. Rul. 91-26]

For employment tax purposes, when contributions are made by an S corporation to an HSA of a two-percent shareholder-employee, the two-percent shareholder-employee is treated as an employee subject to regular social security and Medicare (FICA) tax and not as an individual subject to self-employment (SECA) tax. [IRS Ann. 92-16, 1992-5 I.R.B. 53] However, contributions to an HSA of a two-percent shareholder-employee are not wages subject to FICA tax, even though the amounts must be included in wages for income tax withholding purposes. [IRC § 3121(a)(2)(B)]Assuming he or she meets the eligibility requirements, the two-percent shareholder-employee can deduct the amount of the contributions as an adjustment to gross income on his or her federal income tax return. [IRS Notice 2005-8; 2005-4 IRB 1]

Q 9:57 How are distributions from an HSA taxed?

Distributions from an HSA used exclusively to pay for qualified medical expenses of the account beneficiary, his or her spouse, or dependents are excludable from gross income. [IRC § 223(f)]In general, amounts in an HSA can be used for qualified medical expenses and will be excludable from gross income even if the individual is not currently eligible for contributions to the HSA. What's more, the exclusion applies to distributions for qualified expenses of a spouse or dependent who is not covered by the HDHP or is covered under another plan that is not an HDHP. [IRS Notice 2004-50]

However, any amount of the distribution not used exclusively to pay for qualified medical expenses of the account beneficiary, spouse or dependents is includable in gross income of the account beneficiary and is subject to an additional 10 percent tax on the amount. The penalty tax does not apply to distributions made after the account beneficiary's death, disability, or attaining age 65.

Q 9:58 What are the "qualified medical expenses" that are eligible for tax-free distributions?

The term "qualified medical expenses" are expenses paid by the account beneficiary, his or her spouse or dependents for medical care (including nonprescription drugs as described in Revenue Ruling 2003-102), but only to the extent the expenses are not covered by insurance or otherwise.

The qualified medical expenses must be incurred only after the HSA has been established.

Generally, health insurance premiums are not qualified medical expenses except for the following:

- Qualified long-term care insurance,

- COBRA health care continuation coverage, and

- Health care coverage while an individual is receiving unemployment compensation.

In addition, for individuals over age 65, premiums for Medicare Part A or B, Medicare HMO, and the employee share of premiums for employer-sponsored health insurance, including premiums for employer-sponsored retiree health insurance can be paid from an HSA. [IRS Notice 2004-50] Premiums for Medigap policies are not qualified medical expenses.

Q 9:58

Q 9:59 What are the income tax consequences after the HSA account beneficiary's death?

Upon death, any balance remaining in the account beneficiary's HSA becomes the property of the individual named in the HSA instrument as the beneficiary of the account. If the account beneficiary's surviving spouse is the named beneficiary, the HSA becomes the HSA of the surviving spouse. The surviving spouse is subject to income tax only to the extent distributions are not used for qualified medical expenses.

If the HSA passes to a person other than the account beneficiary's surviving spouse, the HSA ceases to be an HSA as of the date of the account beneficiary's death, and the person is required to include in gross income the fair market value of the HSA assets as of the date of death.

Q 9:60 What nondiscrimination rules apply to HSAs?

If an employer makes HSA contributions, the employer must make available comparable contributions on behalf of all "comparable participating employees" (i.e., eligible employees with comparable coverage) during the same period. [IRC §4980G; Reg. Sec. 54,4980G-0 through 54,4980G-5]Contributions are considered comparable if they are either the same amount or same percentage of the deductible under the HDHP.

Key exception: For tax years beginning after 2006, the 2006 Tax Relief and Health Care Act carved out an exception to the comparability rules enabling employers to make larger HSA contributions for nonhighly compensated employees (NHCEs) than for highly compensated employees (HCEs) (as defined in IRC § 414(q)). The new rule provides that HCEs are not treated as comparable participating employees for purposes of applying the comparability rules to an employer's contributions for non-HCEs. [IRC § 4980G(d)]

On the other hand, NHCEs must be included when testing the comparability of contributions for HCEs. Moreover, the comparability rules apply to the contributions made for non-HCEs. The employer must make available comparable contributions for non-HCEs with comparable coverage.

So, for example, an employer could make contributions for all comparable NHCEs without making any contributions (or making smaller, but not larger, contributions) for HCEs. If employer contributions do not satisfy the comparability rules for a calendar year, the employer is subject to an excise tax equal to 35% of the aggregate amount contributed by the employer to HSAs for that period. However, if an employer's failure to satisfy the comparability rules is due to reasonable cause and not to willful neglect, all or part of the excise tax may be waived to the extent payment of the tax would be excessive relative to the failure involved.

Comparable employees: As a general rule, employees are divided into three categories for comparability testing:

1. Current full-time employees;

2. Current part-time employees; and

3. Former employees (other than former employees with COBRA coverage).

Employees are considered part-time if they are customarily employed for fewer than 30 hours per week.

Employees who are covered by a bona fide collective bargaining agreement are not comparable participating employees if health benefits were the subject of good-faith bargaining. Former employees covered by a collective bargaining agreement also are not comparable participating employees.

The three categories of employees are further broken down according to type of HDHP coverage. As a general rule, there are two categories of coverage:

- Self-only HDHP coverage, and
- Family HDHP coverage.

So, for example, full-time employees with self-only HDHP coverage, part-time employees with self-only HDHP coverage, full-time employees with family coverage, and part-time employees with family coverage are all separate categories of employees and different amounts can be contributed to the HSAs for each category.

However, the IRS regulations allow a further breakdown of employees with family coverage into (1) self plus one, (2) self plus two, and (3) self plus three or more if the employer's plan provides different coverage options for such categories. Note, however, that if an HDHP has more than one coverage category that provides coverage for the same number of individuals, those categories must be treated as a single category for comparability testing. So, for example, employees covered under a category called "employee plus spouse" and employees covered under a category called "employee plus dependent" must be grouped together since both categories provide coverage for two individuals (i.e., self plus one coverage).

Example 9-15: Mammoth Corp. maintains an HDHP and contributes to the HSAs of eligible employees who elect coverage under the HDHP. The HDHP has six coverage options:

1. Self-only;

2. Self plus spouse;

3. Self plus dependent;

4. Self plus spouse plus one dependent;

5. Self plus two dependents; and

6. Self plus spouse and two or more dependents.

However, the plan has only four categories of coverage for comparability testing:

1. Self only;

2. Self plus one (including employees with self plus spouse and self plus dependent coverage);

3. Self plus two (including employees with self plus spouse plus one dependent and self plus two dependents coverage);

4. Self plus three or more (employees with self plus spouse and two or more dependents coverage)

Independent contractors, self-employed individuals, and partners in a partnership are not considered employees and are not subject to the comparability rules. Consequently, a self-employed individual may make contributions to his or her own HSA without making contributions for employees. Similarly, a partnership can make contributions to a partner's HSA without making comparable contributions for other partners or for non-partner employees. However, if contributions are made to any regular employee's HSA comparable contributions must be made for all comparable participating employees.

Non-employer provided HDHP coverage. An employer that contributes only to the HSAs of employees who are eligible individuals with coverage under an employer-provided HDHP is not required to make comparable contributions to HSAs of employees who are covered under a non-employer provided HDHP, even if those employees are otherwise eligible for HSA contributions. However, if the employer contributes to the HSA of any employee who is an eligible individual with coverage under a non-employer provided HDHP, the employer must make comparable contributions to the HSAs of all comparable participating employees whether or not they are covered under the employer's HDHP.

Planning Point: An employer is not necessarily privy to employee's non-employer provided health care coverage. Therefore, the IRS says that an employer that is required to make comparable contributions for employees with non-employer HDHP coverage will satisfy the comparability rule if it makes a reasonable good faith effort to identify all comparable participating employees with non-employer provided HDHP coverage and makes comparable HSA contributions for those employees.

Contributions for spouses. If spouses work for the same employer but only one employee-spouse has family coverage under the employer's HDHP, the employer is required to contribute only to the HSA of the employee-spouse with coverage under the HDHP. The employer is not required to contribute to the HSA of the employee-spouse who is covered under the employer's HDHP because of his or her spouse's coverage. However, if the employer contributes to the HSA of any eligible employee with non-employer provided HDHP coverage, the employer must make comparable contributions to the HSAs of the employee-spouse who is covered under the employee's HDHP because of his or her spouse's coverage (assuming he or she is otherwise eligible).

Planning Note: Bear in mind, however, that an employer's combined contributions for two employee-spouses are not required to exceed the annual contribution limit for individuals with family coverage.

Q 9:60

Contributions for former employees. An employer that is required to make comparable contributions for former employees must take reasonable actions to locate any missing comparable participating former employees. In general, such actions include the use of certified mail, the Internal Revenue Service Letter Forwarding Program or the Social Security Administration's Letter Forwarding Service.

Comparable contributions: Some contributions are not taken into account in applying the comparability rules. The rules do not apply to contributions to the HSAs of independent contractors, sole proprietors, and partners in a partnership. So, for example, a sole proprietor can make contributions to his or her own HSA without making comparable contributions for employees. In addition, the comparability rules do not apply to amounts rolled over by an employee from another HSA or from an Archer MSA. The rules also do not apply to after-tax contributions or to contributions made through a cafeteria plan.

An employer may limit HSA contributions to those employees who are covered under an HDHP sponsored by the employer. In that case, the employer is not required to make comparable contributions for any employee who is covered by an HDHP that is not sponsored by the employer. For example, an employer would not be required to make contributions for an employee who is covered by an HDHP sponsored by his or her spouse's employer.

An employer cannot tie its contributions to the amount of an employee's own contributions by making matching contributions equal to the employee's HSA contribution or a percentage of the employee's contribution. If all employees do not contribute the same amount to their HSAs, they will not receive comparable contributions. Therefore, the contributions will not satisfy the comparability rule.

In addition, an employer's contributions cannot come with strings attached. For example, an employer cannot condition employer contributions to an employee's HSA on participation in health assessments or wellness programs because if all employees do not participate they will not receive comparable contributions. Similarly, an employer cannot make additional contributions to HSAs of employees who have met age or length of service requirements.

Contribution methods: An employer has three options for making HSA contributions. The employer may make "pay-as-you-go" contributions periodically throughout the year (e.g., on a monthly or pay period basis); The employer may make "look-back" contributions by determining the contributions at the end of the calendar year and contributing them to employees' HSAs by April 15 of the following year; or the employer may make "pre-funded" contributions to the HSAs of all employees who are eligible individuals at the beginning of the calendar year. If an employer chooses the "pay-as-you-go" option, it must make contributions for each comparable participating employee who is an employee during the chosen time period. For example, if an employer makes contributions each pay period, it must make HSA contributions for each participating employee who is an employee during the pay period.

Q 9:60

If an employer chooses the "look-back" option, it must make contributions for each employee who was a comparable participating employee for any month in the calendar year.

In the case of "pre-funded" contributions, the employer must make HSA contributions for all employees who are comparable participating employees at the beginning of the year. However, it must also make contributions for all employees who are eligible participating employees for any month during the year, including employees hired after the initial funding date. Contributions for new hires may be made on a pre-funded, pay-as-you-go, or look-back basis.

If an employee has not set up an HSA at the time the employer makes its contributions, the employer will satisfy the comparability rules if it contributes comparable amounts to the employee's HSA when it is established, taking into account each month that the employee was a comparable participating employee. However, an employer is not required to make comparable contributions to an employee's HSA for a calendar year if the HSA is not established by December 31 of that year.

If an employer discovers that the comparability rules are not met for a calendar year, it may not recoup any amounts from an employee's HSA to set things right. An interest in an HSA is nonforfeitable. However, the employer can make additional contributions to satisfy the comparability rules. In other words, if an employer overfunds one employee's HSA it must do the same for all comparable participating employees. Additional contributions to correct non-comparable contributions can be made up until April 15 of the year following the year in which the non-comparable contributions were made. The additional contributions must include reasonable interest.

Penalty tax: If an employer does not satisfy the comparability rule for a calendar year, the employer is subject to an excise tax equal to 35% of the amount contributed by the employer to all HSAs for that year.

Example 9-16: During a calendar year, Alpha Corp. has 8 employees who are eligible individuals with self-only coverage under an HDHP provided by Alpha. The deductible for the HDHP is $2,000. Alpha contributes $2,000 each to the HSAs of two employees and $1,000 each to the HSAs of the other six employees, for total HSA contributions of $10,000. Alpha's contributions do not satisfy the comparability rules. Therefore, Alpha is subject to an excise tax of $3,500 (35% x $10,000).

If a failure to make comparable contributions is due to reasonable cause and not to willful neglect, all or part of the excise tax may be waived to the extent the tax would excessive relative to the failure involved.

Q 9:61 What reporting is required for an HSA?

HSA trustees or custodians must report both contributions and distributions to account holders. In addition, employers must report contributions to an HSA on an employee's Form W-2. Contributions should be reported in box 12 using

Code W—Employer's contribution to an employee's Health Savings Account (HSA).

Employees must report annual contributions to and distributions from an HSA on their federal income tax returns.

Health Care Flexible Spending Accounts

Q 9:62 What is a health flexible spending account?

A health flexible spending account (FSA) is an account set up by an employer to reimburse an employee for out-of-pocket medical expenses. FSAs may be fully funded by employer contributions. However, FSAs are typically set up as salary reduction arrangements under a cafeteria plan. Under this type of arrangement, an employee agrees to contribute a portion of his or her salary to the account on a pre-tax basis. Reimbursements made from the account for qualifying expenses are tax-free to the employee. [Prop. Reg. § 1.125-5]

> **Planning Point:** Health flexible spending accounts are also a tax-saver for employers. Salary reduction contributions are not subject to payroll taxes. Thus, an employer saves the 7.65 percent FICA tax (6.20 percent Social Security tax and the 1.45 percent Medicare tax) for employees who earn less than the Social Security wage base. For employees above the wage base, the employer saves the 1.45 percent Medicare tax.

Q 9:63 What kinds of expenses can be reimbursed from a health flexible spending account?

A health FSA can reimburse those expenses that qualify as medical care under the tax law rules (see Q 9:3), as well as expenses for nonprescription drugs (as described in Revenue Ruling 2003-102), but only to the extent the expenses are not covered by insurance or otherwise. So, for example, a health FSA cannot reimburse an employee for dependent care expenses. In addition, a health FSA cannot treat an employee's premiums for other health care coverage as a reimbursable expense. However, health care premiums may be paid on a salary reduction basis through a cafeteria plan (see Q 9:10).

As a general rule, a health FSA can reimburse an employee for a medical expense only if he or she provides a written statement from an independent third party stating that the expense has been incurred and the amount of the expense. In addition, the employee must provide a written statement indicating that the expense has not been reimbursed and is not eligible for reimbursement under any other health plan coverage. [Prop. Reg. § 1.125-6] However, the use of debit cards to tap FSA funds is permitted provided specific requirements are met (see Q 9:64)

Generally, a health FSA must operate on a pay-as-you-go basis. IRS regulations provide that a health FSA can reimburse an employee for an expense only after the expense has been "incurred." Moreover, the regulations provide that an expense is incurred when the health care is provided, not when the FSA participant is billed or pays for the services. A health FSA cannot make advance reimbursements of future or projected expenses. For certain types of expenses, however, the IRS takes a more flexible approach.

Example 9-17: Employee Janet Jenson's son, Brendan, needs braces. The orthodontic treatment will cost a total of $4,000 and will last for about two years. Jenson's orthodontist requires payment of $2,000 when Brendan begins treatment in September, with the remainder payable over two years. No part of the cost will be covered by insurance. Jenson has contributed $4,000 to her employer's health FSA for the current year.

IRS proposed regulations issued in 2007 provide that a cafeteria plan is permitted, but is not required to, reimburse employees for orthodontia services before the services are provided but only to the extent that the employee has actually made the payments in advance of the orthodontia services in order to receive the services. These orthodontia services are deemed to be incurred when the employee makes the advance payment. [Prop. Reg. § 1.125-5(k)(3)(i)] The IRS says employers can rely on the proposed regulations for current transactions.

Planning Point: Employers should alert employees to the reimbursement policy for these types of expenses. Health FSAs are a use-it-or-lose-it proposition. The employee forfeits funds that are not used for covered expenses by year-end. Therefore, an employee who funds an FSA in anticipation of upfront payments for orthodontia or similar treatments may be out of luck if the employer's policy is to reimburse only on a pay-as-you-go basis.

Q 9:64 Can FSA payments be made by debit or credit card?

Under a traditional flexible spending account arrangement, employees pay for out-of-pocket medical expenses and then submit documentation to the employer to obtain reimbursements. However, the IRS has ruled that employees can be provided with debit, credit, or stored value cards to tap their FSA funds. [Rev. Rul. 2003-43, 2003-21 I.R.B. 935; Notice 2006-69, 2006-31 IRB 107; Notice 2007-2, 2007-2 IRB 254] The previous IRS guidance has been incorporated in proposed regulations issued in 2007. [Prop. Reg. § 1.125-6(c)-(f)] The IRS says that employers can rely on the proposed regulations. The original IRS ruling on the use of cards gives two examples of such arrangements. In one case, an employer issues debit or stored-value cards to employees in amounts equal to the employees' FSA coverage amount. In the other case, the employer uses credit cards issued by a bank with individual credit limits equal to the amount of FSA coverage.

The IRS concluded that medical expense payments made under these arrangements are excludable from employees' incomes provided certain safeguards are in place to ensure that the cards are used only for eligible medical expenses.

On the other hand, the IRS ruled that another employer's debit card program did not satisfy the FSA requirements, because the employer did not require substantiation of all reimbursements made through the card. Instead, the employer used sampling techniques to check up on employees' use of the cards. For example, the employer reviewed 20 percent of dental office transactions paid with the card, but only 5 percent of physician office charges. In addition, the employer did not review small charges or charges in whole dollar amounts, which were assumed to be for copayments. Only those charges sampled were required to be substantiated by submission of receipts. Since the employer did not require substantiation of all charges, the IRS concluded that all payments made with the cards—including charges for legitimate medical expenses—had to be included in employees' wages.

Planning Point: A debit or credit card program has distinct advantages for employees, because they can pay medical expenses directly from their FSA accounts rather than paying the expenses with other funds and then seeking reimbursement from the plan. However, careful attention to the IRS requirements for card programs is imperative to ensure tax-free treatment for employees.

Basic rules: Under the IRS proposed regulations, a health FSA paying or reimbursing medical expenses through a debit, credit, or stored-value card (collectively referred to as debit cards) must meet all of the following requirements:

- Before receiving a debit card, an employee must agree in writing that he or she (1) will only use the card to pay for eligible medical expenses, (2) will not use the debit card for any medical expense that has already been reimbursed, (3) will not seek reimbursement under any other health plan for any expense paid for with the debit card, and (4) will maintain receipts or other documentation for any expense paid with the debit card.

- The debit card includes a statement providing that the employee's agreements are reaffirmed each time the employee uses the card.

- The amount available through the debit card equals the amount elected by the employee for the health FSA for the plan year, and is reduced by amounts paid or reimbursed for medical expenses incurred during the plan year.

- The debit card is automatically cancelled when the employee stops participation in the health FSA.

- The employer limits use of the debit card to eligible medical care providers and stores.

- The employer properly substantiates payments made with the card.

- The employer corrects any improper payments using the debit card.

Eligible medical care providers and stores. Starting in 2008, the IRS rules limit the use of cards to:

- Medical care providers (e.g. physicians, pharmacies, dentists, vision care offices, hospitals, other medical care providers with a health-care related merchant code),

Q 9:64

- Stores with the Drug Stores and Pharmacies merchant category code, and

- Stores with a non-health care merchant category code (e.g., supermarkets, discount stores and wholesale clubs) that have implemented an inventory information approval system.

The IRS provided transition relief for transactions occurring on or before December 31, 2007 to give non-health care merchants time to implement inventory systems. Under the transition rule, merchants that do not have health care merchant codes were treated as an "other medical care provider" with respect to debit card transactions. The same holds true for mail order vendors and web-based vendors that sell prescription drugs. Thus, debit cards could be used for purchases from such businesses. [Notice 2007-2]

Substantiation requirements. The IRS guidance and proposed regs provide for a variety of substantiation methods, depending on the type of payee and the type of payment.

Copayment match substantiation. Copayment match substantiation can be used only for payments to service providers or merchants that have health care related merchant category codes.

A debit or credit amount can be treated as substantiated if it exactly matches the plan's copayment amount for the particular product or services. For example, if an employee debits $10 for a doctor visit under a plan with a $10 copayment for each doctor visit, the debit can be treated as automatically substantiated.

Moreover, automatic substantiation can apply if a debit or credit charge is an exact multiple of a plan copayment (e.g. a debit of $30 for three prescriptions under a plan with a $10 copayment for prescription drugs). The copayment match substantiation method can also be used if a plan has multiple copayments for the same product or service (e.g., different copayments for generic and non-generic drugs). However, automatic substantiation applies only as long as the exact multiple does not exceed five times the maximum copayment.

If the dollar amount of a charge is not an exact multiple of a plan copayment or exceeds five times the copayment, the transaction must be treated as conditional pending additional confirmation, such as receipts.

Example 9-18: A plan requires a $5 copayment for generic drugs and a $10 copayment for non-generic drugs. An employee uses a debit card at a pharmacy to purchase five non-generic prescriptions, for a total debit of $50. Because the transaction is at a pharmacy and the amount of the transaction is an exact multiple that does not exceed five times the maximum copayment for prescriptions, the debit can be treated as substantiated without further review or documentation.

Example 9-19: Same facts as Example 9-18, except the employee uses the card at a pharmacy to purchase three generic prescriptions and three non-generic prescriptions for a total debit of $45. Because the transaction is at a pharmacy and the amount of the transaction is an exact match of a combination of the plan's copayments that does not exceed fives times the maximum copayment, the debit is automatically substantiated.

Example 9-20: Same facts as Example 9-18 except that the employee uses the card at a pharmacy to buy six non-generic prescriptions for a total charge of $60. Because the amount of the transaction exceeds five times the maximum $10 copayment for prescriptions, the debit must be substantiated by a receipt showing that the employee bought prescription drugs, the date of the purchase, and the amount of the purchase.

Example 9-21: Same facts as Example 9-18, except that the employee uses the card at a pharmacy to buy two non-generic prescriptions and a nonprescription medication for a total of $27. Because the debit is not an exact match of a multiple or combination of the copayments prescriptions, the transaction must be further substantiated.

Recurring expenses: An automatic substantiation rule apply to payments recurring expenses that match expenses previously approved as to amount, medical care provider and time period. For example, if an employee refills a prescription drug on a regular basis at the same provider and in the same amount, the payment can be treated as substantiated without the need for submission of a receipt or further review.

Third-party substantiation: If a third party that is independent of the employee and the employee's spouse and dependents (for example, medical care provider, merchant, or pharmacy benefit manager) provides, at the time and point of sale, information to verify to the employer (including electronically by email, the internet, intranet or telephone) that the charge is for an medical expense, the expense is substantiated without the need for further review.

Inventory information approval: If the company that provides debit or credit cards for a plan has a method for approving or rejecting transactions using inventory control information (such as SKUs) against a list of items that qualify as medical expenses, approved transactions can be treated as automatically substantiated. This method can be used for payments to merchants or service providers that do not have health care related merchant category codes, but only if the merchants or provides participate in the inventory information approval system.

Example 9-22: An employer's FSA provides reimbursements for both prescription and nonprescription medications. The employer uses the inventory information approval system for debit card transactions, including transactions at participating stores that sell nonprescription medications but do not have health-related merchant codes. At one participating store, an employee goes to the counter with aspirin, antacid, and cold medicines that cost $20.75, as well as $50 of items that do not qualify as medical expenses. The store's system compares the SKUs for all the times to a list of qualifying medical expenses. The debit for the $20.75 of medical expense items is approved, but the $50 debit for non-medical items is rejected and the employee is asked for an additional payment for that amount. The $20.75 of medical items can be treated as automatically substantiated.

Planning Point: All other charges to a card must be treated as conditional, pending substantiation of the charge through additional independent third-party information describing the goods or services, the date of the service or sale and the amount of the transaction.

Improper payments: If an improper payment (e.g., payment for a nonmedical expense) is made using a debit card, the employer must demand that the employee repay the plan. Moreover, until the improper payment is recovered, the employee's debit card must be de-activated and the employee must request payments or reimbursements of medical expenses from the health FSA through other methods (for example, by submitting receipts or invoices).

If, the employee does not repay the amount of the improper charge, the employer must withholds the amount of the improper charge from the employee's pay or other compensation, to the full extent allowed by applicable law.

If any amount of the improper payment remains outstanding, the employer should use a claims substitution or offset to resolve the problem such as reducing reimbursements for a later substantiated expenses by the amount of the improper payment. So, for example, if an employee has received an improper payment of $200 and subsequently submits a substantiated claim for $250 incurred during the same coverage period, a reimbursement for $50 is made. Finally, if all else fails and the employee remains indebted to the employer for improper payments, the employer should treats the improper payment as it would any other business debt.

Q 9:65 How do employees elect to make salary reduction contributions to a health flexible spending account?

The period of coverage under a health FSA must be 12 months. Employees must elect the amount of coverage under the FSA before the beginning of the coverage period. As a general rule, an employee cannot increase or decrease the amount of coverage during the 12-month period. [Prop. Reg. § 1.125-2] Election changes may be permitted, however, when the employee experiences a "change in status." [Reg. § 1.125-4]Qualifying events include:

- *Changes in legal marital status*, including marriage, death of a spouse, divorce, legal separation, or annulment;
- *Changes in the number of an employee's dependents* as a result of certain events, including birth, adoption, placement for adoption, or death of a dependent;
- *Changes in a dependent's status* that causes the dependent to satisfy or cease to satisfy the eligibility requirements for coverage, such as attainment of age, student status, or similar circumstances;
- *Changes in residence* of the employee, a spouse, or dependent; or
- *Changes in employment status* of the employee, a spouse, or dependent.

[Reg. § 1.125-4(c)]

Q 9:65

An FSA election change is permitted, however, only if it is made on account of and corresponds to the employee's change in status. [Reg. § 1.125-4(c)]

Example 9-23: Magna Corporation offers employees the opportunity to make salary reduction contributions to a health FSA. Before the beginning of the year, Barbara Baker, a single employee, elects to make FSA contributions of $50 per month. During the year, Baker gets married.

Result: Baker may increase her FSA contributions to fund coverage for her new husband. She may not, however, decrease her FSA contributions because a decrease would not correspond to her change in status.

In addition, a health FSA may provide that coverage terminates if an employee does not make the required salary reduction contributions. However, the employee may not be permitted to make a new health FSA election for the remaining portion of the original coverage period.

Q 9:66 What if an employee incurs out-of-pocket medical expenses, but has not yet contributed enough to the health flexible spending account to cover those expenses?

Under the tax law, a health FSA must exhibit the risk-shifting and risk-distribution characteristics of insurance. Therefore, the maximum annual reimbursement under a health FSA must be available to an employee at all times during the period of coverage, even if the employee has not yet made the full contribution for the year. An employer cannot peg reimbursements to an employee's actual contributions.

Example 9-24: Henry Gilmore elects $300 of coverage under Magna Corporation's health FSA for a calendar year. The plan provides that Gilmore must pay the $300 annual premium through salary reduction contributions of $25 per month. Gilmore incurs $250 of medical expenses in January after he has made only one premium payment of $25. Magna must reimburse the full $250 when Gilmore submits a claim for reimbursement.

An employer cannot require acceleration of an employee's contributions based on the employee's incurred claims and reimbursements. In addition, an employee who separates from service during the year cannot be forced to pay additional health FSA contributions even if he or she has received "excess" reimbursements. [Prop. Reg. § 1.125-5(d))]

Example 9-25: Same facts as Example 9-24, except Gilmore terminates employment with Magna and does not make any additional health FSA contributions. Gilmore's coverage under the FSA may be terminated as of the end of January. Therefore, Gilmore will not be entitled to additional reimbursements from the plan. On the other hand, Magna cannot recoup the excess reimbursements from other amounts due to Gilmore.

Q 9:67 Can an employee who separates from service continue coverage under an employer's health FSA?

The regulations provide that, if an employee makes the required contributions for an entire 12-month period, the employer may not terminate the employee's coverage merely because the employee separates from service before the end of the 12-month period. [Prop. Reg. § 1.125-2 Q&A-7(b)(3)] In addition, an employer may be required to offer continued health FSA coverage under the COBRA health care continuation coverage rules (see Q 9:99).

Q 9:68 Can transferred employees continue FSA participation when a business is sold?

The IRS has ruled that following the sale of a business's assets, transferred employees who elected to participate in a health FSA under the seller's cafeteria plan can continue to exclude salary reduction amounts and medical expense reimbursements from gross income without interruption and at the same level of coverage after becoming employees of the buyer if either (1) the seller agrees to continue its existing health FSA for the transferred employees or (2) the buyer agrees to adopt a continuation of the seller's FSA for the transferred employees. [Rev. Rul. 2002-32, 2002-23 I.R.B. 1069]

> **Example 9-26:** Seller Corp. maintains a cafeteria plan that includes a health FSA. To participate in the health FSA, employees elect pre-tax salary reductions in return for the right to receive medical care expense reimbursements up to the amount of their elections for the year. During the plan year, Seller enters into an agreement under which Buyer Corp. acquires a portion of Seller's assets. In connection with the sale, employees of Seller who work with the acquired assets terminate employment with Seller and become employees of Buyer. Buyer agrees to create a cafeteria plan with a health FSA. However, Seller and Buyer agree that the transferred employees will continue to participate in Seller's FSA for a period of time.

> **Example 9-27:** The same facts as Example 9-24, except that, as part of the sale, Buyer agrees to cover the transferred employees under Buyer's health FSA. The transferred employee's existing salary reduction elections will be taken into account for the remainder of Buyer's plan year as if made under Buyer's health FSA. Buyer's plan will reimburse medical care expenses incurred by the transferred employees up to the amount of the employees' elections, reduced by amounts previously reimbursed by Seller. Thus, medical expenses incurred before the closing date of the sale but not previously reimbursed as well as medical expenses incurred after the closing date of the sale will be reimbursed by Buyer's plan.

In addition to approving both plans, the IRS noted that neither plan involves a loss of eligibility for FSA coverage or other change in status. Therefore, transferred employees continue to be subject to their existing FSA elections and may not change those elections unless a change in status event occurs.

Q 9:69 What if an employee has unused funds in a health flexible spending account at year-end?

Health FSAs used to operate on a strict "use-it-or-lose-it" basis. Any unspent funds remaining in an employee's FSA at the end of the plan year were forfeited to the plan.

However, starting with the 2005 plan year, the IRS announced a significant rule change that liberalizes the "use-or-lose-it" rule.

The new rule permits employers to amend their cafeteria plan documents to provide for a grace period of up to 2 1/2 months immediately following the end of the plan year. Qualified medical expenses incurred during the grace period may be paid or reimbursed from any funds remaining in an employee's FSA at the end of the prior plan year. Thus, if an employer opts to include the maximum grace period, employees may have as long as 14 months and 15 days (the 12 months in the plan year plus the 2 1/2 month grace period) to use their FSA funds before any remaining funds are forfeited to the plan.

As under the strict "use-it-or-lose-it" rule, employers may continue to provide for a "run-out" period after the end of the grace period during which qualified expenses incurred during the plan year and the grace period can be paid or reimbursed. [IRS Notice 2005-42, 2005-23 I.R.B. 1]

Q 9:70 What happens if total contributions to a health FSA plan for a year exceed total reimbursements for that year?

If contributions exceed reimbursements, the excess can be used to pay reasonable administrative costs of the plan. Amounts in excess of such expenses—called "experience gains"—may be used to reduce employee contributions for the following year or may be returned to employees. Experience gains must be allocated among employees on a reasonable and uniform basis. For example, gains could be allocated based on employees' coverage levels. However, gains may not be allocated based on employees' claims experience. [Prop. Reg. § 1.125-5(o)]

> **Example 9-28:** Gamma Corporation allows employees to elect health FSA coverage in $100 increments from $500 to $2,000. Gamma's health FSA has $5,000 of experience gains for the year. The $5,000 may be refunded to employees who participated in the plan for the year, with the amount of each employee's refund weighted to reflect his or her level of coverage. Gamma could also use the $5,000 to reduce required premiums for the next plan year (for example, employees might be required to contribute only $480 for $500 of health FSA coverage). Finally, Gamma could use the $5,000 gain to reimburse claims in excess of employees' coverage elections, provided such excess reimbursements are made in a nondiscriminatory manner.

Health Reimbursement Arrangements

Q 9:71 What is a health reimbursement arrangement?

In its simplest form, a health reimbursement arrangement (HRA)—sometimes referred to as a defined contribution health plan—provides each employee with a set sum of money, which the employee uses to acquire health coverage. If the cost of coverage exceeds the amount provided by the employer, the employee makes up the difference.

Employer involvement in an HRA may be minimal—for example, the employer may simply provide the funds and leave the selection of health care up to each employee. At the other end of the spectrum, an employer's plan may offer employees prescreened and preselected health care options through either a single carrier or multiple carriers that are contracted for at group rates.

In addition, an HRA may supplement other medical coverage. For example, an employer may offer health insurance coverage under a high-deductible plan and a maximum annual reimbursement for out-of-pocket medical expenses under an HRA.

Q 9:72 How are HRAs treated for tax purposes?

In a series of revenue ruling and notice, the IRS gave its approval to HRAs that meet certain requirements. [Rev. Rul. 2002-41, 2002-28 I.R.B. 75; Notice 2002-45, 2002-28 I.R.B. 93; Rev. Rul. 2005-24, 2005-16 IRB 892, 04/05/2005] The ruling specifically provides that employer-provided contributions and medical care reimbursements made under a reimbursement arrangement that allows unused amounts to be carried forward are excludable from an employee's gross income.

To qualify for favorable tax treatment, an HRA must be paid for solely by the employer. An HRA may not be provided through a salary reduction arrangement or cafeteria plan. Moreover, an HRA may provide only benefits that reimburse expenses for medical care or for insurance covering qualifying medical care expenses.

On the other hand, unlike other reimbursement arrangements, an HRA may provide reimbursements up to a maximum dollar amount for a coverage period, with any unused portion of the maximum dollar amount carried forward to increase the maximum reimbursement available in later coverage periods.

Each medical expense submitted for reimbursement must be substantiated. Moreover, an HRA cannot reimburse a medical expense that was deducted by the employee in a prior year or that was incurred before the first day the employee became enrolled in the HRA.

An HRA will not qualify if the employee or any other person has the right to receive cash or any other taxable or nontaxable benefit other than the reimbursement of medical care expenses. If an employee or other person has such a right

Q 9:71

either for the current year or a future year, all distributions made from the HRA for the current year will be included in gross income, even if the distributed amounts are used to pay medical expenses. For example, the IRS says that if an arrangement pays a death benefit without regard to medical expenses, no amounts paid under the arrangement will qualify as tax-free reimbursements for medical expenses.

However, an HRA can continue to reimburse former employees or retired employees for medical expenses after termination of employment or retirement. For example, an HRA may provide for reimbursements to a former employee for medical expenses up to the remaining amount in an employee's account at the time of retirement or termination of employment. The plan may also provide that the maximum reimbursement available after retirement or termination of employment be reduced by the administrative cost of continuing the coverage. In addition, an HRA may provide additional employer contributions following an employee's retirement or termination of employment. (*Note:* HRAs are subject to the COBRA continuation coverage requirements. However, a plan may provide for continuation of coverage and additional contributions following retirement or termination even if the employee does not elect COBRA coverage.)

Planning Point: HRAs are similar to medical savings accounts (see Qs 9:24 *et seq.*) and health savings accounts (see Q 9:39 *et seq.*). Each type of arrangement provides funds for reimbursement of an employee's medical expenses and each arrangement permits carryover of unused amounts from year to year. However, there are some significant differences. For example, MSAs and HSAs are available only to individuals with high-deductible health insurance, and contributions to the account are limited to a percentage of the deductible. By contrast, HRA contributions are not limited and can be used to pay the cost of the employee's health insurance itself. In addition, amounts distributed from an MSA or HSA can be used for purposes other than medical expenses (although they are subject to tax and are subject to a 10 percent penalty if the account holder is under age 65). Amounts in an HRA cannot be distributed for purposes other than to pay medical expenses.

HRAs are also akin to health FSAs, which permit employees to set aside salary on a pre-tax basis to pay out-of-pocket medical expenses incurred during the year (see Qs 9:36 *et seq.*). But again, there are significant differences. Most notably, HRAs are not subject to the use-it-or-lose-it rules that apply to FSAs. While FSA funds that are not used by year-end (or during a post-year-end grace period) are forfeited, unused HRA amounts can be carried over from year to year. However, the most significant difference between HRAs and other reimbursement arrangements may be the fact that HRAs must be funded solely by the employer, while other arrangements are typically funded in whole or in part by employee contributions.

Self-Employed Health Insurance

Q 9:73 Can self-employed business owners deduct payments for health insurance for themselves and their employees?

Yes. A self-employed business owner can claim a business expense deduction for amounts paid for health insurance for employees. These payments are deducted on Schedule C, *Profit or Loss from Business*, which the owner files as part of his or her individual income tax return (Form 1040).

However, payments for the self-employed owner's own coverage are not deductible as a business expense. Instead, the tax law provides a special deduction for health insurance costs of self-employed individuals. [IRC § 162(l)] Self-employed health insurance costs are claimed as an above-the-line deduction on the owner's Form 1040. As such, the deduction may be claimed by self-employed individuals who claim the standard deduction as well as by those who itemize deductions.

The self-employed health insurance deduction is equal to 100 percent of the cost of coverage for the business owner, his spouse, and dependents. [IRC § 162(l)]

Furthermore, partners in a partnership and shareholders owning more than 2 percent of an S corporation may also claim the self-employed health insurance deduction. [See Qs 9:13, 9:14.]

In the case of self-employeds, the deduction is available whether the health insurance is purchased in the self-employed's individual name or in the name of the business. [Chief Counsel Advice 200524001] However, the IRS has indicated unofficially that the self-employed health insurance deduction is not available in the case of a policy purchased by an S corporation shareholder-employee in his or her own name.

Q 9:74 Can a business owner claim the self-employed health insurance deduction if he or she is eligible for coverage under another health plan?

The self-employed health insurance deduction is not allowed for any calendar month in which a taxpayer is eligible to participate in a subsidized health plan of an employer of the taxpayer or the taxpayer's spouse. [IRC § 162(l)(2)(B)]

Q 9:75 Are there any limits on the self-employed health insurance deduction?

Yes. The deduction cannot exceed the business owner's earned income from the trade or business providing the health care coverage. [IRC § 162(l)(2)(A)] In addition, the self-employed health insurance deduction is not taken into account in determining the business owner's net earnings from self-employment. Therefore, amounts used to pay the health insurance premiums are subject to Social Security and Medicare (SECA) taxes for self-employed individuals.

Q 9:73

If a self-employed individual has two or more businesses, the profits from one business cannot be netted against the losses of another business for purposes of the earned income test. The deduction is limited to the earned income "derived by the taxpayer from the trade or business with respect to which the plan providing the medical care coverage is established." [Chief Counsel Advice 200524001]

Retiree Health Coverage

Q 9:76 Can an employer provide health coverage for retired employees through its regular health care plan?

Yes. One way to provide health coverage for retired employees is to permit them to continue their participation in the company's regular group health plan for employees following retirement. To qualify for favorable tax treatment, an employer-provided health plan must be provided for the benefit of employees. [IRC §§ 105, 106] However, the IRS has specifically ruled that employees include retired employees and their spouses and dependents. [Rev. Ruls. 62-199, 1962-2 C.B. 38; 75-539, 1975-2 C.B. 45] Therefore, an employer's contributions for health coverage are excludable from a retiree's income. Retirees also qualify for tax-free treatment for benefits paid from the plan to cover medical expenses. [Rev. Rul. 82-2, 1982-1 C.B. 27]

An employer's payments for health coverage for retirees are generally deductible as ordinary and necessary business expenses. [IRC § 162]

Q 9:77 Are retirees taxable on retirement plan distributions that are used to pay for health plan coverage or to reimburse medical expenses?

An IRS ruling makes it clear that distributions from a qualified retirement plan are taxable even if they are used to pay health insurance premiums or are used for other medical expenses [Rev. Rul. 2003-62, 2003-25 I.R.B. 1034].

Example 9-29: Magma Corp. maintains a qualified retirement plan for its employees. Magma also maintains a group health plan for current and former employees and their spouses and dependents. Current employees pay part of the cost of their health insurance by means of salary reduction contributions under Magma's cafeteria plan. In addition, Magma permits retired employees to elect to have a portion of their retirement plan distributions applied to pay for health insurance premiums under the cafeteria plan.

According to the IRS, retirement plan distributions are taxable to retirees and there is no tax law rule that allows retirement plan participants to exclude retirement plan distributions that are applied to purchase benefits under a cafeteria plan. Therefore, a retiree's retirement plan distributions are includible in gross income even if the retiree elects to have the distributions applied to pay health insurance costs under the former employer's cafeteria plan. Moreover, the IRS says the same result applies if retirement plan distributions are applied directly to reimburse medical expenses incurred by a retiree.

Q 9:78 Can an employer provide coverage for retirees through a pension plan?

Generally, an employer cannot use pension funds for purposes other than providing retirement benefits. However, a special tax rule permits a pension or annuity plan to provide health benefits for retirees and their dependents. [IRC § 401(h)]

An employer will qualify for the special rule if all of the following requirements are met:

1. The retiree health benefits are paid out of a separate account;

2. The employer's contributions to the account are reasonable and ascertainable;

3. The benefits provided are subordinate to the retirement benefits provided under the plan;

4. The terms of the plan require that any amount remaining in the plan be returned to the employer upon satisfaction of all liabilities under the plan to provide benefits; and

5. A separate account is established to provide benefits to key employees and their spouses and dependents.

Health and accident benefits are considered subordinate to retirement benefits if the contributions made to provide medical benefits (plus any contributions made to provide life insurance) do not exceed 25 percent of the total contributions to the plan. [IRC § 401(h)]

Q 9:79 Can an employer provide retiree health benefits through a health reimbursement arrangement (HRA)?

Yes. If a retiree was covered by an HRA during his or her working years, the plan may provide for continuing reimbursements of qualifying medical expenses up to the remaining amount in an employee's account following retirement. The plan may also provide for additional employer contributions following an employee's retirement. (see Q 9:72)

In addition, the IRS has ruled that employer contributions of the value of accumulated unused vacation and sick leave to HRAs for retirees are eligible for tax-free treatment, provided payments from the accounts are limited solely to reimbursements of substantiated medical care expenses incurred by the former employees, their spouses, and dependents. [Rev. Rul. 2005-24, 2005-16 I.R.B. 892]

Example 9-30: Alpha Corp. sponsors an HRA that reimburses an employee solely for medical care expenses that are substantiated before the reimbursements are made. The plan reimburses expenses of both current and former employees, including retirees, and their spouses and dependents. The plan also reimburses expenses of the surviving spouse and dependents of a deceased employee. On the death of a deceased employee's surviving spouse and last dependent, any unused reimbursement amount is forfeited.

The plan is paid for solely by the employer. At the end of a plan year, a portion of each employee's unused reimbursement amount is forfeited and the remainder is carried forward. When an employee retires, Alpha automatically contributes an amount to the retiree's account equal to the value of all or a portion of his or her unused vacation and sick leave. These contributions are mandatory, and the retiree may not receive any of the designated amount in cash or other benefits. Result: Amounts contributed to the plan, including the value of unused leave, and amounts paid from the plan are excludable from an retiree's income.

Q 9:80 Do any special rules apply when an employer provides prescription drug benefits to retirees?

The Medicare Prescription Drug, Improvement, and Modernization Act of 2003 [P.L. 108-173] establishes a voluntary prescription drug benefit under Medicare Part D. In conjunction with that change, the Act provides for federal subsidy payments to employers and unions that sponsor qualified retiree prescription drug plans.

Retiree prescription drug plan subsidies are provided for retirees who are eligible for Medicare prescription drug coverage, but who receive drug coverage through an employment-based plan. To receive the subsidy, a plan must offer benefits with an actuarial *value* equal to or greater than Medicare prescription drug benefits, although the benefits need not be identical to the benefits offered by Medicare.

For plan years ending in 2008, the subsidy is 28 percent of prescription drug costs between $275 and $5,600 per eligible individual (i.e., up to $1,568 per individual). The dollar figures are indexed for inflation. The subsidy applies only to costs that are actually paid (net of discounts, chargebacks, and rebates) for prescription drugs; administrative costs are not included in calculating the subsidy. The subsidy is not included in the employer's gross income for federal income tax purposes and does not affect the deductibility of employer contributions to its retiree health plan.

Subsidy applications. The prescription drug subsidy is administered by the Health and Human Services Department's Centers for Medicare and Medicaid Services (CMS). Application for and payment of subsidy is handled electronically through the CMS's RDS Center at http://www.rds.cms.hhs.gov.

An employer seeking the subsidy must complete an electronic application through the RDS Center. The application must be submitted 90 days before each plan year for which the employer intends to seek the subsidy.

An employer may elect to receive subsidy payments on a monthly, quarterly, interim annual, or annual basis. Subsidy payments are made by electronic funds transfer (EFT) to an account designated by the employer. An employer cannot choose to receive payments by check rather than EFT.

Disclosure to employees. All employer that offers prescription drug coverage—including employer that do not apply for the federal subsidy—must disclose to Medicare Part D-eligible plan participants whether or not the plan constitutes creditable coverage. The disclosure requirement applies to all Part D-eligible individuals covered by or applying for coverage under an employer's plan, including active and disabled employees, retirees, and Medicare-eligible dependents.

The purpose of the disclosure requirement is to provide Medicare-eligible individuals with important information necessary to decide whether and when to enroll for Medicare Part D prescription drug coverage. Individuals who do not have other creditable prescription drug coverage generally must enroll when they initially become eligible or face higher premiums when they enroll at a later date. If employer coverage is creditable, an individual can delay enrolling in Part D without incurring a late enrollment penalty.

As a general rule, coverage is creditable if the actuarial value of the coverage equals or exceeds the actuarial value of standard Medicare using a "gross value" test [42 CFR § 423.56(a)].

However, an employer that is *not* claiming the retiree prescription drug subsidy can use a simplified method based on plan design to determine if its plan constitutes creditable coverage. Under the simplified rules, a plan will be deemed to be creditable coverage if it provides:

1. Coverage for brand-name and generic prescriptions;

2. Reasonable access to retail drug providers and, optionally, access to mail order providers;

3. Benefit payments averaging at least 60% of a plan participant's prescription drug expenses; and

4. At least one of the following:

   - Either no annual prescription drug benefit maximum limit or an annual maximum of at least $25,000, or

   - Expected benefits of at least $2,000 per Medicare beneficiary in 2008, or

   - An integrated plan design that covers both medical expenses and prescription drugs with an annual deductible of no more than $250, either no annual benefit maximum or an annual maximum of at least $25,000, and a lifetime combined maximum of at least $1 million.

Employers must also disclose to CMS whether or not their coverage is creditable. However, this disclosure requirement does not apply to employers that apply for the drug subsidy.

Planning Point: The tests for creditable coverage are not identical to the actuarial equivalence tests required to claim the retiree prescription drug

Q 9:80

subsidy. Therefore, an employer plan that constitutes creditable coverage will not automatically qualify for the subsidy.

COBRA Health Care Continuation Coverage

Q 9:81 What is COBRA?

COBRA is an acronym for the Consolidated Budget Reconciliation Act of 1986, the law that introduced the COBRA health care continuation coverage rules.

Q 9:82 What are the basic COBRA requirements?

The COBRA rules require group health plans to provide continued group health plan coverage for certain employees and their family members who would otherwise lose coverage under the plan. [IRC § 4980; Reg. § 4980B-11]

Q 9:83 What plans are covered by COBRA?

Generally, the COBRA continuation coverage requirements apply to any group health plan that is maintained by an employer to provide health care to individuals (or their families) who have an employment-related connection to the employer. Thus, the COBRA rules apply to plans covering employees or former employees. [Reg. § 54.4980B-2]

Q 9:84 What is a group health plan?

The COBRA rules define the term health plan broadly. A plan is a group health plan whether health care is provided directly, by insurance, or through a reimbursement arrangement, such as a flexible spending or health reimbursement arrangement. [Reg. § 54.4980B-2 Q&A-1]

A group insurance policy covering a number of employees is clearly a group health plan. However, the COBRA regulations make it clear that individual insurance policies covering two or more employees will also be treated as a group health plan for COBRA purposes.

An arrangement to provide medical services on a company's business premises will generally be treated as a group health plan. However, the regulations make it clear that an onsite facility that primarily provides first aid to current employees at no charge during working hours is not covered by the COBRA requirements.

Moreover, the regulations provide that the COBRA requirements apply only to employer-sponsored programs that provide medical care and treatment. The rules do not apply to programs that simply further general good health, such as a spa, swimming pool, or fitness center.

In addition, the COBRA requirements do not apply to employer-sponsored plans providing long-term care services. Nor do they apply to amounts contributed by an employer to a medical savings account or health savings account. COBRA, however, covers high deductible health insurance that is provided by an employer in connection with a medical savings account or health savings account.

Q 9:85 Are all employers subject to the COBRA rules?

The COBRA rules generally apply to any employer that maintains a group health plan. However, there is an exception for small employers. A small employer is exempt from the COBRA coverage requirements if it normally employed fewer than 20 employees during the preceding calendar year. Under the COBRA regulations, an employer will qualify as a small employer if it had fewer than 20 employees on at least 50 percent of the typical business days during the prior year. [Reg. § 54.4980B-2 Q&A-4]

For this purpose, only common law employees have to be counted. Self-employed individuals (e.g., the owner of an unincorporated business), independent contractors, and directors do not have to be counted even if they are covered by the same plan as common law employees.

Part-time employees do have to be counted—but they do not count as full employees. Instead, each part-time employee counts as a fraction of an employee equal to the number of hours the part-timer works divided by the number of hours he or she would have to work to be considered full-time. The number of hours necessary to be full-time depends on the employer's normal business practice, but may not be more than 8 hours a day or 40 hours a week.

In addition, instead of counting employees on a day-by-day basis, the regulations permit employers to count employees by pay period and apply that number to each typical business day in the pay period. Whether employees are counted day-by-day or by pay period, the same method must be used for all employees for the entire year. [Reg. § 54.4980B-2, Q&A-5]

A plan that it is not a small-employer plan for a given period remains liable for COBRA coverage that was triggered during that period, even if it later becomes a small-employer plan.

Q 9:86 Does an employer still qualify for COBRA's small employer exception if its workforce increases to 20 or more employees?

As a general rule, an employer is exempt from the COBRA coverage requirements if it normally employed fewer than 20 employees during the prior year. Moreover, that is true even if the employer normally employed 20 or more employees in the current year. However, the rules may be different if the increase in employees is due to acquisition of another business.

Example 9-31: Alpha Co. maintains a group health plan for its employees. Alpha normally employed 15 employees during the prior year. Therefore, as of the beginning of the current year, Alpha's health plan qualifies for COBRA's small employer exception. However, during the current year, Alpha buys all of the stock of Beta Co., which also employed 15 employees in the prior year. After the stock purchase, Alpha and Beta are considered to be a single employer.

Result: The IRS says Alpha's plan no longer qualifies for the small employer exception as of the date of the stock sale. [Rev. Rul. 2003-70, 2003-27 I.R.B. 3] Since Alpha and Beta are treated as a single employer, all employees of both Alpha and Beta must be taken into account in applying the exception. Therefore, because Alpha and Beta combined employed at least 20 employees during the prior year, the small employer exception does not apply to the combined entity following the sale.

Example 9-32: Gamma Co. maintains a group health plan for its employees. During the prior year, Gamma Corp. normally employed 18 employees. Therefore, Gamma's health plan qualified for the small employer exception as of the beginning of the current year. During the current year, Gamma acquired substantially all of the assets of Delta Co., which employed 15 employees throughout the prior year. After the asset acquisition, Gamma continued to operate Delta's former business without interruption or substantial changes.

Result: According to the IRS, Gamma's acquisition of Delta's assets does not cause Gamma and Delta to be treated as a single employer. Therefore, Gamma will continue to qualify for the small employer exception throughout current year. Note, however, that Gamma will become subject to the COBRA coverage requirements in the following year if the addition of the Delta employees causes Gamma to normally employ at least 20 employees in the current year.

Q 9:87 Who is entitled to COBRA coverage?

An employer must provide COBRA coverage to "qualified beneficiaries" who would otherwise lose coverage under a group health plan because of certain triggering events (so-called "qualifying events"). [Reg. § 54.4980B-3]

Q 9:88 Who are qualified beneficiaries?

As a general rule, qualified beneficiaries include any individual who is covered under the plan on the day before a qualifying event as a covered employee, the spouse of a covered employee, or a dependent child of a covered employee. A child who is born to or placed for adoption with a covered employee during a period of COBRA coverage is also a qualified beneficiary. [Reg. § 54.4980B-3, Q&A-1]

For this purpose, a covered employee includes anyone who is covered under a group health plan by virtue of an employment relationship to the employer. For example, a retiree or former employee is a covered employee if he or she is covered by the plan based on his or her former employment with the employer. Unlike the small-employer exception, self-employed individuals, independent contractors, and directors are covered employees if their relationship to the employer makes them eligible to be covered by the plan.

Bear in mind, however, that an employee who is merely eligible for coverage is not a covered employee if he or she is not actually covered under the plan. In general, the reason for the lack of actual coverage (such as having declined participation or having failed to satisfy the plan's conditions for participation) is irrelevant. Similarly, a covered employee's spouse or dependent (other than an after-born or adopted child) is not a qualified beneficiary if he or she is not actually covered by the plan on the day before the qualifying event.

In the case of a cafeteria plan or flexible spending arrangement (FSA), the COBRA coverage requirements apply only to health care benefits that an employee has actually chosen to receive.

Q 9:89 What events trigger COBRA coverage?

There are six different "qualifying events" that can trigger an employer's responsibility to provide COBRA coverage to an employee or an employee's family members:

1. Death of a covered employee;

2. Termination or reduction in hours of a covered employee's employment;

3. Divorce or legal separation of an employee and his or her spouse;

4. Entitlement of a covered employee to Medicare benefits;

5. A child's ceasing to be a dependent who is eligible to be covered under the plan;

6. Bankruptcy of the employer.

To trigger COBRA coverage, a qualifying event must cause the employee or a family member to lose coverage under the employer's health plan. [Reg. § 54.4980B-4]

Q 9:90 What if an employee is still covered by the plan, but the terms and conditions of the coverage have changed?

For purposes of the COBRA rules, a loss of coverage means that the employee or family member is no longer covered under the same terms and conditions that were in effect immediately before the qualifying event. So, for example, an increase in the premium or contribution that must be paid by the employee or family member is considered a loss of coverage if the increase is caused by the qualifying event.

> **Example 9-33:** Betty Finley retires after 30 years with Beta Corp. As a retiree, Finley is required to pay a higher premium for the same group health coverage that she had before retirement.

Result: Finley's retirement is qualifying event—termination of her employment. In fact, she has "lost" coverage because of the higher premium requirement. Therefore, Beta Corp. must offer Finley COBRA continuation coverage.

Caution: This rule may seem somewhat paradoxical. After all, an employer can charge an employee for COBRA coverage and may cut off COBRA coverage after a period of time (see Qs 9:68, 9:80). Therefore, a retiree may get a better deal both price-wise and time-wise if he or she sticks with regular coverage. However, to comply with the rules, an employer must *offer* the COBRA coverage.

Q 9:91 What if health coverage for an employee or family member was reduced or eliminated before a qualifying event?

If the reduction or elimination of coverage was made in anticipation of the event, COBRA coverage is required when the event occurs. For example, COBRA coverage would be required if an employer eliminates an employee's health coverage in anticipation of the employee's termination of employment or an employee drops coverage for a spouse in anticipation of divorce. [Reg. § 54.4980B-4, Q&A-1(c)] The reduction or elimination of coverage must be ignored in determining whether the event results in a loss of coverage.

An IRS revenue ruling makes it clear, however, that a plan is not required to make COBRA coverage available from the date of the employee's anticipatory elimination of coverage for a soon to be ex-spouse. Instead, the plan is required to make COBRA coverage available to the spouse as of the date of the divorce. [Rev. Rul. 2002-88, 2002-52 I.R.B. 995]

Q 9:92 What if the loss of coverage takes place sometime after the qualifying event?

A loss of coverage need not take place simultaneously with the qualifying event, so long as the loss of coverage occurs before the end of the maximum COBRA coverage period for that event (see Q 9:68).

Example 9-34: Gamma Corp. maintains a group health plan for both active employees and retirees (and their families). The coverage for active employees and retirees is identical, and Gamma does not require retirees to pay more for their coverage than active employees. As a result, Gamma is not required to make COBRA coverage available when an employee retires because there is no loss of coverage on termination of employment. However, Gamma subsequently decides to amend the plan to eliminate retiree coverage. At the time the amendment takes effect, several retirees and their spouses have been covered for less than the maximum COBRA coverage period since they terminated employment.

Result: The elimination of retiree coverage is a deferred loss of coverage for those retirees for whom the maximum COBRA period has not expired.

Gamma must make COBRA coverage available to those retirees and their spouses for the balance of the maximum coverage period dating from their termination of employment.

Whereas, if the maximum coverage period has expired at the time a deferred loss of coverage takes place, no COBRA coverage is required.

Q 9:93 Do the COBRA coverage rules apply if an employee is terminated for cause?

Yes, they do. As a general rule, the reasons for an employee's termination of employment are irrelevant. It does not matter if the employee quit voluntarily or was discharged. However, there is one exception: COBRA coverage does not have to be made available if an employee is terminated for gross misconduct.

Planning Point: Employers face stiff penalties for failure to provide COBRA coverage. Therefore, a decision to withhold coverage would be ill advised except in the most extreme cases.

For example, a court upheld an employer's decision not to offer COBRA coverage to an employee who savagely beat a co-worker, even though it occurred off the job. The court concluded that withholding COBRA coverage was justified, because the nature of the conduct was outrageous, and there was a connection between the behavior and the working environment. [*UB Services, Inc. v. Gatson*, U.S. Dist. Ct. (W. Va. 2000)]

Other cases have upheld the employer's determination of gross misconduct where the behavior at issue involved mishandling of employer funds or stealing employer property. [*See, e.g., Burke v. American Stores Employee Benefit Plan*, U.S. Dist. Ct. (N.D. Ill. 1993); *Avina v. Texas Pig Stands, Inc.*, U.S. Dist. Ct. (W.D. Tex. 1991)]

Q 9:94 What is meant by a reduction in hours?

A reduction of hours occurs whenever there is a decrease in the hours that a covered employee is required to work or actually works, as long as there is no immediate termination of employment. Thus, a switch from full-time to part-time work would trigger COBRA coverage if the employee loses health benefits as a result of the change. An absence due to disability or a temporary layoff is also a reduction in hours, even though the employee's hours are reduced to zero.

If a plan measures eligibility for coverage by the number of hours worked in a given time period, such as the preceding month or quarter, an employee who fails to work the requisite hours has experienced a reduction in hours resulting in a loss of coverage. [Reg. § 54.4980B-4, Q&A-1(c)]

Q 9:95 What kind of coverage must be offered under the COBRA rules?

When a qualifying event occurs, each qualified beneficiary who loses coverage must be offered the opportunity to elect to receive the same group health coverage that is provided to similarly situated active employees and their family members who have not experienced a qualifying event (called "non-COBRA beneficiaries"). Ordinarily, this will be the same coverage that the qualified beneficiary had on the day before the qualifying event. [Reg. § 54.4980B-5]

Q 9:96 What if the employer later makes changes in the health plan covering a COBRA beneficiary?

COBRA beneficiaries are basically in the same situation as active employees and their families. Any change in benefits applies equally to both COBRA and non-COBRA beneficiaries. However, an employer cannot cut off coverage for COBRA beneficiaries if it maintains any health plans. If an employer eliminates a plan, any COBRA beneficiaries enrolled in that plan must be offered the option of enrolling in another plan, even if active employees are not offered that option. [Reg. § 54.4980B-7, Q&A-1(a)(3)]

Q 9:97 What if a COBRA beneficiary moves out of the area served by the employer's plan?

Under the COBRA regulations, alternative coverage must be provided if the employer can provide coverage under an existing plan. However, if the employer has no existing plan that serves the employee's new geographic area, the employer is not required to provide alternative coverage.

Q 9:98 How do plan deductibles apply to a COBRA beneficiary?

COBRA beneficiaries are generally subject to the same deductibles as any other plan participant. If COBRA coverage begins during a deductible period, the COBRA beneficiary must retain credit for expenses incurred before the COBRA event occurred. [Reg. § 54.4980B-5, Q&A-2]

If the plan computes deductibles separately for each individual covered by the plan, an individual's remaining deductible on the date COBRA coverage begins is the same as that individual's deductible on the day before the COBRA event.

Example 9-35: Delta Co.'s group health plan applies a separate annual $100 deductible to each individual covered by the plan. Fred Brown dies while working for Delta. At the time of his death, Brown, his wife, and two children were covered by Delta's group health plan. Under Delta's plan, a spouse and dependent children lose their coverage on the last day of the month following the month of a covered employee's death. At that time, Brown's wife had incurred $80 of covered expenses, the Brown's older child had incurred no covered expenses, and the younger child had incurred $120 of covered expenses.

Result: At the beginning of the COBRA coverage period, Brown's wife has a remaining deductible of $20, the older child must still meet the full $100 deductible, and the younger child has no further deductible.

The remaining deductible for a family on the date that COBRA coverage begins depends on the members of the family electing COBRA coverage. In other words, only the expenses of those members who actually elect COBRA coverage need to be taken into account. Moreover, if there is more than one family unit following the qualifying event (for example, in the case of a divorce), the family deductible can be computed separately for each family unit based on the members in that unit.

Example 9-36: Magna's group health plan has a $500 per family annual deductible. The plan also provides that when a covered employee divorces, coverage terminates immediately for the employee's spouse and any dependent children who do not remain in the employee's custody. George Finn, a covered employee with two children, divorces. Finn's ex-wife obtains custody of the younger child, while Finn retains custody of the older child. Finn's ex-wife and the younger child elect COBRA coverage. At the time of the divorce the family had accumulated $420 of covered expenses, including $70 of expenses incurred by Finn, $70 by Finn's ex-wife, $200 by the younger child, and $80 by the older child.

Result: The family unit consisting of Finn's ex-wife and the younger child had accumulated a total of $270 of covered expenses. Thus, the remaining deductible for that family unit is $230. The plan does not have to credit that family unit with the $150 of expenses incurred by Finn and the older child. The remaining deductible for Finn and the older child is not affected because their coverage is not COBRA coverage.

Q 9:99 How does an employer handle limits on plan benefits under the COBRA rules?

Plan limits carry over to the COBRA period in much the same way as plan deductibles, on either an individual or family unit basis. This rule applies both to limits on plan benefits (such as a maximum number of hospital days or a cap on reimbursable expenses) and to limits on out-of-pocket expenses (such as a limits on co-payments or a catastrophic limit).

Example 9-37: Alpha's group health plan pays for a maximum of 150 days of hospital confinement per individual per calendar year. Helen Willis terminated her employment on May 1 and elected COBRA coverage. Willis had been in the hospital for 20 days earlier that year.

Result: Alpha's plan must pay for only 130 days of hospital confinement for Willis for the remainder of the year.

Example 9-38: Beta's health plan reimburses a maximum of $20,000 of covered expenses per family per year. The same limit applies to unmarried covered employees. Jane Hancock and her husband had family coverage under the plan before they divorced. Hancock's ex-husband elected COBRA coverage after the divorce. Before the divorce, the couple had incurred $13,000 of covered expenses—$5,000 for Hancock and $8,000 for her ex-husband.

Result: Alpha's plan must reimburse Hancock's ex-spouse for up to $12,000 of expenses for the remainder of the year—that is, only the ex-spouse's own expenses count against the $20,000 reimbursement cap. Hancock's remaining reimbursement limit is not affected because her coverage is not COBRA coverage.

Q 9:100 Do the COBRA continuation coverage rules apply to health flexible spending accounts?

Health flexible spending accounts (FSAs) allow employees to make salary reduction contributions on a pre-tax basis. The contributions can be withdrawn tax-free to pay out-of-pocket medical expenses. In some plans, the employer also makes contributions to employees' accounts. (See Q 9:36.)

Health FSAs are considered health plans for COBRA purposes. However, the obligation to provide continued coverage under a health FSA may be limited if two conditions are met:

1. Benefits provided under the health FSA are "excepted benefits" [IRC §§ 9831, 9832]; and

2. The maximum amount the employee can be required to pay for a year of COBRA coverage equals or exceeds the maximum benefit available under the FSA for a year.

The IRS says that health FSAs qualify as excepted benefits if: (1) the maximum benefit payable to the employee for the year does not exceed two times the employee's salary reduction election for the year (or, if greater, the amount of the employee's salary reduction election plus $500), and (2) the employer offers other group health plan coverage for the year that is not limited to excepted benefits.

If both of the above conditions are met, a health FSA is not required to make COBRA coverage available for any *subsequent* plan year. In other words, the health FSA can cut off an employee's coverage at the end of the current plan year even if that is short of the normal COBRA coverage period.

In addition, a health FSA is not required to make COBRA coverage available for the *current* plan year unless the benefits available during the remainder of the year will exceed the amount the FSA can charge for the coverage. In other words, COBRA coverage is not required if the plan will simply pay out an amount equal to (or even less than) what it collects from the employee. [Reg. § 54.4980B-2, Q&A-8(b)(c)]

Example 9-39: Omega Corp. offers its employees a major medical plan and a health FSA. The plans operate on a calendar year basis. Before the beginning of each year, employees can elect to reduce their compensation by up to $1,200 and have that amount contributed to the health FSA. Omega matches each employee's health FSA contribution. Thus, the annual benefit available to an employee is two times his or her salary reduction election for the year. Omega has determined that a reasonable estimated cost of providing the coverage for the year is equal to two times an employee's salary reduction for the year. Therefore, Omega can charge 102 percent [IRC § 4980B(f)(2)(C)] of that amount as a COBRA premium. This premium is charged on a monthly basis. So, for an employee who makes the maximum $1,200 salary reduction election, the annual charge is $2,448 (102 percent × $2,400) and the monthly premium is $204.

Helen Arnold, an Omega employee, has elected to make $1,200 of salary reduction contributions to the FSA. Thus, Arnold's maximum benefit for the year is $2,400. Arnold terminates employment with Omega on May 31. As of that date, Arnold had received reimbursements for $300 of health care expenses from the FSA.

Result: Omega's health FSA meets both of the above conditions. The health FSA is an excepted benefit because employees have other group health coverage available and the maximum benefit payable for the year is not greater than two times an employee's salary reduction election for the year. In addition, the maximum amount that can be charged for COBRA coverage exceeds the maximum benefit available for the year. Therefore, Omega's health FSA is not required to make COBRA coverage available to Arnold for any year *after* the current year.

Omega's health FSA is, however, required to offer Arnold COBRA coverage for the current year. After deducting her $300 of reimbursements, Arnold is eligible for an additional $2,100 of benefits in the current year. However, the FSA can charge her only $1,428 for her COBRA coverage for the remainder of the year (7 months × $204). COBRA coverage is required because Arnold's remaining benefits will exceed the cost of her COBRA coverage.

Example 9-40: Same facts as Example 9-30, except Arnold had received $1,000 of reimbursements as of the date she terminated employment.

Result: The plan is not required to offer COBRA coverage for the current year. Arnold's remaining benefit of $1,400 would be less than the $1,428 the plan could charge for the coverage.

Q 9:101 Can a COBRA beneficiary ever change his or her coverage?

Generally, a qualified beneficiary only has a right to continue the coverage he or she had immediately before the qualifying event. However, there are exceptions to this rule. A beneficiary who leaves the area covered by a region-specific plan must be offered alternative coverage under another plan of the employer. In addition, if the employer has an open enrollment period during which similarly situated active employees can switch plans or benefit packages or add or eliminate family members, the same enrollment period rights must be given to the COBRA beneficiary. [Reg. § 54.4980B-5, Q&A-4]

Example 9-41: Omega Corp. has several group health plans for its employees. Employees can pick and choose the plan they want, but all family members must be covered by the same plan. Joan Edmund, her spouse, and her two children are covered by Omega's Plan A. Edmund terminates her employment with Omega.

Result: Each member of Edmund's family must be offered COBRA coverage under Plan A. However, Omega does not have to allow any family member to switch to another plan.

Example 9-42: All members of the Edmunds family elect COBRA coverage under Omega's Plan A. Three months later, Omega has an open enrollment period during which similarly situated active employees are allowed to switch plans or add or eliminate coverage for family members.

Result: During the open enrollment period, each member of the Edmunds family must be offered the opportunity to switch to another plan. For this purpose, each family member is treated as an individual. Thus, each of the Edmunds could choose to be covered under a different plan, even though family members of active employees must all be covered under the same plan as the employee. Bear in mind, however, that Omega could charge each family member separately for his or her COBRA coverage based on the applicable premium for individual coverage.

COBRA beneficiaries may also have the right to add new family members to their coverage (Q 9:54). However, with the exception of a child born to or placed for adoption with a covered employee during the period of COBRA coverage, family members who were not covered at the time of a qualifying event are not themselves qualified beneficiaries. This fact is important if there is another qualifying event during a period of COBRA coverage. (Q 9:71)

Q 9:102 How long does COBRA coverage last?

As a general rule, COBRA coverage lasts for 18 months if the qualifying event was termination of employment or a reduction in hours or 36 months in the case of other qualifying events. [IRC § 4980B(f)(2)(B)]

Q 9:103 Can COBRA coverage be cut off earlier than the end of the maximum coverage period?

Yes. An employer can terminate a COBRA beneficiary's coverage on the *earliest* of the following dates:

- The last day of the maximum COBRA coverage period;
- The first day for which timely payment is not made for the coverage;
- The date the employer ceases to provide any group health plan to any employee;
- The date, after the date of the COBRA election, on which the beneficiary becomes covered by another group health plan;
- The date, after the date of the COBRA election, on which the beneficiary first becomes entitled to Medicare benefits.

[IRC § 4980B(f)(2)(B)]

An employer can terminate a beneficiary's COBRA coverage only if the beneficiary first becomes covered by another health plan *after* the date of the COBRA election. If a COBRA beneficiary first becomes covered under another plan on or before the date of the COBRA election, the other coverage cannot be the basis for terminating the beneficiary's COBRA coverage. [Reg. § 54.4980B-7, Q&A-2]

The regulations make it clear that COBRA coverage can be cut off only if a qualified beneficiary is actually covered by another plan, rather than merely eligible to be covered. In addition, the other plan must not contain any exclusion or limitation with respect to a preexisting condition of the qualified beneficiary (unless the exclusion or limitation is automatically satisfied because of the restrictions on pre-existing condition exclusions imposed by Health Insurance Portability and Accountability Act). (Q 9:94)

Example 9-43: Carol Barnett has coverage under Beta's health plan. She is also covered by a health plan maintained by her husband's employer. Barnett terminates her employment and elects COBRA coverage under Beta's plan.

Result: Beta cannot cut off Barnett's COBRA coverage because of her coverage under her husband's plan.

Example 9-44: Don Simpson works for Magna, Inc. and is covered by Magna's group health plan. Simpson terminates his employment with Magna and elects COBRA coverage. A few months later, Simpson is hired by Gamma Corp. and becomes covered under Gamma's plan. Gamma's plan has no preexisting condition limitations.

Result: Magna can terminate Simpson's COBRA coverage on the date he becomes covered by Gamma's plan.

Example 9-45: Same facts as above, except that Simpson is hired by Gamma and becomes covered by Gamma's plan *before* he elects COBRA coverage under Magna's plan.

Result: Since Simpson became covered by Gamma's plan before the date of his COBRA election, Magna cannot terminate Simpson's COBRA coverage because of his coverage under Gamma's plan.

Similarly, COBRA coverage can be cut-off only if a Medicare-eligible beneficiary is actually enrolled in Medicare. The regulations make it clear that enrollment in either Part A or Part B of Medicare is sufficient for the plan to discontinue COBRA coverage. But as with other employer coverage, the beneficiary must first become enrolled in Medicare *after* the COBRA election. [Reg. § 54.4980B-7, Q&A-3]

Q 9:104 Are there any other circumstances in which an employer can terminate a beneficiary's COBRA coverage?

An employer can terminate a beneficiary's coverage for cause on the same basis that it would terminate the coverage of a non-COBRA beneficiary. For example, if a plan terminates the coverage of active employees who submit fraudulent claims, a qualified beneficiary's coverage can also be terminated for submission of a fraudulent claim.

If an individual who is not a qualified beneficiary has coverage only because of his or her relationship to a qualified beneficiary, that individual's coverage can be terminated whenever the qualified beneficiary's coverage ceases. [Reg. § 54-4980B-7, Q&A-1(c)]

Q 9:105 Is the COBRA coverage period ever extended?

Yes. An initial 18-month COBRA coverage period is extended to 29 months if a qualified beneficiary is determined to be disabled at any time during the first 60 days of COBRA coverage. [IRC § 4980B(f)(2)(B)] An individual who was determined to be disabled before the COBRA coverage period began will qualify if he or she remains disabled on the date COBRA coverage begins. The 29-month coverage period is not limited to the disabled beneficiary. It applies to each qualified beneficiary who is entitled to COBRA coverage because of the same qualifying event.

The 60-day period is measured from the date of the qualifying event (or loss of coverage, if later), not the COBRA election. In the case of a child who is born to or placed for adoption with a covered employee during a period of COBRA coverage, the 60-day period is measured from the date of birth or placement for adoption.

To qualify for the extension, a qualified beneficiary who was affected by the qualifying event must give notice to the plan administrator of the disability determination within 60 days after the date of the determination and before the end of the 18-month COBRA period. [IRC § 4980B(f)(6)]

COBRA coverage under a disability extension can be terminated in the month that is more than 30 days after a final determination that the qualified beneficiary is no longer disabled. [IRC § 4980B(f)(2)(B)(v)] The termination applies to all qualified beneficiaries who received an extension because of the disability of the qualified beneficiary who is no longer disabled. However, COBRA coverage cannot be cut off before the end of the initial 18-month period.

An initial 18-month coverage period (or a 29-month disability coverage period) will be extended to 36 months if a second qualifying event occurs during the COBRA period. [IRC § 4980B(f)(2)(B)(i)(II)] The event must be one that would trigger 36 months of coverage. Thus, a termination of employment following a reduction in hours will not expand the coverage period. The extension applies only to individuals who were qualified beneficiaries at the time of the initial qualifying event and are still qualified beneficiaries at the time of the second event.

> **Example 9-46:** George Henley and his family are covered by Gamma Corp.'s health plan. Henley terminates employment on December 31, 2005. Henley and his family elect COBRA coverage, which will last for 18 months through June 30, 2007. However, Henley dies in January 2007.
>
> *Result:* Because Henley's death would have triggered 36 months of COBRA coverage, Henley's wife and his children are entitled to COBRA coverage for a total of 36 months from the initial qualifying event (i.e., Henley's termination of employment). Their COBRA coverage will last through December 31, 2008.

Q 9:106 If an employer provides non-COBRA coverage for a period of time after a qualifying event, does that extend the COBRA coverage period?

No. The end of the COBRA period is determined from the date of the qualifying event.

Q 9:107 Does a qualified beneficiary have to be offered the right to enroll in a conversion plan at the end of the COBRA period?

Yes. That option must be offered to a qualified beneficiary if it is generally available to similarly situated non-COBRA beneficiaries under the plan. [IRC § 4980B(f)(2)(E)]If a conversion option is not generally available, it need not be offered to a qualified beneficiary.

Q 9:108 How do beneficiaries elect COBRA coverage?

COBRA coverage is not automatic. A health plan can condition the availability of coverage on a timely election of coverage. [Reg. § 54.4980B-7]

The election period must begin no later than the date the beneficiary loses coverage on account of a qualifying event and must not end before the date that is 60 days after the later of: (1) the date the beneficiary loses coverage, or (2) the date notice is given to the beneficiary of the right to elect COBRA coverage. An election is deemed to be made on the date it is sent to the plan administrator. [IRC § 4980B(f)(5)]

> **Example 9-47:** Joe Smith quits his job with Mega Co. on June 1, 2005. Mega's plan provides that employer-provided coverage ends immediately upon termination of employment.
>
> *Result:* Smith's COBRA election period begins on June 1, 2007. Assuming Smith receives notice of his COBRA rights on that date, the election period ends 60 days later on July 31, 2007. However, if Smith does not receive notice until June 15, 2007, the election period will not end until 60 days after the notice date—on August 14, 2007.

Q 9:106

Example 9-48: Same facts as above, except that Mega's plan does not terminate employer-provided health coverage until six months after termination of employment. Thus, Smith does not lose coverage until December 1, 2007.

Result: Smith's election period can begin as late as December 1, 2007, and cannot end until 60 days later on January 30, 2008. Note, however, that Mega can count the six months of employer-provided coverage against Smith's 18 months of COBRA coverage. So Smith can elect an additional 12 months of coverage.

Q 9:109 Does the covered employee or qualified beneficiary have to inform the plan of a qualifying event?

Generally no. The employer or plan administrator is usually responsible for determining if a qualifying event has occurred. However, there are two exceptions: The plan must be informed when a child ceases to be eligible for coverage or when a covered employee divorces or separates. The plan is not required to offer COBRA coverage if the notice is not provided within 60 days after the later of the qualifying event or the date the qualified beneficiary loses coverage on account of the event. [IRC § 4980B(f)(6)]

In the case of a divorce or separation, a single notice given by the covered employee or a qualified beneficiary will preserve the COBRA rights of all qualified beneficiaries who stand to lose coverage.

Q 9:110 Must the plan provide coverage before the COBRA election is made?

If a COBRA election is made at any time during the election period, coverage must generally be provided from the date health plan coverage would otherwise have been lost.

In the case of an insured plan or reimbursement arrangement, the employer can continue the coverage during the election period and cancel it retroactively if the election is not made. Alternatively, if the plan allows for retroactive reinstatement of coverage, the plan can terminate the coverage of a qualified beneficiary and reinstate it when the election is made. [Reg. § 54.4980B-6, Q&A-3]Claims incurred during the election period do not have to be paid before the election is made and any required payment is received by the plan.

If a health care provider (such as a doctor, hospital, or pharmacy) inquires about the beneficiary's coverage during the election period, the plan must give the provider a complete answer regarding the beneficiary's COBRA rights. For example, if the plan provides coverage during the election period subject to retroactive cancellation if no election is made, the plan must inform the provider that the beneficiary is currently covered, but the coverage may be terminated retroactively.

Some plans, such as health maintenance organizations or walk-in clinics, provide health services directly. A beneficiary who seeks services before a COBRA election has been made can be given a choice of electing and paying for COBRA coverage or paying the reasonable and customary charge for the services. If the beneficiary pays for the services, he or she must be reimbursed for the payment within 30 days after the COBRA election is made. Alternatively, the plan can inform the beneficiary that use of the facility will be treated as a constructive COBRA election. In that case, the beneficiary will be required to pay the COBRA premium in order to obtain health services. [Reg. § 54.4980B-6]

Q 9:111 What if a beneficiary waives COBRA coverage before the end of the election period?

A waiver may be revoked at any time before the end of the election period. However, coverage does not have to be provided retroactively. In other words, the beneficiary does not have to be given coverage from the date employer-provided coverage was lost until the date of the revocation of the waiver. [Reg. § 54.4980B-6, Q&A-4]

Q 9:112 Can the employer withhold money or other benefits until a beneficiary makes up his or her mind about COBRA coverage?

No. An employer cannot withhold anything a beneficiary is entitled to in order to compel payment for COBRA coverage or to induce the beneficiary to give up his or her COBRA rights (including the right to make full use of the election period). Moreover, a waiver obtained by means of withholding other benefits or money is invalid. [Reg. § 54.4980B-6, Q&A-5]

Q 9:113 If multiple beneficiaries lose coverage because of a qualifying event, can each one make a separate COBRA election?

Yes. Each beneficiary (including a child who is born to or placed for adoption with a covered employee after the event) must be offered the opportunity to make an independent election to receive COBRA coverage. However, if a covered employee or spouse of a covered employee makes a COBRA election that does not specify whether the election is for self-only coverage, the election is deemed to be for all beneficiaries who lost coverage on account of the same event. [IRC § 4980B(f)(5)]

> **Example 9-49:** Henry Hicks and his wife are covered by Beta's group health plan. Hicks terminates his employment with Beta.
>
> *Result:* Both Hicks and his wife are qualified beneficiaries, and each must be allowed to elect COBRA coverage. Thus, Hicks may elect coverage while his wife declines coverage, or Hicks may elect COBRA coverage for both of them. However, Hicks cannot decline coverage on behalf of his wife. If Hicks does not make an election for his wife, she still has the right to make her own election.

Q 9:111

Q 9:114 How much do beneficiaries pay for COBRA coverage?

An employer can require a qualified beneficiary to pay up to 102 percent of the applicable premium for the COBRA coverage period. The payment may be raised to 150 percent of the applicable premium for any disability extension period. [IRC § 4980B(f)(2)(C); Reg. § 54.4980B-8]

Q 9:115 How does the plan figure the premium?

The applicable premium is what it costs the plan for coverage for similarly situated non-COBRA beneficiaries. [IRC § 4980B(f)(4)]The COBRA premium must be determined in advance of each "determination period." The determination period can be any 12-month period selected by the plan, but the same period must be used from year to year.

Q 9:116 Can the plan charge for the period of coverage before the COBRA election is made?

Yes, the beneficiary may be charged retroactively for the entire period from the date of the loss of coverage. However, the regulations make it clear that a plan can allow a beneficiary to apply the first payment prospectively only. [Reg. § 54.4980B-8, Q&A-4]

Q 9:117 Can the plan increase a beneficiary's premium during the COBRA coverage period?

An increase is permitted only in three situations:

1. If the plan initially charged less than the maximum amount permitted by the COBRA rules, it can raise the premium up to the maximum amount;

2. The increase is made during the disability extension, and the increased premium does not exceed 150 percent of the applicable premium; or

3. The qualified beneficiary makes permitted changes in the coverage being received.

Q 9:118 At what intervals can the plan require premiums to be paid?

The plan must allow payment for COBRA coverage to be made in monthly installments. However, a plan can also allow payments at other intervals (for example, weekly, quarterly, or semiannually). [Reg. § 54.4980B-8, Q&A-3]

Q 9:119 What if the beneficiary does not make a payment or does not make a timely payment?

As noted above, a plan can cancel the coverage for failure to pay on time. However, the regulations make it clear that a payment is timely if it is made within 30 days of the beginning of the coverage period. [Reg. § 54.4980B-8, Q&A-5] A plan can, however, allow a longer grace period.

A beneficiary's initial payment for COBRA coverage cannot be required earlier than 45 days after the COBRA election is made.

If a plan is contacted by a health care provider about a beneficiary's coverage for a period for which the plan has not received payment, the plan must give a complete explanation of the beneficiary's COBRA rights. For example, if the plan cuts off coverage immediately for nonpayment but reinstates it if payment is made by the end of the grace period, the plan must inform the provider that the beneficiary does not currently have coverage but will have retroactive coverage if payment is made.

Q 9:120 What if the beneficiary does not pay in full?

If a payment is not significantly less than the required amount, the payment will be deemed made in full unless the plan notifies the beneficiary of the shortfall and grants a reasonable time for payment of the deficiency. For this purpose, the regulations say 30 days is a reasonable time. [Reg. § 54.4980B-8, Q&A-5(d)]

Q 9:121 How are an employee's COBRA premiums treated for tax purposes?

An individual taxpayer may claim an itemized deduction for health insurance premiums, including COBRA premiums, and other out-of-pocket medical expenses. However, medical expenses are deductible only to the extent they exceed 7.5 percent of the taxpayer's adjusted gross income. [IRC § 213] Therefore, many taxpayers do not actually get a deduction. In addition, a taxpayer who claims the standard deduction and does not itemize deductions cannot claim a medical expense deduction.

Under new rules included in the Trade Act of 2002 (P.L. 107-210), a limited group of COBRA beneficiaries may claim a tax credit for 65 percent of their COBRA premiums. The credit may be claimed by an individual who is certified as eligible for trade adjustment assistance under the Trade Act of 1974 as a result of losing his or her job because of import competition or shifts of production to other countries. The credit may also be claimed by an individual who is at least age 55 and is receiving pension benefits paid by the Pension Benefit Guaranty Corporation (PBGC).

The credit may be claimed for premiums paid for COBRA coverage for the eligible individual and his or her spouse and dependents. The credit may also be claimed for premiums paid for other "qualified health insurance," including coverage provided by any employer or former employer of the individual or the individual's spouse. However, the credit may not be claimed if the employer pays at least 50 percent of the cost of coverage. Therefore, if an employer picks up the tab for a former employee's COBRA coverage, the credit may not be claimed by the employee. As required by the law, the IRS has implemented procedures for advance payment under which eligible individuals can receive

Q 9:120

advance payment of the credit to help pay health care premiums as they come due.

Q 9:122 What notices are required under the COBRA rules?

The COBRA rules impose notice requirements on both employers and employees. These notices include:

- *Initial notice of COBRA rights.* An employer's group health plan must notify employees and their spouses of their COBRA rights when the plan first becomes subject to COBRA or when the employees and spouses first become eligible to participate in the plan. [IRC § 4980B(f)(6)]Final COBRA regulations, issued by the Department of Labor (DOL), generally provide a 90-day window for delivery of the initial COBRA notice beginning with the date on which a covered employee or spouse first becomes covered under the plan (or, if later, the date on which the plan first becomes subject to the COBRA requirements). [DOL Reg. § 2590.606-1; 69 Fed. Reg. 30,083 (May 26, 2004)]

The regulations include a model general notice. An appropriately completed model notice will comply with the COBRA requirements, although use of the model notice is not required.

- *Notice of qualifying events.* The administrator of an employer's group health plan must be notified when an employee or a family member experiences a qualifying event. The obligation to provide this notice may fall on either the employer or the employee, depending on the nature of the qualifying event.

The employer must give notice to the plan administrator within 30 days of the occurrence of a qualifying event concerning (1) the employee's or ex-employee's death, (2) the employee's termination of employment or reduction in hours, (3) the employee's becoming eligible for Medicare, or (4) the commencement of a bankruptcy proceeding by the employer. The 30-day notice period is counted from the date of loss of coverage if the plan provides that the COBRA continuation period will start on the date coverage is lost rather than on the date of the qualifying event. [DOL Reg. § 2590.606-2]

The covered employee or family member must provide to the plan administrator notice of divorce, legal separation, or a dependent child's loss of dependent status under the plan's definition of dependency. The notice must be given within 60 days of the later of (1) the date of the qualifying event, (2) the date that coverage would be lost because of the qualifying event, or (3) the date on which the employee or qualified beneficiary is informed of the notice requirement through the plan's SPD or the initial COBRA notice. [DOL Reg. § 2590.606-3]

- *Notice of COBRA election rights.* Following the occurrence of a qualifying event, the administrator of the employer's group health plan must notify the employee and affected family member of their right to elect COBRA continuation coverage. This notice must be provided within 14 days after the plan administrator receives notice of the qualifying event.

The COBRA notice regulations include a model notice that can be tailored to include plan-specific information. Although the model notice is not mandatory, the DOL says that use of an appropriately completed model notice will be considered good-faith compliance with the contents requirements of the regulations.

- *Notice of disability.* A qualified beneficiary who has been determined to be disabled for Social Security purposes at any time during the first 60 days of continuation coverage because of a qualifying event that was either a termination of employment or a reduction in hours (or who was previously determined to be disabled and remains disabled when COBRA coverage begins) is entitled to a disability extension (see Q 9:104). To qualify for the extension, an individual must notify the plan administrator of the disability determination after the determination is made and before the end of the first 18 months of COBRA continuation coverage. The COBRA notice regulations provide that a plan may require a beneficiary to provide disability notice within 60 days after the latest of (1) the date of the disability determination, (2) the date of the qualifying event, (3) the date on which the qualified beneficiary loses coverage under the plan, or (4) the date on which the qualified beneficiary is informed of the obligation to provide notice. [DOL Reg. § 2590.606-3]Thus, under the regulations, a beneficiary who previously received a disability determination and has not received a subsequent determination that he or she is no longer disabled will have at least 60 days after a qualifying event to provide a disability notice.

- *Notice of unavailability.* If a requirement on plan administrator receives notice of a qualifying event from a plan participant or beneficiary who is not eligible for COBRA coverage under the plan the regulations require the administrator to provide a notice to the individual explaining why he or she is not entitled to coverage. This notice is subject to the same timing requirement as the COBRA election notice—that is, it must be provided within 14 days following the plan administrator's receipt of notice of a qualifying event. [DOL Reg. § 2590.606-4]

The regulations make it clear that a notice of unavailability must be furnished whenever the plan administrator denies coverage after receiving notice from a qualified beneficiary regardless of the reason for the denial and regardless of whether the notice involves a first qualifying event, a second qualifying event, or a request for a disability extension. For example, an unavailability notice would be required if the plan administrator denies coverage because of a determination that no qualifying event has occurred or because the qualified beneficiary did not provide notice in a timely manner or did not provide complete information.

- *Notice of termination.* A plan administrator must provide specific notice in the event COBRA coverage is terminated before the end of the maximum coverage period (e.g., if the employer ceases to offer group health coverage to its employees or the COBRA premium is not timely paid). The notice must be provided as soon as administratively practicable after the termination decision is made, must explain why and when COBRA coverage is being terminated, and

Q 9:122

must describe any rights to other coverage the qualified beneficiaries will have upon termination. [DOL Reg. § 2590.606-4]

The early termination notice is not required to be furnished *before* COBRA coverage can be terminated. However, the DOL says that there may be instances when a plan administrator is able to furnish the notice in advance and would be required to do so under the "as soon as reasonably practicable" standard.

On the other hand, the DOL says that plans can combine furnishing of the early termination notice with the certificate of creditable coverage required under HIPAA (see Q 9:130). That certificate is generally required to be provided within a reasonable time following the cessastion of COBRA coverage.

Q 9:123 What are the penalties for violating the COBRA requirements?

The tax law imposes an excise tax on employers that fail to properly offer COBRA continuation coverage to eligible employees. The tax may also be assessed against other persons, such as an insurer or third-party administrator, who is responsible for providing benefits under the employer's plan. [Reg. § 54.4980B-2, Q&A-10]

The excise tax is $100 per qualified beneficiary for each day of the noncompliance period. However, the penalty tax is capped at $200 per day per family, regardless of the number of qualified beneficiaries affected by the violation. [IRC § 4980B(b)(1), (c)(3)]

The penalty period begins on the date the first COBRA violation occurs. In the case of failure to provide COBRA coverage, the penalty period does not begin until 45 days after the employee or qualified beneficiary makes a written request for COBRA coverage. The penalty period ends on the earlier of: (1) the date the violation is corrected, or (2) six months after the last day of the maximum COBRA continuation period for the employee or qualified beneficiary. A COBRA violation is considered corrected if COBRA coverage is provided retroactively and the employee or beneficiary is placed in as favorable a financial position as he or she would have been if the violation had not occurred. For this purpose, the employer must assume that the employee or beneficiary would have elected the most favorable coverage available.

An employer, however, is not subject to the penalty tax for "inadvertent failures." A failure is considered inadvertent if neither the employer or any other responsible person exercising reasonable diligence knew or should have known of the violation.

Health Care Nondiscrimination and Other Legal Requirements

Q 9:124 What special rules apply to employer-provided group health coverage?

In addition to the tax law rules and COBRA coverage requirements, group health plans are also subject to special requirements that:

- Bar group health plans from using an individual's health status to exclude him or her from coverage;

- Limit the circumstances under which plans can deny coverage for preexisting conditions;

- Grant special enrollment rights when an employee acquires a new dependent or the employee or a dependent loses coverage under another plan;

- Obligate plans to pay for a minimum hospital stay following birth for mothers and newborns if the plan otherwise provides maternity benefits; and

- Require parity of coverage for mental health benefits.

As with failure to meet the COBRA coverage requirements, an employer that violates these rules can be subject to excise tax of $100 per day during the noncompliance period for each beneficiary. [IRC § 4980D] This period begins on the first day a plan does not meet the requirements and ends on the first day the plan meets the requirements and past failures have been corrected.

The excise tax does not apply to any plan maintained by a small employer that provides employee health coverage through a contract with an insurance company. A business is considered a small employer if it employed an average of at least two but not more than 50 employees on business days during the preceding calendar year. If a business was not in operation throughout the preceding calendar year, it will qualify as a small employer if is reasonable to assume that the business will employ an average of at least two but not more than 50 employees on all business days in the current year.

Q 9:125 Can an employer's group health plan impose any requirements for eligibility to participate in the plan?

Yes, a plan can impose eligibility requirements. For example, a plan may require all employees to have worked for the employer for a minimum period of time before becoming eligible to participate in the plan. However, under the Heath Insurance Portability and Accountability Act of 1996 (HIPAA), a group health plan must not base eligibility rules for employees or their dependents on any of the following health factors:

- Health status;

- Medical condition (physical or mental);

Q 9:124

- Claims experience;
- Receipt of health care services;
- Medical history;
- Genetic information;
- Evidence of insurability; or
- Disability.

Evidence of insurability includes conditions arising out of acts of domestic violence as well as participation in such activities as motorcycling, snowmobile riding, all-terrain vehicle riding, horseback riding, or skiing. [IRC § 9802; Reg. § 54.9802-1]

Q 9:126 Can an employer require some employees to pay higher premiums for health coverage?

Employees can be charged higher premiums in some circumstances. For example, an employer can charge employees higher premiums for a higher level of coverage. However, the HIPAA nondiscrimination rules prohibit an employer from charging an employee a higher premium because of a health factor of the employee or a dependent. [IRC § 9802; Reg. § 54.9802-1] See Q 9:89 for a list of health factors that cannot be used in setting premium charges.

Q 9:127 Can a group health plan require an individual to pass a physical examination before enrolling in the plan?

No. A group health plan may not require a physical exam for enrollment. This prohibition applies to late enrollees as well as to those who enroll when they first become eligible.

Example 9-50: An employer sponsors a group health plan that is automatically available to all employees who enroll within the first 30 days of employment. However, employees who do not enroll within 30 days cannot enroll later unless they pass a physical exam.

Result: The rule requiring late enrollees to pass a physical exam impermissibly discriminates based on one or more health factors.

Q 9:128 Can a health plan require individuals to complete a health questionnaire before enrollment?

The HIPAA nondiscrimination rules do not automatically prohibit health questionnaires. Whether a health questionnaire violates the rules depends on how the information is used. For example, scoring a questionnaire for "health points" related to medical conditions or prior medical conditions in order to enroll would constitute impermissible discrimination based on health factors.

Q 9:129 Can a plan exclude an employee from enrolling in a plan because he or she engages in a high-risk activity?

No. An individual cannot be denied enrollment based on evidence of insurability, which includes participation in high-risk activities.

Example 9-51: Under an employer's group health plan, all employees may enroll within the first 30 days of employment. However, employees who participate in certain recreational activities, such as motorcycling or bungee jumping, are excluded from coverage.

Result: By excluding individuals who participate in certain activities, the plan improperly discriminates based on evidence of insurability.

Planning Point: Although a group health plan cannot discriminate among similarly situated individuals when it comes to eligibility, a plan may impose restrictions on benefits as long as they apply uniformly to similarly situated individuals and are not directed at any individual or participant based on a health factor.

Example 9-52: A group health plan provides benefits for head injuries, but has a general exclusion for injuries sustained in specified recreational activities, including bungee jumping. John Egan sustains a head injury while bungee jumping. The plan denies coverage for Egan's injury.

Result: The exclusion does not violate the nondiscrimination rules.

Q 9:130 Can a plan exclude coverage for health conditions that existed prior to enrolling in the plan?

HIPAA imposes limits on exclusions for preexisting conditions and requires plans to give credit for certain periods of previous coverage. [IRC § 9801]

A plan can exclude coverage for a preexisting condition only if the exclusion relates to a condition for which medical advice, diagnosis, care, or treatment was recommended or received within the six-month period ending on the enrollment date. A preexisting condition exclusion may last for no more than 12 months (18 months for a late enrollee) after an employee or dependent enrolls in the employer's plan. In calculating the length of the exclusion, employers must subtract certain periods of "creditable coverage" under another plan.

A plan cannot impose preexisting condition exclusions on newborn and adopted children. Also, pregnancy cannot be treated as a preexisting condition.

Q 9:131 What is creditable coverage?

Creditable coverage is health coverage that an employee or dependent had before he or she enrolled in the employer's plan. Creditable coverage includes coverage under another employer's health plan, other health insurance, public health plans, Social Security, and certain other sources. Creditable coverage does not include coverage that is not general health insurance, such as accident or disability income, liability, workers' compensation, or automobile medical insurance. Also, creditable coverage does not include health coverage for limited benefits, such as limited-scope dental or vision benefits or long-term care plans, and plans under which health benefits are secondary or incidental.

A new employee will generally have a certificate from his or her prior plan showing the extent of his or her prior coverage. Group health plans are required to issue a certificate of creditable coverage when an employee or dependent ceases to be covered under the plan. A certificate must be issued even if an employee or dependent is eligible for COBRA continuation coverage. In addition, a second certificate must be issued when the COBRA coverage is exhausted. A group health plan must issue an additional certificate on request, provided the request is made within 24 months after coverage under the plan or COBRA continuation coverage ceases.

Example 9-53: When John Smithers joins Acme Corporation, he presents a certificate showing that he had four months of creditable coverage under his former employer's group health plan. Acme's group health plan provides that preexisting conditions are excluded from coverage for 12 months following an employee's enrollment in the plan.

Result: When applying the preexisting condition exclusion, Acme must give Smithers credit for four months of prior coverage. Therefore, Smithers will be subject to an eight-month preexisting condition exclusion.

Q 9:132 Suppose a health plan imposes a 12-month pre-existing condition exclusion period, but waives the exclusion after six months for individuals who have not had any claims since enrollment. Is that permissible?

No. A preexisting condition exclusion must be applied uniformly to all similarly situated individuals. In this situation, individuals who experience medical claims in the first six months following enrollment are not treated the same as similarly situated individuals who have no claims during that period.

Q 9:133 When are individuals similarly situated?

Distinctions among groups of individuals may not be based on a health factor. Instead, plans must base any such distinctions on bona fide employment-based classifications that are consistent with the employer's usual business practice.

For example, part-time and full-time employees, employees working in different geographic locations, and employees with different dates of hire or lengths of service could be treated as distinct groups of similarly situated individuals, provided the distinction is consistent with the employer's usual business practice. In addition, a plan may usually treat plan participants and beneficiaries as two separate groups of similarly situated individuals. The plan may also distinguish among beneficiaries based on their relationship to the plan participant (such as spouse or dependent child) or based on the age or student status of dependent children.

Bear in mind, however, that the creation or modification of a classification cannot be directed at individual participants or beneficiaries based on health factors.

Q 9:134 Can a group health plan exclude coverage for a particular medical condition without regard to whether it is preexisting?

Group health plans may exclude coverage for a specific disease, limit or exclude benefits for certain types of treatments or drugs, or limit or exclude benefits for treatments that are determined to be experimental or not medically necessary. However, any benefit restrictions must be applied uniformly to all similar situated individuals and not directed at any participants or beneficiaries based on a health factor.

In addition, some types of exclusions may violate federal nondiscrimination laws. For example, in an administrative decision, the Equal Employment Opportunity Commission (EEOC) held that an employer's failure to provide health insurance coverage for prescription contraceptives while covering a number of other preventive drugs, devices, and services violated Title VII of the Civil Rights Act of 1964, as amended by the Pregnancy Discrimination Act (PDA). [EEOC Decision, Dec. 14, 2000]

Since the EEOC ruling, least two court cases have held that an employer's selective exclusion of contraceptives, while covering other preventive medications, potentially violated the PDA [*Erickson v. Bartell Drug Co.*, 141 F. Supp. 2d 1266 (D. Wash. 2001); In re: Union Pacific Railroad Employment Practices Litigation, (D Neb.2005)] However, one of these cases has been overturned on appeal. The Eighth Circuit, which is the only appellate court to rule on this issue, held that a group health plan that excludes coverage for both male and female contraceptives (other than for medically necessary noncontraceptive purposes) does not violate the PDA. [In re: Union Pacitic Railroad Employment Practices Litigation, (8 Cir. 2007)]

> **Planning Point:** While the Eighth Circuit's decision protects employers within its jurisdiction (North Dakota, South Dakota, Minnesota, Nebraska, Iowa, Missouri, and Arkansas), employers in other state that do not cover prescription contraception still face potential lawsuits. Therefore, they may want to gauge the cost of adding such coverage against the costs of litigation. In addition, employers should check state law. At least 23 states have passed legislation mandating some level of coverage for contraceptives. Most of these states require health insurance policies that cover prescription drugs to also cover prescription contraceptives. A number of states include exemptions for employers who object to contraceptive coverage for religious reasons. Other states exempt "religious employers." However, religious employers do not necessarily include every organization with a religious connection.

Q 9:135 Do any special rules apply when an employee acquires a new spouse or dependent?

Group health plans typically provide that an employee can add coverage for a spouse or dependent only during an open enrollment period. However, HIPAA provides that an employee's new spouse or dependent must be given special enrollment rights.

Special enrollment must be allowed if: (1) the employer's plan offers dependent coverage, (2) the employee is a plan participant or has satisfied all the requirements for participation, and (3) an individual becomes a dependent of the employee because of marriage, birth, adoption, or placement for adoption. The special enrollment period must last for at least 30 days beginning on the date of the marriage, birth, or adoption (including placement for adoption).

During the special enrollment period, the new spouse or dependent may be enrolled in the plan. In addition, in the case of a birth or adoption, the employee may enroll his or her spouse if the spouse was not previously covered by the plan. Moreover, an employee who previously declined coverage may enroll during a special enrollment period if the plan requires the employee to have coverage in order to elect coverage for dependents.

In the case of a new dependent, coverage elected during a special enrollment period must be retroactive to the date of birth, adoption, or placement for adoption. In the case of a new spouse, coverage must become effective no later than the first day of the month following the date the enrollment request is received.

Q 9:136 What special enrollment rules apply if an employee or dependent loses other health coverage?

Under HIPAA, employees and their dependents that declined coverage because they were covered under another plan may be entitled to special enrollment if they lose the other coverage. Special enrollment must be provided only if:

1. The employee or dependent was covered under another plan at the time coverage was initially offered.

2. The employee stated in writing that the other coverage was the reason for declining enrollment—but only if the plan required such a statement and notified the employee of the requirement.

3. The other coverage was either: (a) COBRA continuation coverage that was exhausted, or (b) other health plan coverage that was terminated because of loss of eligibility or termination of employer contributions.

4. The employee requests enrollment within 30 days of exhaustion or termination of the other coverage.

Final HIPAA regulations, which apply for plan years beginning on or after July 1, 2005, make it clear that when an employee's spouse or dependent has special enrollment rights due to a loss of other health coverage, both the spouse or dependent and the employee may enroll in the plan. Moreover, if the employee is already enrolled he or she may change benefit options when a spouse or dependent becomes eligible for special enrollment. [DOL Final Rule 2590.701-6; Reg. § 54.9801-6]

Q 9:137 What special rules apply to newborns and their mothers?

The Newborns' and Mothers' Health Protection Act (NMHPA) requires group health plans that offer maternity benefits to cover a minimum hospital stay for a mother and her newborn following childbirth. A group health plan that provides benefits for a hospital stay in connection with childbirth for a mother and her newborn may not restrict benefits for the stay to less than 48 hours following a vaginal delivery or 96 hours following a delivery by cesarean section.

Planning Point: The NMHPA does not require group health plans to provide maternity benefits. However, if an employer's plan does provide maternity benefits, it must provide benefits for the minimum required time.

If delivery occurs in the hospital, the minimum length of stay for both the mother and newborn begins at the time of delivery. In the case of multiple births, the minimum length of stay begins at the time of the last delivery. If the delivery occurs outside the hospital, the hospital stay begins at the time the mother or newborn is admitted to the hospital as an inpatient in connection with childbirth. The determination of whether the admission is connected to childbirth is a medical decision to be made by the attending health care provider.

Mothers and their newborns don't have to stay for the entire 48-hour or 96-hour period, however. If a decision to discharge a mother or newborn earlier is made by an attending provider, in consultation with the mother (or the newborn's authorized representative), the rules don't apply for the period after the discharge.

A plan may not require a physician or health care provider to obtain authorization from the plan or a health insurance issuer for prescribing the minimum required hospital stay.

Furthermore, a group health plan cannot:

- Deny a mother or newborn eligibility to enroll or renew coverage under the plan to avoid the maternity stay rules;
- Provide payments (including payments in kind) or rebates to a mother to encourage her to accept less than the minimum required benefits;
- Restrict or reduce benefits for any portion of a minimum required hospital stay;
- Penalize an attending health care provider because the provider prescribes the minimum required hospital stay; or
- Provide monetary or other incentives to induce a provider to discharge a mother or newborn early.

However, a group health plan is not prohibited from requiring deductibles, coinsurance, or other cost sharing for maternity benefits—as long as the same benefits are provided throughout the minimum required period.

Q 9:138 What special rules apply to mental health benefits?

Under the Mental Health Parity Act of 1996 (MHPA), if a plan provides both medical and surgical benefits and mental health benefits:

- It cannot impose an annual or aggregate lifetime limit on mental health benefits if it does not impose a limit on substantially all medical and surgical benefits.

- If the plan does provide an annual or aggregate lifetime limit on medical and surgical benefits, the plan must either (1) include mental health benefits under the same limit or (2) use a separate limit for mental health benefits that is at least as much as this limit.

The MHPA is not a permanent provision of the law. It was originally scheduled to expire for benefits related to services furnished on or after September 30, 2001, but has been repeatedly extended by Congress. It is currently scheduled to sunset for benefits related to services furnished on or after December 31, 2007.

Health Benefit Plan Procedures

Q 9:139 Are employers required to provide employees with any special information about their health benefits?

Employees must be provided with a summary plan description (SPD) explaining the benefits provided by the plan and its rules and regulations. An SPD must be furnished to an individual no later than 90 days after he or she becomes a plan participant or begins receiving benefits under the plan. As a general rule, a plan must distribute a new SPD every 10 years. However, a new SPD may be required after five years if there have been material changes in the plan. [ERISA 104(b)(1)]In the interval between SPDs, a plan is required to provide participants with a summary description of any material reduction in covered services or benefits provided by the plan. [ERISA 102(b)]

Q 9:140 Are employers or their health plan administrators required to follow any special rules in processing health benefit claims?

Regulations issued by the Department of Labor (DOL) impose strict time limits for processing medical claims, require plans to establish and maintain claims procedures that meet specified requirements, and impose new requirements and time limits for the review of adverse decisions. [29 CFR 2560.503-1]

Q 9:141 Do employers have to take special steps to protect the privacy of employee's health information?

When it enacted the Health Insurance Portability and Accountability Act in 1996, Congress was concerned that, in an age of electronic health care transactions, additional safeguards were needed to protect individuals' medical privacy. As a result, HIPAA included "administrative simplification" provisions requiring the Secretary of Health and Human Services (HHS) to publish standards for the electronic exchange, privacy, and security of health information. The privacy rules are not limited to electronic transactions, however. The regulations protect medical records or other individually identifiable health information, whether on paper, in computerized form, or communicated orally.

While many of the privacy rules are aimed at doctors and other health care providers, a number of rules affect group health plans and their sponsoring employers. For example, the privacy rules generally require group health plans to establish policies and procedures to protect the confidentiality of protected health information (PHI) about plan participants and beneficiaries, to train employees in their privacy practices, and to provide notice of those practices to plan participants. Moreover, the rules limit the circumstances in which a group health plan may disclose PHI to the employer sponsoring the plan.

The privacy rules apply to "covered entities," which include health plans, health care clearing houses, and any health care provider who transmits health care information in electronic form. [45 C.F.R. 160.102, 160.103] Most employer-sponsored group health plans are covered entities. However, there is one key exception: A group health plan with less than 50 participants that is administered solely by the employer that established and maintains the plan is not a covered entity.

On the other hand, even though an employer that sponsors a group health plan is not technically a covered entity, many of the privacy rule requirements will apply to the sponsoring employer if its employees have access to any PHI. For example, health plan enrollment information is considered PHI. Therefore, if the company employees handle health plan enrollment, the privacy rules must be followed to protect that information.

All covered entities, except *small health plans*, were required to comply with the privacy rules by April 14, 2003. Small health plans had until April 14, 2004, to comply. [45 C.F.R. 164.534] A small health plan is one with annual receipts of not more than $5 million.

Chapter 10

Employee Fringe Benefits

Benefits are a major component of an employee's total compensation package—and a major component of an employer's payroll costs. According to the latest data from the Department of Labor's Bureau of Labor Statistics, benefits account for approximately 30 percent of an employer's total compensation costs.

In many cases, fringe benefits are eligible for favorable tax treatment. For example, some benefits are tax-free to employees and exempt from payroll taxes. However, an employer's benefit plan must generally comply with special tax law rules to qualify for tax-favored treatment. In other cases, taxable fringe benefits are subject to special valuation rules.

This chapter will look at the tax rules governing common fringe benefits.

Basic Rules

Q 10:1 What is a fringe benefit?

A fringe benefit is pay for the performance of services that is provided in a form other than a traditional paycheck. For example, an employer provides a fringe benefit when it gives an employee the use of a company car for personal travel or picks up the tab for an employee's parking at work. Other common fringe benefits include health benefits, dependent care assistance, educational assistance, group term life insurance coverage, and subsidized meals in the company cafeteria.

Q 10:2 Are fringe benefits taxable?

Any fringe benefit provided by an employer is taxable income to an employee and subject to payroll taxes unless the tax law provides a specific exclusion. As a general rule, an employee's taxable compensation includes the fair market value of the fringe benefit less (1) any amount that is excluded from income under the tax law rules and (2) any amount the employee paid for the benefit. [Temp. Reg. §1.61-2T(b)]However, special rules may apply in determining the value of the benefit.

The value of a taxable fringe benefit is also subject to payroll taxes. However, special rules may apply for purposes of withholding, depositing, and reporting payroll taxes on a taxable fringe benefit (see Chapter 14).

Q 10:3 How is the fair market value of a fringe benefit determined?

Generally, the fair market value of a fringe benefit is the amount an employee would have to pay a third party in an arm's-length transaction to buy or lease the benefit. [Temp. Reg. §1.61-2T(b)(2)] This amount is determined based on all the facts and circumstances. The employer's cost to provide the benefit does not determine its fair market value.

Special rules may apply in determining the value of certain fringe benefits.

Q 10:4 Which fringe benefits are eligible for special tax treatment?

The tax law provides special tax treatment for the following fringe benefits:

- Accident and health plans;
- Achievement awards;
- Adoption assistance;
- Athletic facilities;
- Club dues;
- Company cars;
- *De minimis* fringe benefits;
- Dependent care assistance;
- Disability benefits;
- Disaster relief assistance;
- Educational assistance;
- Employee discounts;
- Flights on company aircraft;
- Group long-term care insurance;
- Group term life insurance;
- Lodging on an employer's business premises;
- Meals;
- Moving expense reimbursements;
- No-additional-cost services;
- Split-dollar life insurance;
- Transportation benefits; and
- Working condition fringe benefits.

In many cases, all or a portion of the value of these benefits is excluded from an employee's income and is exempt from income tax withholding. Moreover, in most—but not all—cases, the excluded benefits are exempt from Social Security and Medicare (FICA) or federal unemployment (FUTA) taxes. In other cases, the tax law provides special rules for including the value of a benefit in an employee's income.

Accident and Health Benefits

Q 10:5 What is an accident or health plan?

An accident or health plan is an arrangement that provides benefits for employees, their spouses, and their dependents in the event of personal injury or sickness. [Reg. § 1.105-5(a)]

An accident or health plan may take the form of employer-provided health insurance. In addition, an arrangement to provide direct reimbursements by an employer (a so-called "self-insured" plan) also qualifies an accident or health plan. However, self-insured plans are subject to some special tax rules.

Accident and health plans also include health flexible spending accounts (FSAs), which permit employees to set aside funds on a pre-tax basis to pay for out-of-pocket medical expenses; employer contributions to a health savings account (HSA) or Archer medical savings account (MSA), which can be used to pay for out-of pocket medical expenses in conjunction with high-deductible health insurance coverage; and health reimbursement arrangements (HRAs) that provide funds to employees to be used for health care costs.

The tax treatment of accident and health plans is discussed in detail in Chapter 9.

Q 10:6 How are employee health benefits treated for tax purposes?

As a general rule, an employer's payment for and employee's coverage under an accident or health plan are deductible by the employer and tax-free to the employee. [IRC §§ 162; 106]In addition, amounts received by the employee under the plan as reimbursements for medical care are not included in the employee's income. [IRC § 105]This tax-favored treatment also applies to employer-provided health benefits for an employee's spouse and dependents. Employer-provided health benefits are also exempt from FICA and FUTA taxes.

The tax treatment of accident and health plans is discussed in detail in Chapter 9.

Achievement Awards

Q 10:7 What is an employee achievement award?

An achievement award is an item of tangible personal property that meets all of the following requirements:

- It is given to an employee for length-of-service or safety achievement;
- It is awarded as part of a meaningful presentation; and
- It is awarded under conditions and circumstances that to do not create a significant likelihood that the award represents disguised pay.

[IRC § 274(j)(3)(A)]

Length-of-service award. An employee may not be awarded for length of service until he or she has been employed for at least five years. Moreover, length-of-service awards cannot be provided more frequently than every five years.

An award will not qualify as a length-of-service award if either:

- The employee receives the award during his or her first five years of employment, or
- The employee received another award (other than an award of *de minimis* value) during the year or in any of the prior five years.

[IRC § 274(j)(4)(B)]

Safety achievement award. As its name implies, a safety achievement award is an award to an employee for achieving a certain safety goal. However, awards to managers, administrators, clerical employees, or other professional employees will not qualify as safety achievement awards. In addition, an award will not qualify if, during the tax year, more than 10 percent of employees (excluding employees who are not eligible for such awards) have received safety achievement awards (other than awards of *de minimis* value). [IRC § 274(j)(4)(C)]

Q 10:8 Are employee achievement awards deductible by an employer?

Yes, they are. However, the amount of the deduction depends on whether the employee achievement award is or is not a qualified plan award.

In the case of awards that are not qualified plan awards, the deduction for all such awards made to an employee during a tax year is limited to $400.

In the case of a qualified plan award, the deduction limit is $1,600 less the cost of all other awards (whether or not qualified plan awards) made to the employee during the year. [IRC § 274(j)(2)]

Qualified plan award. A qualified plan award is an achievement award that is given as part of an established written plan or program that does not favor highly compensated employees as to eligibility for benefits. [IRC § 274(j)(3)(B)] For this purpose, highly compensated employees generally include any 5 percent owners and employees with compensation in excess of $80,000 per year (indexed annually for inflation). [IRC § 414(q)] The indexed compensation figure is $105,000 for 2008. [IRS News Release 2007-171, 10/18/2007]

However, no award presented by the employer in a taxable year will be considered a qualified plan award if the average cost of all employee achievement awards during the taxable year under any qualified plan exceeds $400. The average cost is determined by dividing (1) the sum of the costs of all employee achievement awards (without regard to the deductibility of the costs) by (2) the total number of employee achievement awards presented. In determining the average cost, employee achievement awards of nominal value ($50 or less) are not taken into account. [IRC § 274(j)(3)(B); Prop. Reg. § 1.274-8(c)(5)]

Q 10:9 Are employee achievement awards taxable income to employees?

An achievement award is excluded from an employee's wages provided the cost to the employer does not exceed the amount of the employer's deduction (see Q 10:8). Thus, the amount of the exclusion is limited to $400 for awards that are not qualified plan awards and to $1,600 for qualified plan awards.

If the cost of an employee's award is more than the allowable deduction, the employee's wages include the larger of: (1) the excess cost over and above the allowable deduction, or (2) the amount by which the value of the award exceeds the allowable deduction.

Q 10:10 How are employee achievement awards handled for payroll tax purposes?

An achievement award is exempt from income tax withholding, FICA, and FUTA taxes to the extent it is excludable from an employee's wages. However, any amount that is included in an employee's taxable wages is subject to withholding and payroll taxes. [Temp. Reg. § § 31.3121(a)-1T; 31.3306(b)-1T]

Adoption Assistance

Q 10:11 What is an adoption assistance program?

An adoption assistance program is a separate written plan of an employer that meets all of the following requirements:

1. The plan benefits employees under rules that do not favor highly compensated employees or their dependents;

2. The plan does not give more than 5 percent of its payments during the year to shareholders or owners (or their spouses and dependents) who own more than 5 percent of the stock or capital profits interests in the business;

3. The employer gives reasonable notice of the plan to eligible employees; and

4. Employees provide reasonable substantiation that payments or reimbursements are for qualifying expenses.

[IRC § § 137, 127(b)]

Q 10:12 What is the income tax treatment of payments or reimbursements made to an employee for qualified adoption expenses?

Employer-provided payments or reimbursements for qualified adoption expenses generally are excludable from gross income up to a maximum amount per eligible child, subject to an income limitation. In the case of adoption of a child with special needs, the exclusion is allowed regardless of whether the employee has qualifying expenses. The maximum exclusion is $10,000, subject to inflation adjustments for tax years beginning after 2002. For example, for 2008, the maximum exclusion is $11,650 per eligible child. [Rev. Proc. 2007-66, 2007-45 IRB] However, the maximum exclusion applies on a per-adoptee basis, not on an annual basis. [IRC § § 137(a), 137(b)(1)]

According to the Internal Revenue Service (IRS or the Service), if an employee makes an unsuccessful adoption attempt and then successfully adopts an eligible child, the expenses of the unsuccessful adoption are included in maximum exclusion limit for the successful adoption. [Notice 97-9, 1997-1 C.B. 365]

Note: The IRS notice does not address the treatment of employees who make an unsuccessful adoption attempt and then give up. However, the IRS has made it clear that the exclusion is available for expenses connected with a domestic adoption even if the adoption never becomes final. [IRS Pub. No. 968, *Tax Benefits for Adoption*] In the case of foreign adoptions, the tax exclusion for adoption assistance is available only if and when the adoption becomes final.

Reduction of maximum exclusion. The maximum per-adoptee exclusion is reduced for employees with higher incomes and is eliminated entirely for employees with incomes above a specified amount. The full exclusion is available for employees with modified adjusted gross income (AGI) of $150,000 or less and is phased out for employees with modified AGI between $150,000 and 190,000.

Timing of exclusion. Generally, the exclusion for employer-provided adoption assistance is available for the year in which the employer provides the assistance.

In the case of a foreign adoption, employer-provided assistance is excludable from income only if and when the adoption becomes final. If an employer makes adoption assistance payments in a year before the adoption of a foreign child becomes final, the employee must include the payments in taxable income for the year. [IRC §§ 137(e), 23(e); Notice 97-9, 1997-1, C.B. 365] When the adoption becomes final, the employee can make an adjustment to claim the exclusion on that year's return.

The IRS has issued a revenue procedure to establish safe harbor rules for determining the finality of a foreign adoption. The revenue procedure applies to qualified adoption expenses paid or incurred in connection with the adoption of a foreign born child who has received an "immediate relative" (IR) visa from the Department of State. An IR visa is issued only to a foreign-born child who enters the United States pursuant to a decree of adoption or guardianship granted by a court or other government agency (competent authority) with jurisdiction over child welfare matters in the foreign county. The revenue procedure does not apply to the adoption of a child who is already a citizen or resident of the United States when the adoption proceedings begin. IR visas come in three varieties. In addition, the revenue procedure will not apply to adoptions of foreign children to be governed by the Intercountry Adoption Act of 2000, when it takes effect in the United States (see below).

1. An IR-2 visa is issued to a foreign-born child under age 16 who has been in the legal custody of, and has resided with, the adoptive parent or parents for at least two years.

2. An IR-3 visa is issued to a foreign-born child after a full and final adoption has occurred in a foreign country.

3. An IR-4 visa is issued to a child if a foreign country grants legal guardianship or custody to the prospective adoptive parent or parents or to an individual or agency acting on their behalf. An IR-4 visa is also issued if the foreign country grants a simple adoption (in which one or both of the adoptive parents do not see the child before or during the proceedings).

Q 10:12

Under the revenue procedure, a taxpayer may treated the adoption of a foreign born child who receives an IR2 visa, an IR3 visa, or an IR4 visa under a decree of simple adoption as final either:

- In the taxable year in which the foreign court or competent authority enters a decree of adoption; or

- In the taxable year in which a home state court enters a decree of re-adoption or otherwise recognizes the foreign decree, if that taxable year is one of the next two taxable years after the taxable year in which the foreign decree was entered.

In the case of a child who is issued an IR-4 visa under a grant of legal guardianship or custody (as opposed to simple adoption), the adoption may be treated as final in the taxable year in which a home state court enters an adoption decree. [Rev. Proc. 2005-31, 2005-26 IRB 1374]

The Intercountry Adoption Act of 2000 [P.L. 106-279] will implement the Hague Convention on Protection of Children and Co-operation in Respect of Intercountry Adoption. When the Convention enters into force in the United States, the IAA generally will apply to adoptions in which both the sending and the receiving countries are parties to the Convention. A Convention adoption subject to the IAA will be final for federal income tax purposes (1) in the taxable year for which the Secretary of State certifies an adoption as final or (2) in the year in which the state court enters a final decree of adoption.

A married couple must file a joint return to qualify for the exclusion unless they lived apart from each other for the last six months of the taxable year and the individual claiming the credit or the exclusion (1) maintained as his or her home a household for the eligible child for more than one-half of the taxable year, and (2) furnished over one-half of the cost of maintaining that household in that taxable year. For this purpose, an individual legally separated from his or her spouse under a decree of divorce or separate maintenance will not be considered married. [IRC § 137(e)]

Q 10:13 What are qualified adoption expenses?

Qualified adoption expenses are reasonable and necessary adoption fees, court costs, attorney's fees, and other expenses that are directly related to the legal adoption of an "eligible child" by an employee. They include amounts paid or expenses incurred for qualified adoption expenses in connection with any unsuccessful attempt to adopt an eligible child before successfully finalizing the adoption of another eligible child. [Notice 97-9, 1997-1 C.B. 365]

Qualified adoption expenses do not include expenses that are incurred in violation of state or federal law, in carrying out a surrogate parenting arrangement, or in adopting a child of the employee's spouse. [IRC §§ 23(d)(1), 137(d)] Also excluded is any expense (1) for which a deduction or credit is allowed under any other provision of the Internal Revenue Code (IRC or the Code), (2) to the extent that funds for the expense are received under any federal, state, or local program, (3) that is in violation of state or federal law, or (4) that was paid or incurred in a taxable year beginning before 1997. [Notice 97-9, 1997-2 I.R.B. 35]

Q 10:14 Who is an eligible child?

An eligible child is an individual who either:

1. Has not attained age 18; or

2. Is physically or mentally incapable of caring for himself or herself.

[IRC § 23(d)(2)]

The IRS has ruled that, for purposes of the exclusion for employer-provided adoption assistance, a child attains a given age on the anniversary of the date the child was born. For example, a child born on January 1, 1986, attains the age of 18 on January 1, 2004. [Rev. Rul. 2003-72, 2003-33 I.R.B. 346]

Q 10:15 Are there any other tax breaks for adoption expenses?

Yes. Taxpayers may claim a tax credit for eligible adoption expenses. [IRC § 23] Like the exclusion for employer-provided adoption assistance, the credit is $10,000 per adoptee, adjusted for inflation. Thus, for 2008, the maximum credit is $11,650. [Rev. Proc. 2007-66, 2007-45 IRB] The credit for expenses incurred in connection with a domestic adoption can be claimed in the year *following* the year in which the expenses are paid. However, expenses paid or incurred in the year the adoption becomes final can be claimed as a credit in that year. Expenses for a foreign adoption can be claimed as a credit in the year the adoption becomes final. In addition, the credit for adoption of a child with special needs is allowed in the year the adoption becomes final regardless of whether the taxpayer incurred qualifying expenses. The adoption credit in nonrefundable, but unused credits can be carried over for five years.

The adoption credit is phased out at the same income levels as the exclusion for employer-provided adoption assistance (see Q 10:12).

The adoption tax credit and the exclusion for employer-provided adoption assistance are not mutually exclusive. An individual may claim both the maximum allowable credit and the maximum allowable exclusion in connection with a single adoption. [IRC § § 23(d)(1), 137(d)]

Example 10-1: Tom Hill and his wife, Susan, adopted a child. Tom's employer reimbursed $5,000 of eligible adoption expenses under its adoption assistance plan. The Hills paid another $4,000 of eligible expenses out of their own pockets. The Hills modified adjusted gross income was below the phase-out level for the exclusion and the credit.

The Hills may exclude the $5,000 of employer-provided adoption assistance from their income. In addition, the Hills can claim an adoption credit for the $4,000 they paid themselves.

Note: An individual cannot claim both the credit and the exclusion for the same expenses. In addition, an employee cannot claim the credit for any expense reimbursed by his or her employer, whether or not the amount is reimbursed under an adoption assistance plan.

Q 10:16 Is employer-provided adoption assistance subject to income tax withholding and payroll taxes?

Employer-provided adoption assistance is not subject to income tax withholding. However, adoption assistance amounts are subject to Social Security and Medicare taxes (FICA) and federal unemployment tax (FUTA). [Notice 97-9, 1997-1 C.B. 365]

Q 10:17 Must an employer report employer-provided adoption assistance on an employee's Form W-2, Wage and Tax Statement?

Adoption assistance benefits must be reported in box 12 of an employee's Form W-2 using code "T." The amount of the adoption assistance is also included in the totals for Social Security (box 3) and Medicare wages (box 5). However, adoption assistance benefits are not included in the employee's wages (box 1).

Athletic Facilities

Q 10:18 Can the value of an employee's use of an employer's athletic facilities be excluded from the employee's wages?

Yes. Wages do not include the value of an employee's use of an on-premises gym or other athletic facility (e.g., a swimming pool or golf course) if substantially all of its use during the calendar year must be by the employer's employees, their spouses, and dependent children. Thus, the exclusion does not apply if the athletic facility is made available to the general public through membership sales, rental, or similar arrangements. [Reg. § 1.132-1(e)(1)]

Q 10:19 When is an athletic facility considered to be on the premises of an employer?

An athletic facility must be located on premises owned or leased by the employer, but need not be located on the employer's business premises. However, athletic facilities that are facilities for residential use (such as a resort with accompanying athletic facilities) do not qualify. [Reg. § 1.132-1(e)(2)]

Health club, country club, and other memberships do not qualify for the on-premises athletic facility exclusion unless the employer owns or leases and operates the facility and substantially all of the facility's use is by the employer's employees, their spouses, and dependent children. [Reg. § 1.132-1(e)(3)]

Q 10:16

Club Dues

Q 10:20 How is an employer's payment for an employee's club dues handled for tax purposes?

Employer-provided membership in a club organized for business, pleasure, recreation, or other social purposes may be excluded from the employee's gross income as a working condition fringe benefit to the extent the club is used for business purposes. [Reg. § 1.132-5(s)]For example, if a club is used 50 percent for business and 50 percent for personal purposes, 50 percent of the annual dues may be excluded from the employee's income. The other 50 percent must be included in the employee's income as wages.

Club dues may not be deducted as business expenses. [IRC § 274(a)(3)] Therefore, the employer may not claim a deduction for that portion of the dues that is treated as a working condition fringe benefit. However, any dues payments that are treated as compensation to the employee are deductible by the employer. [IRC § 274(e)(2); Reg. § 1.132-5(s)]

Civic and professional clubs. The ban on deduction for club dues does not apply to civic clubs such as Kiwanis or Rotary or to professional groups or similar organizations, including business leagues, trade associations, chambers of commerce, boards of trade, real estate boards, and bar or medical associations. [Reg. § 1.274-2(a)(2)(iii)]

> **Planning Point:** Despite the crackdown on dues deductions, businesses can still deduct out-of-pocket expenses for business-related entertainment at a club, subject to the 50 percent deduction limitation for such expenses (see Chapter 6). For example, guest or greens fees paid to take a client to a country club for golf following a business discussion are deductible. Similarly, the cost of a business meeting held at a club qualifies for a deduction. Consequently, reimbursements to employees for out-of-pocket costs for business-related entertainment at a club can be excluded from an employee's income, provided the reimbursements are made under an accountable plan (see Q 10:93).

Company Cars

Q 10:21 Is the value of an employer-provided vehicle excluded from an employee's income?

The value of a company car that is used strictly for business is fully excludable from an employee's income. However, in many cases, employers permit their employees to use their company cars for personal as well as business driving. In that case, the business use of the car qualifies as a nontaxable working condition fringe benefit, provided the employee properly substantiates the business use. The portion of the value of the employee's use that is attributable to personal driving is treated as compensation to the employee.

An employer may make a special election to treat a car as used 100 percent for personal purposes. Instead of breaking down the employee's car use between business and personal driving, the employer simply reports the full value of the car as taxable compensation to the employee. If an employer takes this option, the value of the car must be determined using the annual lease table valuation method (see Q 10:27). The employee can deduct the business-use portion of the annual value as an employee business expense on his or her individual tax return.

> **Planning Point:** The special election can be a time-saver for an employer because it eliminates the need for records detailing the employee's use of the car in order to determine the portion of the value that is taxable to the employee. On the other hand, there is a catch for the employee. The employee's deduction for the business-use portion of the annual value is treated as a miscellaneous itemized deduction. Miscellaneous itemized deductions are deductible only to the extent the total exceeds 2 percent of the employee's adjusted gross income for the year. Therefore, the employee may not get a dollar-for-dollar offset against the taxable compensation. In addition, as an itemized deduction, the write-off for the value of the business use can be reduced as a result of the itemized deduction phase-out that applies to higher-income taxpayers.

Q 10:22 Is an employee required to substantiate his or her business use of an employer-provided car?

Yes. The value of the use of a company car provided to an employee for use in the employer's business will be treated as a fully taxable fringe benefit unless the employee substantiates the amount of his or her business use. [Reg. § 1.132-5(c)(1); Temp. Reg. § 1.274-5T(a)]

Q 10:23 How is the business use of an employer-provided car substantiated?

The business use of an employer-provided car must be substantiated. To do so, an employee must document:

- The amount of each separate expenditure for the car (e.g., cost of purchase, maintenance, repairs);
- The amount of each business use (i.e., mileage);
- The total use of the car during the taxable period;
- The date of each expenditure relating to the car and the date of each business use; and
- The business purpose for the expense or use.

[Temp. Reg. § § 1.274-5T(b)(6), 1.280F-6T(b)(1)(i)]

Q 10:22

Q 10:24 What kinds of records will be considered adequate for substantiation of business use?

Adequate records must substantiate a deduction for expenses related to the business use of a car. The following items may, singly or in combination, be adequate records: account books, diaries or logs; trip sheets; statements of expense (for example, expense reports); and receipts, paid bills, or similar documentary evidence. [Temp. Reg. § 1.274-5T(c)(2)]

Records generally must be made at or near the time of the expenditure or use—at a time when the taxpayer has full present knowledge of each element of the expenditure or use (such as the amount, time and place, business purpose, and business relationship). Expense account statements prepared from account books, diaries, logs, or similar records made at or near the time of the expenditure or use will also be treated as made at or near the time of the expenditure or use if they are submitted to the employer by the employee in the regular course of good business practice. [Temp. Reg. § 1.274-5T(c)(2)(ii)(A)]

Q 10:25 Are records required if a vehicle is provided for business use only?

Not necessarily. Records of business use are not required if an employer has a written policy statement expressly limiting the use of the vehicle to business use only. [Reg. § 1.132-5(e)]

The employer's policy statement must satisfy five conditions:

1. The vehicle must be owned or leased by the employer and must be provided to one or more employees for use in connection with the employer's trade or business;

2. When not being used in the employer's trade or business, the vehicle must be kept on the employer's business premises except when it is temporarily located elsewhere (for example, for maintenance or repairs);

3. No employee using the vehicle may live at the employer's business premises;

4. No employee may use the vehicle for personal purposes except for *de minimis* personal use (for example, stopping for lunch between two business deliveries); and

5. The employer must reasonably believe that employees do not use the vehicle for personal use (except for *de minimis* use).

[Reg. § 1.132-5(e); Temp. Reg. § 1.274-6T(a)(2)]

Q 10:26 How is the taxable value of an employee's personal use of an employer-provided vehicle calculated?

The taxable value of an employee's personal use of a company car must be included in the employee's gross income. There are four basic valuation methods:

1. Fair market value method (Q 10:26);
2. Annual lease table method (Q 10:27);
3. Cents-per-mile method (Q 10:28); and
4. Commuting value method (Q 10:29).

Once an employer selects a valuation method for a car, IRS regulations impose conditions on when and if the employer can switch methods. [Reg. § 1.61-21(d)(7)]

When applying a special valuation rule for a vehicle that is used by more than one employee at the same time (for example, an employer-sponsored commuting pool), an employer must use the same rule to value the personal use of the vehicle by each employee. The employer must allocate the value among the employees sharing the vehicle based on the relevant facts and circumstances. [Reg. § 1.61-21(c)(2)(ii)(B)]

Q 10:27 How does an employer determine the value of an employee's personal use of a company car using the fair market value method?

The employer determines how much it would cost the employee to lease a comparable car on comparable terms in the geographic area where the employee uses the car. [Reg. § 1.61-21(b)(4)]That cost is then multiplied by the ratio of personal mileage to total miles. The fair market value method may be used for all cars, regardless of value. In addition, the method can be used for any year the car is in service, even if the employer used other methods in prior years.

Q 10:28 How does the annual lease table valuation method work?

The annual lease value of a car is determined from an IRS table of lease values based on the fair market value (FMV) of a car. The employee's personal use percentage is multiplied by the table value to determine the taxable value of the employee's personal use.

The annual lease value is determined using the FMV of the car as of the first day it is made available to the employee for personal use. [Reg. § 1.61-21(d)] There are two safe harbors for determining FMV:

1. *Employer-owned car.* The FMV is the employer's cost to buy the car, including sales tax, title, and other sale expenses.

2. *Employer-leased car.* The FMV is either: (1) manufacturer's suggested retail price (including sales tax, title, etc.) less 8 percent; (2) the value recognized by nationally known pricing sources; or (3) the manufacturer's invoice price (including options) plus 4 percent.

The table can be used to determine the annual lease value of any car with an FMV up to $59,999. If the car's FMV exceeds $60,000, the annual lease value is $500 plus 25 percent of FMV.

The table provides values for a full year of car use. If the car is made available to an employee for a continuous period of 30 or more days but less than a full year, the table value is prorated. If a car is provided to an employee for a continuous period of less than 30 days, the value is determined using the daily lease value. The daily lease value is calculated by multiplying the annual lease value by a fraction, using four times the number of days of availability as the numerator and 365 as the denominator. Alternatively, an employer can apply a prorated annual lease value for a period of less than 30 days by treating the automobile as if it had been provided for 30 days if that would result in a lower value than the daily lease value.

> **Caution:** Once the lease table method is elected to value an employee's personal use of a particular car, an employer cannot switch to the cents-per-mile method to value it in a subsequent year. An employer can switch only to the fair market value or commuting use method. [Reg. § 1.61-21(d)(7)]

If an employer has a fleet of 20 or more automobiles and certain requirements are satisfied, the employer may use a fleet-average value for purposes of calculating the annual lease values of the automobiles in the fleet. [Reg. § 1.61-21(d)(5)(v)]

Q 10:29 How does the cents-per-mile valuation method work?

The cents-per-mile valuation method may be used to value an employee's personal use of an employer-provided vehicle when the following requirements are met:

1. The employer reasonably expects the vehicle will be regularly used in the employer's trade or business throughout the calendar year (or a shorter period of ownership); or

2. The vehicle is primarily used by employees during the calendar year and is actually driven at least 10,000 miles in that calendar year.

However, the cents-per-mile valuation rule cannot be used for higher priced vehicles. The cut-off values for use of the cents-per-mile method are adjusted annually. In the case of vehicles placed in service in 2007, the cents-per-mile method cannot be used for passenger cars with a value of more than $15,100 or light trucks or vans (including minivans and SUVs built on a truck chassis) with a value of more than $16,400. [Rev. Proc. 2007-11, 2007-2 I.R.B. 261]

Under the cents-per-mile rule, the value of the employee's personal use is equal to the standard mileage rate for the year multiplied by the number of personal miles that the employee has driven (that is, for personal purposes). The standard mileage rate is adjusted annually. For example, for 2007, the standard mileage rate is 48.5 cents per mile. [Rev. Proc. 2007-11, 2007-2 I.R.B. 261]

Whether the car or vehicle is regularly used in the employer's trade or business will be determined based on the facts and circumstances. The car will be treated as being used in such a manner if the following is the case:

1. At least 50 percent of the car's total annual mileage is for the employer's business; or

2. The car is generally used each workday to transport at least three of the employer's employees to and from work in an employer-sponsored commuting vehicle pool.

[Reg. § 1.61-21(e)(1)(iv)]

If, a vehicle is used only infrequently for business use, such as for occasional trips to the airport or between the employer's multiple business premises, that use does not count as use in the employer's trade or business. [Reg. § 1.61-21(e)(1)(iv)(B)]

When valuing the use of a vehicle using the cents-per-mile method, the fair market value of maintaining and insuring the vehicle is included. If the employer does not provide fuel, however, the cents-per-mile rate can be lowered by up to 5.5 cents. [Reg. § § 1.61-21(e)(1), (3)] So, for example, the 48.5 cents-per-mile rate for 2007 would be lowered to 43 cents per mile if the employee paid for the gas.

Q 10:30 How does the commuting value method work?

Under the commuting value rule, an employee's use of vehicle is valued at $1.50 per one-way commute (for example, from home to work or from work to home) or $3 per round trip. Those rates apply to each employee regardless of how many employees commute in the same car.

The commuting value rule may be used only if the following conditions are met:

1. The vehicle is owned or leased by the employer;

2. The vehicle is provided to one or more employees for use in connection with the employer's trade or business and is used in the employer's trade or business;

3. The employer requires the employee to commute to or from work (or both) in the vehicle for bona fide noncompensatory business reasons;

4. The employer has established a written policy forbidding use of the vehicle for personal purposes other than commuting or *de minimis* personal use (for example, stopping for a personal errand on the way between a business delivery and the employee's home);

5. The employee does not use the vehicle for any personal purpose other than commuting and *de minimis* personal use; and

6. The employee is not a control employee, including an owner of one percent or more of the business, a shareholder, an officer of the employer with compensation of $50,000 (indexed) or more, or a non-officer employee with compensation of $100,000 (indexed) or more. For 2008, the indexed compensation levels are $90,000 and $185,000, respectively. [IR 2007-171, 10/18/2007] (This limitation only applies if the vehicle is an automobile.)

[Reg. § 1.61-21(f)]

Q 10:30

Q 10:31 How does the commuting value method work for unsafe conditions?

The value of commuting transportation provided to a qualified employee solely because of unsafe conditions is $1.50 for each one-way commute. Unsafe conditions exist if, under the facts and circumstances, a reasonable person would consider it unsafe for the employee to walk or use public transportation at the time of day the employee must commute. One factor indicating whether unsafe conditions exist is the history of crime in the area surrounding the employer's workplace or the employee's home at the time of day the employee commutes.

The unsafe commuting rule may be used if all of the following requirements are met:

1. The employee would ordinarily walk or use public transportation for commuting.
2. The employer has a written policy under which transportation for personal purposes is not provided other than because of unsafe conditions.
3. The employee does not use employer-provided transportation for personal purposes other than because of unsafe conditions.

The unsafe commuting rule applies only to rank-and-file employees. A qualified employee is one who:

1. Performs services for the employer during the year;
2. Is paid on an hourly basis;
3. Is not exempt from the minimum wage and maximum hour provisions of the federal Fair Labor Standards Act (FLSA);
4. Is within a classification of employees to whom the employer pays overtime at one-and-one half times the regular rate of pay as provided in the FLSA; and
5. Receives pay of not more than $75,000 during the year. [Reg. § 1.61-21(k)]

An employee will not be considered a qualified employee if the employer does not comply with the FLSA's record keeping requirements concerning the employee's wages, hours, and other conditions of employment.

De Minimis Fringe Benefits

Q 10:32 What is a de minimis fringe benefit?

A *de minimis* fringe benefit is any property or service provided to an employee that has so little value (after taking into account the frequency with which similar benefits are provided to employees) that it would be unreasonable or administratively impractical to account for it. [IRC § 132 (e)(1)]

Examples of *de minimis* fringe benefits include:

- Occasional personal use of a company copy machine, provided the employer sufficiently controls access to the machine so that at least 85 percent of the total use is for business purposes.
- Holiday gifts, other than cash, with a low fair market value.
- Group term life insurance payable on the death of an employee's spouse or dependent if the face amount is not more than $2,000.
- Occasional parties or picnics for employees and their guests.
- Occasional tickets for entertainment or sporting events.
- Occasional typing of personal letters by a company secretary.

Cash, no matter how little, is never treated as a *de minimis* fringe benefit, except for occasional meal money (see Q 10:62) or transportation fare (Q 10:82). In addition, the IRS has ruled that cash equivalents, such as gift certificates, do not qualify as *de minimis* fringe benefits because it is not unreasonable or administratively impracticable to account for them. [TAM 200437030]

Q 10:33 How are *de minimis* fringe benefits handled for income and payroll tax purposes?

The value of a *de minimis* fringe benefit is excludable from an employee's wages for both income and payroll tax purposes. [IRC § 132(e)(1)]

Dependent Care Assistance

Q 10:34 What is a dependent care assistance plan?

A dependent care assistance plan is a program sponsored by an employer to provide care for employees' dependents. Benefits may take the form of employer-provided cash, cash reimbursement for dependent care expenses incurred by the employee, or both. [IRC § 129]

A dependent care assistance plan must be in writing and must operate for the exclusive benefit of employees. [IRC § 129(d)(1)]

Q 10:35 Are employees taxed on benefits received from an employer-provided dependent care assistance program?

If the dependent care assistance program satisfies certain tax law requirements, dependent care is excludable from an employee's income up to specified limits. [IRC § 129] The maximum annual exclusion is $5,000 if the employee is single or is married and files a joint tax return, or $2,500 if the employee is married and files a separate tax return. However, the exclusion cannot exceed the earned income of the employee if he or she is single. If the employee is married, the exclusion cannot exceed the earned income of the spouse who earned the lesser amount during the calendar year. [IRC § § 129(a)(2), (b)]

If an employee's spouse does not work, the earned income limit would ordinarily prevent an employee from qualifying for tax-free treatment of any amount of dependent care assistance. However, a spouse who is incapacitated or who is a full-time student for at least five months during the calendar year is treated as having earned income of not less than $250 per month if there is one qualifying dependent and not less than $500 per month if there are two or more qualifying dependents. [IRC §§ 121(d), 129(b)(2), 129(e)(2)]Therefore, the employee will qualify for up to $3,000 of tax-free assistance for the care of one dependent and up to $6,000 for the care of two or more dependents.

An employer cannot exclude dependent care assistance from the wages of a highly compensated employee if the plan discriminates in favor of the highly compensated. Failure to satisfy the nondiscrimination rules does not affect the exclusion for benefits provided to employees who are not highly compensated. [IRC § 129(d)]

Highly compensated employees include: (1) any employee who was a 5 percent owner at any time during the year, and (2) employees who earned more than an annually adjusted amount (e.g., $105,000 for 2007 [IRS News Release 2007-171, 10/18/2007]) during the preceding year. However, an employer can ignore the second test if the employee was not in the top 20 percent of employees when ranked by pay for the preceding year.

Q 10:36 What are the nondiscrimination tests?

A dependent care assistance plan must pass four nondiscrimination tests to ensure that benefits provided to highly compensated employees qualify for tax-favored treatment.

1. *Eligibility.* The program must benefit employees who qualify under a classification that does not discriminate in favor of highly compensated employees or their dependents.

2. *Benefits test.* The contributions or benefits under the program cannot discriminate in favor of highly compensated employees or their dependents.

3. *25 percent concentration test.* Not more than 25 percent of the amounts the employer pays or incurs for dependent care assistance during the year may be provided for more than 5 percent owners (or their spouses or dependents).

4. *55 percent concentration test.* The average benefits provided to non-highly compensated employees must be at least 55 percent of the average benefits provided to highly compensated employees.

[IRC §§ 129(d)(2), (3), (4), (8)]

Planning Point: An employer has control over the first two tests; the eligibility and benefits requirements will be met if the plan is properly designed. However, when it comes to the last two tests, employees are in control. If the plan is used by highly compensated employees but passed up by non-highly compensated employees, the plan may fail those two tests. Therefore, an employer may want to "sell" the plan to non-highly compensated employees in order to ensure tax-free treatment for benefits provided to highly compensated employees.

Q 10:37 How are an employer's payments for dependent care assistance treated for tax purposes?

Employers generally may deduct amounts paid or incurred under a dependent care assistance program as ordinary and necessary business expenses. For employer-sponsored day care centers, this applies to operating expenses rather than capital expenditures. [IRC §§129, 162; Reg. §1.162-10; Rev. Rul. 73-348, 1973-2 C.B. 31]

Q 10:38 Who is a qualifying dependent?

To be excludable, dependent care assistance must be used for the care of a "qualifying individual." This includes any individual falling into one of the following three categories:

1. A dependent of the employee who is under the age of 13 and for whom the employee can claim a dependent tax deduction (personal exemption);

2. A dependent of the employee who is physically or mentally incapable of caring for himself or herself; or

3. The spouse of the employee, if the spouse is physically or mentally incapable of caring for himself or herself.

[IRC §21(b)(1)]

The IRS has ruled that, for purposes of the exclusion for employer-provided dependent care assistance, a child attains a given age on the anniversary of the date the child was born. For example, a child born on January 1, 1994, attains the age of 13 on January 1, 2007. [Rev. Rul. 2003-72, 2003-33 I.R.B. 346]

Planning Point: Employers have flexibility in designing dependent care assistance programs. The program's benefits can be limited to childcare or can be broadened to include care of employees' incapacitated adult dependents, such as elderly parents. Expanding the program to include adult dependents may be beneficial from an employee-relations standpoint since a common complaint of single and childless employees is that employee benefits (e.g., health benefits and adoption assistance) are skewed in favor of married employees with children.

Q 10:39 What types of dependent care expenses can a dependent care assistance program cover?

The expenses must be for care of qualifying dependents and related household service. The expenses must be incurred to enable the employee to be gainfully employed. Examples of expenses that may be paid for or reimbursed under a dependent care assistance program include:

- At-home childcare;

- Household services related to the care of elderly or disabled adults living with the employee who are "qualifying individuals";

- Care at licensed nursery schools;

- Dependent care centers meeting state or local government requirements and providing day care for more than six individuals (but not overnight or sleep-away camps).

Regulations specifically provide that the full amount paid to a nursery school in which a qualifying child is enrolled is considered to be for the care of the child, even though the school also furnishes lunch and educational services. By contrast, the regulations provide that school expenses incurred for a child in the first or higher grades are not dependent care expenses. [Reg. § 1.44A-1(c)(3)] The regulations do not specifically mention kindergarten. However, new regulations dealing with the credit for dependent care expenses, which mirrors the exclusion, specifically provide that expenses for a child in kindergarten or a higher grade do not qualify because they are for education, not for child care. [Reg. § 1.21-1(d)(5)]

In the case of qualifying individuals other than dependent children under the age of 13, dependent care expenses that are incurred outside the home can be taken into account only if the qualifying individual regularly spends at least eight hours a day in the employee's household. [IRC § 21(b)(2)(B)]

In order to be reimbursed for dependent care expenses under an employer-provided dependent care assistance program, an employee must provide the name, address, and taxpayer identification number (TIN) of the person performing the services (or if the service provider is a tax-exempt organization such as an educational organization, the name and address of the entity). [IRC § 129(e)(9)]

> **Planning Point:** As a result of this requirement, an employee generally cannot obtain reimbursement for a nanny or housekeeper who is an illegal alien and does not have a Social Security number or a caregiver who is being paid "under the table" without withholding or payment of Social Security taxes. To avoid employee misunderstanding, employers should include the requirement to provide a tax ID number in the descriptive materials relating to the employer's dependent care assistance program.

Q 10:40 What information is an employer required to give employees about a dependent care assistance program?

The sponsoring employer must provide reasonable notification of the availability and terms of its program to eligible employees. [IRC § 129(d)(6)] The plan must furnish each employee who has received benefits in the preceding calendar year with a written statement by January 31 showing the amounts paid or expenses incurred by the employer in providing dependent care assistance to the employee. [IRC § 129(d)(7)]Reporting the amount of dependent care assistance to each employee on the employee's annual W-2 form satisfies this second requirement. [IRC § § 129(d), 6051(a)(9)]

Q 10:41 Can an employee who receives dependent care assistance also claim a dependent care tax credit on his or her tax return?

The tax law provides a credit for certain dependent care assistance expenses incurred by a taxpayer to enable him or her to be gainfully employed. [IRC § 21] An employee is entitled to a tax credit for amounts paid for the care of dependents under the age of 13, disabled dependents, or a disabled spouse (qualified dependents). However, benefit payments received under an employer-provided dependent care assistance program reduce the amount of expenses that may be taken into account in computing the credit for dependent care expenses on a dollar-for-dollar basis. [IRC § 21(c)]

Nonetheless some employees may qualify for both tax breaks. The maximum amount of creditable dependent care expenses is $3,000 for one individual and $6,000 for two or more individuals. As a result, an employee who receives the maximum of $5,000 in dependent care assistance benefits for the care of two or more individuals will be eligible to claim a tax credit for up to $1,000 of additional expenses ($6,000 maximum creditable expenses less $5,000 employer-provided benefits.

> **Planning Point:** Employers' communication materials regarding dependent care assistance programs should include a brief mention of the availability of the tax credit and the effect of plan benefits on the amount of the credit available.

Q 10:42 Are benefits provided under a dependent care assistance program subject to income tax withholding or payroll taxes?

As long as it is reasonable for the employer to believe that payments from a dependent care assistance program are excludable from the employee's gross income, the payments are not subject to FICA tax, FUTA tax, or federal income tax withholding requirements. [IRC § § 3121(a)(18), 3306(b)(13), 3401(a)(18)]

Disability Income Benefits

Q 10:43 What is a disability income plan?

A disability income plan is a plan that provides income replacement benefits to employees who are unable to work because of illness or accident. This type of plan does what its name implies: It "replaces" a portion of the income or compensation lost while the employee is disabled. Thus, the level of benefits generally is dependent on the employee's income before becoming disabled, not on the nature and extent of the employee's particular disability.

Q 10:44 Are employees taxed on the cost of employer-provided disability coverage?

No. The tax law provides an income exclusion for the cost of disability insurance coverage received from an employer. [IRC §§ 61(a)(1), 104(a)(3), 105(a), 106]

> **Planning Point:** An employer may, however, include the amounts of its premium payments for disability insurance coverage in employee's taxable wages for the year. Whether this is done unilaterally by the employer or at the employee's election, the inclusion of premium payments in the employees' incomes will affect the income tax treatment of disability benefits paid to the employee (see Q 10:46).

Q 10:45 Are employer payments for an employee's disability coverage deductible for federal income tax purposes?

Yes, provided that they are ordinary and necessary business expenses. [IRC § 162(a); Reg § 1.162-10]

Q 10:46 Are disability benefits taxable to an employee?

The tax treatment of disability income benefits received by an employee depends on who paid the premiums for the disability coverage. To the extent that the disability income benefits are attributable to employer contributions or payments, they are taxable. However, to the extent that the disability income benefits are attributable to the employee's own contributions, they are not taxed. [IRC §§ 104(a)(3), 105(a)] If both the employer and the employee contribute toward the cost of the coverage, the portion of the disability benefits attributable to employer contributions is taxable, while the portion attributable to employee contributions is tax-free. The taxable and tax-free portions of the benefits are determined by applying a three-year lookback rule. Benefits are generally taxable to the employee to the extent that premiums were paid by the employer within three years preceding the employee's disability.

> **Planning Point:** In the past, it was assumed that this three-year lookback rule also applied when a plan switched from an employer-paid to an employee-paid arrangement. However, an IRS ruling makes it clear that the three-year lookback rule applies only when both the employer and the employee contribute to the cost of coverage in the year in which the employee becomes disabled. According to the rulings, LTD benefits payable to an employee who pays the premiums for coverage *for the plan year in which he or she becomes disabled* are excludable from income, even if the employer paid the premiums in prior years. [Rev. Rul. 2004-55, 2004-34 I.R.B. 319]

The IRS revenue ruling also makes it clear that when an employee elects to have disability coverage paid for by the employer on a pretax basis (i.e., the premiums paid by the employer are excluded from the employee's income), the premiums are treated as paid by the employer and disability benefits received by the employee are includible in the employee's gross income. On the other hand, if an employee elects to have disability coverage paid for by the employer on an after-tax basis (i.e., the premiums paid by the employer are taxed to the employee), the premiums are treated as paid by the employee and disability benefits received by the employee are excludable from the employee's gross income.

Disaster Relief Assistance

Q 10:47 Is employer-provided disaster relief assistance includable in an employee's gross income?

The IRS has ruled that "qualified disaster relief payments" received from an employer are excludable from an employee's gross income under Code Section 139. [Rev. Rul. 2003-12, 2003-3 I.R.B. 283] The IRS ruling dealt with employer-provided flood relief, but the reasoning of the ruling is equally applicable to other "qualified disasters."

Section 139 was added to the Code by the Victims of Terrorism Tax Relief Act of 2001. [P.L. 107-134]Code Section 139 provides that gross income does not include any amount received by an individual as a qualified disaster relief payment. A qualified disaster relief payment means any amount paid to or for the benefit of an individual:

1. To reimburse or pay reasonable and necessary personal, family, living, or funeral expenses incurred as a result of a qualified disaster; or

2. To reimburse or pay reasonable and necessary expenses incurred for the repair or rehabilitation of a personal residence or repair or replacement of its contents to the extent that the need for such repair, rehabilitation, or replacement is attributable to a qualified disaster.

Because of the extraordinary circumstances surrounding a disaster, individuals are not required to account for actual expenses in order to qualify for the exclusion. However, the amount of disaster relief payments must be reasonably expected to be commensurate with the expenses involved. In addition, the exclusion applies only to the extent an expense covered by a disaster payment is not otherwise compensated for by insurance or otherwise.

Q 10:48 What is a qualified disaster?

Qualified disaster relief payments may be made in the event of the following qualified disasters:

1. A disaster that results from a terrorist or military action;

2. A presidentially declared disaster; or

3. A disaster resulting from any event that the Secretary of Treasury determines to be of a catastrophic nature.

[IRC § 139(c)]

Q 10:47

Education Assistance

Q 10:49 What is an education assistance plan?

A tax-qualified education assistance plan (EAP) can provide each employee with up to $5,250 per year of tax-free educational assistance. [IRC § 127]

Education assistance is a popular perk for employees, but in the past these plans were problematic for employers. Although the tax break for EAPs was originally enacted more than 20 years ago, it was a "temporary" provision that required periodic reenactment by Congress. Fortunately, a 2001 law change ended the on-again, off-again status of EAPs. [P.L. 107-16 § 411(a)(2001)] EAPs are now a permanent part of the tax law.

Q 10:50 What are the requirements for a tax-qualified EAP?

An EAP must be a separate written plan that provides assistance only to employees. An EAP will qualify only if all of the following tests are met:

1. The plan benefits employees under rules that do not favor highly compensated employees.

2. The plan does not provide more than 5 percent of its benefits during the year to shareholders or owners who own more than 5 percent of the stock or capital or profits interest of the business.

3. The plan does not allow employees to choose to receive cash or taxable benefits instead of education assistance.

4. The employer gives reasonable notice of the plan to eligible employees.

[IRC § 127]

Q 10:51 What types of educational assistance can the employer's program cover?

Qualifying educational assistance includes tuition, fees and similar payments, and the cost of books, supplies, and equipment. It does not include the cost of tools or supplies that may be retained after completion of a course; meals, lodging, or transportation; or any payment for any course or other education involving sports, games, or hobbies—unless such education involves the business of the employer or is required as part of a degree program. [IRC § 127(c)(1); Reg. § 1.127-2(c)(3)(iii)]

EAP benefits may be provided for both undergraduate and graduate-level courses.

Q 10:52 Are EAP benefits subject to income tax withholding and payroll taxes?

No. As long as it is reasonable for the employer to believe that payments from its Code Section 127 educational assistance program are excludable from the employee's gross income, such program payments are not subject to FICA tax, FUTA tax, or federal income tax withholding requirements. [IRC §§ 3121(a)(18), 3306(b)(13), 3401(a)(18)]

Q 10:53 What if employer-provided education assistance exceeds $5,250 for a year?

Educational benefits that do not qualify for the EAP exclusion generally are taxable. However, if the educational expense incurred by the employee is job-related, the expense may be excludable from the employee's gross income as a working condition fringe benefit.

An education expense is considered job-related if it maintains or improves skills that are required by the employee's job or that are required by the employer or by law as a condition of employment. [Reg. § 1.162-5(a)] Courses taken to meet the minimum education requirements of the employee's job or to prepare the employee for a new trade or business do not qualify as job-related. These courses may, however, be covered by an EAP.

Q 10:54 Can an employer assist employees with the cost of a child's education?

Yes. Moreover, if an employer's workforce includes a number of employees with young families, this type of benefit may prove to be an extremely popular perquisite.

One option is to provide direct assistance in the form of tax-free scholarships for deserving students (see Q 10:55). Alternatively, an employer can help employees boost their education savings by contributing to education savings accounts for employees' children (see Q 10:56) or by sponsoring a Section 529 college saving plan for employees (see Q 10:57).

Q 10:55 When do employer-provided scholarships for employees' children qualify for tax-free treatment?

The tax law provides that gross income does not include any amount received as a qualified scholarship by an individual who is a candidate for a degree at an educational institution, except to the extent the amount represents payment for services rendered. [IRC § 117(c)]

A qualified scholarship generally includes any amount received by an individual as a scholarship or fellowship grant to the extent the individual establishes that, in accordance with the conditions of the grant, the amount was used for qualified tuition and related purposes. [IRC § 117(b)(1); Prop. Reg. § 1.117-6(c)(1)]

However, to qualify for tax-free treatment, scholarships for employees' children must meet the following additional requirements:

Q 10:53

- The scholarship program is not used to recruit employees or induce them to stay;

- The scholarships are awarded by an independent committee;

- There are identifiable minimum requirements for eligibility;

- There is an objective basis for selecting recipients;

- Scholarships cannot be terminated because a recipient's parent leaves the company;

- Scholarships are not limited to a course of study of particular benefit to the employer; and

- Scholarships are not awarded to more than (1) 10 percent of the number of employees' children who are eligible to receive them or (2) 25 percent of employees' children who were eligible and who actually applied for the scholarships and were considered by the selection committee.

[Rev. Rul. 76-47, 1976-2 C.B. 670]

Q 10:56 What is an education savings account?

Education savings accounts (formally called Coverdell education savings accounts) are trusts or custodial accounts set up to pay qualified education expenses of an eligible beneficiary. [IRC § 530]Contributions to an education savings account are not deductible by the contributor. However, contributions are not included in the beneficiary's income, and distributions for qualifying educational purposes are tax-free. As a general rule, contributions to an account are phased out for higher-income taxpayers and are not permitted once income exceeds a ceiling amount. However, the contribution phaseout does not apply to corporations or other entities. [IRC § 530(c)(1)]Thus, a corporation can make a full annual contribution to a child's education savings account regardless of its income.

> **Planning Point:** A company's contribution to an education savings account is *not* a tax-free fringe benefit. The contribution will be treated as additional compensation to the employee for both income tax and payroll tax purposes. Nonetheless, company contributions to education savings accounts may prove to be a popular perquisite, especially for highly paid employees who do not qualify to make their own contributions because their incomes are above the phaseout limits.

An education savings account may be established to pay the education expenses of any beneficiary under age 18. No contributions may be made on behalf of a child after he or she reaches age 18. [IRC § 530(b)(1)(a)(ii)] However, the account may remain in existence to pay qualifying education expenses of the beneficiary until he or she reaches age 30. At that time, the balance in the account must be distributed to the beneficiary, unless the balance is rolled over to an account for another eligible beneficiary. [IRC § § 530(5)(8), 530(d)(8)]

Any individual or entity can contribute to an education savings account on behalf of an eligible beneficiary. The maximum annual contributions made on behalf of a beneficiary cannot exceed $2,000. [IRC § 530(b)(1)(a)(iii)]

Individual contributors are subject to a contribution phaseout. The maximum allowable contribution is phased out for individuals with adjusted gross income between $95,000 and $110,000 on a single return or $190,000 and $220,000 on a joint return. However, as noted above, the contribution phaseout does not apply to corporations or other entities.

Distributions from an education savings account are excluded from a beneficiary's gross income if they are used to pay qualified education expenses. Distributions for other purposes are taxable to the extent they represent untaxed earnings. Taxable distributions are also generally subject to a 10 percent penalty. However, the penalty does not apply if the distribution is made on account of the death or disability of the account beneficiary or the beneficiary's receipt of a scholarship. [IRC § 530(d)]

Qualified education expenses include tuition, fees, books, supplies, equipment, and certain room and board expenses for graduate or undergraduate education. The beneficiary can be enrolled full-time, half-time, or less than half-time. However, room and board expenses are considered qualified expenses only if the beneficiary is enrolled on at least a half-time basis. Qualified expenses also include elementary and secondary school expenses. [IRC §§ 530(b)(2), 530(b)(3)]

Q 10:57 What is a Section 529 college savings plan?

A Section 529 college savings plan allows contributors to save for a designated child's college education on a tax-favored basis. Contributions to the account are not deductible. However, earnings are not taxable while they remain in the account. In addition, amounts withdrawn from the account (including earnings) are not taxable to the extent they are used to pay qualifying higher education expenses of the designated beneficiary.

Planning Point: Although employees can set up and contribute to Section 529 plans on their own, employer-sponsored plans are emerging as a popular employee benefit because they permit employees to make contributions to the plan through payroll deductions. Amounts contributed to a Section 529 plan through payroll deductions are not excludable from income. The amounts are treated as compensation paid to the employee and are subject to payroll taxes.

Qualified higher education expenses include tuition, fees, books, supplies, and equipment required for attendance at a higher educational institution. Qualified expenses also include room and board for a student who is enrolled at least half time. In the case of a special needs beneficiary, qualified expenses also include other expenses that are necessary in connection with his or her college enrollment.

Unlike education savings accounts, there are no income limits for employee contributors or fixed dollar limits on contributions to Section 529 education savings plans. However, Section 529 requires a plan to establish safeguards to prevent contributions in excess of the amount necessary to fund a child's college expenditures. The IRS says that a plan will meet this requirement if contributions are limited to the amount determined actuarially that will pay tuition, fees, and room and board for five years of undergraduate enrollment at the highest-cost college allowed by the plan. [Prop. Reg. § 1.529-2(i)] The plan must prohibit additional contributions once that limit is reached.

Distributions from an education savings account are not eligible for tax-free treatment if they are not used for qualifying expenses. In addition, the law imposes a 10 percent penalty tax on the amount of a distribution from a qualified tuition plan that is includable in gross income. However, unused amounts in one child's account can be rolled over to an account for another beneficiary who is a member of the same family.

Employee Discounts

Q 10:58 What is an employee discount?

An employee discount is the price at which an employer offers property or services for sale to customers minus the price at which the property or service is offered to the employee. [IRC § 132(c)(3); Reg. § 1.132-3(b)(1)]

A *qualified* employee discount is a discount that meets certain requirements. If those requirements are met, the value of a discount is excluded from the employee's gross income. [IRC § 132; Reg. § 1.132-3(a)(1)]

Q 10:59 Are there any limits on the amount of a qualified employee discount?

The portion of an employee discount that qualifies for exclusion from gross income depends on whether the discount is on property or services.

Property. For property sold to an employee at a discount, the maximum excludable portion of the discount is the price at which the property is being offered to non-employee customers in the ordinary course of the employer's line of business multiplied by the employer's gross profit percentage.

An employer's gross profit percentage is based on all property offered to customers (including employee customers) during the tax year preceding the tax year in which the employee discount is available. To determine the gross profit percentage, subtract the total cost of the property from the total sales price of the property and divide the result by the total sales price of the property.

Services. For services sold to an employee at a discount, the maximum excludable portion of the discount is 20 percent of the price at which the services are being offered to non-employee customers. [IRC § 132(c)(1); Reg. § 1.132-3(a)(1)]

The portion, if any, of a discount exceeding those limits is required to be included in an employee's gross income. [Reg. § 1.132-3(e)]

Q 10:60 What form can a qualified employee discount take?

A qualified employee discount may consist of price reductions, cash rebates from the employer, or cash rebates from a third party. The exclusion will apply regardless of whether the property or service is provided at a reduced charge or at no charge at all. [Reg. § 1.132-3(a)(4)]However, any portion of the discount exceeding the allowable limit must be included in the gross income of the employee. [Reg. § 1.132-3(e)]

Q 10:61 Do all types of property qualify for tax-free employee discounts?

As a general rule, a discount on any property offered for sale to customers in the ordinary course of an employer's line of business in which an employee performs substantial services will qualify for the exclusion. However, the exclusion does not apply to real property and personal property (whether tangible or intangible) of a kind commonly held for investment. [Reg. § 1.132-3(a)(2)] Thus, employee discounts on the purchase of securities, commodities, or currency, or of either residential or commercial real estate, are not qualified employee discounts and are not excludable from gross income. [IRC § 132(c)(4); Reg. § 1.132-3(a)(2)(ii)]

Q 10:62 Can an employee's family members also receive tax-free employee discounts?

Yes. For purposes of the qualified employee discount, the term employee is broadly defined to include the following:

1. Current employees in the employer's line of business;
2. Former employees who have separated from service in the employer's line of business by reason of retirement or disability;
3. Any widow or widower of an employee who either died while employed in the employer's line of business or separated from service in the employer's line of business as the result of retirement or disability; and
4. The spouse and dependent children of any of the above (a dependent child includes a son, stepson, daughter, or stepdaughter who is also a dependent of the employee or whose parents are both deceased and who has not attained age 25). [Reg. § § 1.132-1(b)]

Q 10:63 Are there nondiscrimination rules for qualified employee discounts?

In order for the value of an employee discount to be excluded from a highly compensated employee's gross income, the benefit must be available on substan-

Q 10:60

tially the same terms to all employees or to a group of employees under a reasonable classification set up by the employer that does not discriminate in favor of highly compensated employees. [IRC § 132(j)(1); Reg. § 1.132-8]

Flights on Company Aircraft

Q 10:64 If any employee takes a personal flight on a company aircraft, is the value of the flight taxable to the employee?

When an employee uses an employer-owned, leased, or chartered aircraft for a personal trip, the employer must value and tax the flight for federal income tax withholding, FICA, and FUTA purposes using the Standard Industry Fare Level (SIFL) formula.

The formula works as follows:

Step 1. Multiply the mileage of the flight by the SIFL cents-per-mile rate that applies to the distance of the flight for the period the flight was taken;

Step 2. Multiply the Step 1 result by the appropriate aircraft multiple;

Step 3. Add the terminal charge in effect at the time of the flight.

The aircraft multiples are constant from year to year. They depend on the weight of the aircraft and the employee's rank in the company:

Maximum certified takeoff weight of the aircraft	*Key employee*	*Non-key employee*
6.000 lbs or less	62.5 percent	15.6 percent
6,001-10,000 lbs.	125 percent	23.4 percent
10,001-25,000 lbs	300 percent	31.3 percent
25,001 lbs. or more	400 percent	31.3 percent

The mileage rates and terminal charge change twice a year and are announced by the IRS in an official revenue ruling.

Group Long-Term Care Insurance

Q 10:65 What is long-term care insurance?

Long-term care insurance generally provides financial protection against potentially devastating costs associated with long-term care for functionally disabled individuals who are unable to care for themselves because of a chronic or irremediable physical or mental condition. Long-term care covers both medical and nonmedical support services provided in a setting other than an acute care unit of a hospital.

However, to receive favorable tax treatment, long-term care insurance must meet specific qualification requirements contained in the Internal Revenue Code.

Q 10:66 What are the tax requirements for a qualified long-term care insurance contract?

In order to be treated as a qualified long-term care insurance contract for tax purposes, the contract must meet all of the following requirements:

1. The only insurance protection provided under the contract is coverage of "qualified long-term care services";

2. The contract does not pay or reimburse expenses covered by Medicare (including Medicare deductibles or coinsurance amounts) except where Medicare is secondary or the contract makes per diem or other periodic payments without regard to expenses;

3. The contract is guaranteed renewable;

4. The contract does not provide for a cash surrender value or other money that can be borrowed or paid, pledged, or assigned as collateral for a loan (this does not prohibit a refund on the death of the insured or on a complete surrender or cancellation of the contract if the refund does not exceed the premiums paid under the contract);

5. All premium refunds and policyholder dividends must be applied as a reduction in future premiums or to increase future benefits; and

6. The contract complies with a number of consumer protection provisions.

[IRC § 7702B]

Qualified long-term care services are necessary diagnostic, preventive, therapeutic, curing, treating, mitigating, rehabilitative, maintenance, and personal care services that are (1) required by a chronically ill individual and (2) provided pursuant to a plan of care prescribed by a licensed health care practitioner. [IRC § 7702B(c)(1)]

Q 10:67 Are employees taxed on the value of employer-paid group long-term care insurance?

Group long-term care insurance is treated as accident and health insurance. Therefore, the value of employer-paid coverage is excludable from an employee's income as contributions to an accident and health plan. [IRC § 106]

Q 10:68 Can employees deduct premiums they pay for group long-term care insurance?

An employee's premium payments for qualified long-term care insurance are treated as deductible medical expenses. However, the deductible amount is subject to annual dollar limitations based on the individual's attained age at the end of the taxable year of payment. These limits are adjusted annually for inflation. For example, the limits for 2007 are as follows:

Q 10:66

Age	Limit
Age 40 or less	$290
More than 40 but not more than 50	550
More than 50 but not more than 60	1,110
More than 60 but not more than 70	2,950
More than 70	3,680

[Rev. Proc. 2006-53, 2006-48 IRB]

In addition, a medical expense deduction is available only to the extent that the total of long-term care premiums and other qualifying expenses exceed 7.5 percent of adjusted gross income and have not been compensated for by insurance or otherwise. [IRS Notice 97-31, 1997-21 I.R.B. 5]

Q 10:69 Can an employer deduct the cost of group long-term care insurance for its employees?

Qualified long-term care insurance is treated as accident and health insurance for tax purposes. Therefore, an employer is entitled to deduct its contributions as a business expense in the same manner as employer contributions for other accident and health insurance (i.e., medical or disability benefit insurance).

Q 10:70 How are employees taxed on benefits received under group long-term care insurance?

Amounts received as benefits under a qualified long-term care insurance contract generally are treated as amounts received for personal injuries and sickness and as reimbursements for expenses incurred for medical care. [IRC § 7702B(a)(2)]Therefore, they are generally excludable from income. [IRC § 105]However, special exclusion limits may apply if the contract pays benefits on a per diem basis without regard to the actual costs of the qualified long-term care services. [IRC § § 7702B(d)(1), 7702B(2)]

Group Term Life Insurance

Q 10:71 Is employer-provided group term life insurance taxable to an employee?

The cost of employer-paid premiums for up to $50,000 of coverage is not includable in employee's income or subject to federal income tax withholding, FICA, or FUTA taxes. The cost of excess coverage over $50,000 must be included in income on the employee's Form W-2 and is subject to FICA, but not federal income tax withholding or FUTA. [IRC § § 3121(a)(2)(C), 3306(b)(2)(C), 3401(a)(14)]

The exclusion does not apply to insurance provided to 2-percent shareholders of an S corporation. In addition, if an employer's plan favors key employees as to participation and benefits, the entire cost of the insurance provided to key employees is ineligible for the exclusion. In each case, the cost of the insurance is subject to FICA tax and must be reported as wages on Form W-2. However, the cost is not subject to income tax withholding or FUTA tax. (See Q 10:59 for special rules relating to coverage for key employees.)

Q 10:72 What are the requirements for group term life insurance to qualify as an excludable fringe benefit?

This exclusion applies to life insurance coverage that meets all the following conditions:

1. It provides a general death benefit that is not included in income.

2. Insurance coverage is provided to a group of employees.

3. Each employee is provided with an amount of insurance based on a formula that prevents individual selection. This formula must use factors such as the employee's age, years of service, pay, or position.

4. The insurance is provided under a policy carried directly or indirectly by the employer.

Q 10:73 How does the employer figure the taxable value of group term coverage that exceeds the $50,000 exclusion limit?

The taxable "cost" of group term coverage in excess of $50,000 is determined by using the IRS table reproduced below, regardless of what the employer actually paid for the coverage. The taxable value of the coverage is reduced to the extent the employee made after-tax contributions toward the coverage cost. [Reg. §§ 1.79-1—1.79-3]

Cost Per $1,000 of Protection for One Month

Age	Cost
Under	$ .05
25 through 29	.06
30 through 34	.08
35 through 39	.09
40 through 44	.10
45 through 49	.15
50 through 54	.23
55 through 59	.43
60 through 64	.66
65 through 69	1.27
70 and older	2.06

When using this table, the employee's age is the age attained on the last day of the calendar year. [Reg. § 1.79-3(d)(2)]

Q 10:72

Example 10-2: Dawson, age 49, receives $300,000 of employer-paid group term life insurance coverage for the year. He contributes $25 per month, after taxes, toward the cost of his coverage. The taxable value of his coverage is determined as follows:

Amount of taxable coverage: $300,000 - $50,000	=	$250,000
Annual cost per $1,000 of coverage: 12 months × 15	=	$1.80
Total annual cost of excess coverage: $1.80 × 250	=	$450
Less Dawson's after-tax contributions 12 × $25	=	$300
Dawson's taxable group term benefit $450 - $300	=	$150

Q 10:74 What if an employer provides life insurance coverage for an employee's spouse or dependents?

If the face amount of the coverage does not exceed $2,000, the coverage is deemed a *de minimis* fringe benefit and is not taxable or included in the employee's income. [Notice 89-100, 1989-2 C.B. 447]

If the face amount exceeds $2,000, the cost of all coverage (including the initial $2,000) is included in the employee's income on Form W-2. The cost of the coverage is subject to federal income tax withholding, FICA, and FUTA to the extent the employee did not pay for the coverage with after-tax contributions. IRS Table I is used to figure the taxable cost based on the spouse's or dependent's age. [Reg. §§ 1.61-2(d)(2)(ii)(b); 1.132-6(e)(2); 31.3401(a)(14)-1; Notice 89-110 C.B. 1989-2, 447]

Q 10:75 Can an employer provide group term life insurance for retired or former employees?

Retired or terminated employees can receive up to $50,000 of group term coverage tax-free. [IRC § 79(a); Reg. § 1.79-0] The cost of coverage in excess of $50,000 is included in income in the year coverage is provided. Each ex-employee's portion of FICA tax owed on the excess coverage must be listed separately on Forms W-2 so the ex-employee can enter it on his or her personal income tax return and pay the FICA tax directly to the IRS.

The value of the excess coverage provided to retirees or terminated employees is not taxable if any of the following apply:

- Coverage is provided as part of a qualified pension, profit-sharing, stock bonus, or annuity plan. [Reg. § 1.79-2(d)]

- The insurance covers former employees who terminated employment with a total and permanent disability. (For the year in which the employee becomes disabled, the exclusion applies to that part of the year during which the employee is disabled.) [Reg. § 1.79-2(b)(2)]

- The insurance plan was in existence on January 1, 1984 (or the plan is a comparable successor plan) with respect to those who (1) retire or separate from service under the plan, (2) were employed during 1983 by the employer maintaining the plan, and (3) reached age 55 on or before January 1, 1984. [IRC § 79(e)]

- The employer or a charity is the sole beneficiary of the insurance policy or the portion of the policy in excess of $50,000. [Reg. § 1.79-2(c)(3)]

Q 10:76 What special rules apply to coverage for key employees?

If an employer's group term life insurance plan discriminates in favor of key employees—either regarding eligibility for coverage or benefits provided—the key employees are taxed on the entire value of their coverage, including the first $50,000. Furthermore, the employer calculates the taxable value of key employees' coverage using *the higher* of the actual premiums the employer paid or the cost from the IRS table. Non-key employees do not lose the $50,000 exclusion or the Table I advantage. [IRC § 79(d)(1)]

Key employees. These are employees listed in IRC § 416(i), plus any former employee who was a key employee at retirement or separation.

Plan requirements. An employer's plan must meet certain eligibility requirements to be nondiscriminatory. At least one of these four tests must be met:

- At least 70 percent of all employees benefit from the plan;
- At least 85 percent of all employees participating are not key employees;
- Participants make up a group that the IRS determines is not discriminatory; or
- The plan is part of cafeteria plan that meets the requirements of Internal Revenue Code (IRC or the Code) Section 125.

Key employees can get bigger death benefits under a plan as long as benefit levels for all employees bear a uniform relationship to compensation. [IRC § 79(d)]

When applying these tests, employees can be excluded if they (1) have not completed three years of service; (2) are part-time or seasonal; (3) are nonresident aliens who have not earned U.S. source income from the employer; or (4) are covered by a collective bargaining agreement in which benefits under the plan were subject to good faith bargaining. [IRC § 79(d)(3)]

Lodging on an Employer's Business Premises

Q 10:77 Is employer-provided lodging taxable to an employee?

The value of employer-provided lodging is excluded from an employee's wages if the lodging meets the following tests:

1. It is furnished on the employer's business premises;
2. It is furnished for the employer's convenience; and
3. The employee must accept the lodging as a condition of employment.

[IRC § 119(a)]

This exclusion does not apply if the employee can choose to receive additional pay instead of lodging.

Key exception. A more than 2-percent shareholder of an S corporation is not treated as an employee for purposes of the lodging exclusion. Therefore, the value of lodging provided by the corporation is subject to income and payroll taxes. [IRC § 1372(a)]

Business premises. For purposes of the exclusion, an employer's business premises are generally the employee's place of work.

For the employer's convenience. Whether lodging is furnished for the convenience of the employer depends on all the facts and circumstances. The employer must have a substantial business reason for providing the lodging other than to provide the employee with additional pay.

Condition of employment. Lodging meets this test if an employer requires employees to accept the lodging because they need to live on premises to be able to properly perform their duties. Examples include employees who must be available at all times and employees who could not perform their required duties without being furnished the lodging.

Example 10-3: A hospital gives Joan, an employee of the hospital, the choice of living at the hospital free of charge or living elsewhere and receiving a cash allowance in addition to her regular salary. If Joan chooses to live at the hospital, the hospital cannot exclude the value of the lodging from her wages because she is not required to live at the hospital to properly perform her duties.

Meals

Q 10:78 Are employer-provided meals taxable income to employees?

The tax law carves out income exclusions for three types of employer-provided meals:

1. *De minimis* meals (Q 10:79);

2. Meals provided at an employer-operated eating facility (Q 10:79); and

3. Meals provided on the employer's business premises for the convenience of the employer (Q 10:83).

Q 10:79 When are meals excludable as *de minimis* meals?

The exclusion applies to any meal or meal money provided to an employee that has so little value (taking into account how frequently meals are provided to employees) that accounting for it would be unreasonable or administratively impracticable. [Reg. § 1.132-6(d)]For example, the exclusion applies to the following items:

- Coffee, doughnuts, or soft drinks.
- Occasional meals or meal money provided to enable an employee to work overtime. (However, the exclusion does not apply to meal money figured on the basis of hours worked.)
- Occasional parties or picnics for employees and their guests.

Planning Point: If food or beverages furnished to employees qualify as a *de minimis* benefit, the employer can deduct their full cost. The 50 percent limit on deductions for the cost of meals does not apply. (See Chapter 6 for a discussion of the meal deduction limit.)

Q 10:80 What is an employer-operated eating facility for employees?

An employer-operated facility for employees is any facility that:

1. Is owned or leased by the employer;
2. Is operated by the employer;
3. Is located on or near the employer's business premises; and
4. Furnishes meals that are provided before, during, or immediately after the employee's workday.

Meals include food, beverages, and related services provided at the facility.

[Reg. § 1.132-7(a)(2)]

Q 10:81 When are meals provided to employees at an employer-operated eating facility excludable from an employee's income?

The value of free or discounted meals provided to employees in employer-subsidized cafeterias, dining rooms, and other eating facilities are treated as excludable *de minimis* fringe benefits if the annual revenue from the facility equals or exceeds the direct operating costs of the facility. [Reg. § 1.132-7(a)(1)(i)]

For this purpose, the revenue from providing a meal is considered equal to the facility's direct operating costs to provide the meal if the meal's value can be excluded from an employee's wages under the rules for meals provided on the employer's business premises for the convenience of the employer (see Q 10:66). In other words, the employee will be treated as having paid cost for the meal.

The exclusion is available to highly compensated employees only if access to the facility is available on substantially the same terms to each member of a group of employees that is defined under a reasonable classification set up by the employer, which does not discriminate in favor of highly compensated employees. [Reg. § 1.132-7(a)(1)(ii)]Therefore, the exclusion generally would not apply to meals provided at an executive dining room.

Planning Point: The issue of whether meals qualify as *de minimis* fringe benefits is significant for employers as well as employees. As a general rule, an employer's deduction for meals provided to employees is limited to 50 percent of the cost. [IRC § 274(n)(1)]However, an employer can claim a full

Q 10:80

deduction for meals that qualify as *de minimis* fringe benefits. [IRC § 274(n)(2)(B)]

Q 10:82 How are employees taxed on meals that do not qualify for exclusion from income?

If meals do not qualify for exclusion from income, the employee is taxed on the fair market value of the meals less the amount (if any) paid for the meals. [Reg. § 1.132-7(c)]

Q 10:83 When are meals furnished on an employer's business premises excludable from an employee's income?

The value of meals furnished to an employee can be excluded from the employee's gross income if:

1. The meals are furnished on the business premises of the employer; and

2. The meals are furnished for the convenience of the employer. [IRC § 119(a)]

A meal is considered furnished for the convenience of the employer if the employer has substantial noncompensatory business reasons for furnishing the meal. The fact that an employer may charge for meals or that an employee may decline a meal is not taken into account in determining whether a meal is furnished for the convenience of the employer. [IRC § 119(b)(2)]

If meals furnished to more than half of all employees who are furnished meals satisfy the convenience of the employer test, meals furnished to other employees will also be deemed to satisfy the test. [Reg. § 1.119-1(a)(2)(ii)(E)]

A more than 2-percent shareholder of an S Corporation is not treated as an employee for purposes of the exclusion for employer-provided meals. [IRC § 1372(a)]

Q 10:84 What are some examples of meals that will be treated as furnished for the convenience of the employer?

The IRS gives the following examples of meals that will be treated as furnished for the convenience of the employer:

- Meals furnished to food service employees during, or immediately before or after, working hours.

- Meals furnished during working hours so that an employee will be available for emergency call during the meal period, provided the employer can show that emergency calls have occurred or can reasonably be expected to occur.

- Meals furnished during working hours if the nature of the employer's business restricts the employee to a short meal period (such as 30 or 45 minutes) and the employee cannot be expected to eat elsewhere in such a short time.

- Meals furnished during working hours if the employee could not otherwise eat proper meals elsewhere within a reasonable period of time (for example, if there are insufficient eating facilities in the area).

[IRS Pub. No. 16-B, *Employer's Tax Guide to Fringe Benefits*]

Moving Expense Reimbursements

Q 10:85 Are moving expense reimbursements taxable to employees?

A qualified moving expense reimbursement received by an employee in connection with a job-related move is tax-free to the extent it covers expenses that would be deductible by the employee on his or her own tax return if the employee paid the expenses. Tax-free treatment also applies to qualified expenses paid directly by the employer to a third party and the value of moving services provided by the employer. [IRC § § 132(g), 217] A reimbursement is not tax-free if it covers expenses that would not be deductible if paid by the employee.

Job-related moving expenses are deductible only if an employee's new work location is at least 50 miles farther from the employee's old home than was the old work location. For example, if the employee's former principal place of work was 10 miles from the old residence, the new principal place of work must be at least 60 miles from the old residence. If an employee had no former principal place of work, the new principal place of work must be at least 50 miles from the old residence. [IRC § 217(c)(1)]In measuring the distance, the shortest of the more commonly traveled routes between the two points is used. [IRC § 217(c)]

In addition, the employee must work full time or at least 39 weeks during the first 12 months after the employee's arrival in the general area of the new principal place of work. Failure to satisfy the work-time test is excused, however, if the employee is unable to satisfy the requirement because of death or disability or because of an involuntary separation from employment (other than for willful misconduct) or transfer for the benefit of the employer. [IRC § § 217(c)(2), (d)(1)]

Q 10:86 What are deductible moving expenses?

Deductible moving expenses include reasonable expenses for the following:

1. Moving household goods and personal effects from the former residence to the new residence (including the cost of storing and insuring household goods and personal effects for up to 30 consecutive days); and

2. Traveling (including lodging but excluding meals) from the former residence to the new place of residence.

[IRC § 217(b)]

In the case of a foreign move, reasonable moving expenses also cover the following:

1. Moving household goods and personal effects to and from storage; and

2. Storing the goods and effects for part or all of the period during which the foreign place of work is the principal place of work.

[IRC §§ 217(b), 217(h)]

Q 10:87 What moving expenses are not tax deductible?

Nondeductible moving expenses include the following:

- House-hunting expenses;
- Temporary living expenses;
- Expenses for the sale or purchase of a house;
- Expenses to obtain or break a lease; and
- Meal expenses.

Planning Point: An employer can reimburse any expenses for a job-related move. However, expenses that would not qualify for a deduction if paid by the employee cannot be reimbursed on a tax-favored basis. Reimbursements for those expenses must be treated as compensation to the employee, subject to income tax withholding and payroll taxes.

Q 10:88 What withholding and reporting requirements apply to moving expense reimbursements?

Qualified moving expense reimbursements are excludable from an employee's wages. If the expenses were paid directly to the employee, they must be reported on the employee's W-2 form. Payments to a third party and the value of moving services provided by the employer are not reported on Form W-2. In addition, the employer must provide the employee with an itemized list of moving expense reimbursements. [IRS Pub. No. 15-B, *Employer's Tax Guide to Fringe Benefits*] IRS Form 4782, *Employee Moving Expense Information*, may be used for this purpose.

If an employer's payments are not qualified moving expense reimbursements, they are wages subject to FICA, FUTA, and federal income tax withholding. [IRC §§ 3121(a)(11), 3306(b)(9), 3401(a)(15)]

No-Additional-Cost Services

Q 10:89 What is a no-additional-cost service?

A no-additional-cost service is any service provided by an employer to an employee for the employee's personal use that meets the following requirements:

1. The service is offered for sale to non-employee customers by the employer in the ordinary course of its line of business;

2. The employee performs substantial services in that same line of business; and

3. No substantial additional cost is incurred by the employer in providing the service to the employee.

[IRC § 132(b)]

The value of a no-additional-cost service is excluded from an employee's gross income. [IRC §§ 132(a), (b); Reg. §§ 1.132-1(a)(1), -2(a)(1)] The exclusion applies regardless of whether the service is provided at no charge or at a reduced price. The benefit may also be provided through a partial or total rebate of the price the employee pays for the service. [IRC § 132(b); Reg. §§ 1.132-2(a)(1)(ii), (3)]

No-additional-cost services may be provided to both current and former employees and to their family members on a tax-favored basis. [Reg. § 1.132-1(b); IRC § 132(h)]

Line of business requirement. An employee can exclude from gross income only those no-additional-cost services or qualified employee discounts in the line of business in which he or she performs substantial services. If an employee performs services directly benefiting more than one line of business, he or she is treated as performing substantial services for all such lines of business; thus, the employee could qualify to receive no-additional-cost services or qualified employee discounts from all of them. [Reg. § 1.132-4(a)(1)]

Q 10:90 What types of services qualify as no-additional-cost services?

No-additional-cost services are excess capacity services, such as lodging provided by an employer that operates a hotel; transportation by aircraft, train, bus, subway, or cruise line if the employer is in one of those lines of business; and telephone services provided by a telephone company. [Reg. § 1.132-2(a)(2)]

On the other hand, the exclusion for no-additional-cost services does not apply to non-excess capacity services, such as the facilitation by a stock brokerage firm of stock purchases. (An employer may, however, give an employee a discount on non-excess capacity services. See Q 10:74 *et seq.*) [Reg. § 1.132-2(a)(2)]

For the exclusion to apply, the employer cannot incur substantial additional cost (including revenue that is foregone because the service is provided to an employee rather than to a non-employee customer) in providing the service to the employee.

Q 10:91 Can employers team up to provide no-additional-cost services?

Yes. An employee of one employer can receive tax-free no-additional-cost services from a second, unrelated employer. In order to do so, the following three requirements must be satisfied:

Q 10:90

1. The two unrelated employers must have a written reciprocal agreement permitting each employer's employees performing substantial services in the same line of business to receive no-additional-cost services from the other employer;

2. The service received by the employee from the unrelated employer is the same type of service generally provided to non-employee customers in the line of business in which the employee works and in the line of business from which the employee receives the service (so that it would be a no-additional-cost service to the employee if provided directly by the employee's own employer); and

3. Neither employer incurs substantial additional cost either in providing such service to the other employer's employees or under the agreement.

[IRC § 132(i); Reg. § 1.132-2(b)]

Q 10:92 Are no-additional-cost services subject to nondiscrimination requirements?

In order for the value of a no-additional-cost service to be excluded from a highly compensated employee's gross income, the benefit must be available on substantially the same terms to all employees of the employer, or to a group of employees under a reasonable classification set up by the employer that does not discriminate in favor of highly compensated employees. [IRC § 132(j)(1); Reg. § 1.132-8(a)(1)]For this purpose, the definition of highly compensated employee contained in Code Sections 414(q), 414(s), and 414(t) is used. [IRC § 132(j)(6); Reg. § 1.132-8(f)]

If a no-additional-cost benefit is provided on a discriminatory basis, the value of the service is not excludable from income of the highly compensated employees. [Reg. § 1.132-8(a)(2)]

Transportation Benefits

Q 10:93 What are qualified transportation fringe benefits?

Qualified transportation fringe benefits are assistance for commuting costs that may excluded from employees' incomes. There are three types of qualified transportation benefits:

1. Transportation in a commuter highway vehicle (van pooling) between an employee's home and the workplace.

2. Transit passes.

3. Qualified parking.

[IRC § 132(f)(1)]

The exclusion applies whether an employer provides one or a combination of qualified benefits to an employee. [IRC § 132(f)]

The exclusions for transit passes and qualified parking are subject to dollar limits, which apply on a monthly basis (see Q 10:97).

Q 10:94 What is a commuter highway vehicle?

A commuter highway vehicle is any highway vehicle that seats at least six adults (not including the driver) For a vehicle to qualify, the employer must reasonably expect that at least 80 percent of the mileage will be for transporting employees between their homes and the workplace with employees occupying at least one-half the vehicle's seats (not including the driver's seat). [IRC § 132(f)(5)(B); Reg. § 1.132-9 Q&A-2]

Q 10:95 What is a transit pass?

A transit pass is any pass, token, fare card, voucher, or similar item entitling a person to ride free of charge or at a reduced rate on mass transit (e.g., a bus, train, or ferry) or in a highway vehicle with a seating capacity of at least six adults (excluding the driver) that is operated for hire. [IRC § 132(f)(5)(A); Reg. § 1.132-9 Q&A-3]

Q 10:96 What is qualified parking?

Qualified parking is parking provided to an employee on or near the business premises of an employer. It also includes parking or on or near a location from which the employee commutes to work by means of mass transit, a vehicle for hire, a vanpool, or a carpool. Qualified parking does not include any parking at or near the employee's home. [IRC § 132(f)(5)(C); Reg. § 1.132-9, Q&A-4]

> **Example 10-4:** Diane, an employee of Bigco, drives from her home to a commuter railway station, parks her car, and takes the train to work. If Bigco pays for the cost of parking at the railway station, it is a qualified transportation fringe benefit. In addition, Bigco can pick up the cost of Diane's train travel.

Qualified parking includes parking at or near a work location at which the employer provides services for the employer. However, it does not include the value of parking that is excludable from gross income as a working condition fringe benefit, nor does it include business expense reimbursements to an employee for parking that are excludable from income as made under an accountable plan (see Q 10:79). So, for example, reimbursements for parking expenses incurred by an employee on a business trip for the employer are not treated as qualified parking and do not count toward the monthly limit on parking benefits.

Parking is considered provided by an employer if the parking is on property owned or leased by the employer, the employer pays for the parking, or the employer reimburses the employee for parking expenses.

Q 10:94

Q 10:97 What are the dollar limits on qualified transportation fringe benefits?

In the case of transportation in a commuter highway vehicle or transit passes, the monthly dollar limit is $100 a month adjusted annually for inflation. The dollar limit for 2008 is $115 per month. [Rev. Proc. 2007-66, 2007-45 I.R.B.] For 2007, the limit was $110. [Rev. Proc. 2006-53, 2006-48 IRB]

If an employee receives both benefits, the monthly limit applies to the combined benefits.

> **Example 10-5:** In 2007, Brendan, an employee of Bigco, is provided with transportation in a commuter highway vehicle at a cost of $40 a month and with a transit pass costing $85 a month—a total of $125 of benefits. The dollar limit for 2008 is $115 per month. Thus, Brendan has gross income of $10 each month.

In the case of qualified parking, the dollar limit on the exclusion from income is $175 per month indexed for inflation. [IRC § 132(f)(2)] The dollar limit for 2008 is $220 per month. [Rev. Proc. 2007-66, 2007-45 I.R.B.] For 2007, the limit was $215. [Rev. Proc. 2006-53, 2006-48 IRB]

Q 10:98 Can an employer offer employees a choice between cash or qualified transportation benefits?

An employer may offer employees a choice between cash or qualified transportation fringe benefits. An employee will not have any amount included in gross income solely because he or she was provided with such a choice between cash and transportation benefits. [IRC § 132(f)(3)]

The employee's election to receive benefits in lieu of cash compensation must be in writing or another permanent form, such as electronic media. The election must contain the date of the election, the amount of the compensation to be reduced, and the period for which the benefit will be provided. The election must relate to a fixed dollar amount or fixed percentage of compensation. [Reg. § 1.132-9, Q&A-12)]

The compensation reduction election must be made before the employee is able currently to receive the cash. The compensation reduction may not exceed the monthly limits for transportation benefits the employee elects to receive.

Q 10:99 Can an employer reimburse an employee in cash for the cost of a qualified transportation fringe benefit?

An employer can provide cash reimbursements to an employee for expenses incurred or paid by the employee for transportation in a commuter highway vehicle or qualified parking.

However, despite strenuous objections from employer groups, the transportation fringe benefit regulations provide that cash reimbursement for transit passes is permitted only if a voucher or similar item that may be exchanged only for a transit pass is not readily available for direct distribution by the employer to the employee. [IRC § 132(f)(3); Reg. § 1.132-9, Q&A-16]

Employers that make cash reimbursements for parking or transportation in a commuter highway vehicle must establish a bona fide reimbursement arrangement to ensure that employees have actually incurred transportation expenses. [Reg. § 1.132-9, Q&A-16(a)] The arrangement must include reasonable procedures to ensure that an amount equal to the reimbursement was incurred for qualified transportation expenses. In addition, the expense must be substantiated within a reasonable period of time.

Substantiation within 180 days will be considered reasonable. [Reg. § 1.132-9, Q&A-16(c)]Reasonable substantiation procedures may include presentation of a parking receipt or a used or unused time-sensitive transit pass (such as a monthly pass). If receipts are not provided in the ordinary course of business (for example, if the employee uses metered parking or transit passes that are not returned to the user), it is reasonable for the employer to accept the employee's certification of the type and amount of expenses incurred, provided the employer has no reason to doubt the employee. [Reg. § 1.132-9, Q&A-16(d)]

Q 10:100 What special rules apply to transit passes?

Transit passes must be distributed in-kind unless vouchers or similar items that may be redeemed only for passes are not readily available for direct distribution by the employer. If passes or vouchers are readily available, the in-kind distribution requirement is satisfied if distribution is made by the employer or by another person on behalf of the employer. For example, the in-kind distribution will be met if a transit operator credits amounts to employees' fare cards as a result of payments made to the operator by the employer. [Reg. § 1.132-9, Q&A-16(b)(1)]

A voucher or similar item is readily available for direct distribution unless:

1. The average annual fees that the employer must pay to obtain the vouchers (excluding reasonable and customary delivery charges that do not exceed $15 per order) are more than 1 percent of the average annual value of the vouchers.

2. Other nonfinancial restrictions cause vouchers not to be readily available.

Nonfinancial restrictions may include advance purchase requirements, purchase quantity requirements, or limits on voucher denominations. For example, a requirement that vouchers may be purchased only once a year may effectively prevent an employer from obtaining vouchers for distribution to employees. However, a requirement that vouchers can be purchased no more frequently than monthly does not effectively prevent the employer from obtaining vouchers for direct distribution to employees. Similarly, vouchers would not be considered readily available if the voucher provider requires a $1,000 minimum purchase and the employer needs only $200 of vouchers.

Q 10:100

Planning Point: An employer's internal administrative cost of providing the vouchers is not taken into account in determining whether vouchers are readily available.

Q 10:101 Are qualified transportation fringe benefits subject to income tax withholding and payroll taxes?

If a qualified transportation fringe benefit is excludable from an employee's income, it is not subject to income tax withholding or to FICA or FUTA taxes. However, benefits that exceed the dollar limits are subject to income tax withholding, FICA, and FUTA taxes. [IRC §§ 3401(a)(19), 3121(a)(20), 3306(b)(16)]

Q 10:102 Are qualified transportation fringes calculated on a monthly basis?

Yes. The value of transportation in a commuter highway vehicle, transit passes, and qualified parking is calculated on a monthly basis to determine whether the value of the benefit has exceeded the applicable statutory monthly limit on qualified transportation fringes. Except in the case of a transit pass, the applicable statutory monthly limit applies to qualified transportation fringes used by the employee in a month. In the case of a transit pass, the applicable statutory monthly limit applies to the transit passes provided by the employer to the employee in a month for that month or for any previous month in the calendar year.

In the case of transit passes, the exclusion is available to the extent passes distributed do not exceed the cumulative monthly limit for the year. [Reg. § 1.132-9(b)]

> **Example 10-6:** XYZ Company does not give any transit passes to Peter Nolan until the end of February 2006. At that time, XYZ gives Nolan $200 worth of passes. Since the value of the passes does not exceed the monthly limit figured cumulatively (2 months at $105), the passes are tax-free. Note, however, that if Nolan did not join the company until February, $95 would be taxable.

Q 10:103 Can employers distribute transit passes in advance?

Yes. Employers can distribute transit passes in advance for more than one month, but not for more than 12 months. [Reg. § 1.132-9, Q&A-9(b)] The value of the passes is excludable provided they do not exceed the combined monthly limits for all months in which they will be used.

If an employee terminates employment after receiving an advance distribution of transit passes, the value of passes provided for any month following the termination must be reported as wages for income tax purposes. However, if passes are provided in advance for no more than three months (e.g., for a calendar quarter) and an employee terminates employment before the last month of the period, the employer may exclude the value of the passes from wages for payroll taxes and income tax withholding. This rule does not apply if, at the time the passes were distributed, there was an established date for the employee's termination of employment (for example, if the employee had given notice of retirement). [Reg. § 1.132-9(c)]

Q 10:104 Can qualified transportation fringe benefits be provided to individuals who are not employees?

No. An employer may provide qualified transportation fringe benefits only to current employees. [Reg. § 1.132-9, Q&A-5]

Self-employed individuals are not employees for purposes of qualified transportation fringe benefit rules. Therefore, individuals who are partners, sole proprietors, 2 percent shareholders of S corporations (who are treated as partners for fringe benefit purposes), or independent contractors are not eligible for qualified transportation fringe benefits. [Reg. § 1.132-9, Q&A-24]

Working Condition Fringe Benefits

Q 10:105 What are working condition fringe benefits?

Working condition fringe benefits are property or services provided to an employee so that the employee can perform his or her job. The value of a working condition fringe benefit is excluded from the employee's if the employee could have deducted it as a business or depreciation expense if he or she had paid the cost. [IRC § 132(d); Reg. § 1.132-5(a)]The employee's use of the property or service must be related to the employer's trade or business and must be substantiated by adequate records or other evidence. [IRC §§ 162, 167; Reg. § 1.132-5]

The exclusion also applies to cash reimbursements to employees for qualifying expenses. However, the reimbursement must be made under an accountable reimbursement plan (see Q 10:118 *et seq.*)

Examples of excludable working condition fringe benefits include:

- Cars used for business or demonstration;
- Chauffeur services;
- Transportation required because of security concerns (such as terrorist activity, death threats, and threat of kidnapping or serious bodily harm);
- Airplanes and air transportation;
- Bodyguards;
- Use of consumer goods for product testing and evaluation;
- Travel expenses, including meals and lodging;
- Word processors and computers;
- Entertainment; and
- Club dues.

The exclusion does not apply to a physical examination program provided by the employer, even if participation is mandatory. [Reg. § 1.132-5(a)(1)(iv)]

Q 10:106 Are working condition fringe benefits subject to nondiscrimination requirements?

Except for product testing programs, the tax law does not impose any nondiscrimination rules on the availability of the exclusion for working condition fringe benefits. Therefore, an employer can make working condition fringe benefits available to selected employees if it wishes. [Reg. § 1.132-5(q)]

Split-Dollar Life Insurance

Q 10:107 What is split-dollar life insurance?

In a split-dollar life insurance arrangement, both the employer and the employee have interests in permanent life insurance policy coverage on the employee's life. At the employee's death, the employer receives a specified portion of the death benefit proceeds, and the employee's estate or beneficiary receives the balance.

Under a traditional split-dollar plan, the employer pays the portion of the annual policy premium that equals the increase in the policy's cash value for the year, and the employee pays the remainder of the premium. At the employee's death, the employer receives the cash surrender value of the policy (thus recouping most or all of its cost for the policy), and the employee's estate or beneficiary receives the remainder of the death benefit proceeds.

There are, however, a number of variations on the traditional split-dollar plan. These include equity split-dollar arrangements, which have become increasingly popular in recent years.

Under an equity split-dollar arrangement, the death benefit that goes to the employee's beneficiaries is not limited to what is left over after the employer gets the cash value; the beneficiaries get a portion of the cash value as well. The employer generally recovers only an amount equal to the cumulative premiums it paid. The remainder of the death benefit is paid to the beneficiaries. During the life of the policy, when the cash value buildup exceeds the cumulative premiums paid by the employer, the employee is considered to have an equity interest in the policy. If the policy is surrendered, the employee will receive a portion of the cash value.

Ownership of the policy generally takes one of two forms—endorsement method and collateral assignment method. Under the endorsement method, the employer is the owner of record, and an endorsement is added to the policy to identify the employee's beneficial interest in the policy. Under the collateral assignment method, the employee is the owner of record, but a collateral assignment of the policy is made to the employer to evidence the employer's beneficial interest in the life insurance.

Q 10:108 Can an employer deduct its premium payments under a split-dollar plan?

No. An employer cannot deduct premiums on a life insurance policy covering the life of an officer or employee if the employer is a beneficiary, directly or indirectly, under the policy, as is the case under a split-dollar plan. [IRC §§ 264(a)(1)]

Q 10:109 Does an employer's payment of part or all of the annual premium under a split-dollar insurance plan result in taxable income to the employee?

Yes. An employee is taxed on the value provided by the employer.

In the case of a traditional split-dollar arrangement, the employee is taxed on the death benefit coverage provided by the employer valued using an IRS table (currently Table 2001), based on the cost of one year of term insurance.

The tax treatment of an equity split-dollar life insurance arrangement depends on whether the employer or the employee is the owner of the policy.

When the employer is the owner of the policy, the employer is treated as providing an economic benefit to the employee that is taxable to the employee. The economic benefit is includes the value of the death benefit as well as any interest in the policy cash value to which the employee has current access (e.g., through withdrawals, borrowings, or surrender of the policy). When the employee is the owner, the tax treatment depends on whether the employee is obligated to repay the premiums paid by the employer. If no repayment is required, the full value of the employer-advanced premiums are included in the employee's income each year. If the employee is obligated to repay, each premium payment is treated as a separate loan by the employer to the employer. If the loan under the split-dollar arrangement is not a below-market loan, the general rules for loans apply. The employee may not deduct any interest paid on the split-dollar loan because it is personal interest. If the loan is a below market loan, the imputed interest will generally be treated as taxable compensation to the employee. [Reg. § 1.61-22]

Q 10:110 How are death benefit proceeds under a split-dollar plan treated for tax purposes?

The death benefits paid under a split-dollar life insurance plan are proceeds of life insurance; therefore, the amounts received by both the employer and the employee's estate or beneficiary generally are fully exempt from income tax. [IRC § 101(a)]

Q 10:108

Cafeteria Plans

Q 10:111 What is a cafeteria plan?

A cafeteria plan is written plan that offers participants the opportunity to choose between taxable benefits and cash and one or more qualified employee benefits that are excludable from income. [IRC § 125] Thus, employees have the opportunity to personalize their benefits to best suit their individual needs.

Salary reduction contributions are treated, for tax purposes, as employer contributions toward qualified benefits. Thus, a cafeteria plan can offer employees a choice between (1) salary or (2) reduced salary plus one or more qualified benefits.

> **Example 10-7:** Bigco offers its employees a plan under which they have the opportunity to have medical coverage if they reduce their salary by the amount of the employee premiums. This is a cafeteria plan. Employees have the choice of receiving salary only or a reduced salary plus medical coverage.

Q 10:112 What are qualified benefits?

Qualified benefits that can be offered on a pretax basis through a cafeteria plan include the following:

- Accident or health insurance coverage that is excludable from income (see Chapter 9);
- Adoption assistance (see Q 10:11 *et seq.*);
- Group term life insurance coverage (see Q 10:71 *et seq.*);
- Dependent care assistance (see Q 10:34 *et seq.*);
- Participation in a 401(k) retirement plan;
- Any other benefit permitted under IRS regulations, including vacation days.

[IRC § 125(f); Temp. Reg. § 1.125-2T; Prop. Reg. § § 1.125-1, Q&As 5, 7, 1.25-2, Q&As 4, 5]

Q 10:113 How must cafeteria plan elections be structured to ensure that qualified benefits do not lose their favorable tax treatment?

An employer must adopt certain procedures for benefit elections to ensure that cafeteria plan participants are not deemed to have constructively received—and therefore owe tax on—the cash compensation that they have elected not to receive. To do this, the employer plan must make certain that the choice of benefits is made before the cash becomes currently available. [Prop. Reg. § § 1.125-1, Q&As 9, 15; 1.125-2, Q&A 2]

Q 10:114 What if an employee wants to change an election in midstream?

As a general rule, cafeteria plan elections must be made before the beginning of the plan year—and cannot be changed later on. So, for example, if an employee wants to increase his 401(k) plan contributions in midyear, he is out of luck. The same holds true for an employee who passed up a benefit but later regrets that choice.

However, the regulations do authorize midyear election changes that involve more than just second-guessing. The regulations permit employees to change their benefit choices when they experience one of the following changes in status:

1. Changes in legal marital status, such as marriage, death of a spouse, divorce, legal separation, or annulment.

2. Changes in the number of an employee's dependents as a result of certain events, including birth, adoption, placement for adoption, or death of a dependent.

3. Changes in employment status, including the loss of a job or start of a new job by the employee, spouse, or a dependent.

4. Changes in work schedule that reduce or increase the work hours of the employee, spouse, or a dependent, including a switch from part-time to full-time work, a strike or lockout, or return from an unpaid leave of absence.

5. Changes in a dependent's status that make the dependent newly eligible or ineligible for benefits, such as attainment of age by a minor, a change in student status, or similar circumstances.

6. Changes in residence or worksite by the employee, spouse, or a dependent.

[Reg. § 1.125-4]

Planning Point: Whether a particular change in status will trigger an election change depends on the type of benefit involved. For example an employee's change in residence may trigger a health benefit election change if the employee originally opted for a region-specific plan. On the other hand, a change in residence would not normally justify a change in life insurance benefits or adoption assistance.

In addition, an election change must generally correspond to the employee's change in status. For example, if an employee's child reaches the age when he or she can no longer be covered as a dependent under the plan, an election change to drop the coverage for the child would be consistent with the change of status. However, an election to drop the employee's own health coverage would not be permitted.

In addition to changes triggered by a change in status, a cafeteria plan may also allow election changes when there are significant changes in the cost or coverage provided by a particular cafeteria plan benefit. [Reg. § 1.125-4(f)]

Q 10:114

Planning Point: An employer may permit midyear election changes that are authorized by the regulations—but an employer is not required to do so. Therefore, the circumstances under which changes will be permitted should be spelled out in the cafeteria plan document.

Q 10:115 What must be included in the cafeteria plan document?

The plan document for a cafeteria plan must include all of the following information:

1. Eligibility requirements for participation in the plan.

2. Procedures for making benefit elections under the plan, including the time period for making elections; the extent to which elections are irrevocable; and how long elections will remain effective.

3. Benefits available under the plan and the periods during which benefits will be provided.

4. The time periods during which benefits will be provided.

5. The type of employer contributions that will be made to the plan (for example, salary reduction or employer contributions or both).

6. The maximum amount of elective (or salary reduction) contributions that may be made by an employee.

7. The plan year of the cafeteria plan.

If a cafeteria plan includes the option to receive benefits contained in other separate written plans, such as a group term life insurance plan or a medical plan, the benefits under those other plans do not have to be described in detail in the cafeteria plan document. Instead, the cafeteria plan can incorporate them by reference. However, if the cafeteria plan offers different maximum levels of coverage, for example, those differences must be described in the cafeteria plan document. [Prop. Reg. §§ 1.125-1, Q&A 3; 1.125-2, Q&A 3]

Planning Point: The cafeteria plan rules recognize two types of cafeteria plans: an integrated plan, in which all of the benefits are described, and a "spider-type" plan that refers to other, freestanding plans. (The name comes from the fact that a diagram of this type of plan would look like a spider's legs reaching out from a main body).

Q 10:116 Who can participate in a cafeteria plan?

All participants in a cafeteria plan must be employees. [IRC § 125(d)(1)(A); Prop. Reg. § 1.125-1, Q&A 4] A cafeteria plan cannot cover self-employed individuals and more than 2 percent shareholders in S corporations.

Q 10:117 Is a cafeteria plan required to satisfy nondiscrimination rules?

Yes. A cafeteria plan cannot discriminate in favor of highly compensated employees as to eligibility to participate in the plan or actual benefits provided under the plan. [IRC § 125(b)(1)]If the plan does discriminate, the highly compensated employees are not eligible for favorable tax treatment. The value of any cash or taxable benefits they could have received must be included in wages. However, the tax treatment of rank-and-file employees is not affected.

In addition, the tax law provides that if a cafeteria plan favors key employees (including highly paid officers and certain owners), those employees will be taxed on the cash or taxable benefits they could have received in lieu of qualified benefits. A plan favors key employees if more than 25 percent of the total nontaxable benefit provided for all employees goes to key employees. [IRC § 125(a)(2)]

Accountable Plans

Q 10:118 What is an accountable reimbursement plan?

When an employer reimburses an employee for business-related expenses, the reimbursement is not taxable income to the employee—provided it is made under an accountable plan. [IRC § 62(a)(2)(A); Reg. § 1.62-2]

A reimbursement arrangement must meet four requirements to qualify as an accountable plan.

1. *Business connection.* The reimbursement must be for job-related expenses that would be deductible by the employee if he or she were not reimbursed. An advance to an employee will qualify only if it is for expenses the employee is reasonably expected to incur.

2. *Substantiation.* The employee must provide the employer with the same detailed expense records that would be required to claim the deduction on his or her return. As a general rule, these records must substantiate the amount of the expenses and the time, place, and business purpose. There are, however, substantiation shortcuts for certain expenses. For example, per diem allowances for travel expenses that stay within IRS-approved rates will be deemed substantiated if the employee substantiates the time, place, and business purpose of the trip; the employee does not have to account for his or her actual expenses. Similarly, a mileage allowance for business car trips that does not exceed the IRS-approved rate for the year will be deemed substantiated if the employee accounts for the time, place, and business purpose of the trip and the number of miles driven.

3. *Return of unspent amounts.* If an employer advances funds to cover business expenses, the employer must require the employee to return any unspent amounts. If the employee does not do so, the arrangement will still qualify as an accountable plan to the extent of substantiated expenses. Only the excess amount is taxable.

4. *Timeliness.* The employee must substantiate the expenses and return any unspent amounts within a reasonable period of time after the expenses are incurred.

Q 10:119 What if a reimbursement arrangement does not meet the accountable plan requirements?

If an expense arrangement does not meet the accountable plan requirements, the reimbursements and advances are taxable income to the employee. The employee can deduct the expenses as employee business expenses (provided the employee can meet the substantiation requirements). However, employee business expenses are treated as a miscellaneous itemized deduction. Thus, the employee will not benefit from the deduction if the employee does not itemize deductions. Moreover, even if the employee does itemize, miscellaneous itemized deductions are deductible only to the extent the total exceeds 2 percent of the employee's adjusted gross income. [IRC § 67]

Chapter 11

Retirement Plans

Employer-sponsored retirement plans are a form of deferred compensation and basically fall into two categories: qualified and nonqualified. Qualified plans offer more tax advantages but must meet stringent requirements. For example, qualified plans generally cannot discriminate against rank-and-file employees in terms of benefits. Nonqualified plans are more flexible and are often used by employers to reward key employees as a supplement to qualified plans.

Individual retirement accounts (IRAs) are set up by individuals outside of the employer-employee context and are available to anyone with earnings from employment or self-employment.

Qualified Plans—The Basics

Q 11:1 What are qualified retirement plans?

A qualified retirement plan is a deferred compensation arrangement that meets the qualification standards of Internal Revenue Code (IRC or Code) Section 401. By meeting these standards, the plan is accorded special tax treatment.

Q 11:2 What is the special tax treatment available to qualified retirement plans?

Employees do not include qualified plan benefits in gross income until the benefits are distributed even though the plan is funded and the benefits are nonforfeitable. [IRC § 402]Tax deferral is provided under qualified plans from the time contributions are made until the time benefits are received. The employer is entitled to a current deduction (within limits) for contributions to a qualified plan even though an employee's income inclusion is deferred. [IRC § 404]Contributions to a qualified plan are held in a tax-exempt trust. [IRC § 501(a)]

A primary purpose of the qualification standards and related rules governing qualified plans is to ensure that qualified plans benefit an employer's rank-and-file employees as well as highly compensated employees. They also define the rights of plan participants and beneficiaries and provide some limit on the tax benefits for qualified plans.

Q 11:3 What types of qualified retirement plans are available?

Qualified plans are broadly classified into two categories based on the nature of the benefits provided: defined contribution plans and defined benefit pension plans.

Under a defined benefit pension plan, benefit levels are specified under a plan formula. The general assets of the trust established under the plan fund the benefits under a defined benefit plan; individual accounts are not maintained for employees participating in the plan. [IRC § 414(j)] The typical pension plan is a defined benefit plan.

Benefits under defined contribution plans are based solely on the contributions (and earnings thereon) allocated to separate accounts maintained for each plan participant. [IRC § 414(i)]There are several different types of defined contribution plans, including money purchase pension plans, target benefit plans, profit-sharing plans, stock bonus plans, and employee stock ownership plans (ESOPs). A profit-sharing plan or stock bonus plan may include a qualified cash or deferred arrangement (a "section 401(k)" plan; see below).

The various different types of plans are in part historical and reflect the various different ways in which employers structure deferred compensation programs for their employees.

Q 11:4 What is a qualified profit-sharing plan?

Employer contributions to a profit-sharing plan are ordinarily based on profits. The employer is not required to contribute any particular percentage of profits, but contributions must be substantial and recurring. A profit-sharing plan must have a definite written formula for allocating profits among individual accounts maintained for employees. [Reg. § 1.401-1(b)(1)(ii)]

Q 11:2

Q 11:5 What is a money purchase plan?

A money purchase pension plan is like a profit-sharing plan except that an employer's contributions are not discretionary. The plan must have a contribution formula. [Reg. § 1.401-1(b)(1)(i)]

Q 11:6 What are stock bonus and ESOP plans?

A qualified stock bonus plan provides benefits in the form of stock in the employer corporation. Stock bonus plans generally must satisfy the requirements that apply to profit-sharing plans.

An ESOP is a qualified stock bonus plan or a combination stock bonus and money purchase plan that invests primarily in employer securities. [IRC § 4975(e)(7)] The ESOP designation offers certain advantages. For example, an ESOP can qualify for an exemption from the prohibited transaction rules that apply to loans (see below).

Q 11:7 What is a cash or deferred arrangement?

Cash or deferred arrangements, often called 401(k) plans, allow an employee to choose between (1) taking compensation in cash or (2) having the employer contribute the amount to a profit-sharing or stock bonus plan on the employee's behalf. If the employee elects to have the amount contributed to a plan, the contribution is excludable from the employee's income. [IRC § § 401(k); 402(e)(3)]

Beginning in 2006, a plan may permit an employee who makes elective contributions under a qualified 401(k) plan to designate some or all of those contributions as "Roth" contributions. Although designated Roth contributions are elective contributions under a qualified cash or deferred arrangement, unlike pre-tax elective contributions, they are currently *includible* in gross income. However, a qualified distribution of designated Roth contributions is *excludable* from gross income. [IRC § § 402A]For more details on Roth 401 (k) arrangements, see Q 11:78.

Coverage and Nondiscrimination Requirements for Qualified Plans

Q 11:8 Do qualified retirement plans have to meet coverage and nondiscrimination requirements?

Yes. They are designed to ensure that qualified plans benefit a significant portion of an employer's rank-and-file employees compared to the portion of highly compensated employees benefiting under the plan.

These rules include numerical minimum coverage rules, [IRC § 410(b)] a minimum participation rule requiring that a defined benefit pension plan benefit a minimum number of employees, [IRC § 401(a)(26)] and a general nondiscrimination requirement. [IRC § 401(a)(4)]

Special nondiscrimination rules apply to 401(k) plans, employer-matching contributions, after-tax employee contributions, and to "top-heavy" plans.

For purposes of applying the nondiscrimination rules, the maximum amount of compensation that may be taken into account is $210,000 (for 2005). [IRC § 404(l)]

Q 11:9 What is the minimum coverage requirement?

The group of employees covered under a qualified retirement plan must include a minimum percentage of the employer's non-highly compensated employees. The minimum percentage is generally determined by reference to the percentage of highly compensated employees who benefit under the plan. Two tests are available for satisfying the minimum coverage requirement: the ratio percentage test and the average benefits test.

Ratio percentage test. Under the ratio percentage test, the percentage of the employer's non-highly compensated employees who benefit under the plan and the percentage of the employer's highly compensated employees who benefit under the plan are determined. The ratio of the two percentages (ratio percentage) is determined by dividing the non-highly compensated employee percentage by the highly compensated employee percentage. If the ratio percentage is at least 70 percent, the plan satisfies the ratio percentage test and, therefore, the minimum coverage requirement. [IRC § 410(b)(1)(A)]

The ratio percentage test can be most easily understood using an example of a plan that covers all the employer's highly compensated employees. In that case, the percentage of highly compensated employees covered is 100 percent. As long as the plan covers at least 70 percent of the employer's non-highly compensated employees, the plan's ratio percentage will be at least 70 percent, and the plan will satisfy the ratio percentage test. However, if a plan covering 100 percent of the highly compensated employees covers less than 70 percent of the non-highly compensated employees, the plan will not satisfy the minimum coverage requirements by means of the ratio percentage test.

Average benefits test. If a plan does not satisfy the ratio percentage test, it must satisfy the average benefits test, which includes several components. First, the classification of employees covered by the plan (such as hourly employees or employees of a particular division) must be reasonable and reflect objective business criteria.

In addition, the ratio percentage of the plan must exceed a threshold established under the regulations. The threshold depends on the percentage of non-highly compensated employees in the employer's workforce as a whole (non-highly compensated employee concentration percentage). The higher the non-highly compensated employee concentration percentage, the lower the required ratio percentage for the plan. In some cases, additional facts and circumstances must be considered.

Q 11:9

The last component, called the "average benefit percentage test" under the regulations, requires an analysis of the benefits provided to employees under the employer's qualified retirement plans.

The average benefit percentage test involves three determinations: (1) individual benefit percentages for the employees, that is, the employee's benefits as a percentage of the employee's compensation; (2) average benefit percentages for the group of non-highly compensated employees and the group of highly compensated employees; and (3) the ratio of the average percentages for the groups. For this purpose, benefits provided under all of the employer's plans and all of the employees in the workforce, even those not covered by any plan, are taken into account. The test requires that the average benefit percentage of the non-highly compensated employees must be at least 70 percent of the average benefit percentage of the highly compensated employees. [Reg. § 1.410(b)-2, -4, and -5]

Q 11:10 What is the minimum participation requirement?

A defined benefit plan is not a qualified plan unless it benefits no fewer than the *lesser* of (1) 50 employees of the employer or (2) the *greater* of (a) 40 percent of all employees of the employer or (b) 2 employees (1 employee if there is only 1 employee). [IRC § 401(a)(26)]

Q 11:11 What is the general nondiscrimination requirement?

The contributions or benefits provided under a qualified retirement plan must not discriminate in favor of highly compensated employees. [IRC § 401(a)(4)] The regulations provide detailed and exclusive rules for determining whether a plan satisfies the general nondiscrimination requirement. Under the regulations, the amount of contributions or benefits provided under the plan; all benefits, rights, and features offered under the plan; and the timing of plan amendments must be tested. The regulations provide that both the form of the plan and the effect of the plan in operation determine whether the plan is nondiscriminatory.

Safe harbors and general tests. The regulations offer several plan designs that satisfy the general nondiscrimination rules on a safe-harbor basis so that little or no testing is required. [Reg. § 1.401(a)(4)-1 through 1.401(a)(4)-13] The safe harbors for defined contribution plans and defined benefit plans involve plan designs that generally provide contributions or benefits that are a uniform percentage of compensation.

If a plan does not satisfy one of the safe harbors, it is subject to the general tests provided in the regulations. [Reg. §§ 1.401(a)(4)-2(c); 1.401(a)(4)- 3(c)]These general tests are very complicated. Like the average benefit percentage test, they involve a determination of individual contribution or benefit rates for employees in the plan and a comparison of the rates of the highly compensated employees and the non-highly compensated employees. Although average benefit rates for the two groups are compared under the average benefit percentage test, the general nondiscrimination tests compare the rates for individual employees.

A plan passes the general test if, for each contribution or benefit rate that applies to a highly compensated employee, the same rate (or a higher rate) applies to a sufficient number of non-highly compensated employees to make up a group that satisfies the minimum coverage requirements. In the case of a defined benefit plan, the general test applies twice, once on the basis of the normal retirement benefits provided under the plan and again on the basis of the other benefits (such as early retirement benefits) that are actuarially the most valuable benefits provided under the plan.

Generally, the general test for contribution rates applies to a defined contribution plan, and the general test for benefit rates applies to a defined benefit plan. However, the regulations also permit a defined contribution plan to be tested on an equivalent benefits basis or a defined benefit plan to be tested on an equivalent contributions basis. [Reg. § 1.401(a)(4)-8]

Q 11:12 Can an employer exclude certain employees?

Yes. An employer is permitted to exclude from a plan employees who either are under age 21 or have been employed for less than a year. [IRC § 410(a)(1)(A)] Alternatively, the employer may use a lower age or service requirement, or none at all, to determine eligibility for the plan. For example, the employer may cover all employees age 21, regardless of their service, or the employer could cover all employees who have been employed for six months, regardless of their ages.

If the employer does not cover excludable employees in the plan, they are disregarded in applying the minimum coverage requirements and the general nondiscrimination rules. If the employer covers any excludable employees in the plan, two options apply. First, test the plan by taking into account all employees in the workforce who meet the plan's eligibility requirements. Second, test the portion of the plan covering nonexcludable employees, taking into account all the nonexcludable employees in the workforce; the portion of the plan covering excludable employees is tested separately, taking into account all the excludable employees in the workforce who meet the plan's eligibility requirements. [Reg. § 1.401(a)(26)-6]

Q 11:13 Does a special nondiscrimination test apply to elective contributions under 401(k) plans?

Yes. A special nondiscrimination test applies to the elective deferrals of employees. The test is satisfied if the actual deferral percentage for eligible highly compensated employees for a plan year is equal to or less than either (1) 125 percent of the actual deferral percentage of all non-highly compensated employees eligible to defer under the arrangement or (2) the lesser of 200 percent of the actual deferral percentage of all eligible non-highly compensated employees or the actual deferral percentage for all eligible non-highly compensated employees plus 2 percentage points. [IRC § 401(m)(2)]

For example, if the actual deferral percentage for non-highly compensated employees is 5 percent, then the actual deferral percentage for highly compensated employees cannot exceed 6.25 percent under the first test (5 + 1.25), or 7 percent under the second test (the lesser of 5 + 2 or 5 × 200 percent).

The actual deferral percentage for a group of employees is the average of the ratios (calculated separately for each employee in the group) of the contributions paid to the plan on behalf of the employees to the employees' compensation. The maximum permitted actual deferral percentage for highly compensated employees for a year is generally determined by reference to the actual deferral percentage for non-highly compensated employees for the preceding year (although testing may be done on a current-year basis).

If a 401(k) plan satisfies the special nondiscrimination test, it is treated as satisfying the general nondiscrimination rules with respect to the amount of elective deferrals. However, the group of employees eligible to participate in the arrangement is still required to satisfy the minimum coverage test.

Safe harbor. As an alternative to the special nondiscrimination test, a 401(k) plan may satisfy a design-based safe harbor. [IRC § 401(k)(12)]Under the safe harbor rule, a plan satisfies the contribution requirements for a 401(k) plan if the employer either (1) satisfies certain matching contribution requirements or (2) makes nonelective contributions to a defined contribution plan of at least 3 percent of an employee's compensation on behalf of each non-highly compensated employee who is eligible to participate in the arrangement without regard to whether the employee makes elective contributions under the arrangement. In addition, under the safe harbor rule, the plan must satisfy a notice requirement. The notice requirement is satisfied if each employee eligible to participate in the 401(k) plan is given written notice, within a reasonable period before any year, of the employee's rights and obligations under the arrangement.

IRS regulations make it clear that employers have considerable flexibility in applying the nondiscrimination rules. For example, an employer may switch from numerical nondiscrimination testing to the design-based safe harbor. However, the regulations also make it clear that the rules are intended to be applied by employers in a manner that does not make use of changes in plan testing procedures or other plan provisions to inappropriately inflate the actual deferral percentage of non-highly compensated employees in order to increase contributions by highly compensated employees. According to the IRS, the nondiscrimination requirements are part of an overall requirement that benefits or contributions cannot discriminate in favor of highly compensated employees. Therefore, a plan will not be treated as satisfying that requirement if there are repeated changes that have the effect of distorting the deferral percentages of non-highly compensated employees in order to increase contributions by highly compensated employees. [Reg. § § 1.401(k)-1 through 1.401(k)-6, 12/28/04]

Q 11:14 Does a special nondiscrimination rule apply to employer matching contributions and employee contributions under a defined contribution plan?

Yes. This special nondiscrimination test is similar to the special nondiscrimination test applicable to 401(k) plans. [IRC § 401(m)] Contributions that satisfy the special nondiscrimination test are treated as satisfying the general nondiscrimination rules with respect to the amount of contributions.

For this purpose, the term "employer matching contributions" means any employer contribution made on account of (1) an employee contribution or (2) an elective deferral under a 401(k) plan. [IRC § 401(m)(4)]

Q 11:15 For purposes of the nondiscrimination rules, who is a "highly compensated" employee?

A highly compensated employee is an employee who (1) was a 5 percent owner of the employer at any time during the current or prior year, or (2) for the prior year, received more than $105,000 (for 2008; $100,000 for 2007) in compensation from the employer, and, if the employer elects, was among the top 20 percent most highly compensated employees. [IRC § 414(q)]

Q 11:16 What happens if a qualified retirement plan fails to comply with the nondiscrimination requirements?

If a plan fails to meet the nondiscrimination requirements (or other qualification standards), then the special tax benefits for qualified plans do not apply, and benefits and contributions are taxed under normal income tax rules.

In general, this means that contributions to the plan are includible in the employees' gross income when such contributions are no longer subject to a substantial risk of forfeiture. [IRC § § 402(b), 83] Amounts actually distributed or made available to an employee are generally includible in income in the year distributed or made available under the rules applicable to taxation of annuities. [IRC § 72]. Special sanctions apply in the case of failure to meet certain qualification rules (e.g., 10 percent penalty tax on excess contributions to a qualified plan). [IRC § 4979]

Other Qualified Plan Requirements

Q 11:17 Are there limits on contributions made to and benefits received from qualified retirement plans?

Yes. Limits apply to contributions made to a defined contribution plan and benefits received under a defined benefit plan, [IRC § 415] the amount of compensation that may be taken into account under a plan for determining contributions and benefits, [IRC § 401(a)(17)]and the maximum amount of elective deferrals that an individual may make to a 401(k) plan. [IRC § 402(g)]

Q 11:14

The Code now allows certain plan participants to make "catch-up" contributions in excess of the standard contribution limit (see below).

Q 11:18 What is the contribution limit for a defined contribution plan?

Under a defined contribution plan, the annual additions to the plan with respect to each plan participant cannot exceed the lesser of (1) 100 percent of compensation or (2) $40,000 for plan years beginning after 2001. [IRC § 415(c)(1)] The $40,000 limit is indexed in $1,000 increments for inflation occurring after July 1, 2001. For 2008, the dollar limit is $46,000 ($45,000 for 2007).

Annual additions are the sum of employer contributions, employee contributions, and forfeitures with respect to an individual under all defined contribution plans of the same employer.

Q 11:19 What is the benefit limit for defined benefit plans?

Under a defined benefit plan, the maximum annual benefit payable at retirement is generally the lesser of (1) 100 percent of average compensation for the three consecutive years for which compensation is the highest, or (2) $160,000. The benefit limit is indexed in $5,000 increments for inflation occurring after July 1, 2001. [IRC § 415(b)(1)] For 2008, the dollar limit is $185,000 ($180,000 for 2007). In the case of a participant who has retired or otherwise terminated employment with a vested benefit, the high three compensation limitation is also subject to a cost-of-living adjustment. [IRC § 415(d)] Each year, the IRS issues an adjustment factor that increases the prior year's adjusted high three years compensation limit (e.g., see IRS News Release IR-2007-171, October 18, 2007). Recently finalized regulations limit the participant's high-three compensation to the maximum compensation that may be taken into account under Internal Revenue Code Section 401(a)(17) (see next question). [Reg. § 1.415(b)-1(a)(5)]

Q 11:20 Is there a limit on the amount of compensation on which contributions and benefits can be based?

Yes. The annual compensation of each participant that may be taken into account in determining contributions and benefits under a plan is limited to $225,000 for 2007 and $230,000 for 2008. [IRC § 401(a)(17)]

Q 11:21 What is the limit on elective deferrals to a 401(k) plan?

The IRC imposes an annual dollar limit on an employee's elective deferrals to a 401(k) plan. The limit is $15,500 in 2007 and 2008. [IRC § 402(g)(1)]The limit is indexed for inflation, but only in $500 increments.

Q 11:22 What are "catch-up" contributions?

Catch-up contributions allow employees to make additional retirement plan contributions as they near retirement. This is aimed at employees who did not contribute sufficient amounts in their younger days and now have to "catch up." However, the tax rules make no distinction between those who have contributed the maximum all along and those who did not—all "catch-up eligible participants" can make catch-up contributions.

An employee is a catch-up eligible participant if he or she is otherwise eligible to contribute to the plan and will be age 50 or older before the end of his or her tax year (normally, the calendar year). If the plan does not operate on the calendar year, an employee is treated as a catch-up eligible participant beginning on January 1 of the calendar year that includes his or her 50th birthday, without regard to the plan year. [Reg. § 1.414(v)-1(g)(3)]

Under the catch-up provision, the otherwise applicable dollar limit on elective deferrals under a Section 401(k) plan (as well as those for SEP and SIMPLE plans; see below) is increased for eligible participants. [IRC § 414(v)(2)] The catch-up contribution provision does not apply to after-tax employee contributions.

The additional amount of elective contributions that may be made by an eligible individual participating in such a plan is the lesser of (1) the "applicable dollar amount" or (2) the participant's compensation for the year reduced by any other elective deferrals of the participant for the year. The applicable dollar amount under a Section 401(k) plan is $5,000 for 2007 and 2008. The $5,000 amount is adjusted for inflation in $500 increments.

An eligible employee's contributions are treated as catch-up contributions to the extent they exceed the normal plan contribution limits and do not exceed the maximum limit on catch-up contributions. [Reg. § 1.414(v)-1(a)] In other words, the last dollars contributed for the year are considered catch-up contributions.

Catch-up contributions are not subject to any other contribution limits and are not taken into account in applying other contribution limits. So, for example, the catch-up contributions can be made even if they push total annual additions to a defined contribution plan over the $46,000 limit for 2008.

In addition, catch-up contributions are not subject to the Code's nondiscrimination rules. However, a plan will fail the nondiscrimination tests unless the plan allows all eligible individuals participating in the plan to make the same election for catch-up contributions. [Reg. § 1.414(v)-1(e)]

An employer is permitted to make matching contributions with respect to catch-up contributions. Any such matching contributions are subject to the normal applicable rules.

Example 11-1: Employee *A* is a highly compensated employee who is over age 50 and who participates in a Section 401(k) plan sponsored by *A*'s employer. The maximum annual deferral limit is $15,500 for 2008. After application of the special nondiscrimination rules applicable to Section 401(k) plans, the maximum elective deferral *A* may make for 2008 is $10,000. Under the catch-up provision, *A* is able to make additional elective deferrals of $5,000.

Q 11:22

Example 11-2: Employee *B*, who is over 50, is a participant in a Section 401(k) plan. *B*'s compensation for the year is $30,000. The maximum annual deferral limit is $15,500 for 2008. Under the terms of the plan, the maximum permitted deferral is 10 percent of compensation or, in *B*'s case, $3,000. *B* can contribute up to $8,000 for the year ($3,000 under the normal operation of the plan, and an additional $5,000 under the catch-up provision).

Q 11:23 How quickly must contributions and benefits vest in qualified plans?

A plan is not a qualified retirement plan unless a participant's employer-provided benefit vests at least as rapidly as under one of two alternative minimum vesting schedules: (1) "cliff" vesting or (2) graduated vesting. [IRC § 411(a)(2)] For tax years generally beginning before 2007, accelerated vesting schedules apply to benefits attributable to employer matching contributions. For tax years generally beginning after December 31, 2006, the accelerated vesting schedules apply to benefits attributable to all employer contributions to defined contribution plans, and the slower vesting schedules apply to benefits attributable to all employer contributions to defined benefit plans.

Cliff Vesting. In cliff vesting, an employee's rights in accrued benefits derived from employer contributions fully vest after a set period of service. Vesting is keyed to length of service with the employer, not length of participation in the plan. If employees become fully vested after the applicable period of service, a plan may provide for no vesting at all before the completion of that period of service.

Graduated Vesting. As an alternative to cliff vesting a plan may adopt graduated vesting. In graduated vesting, a set portion of accrued benefits attributable to employer contributions must vest as an employee completes a set period of service. There are two statutory schedules for graduated vesting: two-to-six year vesting, and three-to-seven year vesting.

2 to 6 Year Vesting

Years of Service	Nonforfeitable Percentage
2	20%
3	40%
4	60%
5	80%
6 or more	100%

3 to 7 Year Vesting

Years of Service	Nonforfeitable Percentage
3	20%
4	40%
5	60%
6	80%
7 or more	100%

Plan years beginning before 2007. For plan years generally beginning before 2007, the applicable vesting schedule is determined by whether the employer contributions are matching or nonmatching. These rules operate as follows:

- Cliff vesting. In both defined benefit plans and defined contribution plans, accrued benefits attributable to employer matching contributions must vest after the employee has completed three years of service. Other employer contributions (non-matching contributions) must vest after the employee has completed five years of service.

- Graduated vesting. in both defined benefit plans and defined contribution plans, the two-to-six year vesting schedule applies to employer matching contributions; and the three-to-seven-year vesting schedule applies to other employer contributions (non-matching contributions).

Plan years beginning after 2006. For plan years generally beginning after 2006, the applicable vesting schedule is determined by whether the plan is a defined contribution plan or a defined benefit plan. These rules operate as follows: [IRC § 411(a)(2)]

- Cliff vesting. In a defined contribution plan, accrued benefits derived from all employer contributions, both matching and non-matching, must vest after an employee has completed three years of service. In a defined benefit plan, accrued benefits derived from all employer contributions, both matching and non-matching, must vest after an employee has completed five years of service.

- Graduated vesting. In a defined contribution plan, the two-to-six-year vesting schedule applies to all employer contributions, both matching and non-matching. In a defined benefit plan, the three-to-seven-year vesting schedule applies to all employer contributions, both matching and non-matching.

Q 11:24 Does the IRC impose restrictions on the transactions a qualified plan may engage in?

Yes. The Code imposes an excise tax on certain prohibited transactions between a plan and a "disqualified" person. [IRC § 4975 (c)] Prohibited transactions generally include the following:

- A transfer of plan income or assets to, or use of them by or for the benefit of, a disqualified person.

- Any act of a fiduciary by which he or she deals with plan income or assets in his or her own interest.

Q 11:24

- The receipt of consideration by a fiduciary for his or her own account from any party dealing with the plan in a transaction that involves plan income or assets.

- Any of the following acts between the plan and a disqualified person: (1) selling, exchanging, or leasing property; (2) lending money or extending credit; and (3) furnishing goods, services, or facilities.

Some transactions are exempt from the prohibited transaction restrictions. For example, a prohibited transaction does not take place if a disqualified person receives any benefit to which he or she is entitled as a plan participant or beneficiary. However, the benefit must be figured and paid under the same terms as for all other participants and beneficiaries. An exemption also applies to certain loans from a plan (see below).

Q 11:25 Who are "disqualified persons"?

Disqualified persons include:

1. A fiduciary of the plan;

2. A person providing services to the plan;

3. An employer, any of whose employees are covered by the plan;

4. An employee organization, any of whose members are covered by the plan;

5. Any direct or indirect owner of 50 percent or more of any of the following: (a) the combined voting power of all classes of stock entitled to vote, or the total value of shares of all classes of stock of a corporation, (b) a capital interest or profits interest of a partnership, (c) the beneficial interest of a trust or unincorporated enterprise that is an employer or an employee organization described in (3) or (4);

6. A member of the family of any individual described in (1), (2), (3), or (5) (a member of a family is the spouse, ancestor, lineal descendant, or any spouse of a lineal descendant);

7. A corporation, partnership, trust, or estate of which (or in which) any direct or indirect owner holds 50 percent or more of the interest described in 5(a), (b), or (c);

8. An officer, director (or an individual having powers or responsibilities similar to those of officers or directors), a 10 percent or more shareholder, or highly compensated employee (earning 10 percent or more of the yearly wages of an employer) of a person described in (3), (4), (5), or (7); and

9. A 10 percent or more (in capital or profits) partner or joint venturer of a person described in (3), (4), (5), or (7).

[IRC § 4975 (c)(2)]

Q 11:26 What is the excise tax on prohibited transactions?

The initial tax on a prohibited transaction is 15 percent of the amount involved for each year (or part of a year) in the taxable period. If the transaction is not corrected within the taxable period, an additional tax of 100 percent of the amount involved is imposed. [IRC § 4975(b)]

Both taxes are payable by any disqualified person who participated in the transaction (other than a fiduciary acting only as such). If more than one person takes part in the transaction, each person can be jointly and severally liable for the entire tax.

The amount involved in a prohibited transaction is the greater of the following amounts:

- The money and fair market value of any property given; or
- The money and fair market value of any property received.
- If services are performed, the amount involved is any excess compensation given or received.

The taxable period starts on the transaction date and ends on the earliest of the following days:

- The day the IRS mails a notice of deficiency for the tax;
- The day the IRS assesses the tax; or
- The day the correction of the transaction is completed.

Q 11:27 Can a disqualified person who is also a plan participant get a loan from the plan?

Yes. The Code carves out an exemption to the prohibited transaction rules for loans between a qualified plan and disqualified persons who are plan participants. Loans to participants are permitted if loans are available to all participants on a reasonably equivalent basis, are not made available to highly compensated employees in amounts greater than are made available to other employees, are made under specific provisions in the plan, bear a reasonable rate of interest, and are adequately secured. [IRC § 4975(d)(1)](A loan may be treated as a taxable distribution unless it meets certain requirements; see below.) This exemption from the prohibited transaction rules applies to loans to sole proprietors and partners as well as common-law employees. [IRC § 4975(f)(6)(B)]

Q 11:28 Is there any way to correct problems with a qualified retirement plan?

The Service's Employee Plans Compliance Resolution System (EPCRS) permits employers to correct technical and administrative problems with the plans in order to retain tax-favored status. [Rev. Proc. 2006-27, I.R.B. 2006-22] EPCRS may be used by most qualified plans, including simplified employee pensions (SEPs) and SIMPLE IRA plans.

There are three components of ECPRS:

- The Self-Correction Program (SCP) permits a plan sponsor to correct "insignificant operational failures" in certain simple plans, such as 403(b) plans, SEPs or SIMPLE IRA plans. These corrections can be made without having to notify the IRS and without paying any fee or sanction.

- The Voluntary Correction Program (VCP) allows a plan sponsor, at any time before an audit, to pay a limited fee and receive the IRS's approval for a correction of a qualified plan, a 403(b) plan, SEP or SIMPLE IRA plan.

- The Correction on Audit Program (Audit CAP) allows a sponsor to correct a failure or an error that has been identified on audit and pay a sanction based on the nature, extent and severity of the failure being corrected.

Plan sponsors who fail to take advantage EPCRS will not receive the favorable tax treatment available in EPCRS programs if the problems are discovered upon examination. EPCRS is unavailable in cases where either the plan or the plan sponsor has been a party to an abusive tax avoidance transaction and the plan failure is directly or indirectly related to the abusive tax avoidance transaction.

Top-Heavy Plans

Q 11:29 What is a top-heavy plan?

A top-heavy plan is a qualified plan where the bulk of benefits and contributions go to the owners and officers of the employer. The Code imposes additional restrictions on owner-dominated plans to insure that a plan's delivery of contributions and benefits is not "top-heavy" in favor of owners and officers. [IRC §416]

Important differences exist between the top-heavy rules and the general nondiscrimination and vesting rules that apply to other qualified plans. Top-heavy rules differ from the general nondiscrimination rules in:

- How they measure or test whether top employees receive a disproportionate share of contributions or benefits, compared with rank-and-file workers; and

- Requiring top-heavy plans to meet more generous minimum standards for benefits to workers, including (1) higher minimum benefits than the general nondiscrimination rules may require and (2) a shorter length of time the employee must work before acquiring vested, or nonforfeitable, rights to benefits.

Q 11:30 What plans are subject to the top-heavy rules?

A defined benefit plan is a top-heavy plan if more than 60 percent of the cumulative accrued benefits under the plan are for "key employees." A defined contribution plan is top heavy if the sum of the account balances of key employees is more than 60 percent of the total account balances under the plan. [IRC § 416(g)(1)] For each plan year, the determination of top-heavy status generally is made as of the last day of the preceding plan year (the determination date).

For purposes of determining whether a plan is a top-heavy plan, benefits derived both from employer and employee contributions, including employee elective contributions, are taken into account. However, starting in 2002, a Section 401(k) plan that satisfies the design-based safe harbor requirements will not be a top-heavy plan. [IRC § 416(g)(4)]

The accrued benefit of a participant in a defined benefit plan and the account balance of a participant in a defined contribution plan includes any amount distributed within the one-year period ending on the determination date (within a five-year period for in-service withdrawals).

In some cases, two or more plans of a single employer must be aggregated for purposes of determining whether the group of plans is top heavy. The following plans must be aggregated: (1) plans that cover a key employee (including collectively bargained plans); and (2) any plan upon which another plan covering a key employee depends for purposes of satisfying the Code's nondiscrimination rules. The employer may be required to include terminated plans in the required aggregation group. In some circumstances, an employer may elect to aggregate plans for purposes of determining whether they are top heavy. [IRC § 416(g)(2)]

Q 11:31 Who is a "key employee"?

An employee will be considered a key employee if, during the prior year, the employee was:

1. An officer with compensation in excess of $150,000 in 2008 ($145,000 in 2007);

2. A 5 percent owner; or

3. A 1 percent owner with compensation in excess of $150,000.

[IRC § 416(i)(1)(A)]

A family ownership attribution rule applies to the determination of 1 percent owner status and 5 percent owner status. Under this attribution rule, an individual is treated as owning stock owned by the individual's spouse, children, grandchildren, or parents. [IRC §§ 416(i)(1)(B), 318]

Q 11:30

Q 11:32 What is the minimum benefit that a top-heavy plan must provide?

A minimum benefit generally must be provided to all non-key employees in a top-heavy plan. In general, a top-heavy defined benefit plan must provide a minimum benefit equal to the lesser of (1) 2 percent of compensation multiplied by the employee's years of service, or (2) 20 percent of compensation. A top-heavy defined contribution plan must provide a minimum annual contribution equal to the lesser of (1) 3 percent of compensation, or (2) the percentage of compensation at which contributions were made for key employees (including employee elective contributions made by key employees and employer matching contributions). [IRC § 416(c)]

Q 11:33 What is the vesting requirement for a top-heavy plan?

Benefits under a top-heavy plan must vest at least as rapidly as under one of the following schedules:

- Three-year cliff vesting, which provides for 100 percent vesting after three years of service; or
- Two-six-year graduated vesting, which provides for 20 percent vesting after two years of service, and 20 percent more each year thereafter so that a participant is fully vested after six years of service.

[IRC § 416(b)]

Note: For plan years beginning after 2006, the vesting schedule for top-heavy defined contribution plans is the same as for defined contribution plans that are not top heavy (see Q 11:23). However, for defined benefit plans, the vesting schedule for top-heavy plans remains more accelerated than the schedule for non-top-heavy plans.

Employer Deductions for Qualified Plan Contributions

Q 11:34 Can an employer deduct contributions to a qualified retirement plan?

Yes. Employer contributions to qualified retirement plans are deductible subject to certain limits. In general, the deduction limit depends on the kind of plan (see below). Subject to certain exceptions, nondeductible contributions are subject to a 10 percent excise tax. [IRC § 4972]

Q 11:35 Is there a limit on deductions for contributions to a defined contribution plan?

Yes. An employer's deduction for contributions to a defined contribution plan cannot exceed 25 percent of the aggregate compensation paid or accrued during the tax year for all employees participating in the plan. [IRC

§ 404(a)(3)(A)] Elective deferrals to a 401(k) plan are not subject to the 25 percent cap. [IRC § 404(n)]

The IRS has ruled that restorative payments to make up for losses due to a breach of fiduciary duty are also not included in applying the deduction limit. [Rev. Rul. 2002-45, 2002-29 I.R.B. 116]

> **Example 11-3:** Magma Corp. maintains a defined contribution retirement plan for its employees. Magna invested a large portion of the plan assets in a high-risk investment that later turned out to be worthless. A group of employees sued Magma for breaching its fiduciary duty. Magma and the employees agreed to a court-approved settlement that required Magma to repay the losses (plus earnings) to the plan. The repayment was allocated proportionately among plan participants. Magma's payment is a restorative payment that is not taken into account for purposes of the annual deduction limit.

The IRS also ruled that payments made in reasonable anticipation of a lawsuit for breach of fiduciary duty will be treated as restorative payments. On the other hand, payments to a plan to make up for losses due to market fluctuations will generally be treated as contributions, not as restorative payments.

Q 11:36 Is there a limit on deductions for contributions to a defined benefit plan?

Yes. Contributions in excess of the "full funding limit" are not deductible. [IRC § 404(a)], Beginning with 2004, the full funding limit is equal to the excess, if any, of the accrued liability under the plan over the value of plan assets. [IRC § 412(c)(7)]

Distributions

Q 11:37 When must a plan make distributions to plan participants?

A qualified plan must provide that benefit payments begin (unless otherwise elected by a participant) no later than the 60th day after the plan year in which occurs the latest of (1) the date the participant reaches age 65, (2) the 10th anniversary of the employee's participation in the plan, or (3) the date the participant terminates his or her employment. [IRC § 401(a)(14)]

Q 11:38 Can a qualified retirement plan permit distributions before retirement?

The Code limits the circumstances under which plan participants may obtain pre-retirement withdrawals from a qualified plan. In general, these restrictions recognize that qualified plans are intended to provide retirement income.

The least restrictive withdrawal rules apply to profit-sharing plans and stock bonus plans. Amounts may generally be withdrawn from such plans after they have been in the plan for two years. Distributions before the expiration of the two-year period may also be made in the event of retirement, death, disability, other separation from service, or hardship [Reg. § 1.401-1(b)(1)(ii); Rev. Rul. 71-224, 1971-1 C.B. 12]

Distributions from qualified pension plans (i.e., defined benefit pension plans and money purchase pension plans) may generally be made only in the event of retirement, death, disability, or other severance from employment. However, starting in 2007, pension plans may begin paying benefits to workers at age 62; even if they continue to work. [IRC § 401(a)(36)]

Special rules apply to Section 401(k) plans. Elective deferrals under a qualified cash or deferred arrangement (and earnings thereon) may only be distributed on account of severance of employment, death, or disability, or attainment of age 59-1/2. Elective deferrals (but not earnings thereon) may also be distributed on account of a hardship of the employee. [IRC § 401(k)(2)(B)]

Q 11:39 What are the minimum distribution rules?

The Code provides that the distribution of a minimum level of benefits must begin no later than the required beginning date. [IRC § 401(a)(9)] Minimum distribution rules also apply to benefits payable with respect to a plan participant who has died. Failure to comply with the minimum distribution rules results in an excise tax imposed on the payee equal to 50 percent of the required minimum distribution not distributed for the year. In addition, the failure of a qualified retirement plan to provide for compliance with the minimum distribution rules results in disqualification of the plan. [Reg. § 54.4974-2]

Q 11:40 What are the minimum distribution rules that apply prior to the death of the plan participant?

In the case of distributions prior to the death of the plan participant, the minimum distribution rules are satisfied if either (1) the participant's entire interest in the plan is distributed by the required beginning date, or (2) the participant's interest in the plan is to be distributed beginning not later than the required beginning date, over a permissible period. The permissible periods are (1) the life of the participant, (2) the lives of the participant and a designated beneficiary, (3) the life expectancy of the participant, or (4) the joint life and last survivor expectancy of the participant and a designated beneficiary. The required beginning date is April 1 of the calendar year following the later of (1) the calendar year in which the employee attains age 70-1/2 or (2) the calendar year in which the employee retires. However, in the case of a 5 percent owner of the employer, distributions are required to begin no later than April 1 of the calendar year following the year in which the 5 percent owner attains age 70-1/2. [Reg. § 1.401(a)(9)-2]

If commencement of benefits is delayed beyond age 70-1/2, then the accrued benefit of the employee must be actuarially increased to take into account the period after age 70-1/2 in which the employee was not receiving benefits under the plan. [IRC § 401(a)(9)(C)]

IRS regulations contain mortality tables for calculating required minimum distributions. [Reg. § 1.401(a)(9)-9]

Q 11:41 What are the minimum distribution rules that apply after the death of the plan participant?

In general, if the participant dies after minimum distributions have begun, the remaining interest must be distributed at least as rapidly as under the minimum distribution method being used as of the date of death.

If the participant dies before minimum distributions have begun and the participant has a designated beneficiary, the life expectancy rule of IRC Section 401(a)(9)(B)(ii) applies. Thus, absent a plan provision or election of the five-year rule, the life expectancy rule applies in all cases in which the participant has a designated beneficiary. Under the life expectancy rule, any portion of a participant's interest payable to (or for the benefit of) a designated beneficiary must be distributed, beginning within one year of the participant's death, over the life of such designated beneficiary or over the life expectancy of such designated beneficiary. If the participant does not have a designated beneficiary, the five-year rule applies, and the entire remaining interest must generally be distributed within five years of the participant's death. [Reg. § 1.401(a)(9)-3]

A surviving spouse beneficiary is not required to begin distribution until the date the deceased participant would have attained age 70-1/2. In addition, a surviving spouse who receives an eligible rollover distribution from a tax-favored retirement plan may roll over the distribution to an IRA that is treated as owned by the surviving spouse. [Reg. § 1.401(a)(9)-3]

Q 11:42 How are distributions from a qualified plan taxed?

A distribution of benefits from a qualified retirement plan generally is includible in gross income in the year it is paid or distributed under the rules relating to taxation of annuities. This means that any amount distributed is fully includible in gross income unless the employee has made after-tax contributions and, therefore, has a tax basis in the plan benefits (i.e., basis). [IRC §§ 72, 402]

Special rules apply in the case of certain lump-sum distributions from a qualified plan, distributions that are rolled over to an IRA or another qualified plan, and distributions of employer securities (see below).

Distributions before age 59-1/2 from qualified plans are subject to a penalty tax unless an exception applies. [IRC § 72(t)]

Q 11:41

Q 11:43 How is a distribution taxed if the employee has made after-tax contributions?

In general, when an employee has a tax basis, the amount of a distribution from a qualified retirement plan that is includible depends on: (1) whether the distribution is a periodic payment or a nonperiodic payment; and (2) in the case of a nonperiodic payment, whether it is made before or on or after the annuity starting date.

In the case of periodic payments, basis is generally recovered on a pro-rata basis as payments are made. That is, each payment is treated in part as a return of basis and in part as taxable income. [IRC § 72(b)(1)]

In the case of nonperiodic payments, the pro-rata basis recovery rule generally applies to amounts received before the annuity starting date. In the case of nonperiodic payments received after the annuity starting date, the distribution is generally fully includible in income (i.e., no portion of the payment is treated as a return of basis). [IRC § 72(e)]

A payment is considered a periodic payment only if it meets all of the following three requirements: (1) the payment is received on or after the annuity starting date; (2) the payment is one of a series of payments payable in periodic installments at regular intervals (e.g., annually, semiannually, quarterly, monthly, or weekly) over a period of more than one year; and (3) subject to certain exceptions, the total amount payable is determinable at the annuity starting date either directly under the terms of the contract or plan or indirectly by the use of mortality tables or compound interest calculations in accordance with sound actuarial theory. [Reg. § 1.72-2(b)(2)]

Common types of periodic payments include the following:

- Single life annuities, which pay a fixed amount at regular intervals for the lifetime of a single individual;

- Joint and survivor annuities, which pay a fixed amount at regular intervals for the lifetime of a single individual and, following the death of such individual, a fixed amount at regular intervals for the lifetime of another individual; and

- Term-certain annuities, which pay a fixed amount at regular intervals over a specified period (e.g., 10 years).

A nonperiodic payment is any payment that is not a periodic payment.

Q 11:44 What are the special rules for a lump-sum distribution from a qualified plan?

A plan participant who was born before 1936 may make special elections for pre-1974 capital gain treatment and/or ten-year averaging on a lump-sum distribution from a qualified plan A lump-sum distribution is a distribution within one tax year of the balance to the credit of the participant that is made (1) on account of the participant's separation from service with the employer (not available to self-employed individuals), (2) after the participant reaches age

59-1/2, (3) on account of the participant's death, or (4) in the case of self-employed individuals, on account of disability. [IRC § 402(e)]

Under the special elections, a participant who has reached age 50 before 1986 can elect to (1) have amounts attributable to pre-1974 participation taxed at the flat 20 percent capital gains rate, and (2) have amounts attributable to post-1973 participation taxed as if it were received over a 10-year period by a single taxpayer using the tax rates in effect in 1986.

Q 11:45 What are the special rules for a distribution of employer securities?

A plan participant is not required to include in gross income amounts received in the form of a lump-sum distribution to the extent that the amounts are attributable to net unrealized appreciation in employer securities. Such unrealized appreciation is includible in gross income when the securities are disposed of in a taxable transaction. [IRC § 402(e)(4)]Basically this means that, in the year of the distribution, the employee includes in income only that portion of the distribution representing the plan's original cost for the employer securities.

In addition, gross income does not include net unrealized appreciation on employer securities attributable to after-tax employee contributions, regardless of whether the securities are received in a lump-sum distribution. Such appreciation is includible in income when the securities are disposed of in a taxable transaction.

Q 11:46 What are the special rules for rollover distributions?

An "eligible rollover distribution" from a qualified plan may be rolled over tax-free to certain IRAs or another qualified plan. [IRC § 402(c)(1)] An "eligible rollover distribution" generally means any distribution to an employee of all or any portion of the balance to the credit of the employee in a qualified plan. It does *not* include:

- Any distribution that is one of a series of substantially equal periodic payments made (1) for the life (or life expectancy) of the employee or the joint lives (or joint life expectancies) of the employee and the employee's designated beneficiary, or (2) for a specified period of 10 years or more;

- Any distribution to the extent such distribution is required under the minimum distribution rules; and

- Any hardship distribution from a 401(k) plan.

[IRC § 402(c)(4)]

A plan must provide that employees have the option to elect to have an eligible rollover distribution transferred directly to an IRA or another qualified plan. If the employee elects not to make such a transfer, then the distribution is subject to withholding at a flat rate of 20 percent.

An eligible rollover distribution includes a distribution of after-tax contributions to a qualified plan. Rollovers of after-tax contributions may be made to a defined contribution employer plan (provided the plan accepts such rollovers) or to an IRA. A rollover of after-tax contributions must be made by a direct trustee-to-trustee transfer. [IRC § 402(c)(2)] Starting in 2007, after-tax distributions from a defined contribution plan may be rolled over to defined benefit plan. [IRC § 402(c)(2)(A)]

Generally, a rollover must be completed no later than the 60th day following the date the distribution is received. [IRC § 402(c)(3)] If a rollover is not completed within the required time, the amount of the distribution is included in gross income. In addition, a 10 percent penalty tax applies unless the employee is over age 59-1/2 or another exception applies (see below). [IRC § 72(t)]

However, the IRS may waive the 60-day rollover requirement "where the failure to waive such requirement would be against equity or good conscience." The IRS has issued a revenue procedure, explaining how and when it will grant a waiver. [Rev. Proc. 2003-16, 2003-4 I.R.B. 359]

The Service says that it will automatically waive the 60-day rollover time limit in certain cases where failure to meet the deadline was due to errors on the part of a financial institution. Taxpayers who qualify for an automatic waiver do not have to apply to the IRS. An automatic waiver will be granted if a taxpayer followed all the procedures set forth by the financial institution for depositing the funds into an eligible retirement plan within the 60-day period (including giving deposit instructions) but the funds were not deposited on time solely because of an error on the part of the financial institution.

An automatic waiver will be granted only if (1) the funds are deposited into an eligible plan within one year from the beginning of the 60-day rollover period and (2) the original rollover would have been valid if the financial institution had deposited the funds as directed. In all other circumstances, taxpayers must apply to the IRS for a private letter ruling to obtain a waiver of the 60-day time limit. The IRS says that it will issue a favorable ruling in cases involving disasters or other circumstances beyond the reasonable control of the taxpayer.

Q 11:47 What is the penalty tax on early distributions?

If a distribution is made to an employee under a qualified plan before he or she reaches age 59-1/2, the employee may have to pay a 10 percent additional tax on the distribution. [IRC § 72(t)] This tax applies to the amount received that the employee must include in income.

The 10 percent tax will not apply if distributions before age 59-1/2 are made in any of the following circumstances.

- Made to a beneficiary (or to the estate of the employee) on or after the death of the employee;

- Due to the employee having a qualifying disability;

- Part of a series of substantially equal periodic payments beginning after separation from service and made at least annually for the life or life expectancy of the employee or the joint lives or life expectancies of the employee and his or her designated beneficiary. (The payments under this exception, except in the case of death or disability, must continue for at least five years or until the employee reaches age 59-1/2, whichever is the longer period.);

- Made to an employee after separation from service if the separation occurred during or after the calendar year in which the employee reached age 55;

- Made to an alternate payee under a qualified domestic relations order (QDRO); or

- Made to an employee for medical care up to the amount allowable as a medical expense deduction (determined without regard to whether the employee itemizes deductions).

[IRC § 72(t)(2)]

The Pension Protection Act of 2006 also exempts distributions to activated reservists from the 10% penalty. [IRC § 72(t)(2)(G)(iii)]

Q 11:48 Can employees borrow from a qualified retirement plan?

One of the most highly touted features of 401(k) and other defined contribution retirement plans is the ability to borrow money from the plan when the need arises. However, plan loans must meet specific tax law requirements.

The general rule is that if an employee borrows from his or her retirement plan account, the amount borrowed is treated as a "deemed distribution," which is subject to income tax and possible penalties. [IRC § 72(p)] However, a loan will not be treated as a deemed distribution if it meets the following four requirements:

1. Repayment terms—The loan is required to be repaid within five years (unless the loan is used to acquire a principal residence).

2. Level amortization—The repayments are substantially level and made at least quarterly.

3. Amount limitation—The loan, plus any other outstanding loans from the plan, does not exceed the lesser of $50,000 or 50 percent of the employee's plan account. The $50,000 limit is reduced by the difference between the highest total loan balance during the preceding one year and the loan balance on the date of the new loan.

4. Enforceability—The loan is evidenced by a legally enforceable agreement that spells out the amount of the loan, the term of the loan, and the repayment schedule. The agreement must be in writing or in an electronic medium that meets certain standards. [Reg. § 1.72 (p)-1, Q&A 3]

Q 11:48

A deemed distribution can occur in two situations: (1) if the loan is not set up correctly and fails to meet the tax law requirements or (2) if the employee fails to make the loan repayments on schedule.

If a loan fails to satisfy the requirements for non-deemed distribution treatment at the outset, the employee is treated as having received a deemed distribution of the entire loan amount when the loan is made. If the employee does not repay on schedule, the outstanding loan balance is deemed distributed when a payment is missed. A plan may provide for a grace period, but it cannot last beyond the end of the calendar quarter following the calendar quarter in which the missed payment was due.

A deemed distribution is treated like any other plan distribution for purposes of determining the amount that is taxable to the employee. Thus, if the employee's account includes after-tax contributions, part of the deemed distribution may be taxable and part may be tax-free. Similarly, the 10 percent early withdrawal penalty applies to a deemed distribution just like any other distribution.

IRS regulations address some key issues regarding plan loans. [Reg. § 1.72(p)-1]

Multiple loans. The IRS states that there is no specific authority in the tax law for limiting the number of plan loans. Moreover, it noted that some plan participants, such as a parent facing multiple college tuition bills, might have a need for multiple borrowings in a year. On the other hand, the IRS noted that some plans include provisions under which a participant cannot have more than two outstanding loans at one time. Therefore, participants will have to check the specific terms of their employer's plan.

Loans following a deemed distribution. An employee is not barred from further borrowings after a deemed distribution. However, the regulations provide that if an employee has a deemed distribution on a loan and the loan has not been repaid, a subsequent loan will be treated as a deemed distribution unless (1) there is an arrangement between the plan, the employee, and the company that loan repayments will be made through payroll deductions, or (2) the plan receives adequate security for the loan from a source other than the employee's plan account.

If one of these conditions is met initially, but later is not (e.g., the employee revokes consent to payroll deductions), the amount outstanding on the loan will be treated as a deemed distribution.

Loan refinancings. The IRS regulations permit an employee to refinance an existing plan loan and borrow additional amounts at the same time. Both the old and new loans must meet the repayment term (i.e., five years unless the loan is a home loan) and level amortization requirements. But there is a catch: If the repayment date for any portion of the refinanced loan extends beyond the latest permissible date for repaying the original loan, the two loans combined cannot exceed the borrowing cap. For this purpose, the latest permissible date for repaying the original loan is five years from the date the loan was taken out (assuming the loan is not a home loan), even if the loan was actually due in less than five years.

Example 11-4: Joan Pierce borrows $40,000 from her company's plan on January 1, 2008, to be repaid in 20 quarterly installments of $2,491 each. Thus, the term of the loan ends on December 31, 2012. On January 1, 2009, when the outstanding balance is $33,322, the loan is refinanced and replaced by a new $40,000 loan to be repaid in 20 quarterly installments of $2,491 each. Thus, the term of the refinance loan ends on December 31, 2013.

Under the IRS regulations, the balance on the old loan plus the amount of the new loan cannot exceed $50,000 reduced by the difference between (1) the highest outstanding loan during the one-year period ending on December 31, 2008 and (2) the outstanding balance of all loans on January 1, 2009, immediately before the new loan is taken out. The amount of the new loan is $40,000; the outstanding balance of the old loan on January 1, 2009, is $33,322; and the highest outstanding balance during 2008 was $40,000. Therefore, the new loan and the January 1, 2009 balance on the old loan cannot exceed $43,322 ($50,000 reduced by the difference between $40,000 and $33,322). However, the two loans combined come to $73,322. So Pierce has a deemed distribution of $30,000 on January 1, 2009.

On the other hand, the rule combining the old and new loans for purposes of the $50,000 loan limit does not apply if the term of the new loan does not extend beyond the latest permissible date for repaying the old loan. For example, if the term of Pierce's new loan ended on December 31, 2012, instead of 2013, there would be no deemed distribution.

In addition, even if the new loan has a term that extends beyond the latest permissible date for repaying the old loan, there is still no problem as long as the portion of the new loan equal to the balance on the old loan will be paid off within a period ending on the last permissible date for repaying the old loan.

Example 11-5: Same facts as Example 11-4, except that Pierce must pay off $33,322 of the new loan—an amount equal to the balance on the old loan— by December 31, 2012, the original due date for the old loan. The new loan agreement specifies that Pierce's first 16 loan installments (through the end of 2012) will be $2,907 each. That is the sum of the $2,491 installments Pierce was making on the old loan plus an extra $416 required to amortize the additional $6,678 she borrowed over a five-year period. The final four installments in 2013 are set a $416 each. Since Pierce will pay off the refinanced portion of the old loan over the original five-year term, there will be no deemed distribution.

Q 11:48

Small Business Retirement Plans: SEP and SIMPLE Plans

Q 11:49 What is an SEP plan?

A simplified employee pension (SEP) is a written plan that allows an employer to make contributions to employees' accounts without getting involved in the more complex requirements for qualified plans. On the other hand, some advantages available to qualified plans, such as the special tax treatment that may apply to qualified plan lump-sum distributions, do not apply to SEPs.

Under a SEP, an employer makes contributions to a traditional individual retirement arrangement (called a SEP-IRA) set up by or for each eligible employee. SEP-IRAs are owned and controlled by the employee, and the employer makes contributions to the financial institution where the SEP-IRA is maintained. [IRC § 408(k)]

An employer does not have to make contributions every year to SEP-IRAs. But if an employer does not contributions, it must not discriminate in favor of highly compensated employees. [IRC § 408(k)(3)(A)]

A SEP-IRA cannot be designated as a Roth IRA. Employer contributions to a SEP-IRA will not affect the amount that an individual can contribute to a Roth IRA.

An employer cannot prohibit distributions from a SEP-IRA. Also, an employer cannot make contributions on the condition that any part of them must be kept in the account.

Distributions from a SEP-IRA are subject to the IRA rules (see below).

Q 11:50 Which employees must be covered by an SEP?

SEP-IRAs must be set up for, at a minimum, each eligible employee. An eligible employee is an individual who has:

- Reached age 21;
- Worked for the employer for at least three of the last five years; and
- Received at least $500 in compensation (for 2007 and 2008).

[IRC § 408(k)(2)]

Q 11:51 Must an SEP plan be in writing?

Yes. An employer must execute a formal written agreement to provide benefits to all eligible employees under a SEP. The employer can satisfy the written agreement requirement by adopting an IRS model SEP using Form 5305-SEP. An employer cannot use Form 5305-SEP if any of the following apply:

- The employer currently maintains any other qualified retirement plan;
- The employer has maintained a defined benefit plan, even if it is now terminated; or
- There are eligible employees for whom IRAs have not been set up.

Q 11:52 How much can an employer contribute to an SEP?

The Code limits contributions for a year to an employee's SEP-IRA to the smaller of 25 percent of the employee's compensation or the dollar limit for additions to a defined contribution plan account ($46,000 for 2008). [IRC § 402(h)(2)] *Note:* When computing contributions to a SEP, no more than $230,000 (for 2008) of an employee's compensation can be taken into account.

A "catch-up eligible participant" may make a contribution to an SEP over and above the regular contribution limit. An employee is a catch-up eligible participant if he or she is otherwise eligible to contribute to the plan and will be age 50 or older before the end of his or her tax year (normally, the calendar year). If the plan does not operate on the calendar year, an employee is treated as a catch-up eligible participant beginning on January 1 of the calendar year that includes his or her 50th birthday, without regard to the plan year. [Reg. § 1. 414(v)-1(g)(3)]

The amount of catch-up contributions that may be made to an SEP is the lesser of (1) the "applicable dollar amount" or (2) the participant's compensation for the year reduced by any other elective deferrals of the participant for the year. The applicable dollar amount is $5,000 for 2007 and 2008.

Q 11:53 What is a SIMPLE Plan?

A SIMPLE plan, a "savings incentive match plan for employees," is a 401(k)-type plan designed for small businesses.

SIMPLE plans can be adopted by employers who:

- Employ 100 or fewer employees who received at least $5,000 in compensation during the preceding year; and

- Do not provide contributions or benefits for the year under another employer-sponsored retirement plan.

[IRC § 408(p)(2)(C)]

SIMPLE plans can be set up in one of two ways: (1) using SIMPLE-IRAs (SIMPLE-IRA plan), or (2) as part of a 401(k) plan (SIMPLE 401(k) plan).

Q 11:54 What is a SIMPLE-IRA plan?

A SIMPLE-IRA plan involves the establishment of SIMPLE-IRAs for each eligible employee. SIMPLE-IRAs are the individual retirement accounts or annuities into which contributions are deposited.

Contributions are made up of (1) salary reduction contributions and (2) employer contributions. The employer must make either matching contributions or nonelective contributions. No other contributions can be made to the SIMPLE-IRA plan.

Salary reduction contributions. The amount the employee chooses to have the employer contribute on his or her behalf cannot exceed $10,500 in 2007 and 2008. [IRC § 408(p)(2)(A)] These contributions must be expressed as a percentage of the employee's compensation unless the employer permits the employee to express them as a specific dollar amount.

Employer matching contributions. An employer is generally required to match each employee's salary reduction contributions on a dollar-for-dollar basis up to 3 percent of the employee's compensation. This requirement does not apply if the employer makes nonelective contributions (see below).

> **Example 11-6:** John Rose earns $25,000 during the year and chooses to defer 5 percent of his salary to a SIMPLE-IRA. His employer makes a 3 percent matching contribution. The total contribution the employer makes for John is $2,000—a $1,250 salary reduction contribution and a $750 employer matching contribution.

An employer can elect to make a matching contribution of less than 3 percent, but the percentage must be at least 1 percent. An employer cannot choose a percentage less than 3 percent for more than two years during the five-year period that ends with (and includes) the year for which the election is effective.

Nonelective contributions. Instead of matching contributions, an employer can choose to make nonelective contributions of 2 percent of compensation on behalf of each eligible employee who has at least $5,000 of compensation for the year. [IRC § 408(p)(2)(B)]

> **Example 11-7:** Same facts as before, except that Rose's employer chooses to make a 2 percent nonelective contribution. Rose's employer contributes a total of $1,750 to Rose's SIMPLE-IRA for the year—a $1,250 salary reduction contribution and a $500 nonelective contribution.

Catch-up contributions. A "catch-up eligible participant" may make additional contributions to a SIMPLE-IRA. An employee is a catch-up eligible participant if he or she is otherwise eligible to contribute to the plan and will be age 50 or older before the end of his or her tax year (normally, the calendar year). If the plan does not operate on the calendar year, an employee is treated as a catch-up eligible participant beginning on January 1 of the calendar year that includes his or her 50th birthday, without regard to the plan year. [Reg. § 1. 414(v)-1(g)(3)]

The additional amount of catch-up contributions that may be made by an eligible participant is the lesser of (1) the "applicable dollar amount" or (2) the participant's compensation for the year reduced by any other contributions for the year. The applicable dollar amount adjusted for inflation in $500 increments in 2007 and later years. For 2007 and 2008, the applicable dollar amount is $2,500.

Q 11:55 Who are "eligible employees" for SIMPLE-IRA purposes?

Any employee who received at least $5,000 in compensation during any two years preceding the current calendar year and is reasonably expected to earn at least $5,000 during the current calendar year is eligible to participate in a SIMPLE-IRA plan. [IRC §408(p)(4)(A)] An employer can use less restrictive eligibility requirements (but not more restrictive ones) by eliminating or reducing the prior year compensation requirements, the current year compensation requirements, or both. For example, an employer can allow participation for employees who received at least $3,000 in compensation during any preceding calendar year.

Q 11:56 How does an employer set up a SIMPLE-IRA plan?

An employer can use IRS Form 5304-SIMPLE or Form 5305-SIMPLE to set up a SIMPLE-IRA plan. Each form is a model SIMPLE plan document. Which form is used depends on whether the employer selects a financial institution or the employees select the institution that will receive the contributions.

Form 5304-SIMPLE is used if the employer allows each plan participant to select the financial institution for receiving his or her SIMPLE-IRA plan contributions. Form 5305-SIMPLE if used if the employer requires that all contributions under the SIMPLE-IRA plan be deposited initially at a designated financial institution.

The SIMPLE-IRA plan is considered adopted when all appropriate boxes and blanks on the form are filled in and the form has been signed. The employer keeps the original form; it is not filed with the IRS.

Q 11:57 How are SIMPLE-IRA contributions treated for tax purposes?

An employer can deduct contributions and employees can exclude these contributions from their gross income. [IRC §404(m)(1)]SIMPLE-IRA contributions are not subject to federal income tax withholding. However, salary reduction contributions are subject to social security, Medicare, and federal unemployment (FUTA) taxes. Matching and nonelective contributions are not subject to these taxes.

Q 11:58 What is a SIMPLE 401(k) plan?

A SIMPLE 401(k) plan generally must satisfy the rules that apply to a regular 401(k) plans (see above). However, contributions and benefits under a SIMPLE 401(k) plan will be considered not to discriminate in favor of highly compensated employees provided the plan meets the following conditions: [IRC §401(k)(11)(A)]

- Under the plan, an employee can choose to make salary reduction contributions for the year to a trust in an amount expressed as a percentage of the employee's compensation, but not more than $10,500 (for 2007 and 2008);

- The employer makes either (1) matching contributions up to 3 percent of compensation for the year, or (2) nonelective contributions of 2 percent of compensation on behalf of each eligible employee;

Q 11:56

- No other contributions can be made to the plan;
- Contributions are made, and no benefits accrue, during the year under any other qualified retirement plan of the employer on behalf of any employee eligible to participate in the SIMPLE 401(k) plan; and
- The employee's rights to any contributions are nonforfeitable.

Nonqualified Retirement Plans

Q 11:59 What is a nonqualified retirement plan?

Like a qualified retirement plan, a nonqualified plan is a deferred compensation arrangement designed primarily to provide benefits at retirement. However, unlike a qualified plan, a nonqualified plan is not subject to the special restrictions (e.g., nondiscrimination rules, contribution and benefit limits, vesting) that apply to qualified plans. By the same token, a nonqualified plan does not enjoy the same tax benefits as qualified plans.

Nonqualified plans are commonly used to provide retirement benefits to highly compensated and other key employees, often as a supplement to benefits under a qualified plan. For example, an employer may set up a nonqualified salary reduction plan in addition to qualified 401(k) plan to provide retirement benefits in excess of those permitted by the 401(k) rules.

Nonqualified retirement plans generally fall into two categories: funded and unfunded. An unfunded plan may simply involve a mere promise to pay an employee a certain amount at retirement. With a funded plan, amounts are set aside currently by the employer, typically in a trust or similar arrangement, to provide future benefits.

Q 11:60 When is an employee taxed on benefits from an unfunded nonqualified retirement plan?

Nonqualified deferrals of compensation made after December 31, 2004, are subject to Section 409A. Under Section 409A, amounts that are deferred under a nonqualified deferred compensation arrangement, including a nonqualified retirement plan, and that are not subject to a substantial risk of forfeiture must be currently included in the employee's income, unless the plan meets certain requirements. [IRC § 409A(a)(1)(A)(i)] Any amount included in gross income will be subject to interest and an additional income tax.

To avoid immediate inclusion of deferrals, a nonqualified plan must:

1. allow distributions no earlier than when the employee separates from service, becomes disabled, or dies, at a time specified under the plan, or when there is a change in control event;

2. not allow acceleration of benefits, except as provided by regulations; and

3. comply with certain rules limiting the elections available under the plan. [IRC § 409A(a)(2), (3) and (4)]

The plan language must require these rules to be followed and they must be followed in practice.

Any amount deferred under a nonqualified retirement plan will not be includible if it is still subject to a substantial risk of forfeiture or was previously included in gross income. [IRC. § 409A(a)(1)(A)(i)]

The IRS has released final regulations regarding the application of Code Sec. 409A to nonqualified retirement plans and other deferred compensation arrangements. [Reg. § § 1.409A-1 through 1.409A-6]. The effective date of the regulations has been postponed until after December 31, 2008. [Notice 2007-86, 2007-46 I.R.B] Until then, employers and employees can rely on the final regulations, or operate according to a good faith interpretation of Section 409A.

Q 11:61 What is a "substantial risk of forfeiture"?

There is a substantial risk of forfeiture if (1) the employee's right to the deferred amount is conditioned on the performance of substantial future services by any person or the occurrence of a condition related to a purpose of the compensation, and (2) the possibility of forfeiture is substantial. [Reg. § 1.409A-1(d)(1)]

A condition related to a purpose of the compensation must relate to the employee's performance for the employer or for its business activities or goals (e.g., the attainment of a prescribed level of earnings, equity value or a liquidity event).

An amount is not subject to a substantial risk of forfeiture merely because the right to the amount is conditioned, directly or indirectly, upon the refraining from performance of services. An amount will not be considered subject to a substantial risk of forfeiture beyond the date or time at which the employee otherwise could have elected to receive the amount of compensation, unless the amount subject to a substantial risk of forfeiture is considerably greater than the amount the employee otherwise could have elected to receive. For example, a salary deferral generally may not be made subject to a substantial risk of forfeiture. However, where a bonus arrangement provides an election between a cash payment of a certain amount or restricted stock units with a materially greater value that will be forfeited absent continued services for a period of years, the right to the restricted stock units generally will be treated as subject to a substantial risk of forfeiture. [Reg. § 1.409A-1(d)(1)]

Q 11:62 What is a "nonqualified deferred compensation arrangement"?

A nonqualified deferred compensation plan is generally any nonqualified plan that provides for the deferral of the payment of compensation owed to an employee to a time more than two and one half months after the end of the year in which the compensation ceases to be subject to a substantial risk of forfeiture. The term nonqualified deferred compensation plan does not include a qualified retirement plan, tax-deferred annuity, simplified employee pension, or SIMPLE plan. It also does not include any bona fide vacation leave, sick leave, compensatory time, disability pay or death benefit plan or any Archer Medical Savings Account, any Health Savings Account, or any other medical reimbursement arrangement. [IRC § 409A(d)(1); Reg. § 1.409A-1(a)]

There is a deferral only if the employee has a right to compensation during a tax year that has not been actually or constructively received and is payable to him in a later year. An employee does not have a legally binding right to compensation if that compensation may be unilaterally reduced or eliminated by the employer after the services giving rise to the right to compensation have been rendered. If the facts and circumstances indicate that the employer's discretion to reduce or eliminate compensation is available or exercisable *only upon* a condition, or the discretion to reduce or eliminate the compensation lacks *substantive significance*, an employee will be considered to have a legally binding right to the compensation. [Reg. § 1.409A-1(b)(1)]

Short term deferrals. Compensation is not deferred if it is actually or constructively received by the employee within two and a half months from the end of the first tax year (of the employee or the employer) in which the amount is no longer subject to a substantial risk of forfeiture. [Reg. § 1.409A-1(b)(4)(i)]

Example 11-8: An employer with a calendar year tax year who on November 1, awards a bonus so that an employee is considered to have a legally binding right to the payment as of November 1, will not be considered to have provided for a deferral of compensation if, absent an election to otherwise defer the payment, the amount is paid to the employee on or before the following March 15.

Stock options. The grant of a tax-favored "incentive" stock option to an employee is not considered a deferral of compensation. The grant of a nonqualified stock is also generally not considered a deferral of compensation if:

1. The exercise price for the stock option is not less than the stock's fair market value on the date the option is granted,
2. The number of shares is fixed as of the date the option is granted,
3. The receipt, transfer or exercise of the option is taxable as a receipt of property for services, and
4. The option does not include any deferral feature other than the deferral of recognition of income until the later of exercise or disposition of the option, or the time the stock acquired pursuant to the exercise of the option first becomes substantially vested.

[Reg. § 1.409A-1(b)(5)(i)(A)].

Q 11:63 If deferred compensation is not subject to a substantial risk of forfeiture, what requirements must be met to avoid current income inclusion?

As noted above, there are three basic requirements that must be met:

1. Distributions. A nonqualified deferred compensation plan must provide that compensation deferred under the plan cannot be distributed earlier than:

a. the date of the employee's separation from service (or six months after the date of the employee's separation from service, in the case of a "specified employee"), becoming disabled, or dying;

b. a time specified under the plan at the time of the deferral election;

c. the time of a change in the ownership or effective control of the employer or in the ownership of a substantial portion of the assets of the employer , or

d. the occurrence of an unforeseeable emergency. [IRC § 409A(a)(2)(A)]

A nonqualified deferred compensation plan must provide that "specified employees" cannot receive a distribution made on account of their separation from service until six months after the date of separation. A specified employee is an employee of any publicly traded corporation who is an officer of the corporation having annual compensation in excess of $130,000 (adjusted for inflation), is a five-percent owner of the corporation, or is a one percent owner of the corporation and has annual compensation in excess of $150,000. [Reg. § 1.409A-1(i)(l)].

For purpose of the distribution rules, an unforeseeable emergency is a severe financial hardship to the employee resulting from an illness or accident of the employee, the employee's spouse or a dependent of the employee; a loss of the employee's property due to casualty; or other similar extraordinary and unforeseeable circumstances beyond the control of the employee. The amount of a distribution made because of an unforeseeable emergency cannot exceed the amount necessary to satisfy the emergency plus the amount necessary to pay taxes reasonably anticipated as a result of the distribution. The amount necessary to satisfy the emergency must be reduced to take into account the extent to which the hardship can be relieved through reimbursement or compensation by insurance or otherwise or by liquidation of the employee's other assets. [Reg. § 1.409A-3(i)(3)]

2. Acceleration of benefits. No accelerations of distributions is generally allowed. Among the exceptions are the following:

- *Domestic relations order.* A plan may permit the acceleration of the time or schedule of a payment to an individual other than the plan participant as may be necessary to fulfill a domestic relations order.

- *Conflicts of interest.* A plan may permit the acceleration of the time or schedule of a payment under the plan as may be necessary to comply with ethics laws or federal Office of Government Ethics conflict of interest requirements.

- *Payment of employment taxes.* A plan may permit the acceleration of the time or schedule of a payment to pay the Federal Insurance Contributions Act tax on compensation deferred under the plan (the FICA amount). A plan may also permit the acceleration of the time or schedule of a payment to pay the income tax withholding imposed on the FICA amount, and to pay the additional income tax withholding attributable to the pyramiding wages and taxes. However, the total payment under this acceleration provision must not exceed the sum of the FICA amount and the income tax withheld on the FICA amount.

- *Payments upon income inclusion under IRC. § 409A.* An arrangement may permit the acceleration of the time or schedule of a payment to an employee under the plan at any time the arrangement fails to meet the requirements of Sections 409A.

- *Cancellation of deferrals following an unforeseeable emergency or hardship distribution.* An arrangement may permit a cancellation of an employee's deferral election due to an unforeseeable emergency or a hardship distribution. The deferral election must be cancelled, and not postponed or otherwise delayed, such that any later deferral election will be subject to the provisions governing initial deferral elections.

- *Arrangement terminations.* An arrangement may permit an acceleration of the time and form of a payment where the right to the payment arises due to a termination of the arrangement in accordance with certain conditions.

- *Payment of state, local, or foreign taxes.* A plan may provide for an acceleration to reflect payment of state, local, or foreign tax obligations arising from participation in the plan that apply to an amount deferred under the plan before the amount is paid or made available to the participant.

- *Cancellation of deferral elections due to disability.* A plan may provide for a cancellation of an employee's deferral election, or a cancellation of such election may be made, where such cancellation occurs by the later of the end of the employee's tax year or the 15th day of the third month following the date the employee incurs a disability.

- *Offset of debt.* A plan may provide for an acceleration as satisfaction of a debt of the employee to the employer, where such debt is incurred in the ordinary course of the employment relationship, the entire amount of reduction in any of the employer's tax years does not exceed $5,000, and the reduction is made at the same time and in the same amount as the debt otherwise would have been due and collected from the employee. [Reg. § 1.409A-3(j)(4)]

   3. Elections. A nonqualified deferred compensation plan must meet certain requirements regarding the employees' elections to defer compensation and to receive distributions.

- *Initial deferral decisions.* A plan must provide that compensation for services performed during a tax year can be deferred only if the employee's deferral election is made before the close of the preceding tax year. In the case of the first year in which an employee becomes eligible to participate in the plan, the election may be made within 30 days after the date the employee becomes eligible to participate. That election is effective only for compensation with respect to services performed after the election is made. In the case of any performance-based compensation that is based on services performed over a period of at least 12 months, the election may be made no later than six months before the end of the period [Reg. § 1.409A-2] Performance-based compensation means compensation contingent on the satisfaction of preestablished organizational or individual performance criteria relating to a performance period of at least 12 consecutive months in which the employee performs services.

- *Subsequent elections.* A plan may permit subsequent elections to delay or change the form of payments under the plan. If it does permit such elections, a plan must require that the new election cannot take effect until at least 12 months after it is made. A subsequent election to further defer a distribution to be made after the employee's separation from service, on a predetermined date or schedule, or upon a change of ownership of the employer must defer any payment to which it applies (not just the first payment) for at least five years. A subsequent election relating to a payment to be made on a predetermined date or schedule cannot be made less than 12 months prior to the first scheduled payment. [IRC § 409A(a)(4)(C)]

Q 11:64 When can an employer deduct payments under a nonqualified plan?

An employer can claim a deduction for payments made under a nonqualfied plan only in the year they are includible in the gross income of the employee. [IRC § 404(a)(5)]

Individual Retirement Accounts

Q 11:65 What is an individual retirement account?

An individual retirement account (IRA) is a tax-exempt trust or custodial account set up for the exclusive benefit of the account owner and beneficiaries (individual retirement annuities can also be purchased from insurance companies). [IRC § 408(a)] The account is created by a written document. The document must show that the account meets all of the following requirements.

- The trustee or custodian must be a bank, a federally insured credit union, a savings and loan association, or an entity approved by the IRS to act as trustee or custodian.

- The trustee or custodian generally cannot accept contributions of more than $54,000 for 2008 ($4,000 for 2007). However, rollover contributions are not subject to the limit (see below).

- Contributions, except for rollover contributions, must be in cash.

- No part of the trust funds will be invested in life insurance contracts.

- Funds in the account are nonforfeitable at all times.

- The account owner must start receiving distributions by April 1 of the year following the year in which he or she reaches age 70-1/2.

[IRC § 408(a)]

There are two types of IRAs: the regular or traditional IRA and the Roth IRA. Qualifying taxpayers are entitled to deduct contributions to a regular IRA, but withdrawals are taxable. Contributions to a Roth IRA are nondeductible but distributions may qualify for a full tax exemption.

Q 11:66 Who can set up a traditional IRA?

A taxpayer can set up and contribute to a traditional IRA if he or she (1) has taxable compensation for the year (including net earnings from self-employment) or, in the case of joint return filers, if his or her spouse has taxable compensation, and (2) has not reached age 70-1/2 by the end of the year.

Q 11:67 How much can be contributed to a traditional IRA?

The maximum contribution, other than a rollover contribution, for all IRAs maintained by a taxpayer in any year is the lesser of:

- The taxpayer's compensation that must be included in gross income for the year; or
- $54,000.

[IRC § 219(b)]

The $54,000 limit will be adjusted for inflation after 2008. Taxpayers age 50 and over can make "catch-up" contributions over and above the annual maximum. Catch-up contributions are limited to $1,000 in 2006 and after.

If a taxpayer files a joint return and has less taxable compensation than his or her spouse, the maximum allowable IRA contribution for the taxpayer in 2008 is the lesser of the following two amounts:

- $54,000 ($6,000 if age 50 or over); or
- The total compensation includable in the gross income of both the taxpayer and spouse reduced by the spouse's IRA contribution for the year.

This means that the total combined contributions that can be made for the year to the taxpayer's IRA and his or her spouse's IRA can be as much as $10,000 (or $11,000 if one spouse is 50 or older, or $12,000 if both spouses are 50 or older).

Example 11-9: Christine, a full-time student with no taxable compensation, marries Jeremy during 2008. For the year, Jeremy has taxable compensation of $45,000. He plans to contribute $54,000 to a traditional IRA. If he and Christine file a joint return, each can contribute $54,000 to a traditional IRA. This is because Christine, who has no compensation, can add Jeremy's compensation, reduced by the amount of his IRA contribution, ($45,000 – $4,000 = $41,000) to her own compensation (-0-) to figure her maximum contribution to a traditional IRA. In her case, $54,000 is her contribution limit, because $54,000 is less than $41,000 (her compensation for purposes of figuring her contribution limit).

Q 11:68 How much can be deducted for a contribution to a regular IRA?

If neither the IRA owner nor his or her spouse is covered by a qualified retirement plan, the contribution is deductible up to amount of the maximum allowable contribution. If the IRA or spouse is covered by a qualified plan, the deduction may be reduced or eliminated. [IRC § 219(g)]

For this purpose, an individual is considered covered by a defined contribution plan if amounts are contributed or allocated to his or her account for the plan year that ends with or within the individual's tax year. If an amount is allocated to the individual's account for the plan year, he or she is deemed covered by the plan even if the individual has no vested interest in the account.

In the case of a defined benefit plan, an individual is considered covered by the plan if he or she is eligible to participate in the plan for the plan year ending within the individual's tax year. This rule applies even if the individual declined to participate in the plan or did not perform the minimum service required to accrue a benefit for the year. [Reg. § 1.219-2(b)]

Q 11:69 How much can be deducted when the owner of an IRA is covered by a qualified plan?

That depends on the IRA owner's income and filing status. The deduction begins to decrease (phase out) when the owner's income rises above a certain amount and is eliminated altogether when it reaches a higher amount. These amounts vary depending on the IRA owner's filing status.

If the owner files a joint return, the IRA deduction begins to decrease when adjusted gross income reaches $80,000, and the deduction is eliminated completely when adjusted gross income reaches $100,000. For an IRA owner filing as a single taxpayer or as a head of household, the phase-out starts at $50,000 and ends at $60,000. So, for example, if a joint filer belongs to retirement plan at work and has an adjusted gross income of $90,000, the maximum IRA deduction for 2008 is $2,500 ($10,000/$20,000 × $54,000).

The phase-out range is higher for an IRA owner who is not covered by a qualified retirement plan, but whose spouse is covered. In this case, the deduction starts to decrease once adjusted gross income reaches $150,000, and the deduction is eliminated when adjusted gross income reaches $160,000. [IRC § 219(g)(7)]

An individual may make nondeductible contributions to a traditional IRA, up to the allowable maximum contribution limits (less any contributions for which a deduction is claimed). [IRC § 408(o)). So, for example, if an individual participates in a qualified retirement plan and his or her income exceed the adjusted gross income limits outlined above, nondeductible contributions can still be made.

Q 11:68

Q 11:70 What is a rollover contribution?

Generally, a rollover is a tax-free distribution of cash or other assets from one retirement plan that is subsequently contributed to another retirement plan. The contribution to the second retirement plan is called a "rollover contribution."

An IRA owner can transfer, tax-free, assets from a qualified retirement plan into an regular IRA, from one regular IRA to another regular IRA, and from a regular IRA into a qualified plan (if the plan permits it). [IRC §§ 408(d)(3), 402(c)(5)](Transfers can also be made between regular IRAs and Roth IRAs; see below.)

Transfers can also be made directly from one trustee to another—a "direct rollover." However, this is not a true rollover because there is no distribution to the taxpayer.

No deduction is allowed for rollover contributions. Also, the rollover must be completed by the 60th day after the day the taxpayer receives the distribution to retain the rollover's tax-free status.

If a taxpayer makes a tax-free rollover of any part of a distribution from a traditional IRA, he or she cannot make a tax-free rollover of any later distribution from that same IRA within a one-year period. [IRC § 408(d)(3)] The taxpayer also cannot make a tax-free rollover of any amount distributed, within the same one-year period, from the IRA into which he or she made the tax-free rollover. The one-year period begins on the date of the distribution, not on the date it is rolled over. The one-year limit does not apply to trustee-to-trustee transfers.

If an eligible rollover distribution is paid to directly to the taxpayer, the payer must withhold 20 percent of it. This applies even if the taxpayer plans to roll over the distribution to a traditional IRA. The withholding can be avoided by choosing the direct rollover option.

Planning Point: The rollover provision allows IRA owners to tap their IRAs for funds on a temporary basis—a short-term, interest-free loan from the IRA to the owner. The owner can withdraw the funds, have the use of them for 60 days, and then redeposit them in an IRA with no tax consequences. However, this can be done no more than once a year.

Generally, a rollover must be completed no later than the 60th day following the date the distribution is received. [IRC § 408(d)(3)] However, the IRS may waive the 60-day rollover requirement "where the failure to waive such requirement would be against equity or good conscience." In a revenue procedure, the IRS explained how and when it will grant a waiver. [Rev. Proc. 2003-16, 2003-4 I.R.B. 359] The IRS says that it will automatically waive the 60-day rollover time limit in certain cases where failure to meet the deadline was due to errors on the part of a financial institution. Taxpayers who qualify for an automatic waiver do not have to apply to the IRS.

An automatic waiver will be granted if a taxpayer followed all the procedures set forth by the financial institution for depositing the funds into an eligible retirement plan within the 60-day period (including giving deposit instructions) but the funds were not deposited on time solely because of an error on the part of the financial institution. An automatic waiver will be granted only if (1) the funds are deposited into an eligible plan within one year from the beginning of the 60-day rollover period and (2) the original rollover would have been valid if the financial institution had deposited the funds as directed.

In all other circumstances, taxpayers must apply to the IRS for a private letter ruling to obtain a waiver of the 60-day time limit. The IRS says that it will issue a favorable ruling in cases involving disasters or other circumstance beyond the reasonable control of the taxpayer.

Q 11:71 When can an IRA owner make withdrawals from an IRA?

Distributions can commence without penalty once the IRA owner reaches age 59-1/2. Distributions must begin once the IRA reaches age 70-1/2. The minimum distributions that apply to qualified plan participants (see above) also apply to IRA owners. [IRC § 408(a)(6)]However, like 5 percent owners who participate in a qualified plan, an IRA owner cannot defer minimum distributions beyond age 70-1/2, even if he or she has not retired.

Q 11:72 How are distributions from a regular IRA taxed?

Distributions (other than rollover distributions) from a regular IRA are fully taxable ordinary income if only deductible contributions were made to the IRA. Because the IRA owner has no basis in the IRA, any distributions are fully taxable when received. [IRC § § 408(d), 72]

If the IRA owner made nondeductible contributions to the IRA, he or she has a cost basis equal to the amount of those contributions. These nondeductible contributions are not taxed when they are distributed. They are a return of the IRA owner's investment in the IRA.

Distributions before age 59-1/2 are generally also subject to a 10 percent early withdrawal penalty unless it qualifies under one of several exceptions.

- The IRA owner has unreimbursed medical expenses that are more than 7.5 percent of adjusted gross income.

- The distributions are not more than the cost of medical insurance, and the IRA owner is unemployed.

- The IRA owner is disabled.

- The distribution is one of a series of substantially equal periodic distributions spread over the life of the IRA owner or the joint lives of the owner and his or her beneficiary.

- The distributions do not exceed qualifying higher education expenses.

- The distributions are used to buy, build, or rebuild a first home.

[IRC § 72(t)(1)]

Q 11:73 What is a Roth IRA?

A Roth IRA is simply an IRA that is designated as a Roth IRA. [IRC § 408A(b)] It is treated like a regular IRA except to the extent that special rules apply. No deduction is allowed for contributions to a Roth IRA, but qualifying distributions are tax-free.

Unlike traditional IRAs, contributions can be made to a Roth IRA after age 70-1/2, and the IRA minimum distribution rules do not apply to Roth IRA owners before death.

Q 11:74 How much can be contributed to a Roth IRA?

For 2007, an individual can contribute up to the lesser of: (1) $4,000 or (2) 100 percent of compensation. [IRC § 408A(c)(1)] For 2008, the dollar limit increases to $5,000. As with a traditional IRA, taxpayers age 50 or over may make catch-up contributions to a Roth IRA (see above). The maximum contribution is reduced by any amount contributed to a traditional IRA for the year. For 2007, allowable contributions are also phased out ratably over the following levels of adjusted gross income: $150,000 to $160,000 for joint filers and $95,000 to $110,000 for single filers and heads of households. Thus, an individual with adjusted gross income of more than $160,000 on a joint return or $110,000 on a single or head-of-household return cannot make a Roth IRA contribution for the year (but see next question). For 2008, the corresponding phaseout ranges are $159,000 to $169,000 for joint filers and $101,000 to $116,000 for single filers and heads of households.

Q 11:75 Can a traditional IRA be converted to a Roth IRA?

Yes. The conversion can take place in one of three ways: (1) by rolling over funds in the traditional IRA to a Roth IRA, (2) by a direct transfer from the trustee of the traditional IRA to the trustee of the Roth IRA, or (3) by a trustee transferring funds from a traditional IRA to a Roth IRA. [IRC § 408A(c)(3)]

The conversion is subject to income tax as if it were a distribution from the traditional IRA that was not rolled over. However, the conversion is not subject to the 10 percent penalty tax on early withdrawals. Conversions are currently allowed only for taxpayers with adjusted gross incomes of $100,000 or less.

For tax years beginning after December 31, 2009, the $100,000 adjusted gross income limitation of traditional-to-Roth IRA conversions is repealed. [IRC § 408A(c), as amended by the Tax Increase Prevention and Reconciliation Act of 2005 (P.L. 109-222)]. For conversions in 2010, the taxpayer can elect to recognize the conversion amount ratably in 2011 and 2012.

Planning Pointer: The income limits on both kinds of IRAs have prevented higher income taxpayers from making deductible contributions to traditional IRAs or any contributions to Roth IRAs. They could always make nondeductible contributions to a traditional IRA, but such contributions have a limited benefit (no current deduction; tax on account income is deferred rather than eliminated; required minimum distributions). A taxpayer could avoid these problems by making nondeductible contributions to a traditional IRA and then converting it to a Roth IRA, but this option was not available for upper income taxpayers who would have the most to benefit from such a conversion. With the elimination of the income limit for tax years after December 31, 2009, higher income taxpayers can begin now to make nondeductible contributions to a traditional IRA and then convert them to a Roth IRA in 2010. In all likelihood, there will be little to tax on the converted amount. They could continue making nondeductible IRA contributions in the future and roll them over into a Roth IRA periodically. Thus, the elimination of the income limit for converting to a Roth IRA also effectively eliminates the income limit for contributing to a Roth IRA.

Q 11:76 How are distributions from a Roth IRA taxed?

Distributions from a Roth IRA are not taxable to the extent that they are rolled over into another Roth IRA or to the extent that they represent a return of the IRA's nondeductible contributions. Most importantly, "qualified" distributions from a Roth IRA are also exempt from tax. [IRC § 408(d)(1)]

A qualified distribution is any payment or distribution from a Roth IRA that meets the following requirements.

- It is made after the 5-year tax period beginning with the first tax year for which a contribution was made to a Roth IRA set up for the taxpayer's benefit; and

- The payment or distribution is made: (1) on or after the date the taxpayer reaches age 59-1/2, (2) because the taxpayer is disabled, (3) to a beneficiary or to the taxpayer's estate after his or her death, or (4) because of the purchase of a first-time home (up to a $10,000 lifetime limit).

Nonqualifying distributions are treated as first coming from the taxpayer's nondeductible contributions, [IRC § 408(d)(4)]so distributions become taxable only after all contributions have been recovered. Taxable distributions are subject to the 10 percent penalty on early withdrawals unless one of the exceptions applies (see above).

Q 11:77 Can an employer sponsor IRAs for employees?

Yes. There are two ways an employer can assist employees in making contributions to an IRA.

The simplest approach is to permit employees to contribute to a regular or Roth IRA through payroll deductions. Both the Service and the Department of Labor (DOL) have approved payroll deduction IRA arrangements. [IRA Ann 99-2; 29 CFR 2509.99-1]With a payroll deduction arrangement, the employer's involvement is generally limited to permitting an IRA sponsor to publicize its program to employees, collect contributions through payroll deductions, and remit the contributions to the IRA sponsors. Therefore, the DOL has ruled that simply gives employees the opportunity to contribute to an IRA through payroll deductions and the employer has not established a "pension plan" and is not subject to the extensive requirements of the Employee Retirement Income Security Act (ERISA).

Alternatively, for 2003 and later years, an employer can take a more active role by sponsoring "deemed IRAs" in conjunction with a qualified retirement plan. Deemed IRAs are separate accounts in an employer plan to which employees make voluntary contributions. The accounts will be treated as traditional IRAs or Roth IRAs if they are established under the plan and meet the requirements applicable to either traditional IRAs or Roth IRAs. [IRC §§ 219, 408, and 408A] IRS regulations provide that the qualified plan and the deemed IRAs are generally treated as separate entities, subject to separate tax law rules. [Reg. § 1.408(1)-1]For example, issues regarding eligibility to make deemed IRA contributions and the deductibility of those contributions are determined under the rules applicable to IRAs. In addition, the nondiscrimination rules for qualified plans do not apply to deemed IRAs.

On the other hand, the regulations provide that deemed IRA funds may be commingled with qualified retirement plan funds for investment purposes, provided gains and losses are separately allocated to employees' deemed IRA and qualified plan accounts.

As noted above, a deemed IRA may be either a traditional IRA or a Roth IRA. However, because contributions to deemed IRAs are limited to employee contributions, SIMPLE IRAs or SEPs that receive employer contributions will not qualify as deemed IRAs.

Q 11:78 What is a Roth 401(k) arrangement?

For tax years beginning after December 31, 2005, employers can offer Roth 401(k)s. Like a Roth IRA, contributions to a Roth 401(k) are made with after-tax funds. Earnings in, and qualified distributions from, a Roth 401(k) are tax-free. Designated Roth contributions are limited to a participant's elective deferrals. Employer-matching contributions and non-elective contributions are not permitted to be designated as after-tax Roth contributions.

Unlike Roth IRAs, Roth 401(k)s have no income limitations. They are available to everyone who is a participant in a 401(k) (plan that allows the contributions [IRC § 402A]. Employees with high earnings will benefit most from the new plan since there are no income limits and their tax brackets tend to rise with age.

A designated Roth contribution is an elective contribution under a qualified cash or deferred arrangement that is:

1. Designated irrevocably by the employee at the time of the cash or deferred election as a designated Roth contribution;

2. Treated by the employer as not excludible from the employee's income; and

3. Maintained by the plan in a separate account. [Reg. § 1.401(k)-1(f)(1)]

Designated Roth contributions are subject to the nonforfeitability and distribution restrictions applicable to elective contributions and are taken into account under the actual deferral percentage test of Internal Revenue Code Section 401(k) (see above) in the same manner as pre-tax elective contributions. Similarly, designated Roth contributions may be treated as catch-up contributions and serve as the basis for a participant loan. [Reg. § 1.401(k)-1(f)(4)]

Roth 401(k)s are a separate kind of employee elected deferral. They can only be offered in conjunction with a regular 401(k) plan: Roth-only plans are prohibited. Any 401(k) plan offering a Roth option must offer pre-tax elective contributions.

Contributions and withdrawals of designated Roth contributions are credited and debited to a designated Roth contribution account. The account is maintained for the employee who made the designation, and the plan must maintain a record of the employee's investment. Gains, losses, and other credits or charges are separately allocated on a reasonable and consistent basis to the designated Roth contribution account and other accounts under the plan. Forfeitures are not allocated to the designated Roth contribution account. No contributions other than designated Roth contributions and rollover contributions are permitted to be allocated to a designated Roth account. The separate accounting requirement applies at the time the designated Roth contribution is contributed to the plan and must continue to apply until the designated Roth contribution account is completely distributed. [Reg. § 1.401(k)-1(f)(3)]

Chapter 12

Owner-Corporation Transactions

Regularly taxed C corporations and their shareholders often engage in a variety of dealings. Of course, probably the most common transaction is the corporation's payment of dividends to the shareholders (see Chapter 3). But, with closely held corporations, there may be many other types of transactions. For example, a shareholder may lend money to the corporation—or the corporation may lend money to the shareholder. A shareholder may make additional capital contributions to the corporation when it is going through a rough spot or when it is expanding. A shareholder may lease or sell property to the corporation—or vice versa. Furthermore, in many closely held corporations, shareholders are also employees and receive salaries and fringe benefits.

Shareholders of closely held corporations may view their corporations as their alter egos—and these transactions are merely seen as shifting money from one pocket to another. But the tax code treats corporations and their owners as separate taxpayers, and these transactions can often raise various unforeseen tax complications.

Lending and Borrowing Money

Q 12:1 Are there any tax consequences when a shareholder lends money to or borrows money from a corporation?

Generally, there are no tax consequences to a transfer of money between a shareholder and his or her corporation as long as (1) the transaction is a bona fide loan and not some other type of transaction disguised as a loan and (2) interest is charged and paid at a market rate. [IRC § 7872] The proceeds will not be taxable to the borrower and the repayment will not be taxable to the lender, just as if the corporation and the shareholder were strangers.

Q 12:2 Can a shareholder deduct interest paid on a loan from his or her corporation?

A shareholder can deduct interest on a corporate loan to the same extent that it would be deductible on a loan from another source. For example, if the loan proceeds were used for personal purposes, the interest would generally be nondeductible. [IRC § 163(h)(1)]On the other hand, if a shareholder borrowed funds from the corporation for use in a trade or business (other than the business of being an employee), the interest would be fully deductible.

Q 12:3 Can a shareholder deduct interest paid on debt incurred to acquire stock in a corporation?

Yes. Interest paid on a loan to buy stock will generally be treated as investment interest under the Code. Investment interest is deductible up to the amount of the shareholder's net investment income for the year. [IRC § 163(d)]

Net investment income is the excess of investment income over investment expenses. Interest in excess of net investment income can be carried over to future years and deducted up to the amount of net investment income for those years.

"Investment interest" is interest paid on debt connected with property held for investment. [IRC § 163(d)(3)(A)] Moreover, the phrase "held for investment" includes any property that produces dividend income. [IRC § 469(e)(1)]

The interest paid will generally not be treated as fully deductible business interest under the Code. Even if the shareholder is the sole owner of the corporation and considers the corporation to be his or her "business" the loan will be considered an investment loan. For example, in Revenue Ruling 93-68 [1993-2 C.B. 72], the IRS considered the situation where a taxpayer borrowed money to buy stock in a C corporation to protect his job with the corporation. The IRS ruled that the interest paid on the loan was not business interest unless the taxpayer was a dealer or trader in stock or securities. Regardless of the motives of the shareholder in buying the stock, the stock was considered investment property for purposes of the interest deduction.

Q 12:4 What happens if a shareholder borrows money from a corporation at an interest rate below the going market rate?

Below-market loans are governed by a special provision of the Code. [IRC §7872] For this purpose, a below-market loan is a loan on which no interest is charged or on which the interest is charged at a rate below the "applicable federal rate."

The Internal Revenue Service (IRS or the Service) publishes the applicable federal rates (AFR) each month in the Internal Revenue Bulletin. Internal Revenue Bulletins are available on the IRS Web site at *www.irs.gov*. The rates can also be obtained at IRS offices.

Under IRC Section 7872, a below-market loan is recast as a two-step transaction (1) a loan from the lender at the AFR, and (2) a payment from the lender to the borrower equal to the amount of the foregone interest which the borrower then uses to repay the lender. [IRC §7872(a)(1)] The foregone interest for any period is the difference between the interest that would have been charged at the AFR and the interest (if any) that was actually charged.

The tax treatment of step (2) depends on the substance of the transaction. In the case of a loan to a shareholder, the deemed payment from the corporation is a dividend, which would generally be taxable to the shareholder and not deductible by the corporation (see Chapter 3). The deemed interest payment by the shareholder would be deductible or nondeductible depending on the use of the proceeds (see above). The corporation reports both the actual and foregone interest income.

If the loan to the shareholder is payable on demand, the deemed payment to the shareholder and the deemed repayment to the corporation are treated as if they occur annually. In the case of a term loan, the deemed payment to the shareholder occurs once, when the loan is made. The deemed payment is equal to the loan amount less the present value of all payments due under the loan. The deemed repayment by the shareholder is spread out over the term of the loan. In other words, the shareholder will realize all of the dividend income upfront, while the interest repayments are deemed paid with the passage of time.

The special below-market loan provision does not apply to loans of $10,000 or less between a shareholder and a corporation if tax avoidance is not a principal purpose of the interest arrangement. [IRC §7872(c)(2)]

Q 12:5 What happens if a shareholder lends money to his or her corporation at a below-market rate?

Again, the loan will be recast as a two-step transaction (see Q 12:4 above), except that the tax consequences will be different. The shareholder-lender will be deemed to make a payment to the corporation, which it, in turn, uses to pay the foregone interest. The deemed payment to the corporation will be treated as a capital contribution (see Chapter 3), which is nondeductible by the shareholder.

[Reg. §1.7872-4(d)]The deemed repayment of interest will be deductible by the corporation and taxable to the shareholder.

Q 12:6 When will a loan from a shareholder to a corporation be treated as "bona fide"?

The IRS and the courts are concerned that an equity investment in a corporation may be disguised as a debt. Debts enjoy more favorable tax treatment than equity investments. For example, a corporation can deduct the interest it pays a shareholder on a debt; dividends paid on equity investments are not deductible by the corporation.

It should be noted that the Jobs and Growth Tax Relief Reconciliation of 2003 [P.L. 108-27]and the Tax Increase Prevention and Reconciliation Act of 2005 have temporarily narrowed the advantage that debt holds over an equity investment. While dividends are still nondeductible by the corporation, they are more favorably treated at the shareholder level than interest. Through 2010, dividends are generally taxed to shareholders at the same rate as net capital gain, while interest is taxed at ordinary income rates (see Chapter 3).

No single test determines whether a transfer of funds to a corporation is a debt or a disguised equity investment. The ultimate question is: Do the rights conferred more closely resemble those of a shareholder or those of a creditor? For the answer, the IRS and the courts weigh a number of factors. The factors can be dividend into two categories: (1) the formalities of the transaction, and (2) the realities of the transaction.

The formalities. The first group of factors concerns the formal nature of the certificate the shareholder gets in return for the for the transfer of funds:

- Name given to the certificate—*Stock* indicates equity. *Bonds, debentures,* or *notes* are debt. Some questions the courts ask include: Is the transfer treated as a loan on the corporation's books and tax returns? Are sums the shareholder receives from the corporation treated as interest on the shareholder's tax return? Is the promissory note drafted in a formal manner? Does the agreement creating the obligation refer to the transfer as a *debt* or a *loan* rather than a *contribution to capital*? Are words associated with debt, such as *principal, interest, due date,* and *collection,* used throughout the agreement?

- Maturity date—A *fixed maturity,* when the lender can demand payment, used throughout the agreement without regard to earnings, will strengthen the argument that the transfer created a loan. But a demand note does not have a fixed maturity date. Also, a shareholder advance made with the understanding that it would be repaid when the corporation liquidates has been held not to have a fixed maturity date. [*Alexander & Baldwin, Ltd. v. Kanne,* 190 F.2d 15 (9th Cir. 1951)] A maturity date of more than 15 years also suggests the shareholder is not serious in expecting repayment.

- Interest rates—Payment of a reasonable rate of interest suggests debt.

Q 12:6

- Unconditional interest payments—A shareholder has no right to dividends until they are declared. Whereas, a creditor may demand interest even if the corporation has no profits.

- Relationship to debts owed outside creditors—If the shareholder's right to repayment is subordinate to the rights of outside creditors, courts are more likely to think of the advance as equity. If, however, the shareholder can show that the advance was secured in some way, the argument that it is a loan is stronger.

The realities. The second group of factors looks at the business reality of the borrower-lender relationship:

- Capitalization level—Debt cannot solely finance a corporation. In determining whether an advance is capital or debt, the courts look at the overall ratio of the corporation's debt to stock equity. A thinly capitalized corporation has a high ratio of debt to equity. Debt that is no more than three times equity is often regarded as acceptable.

- Balance of interest between creditor and stockholder—Stockholders advancing funds in proportion to their ownership interests signifies equity contributions. Some courts have required that, for advances to be considered debt, shareholders must show they are in a substantially different position after making the advances. If some investors take debt and others take stock and debt, different rights have been created among the shareholders—a sign the courts view favorably.

- Company's ability to get financing from outside—If a corporation could borrow from outsiders after issuing debt to its shareholders, a loan from shareholders looks more legitimate. It is also helpful to show that amounts and terms of the loan would have been acceptable to a non-shareholder lender.

- Expectation of payment—In some cases, courts have asked whether the corporation's prospects when the transfers were made affected the likelihood that the money would be repaid. When a corporation has a history of losses and defaults, the funds transferred are placed at the risk of the business. Courts are then more likely to view the transfer as a contribution to capital.

- Record of payment—Courts look at how the parties treated the debt after it was created. As evidence that debt exists, the courts like to see consistent and timely principal and interest payments. The shareholder should report such interest payments as taxable income on his or her personal tax return.

- Use of the funds—Courts look at how the funds were used. If the funds are added to a corporation's daily operating expenses, it looks like debt. Funding for purchase of capital assets looks like equity.

- Sinking fund—Money put aside to provide repayment helps convince the IRS and the courts that the corporation views the contribution as a loan that must be repaid.

Q 12:6

The key point to keep in mind is that presence or absence of a promissory note is not decisive by itself. For example, in one recent case before the Sixth Circuit Court of Appeals, the corporate taxpayer executed promissory notes in some years, but not in others. Nevertheless, the court held that the advances made to the corporation by its shareholders constituted bona fide debts and the corporation's deductions for its interest payments should be upheld.

The case involved Indmar, a Tennessee manufacturer of marine engines. Beginning in 1987, the shareholders began to make advances to Indmar on a periodic basis. While the advances were not initially represented by promissory notes, the corporation began executing notes in 1993.

Indmar treated all of the advances as loans from shareholders in the corporate books and records, and made monthly payments calculated at 10% of the advanced funds. Indmar reported the payments as interest expense deductions on its federal income tax returns and the shareholders reported the payments as interest income on their individual income tax returns.

The appeals court found that overall the facts of the case favored treating the advances as debts and not equity investments. For example:

- The fixed rate of interest and regular interest payments indicate that the advances were bona fide debt.

- The parties structured the advances as demand loans. While the loans advances did not have fixed maturity dates, they did have ascertainable maturity dates controlled by the shareholders.

- Indmar always went to a bank for funds to buy capital equipment. The shareholder advances were used for working capital.

- Indmar had sufficient external financing available to it.

- Indmar was adequately capitalized.

- The shareholders did not make the advances in proportion to their respective equity holdings.

The court did acknowledge that a few of the relevant factors weighed against the existence of debt. For example, Indmar did not set up a sinking fund for debt repayment. But the court noted that sinking funds are usually required by lenders when the risk of repayment will likely be high. When a company has sound capitalization, as Indmar did, there is less need for a sinking fund. In any case, the majority of the relevant factors indicated that the advances should be considered bona fide debts. [*Indmar Products Co. Inc.*, CA-6, 2006-1 USTC ¶50,270, rev'g 89 TCM 795, Dec. 55,936(M), TC Memo. 2005-32]

Q 12:7 When will a loan from a corporation to a shareholder be considered "bona fide"?

When a corporation transfers funds to a shareholder, the issue is: Is the transfer a bona fide loan or is it a disguised dividend? The IRS and the courts look at objective factors to determine if there was a bona fide intention to repay.

Q 12:7

In *Weigel v. Commissioner*, [T.C. Memo 1996-485]Raymond Weigel was the sole shareholder of Goshorn Construction & Pipeline, Inc., a Denver pipeline construction company. During one tax year, the company made cash transfers of about $350,000 to or on behalf of Weigel. By year's end, however, Goshorn's books showed that the outstanding balance Weigel owed had been reduced to a little more than $181,000. Goshorn reported retained earnings of $990,000.

For its tax year ending October 31, 1989, Goshorn transferred $126,000 to Technical Packaging, Inc. Technical was an S corporation with Weigel as its sole shareholder. Goshorn also recorded a transfer of almost $148,000 to Weigel, personally. Weigel leased property to Goshorn, and $45,000 of the rent due was used to reduce the balance to around $103,000.

Goshorn's "accounts receivable" from Technical was reduced to $21,000 at the end of the third year and to zero by the end of the fourth year.

On audit, the IRS determined that these cash transfers were in fact dividends to Weigel. When the case came before the Tax Court, Weigel testified that the transfers were intended to be loans.

The court looked at a number of factors to make its decision. There were both positives in Weigel's favor and negatives that worked against him:

Negatives:

- Degree of control—Weigel had exclusive, unfettered control over Goshorn. He was involved in all phases of the business, including participation in the Service's audit.

- Restrictions on disbursements—During the years at issue, Weigel's "loan" account went from zero to almost $380,000. There was no evidence of any ceiling on the amount he could borrow.

- Corporate earnings and dividends—The loans to Weigel were never greater than Goshorn's retained earnings. Besides that, during the years Weigel owned Goshorn, the company never declared a dividend.

- Use of loan documentation—Weigel did not execute any notes to Goshorn showing his obligation to repay the transfers. Also, Goshorn did not receive any collateral for the "loans."

- Ability of shareholder to repay—Weigel testified that he owned a number of properties that could have been sold to pay his Goshorn debts. But the court noted that Weigel provided no evidence to support the high values he placed on these properties. What is more, Weigel had other debts to pay off, including a $400,000 debt for unpaid unemployment taxes.

- Creation of legal obligation—There was no definite maturity date due to the lack of documentation, and repayments were made irregularly.

- Corporation's attempt to enforce payment—There was no evidence that Goshorn took any steps to enforce repayment.

Positives:

- Treatment of disbursements on corporate records—Goshorn recorded the transfers to Weigel as loans on its corporate books. The transfers were disclosed to Goshorn's bank during the loan-negotiation process.

- Shareholder attempts to repay—Weigel made numerous repayments over the years. Weigel's largest credits against his "loan account" came from rent that Goshorn owed him. But Weigel also had been repaying a number of Goshorn's liabilities. For example, in one year Weigel and his wife took out a personal note from a bank to pay off a note Goshorn owed the bank.

Despite Weigel's testimony that loans were intended, the court ruled that the objective factors required a finding of dividend treatment.

Indirect loans. The dividend issue is not limited to situations where a shareholder is the direct borrower of a loan. A shareholder may be in receipt of a constructive dividend if a corporate loan merely accrues to the shareholder personal benefit.

A recent federal appeals court case is a good illustration of this point. Five individuals owned and controlled a family trust that owned all of the shares of a corporation (Corp). The owners of the trust also owned controlling interests in a limited liability company (LLC) engaged in real estate development.

LLC planned to develop condominiums but was unable to obtain construction financing. Corp "loaned" $2.4 million to LLC as initial financing and received a promissory note. The note had no maturity date, was not secured, required no guarantees from the owners of LLC, and was a demand note without any scheduled payments of interest or principal. Only $44,000 was ever paid on the note. The condominium development failed and Corp received no other interest or principal on the "loan."

The Sixth Circuit Court of Appeals ruled that the payment to the LLC was a constructive dividend. Corp's payment to LLC benefited LLC's owners, who were the same as Corp's owners (attributing ownership through the family trust). [*Hubert Enterprises*, U.S. Ct. App. (6th Cir., 2007)]

Sale and Lease of Property

Q 12:8 Are the tax consequences of a sale of property between a corporation and a shareholder the same as those for unrelated parties?

Generally, yes. However, if a corporation sells property to a shareholder for an amount that is less than its fair market value, the shareholder will be treated as having received a dividend to the extent of the corporation's accumulated earnings and profits. The amount of the dividend is generally equal to the difference between the amount paid for the property and its fair market value if the amount paid exceeds the corporation's basis for the property. [Reg. § 1.301-1(j)]

Q 12:8

Example 12-1: XYZ sells property to its owner for $10,000. The fair market value of the property is $15,000, and the corporation's adjusted basis for the property is $8,000. The owner has received a dividend of $5,000.

If property is sold to an individual shareholder, the same rule applies when the sales price is less than the fair market value and also less than the corporation's basis. Whereas, a different rule applies when the property is sold to a corporate shareholder for an amount less than the property's fair market value and less than the selling corporation's basis. In this situation, if the fair market value equals or exceeds the selling corporation's basis, the distribution equals the difference between: (1) the selling corporation's adjusted basis, increased by any gain recognized on the sale, and (2) the selling price. Where the fair market value of the property is less than the selling corporation's basis, the amount of the distribution is the excess of the fair market value over the amount paid for the property. [Reg. § 1.301-1(j)]

Q 12:9 What are the tax consequences if a shareholder leases property to or from a corporation?

As with a sale to a shareholder, the transaction is treated like a lease between unrelated parties as long as the rent paid equals the fair rental value of the property.

However, if a corporation pays an excessive rent on property leased from the shareholder, the excess rent may be treated as a disguised dividend to the shareholder. [e.g., *McKeever v. Eaton,* 6 F. Supp. 697 (DC CT 1934)] The result would be the same if the corporation leased property to a shareholder at a bargain rental—the difference between the fair market rental and the actual rent paid would be a constructive dividend. [e.g., Rev. Rul. 58-1, 1958-1 C.B. 173]

Compensation for Shareholder-Employees

Q 12:10 If a shareholder is also an employee of the corporation, are compensation payments to the shareholder-employee deductible by the corporation?

Yes, compensation paid to shareholder-employees for services rendered is deductible by the corporation as long as it is considered "reasonable." [Reg. § 1.162-7(b)(3)] Compensation is considered reasonable if it does not exceed amounts that ordinarily would be paid for similar services by similar businesses in similar circumstances. However, the IRS scrutinizes compensation arrangements in closely held corporations to see if the corporation and shareholder are attempting to convert nondeductible dividends into deductible compensation. If a corporation pays a shareholder-employee an amount in excess of what is considered reasonable, the IRS may characterize the excess as a dividend.

It is important to keep in mind that the Jobs and Growth Tax Relief Reconciliation Act of 2003 and the Tax Increase Prevention and Reconciliation

Act of 2005 provide that qualified dividend income is taxed at the same rates that apply to net capital gain through 2010. [IRC § 1(h)(11)] Furthermore, the same tax laws generally cap the tax rate on net capital gain at 15 percent through 2010 for taxpayers in the higher brackets.

In a few situations, these tax laws almost turn the "reasonable" compensation issue on its head. Owner-employees of C corporations may sometimes be better off *reducing or eliminating* their compensation and receiving most or all of the payments from their corporations in the form of dividends.

> **Example 12-2:** Paul Smith is the president and sole owner of XYZ Inc., a C corporation. He has $75,000 of profits that he can pay out as compensation or dividends. If the profits are paid out as dividends, XYZ will owe a corporate tax of $13,750. That leaves $61,250 to be distributed to Smith. At a 15 percent tax rate, Smith will net $52,062. On the other hand, if the $75,000 of profits is paid out as compensation, XYZ will owe no corporate tax, but the compensation will be taxable at ordinary income rates. If Smith is in the 28 percent tax bracket, he will be left with $54,000 after income taxes. But then there is the FICA tax: $5,738 will have to be deducted from Smith's paychecks for Social Security and Medicare taxes (and XYZ will have to pay a like amount). So, by going the compensation route, Smith will net only $48,262, almost $4,000 below what he would get with a straight dividend payout.
>
> This is an extreme example to be sure. For example, if XYZ were in a higher tax bracket, the dividend payout after taxes would be smaller. Alternatively, if Smith were already paid a $200,000 salary, reducing the salary and paying $100,000 out as dividends would not save much in FICA tax. That is because Smith and the company only pay the Medicare portion of FICA in the $100,000-$200,000 range. The point is, however, that all compensation packages between owners and their closely-held corporations should be reviewed to see if the owners are receiving the "best" compensation from a tax standpoint.
>
> While the changes in the 2003 and 2005 acts certainly affect an owner's perspective on the reasonable-compensation issue, they will also affect the Service's. In some cases, it may be to the Service's benefit to argue that an owner is being paid an unreasonably *low* compensation and is receiving too much in the form of dividends. While this argument would represent a departure from the Service's traditional position, the Service has argued this before in dealing with owners of S corporations (see Chapter 4).

Q 12:11 How does a shareholder-employee determine whether or not his or her salary is "reasonable"?

There is no clear-cut answer. It depends on the particular facts of the situation. There are several key indicators, such as the following, that courts have used to determine whether or not a shareholder-employee's compensation is reasonable:

- The nature, extent, and scope of the shareholder-employee's work;
- The shareholder-employee's qualifications;
- The size and complexity of the corporation's business;
- A comparison of salaries paid with sales, gross income, and capital value;
- General economic conditions;
- A comparison of salaries to distributions to shareholders and retained earnings;
- The corporation's salary policy for all employees;
- The corporation's financial condition; and
- Whether independent investors contemplating purchase of the company would be willing to pay the compensation.

For example, in a recent case, the Tax Court looked at the compensation Miller & Sons, Inc. paid its president and CEO, Darle Miller. [*Miller & Sons, Inc.*, T.C. Memo. 2005-114] Miller & Sons' primary business was interior wall construction. It was awarded construction jobs from general contractors by submitting the lowest bid to complete a specific job.

Darle Miller performed many duties as CEO, including preparing and submitting job bids, scheduling projects and jobs, hiring and coordinating employees, coordinating activities between the company and the general contractors, ordering supplies, dealing with payroll issues, and confronting any problems that arose.

Darle Miller's compensation consisted of a base salary plus bonuses. During the period 1996 through 2000, his total compensation ranged from $282,501 to $440,000.

The IRS challenged Miller and Sons' deduction for Darle Miller's compensation on the ground that it was unreasonable. But the Tax Court ruled in the company's favor.

Factors that aided the company include:

Employee qualifications. The company obtained jobs primarily by submitting the lowest bid to a general contractor, and Darle was solely responsible for preparing each bid. He therefore deserved high compensation because of his knowledge and experience.

Nature, extent, and scope of an employee's work. Again, this worked in the company's favor. Miller & Sons' success depended on two things: (1) accurately estimating the cost of completing a job, and (2) completing the job within budget. Darle was the sole individual responsible for preparing these bids. In addition to performing his duties as CEO, he performed many other tasks. The Tax Court believed that Darle was irreplaceable to the company.

Size and complexity of the business. While the drywall business does not require any significant technical knowledge and could be started with a very small investment, a number of Miller and Sons' competitors have failed since it started up. In a competitive industry such as this, the company's development of business methods and techniques directly related to its success. The successful execution of these methods was complex or, at a minimum, difficult. Consequently, the Tax Court found that this factor also favored the company.

Comparison of salaries with distributions to stockholders and retained earnings. If a corporation never pays dividends, compensation paid to shareholder-employees may be a form of disguised dividends. However, a shareholder's return on an investment doesn't have to be in dividends; it can come in the form of retained earnings that increase the value of the shareholder's investment. Miller and Sons' return on earnings average 15 percent, which the Tax Court found to be reasonable.

Most reasonable compensation cases involve individuals who are the "heart-and-soul" of their corporations. However, in family corporations, the issue can arise when a shareholding family member performs relatively little services for the corporation. The most obvious abuse would be where a corporation pays a family member for a "no-show" job. Nevertheless, even when the family member performs some services, the question may arise: Is he or she being compensated for the services—or simply for being a relative and a shareholder?

For example, in one Tax Court case [*E.J. Harrison and Sons, Inc. v Comm'r,* T.C. Memo 2003-239], the issue was the reasonableness of the compensation paid to the widow of the corporation's CEO. Elmo Harrison was the founder and president of E.J. Harrison and Son's Inc., which operated a trash hauling business. Harrison died in 1991. After his death, his three sons (who had joined the business in the 1960s) and his widow, Myra Harrison, made up the company's board of directors. Myra owned 46 percent of the company's outstanding stock.

Shortly after Elmo Harrison's death, the board of directors elected Myra president of the company. Her three sons served as vice-presidents of the company and one held the title "secretary and treasurer."

Prior to Elmo Harrison's death, Myra had kept "the books", basically keeping track of payments and collections. She also paid certain bills and attended contract negotiation meetings with Elmo. After his death, Myra's principal activities consisted of (1) attending board meetings and voting on major proposals put forward by her sons, who were responsible for the day to day operations of the company; (2) engaging in extensive public relations activities on behalf of the company; and (3) acting as a co-guarantor (together with her sons) of bank loans to the company for major capital equipment purchases.

For the years 1995-1997, Myra was paid $860,000, $818,000, and $600,000, respectively, as compensation for her services. During those years, Myra was in her company office an average of two to three times per week. On occasion, she also took work home. Her work consisted in part of filing and maintaining historic company records.

Myra also looked over proposed trash hauling contracts before signature, and she reviewed bills and signed checks prepared by others in payment of those bills. On occasion, she attended meetings arranged by one or more of her sons with drivers or other employees where her fluency in Spanish was of use. In addition, she met with bankers in connection with her loan guaranties. Including her public relations activities, Myra Harrison worked 40 or more hours per week on the company's behalf. In 1997, Myra was 81 years old.

The IRS disallowed the corporation's deduction for most of Myra's compensation during 1995-1997. The IRS contended that anything in excess of $54,000 (in 1995), $56,000 (in 1996), and $58,000 (in 1997) was "unreasonable and excessive compensation." The IRS considered Myra's services equivalent to no more than those provided by an outsider serving as chair of a corporation's board of directors. The excess amounts were intended to be disguised dividends to Myra rather than payments for services rendered.

Basically, the Tax Court agreed with the IRS that Myra's activities on the company's behalf were like the duties performed by an outside board chair. Factors that influenced the court included:

- Myra's role as a member of the board was limited to the review and approval of proposals developed by her sons. Her titles of president and chairman of the board were titular and not reflective of her actual status within the company.

- Although Myra was instrumental in helping the company project a positive corporate image in the communities it served, there was nothing to indicate her public relations activities contributed directly to the company's sales and profits.

- In these circumstances, Myra's guaranties of corporate loans were a means of protecting her ownership interests in the company, not a function of her employment by the company.

- Because the company's overall profits for 1995-1997 were primarily attributable to the efforts of Myra's sons, and not her, an independent investor in the company would object to the size of Myra's compensation.

The Tax Court did find, however, that Myra's efforts were more valuable than those normally provided by an outside board chair. Her lifetime devotion to the business, the respect for her judgment accorded by her sons who actually ran the business on a day-to-day basis, and her dedication in the performance of her public relations function provided extra benefits. So the court authorized an 80 percent premium over and above the usual compensation paid to an outside board chair. The court held that the company's allowable deductions for Myra's compensation for 1995, 1996, and 1997 were $98,000, $101,000, and $106,000 respectively. [*Harrison and Sons, Inc.*, T.C. Memo. 2003-239]

Q 12:12 Is there anything a shareholder-employee can do in advance to head off an IRS attack on his or her compensation?

Yes. The key to protecting a compensation package is proof—proof that the shareholder-employee deserves every penny of compensation the corporation pays. Here are some suggested steps a shareholder-employee may want to take:

1. Find out what comparable-sized companies in similar lines of business are paying their owners.

2. Get financial data on the performance of the industry the corporation is in and see how the corporation compares. The better the corporation is doing in comparison with similar companies, the more compensation can be justified.

3. Keep a record of the shareholder-employee's job responsibilities. If he or she does work that exceeds the normal responsibilities of someone with the same title, that warrants higher pay.

4. If the corporation is accumulating profits instead of paying out dividends, spell out the reasons in the corporate minutes (e.g., specific plans for expansion).

5. The shareholder-employee may want to formally tie his or her compensation into the corporation's performance. For example, a bonus plan could be set up for the shareholder-employee that increases in relation to the corporation's net sales.

6. Corporate minutes or resolutions should be used to record compensation agreements between the shareholder-employee and the corporation. They should explicitly state the value of the services and abilities in establishing the pay levels. If current compensation is intended to make up for past sacrifices, those sacrifices should be detailed in writing.

7. If the shareholder-employee's bonus is tied to profits, the amount should be set early in the year, it should depend on results, and the percentage should remain constant. Increasing a percentage at the end of a year of high earnings raises the IRS's suspicions of unreasonable compensation.

Planning Point: Some corporations try to protect themselves against an unfavorable IRS audit through payback or hedge agreements. The shareholders promise to repay any part of their compensation for which the company is denied a deduction. The shareholders get a tax deduction for the repayment. But the payback agreement can create its own problems. Its existence suggests to the IRS that even the shareholder-employees question the reasonableness of their compensation.

Bad Debts and Worthless Stock

Q 12:13 If a shareholder lends money to a corporation and the corporation is unable to repay the loan, is the shareholder entitled to a loss deduction?

If a shareholder makes a "business" loan to his or her corporation, the shareholder can claim a loss deduction in the year the debt becomes partially or totally worthless. If a shareholder makes a "nonbusiness" loan to the corporation, a loss deduction is allowed only in the year it becomes totally worthless.

Deductions for business bad debts are ordinary losses fully deductible against ordinary income. [IRC § 166(a)]Nonbusiness bad debts are capital losses, deductible only against capital gain and up to $3,000 of ordinary income annually. [IRC § 166(d)]

Q 12:14 What is the difference between a "business" bad debt and a "nonbusiness" bad debt?

A business bad debt is a debt that was either:

1. Created or acquired in the taxpayer's business; or

2. Closely related to the taxpayer's business when it became partly or totally worthless.

[Reg. § 1.166-5(b)]

Any other type of debt is a nonbusiness bad debt.

Q 12:15 Are losses arising from loans from shareholders to their corporations typically considered business bad debts?

A nonemployee-shareholder generally cannot claim a business bad debt deduction when the corporation is unable to repay the loan. The business of a corporation is not attributable to the shareholder, so the fact that the debt arose out of the corporation's business does not mean that it arose out of the shareholder's business. However, a shareholder can treat a bad debt as a business bad debt if the shareholder can show that the debt was related to his or her own business. [e.g., *Albert G. Wade*, T.C. Memo 1963-50 (1963)]

For example, in one Tax Court case, a writer advanced money to his corporation. The corporation published the writer's work to promote his literary reputation. The court ruled that he was entitled to a business bad debt deduction. [*Funk v. Comm'r*, 35 T.C. 42 (1960)]In another case, a taxpayer in the produce business could not obtain a reliable supply of bananas, so she set up a corporation to engage in the banana trade and loaned money to the corporation. The Tax Court ruled that she could claim a business bad debt deduction. [*Dorminey v. Comm'r*, 26 T.C. 940 (1956)]

The IRS may also scrutinize claims for business bad debt deductions to see if they are bona fide debts, or in reality an equity investment. For example, the IRS recently disallowed a couple's business bad debt deduction for transfers to a corporation in which they were majority shareholders. The couple did not receive a promissory note for the transfers, but they were carried on the corporation's books as "loans from shareholders."

The Tax Court upheld the Service's disallowance. The court noted that there was no fixed repayment schedule and no record of actual repayments by the corporation. The couple never demanded repayment of the transfers, and their continued lending of additional funds tended to refute the existence of a valid debtor-creditor relationship. [*Dunnegan*, T.C. Memo. 2002-119]

Q 12:16 If the shareholder is also an employee of the corporation, can he or she deduct a bad debt owed by the corporation as a business bad debt?

An employee may be able to claim a business bad debt deduction when the debt was created in order to protect his or her job and source of income. When an employee is also a shareholder, the question becomes: Was the loan made to protect the shareholder-employee's job or to protect his or her investment in the corporation? Whether a business bad debt deduction is allowed depends on which was the dominant motive for making the loan. For example, when the shareholder-employee's salary is large and his or her investment in the corporation is relatively small, a loan to protect employment seems reasonable. But when the salary is smaller, the shareholder-employee has other substantial sources of income, and he or she can easily find another job, then a business bad debt deduction is more doubtful.

Q 12:17 If a corporation's business fails, can a shareholder deduct the loss from his or her investment?

A shareholder may deduct a loss from the worthlessness of his or her stock in the corporation. [IRC § 165(a)]The loss is generally a capital loss unless the stock qualifies for special treatment under Section 1244 (see below).

The loss is deductible only in the year the stock becomes totally worthless. No deduction is allowed for a mere decline in the value of stock, no matter how big the decline. [Reg. § 1.165-5]To claim a deduction the shareholder must show that the stock had at least some value at the end of the prior year and that there was an identifiable event during the year that made it worthless.

Q 12:18 What special tax treatment is available under Section 1244?

A loss recognized when stock becomes worthless (or when it is sold or exchanged) can be claimed as a fully deductible ordinary loss if the stock qualifies as "small business corporation" stock under IRC Section 1244.

The amount that can be deducted as an ordinary loss is limited to $50,000 each year. On a joint return the limit is $100,000, even if only one spouse has this type of loss. [IRC § 1244(b)]So, for example, if one spouse has a loss of $110,000 and the other spouse has no loss, the couple can deduct $100,000 as an ordinary loss on a joint return. The remaining $10,000 is a capital loss.

Q 12:19 What stock qualifies for Section 1244 treatment?

To qualify for ordinary loss treatment, the following requirements must be met:

- The owner of the stock must be the original purchaser of the stock. Transferees cannot qualify. [IRC § 1244(a)]

- The stock must have been acquired for money or property (other than stock and securities). If the stock was acquired in exchange for services rendered, the ordinary loss deduction is not available.
- The corporation must be a domestic "small business corporation."
- During its five most recent tax years before the loss, the corporation must have derived more than 50 percent of its gross receipts from income other than royalties, rents, dividends, interest, annuities, and gains from sales and trades of stocks or securities. If the corporation was in existence for at least one year, but less than five years, the 50 percent test applies to the tax years ending before the loss. If the corporation was in existence less than one year, the 50 percent test applies to the entire period the corporation was in existence before the day of the loss. [IRC § 1244(c)]

Q 12:20 What is a "small business corporation"?

A corporation is a small business corporation if its capital receipts do not exceed $1 million when the stock is issued. Capital receipts are the aggregate amounts of money and property received by the corporation for stock, as a contribution to capital, and as paid-in surplus. [IRC § 1244(c)]

Expenses Incurred for the Corporation

Q 12:21 Can an owner claim a deduction for business expenses incurred on behalf of the corporation?

No. IRC § 162 allows a deduction for "ordinary and necessary" business expenses. Generally, to be deductible as a business expense, an expenditure must be "directly connected with or pertaining to the taxpayer's trade or business." [Reg. § 1.162-1(a)] Therefore, only the taxpayer carrying on the business for which the expenditure is made is entitled to the deduction.

It is also well established that a corporation and its shareholders are separate taxable entities. So a corporate taxpayer may only deduct expenses paid or incurred in its business. Conversely, a shareholder is not entitled to deduct expenses directly related to the corporation's business even if he or she pays such expenses from personal funds without being reimbursed by the corporation. [e.g., *Leamy* 85 T.C. 798 (1985)] These expenditures generally are treated as capital contributions or loans from the shareholder to the corporation and are amortizable or deductible, if at all, only by the corporation.

IRC § 212 provides that investors can claim a deduction for expenses paid or incurred during the tax year for the production of income. But here again the expense must be "ordinary and necessary" and it must be such an expense as is personal to the taxpayer and immediately related to his or her own income or property. A shareholder's expenditures on behalf of the corporation's might cause the corporation to prosper but it would be the income and property of the corporation that would be immediately benefited. Any incidental benefit to an investor as a shareholder of the corporation is too remote. [*Deputy v. du Pont* 308 U.S. 488 (1940)]

Q 12:22 If an owner of a corporation is also an employee, can expenses incurred on behalf of the corporation be deducted as employee business expenses?

It depends. An employee who voluntarily incurs corporate expenses is not entitled to a deduction because they are not considered necessary employee expenses. On the other hand, where, as a condition of employment, an employee incurs unreimbursed expenses on behalf of the corporate employer, the employee may generally deduct those expenses. [Rev. Rul. 57-502 , 1957-2 C. B. 118]

For example, a recent Tax Court case involved an individual who was a 50% owner and vice-president of a corporation. The corporation adopted a resolution requiring the corporate officers to incur expenses as may be necessary and stating that they shall not be reimbursed by the corporation for these expenses. The resolution states that the vice president "shall also be responsible for supplying office space and his own vehicle for his business services and shall not be reimbursed therefor by the Corporation."

The Tax Court upheld the vice-president's deduction for expenses he incurred on behalf of the corporation. The resolution enacted by the corporation required the vice-president to assume certain expenses including providing office space and a vehicle. According to the Tax Court, this meant that the expenses covered by the corporate resolution were the vice-president's expenses and not the corporation's. [*Craft*, TC Memo. 2005-197]

Chapter 13

Sales and Other Dispositions of Business Assets

Most business owners are probably well aware that when they sell a business asset, such as a piece of machinery or a business building, they will have gain or loss on the sale. However, other types of dispositions can also result in a gain or loss. For example, a business owner may realize a gain or loss when property is exchanged for other property, when property is condemned, or when a business property is simply abandoned. Moreover, some transactions that are not technically labeled as sales may be treated as sales for tax purposes. For example, a lease of business property may actually be a conditional contract for the sale of property.

On the other hand, not every sale or disposition is a taxable event. In some cases, the tax law provides that a realized gain or loss is not recognized for tax purposes. For example, no gain or loss is recognized when business or investment property is exchanged for like-kind property.

In addition, not all recognized gains and losses receive the same tax treatment. Gains or losses may be ordinary or capital depending on the nature of the asset and the type of transaction involved. Capital gains may be taxed at a lower rate than ordinary income. On the other hand, deductions for capital losses may be limited.

This chapter will explore various types of transactions that are treated as sales or exchanges. In addition, this chapter will explain how to figure the gain or loss on a sale or exchange, how the gain or loss is treated for tax purposes, and the reporting requirements for sales and exchanges.

Sales and Exchanges

Q 13:1 What is a sale or exchange?

A sale is a transfer of property for money, or a mortgage, note, or other promise to pay money. An exchange is a transfer of property for other property or services, although it may involve a transfer of money to equalize values. [IRS Pub. No. 544, *Sales and Other Dispositions of Assets*]

Q 13:2 When is a lease of property treated as a sale?

In some cases, a transaction that is structured as a lease may actually be a conditional sales contract. Payments made under a conditional sales contract are not deductible as rent by the lessee, and amounts received by the lessor (other than amounts that represent interest) are treated as proceeds from the sale of the property.

Whether an agreement is a conditional sales contract depends on the intent of the parties. No single test, or special combination of tests, always applies. However, in general, an agreement may be considered a conditional sales contract rather than a lease if any of the following is true:

- The agreement applies part of each payment toward equity to be acquired by the lessee;
- The lessee will acquire title to the property after payment of a stated amount of required payments;
- The total amount the lessee must pay to use the property for a short time represents a large part of the amount the lessee would pay to obtain title to the property;
- The lessee must pay much more than the current fair rental value of the property;
- The agreement gives the lessee an option to buy the property at a nominal price compared to the value of the property at the time the option may be exercised;
- The lessee has an option to buy the property at a nominal price compared to the total payment amount required under the agreement; or
- The agreement designates part of the payments as interest, or a portion of the payments is readily recognizable as the equivalent of interest.

Q 13:1

The fact that the lease agreement does not provide for the transfer of title to the lessee or specifically precludes the transfer of title will not necessarily prevent the agreement from being treated as a sale. Moreover, an agreement generally will be presumed to be a sale if the total rental payment and any additional option price is approximately the price at which the property could have been purchased at the time the agreement was entered into, plus interest and carrying charges. [Rev. Rul. 55-540, 1955-2 C.B. 39]

Q 13:3 What other kinds of transactions are treated as sales or exchanges?

A number of transactions that are not technically labeled as sales or exchanges are treated as such for tax purposes. Examples include:

- *Cancellation of a lease.* Payments received by a tenant for the cancellation of a lease are treated as an amount realized from the sale of property. [IRC § 1241]

- *Copyrights.* Payments for granting the exclusive use of a copyright are treated as amounts received from the sale of property. [IRC § § 1221; 1231] The payments may be either a fixed amount; a percentage of receipts from the sale, performance, exhibition, or publication of the copyrighted work; or an amount based on the number of copies sold, performances given, or exhibitions made.

- *Easements.* The amount received for granting an easement is subtracted from the basis of the property. If only a specific part of a tract of property is affected by the easement, only the basis of that part is reduced by the amount received. If it is impossible or impractical to separate the basis of the part of the property on which the easement is granted, the basis of the whole property is reduced by the amount received. Any amount received that is more than the basis to be reduced is a treated as gain from the sale of property. An easement on property (for example, a right-of-way over it) that is granted under condemnation or threat of condemnation is treated as a forced sale, even though the owner keeps the legal title to the property.

- *Transfers to satisfy debt.* A transfer of property to satisfy a debt is an exchange. [See, e.g., Rev. Rul. 76-111, 1976-1 C.B. 214]

- *Foreclosures and repossessions.* If a borrower does not make payments on a loan secured by property, the lender may foreclose on the loan or repossess the property. The foreclosure or repossession is treated as a sale or exchange. The same holds true if the borrower voluntarily returns the property to the lender.

- *Abandonment of property.* Although not technically a sale or exchange, an abandonment of business property is a disposition that is recognized for tax purposes. The amount of the loss from abandonment is the adjusted basis of the property.

- *Involuntary conversions.* An involuntary conversion occurs when property is destroyed, stolen, condemned, or disposed of under threat of condemnation, and the owner receives property or money in payment, such as insurance or a condemnation award. An involuntary conversion is treated as a forced sale or exchange of the property. [IRC § 1231]

- *Property as compensation.* An employer's transfer of property as compensation, or as a contribution to an employee's trust, is also considered a taxable disposition of property. [Rev. Rul. 73-345, 1973-2 C.B. 11]

Gain or Loss

Q 13:4 When is gain or loss realized?

Gain or loss is usually realized when property is sold, exchanged, or disposed of in a taxable transaction. [IRC § 1001]

Q 13:5 How is gain or loss figured?

A gain is the amount realized from a sale or other disposition that exceeds the adjusted basis of the property. A loss is the excess of the adjusted basis of the property over the amount realized from the sale or disposition.

The adjusted basis of property is the original cost or other basis plus certain additions and minus certain deductions, such as depreciation and casualty losses. [IRC §§ 1012, 1016] In determining gain or loss, the costs of transferring property to the new owner, such as selling expenses, are added to the adjusted basis of the property. For further details on calculating basis, see Q 13:8 *et seq.*

The amount realized from a sale or disposition is the total of all money received plus the fair market value (FMV) of all property or services received. [IRC § 1001(b)]The amount realized also includes the amount of liabilities from which the transferor is discharged as a result of the sale or disposition. [Reg. § 1.1001-2]For example, the amount realized on a sale or disposition includes any liabilities that are assumed by the buyer and any liabilities to which the transferred property is subject, such as a mortgage, that are assumed by the buyer. Real estate taxes owed by the seller on the date of the sale that are assumed by the buyer are included in the amount realized. [IRC § 1001(b)(2); Reg. § 1.1001-1(b)]

The fair market value of property received in an exchange is the price at which the property would change hands between a willing buyer and a willing seller who both have reasonable knowledge of all relevant facts. If parties with adverse interests place a value on property in an arm's-length transaction, that price is strong evidence of fair market value. If there is a stated price for services received in an exchange, that price will be treated as the fair market value of the services absent evidence to the contrary.

Q 13:4

Example 13-1: Joe Black owns a business building that costs $70,000. Over the years, Black has made permanent improvements to the building, which cost $20,000, and claimed depreciation deductions of $10,000. Black sold the building in exchange for $100,000 plus property with a fair market value of $20,000. The buyer also assumed real estate taxes of $3,000 and a mortgage of $17,000. Black's selling expenses were $4,000.

Black's amount realized from the sale is $140,000—the sum of the $100,000 cash received, the $20,000 fair market value of the property received, and the $20,000 in real estate taxes and mortgage obligations assumed by the buyer. Black's adjusted basis for the building is $84,000—the $70,000 original cost plus the $20,000 cost of improvements and the $4,000 of selling expenses less the $10,000 of depreciation. Therefore, Black's realized gain on the sale is $56,000— the $140,000 amount realized less his adjusted basis of $84,000.

Q 13:6 What if property is sold or exchanged for less than its fair market value?

A sale for less than fair market value may simply be a bad deal. However, if a taxpayer sells property for less than fair market value with the intention of making a gift of part of the property, the transaction is a bargain sale, which is treated as part sale and part gift. The taxpayer has gain if the amount realized is more than the adjusted basis of the property. There is no loss, however, if the amount realized is less than the adjusted basis of the property. [Reg. § 1.1001-1(e)]

A bargain sale to a charity is treated as part sale or exchange and part charitable contribution. If a deduction for the contribution is allowable, the adjusted basis of the property must be allocated between the part sold and the part contributed based on fair market value. The adjusted basis of the part sold is calculated using the following formula:

$$\text{Adjusted basis of Part Sold} = \text{Adjusted basis of Entire Property} \times \frac{\text{Amount Realized}}{\text{FMV of Entire Property}}$$

Because of this allocation, there may be a gain even if the amount realized on the bargain sale does not exceed the adjusted basis of the property.

Example 13-2: Ellen Smith, a self-employed business owner, sold some business inventory to a charitable organization at a bargain price. Smith can claim a deduction for the contribution portion of the transaction. The property had a fair market value of $10,000, and Smith's basis in the property was $4,000. The charity paid $2,000 for the property.

Smith's basis for the portion sold is $800 ($4,000 adjusted basis of the entire property × $2,000 amount realized /$10,000 fair market value of the entire property). Therefore, she has a gain on the sale portion of the transaction of $1,200 ($2,000 amount realized less $800 adjusted basis of the part sold).

A charitable deduction for a donation of inventory is generally limited to the basis of the property. [Reg. § 1.170A-4(a)(1)]Therefore, Smith may claim a charitable deduction equal to her $3,200 basis in the donated portion of the inventory ($4,000 total adjusted basis less $800 allocable to the portion sold).

Note: A special rule applies to inventory donations by corporations. If the donation is used for the care of the ill, needy, or infants, then the corporation may qualify for a deduction equal to the lesser of: (1) the adjusted basis of the inventory plus one-half of the profit had the inventory been sold for its fair market value, or (2) twice the basis of the inventory. [IRC § 170(e)(3)]

Q 13:7 How is gain or loss figured if a property was used partly for business and partly for personal purposes?

When a sale or exchange involves property that was used partly for business or rental purposes and partly for personal purposes, gain or loss must be figured as if the taxpayer sold two separate pieces of property. The amount realized, selling expenses, and the basis of the property must be divided between the business or rental portion and the personal portion. Depreciation claimed on the business portion is subtracted from the basis allocated to that portion.

Gain or loss on the business or rental part of the property may be a capital gain or loss or an ordinary gain or loss (see Q 13:16). Any gain on the personal part of the property is a capital gain. A loss on the personal portion is not deductible.

Basis

Q 13:8 How is the original basis of property determined?

The original basis of property is generally its cost. The cost of property is the amount paid for it, either in cash or other property, plus commissions and other expenses connected with the purchase. [IRC § 1012; Reg. § 1.1012-1(a)] The basis of mortgaged property includes the amount of the indebtedness. Real estate taxes are part of the cost of property if the buyer assumes the seller's obligation to pay them. [Reg. § 1.1012-1(b)]

If property is acquired in a taxable exchange, basis may be determined in one of two ways.

Some rulings have ascertained the cost basis of the property received in an exchange to be the fair market value of the property received. [See, e.g., Rev. Rul. 57-535, 1957-2 C.B. 513]

Other decisions have computed the cost basis of property received in an exchange by increasing the FMV of the property exchanged by payments made or decreasing the FMV by payments received to compensate for unequal values of the exchanged properties. [See, e.g., *Est. of Myers*, 1 T.C. 100 (1942)]

Planning Point: In most cases, the result will be the same under both methods. The result may differ, however, if the value of the property received is not equal to the value of the property given up, and no equalizing payments are made.

In some cases, an exchange of property is not a taxable event. For example, gain or loss on an exchange of "like-kind" properties is not recognized for tax purposes (see Q 13:30 *et seq.*). Similarly, gain is not recognized on an involuntary conversion if the taxpayer receives property that is similar or related in service or use to the converted property (see Q 13:25 *et seq.*). The basis of property received in a nontaxable exchange is the same as the basis for the property given up in the exchange. [IRC §§ 1031(d), 1033(b)] However, if the exchange also involves money or property that is not like kind, adjustments must be made to basis. The rules for determining the basis of property received in an involuntary conversion or a like-kind exchange are discussed in detail later in this chapter.

If a taxpayer builds property or has property built by a contractor, the basis of the property includes construction expenses. These construction expenses may include the cost of land, labor and materials, architect's fees, building permit charges, payments to contractors, payments for renting construction equipment, and inspection fees. [IRC Sec. 263(a); Reg. § 1.263(a)-1; Reg. § 263(a)-2]

If a business owner uses his or her own employees and equipment to construct property, the basis of the property includes wages paid to the employees for construction work, depreciation on equipment while it is used in construction, operating and maintenance costs for the equipment, and the cost of supplies and materials that are used in the construction.

Note: Construction-related costs cannot be deducted as business expenses. They must be capitalized as part of the basis of the constructed property.

Q 13:9 How is the cost basis figured if more than one asset is purchased for a single sum?

If a business owner buys multiple assets for a lump sum, the amount paid must be allocated among the assets. As a general rule, a specific allocation agreed to by a buyer and a seller in an arm's-length transaction will be accepted for tax purposes. If the buyer and seller do not agree to a specific allocation, the allocation should be made according to the relative value of each asset in relation to the whole. [*C.D. Johnson Lumber Corp. v. Comm'r*, 12 T.C. 348, *acq.* 1950 C.B. 3] If it is not possible to make an allocation, no gain or loss will be recognized on the sale of any of the assets until the entire cost has been recovered. [*Atwell v. Comm'r*, 17 T.C. 1374, *acq.* 1953-1 C.B. 6]

Q 13:10 How is the basis of individual assets determined when a taxpayer buys an ongoing business?

The price paid for the business must be allocated among the acquired assets. The price paid is generally reduced by any cash and general deposit accounts (including checking and saving accounts) received by the buyer. The remaining amount is allocated to other assets in proportion to (but not in excess of) their fair market values in the following order:

1. Certificates of deposit, U.S. Government securities, foreign currency, and actively traded personal property, including stock and securities.

2. Accounts receivable, other debt instruments, and assets that are marked-to-market at least annually for federal tax purposes (e.g., commodities held by a dealer).

3. Property of a kind that would be included in inventory if on hand at the end of the tax year or property held primarily for sale to customers.

4. All other assets except goodwill, going concern value of the business, and other Internal Revenue Code (IRC or the Code) Section 197 intangibles (e.g., patents, copyrights, trademarks, trade names, franchises, licenses and permits, business operating systems and information bases).

5. Section 197 intangibles other than goodwill and going concern value.

6. Goodwill and going concern value. [IRC § 1060; Reg. § 1.1060-1]

The buyer and seller can enter into a written agreement specifying the allocation of the purchase price among the assets. The agreement will be binding on both parties, unless the Internal Revenue Service (IRS or the Service) determines the amounts are not appropriate.

Both the buyer and seller must report to the IRS on the allocation of the sales price among the business assets. The buyer and seller should each attach Form 8594, *Asset Acquisition Statement*, to their returns for the year of the sale.

Q 13:11 How is the fair market value of inventory established when a taxpayer is determining the basis of inventory acquired as part of the purchase of an ongoing business?

The IRS has issued guidance on how to value inventory when a business is purchased. [Rev. Proc. 2003-51, 2003-29 I.R.B. 121] The IRS says that three basic methods can be used to determine the fair market value of inventory: (1) the replacement cost method, (2) the comparative sales method, and (3) the income method.

Replacement cost method. This method generally provides a good indication of fair market value if inventory is readily replaceable in a wholesale or retail business but generally should not be used in establishing the fair market value of the work in process or finished goods of a manufacturing concern.

In valuing a bulk inventory of raw materials or goods purchased for resale under this method, the determination of the replacement cost of the individual items should only be the starting point and may need an adjustment. For example, the fair market value must be determined in light of what a willing purchaser would pay and a willing seller would accept for the inventory. A willing purchaser might be expected to pay (and a willing seller might be expected to demand) a price for inventory that would compensate the seller not only for the current replacement cost but also for a fair return on expenditures in accumulating and preparing the inventory for distribution. Thus, an amount equal to the fair value of the related costs that the taxpayer would have incurred in acquiring and accumulating the same quantity of goods had the goods been purchased separately (e.g., purchasing, handling, transportation, and off-site storage costs) should be added to the base replacement cost.

In addition, in valuing a particular inventory under this method, other factors may be relevant. For example, a well-balanced inventory available to fill customers' orders in the ordinary course of business may have a fair market value in excess of its cost of replacement, because it provides a continuity of business, whereas an inventory containing obsolete merchandise unsuitable for customers may have a fair market value of less than the cost of replacement.

Comparative sales method. The comparative sales method uses as the starting point the actual or expected selling prices of finished goods to customers in the ordinary course of business. The inventory to be valued may represent a larger quantity than the normal trading volume. The IRS says that expected selling price is a valid starting point only if the inventory is expected to be used to fill customers' orders in the ordinary course of business.

If the expected selling price is used as a basis for valuing finished goods inventory, the base amount must be adjusted for such factors as:

1. The time that would be required to dispose of this inventory;

2. The expenses that would be expected to be incurred in the disposition (e.g., all costs of disposition, applicable discounts, sales commissions, and freight and shipping charges);

3. A profit commensurate with the amount of investment in the assets and the degree of risk.

Income method. According to the IRS the income method, when applied to fair market value determinations for finished goods, recognizes that finished goods must generally be valued in a profit-motivated business. As the amount of inventory may be large in relation to normal trading volume, the highest and best use of the inventory will be to provide for a continuity of the marketing operation of the ongoing business. In addition, the finished goods inventory will usually provide the only source of revenue of an acquired business during the period it is being used to fill customers' orders. The historical financial data of an acquired company can be used to determine the amount that could be attributed to finished goods in order to pay all costs of disposition and provide a return on the investment during the period of disposition.

Work in process. The IRS says that the fair market value of work in process should be based on the same factors used to determine the fair market value of finished goods. However, there must be a reduction for the expected costs of completion.

Q 13:12 What is the basis of property that is converted from personal to business or rental use?

When property is converted from personal to business or rental use, the basis for depreciation is the lesser of: (1) the fair market value of the property on the date of the conversion, or (2) the adjusted basis of the property on that date. [Reg. § 1.165-9(b)]

> **Example 13-3:** Harriet Block paid $160,000 to have a home built on a lot that cost $25,000. Block paid $18,000 for permanent improvements to the home. Block converted the home to rental use. Block's adjusted basis for the property at the time of the conversion to rental was $178,000 ($160,000 plus $18,000 improvements). On the conversion date, the property had a fair market value of $180,000 of which $15,000 was for the land and $165,000 for the house. The cost of the land is not included in determining Block's basis for depreciation because land is not depreciable.
>
> *Result:* Block's basis for figuring depreciation is the $165,000 fair market value on the date of the conversion because that is less than her adjusted basis for the property.

However, if the converted property is later sold or disposed of, two sets of basis rules apply.

1. The basis for figuring gain is the adjusted basis of the property on the date of the sale or disposition, including the cost of the land. [Reg. § 1.165-9(b)]

> **Example 13-4:** Same facts as Example 13-3, except that Block sold the property at a gain after claiming depreciation deductions of $37,500. Block's adjusted basis for figuring gain is $165,500 ($178,000 adjusted basis on conversion plus $25,000 cost of the land less $37,500 depreciation).

2. The basis for calculating a loss is the lesser of the adjusted basis or fair market value of the property at the time of the conversion (including the land), adjusted for the period after the conversion. [Reg. § 1.165-9(b)]

> **Example 13-5:** Same facts as Example 13-4 except that Block sold the property at a loss after claiming depreciation deductions of $37,500. Block's starting point for calculating basis is the fair market value on the date of the conversion to rental use ($180,000) because that was less than her adjusted basis of $203,000 ($178,000 of the house and improvements plus $25,000 cost of land). The fair market value of the property ($180,000) is then reduced by the depreciation deductions ($37,500), giving Block a basis of $142,500.

If the taxpayer has a loss when using the basis for gain and a gain when using the basis for loss, neither gain nor loss is realized on the sale or disposition.

Planning Point: The effect of the loss basis calculation is to limit a loss deduction to the decline in value (net of any basis adjustments) following the conversion.

Q 13:13 How is the adjusted basis of property determined?

The cost or other basis of property is only the starting point for determining basis at the time of a sale or exchange. Certain additions and subtractions must be made to determine the adjusted basis of the property, which is used to calculate gain or loss. [IRC § 1016]

Additions to basis include capital expenditures for improvements to the property, purchase commissions, sales tax, freight charges to obtain the property, installation charges, legal costs to defend or perfect title to the property, title insurance, survey expenses, and recording fees. However, no adjustment may be made for any expenditure that is currently deductible. [Reg. § 1.1016-2(a)]

Subtractions from basis are made for items that represent a return of part of the cost of the property. Items that reduce basis include depreciation or Section 179 expensing deductions, depletion and amortization, casualty and theft loss deductions and insurance reimbursements, and cancellation of debt that is excluded from income (e.g., cancellation in bankruptcy or when a taxpayer is insolvent).

Q 13:14 Do any other special rules apply in calculating the basis of business property?

Yes. The uniform capitalization (UNICAP) rules require capitalization of direct costs and an allocable portion of most indirect costs associated with production and resale activities. [IRC § 263(a)]The costs must be added to the basis of property and cannot be deducted currently. The UNICAP rules are discussed in Chapter 5.

Gain and Loss Recognition

Q 13:15 When is gain or loss from a sale or exchange reported for tax purposes?

As a general rule, gain or loss realized from a sale or exchange of property is recognized for tax purposes in the year of the sale or exchange. [IRC § 1001(c)]Recognized gains must be included in gross income. Recognized losses are deductible from gross income.

There are some important exceptions to the general rule that realized gain or loss is recognized for tax purposes. For example, a loss on personal property is not deductible. In addition, the following exchanges may qualify for tax-free (or partially tax-free) treatment:

- Involuntary conversions (Q 13:24 *et seq.*); and
- Like-kind exchanges (Q 13:29 *et seq.*).

Q 13:16 How is gain or loss from a sale or exchange of business property classified for tax purposes?

A gain or loss is classified as either ordinary or capital for tax purposes. In addition, capital gains or losses are classified as either short- or long-term, depending on whether the property is held for one year or less or for more than one year. In the case of personal or investment property, capital assets produce capital gain or loss, while noncapital assets produce ordinary income or loss. Capital gains and losses are netted to determine whether the taxpayer has net gain or loss for the year. [IRC § 1222]

- A net short-term or long-term capital gain of a corporation and a net short-term gain of a noncorporate taxpayer is taxable at the same rate as ordinary income.

- If there is a net capital loss, a noncorporate taxpayer may claim a deduction of up to $3,000 for the year. [IRC § 1211(b)] Corporations can deduct capital losses only to the extent of capital gains. [IRC § 1211(a)]Individual taxpayers can carry over capital losses indefinitely, and the losses retain their character as short- or long-term in the succeeding years. Corporations can carry a net loss back three years and can carry a net loss forward five years as a short-term loss. [IRC § 1212]

- A net long-term capital gain of a noncorporate taxpayer is generally taxed at a more favorable rate than ordinary income. [IRC § 11(h)]The maximum tax rate for long-term capital gains is generally 15 percent (5 percent for taxpayers whose regular tax rate is 15 percent or less). Under the Jobs and Growth Tax Relief Reconciliation Act of 2003 [P.L. 108-27], these rates generally expire at the end of 2008 (except that the 5 percent rate is reduced to 0 percent for 2008). However, the Tax Increase Prevention and Reconciliation Act of 2005 [P.L. 109-222] extends the rates (including the 0 percent rate for taxpayers whose regular tax rate is 15 percent or less) through 2010.

The 15/5 percent maximum capital gain tax rates do not apply to certain capital gains. A 28 percent maximum rate applies to gains from collectibles and certain gains from the sale of small business stock (see Q 13:44 *et seq.*), while a 25 percent maximum rate applies to certain unrecaptured depreciation (see Q 13:23 *et seq.*). Corporations do not get a tax rate reduction for capital gains. [IRC § 1201(a)]

The rules, however, are different for sales or exchanges (including involuntary conversions) of property held longer than one year that is either used in a trade or business or held for the production of rents and royalties. These sales or exchanges—which are called Section 1231 transactions—go through a separate netting process to determine if there is net Section 1231 gain or loss for the year. A net Section 1231 loss is treated as an ordinary loss, while a net Section 1231 gain is treated as long-term capital gain. [IRC § 1231 (a)]

Another set of rules comes into play, however, if the property disposed of was depreciable: if so, all or part of the gain may be treated as ordinary income under the tax law's depreciation recapture rules (see Q 13:20 *et seq.*).

Q 13:17 What sales or exchanges qualify as Section 1231 transactions?

The following transactions result in gain or loss subject to Section 1231 treatment:

- Sales or exchanges of real property or depreciable personal property that was used in a trade or business and held longer than one year. For this purpose, property held for the production of rents or royalties is "used in a trade or business."

- Sales or exchanges of leaseholds used in a trade or business and held longer than one year.

- Sales or exchanges of cattle and horses held for draft, breeding, dairy, or sporting and held for two years or longer.

- Sales or exchanges of other livestock (not including poultry) held for draft, breeding, dairy, or sporting and held for one year or longer.

- Sales or exchanges of unharvested crops provided the crops and land are sold, exchanged, or involuntarily converted at the same time and to the same person and the land was held longer than one year.

- Cutting of timber or disposal of timber, coal, or iron ore that is treated as a sale.

- Condemnations of business property or a capital asset held in connection with a trade or business or a transaction entered into for profit (e.g., investment property held longer than one year).

- Casualties and thefts affecting business property, property held for the production of rents and royalties, or investment property held longer than one year.

[IRC § 1231(b)]

A sale, exchange, or involuntary conversion of inventory or other property held mainly for sale to customers is not a Section 1231 transaction. If a business will get back all, or nearly all, of the investment in the property by selling it rather than by using it up in the business, it is property held mainly for sale to customers.

Example 13-6: Wire Co. manufactures and sells steel cable, which is delivered on returnable reels that are depreciable property. Customers make deposits on the reels, which are refunded if the reels are returned within a year. If a reel is not returned, Wire Co. keeps the customer's deposit as the agreed-upon sales price for the reel. However, most reels are returned within the one-year period. Under these circumstances, the reels are not property held for sale to customers in the ordinary course of business. Any gain or loss resulting from a reel not being returned may be capital or ordinary, depending on Wire Co.'s other Section 1231 transactions.

Intangible property. The IRS recently ruled that intangible property, amortizable under Internal Revenue Code Section 197 (see Chapter 7) may also qualify for Section 1231 treatment. The ruling involved an automobile manufacturer that was ceasing production. The manufacturer paid amounts to auto dealers to terminate their distributor agreements.

The IRS said that the cancellation of a distributor agreement between a manufacturer and a distributor of the manufacturer's products is a sale or exchange of property if the distributor made a substantial capital investment in the distributorship and the investment is reflected in physical assets. Recognized gain from the cancellation Section 1231 gain and may be treated as capital if the agreement is property of a character subject to the allowance for depreciation. For this purpose, property is treated as being of that character if it is amortizable under Section 197. [Rev. Rul. 2007-37, 2007-24 I.R.B]

Q 13:18 Are any gains on Section 1231 transactions excluded from the calculation of overall Section 1231 gain or loss?

Yes. Gains or losses from a transaction are included in the Section 1231 calculation only to the extent they are taken into account in figuring taxable income for the year. [IRC § 1231(a)(4)(A)]Therefore, tax-free, like-kind exchanges and involuntary conversions on which gain is not recognized are not factored into the calculations.

In addition, gain that must be recaptured as ordinary income under the depreciation recapture rules is not included in the calculation (see Q 13:20 *et seq.*)

Finally, a special rule applies to gains and losses from casualties or thefts. If casualty or theft losses exceed casualty or theft gains, neither the gains nor the losses are taken into account in the Section 1231 computation. [IRC § 1231 (a)(4)(B)]Instead, all casualty or theft losses are treated separately as ordinary income or deductible losses.

Q 13:19 How is net Section 1231 gain or loss calculated?

The following steps are used to determine net Section 1231 gain or loss:

Step 1. Determine the amount of gain to be recaptured as ordinary income under the depreciation recapture rules. These amounts are not included in further calculations.

Step 2. Figure the net gain or loss from casualties or thefts of business property. If the net figure is a loss, neither the gains nor the losses are included in further calculations.

Step 3. Net all remaining Section 1231 gains and losses.

If the result is a net Section 1231 loss, it is treated as an ordinary loss. If there is a net Section 1231 gain, it is treated as ordinary income up to the amount of nonrecaptured Section 1231 losses from prior years. [IRC § 1231(c)] Any remaining gain is treated as long-term capital gain. [IRC § § 1231(a)(1), (2)]

Q 13:18

Nonrecaptured Section 1231 losses are net Section 1231 losses from the previous five years that have not been applied against net Section 1231 gain by treating the gain as ordinary income. Nonrecaptured losses are applied against net Section 1231 gain beginning with the earliest loss in the five-year period.

Example 13-7: Fabcor, Inc. is a calendar-year corporation. In Year 1, Fabcor had a net Section 1231 loss of $8,000. Fabcor had a net Section 1231 gain of $5,250 for Year 4 and $4,600 for Year 5. In Year 4, Fabcor treated its entire net Section 1231 gain as ordinary income by recapturing $5,250 of its $8,000 nonrecaptured Section 1231 loss from Year 1. For Year 5, the company recaptures the remaining loss from Year 1 by reporting $2,750 ($8,000 - $5,250) of its net Section 1231 gain as ordinary income. The remaining $1,850 ($4,600 - $2,750) of net Section 1231 gain is treated as long-term capital gain.

For noncorporate taxpayers, nonrecaptured losses are treated as coming first from net Section 1231 gain that would otherwise be taxed at 28 percent, then from gain that would be taxed at 25 percent, and finally from gain that would be taxed at the 15 percent or 5 percent rate.

Example 13-8: Use the same facts as Example 13-7, except that an individual operates the business as a sole proprietorship. The $4,600 gain for Year 5 consists of a $1,000 that would normally be taxed at 28 percent and $1,750 of gain that would normally be taxed at 15/5 percent. Therefore, the $2,750 that is treated as ordinary income consists of the entire $1,000 of gain in the 28 percent rate group and $1,750 of gain in the 15/5 percent group. The remaining $1,850 of gain is treated as capital gain eligible for the 15/5 percent rates.

Depreciation Recapture

Q 13:20 What is depreciation recapture?

When depreciated property is sold, gain on the sale is "recaptured" as ordinary income to the extent of previously claimed depreciation deductions. The amount of depreciation recapture depends on whether the property is:

- Section 1245 property (see Q 13:21 *et seq.*); or
- Section 1250 property (see Q 13:23 *et seq.*).

Q 13:21 What is Section 1245 property?

Section 1245 property includes any property that is or has been subject to an allowance for depreciation or amortization and that falls into any of the following categories:

1. Personal property (either tangible or intangible).
2. Other tangible property (except buildings and their structural components) used as an integral part of manufacturing, production, or extraction, or of furnishing transportation, communications, electricity, gas,

water, or sewage disposal services, including research and storage facilities.

3. That part of any real property (not included in (2)) with an adjusted basis that was reduced by certain amortization deductions (including those for certified pollution control facilities, child-care facilities, removal of architectural barriers to persons with disabilities and the elderly, or reforestation expenses) or a Section 179 expensing deduction.

4. Single-purpose agricultural (livestock) or horticultural structures.

5. Storage facilities (except buildings and their structural components) used in distributing petroleum or petroleum products.

[IRC § 1245(a)(3)]

Section 1245 property does not include buildings and structural components. For this purpose, structures that are essentially items of machinery or equipment should not be treated as buildings and structural components. Also, buildings do not include structures that house Section 1245 property if the structure's use is so closely related to the property's use that the structure must be replaced when the property it initially houses is replaced. The fact that the structure is specially designed to withstand the stress and other demands of the property and the fact that the structure cannot be used economically for other purposes indicates that the structure is closely related to the use of the property it houses. Structures such as oil and gas storage tanks, grain storage bins, silos, fractionating towers, blast furnaces, basic oxygen furnaces, coke ovens, brick kilns, and coal tipples are not treated as buildings. [Reg. § 1.48-1(e)]

A storage facility is a facility used mainly for the bulk storage of fungible commodities. [Reg. § 1.48-1(d)(5)]Bulk storage means the storage of a commodity in a large mass before it is used. For example, if a facility is used to store oranges that have been sorted and boxed, it is not used for bulk storage. To be fungible, a commodity must be such that one part may be used in place of another. Stored materials that vary in composition, size, and weight are not fungible. One part cannot be used in place of another part, and the materials cannot be estimated and replaced by simple reference to weight, measure, and number. For example, the storage of different grades and forms of aluminum scrap is not storage of fungible commodities.

Q 13:22 How is the gain on Section 1245 property treated for tax purposes?

A gain on the disposition of Section 1245 property is treated as ordinary income to the extent of the depreciation allowed or allowable on the property.

The amount of gain treated as ordinary income is the lesser of:

1. The depreciation and amortization allowed or allowable on the property; or

2. The gain realized on the disposition (the amount realized from the disposition minus the adjusted basis of the property).

[IRC § 1245(a)]

Q 13:22

Depreciation and amortization that must be recaptured as ordinary income includes ordinary depreciation deductions, Section 179 expensing deductions, deductions for removing barriers to the disabled and elderly (IRC Section 190), and various amortization deductions (e.g., the costs of acquiring a lease, lease improvements, or Section 197 intangibles).

The Job Creation and Worker Assistance Act of 2002 allowed taxpayers to claim an optional 30-percent first-year depreciation allowance on certain property placed in service on or after September 11, 2001, and before January 1, 2005. The Jobs and Growth Tax Relief Reconciliation Act of 2003 provided an optional 50-percent first-year allowance for certain property placed in service after May 5, 2003, and before January 1, 2005. [IRC § 168(k)] The IRS says that an optional first-year allowance is considered to be depreciation and is subject to recapture. [Temp. Reg. § 1.168(k)-1T(f)(3)]

Amounts subject to recapture may also include depreciation and amortization claimed on other property or claimed by other taxpayers. For example, depreciation recapture on Section 1245 property that was acquired in a tax-free like-kind exchange or involuntary conversion includes depreciation claimed on the exchanged or converted property. In addition, depreciation claimed by a previous owner of the Section 1245 property must be recaptured if a taxpayer's basis is determined with reference to the previous owner's basis (for example, the donor's depreciation deductions on property that was received as a gift).

Example 13-9: Ken Billings, a sole proprietor, files his tax returns on a calendar-year basis. In Year 1, Billings bought and placed in service a used light-duty truck (5-year property) that cost $10,000. The truck is used 100 percent for business. Billings claimed depreciation deductions of $2,000 in Year 1 and $3,200 in Year 2. Billings sells the truck in Year 3 for $7,000. The depreciation deduction for Year 3, the year of sale, is $960. The amount of gain treated as ordinary income is calculated as follows.

1.	Amount realized	$ 7,000
2.	Cost (Year 1)	$10,000
3.	Depreciation ($2,000 + $3,200 + $960)	6,160
4.	Adjusted basis (line 2 less line 3)	$ 3,840
5.	Gain realized (line 1 less line 4)	$ 3,160
6.	Gain treated as ordinary income (lesser of line 3 or line 5)	$ 3,160

Depreciation recapture is figured using the greater of the depreciation allowed or allowable for the property. However, if a taxpayer has consistently taken proper deductions under a particular depreciation method, the amount of depreciation will not be increased even though a greater amount would have been allowed under another depreciation method. If taxpayer did not take any deductions at all for depreciation, adjustments to basis for depreciation allowable are figured by using the straight-line method. [Reg. §§1.1245-2(a)(7); 1.1016-3(a)(2)]

Q 13:23 What is Section 1250 property?

Section 1250 property includes all real property that is subject to an allowance for depreciation and that is not and never has been Section 1245 property. [IRC §1250(c)]It includes leaseholds of land or Section 1250 property subject to an allowance for depreciation. A fee simple interest in land, however, is not included because it is not depreciable.

Q 13:24 How is gain recaptured on Section 1250 property?

Gain on the disposition of Section 1250 property is treated as ordinary income only to the extent of "additional depreciation"—that is, depreciation in excess of straight-line depreciation—allowed or allowable on the property. [IRC §1250]

Residential rental property and nonresidential real property placed in service after 1986 must be depreciated under the straight-line method. [IRC §168(b)(3)]Therefore, no depreciation recapture is required because no additional depreciation in excess of straight line was allowed or allowable. However, a the Job Creation and Worker Assistance Act of 2002 and the Jobs and Growth Tax Relief Reconciliation Act of 2003 allowed taxpayers to claim an additional 30 or 50 percent first-year depreciation allowance on certain property placed in service before January 1, 2005. [IRC Sec. 168(k)] The additional depreciation allowance was available for "qualified leasehold improvements" to the interior of a nonresidential building, provided the improvement is placed in service more that three years after the building was first placed in service. Because the additional first-year allowance effectively accelerates depreciation of the improvement, depreciation recapture may be required when the building is sold.

A special tax rate applies to gain attributable to depreciation allowed or allowable on the property. This unrecaptured Section 1250 gain is taxed at a maximum capital gain rate of 25 percent (rather than the 15/5 percent rates that apply to most long-term capital gain). [IRC §1(h)]

> **Example 13-10:** Phil Brown, who is in the top individual income tax bracket, bought an office building three years ago for $100,000. The area underwent a boom, and Brown doubled his money, selling the building for $200,000. Brown claimed $30,000 of straight-line depreciation on the building. Therefore, his basis for the building is $70,000 ($100,000 cost less $30,000 depreciation), and his gain on the sale is $130,000. No depreciation recapture is required. However, Brown's unrecaptured Section 1250 gain of $30,000 is taxed at a 25 percent rate. The remaining $100,000 of gain is taxed at a 15 percent rate (assuming Brown's regular tax bracket is above 15 percent).

For property placed in service before 1986, a portion of the gain representing additional depreciation on the property may be recaptured as ordinary income.

For real property that is not residential rental property, 100 percent of the additional depreciation for periods after 1969 is subject to recapture. There is no recapture of additional depreciation for periods before 1970.

For residential rental property, 100 percent of the additional depreciation for periods after 1975 is subject to recapture. There is no recapture for of additional depreciation for periods before 1976. Special rules apply to residential rental property that is low-income housing. [IRC § 1250(a)(1)(B)]

Involuntary Conversions

Q 13:25 What is an involuntary conversion?

An involuntary conversion occurs when property is destroyed, stolen, condemned, or disposed of under the threat of condemnation, and the property owner receives other property or money in payment, such as insurance or a condemnation award. Involuntary conversions are also called involuntary exchanges.

Casualty and theft. A casualty occurs when property is destroyed by fire, storm, accident, or some other sudden, unexpected, or unusual event. Theft includes larceny, embezzlement, and robbery. [Reg. § 1.155-8(d)]

Condemnation. A condemnation is the process by which private property is legally taken for public use without the owner's consent. The federal government, a state government, a political subdivision, or a private organization that has the legal power to take the property may force a condemnation. The owner receives a condemnation award (money or property) in exchange for the property taken. A condemnation is like a forced sale, the owner being the seller and the condemning authority being the buyer.

Example 13-11: A local government informed Karen Henderson that it wanted to acquire her business property for a public park. After the local government took action to condemn the property, Henderson went to court to keep it. However, the court decided in favor of the local government, which took the property under its power of eminent domain and paid Henderson an amount fixed by the court. The taking of Henderson's property was a condemnation of private property for public use.

Threat of condemnation. A threat of condemnation exists if a representative of a governmental body or a public official authorized to acquire property for public use informs a property owner that the governmental body or official has decided to acquire his or her property. A sale under threat of condemnation qualifies as an involuntary conversion, provided the property owner has reasonable grounds to believe that, if he or she does not sell voluntarily, his or her property will be condemned.

Example 13-12: Bill Finley owns business property that borders public utility lines. The utility company has the authority to condemn property. The company informs Finley that it intends to acquire his property either by negotiation or condemnation. A threat of condemnation exists when Finley receives the notice.

The IRS recently ruled that a condemnation was "threatened" even though the taxpayer hadn't been formally notified of that fact by a government agency. The taxpayer's local planning board had approved a redevelopment plan that included the taxpayer's property. The plan specifically provided that public works and utilities facilities would be located on the taxpayer's property. The taxpayer received an offer from a third-party to purchase the property. The IRS ruled that the sale would qualify as an involuntary conversion because it was reasonable to conclude that the property was currently "subject to an actual and realistic threat or imminence of condemnation." [Ltr. Rul. 200518066]

Q 13:26 Is gain or loss from an involuntary conversion of business property recognized for tax purposes?

Gain or loss from an involuntary conversion of business property is generally recognized for tax purposes. However, there are two key exceptions:

1. *Direct conversion.* If property is converted directly into other property that is similar or related in service or use, a gain on the conversion will not be recognized. [IRC § 1033(a)(1)]This may happen, for example, if property is condemned and the condemning authority replaces it with other property, rather than providing a monetary award.

2. *Replacement.* A taxpayer may elect nonrecognition of gain on an involuntary conversion if replacement property that is similar or related in service or use is acquired within set time limits, and the cost of the replacement property equals or exceeds the amount realized on the conversion. [IRC § 1033(a)(2)(A)] In addition, nonrecognition applies if a taxpayer buys a controlling interest of at least 80 percent in a corporation owning property that is similar or related in service or use to the converted property. Gain is recognized, however, if the amount realized on the conversion exceeds the cost of the replacement property.

Example 13-13: Tom Hawk bought office machinery for $1,500 two years ago and deducted $780 depreciation. This year a fire destroyed the machinery, and Hawk received $1,200 from his fire insurance company, realizing a gain of $480 ($1,200 - $720 adjusted basis). Hawk elects nonrecognition treatment for the gain. However, replacement machinery costs only $1,000. Hawk's taxable gain is limited to the remaining $200 insurance payment. Hawk's gain is treated as ordinary income under the depreciation recapture rules (see Q 13:20 *et seq.*).

Q 13:27 What property qualifies as replacement property?

To avoid recognition of gain on an involuntary conversion, the proceeds must be reinvested in property that is similar or related in service or use to the converted property or in a controlling interest in a corporation that owns such property. [IRC § 1033(a)(2)]

To qualify as similar or related property, the nature of the replacement property's service or use must be the same as the converted property. The replacement property does not have to be identical to the converted property as long as it has the same general characteristics and is functionally the same as the converted property. For example, a business vehicle must be replaced with another vehicle that performs the same functions.

However, a more liberal rule applies to the replacement of real property that is held for investment or used in a trade or business that is condemned or sold under a threat of condemnation. [IRC § 1033(g)] To qualify for nonrecognition treatment of the gain, the property must be replaced with "like-kind" property.

Like kind has the same meaning as under the rules for like-kind exchanges of business or investment property. (See Q:13:32.) For example, improved and unimproved realty is like kind.

Q 13:28 What are the time limits for acquiring replacement property?

As a general rule, the period for acquiring replacement property begins on the date of the involuntary conversion or, in the case of condemned property, the earlier date on which the threat or imminence of condemnation began. The replacement period ends two years after the close of the tax year in which any portion of the gain on the conversion is realized. [IRC § 1033(c)] However, for real property placed in a trade or business, the replacement period is three years. [IRC § 1033(g)(4)]

Q 13:29 What is the basis of property acquired in an involuntary conversion?

The nonrecognition rules for gain on involuntary conversions do not permanently exclude gain from taxation—they defer the gain until there is a taxable sale or exchange of the replacement property. Therefore, the basis of the replacement property reflects the nonrecognized gain. Here is how the basis of replacement property is determined:

Direct conversion. If gain is not recognized because property was converted directly into other property that is similar or related in service or use, the basis of the replacement property is the same as the adjusted basis of the converted property. [IRC § 1033(b)(1)]

> **Example 13-14:** Fred Finn owned land with a basis of $50,000. A governmental authority condemned the land, and Finn received similar land as a replacement. The basis of the replacement land is $50,000.

No gain recognized on replacement. If gain is not recognized on a conversion because the cost of replacement property exceeds the amount realized, the basis of the replacement property is equal to its cost less the gain not recognized. [IRC § 1033(b)(2)]

Example 13-15: Machine Co. owned a piece of equipment with a basis of $100,000. The machine was destroyed by fire, and Machine Co. received insurance proceeds of $125,000. Therefore, Machine Co. realized a gain on the conversion of $25,000. However, Machine Co. bought a replacement machine for $130,000. Therefore, no gain is recognized because the cost of the replacement machine exceeded the amount realized on the conversion. The basis of the new machine is $105,000 ($130,000 cost of the new machine less $25,000 of gain not recognized).

Gain recognized on replacement. If gain is recognized on a conversion because the amount realized exceeds the cost of replacement property, the basis of the replacement property is also equal to its cost less any gain not recognized.

Example 13-16: Same facts as Example 13-15, except Machine Co. bought a replacement machine for $110,000. Because the $110,000 cost of the replacement machine was less than the $125,000 amount realized, Machine Co. must recognize a gain of $15,000; $10,000 of gain is not recognized. The basis of the new machine is $100,000 ($110,000 cost less $10,000 gain not recognized).

Like-Kind Exchanges

Q 13:30 What is a like-kind exchange?

Like-kind exchange rules permit a taxpayer to make a tax-free swap of business or investment property; the property is exchanged for like-kind property. [IRC § 1031(a)(1)]

The gain or loss that is not recognized on a like-kind exchange is tax-deferred, not tax-exempt. The property received in the exchange has the same basis as the property transferred. Therefore, the deferred gain or loss will be recognized when the taxpayer disposes of the new property. In addition, the holding period of the property received in the exchange includes the holding period of the property transferred. [IRC § 1223(1)]

To qualify for tax-deferred treatment, all of the following conditions must be met:

1. There must be an exchange of properties (Q 13:30);

2. The properties exchanged must be property held for productive use in a trade or business, or held for investment, that are eligible for like-kind exchange treatment (Q 13:31);

3. The properties exchanged must be like kind (Q 13:32); and

4. The property received in the exchange must be identified and the exchange completed within a prescribed time limit (Q 13:34).

Q 13:30

Q 13:31 What transactions qualify as an exchange of properties?

To qualify for tax-deferred treatment there must be an actual exchange of properties. A transaction will not qualify for like-kind exchange treatment if the taxpayer exchanges property for money, which is then used to acquire like-kind property. However, a party to the transaction may transfer money—called "boot"—to even up the exchange (see Q 13:40).

In its simplest form, a like-kind exchange involves simultaneous transfers of properties by two parties. However, an exchange need not be simultaneous to qualify for like-kind exchange treatment (see Q 13:34). Moreover, a like-kind exchange may involve multiple parties (see Q 13:37 *et seq.*).

Q 13:32 What property is eligible for like-kind exchange treatment?

In a like-kind exchange, both the property transferred and the property received must be held by the taxpayer for investment or for productive use in a trade or business. [IRC § 1033(a)(1)]Machinery, buildings, land, trucks, and rental houses are examples of property that may qualify.

However, the like-kind exchange rules do not apply to exchanges of the following property:

- Property used for personal purposes, such as a home or family car;
- Stock in trade or other property held primarily for sale, such as inventories, raw materials, and real estate held by dealers;
- Stocks, bonds, notes, or other securities or evidence of indebtedness, such as accounts receivable;
- Partnership interests;
- Certificates of trust or beneficial interest; or
- Chooses in action.

[IRC § 1031(a)(2)]

Q 13:33 What is like-kind property?

Like-kind properties are properties of the same nature or character, even if they differ in grade or quality. [Reg. § 1.1031(a)-1(b)]

The exchange of real estate for real estate and the exchange of personal property for similar personal property are exchanges of like-kind property. [Reg. § § 1.1031(a)-1(b), (c)] For example, a swap of land improved with an apartment house for land improved with a store building, or a panel truck for a pickup truck, is a like-kind exchange.

An exchange of personal property for real property does not qualify as a like-kind exchange. For example, an exchange of a piece of machinery for a store building does not qualify. Nor does the exchange of livestock of different sexes qualify. [Reg. § 1.1031(e)-1]

An exchange of city property for farm property, or improved property for unimproved property, is a like-kind exchange. In addition, the exchange of real estate owned by a taxpayer for a real estate lease that runs 30 years or longer is a like-kind exchange.

Depreciable tangible personal property can be either "like kind" or "like class" to qualify for nonrecognition treatment. Like-class properties are depreciable tangible personal properties within the same General Asset Class or Product Class. Property classified in any General Asset Class may not be classified within a Product Class. [Reg. § 1.1031(a)-2]

General Assets Classes describe types of property frequently used in many businesses. For example:

- Office furniture, fixtures, and equipment (Asset Class 00.11);
- Information systems, such as computers and peripherals (Asset Class 00.12);
- Data handling equipment other than computers (Asset Class 00.13);
- Automobiles and taxis (Asset Class 00.22); and
- Light, general-purpose trucks (Asset Class 00.241).

Product Classes list depreciable tangible personal property under four-digit Standard Industrial Classification (SIC) codes. Copies of the product class manual may be obtained from the National Technical Information Service, an agency of the U.S. Department of Commerce, at *www.ntis.gov/*.

Example 13-17: Nora Wilson swaps a personal computer used in her business for a computer printer to be used in the business. The properties fall within the same General Asset Class and, therefore, qualify for like-kind exchange treatment.

If intangible personal property or nondepreciable personal property is exchanged for like-kind property, no gain or loss is recognized on the exchange. However, there are no like classes for intangible properties. The tax treatment of like-kind exchanges of intangibles requires specificity and the analysis of exchanges on an item-by-item basis. The IRS emphasized this in a recent ruling when it rejected a taxpayer's like-kind exchange of patents, trademarks and other intangible property. [TAM 200602034]

The taxpayer in the new ruling proposed a matching scheme that would group all patents into four broad categories of underlying property (Process, Machine, Manufacture, and Composition of Matter). For example, a machine patent could be like-kind to any other machine patent and a process patent would be like-kind to any other process patent. The taxpayer also claimed like-kind treatment for trademarks and trade names.

The IRS said that a two prong analysis must be used, which requires the matching of the:

1. Nature or character of the rights involved; and

2. Nature or character of the underlying property to which the intangible personal property relates.

The IRS noted, "Whenever possible, the underlying tangible personal properties to which the intangible asset relates should be compared using the General Asset Classes and the Product Classes already afforded for testing whether personal properties are of like class."

Generally, the nature or character of rights under one patent is the same as the nature or character of rights under a different patent even if the underlying property may differ. The first prong of the test is satisfied if a patent exists on both sides of the exchange. Matching by General Asset Class and the Product Classes is reasonable to satisfy the second prong, the IRS explained. However, in this case, the IRS found no authority for the taxpayer's proposed matching scheme.

The IRS also rejected the taxpayer's argument that all trademarks and trade names exchanged in the transactions be considered of like-kind. This approach, the IRS explained, would improperly treat any trademark or trade name as like-kind regardless of use, appearance, form, or origin. All trademarks and trade names are not alike and should not be considered of like-kind for purposes of the tax-free exchange rules.

Q 13:34 What is a deferred exchange?

In a deferred exchange, a taxpayer transfers property used in business or held for investment and later receives replacement like-kind property to be used in business or held for investment.

To qualify for tax-free treatment, the transaction must be an exchange (that is, a property-for-property swap) rather than a transfer of property for money that is later used to buy replacement property. If, before acquiring the replacement property, a taxpayer actually or constructively receives money or unlike property in full payment for the property transferred, the transaction will be treated as a sale rather than a deferred exchange. In that case, gain or loss is recognized even if the taxpayer later acquires like-kind replacement property. (It would be treated as if taxpayer purchased the property.)

Money or unlike property is constructively received if it is credited to a taxpayer's account or otherwise made available to the taxpayer. However, certain arrangements that are designed to ensure that the other party to the exchange carries out the obligation to transfer replacement property are not treated as constructive receipt of money or unlike property. For example, securing the other party's obligation by a mortgage or by cash in a qualified escrow account is not treated as constructive receipt. [Reg. § 1.1031(k)-1(g)]

Q 13:35 What are the time limits for completing a deferred exchange?

The property to be received in the exchange must be identified within 45 days of the date the property relinquished in the exchange is transferred. The replacement property must be received by the earlier of: (1) the 180th day after the date the property given up in the exchange is transferred, or (2) the due date, including extensions, for the tax return for the year in which the transfer occurs. [IRC § 1031(a)(3)]

If a transfer involves multiple properties that are transferred at different times, the identification and receipt periods begin on the date of the earliest transfer. [Reg. § 1.1031(k)-1(b)(2)(iii)]

Q 13:36 How is replacement property identified?

A transferor must identify the replacement property in a signed written document and deliver it to the other party to the exchange. [Reg. § 1.1031(k)-1(c)] The document must clearly describe the replacement property—for example, by giving the legal description or street address for real property or the make, model, and year for a car. Identification of a replacement property can be cancelled in a signed written document executed during the identification period.

A transferor can identify more than one possible replacement property—within limits. The maximum number of identified replacement properties is limited to the larger of: (1) three properties, or (2) any number of properties whose total fair market value (FMV) at the end of the identification period is not more than double the total fair market value of the properties transferred.

Q 13:37 Can a like-kind exchange be handled through a third party?

A like-kind exchange of properties can be made through a qualified intermediary. [Reg. § 1.1031(k)-1(g)(4)]

A qualified intermediary is a person who enters into a written exchange agreement with the transferor to acquire and transfer the relinquished property and to acquire the replacement property and transfer it to the transferor. A qualified intermediary may not be the transferor's agent (e.g., an employee, attorney, accountant, investment banker or broker, or real estate agent or broker) at the time of the transfer or have served as the transferor's agent within the two-year period before the exchange. [Reg. § 1.1031(k)-1(k)]

Q 13:38 Can a transferor acquire replacement property before transferring the property to be given up in the exchange?

Generally, the like-kind exchange rules do not apply to this type of reverse exchange. However, a reverse exchange can be set up through a qualified exchange accommodation arrangement (QEAA). [Rev. Proc. 2000-37, 2000-2 C.B. 308]

Under a QEAA, either the replacement property or the relinquished property is transferred to an exchange accommodation titleholder (EAT), discussed below, who is treated as the beneficial owner of the property for federal income tax purposes. If the property is held in a QEAA, the IRS will accept the qualification of property as either replacement property or relinquished property and the treatment of an EAT as the beneficial owner of the property for federal income tax purposes.

Q 13:39 What are the requirements for a QEAA?

Property is held in a QEAA only if all the following requirements are met:

- The arrangement is evidenced by a written agreement;
- The time limits for identifying and transferring the property are met;
- Qualified indications of ownership of property (e.g., legal title or contract of deed) are transferred to the EAT;
- The EAT holds the property for the benefit of transferor in order to facilitate a like-kind exchange;
- The transferor and the EAT agree to report the acquisition, holding, and disposition of the property in a manner consistent with the agreement; and
- The EAT is treated as the beneficial owner of the property for all federal income tax purposes.

Under a QEAA, the property to be given up in the exchange must be identified no later than 45 days after the transfer of qualified indications of ownership of the replacement property to the EAT, and the exchange must be completed within 180 days after the transfer of qualified indications of ownership of the property to the EAT. [Rev. Proc. 2000-37, 2000-2 C.B. 308]

Q 13:40 What if a like-kind exchange also involves money or property that is not like kind?

If a party to a like-kind exchange also receives money or property that is not like kind (referred to as "boot"), gain is taxable to the extent of the money and the fair market value of the property that is not like kind. For this purpose, liabilities assumed by the other party to the exchange are treated as cash received. [Reg. § 1.1031(b)-1(c)]

Example 13-18: Sam Smith exchanges real estate held for investment with an adjusted basis of $8,000 for other real estate to be held for investment. The fair market value of the real estate Smith receives is $10,000. Smith also receives $1,000 in cash. Although the total gain realized on the transaction is $3,000, only $1,000 (the amount of cash received) is recognized.

If a party to a like-kind exchange transfers money in addition to like-kind property, no gain or loss is recognized. However, the basis of the property received in the exchange is equal to the basis of the property transferred increased by the money paid.

If like-kind exchange also involves a transfer of property that is not like kind, gain or loss is recognized on the non-like-kind property. The gain or loss is equal to the difference between the fair market value of the property and its adjusted basis.

> **Example 13-19:** Jean Knox exchanges stock and real estate she held for investment for real estate to be held for investment. The stock has a fair market value of $4,000 and an adjusted basis of $1,000. The real estate transferred has a fair market value of $16,000 and an adjusted basis of $10,000. The real estate received has a fair market value of $20,000. Knox does not recognize gain on the exchange of the real estate because it qualifies as a like-kind exchange. However, Knox must recognize a $3,000 gain on the stock because it is not like-kind property.

Q 13:41 What is the basis of property received in a like-kind exchange?

In a straight like-kind property swap, the basis of the property received in the exchange is equal to basis of the property transferred. [IRC § 1031(d)]

The total basis for all properties (other than money) received in a partial like-kind exchange is the total adjusted basis of the relinquished properties, increased by any costs incurred and any gain recognized and reduced by any money received and any loss recognized. Basis is allocated first to property that is not like kind, other than money, up to its fair market value on the date of the exchange. Any remaining amount is the basis of the like-kind property. [Reg. § 1031(d)-1]

Q 13:42 Can related parties enter into a like-kind exchange?

Yes. However, special rules apply to related-party exchanges. Under those rules, if either party disposes of the like-kind property within two years after the exchange, the exchange is disqualified from tax-free treatment. Gain or loss on the original exchange must be recognized as of the date of the disposition. [IRC § 1031(f)]

For this purpose, related parties include certain family members (including a spouse, brother, sister, parent, or child), a corporation or partnership, and a more-than-50 percent owner, or two partnerships in which the same person owns more than 50 percent of the capital interests or profits.

The required two-year holding period begins on the date of the last transfer of property that was part of the exchange.

> **Example 13-20:** John Crandall used a panel truck in his house painting business. John's sister, Joan, used a station wagon in her landscaping business. In December of Year 1, John exchanged his truck plus $200 for Joan's station wagon. At that time, the fair market value of the truck was $7,000, and its adjusted basis was $6,000. The fair market value of the station wagon was $7,200, and its adjusted basis was $1,000. John realized a gain of $1,000 on the exchange (the $7,200 fair market value of the station wagon minus the $200 cash paid minus the $6,000 adjusted basis of the truck). Joan realized a

gain of $6,200 (the $7,000 fair market value of John's truck plus the $200 Joan received minus the $1,000 adjusted basis of the station wagon).

However, under the like-kind exchange rules, John did not recognize any gain. His basis in the station wagon was $6,200 (the $6,000 adjusted basis of the truck plus the $200 he paid). Joan recognized gain only to the extent of the money she received, $200. Her basis in the truck was $1,000 (the $1,000 adjusted basis of the station wagon minus the $200 received, plus the $200 gain recognized).

In December of Year 2, John sold the station wagon to a third party for $7,000. Because it was sold within two years after the exchange with Joan, the exchange was disqualified from tax-free treatment. On his tax return for Year 2, John must report the $1,000 gain on the prior year's exchange. He will also report a $200 loss on the sale (the adjusted basis of the station wagon, $7,200 (its $6,200 basis plus the $1,000 gain recognized) minus the $7,000 realized from the sale).

In addition, Joan must report the $6,000 gain from the exchange with John that was not recognized in Year 1. Her adjusted basis in the truck is increased to $7,000 (its $1,000 basis plus the $6,000 gain recognized).

The nonrecognition provision for like-kind exchanges does not apply to any exchange that is part of a transaction (or a series of transactions) structured to avoid the related party rule. [IRC § 1031(f)(4)] For example, if a taxpayer, pursuant to a prearranged plan, transfers property to an unrelated party who then exchanges the property with a party related to the taxpayer within two years of the previous transfer, the related party will not be entitled to nonrecognition treatment. [H.R. Rep. No. 247, 101st Cong. 1st Sess. 1341 (1989)]

The IRS has ruled that the related party rule cannot be avoided by using a qualified intermediary (see Q 13:37).

Example 13-21: Bob Smith owns Property A with a fair market value of $150,000 and an adjusted basis of $50,000. Bob's brother, Ted Smith, owns Property B with a fair market value of $150,000 and an adjusted basis of $150,000. Both property A and B are held for investment. Nina Black, who is not related to Bob and Ted, wants to buy Property A from Bob. Bob enters into an agreement with Ted and Nina to transfer Property A and Property B to a qualified intermediary. Pursuant to their agreement, on January 6 of Year 1, Bob transfers Property A to the qualified intermediary and the intermediary transfers Property A to Nina in exchange for $150,000. On January 13 Ted transfers Property B to the qualified intermediary and receives the $150,000 cash paid by Nina. The qualified intermediary transfers Property B to Bob.

According to the IRS, Bob is using a qualified intermediary to circumvent the purposes of the related party rule. The result is effectively the same as if Bob and Ted had swapped properties and Ted had sold his property to Nina within two years. That would have violated the related party rule, and the use of a qualified intermediary does not change the situation. Therefore,

Bob's exchange does not qualify for nonrecognition treatment, and he has a taxable gain of $100,000. [Rev. Rul. 2002-83, 2002-49 I.R.B. 927]

Q 13:43 How do taxpayers elect like-kind exchange treatment?

Nonrecognition on a like-kind exchange is not elective; it is mandatory if the requirements are satisfied. Moreover, the IRS will recharacterize a sale and purchase as a like-kind exchange in certain circumstances. [IRS Pub. No. 544, Sales and Other Dispositions of Assets]

> **Example 13-22:** Susan Baker used a car in her business for two years. The adjusted basis of the car is $3,500 and its trade-in value is $4,500. Baker is interested in a new car that costs $20,000. Ordinarily, Baker would trade in the old car for the new one and pay the dealer $15,500. Thus, under the like-kind exchange rules, Baker's basis for depreciation of the new car would then be $19,000 ($15,500 plus $3,500 adjusted basis of her old car).
>
> However, to increase her basis for depreciation of the new car, Baker arranges to sell her old car to the dealer for $4,500. She then buys the new car for $20,000 from the same dealer.
>
> *Result:* The IRS says Baker will be treated as having exchanged her old car for the new one because the sale and purchase are reciprocal and mutually dependent. Her basis for depreciation for the new car will be $19,000, the same as if she traded in the old car.

Sales of Small Business Stock

Q 13:44 Are there any tax breaks for gain on the sale of small business stock?

Yes, the tax law provides an exclusion for 50 percent of the gain on "qualified small business stock" that has been held for more than five years. [IRC § 1202] The 50 percent of the gain that is taxable does not qualify for the standard 15/5 percent tax rate on capital gain. Instead, like collectibles, the taxable 50 percent is taxed at the lesser of 28 percent or the taxpayer's regular tax rate. [IRC § 1(h)(4)] Thus, for a taxpayer whose regular tax rate is 28 percent or above, the effective tax rate on the gain from small business stock is 14 percent (50 percent of 28 percent).

The Internal Revenue Code provides another benefit for qualified small business stock. Gain from the sale or exchange of qualified stock held for more than six months is tax-free if the proceeds from the sale are rolled over into other qualified small business stock. [IRC § 1045]

These tax breaks are available only to individuals and pass-through entities (partnerships, S corporations, and trusts or estates). The tax breaks are not available to C corporations.

Q 13:45 Are there any limits on the exclusion of gain from the sale of qualified small business stock?

There is an annual dollar limit on the exclusion for gain from the sale of qualified small business stock. The limit is the greater of $10 million per shareholder or 10 times the amount the shareholder paid for the stock. [IRC § 1202(b)]The $10 million dollar figure is reduced by the amount of any gain excluded in prior years.

Q 13:46 What are the requirements for a rollover of gain from the sale of qualified small business stock?

To qualify for rollover treatment, proceeds from the sale of qualified small business stock must be used to purchase other qualified small business stock within 60 days of the sale. [IRC § 1045(a)] Gain on the sale is recognized only to the extent the amount realized on the sale exceeds the cost of qualified replacement stock within the 60-day period.

Any gain not recognized reduces the basis of the replacement stock. The basis adjustment is applied to replacement stock in the order in which it is purchased. [IRC § 1045(b)(3)]As a general rule, the holding period for the replacement stock includes the holding period of the stock sold. [IRC § 1045(b)(4)]

Planning Point: Qualified small business stock acquired in a rollover will qualify for the 50 percent exclusion for gain when the stock is sold (assuming all the requirements are met at the time of the sale). Moreover, because the holding period of the replacement stock includes the holding period of the original stock, the minimum five-year holding period will be measured from the date the original stock was acquired.

Q 13:47 What is qualified small business stock?

Qualified small business stock is stock in a "qualified small business" that is engaged in an "active business." [IRC § 1202(c)] In addition, the stock must meet the following requirements:

- The stock is in a C corporation;
- The stock was originally issued after August 10, 1993; and
- The issuing corporation had total gross assets of $50 million or less at all times after August 9, 1993 and before the stock was issued and immediately after the stock was issued.

[IRC § 1202(d)]

Q 13:48 What is a qualified small business?

A qualified small business includes any business other than:

- A business involving services in the fields of health, law, engineering, architecture, accounting, actuarial science, performing arts, consulting, athletics, financial services, or brokerage services;
- A business whose principal asset is the reputation or skill of one or more employees;
- A banking, insurance, financing, leasing, investing, or similar business;
- A farming business (including the raising or harvesting of trees);
- A business involving the production of products for which percentage depletion can be claimed; and
- A business operating a hotel, motel, restaurant, or similar establishment.

[IRC § 1202(e)(3)]

Q 13:49 What is the active business requirement?

Stock qualifies for the exclusion of gain only if the corporation is engaged in an active business for substantially all of the time the stock was held. [IRC § 1202(c)(2)(A)]In the case of a rollover, the company issuing the replacement stock must meet the active business requirement for six months following the purchase. [IRC § 1045(b)]

A corporation will meet the active business requirement if it uses 80 percent or more of its assets (by value) in one or more businesses other than disqualified businesses (see Q 13:48). [IRC § 1202(e)(3)] Assets that are held to meet the working capital needs of the business or assets that are held for investment and are used within two years to finance research count toward the 80 percent requirement.

A corporation will not meet the active business requirement if it has significant assets invested in real estate or securities. The value of real estate that is not used in the business cannot exceed 10 percent of total assets. [IRC § 1202(e)(7)]The value of securities cannot exceed 10 percent of net assets. [IRC § 1202(e)(5)(B)]

The active business requirement does not apply to a specialized small business investment company (SSBIC) that is licensed by the Small Business Administration. [IRC § 1202(c)(2)(B)]

Chapter 14

Payroll Taxes

In the past three decades, employers have seen payroll taxes grow from a minor expense to a major cost—and payroll taxes continue to rise. In 1975, employers and employees each paid a 5.85 percent FICA tax (4.95 percent Social Security and 0.9 percent Medicare) on the first $14,100 of earnings. So employers and employees each paid a maximum tax of $824.50. By 2007, the Social Security portion of the tax had climbed to 6.2 percent and the taxable wage base has increased to a whopping $97,500—resulting in a maximum tax for both employers and employees of $6,045. In addition, Congress eliminated the wage base for the Medicare tax starting in 1994. So, employers and employees each owe the 1.45 percent Medicare tax on an unlimited amount of wages.

In addition to rising tax rates, payroll taxes have become increasingly complex. New types of compensation and fringe benefits have spawned new—and complex—payroll tax rules. In addition, changes in the relationship between employers and employees—such as the outsourcing of work traditionally performed by employees—has resulted in an increasing number of disputes between employers and the Internal Revenue Service (IRS or the Service) over payroll tax responsibilities.

This chapter will guide the reader through the maze of today's federal payroll tax rules and regulations.

Payroll Tax Basics

Q 14:1 What are an employer's basic payroll tax responsibilities?

Employers have a variety of payroll tax responsibilities. Each employer must:

- Withhold income taxes from wages and other compensation paid to employees;

- Withhold and pay Social Security and Medicare (FICA) taxes;

- Pay federal unemployment (FUTA) tax;

- Make timely and accurate payroll tax deposits;

- File quarterly and annual payroll tax returns; and

- Provide employees with annual statements of their compensation and payroll taxes.

Income Tax Withholding

Q 14:2 What types of payments to an employee are subject to income tax withholding?

An employer must withhold income taxes from basic wage payments to employees. In addition, withholding is required for other types of compensatory payments such as bonuses, retirement plan benefits, and taxable fringe benefits.

Q 14:3 How does an employer know how much to withhold from an employee's wages?

The starting point for determining the amount to withhold from an employee's wages is Form W-4, *Employee's Withholding Allowance Certificate*, which must be submitted by each employee. [IRC §§ 3401(e), 3402(f), 3402(m); Reg. §§ 31.3401(e)-1; 31.3401(f)(1)-1 through (f)(6)-1; 31.3402(m)-1]

An employee's Form W-4 indicates the employee's withholding status as a married or single individual. In addition, Form W-4 indicates the number of withholding allowances the employee may claim. This information is necessary to calculate withholding using tables issued by the IRS.

Each withholding allowance claimed on an employee's W-4 represents an amount of income that is exempt from withholding for the year. For example, for 2007, each withholding allowance was worth $3,400; for 2008, it's worth $3,500 [Form W-4, *Employee's Withholding Allowance Certificate*]

Q 14:1

In general, an employee's withholding allowances mirror the allowances that will be used to figure his or her income tax liability. For example, an employee can claim a personal withholding allowance unless the he or she can be claimed as a dependent on another person's tax return. In addition, an employee can claim allowances for a spouse and for each dependent the employee expects to claim on his or her tax return. [IRC § 3402(f)]

Employees may also be entitled to additional withholding allowances under certain circumstances. For example, a single employee who has only one job or a married employee who has only one job and whose spouse does not work outside the home is entitled to an additional allowance. Additional withholding allowances may also be claimed to take into account estimated deductions, adjustments to income, and tax credits that will be claimed when the employee files his or her tax return. [IRC § 3402(m)]

If an employee's income tax liability will exceed his or her withholding for the year, the employee may claim fewer withholding allowances than he or she is entitled to. In addition, the employee's W-4 can request that additional amounts be withheld for each pay period. Increased amounts that the employee voluntarily asks to have withheld are treated as tax that is required to be withheld and remitted by the employer. [IRC § 3402(I); Reg. § 31.3402(I)-1]

In some cases, an employee's form may indicate that he or she is exempt from withholding. An employee can claim exemption from withholding if he or she had no tax liability for the prior year and expects to incur no tax liability for the current year. An employee who can be claimed as a dependent on someone else's tax return generally cannot claim exemption from withholding in 2008 if he or she has more than $900 of income that includes more than $300 of unearned income. [Rev. Proc. 2007-66 I.R.B. 2007-45]

Q 14:4 When must an employer obtain Form W-4 from an employee?

An employer should obtain a W-4 form from an employee on or before the employee's first day of work. [Reg. § 3402(f)(2)-1]

An employer is not required to verify the accuracy of an employee's Form W-4. However, if an employee alters or makes unauthorized additions to the form it is invalid. In addition, if an employee indicates, either orally or in writing that the information on the form is false, it must be treated as invalid. In either case, the employer should ask the employee for a new form.

If an employee does not submit a valid Form W-4, the employer must withhold from the employee as a single individual claiming zero tax withholding allowances. If an employee submits an invalid W-4 to replace one already on file, the employer should continue to withhold on the basis of the original certificate until the employee submits a valid replacement. [Reg. § 31.3402(f)(2)-1(e)]

Q 14:4

Q 14:5 Does the tax law permit employers to obtain and maintain Forms W-4 electronically?

W-4 forms have traditionally been submitted on paper. However, the IRS rules permit an employer to establish an electronic system for filing and maintaining W-4 forms. [Reg. § 31.3402(f)(5)-1]

The electronic system must ensure that the information received is the information that was submitted by the employee, and must document all occasions of employee access that result in the filing of a Form W-4. The design and operation of the system, including access procedures, must make it reasonably certain the person accessing the system is the employee identified in the W-4 form. The system must provide the employer with exactly the same information as a paper Form W-4.

The employee must sign the W-4 form under penalties of perjury. To meet that requirement, the electronic W-4 must contain the jurat statement that appears on the paper W-4 and must inform the employee that he or she is signing electronically under penalties of perjury. The electronic signature may be in any form that identifies the employee and authenticates and verifies the filing. The electronic signature must be the last item on the electronic W-4.

Upon request by the IRS, the employer must supply a hardcopy of the electronic Form W-4 and a statement that, to the best of the employer's knowledge, the named employee filed the electronic form. The hardcopy of the electronic W-4 must contain exactly the same information as a paper Form W-4, but need not be a facsimile of the paper form. [Reg. § 31.3402(f)(5)-1]

The IRS says that employers must make filing on paper reasonably available to an employee who has a serious objection to using the electronic system or whose access to or ability to use the system is limited. Telling the employee how to get a paper form and how to submit it will generally satisfy this requirement. However, the IRS cautions employers that further steps may be required under the Americans with Disabilities Act if the employee is unable to use the electronic system because of a disability.

Q 14:6 Is an employer required to file employee's W-4 forms with the IRS?

As a general rule, W-4 forms do not have to be filed with the IRS. They must be kept on file and made available if the IRS wishes to inspect them.

Under prior rules, employers were required to forward to the IRS two categories of W-4 forms: (1) forms claiming more than 10 withholding allowances, and (2) forms claiming exemption from withholding if the employee's wages exceeded $200 a week. However, this requirement has been eliminated by the IRS, effective as of April 15, 2005. Instead, employers must now submit copies of W-4s to the IRS only when directed to do so by written notice or as directed in published guidance. [Reg. § 31.3402(f)(2)-1(g)(1)]

Q 14:5

If the IRS determines that an employee has inadequate withholding, it will send the employer and the employee a "lock-in letter." The lock-in letter will specify the maximum number of withholding allowances permitted for the employee and the new rate for withholding.

Employers will receive two copies of the lock-in letter as a backup in case the employee does not receive the lock-in letter. If the employee is still working for the employer, the employer must give the employee copy to the employee within ten days of receiving it. If the employee no longer works for the employer, the employer must notify the IRS through the procedures described in the lock-in letter.

Employees will be given some time before the new lock-in rate is effective to submit directly to the IRS a new Form W-4 and a statement supporting lower income tax withholding.

The employer must withhold tax at the new rate specified in the lock-in letter at the time specified in the letter, which is not supposed to be any sooner than 45 days after the date on the lock-in letter.

The employer may not decrease the rate after the new rate becomes effective. Any new Form W-4 submitted by an employee to an employer after the receipt of a lock-in letter should be disregarded by employers. [Reg. § 31.3402(f)(2)-1(g)(2)]

The IRS has warned employers about ensuring that online systems where employees can change their Form W-4s at anytime online have mechanisms in place to block employees who have been locked-in. If employers do not withhold in accordance with the lock-in letter, they will be liable for any additional tax owed. Additionally, employers may be liable for a penalty if they do not ensure the lock-in rate is in place by the date specified in the letter.

Before the lock-in letter is received, though, employers do not have to submit any information to the IRS. That is, even if an employer gets a valid Form W-4 from an employee and it appears to the employer that the employee is claiming an incorrect withholding amount, the IRS web site ("Withholding Compliance Questions & Answers") states that an employer should withhold at the rate specified on the employee's Form W-4. But the employer should warn the employee that the IRS may review it and order the employer to lock-in a higher rate.

Q 14:7 Are employees required to submit a new Form W-4 each year?

No—with one exception. A Form W-4 that indicates an employee is exempt from withholding has a cut-off date. To continue the exemption the employee must submit a new Form W-4 by February 15 of each year. If an employer does not receive a new Form W-4 by that date, the employer must withhold as if the employee is single and claims no withholding allowances. [Reg. § 31.3402(f)(4)-2]

Q 14:8 When can an employee submit a new Form W-4?

An employee can submit a new Form W-4 to change his or her withholding at any time. An employee is required to submit a new Form W-4 within 10 days if his or her withholding allowances *decrease* or if he or she is no longer entitled to exemption from withholding.

Planning Point: An employee is not required to submit a new Form W-4 to increase withholding allowances and thus reduce withholding. Moreover, the onus is on the employee to do so. If an employee delays submitting a new W-4, it applies prospectively only. The employee cannot get back amounts that were withheld on the basis of his or her prior withholding certificate.

Q 14:9 When must an employer implement an employee's new Form W-4?

An employer must implement the requested changes no later than the first payroll period ending on or after the 30th day from the day the employer receives the new form. If the employer does not have regular payroll periods, the employer must put a new Form W-4 into effect for the first payment of wages on or after the 30th day from the date the employer receives the form. [Reg. § 31.3402(f)(3)-1]

Q 14:10 When do wages become subject to income tax withholding?

Generally, an employer must withhold on wages when they are actually or constructively paid to the employee. Wages are constructively paid when they are credited to an employee's account or otherwise set apart so that the employee has an unrestricted right to them. [Reg. § 31.3402(a)-1(b)]If there is a substantial restriction on an employee's right to receive wages, they are not subject to withholding until the restrictions lapse or the wages are actually paid to the employee. [Reg. § 31.3402(a)-1]

Q 14:11 How frequently must an employer withhold on wages?

An employer must withhold on wages each payroll period. [IRC § 3402]

Q 14:12 What is a payroll period?

An employer's payroll period is the time for which the employer usually makes wage payments to an employee. Regular payroll periods can be daily, weekly, biweekly, semimonthly, quarterly, semiannual, or annual. [Reg. § 31.3401(b)-1] Any other period is considered a miscellaneous payroll period.

The fact that an employer cuts checks at regular intervals does not necessarily determine the payroll period from which the employee is paid. The payroll period is determined by the period of service for which wages are paid, not by the period between paychecks. [Reg. § 1.3401(b)-1(a)]

Example 14-1: An employer issues payroll checks to all of its employees on Friday of each week. Some employees work five days each week, Monday through Friday. Others work only three days, Monday through Wednesday. The employees who work a full week are on a weekly payroll period, while those who work only three days are not on a weekly payroll period.

As a general rule, the employer should withhold on wages paid to employees who are paid for a period of less than a week using methods for daily or miscellaneous payroll periods (see Qs 14:13, 14:14). If, however, an employee who is paid for a period of less than a week signs a statement under penalties of perjury that he or she is not working for any other employer during the week, the employer may figure the employee's withholding on a weekly payroll period. If the employee subsequently begins to work for someone else, the employee must notify the employer within 10 days. The employer must then withhold on the basis of a daily or miscellaneous payroll period.

These rules stem from the fact that a portion of the value of an employee's withholding allowances is allocated ratably to each payroll period. An employee's wages for the period are subject to withholding only to the extent they exceed the exempt amount for the payroll period. For example, in 2007, when each withholding allowance is worth $3,400, a weekly worker claiming one exemption was entitled to an exemption of $65.38 per week ($3,400/52). On the other hand, if a worker claiming one allowance worked for two different employers during the week, use of a weekly payroll period would double the weekly exemption to $130.76.

Q 14:13 What if an employee is occasionally paid for a longer or shorter period than his or her regular payroll period?

If an employee is generally paid according to a set payroll period, the employer should withhold on that basis even if a particular payment covers a longer or shorter period. [Reg. § 31.3401(b)-1]Employers frequently run into this situation with vacation pay.

Example 14-2: Barbara Penn is normally paid weekly. Penn takes a three-week vacation during the year. Penn's employer cuts one check for Penn's three weeks of vacation pay. The employer should treat the check as payment for three weekly payroll periods.

Calculating Income Tax Withholding

Q 14:14 How does an employer figure the amount of income tax to withhold?

There are two basic methods for calculating income tax withholding:

1. The percentage method (see Q 14:15); and
2. The wage-bracket method (see Q 14:16).

The tax law permits the employer to use other methods to compute wage withholding so long as they produce results that fall within a prescribed range of tolerance. [Reg. § 31.3402(h)(4)-1]An alternative method will be acceptable if the result equals or falls between the results produced by the percentage and wage-bracket methods. In addition, a result that falls within $10 of the annual amount that would be withheld under either of those methods would be acceptable. The IRS has specifically approved two additional withholding methods—the alternative percentage method tables and the wage-bracket percentage method tables—that produce acceptable results for computerized payrolls. [See IRS Pub. No. 493, *Alternative Tax Withholding Methods and Tables*]

In addition, employers may use the following withholding methods under appropriate circumstances:

- The average estimated wage method (see Q 14:17);

- The annualized wage method (see Q 14:18);

- The cumulative withholding method (see Q 14:19); and

- The part-year withholding method.

Q 14:15 What is the percentage method of withholding?

The percentage method may be used for any payroll period, but it *must* be used if the employer pays employees quarterly, semi-annually or annually. [IRC § 3402(b)] The percentage method must also be used if an employee's wages fall above the last wage bracket on the tables that are used to compute withholding under the wage-bracket method.

To figure withholding using the percentage method:

Step 1. Multiply the dollar value of one withholding allowance for a payroll period by the number of allowances claimed on Form W-4 by the employee. The dollar value of a withholding allowance changes from year to year. For example, for 2007, the value of one allowance is $3,400 per year, or $65.38 per week.

Step 2. Subtract that amount from the employee's wages.

Step 3. Figure the amount to be withheld according to the employee's wage level and marital status using the percentage withholding tables in Circular E, *Employer's Tax Guide.*

Example 14-3: Jon Pitt is a single employee who claims two withholding allowances. Jon's gross pay comes to $300 per week for 2007. Since Jon is paid weekly each withholding allowance is worth $65.38 per week ($3,400/52). Since Jon claims two exemptions, his employer subtracts $130.76 (2 × $65.38) from his gross pay. The remaining $169.24 is subject to withholding. Jon's employer uses the Weekly Payroll Period table for Single Persons in Circular E to figure the amount to withhold from each weekly paycheck. Jon's withholding comes to $11.82.

Q 14:16 What is the wage-bracket method of withholding?

Employers who choose to use the wage-bracket method simply find the correct amount to withhold from tables supplied by the IRS. [IRC § 3402(c)] Tables for using the wage-bracket method are found in Circular E, *Employer's Tax Guide*. There are separate tables for married and single persons. The wage-bracket method can be used for weekly, biweekly, semi-monthly, monthly, daily and miscellaneous payroll periods up to certain income levels. If the employee's income for the pay period exceeds the highest bracket amount for the payroll period, the employer must use the percentage withholding method.

To use the wage-bracket tables, the employer simply consults the proper table for the employee's marital status and the appropriate payroll period. There is no need to reduce gross wages by the value of the employee's withholding exemptions—the tables do that automatically for up to 10 exemptions.

Note: The wage-bracket tables can still be used if the employee claims more than 10 withholding allowances. However, the employer must first reduce gross wages by the value of the exemptions in excess of 10 using the appropriate amount for the payroll period.

Example 14-4: Jon Pitt is a single employee who claims two withholding allowances. Jon's gross pay comes to $300 per week for 2007. Jon Pitt's employer chooses to use the wage-bracket method instead of percentage withholding. The employer consults the table for Single Persons—Weekly Payroll Period. Jon's gross wages of $300 fall into the $300-$310 range on the table. Jon's employer consults the column for two withholding exemptions, which produces a weekly withholding amount of $12.

Jon's withholding is $12 using the wage-bracket method, but $11.82 using the percentage method. Why the difference? The wage-bracket tables compute the *average* withholding for a $10 range of gross pay amounts. Thus, the bracket tables will produce a higher withholding amount for gross pay amounts at the bottom of a range and a lower withholding for gross pay amounts at the top of a range.

Q 14:17 What is the average estimated wage method of withholding?

The average estimated wage method permits an employer to withhold tax for a payroll period based on estimated average wages, making necessary adjustments at the end of each quarter. [Reg. § 31.3402(b)(1)-1]An employer may also withhold tax on tips on an estimated basis.

Q 14:18 How does an employer withhold using the annualized wage method?

The annualized wage method is a popular alternative withholding method, especially for computerized payroll systems. [Reg. § 31.3402(h)(2)-1] To use this method, the employer multiplies the amount of the employee's wages for a particular payroll period by the number of payroll periods in the year. The employer then figures an annual withholding amount using the Percentage Method Table for an Annual Payroll Period. The annual withholding amount is divided by the number of payroll periods to determine the amount of withholding for each payroll period.

Q 14:19 When do employers use the cumulative withholding method?

One problem with the traditional withholding methods is that they fail to account for dips and jumps in an employee's wages throughout the year. If an employee earns a great deal during some pay periods of the year, but relatively small amounts during other pay periods, the employee will be over withheld if the percentage or wage-bracket methods are used. One way to get around this problem is using cumulative withholding. [Reg. § 31.3402(h)(3)-1]

Cumulative withholding can be used only if the employee was paid for the same payroll period (weekly, biweekly, etc.) since the beginning of the year. The employee must request cumulative withholding in writing. Here is how it works:

Step 1. Find the average pay per payroll period by dividing the employee's total earnings to date (including wages for the current payroll period) by the number of payroll periods to date including the current period.

Step 2. Figure the withholding on this amount using the percentage method.

Step 3. Multiply the withholding by the number of payroll periods used above.

Step 4. Subtract the total withholding calculated from the total tax withheld to date during the calendar year. The excess is the amount to withhold for the current payroll period. [Rev. Proc. 78-8, 1978-1 C.B. 562]

> **Example 14-5:** Jane Blue is a single employee who claims one withholding allowance. Jane works on a commission basis. Commissions are paid monthly. Blue had no earnings in January and February of 2007. From March through the end of August—the company's busy season—Blue took in $24,000 in commissions—$4,000 each month. Blue's employer withheld $591 a month, using the wage-bracket tables. In September, things slowed down. Blue's commissions dropped to just $1,000 a month for the rest of the year.

If Blue's employer continued to use wage-bracket withholding, Blue would have had $52 withheld from her September check. However, Blue requested cumulative withholding. Here is how her withholding was calculated:

Step 1. Average pay per payroll period ($25,000 ÷ 9)	$2,778
Step 2. Withholding on average pay per payroll period	310
Step 3. Multiply withholding per pay period by total pay periods	2,790
Total withholding less total withheld to date ($2,790 - 3,546)	(756)

Since Blue's employer had already withheld more than her cumulative withholding as of September, the cumulative withholding method cut her September withholding to zero.

Q 14:19

Q 14:20 When can withholding be calculated using the part-year employment method?

The part-year withholding method can avoid overwithholding for employees who are hired for only part of the year, such as summer workers or other seasonal employees who have no other earnings during the year. [Reg. § 31.3402(h)(4)-1(c)]As with cumulative withholding (see Q 14:19), this method must be requested by the employee.

A part-year employee can request use of the part-year employment method provided:

- The employee uses the calendar year accounting period; and

- The employee reasonably anticipates that he or she will be employed for a total of no more than 245 days in all terms of continuous employment during the current calendar year.

[Reg. § 31.3402(h)(4)-1(c)]

The part-year withholding method works pretty much like the cumulative withholding method (see Q 14:19). However, in computing the average pay per payroll period, the employer takes into account only the number of payroll periods for which the employee was actually employed during the year. Here is how withholding is calculated using the part-year method:

Step 1. Add the wages to be paid the employee for the current payroll period to any already paid the employee in the current term of continuous employment.

Step 2. Add the number of payroll periods used in Step 1 to the number of payroll periods between the employee's last employment and current employment. To find the number of periods between the last employment and current employment, divide (a) the number of calendar days between the employee's last day of earlier employment (or the previous December 31, if later) and the first day of current employment by (b) the number of calendar days in the current payroll period.

Step 3. Divide the Step 1 amount by the total number of payroll periods from Step 2.

Step 4. Find the tax in the withholding tax tables on the Step 3 amount. Be sure to use the correct payroll period table and to take into account the employee's withholding allowances.

Step 5. Multiply the total number of payroll periods from Step 2 by the Step 4 amount.

Step 6. Subtract from the Step 5 amount the total tax already withheld during the current term of continuous employment. Any excess is the amount to withhold for the current payroll period.

Q 14:21 How does an employer withhold when an employee receives extra payments in addition to regular wages?

Amounts paid in addition to an employee's regular wages (e.g., bonuses, back-pay, sick leave, severance pay) are treated as supplemental payments. If the employer pays a supplemental amount along with a regular wage payment, the employer can simply combine the two amounts and withhold as if they were a single wage payment for a regular payroll period. However, if a supplemental payment is paid by separate check or separately itemized on a single check, the employer has a choice:

- The employer can combine the supplemental payment with regular wages for the payroll period; or

- The employer can withhold at a flat rate, disregarding any withholding allowances claimed by the employee on his or her W-4.

[Reg. § 31.3402(g)(1)]

The flat rate is generally tied to the third lowest tax rate for singles. [Reg. § 1.3402(g)-1(a)]Prior to the enactment of the Jobs and Growth Tax Relief Reconciliation Act of 2003 (JGTRRA) [P.L. 108-27 (May 28, 2003)], the rate was 27 percent. Under JGTRRA, the rate is 25 percent through 2010. [IRC § 1(i)(2)]A special rule applies to supplemental wage payments in excess of $1,000,000. Section 904 of the American Jobs Creation Act of 2004 [P.L. 108-357]increased the flat withholding rate on these payments to 35 percent, effective for payments made after December 31, 2004.)

Flat-rate withholding will cause overwithholding for employees whose regular wages fall in an income tax rate bracket below 25 percent. On the other hand, aggregating a supplemental payment with regular wages may also be a problem for these employees. A large supplemental payment on top of regular wages could push a low-income worker into a higher withholding bracket. In an extreme case, a worker who has nothing withheld from regular paychecks could have a large amount withheld from a supplemental payment.

The employment tax rules provide a solution—at least for the extreme case. If an employee's regular wage payments are less than the value of withholding allowances claimed, the excess withholding allowances can be used to shelter a supplemental payment. The employer can aggregate the supplemental payment with total wages paid for the period covered by the supplemental payment. The combined amount is averaged over the period covered by the supplemental amount, and withholding is computed on the average amount. [Reg. § 31.3402(g)-1(b)]

Q 14:22 Are employee fringe benefits subject to income tax withholding?

Fringe benefits are subject to income tax withholding and Social Security and Medicare (FICA) taxes unless the tax law specifically excludes them. [IRC § 3121(a), 3401(a)]The amount treated as income is generally the fair market value of the benefit less any amount paid by the employee. The income tax withholding and FICA tax rules for common fringe benefits are discussed in Chapter 10.

Q 14:23 How does an employer withhold on noncash fringe benefits?

Many fringe benefits are provided in kind rather than in cash. For example, an employee may be provided with a company car or may have the use of an employer-owned plane for personal trips. Withholding on these benefits must be made from cash wages due to the employee. [IRC § 3501; Temp. Reg. § 31.3501(a)-1T]

Employers have a great deal of flexibility in withholding tax on noncash fringe benefits. An employer may withhold on noncash fringe benefits on a pay period, quarterly, semiannual, annual, or other basis. A single benefit can be treated as paid on more than one date over the year, even if the employee receives the benefit all at once. In addition, the employer does not have to use the same pay date for all employees or for all benefits.

The employer also has a choice of withholding methods. The employer can add the value of the benefit to wages for a payroll period and withhold on the total using regular withholding rates; or the employer can treat the fringe benefit as a supplemental wage payment and withhold at a flat 28 percent rate (see Q 14:21).

The employer must generally treat all benefits provided during the year as paid no later than December 31. However, the tax law provides a few key exceptions: An employer may use October 31 or any later date in the calendar year as the cutoff for the date for determining noncash fringe benefits provided to an employee during that year. [Ann. 85-113, 1985-31 I.R.B. 31] Therefore, an employer can treat the value of benefits actually received by an employee in November and December as if they were received in the following year.

Only benefits *actually provided* after the cutoff date can be treated as paid in the following year. The rule does not apply to benefits received by employees before the cut off date, even if the employer treats the benefits as paid at year-end for withholding purposes. In addition, the special cutoff rule cannot be used for fringe benefits involving the transfer of real estate or investment property. And it cannot be used to report the value of group term life insurance.

The employer may elect the special rule for some noncash benefits and not for others. In addition, the cutoff date does not have to be the same for all benefits. However, if the employer elects to use the rule for a particular benefit, it must be used for all employees receiving that benefit. [Ann. 85-113, 1985-31 I.R.B. 31]

Example 14-6: Alpha Company provides Harvey Allen with a company car. Alpha Co. reports the full value of the car use as income to Allen (see Q 14:23). Alpha elects to use the special accounting rule with an October 31 cutoff. Alpha treats the value of Allen's car use from January 1 through October 31 as a fringe benefit provided to Allen in the current year. Alpha reports that amount as income to Allen for the current year. However, the value of Allen's car use for November and December is reported as a fringe benefit in the following year.

The employer must notify each affected employee that the employer used the special rule and period for which it was used. The notice must be given between the date of the employee's last paycheck for the year and the date the employer provides the employee with her or W-2 for the year. Reason: The employee's treatment of the benefit must match up with the employer's. The employee must also use the special cutoff rule for all purposes (e.g., deductions related to the fringe benefit) and for the same period.

Q 14:24 Are tips received by employees subject to income tax withholding?

An employer must withhold income tax on cash tips (including credit card charges) of $20 or more received by an employee in a calendar month. [IRC § 3402(k)]Noncash tips and cash tips of less than $20 a month are not subject to income tax withholding. [IRC § 3401(a)(16)] The withholding is made from cash wages payable to the employee or from other funds the employee makes available.

There are, however, some limits on an employer's obligation to withhold on tips.

Reported tips. An employer's obligation to withhold income taxes on tip income extends only to the amount of tips reported by the employee. The tax law requires employees to report tip income to the employer by the 10th of the month following the month in which the tips are received. The report should include tips that were charged by customers and paid over to the employee by the employer as well as cash tips received directly by employees. No report is required for months when an employee's tips are less than $20.

Tip reports can be made on IRS Form 4070, *Employee's Report of Tips to Employer,* or on a similar statement. In addition, an employer is permitted to establish a system for electronic reporting by employees. [Reg. § 1.6053-1] For further details on tip reporting see Q 14:36.

Available funds. Income tax withholding on tip income is required only to the extent that other funds are available from which to withhold. If, by the 10th of the month after the month the employer received the employee's report on tips, there are insufficient employee funds available to deduct the employee tax, the employer is no longer obligated to collect it. If there are some funds available, taxes are withheld in the following order:

1. Taxes on regular wages and other compensation;

2. Social Security and Medicare (FICA) taxes on tip income; and

3. Income taxes on tips.

[Reg. § 31.3402(k)-1(c)]

An employer may treat reported tips as supplemental payments in determining the federal income tax to withhold. Tips may be treated as part of the current or preceding wage payment, or if the tax already has been withheld from the regular wage payment, tax on the tips may be figured using the supplemental rate of 28 percent (see Q 14:21).

Payroll Taxes

Q 14:25 What types of payroll taxes are imposed under federal law?

As a general rule, the tax law imposes three types of payroll taxes on employee earnings:

- Social Security taxes payable by both the employer and employee (see Q 14:26);
- Medicare taxes payable by both the employer and employee (see Q 14:27); and
- Unemployment tax payable by the employer (Q 14:28).

Social Security taxes are imposed by the Federal Insurance Contributions Act and are collectively known as FICA taxes. The Federal Unemployment Tax Act (FUTA) imposes the unemployment tax.

Q 14:26 What is the Social Security portion of the FICA tax?

The Social Security tax funds the old age, survivors, and disability (OASDI) portion of the Social Security program. An employer is required to withhold Social Security tax from employee's wages and to pay a matching amount of tax.

An employer and employee must each pay the 6.2 percent (12.4 percent combined total) Social Security tax on covered wages (including tip income) up to the Social Security wage base for the year. The Social Security wage base is adjusted annually for inflation. For 2007, the wage base was $97,500. Thus, employers and employees were each subject to a maximum tax of $6,045—or a combined total of $12,090. For 2008, the wage base will be $102,000.

Q 14:27 What is the Medicare portion of the FICA tax?

There is no wage base for the Medicare portion of the FICA tax. Employers and employees must each pay the 1.45 percent Medicare tax (2.9 percent combined total) on all covered wages.

Q 14:28 What payments to an employee are subject to FICA tax?

For FICA tax purposes, wages generally mean all compensation for services performed in covered employment. [IRC §3121]Wages subject to FICA tax includes the value of fringe benefits and other noncash compensation unless a specific exemption applies. FICA wages are generally subject to tax when paid regardless of when they are earned.

Whether FICA covers an employee's wages depends on whether he or she is engaged in covered employment. Most professions and industries are covered. However, there are special rules covering some kinds of employment, including self-employed individuals (see Q 14:33), partners in a partnership (see Q 14:34), S corporation shareholders (see Q 14:35), and family members employed in a business (see Q 14:36).

Q 14:29 What is the federal unemployment tax?

Only employers pay the federal unemployment (FUTA) tax. The FUTA rate is nominally set at 6.2 percent on the first $7,000 of wages paid to a covered employee during the tax year. [IRC § 3301] (The 6.2 percent rate includes a 0.2 percent temporary surtax that is scheduled to expire at the end of 2007 unless extended by Congress.) However, the effective rate for employers in most states is far lower than 6.2 percent.

Employers that pay their state unemployment taxes on time can generally claim a credit equal to 5.4 percent of their FUTA wages. [IRC § 3302] In other words, most employers pay a federal tax of only 0.8 percent.

> **Example 14-7:** XYZ Company has 50 employees each of whom earns more than $7,000 during 2007. Thus, XYZ's taxable payroll for FUTA purposes is $350,000 on which it owes a gross FUTA tax of $21,700 (6.2 percent × $350,000). However, XYZ gets a credit against its gross FUTA liability for timely payments of its state unemployment tax liability equal to up to 5.4 percent of its FUTA taxable payroll. So if XYZ paid $18,900 (5.4 percent × $350,000) in state unemployment taxes, the credit would reduce its net FUTA tax to only $2,800 (0.8 percent × $350,000). In other words, XYZ would have a total unemployment tax liability of 6.2 percent—split between the state and federal governments.

However, the credit is actually a better deal than that. An employer can claim a 5.4 percent credit even if its state tax rate is lower than 5.4 percent. The employer gets a credit for what it actually paid the state—and it gets an additional credit equal to the difference between that amount and what it would have paid at the 5.4 percent rate.

Suppose XYZ Company in Example 14-7 pays a state unemployment tax of only 1 percent. It owes the state $3,500 in state unemployment tax. However, it still gets a full 5.4 percent credit against its FUTA tax. So it pays only 0.8 percent—or $2,800—in net FUTA tax for the year. Its combined state and federal taxes rate is only 1.8 percent.

> **Caution:** State employment taxes that are paid late are not eligible for a full credit. The employer can only claim a credit for 90 percent of the amount that would have been allowed if the taxes had been paid on time. [IRC § 3302(a)(3)] Moreover, an employer cannot take any credit at all if it does not pay any state unemployment taxes. Furthermore, the 5.4 percent credit

could be reduced if the employer's state borrowed from the federal government and kept an open balance for more than two years.

Practice Point: The key to keeping unemployment taxes in check is the employer's state unemployment tax rate. The lower the state tax rate, the lower the total state and federal unemployment tax liability. The crucial factor in determining the state tax rate is the employer's experience rating. State unemployment taxes are really premiums that employers pay for unemployment insurance for their workers. As with other insurance, low-risk employers pay lower premiums, while high risks pay higher premiums. The employer's experience rating is an assessment of the risk that employees will call on the state insurance fund for benefits.

While states use different methods for determining an employer's experience rating, in virtually all states keeping a lid on benefits paid to former employees will lead to a lower experience rating. Employers are often reluctant to contest an ex-employee's benefit claim—even if the employer has good cause. However, employers should be aware that undeserved claims could cost them unnecessary payroll tax dollars.

Q 14:30 Which employers are liable for the federal unemployment tax?

In general, employers are liable for FUTA taxes on employee wages if in the current year or the preceding year:

- Wages paid to all employees totaled $1,500 or more in any calendar quarter; or
- The employer employed at least one employee for at least part of a day during 20 weeks of the year. The 20 weeks do not have to be consecutive.

[IRC § 3306(a)(1)]

Q 14:31 How are FICA and FUTA taxes handled if a business is sold during the year?

When an employee works for two employers during the year, each employer must separately pay the 6.2 percent Social Security portion of FICA taxes on the employee's earnings up to the Social Security wage base. Also, each employer must pay FUTA taxes on wages up to the $7,000 FUTA wage base.

The employers must also collect the employee share of Social Security and Medicare taxes on the full amount of wages paid to the employee. However, the employee is entitled to claim a refund for the overpaid FICA tax on his or her income tax return for the year.

Example 14-8: One employer pays an employee $60,000 in the first half of 2008 and another employer pays the same employee $60,000 during the second half of the year. The two employers must pay Social Security taxes on a total of $120,000—even though the 2008 Social Security wage base is $102,000. Each employer pays tax on $60,000.

There is, however, a special relief provision when one employer acquires another employer during the year. The successor employer may be able to combine its wage payments with those of the prior employer in figuring Social Security and FUTA taxes. Therefore, once the employee's *total* earnings for the year reach the Social Security or FUTA wage bases, the successor employer's payroll tax liability is cut off. [Ltr. Rul. 9315007 (Jan. 12, 1993)]

Note: The relief provision does not apply to the Medicare portion of the FICA tax because there is no wage base for that tax. Each employer must pay the 1.45 percent Medicare tax on all wages paid to the employee.

Earnings paid by a prior employer are treated as paid by the successor employer under the following conditions:

- The successor obtains substantially all of the property used in the prior employer's business or a separate unit of the prior employer's business;

- Employees work for the prior employer immediately before the acquisition and for the successor immediately after; and

- The earnings are paid during the calendar year of the acquisition.

[IRC §§ 3121(a)(1), 3306(b)(1)]

Example 14-9: Huge Company owned 13 subsidiary corporations that it wanted to consolidate. Huge formed a limited partnership and named itself as general partner. The limited partnership then absorbed the subsidiaries in a number of ways, including statutory mergers, liquidations, and asset transfers.

The IRS determined that the limited partnership was a successor employer to each of the subsidiaries. Therefore, the partnership got payroll tax credit for wages paid by the subsidiaries. *Reason:* The regulations provide that, for payroll tax purpose, "the method of acquisition by an employer of the property of another employer is immaterial." [Reg. §§ 31.3121(a)-1(b)(3), 31.3306(b)-1(b)(3)] Thus, it made no difference that the partnership acquired some of the subsidiaries through mergers, others through liquidations, and still others through asset transfers.

Furthermore, each subsidiary qualified as a separate unit of Huge Company's business. And the employees of each subsidiary worked for the partnership after the consolidation. So Huge met all of the requirements for a successor employer.

When a successor employer absorbs a prior employer (e.g., in a merger), the successor should provide its acquired employees with a single W-2 that reports wages for the whole year. [Rev. Rul. 62-60, 1962-1 C.B. 186] When the prior and successor employers remain as two distinct entities, however, there is a reporting choice. If the prior and successor employers both agree, the successor may give employees a single W-2 that reports wages for the whole year. Otherwise, the prior and successor employers should provide independent W-2 Forms. [Rev. Proc. 84-77, 1984-2 C.B. 753]

Q 14:31

Q 14:32 How are payroll taxes handled when an employee concurrently works for two related employers?

If an employee works for two or more employers during a year, the combined compensation may exceed the Social Security wage base for FICA tax purposes ($102,000 for 2007). In this case, there will be an overpayment of FICA tax. For example, if an employee is paid $45,000 by one employer and $65,000 by another, the total wages exceed the maximum amount subject to the Social Security portion of FICA (there is no maximum wage base for the Medicare portion of FICA).

The employee is entitled to claim a refund for the FICA tax overpayment on his or her income tax return. However, there is generally no equivalent relief for the two employers. Each employer is responsible for paying up to the maximum Social Security tax for the employee. There is, however, a limited relief provision if the employers are related corporations. When two or more related corporations share employees and one corporation acts as the "common paymaster" for the employees' combined wages, FICA taxes for the shared employees are computed as if they had only one employer. [IRC § 3121(s)] So there will be no FICA tax overpayment by the employers or the employees.

The common paymaster is responsible for filing information and tax returns and issuing Forms W-2 for the employees concurrently employed by the related corporations. [Reg. § 31.3121(s)-1(a)]

Related corporations. Corporations will be considered related corporations for a calendar quarter if they meet any one of the following tests at any time during the quarter:

- The corporations are members of a "controlled group of corporations" connected through 50 percent common stock ownership [IRC § 1563, but substituting a 50 percent common stock ownership for 80 percent];

- In the case of a corporation that does not issue stock (e.g., nonprofit organizations), either (1) 50 percent or more of the members of one corporation's governing body are members of the other corporation's governing body), or (2) the holders of 50 percent or more of the voting power to select such members are concurrently the holders of 50 percent or more of that power with respect to the other corporation;

- 50 percent or more of one corporation's officers are concurrently officers of the other corporation; or

- 30 percent or more of one corporation's employees are concurrently employees of the other corporation.

[Reg. § 31.3121(s)-1(b)(1)]

Example 14-10: X Corporation employs individuals A, B, D, E, F, G, and H. Y Corporation employs individuals A, B, and C. Z Corporation employs individuals A, C, I, J, K, L, and M. X Corporation is the paymaster for all 13 individuals. The corporations have no officers or stockholders in common.

X and Y are related corporations because at least 30 percent of Y's employees are also employees of X. Y and Z are related corporations because at least 30 percent of Y's employees are also employees of Z. X and Z are not related corporations because neither corporation has 30 percent of its employees concurrently employed by the other corporations.

Individual B is treated as having one employer. Individual C has two employers for these purposes, although Y and Z are related corporations, because C is not employed by X Corporation, the common paymaster. Individual A also is treated as having two employers for the purposes of these sections because X and Y Corporations are treated as one employer, and Z Corporation is treated as a second employer (since it is not related to the paymaster, X Corporation). Of course, individuals D, E, F, G, H, I, J, K, L, and M are not concurrently employed by two or more corporations and the common paymaster rules do not apply to them.

Example 14-11: M and N Corporations are both related to Corporation O but are not related to each other. Individual A is concurrently employed by all three corporations and paid by O, their common paymaster. Although M and N are not related, O is treated as the employer for A's employment with M, N, and O.

Common paymaster. A common paymaster of a group of related corporations is whichever member of the group that pays compensation to employees of two or more of those corporations on their behalf and that is responsible for keeping books and records for the payroll with respect to those employees. The common paymaster is not required to pay compensation to all the employees of the related corporations, but the common paymaster rules are not available to any compensation that is not paid through the common paymaster. The common paymaster may pay concurrently employed individuals under this section by one combined paycheck, drawn on a single bank account, or by separate paychecks, drawn by the common paymaster on the accounts of one or more employing corporations. [Reg. § 31.3121(s)-1(b)(2)]

Example 14-12: S, T, U, and V are related corporations with 2,000 employees collectively. Two or more of the corporations currently employ forty of these employees during a calendar quarter. The four corporations arrange for S to pay wages to 30 of these 40 employees for their services. Under these facts, S is the common paymaster of S, T, U, and V with respect to the 30 employees. S is not a common paymaster with respect to the remaining employees.

Concurrent employment. An employee must be concurrently employed by two or more of the related corporations to qualify under the common paymaster rules. This means that there must be a contemporaneous employment relationship with each corporation. If this exists, then the fact that the employee is temporarily inactive vis-a -vis one of the corporations is immaterial. However, employment is not concurrent with respect to one of the related corporations if the employee's employment relationship with that corporation is completely nonexistent during periods when the employee is not performing services for that corporation. An employment relationship is completely nonexistent if all rights and obligations of the employer and employee with respect to employment have terminated, other than those that customarily exist after employment relationships terminate. Circumstances that suggest that an employment relationship has become completely nonexistent include unconditional termination of participation in deferred compensation plans of the employer, forfeiture of seniority claims, and forfeiture of unused fringe benefits such as vacation or sick pay. [Reg. § 31.3121(s)-1(b)(3)]

> **Example 14-13:** M, N, and O are related corporations, which use N as a common paymaster with respect to officers. Their respective headquarters are located in three separate cities several hundred miles apart. A is an officer of M, N, and O, who performs substantial services for each corporation. A does not work a set length of time at each corporate headquarters, and when A leaves one corporate headquarters, it is not known when A will return, although it is expected that A will return. Under these facts, the three corporations concurrently employ A.

> **Example 14-14:** P, Q, and R are related corporations whose geographical zones of business activity do not overlap. P, Q, and R have a common pension plan and arrange for Q to be a common paymaster for managers and executives. All three corporations maintain cafeterias for the use of their employees. B is a cafeteria manager who has worked at P's headquarters for 3 years. On June 1, B is transferred from P to the position of cafeteria manager of R. There are no plans for B's return to P. B's accrued pension benefits, vacation and sick pay, do not change as a result of the transfer. The decision to transfer B was made by Q, the parent corporation. Under these facts, B is not concurrently employed by P and R, because B's employment relationship with P was completely nonexistent during B's employment with R. Furthermore, the common paymaster rules are inapplicable since B also was not employed by Q, the common paymaster.

Q 14:33 Are self-employed business owners subject to FICA and FUTA taxes?

Self-employed business owners do not pay either FICA or FUTA taxes. However, they are subject to Social Security and Medicare taxes under the Self-Employment Contributions Act (SECA) (See Chapter 1). [IRC § 1401]

Q 14:34 Are partners in a partnership subject to FICA and FUTA taxes?

Payments received by a partner from the partnership for services rendered are not "wages" with respect to "employment" and therefore are not subject to the FICA taxes or FUTA taxes. Such remuneration also is not subject to federal income tax withholding. [Rev. Rul. 69-184, 1969-1 C.B. 256]

Partners are, however, generally subject to self-employment tax on their net earnings. A partner's net earnings are his or her distributive share of the partnership's income plus any guaranteed payments. [Reg. § 1.1402(a)-1(a)(2)] Income from a partnership where the partnership's income consisted only of interest, rents, royalties, and long-term capital gains is not subject to self-employment income. [*Pugh v. Comm'r*, T.C. Memo 1981-448]

In computing net earnings from self-employment, the distributive share of income of a *limited* partner is excluded. But this exclusion does not apply to guaranteed payments to that partner for services actually rendered to or on behalf of the partnership. [IRC § 1402(a)(13)]

Periodic payments made by a partnership to a retired partner may be exempt from self-employment tax if made on account of retirement under a written plan of the partnership. The exemption is available only if (1) the retired partner renders no services to the partnership, (2) there is no obligation from the other partners in the partnership to the retired partner other than to make retirement payments under the partnership plan, and (3) the retired partner's share in the capital of the partnership must have been paid in full. [IRC § 1402(a)(10)]

Q 14:35 Are payments to an S corporation shareholder subject to FICA and FUTA taxes?

Unlike a partner in a partnership (see Q 14:31), an S corporation shareholder who performs services for the corporation is considered an employee of the corporation. The IRS has specifically ruled that a shareholder of an S corporation is not subject to self-employment tax. The share of the corporation's income taxed to the shareholder is not considered net earnings from self-employment. [Rev. Rul. 59-221, 1959-1 C.B. 225]

Amounts received by an S corporation shareholder as remuneration for services rendered are considered "wages" for FICA, FUTA, and income tax withholding purposes. On the other hand, dividends received by S corporation shareholders are not taxable wages. However, the IRS may reclassify dividends as wages to prevent payroll tax avoidance.

Example 14-15: Bob Brown and Sam Smith were the sole shareholders of XYZ Inc., an S corporation. Brown and Smith performed services for the corporation. However, to avoid payment of payroll taxes, they drew no salary from the corporation. Instead, they arranged for XYZ to pay them dividends equal to the amount that they would otherwise have received as reasonable compensation for the services they performed.

The IRS ruled that the dividends were compensation for services rendered rather than a distribution of the corporation's earnings and profits. As such, the payments were wages, subject to FICA, FUTA, and income tax withholding. [Rev. Rul. 74-44, 1974-1 C.B. 287]

Q 14:35

Q 14:36 Are wages paid to family members subject to income tax withholding and payroll taxes?

As a general rule, wages paid to a family member, including a spouse, parent, or child, are subject to income tax withholding and payroll taxes, although there are some very narrow exceptions.

Income tax withholding. Wages paid to the following individuals are subject to income tax withholding:

- A child employed by a parent;

- A child employed by partnership, even if the partnership consists solely of the parents;

- A child employed by a corporation, whether it is a regular C corporation or an S corporation;

- A parent employed by a son or a daughter; and

- A spouse employed by his or her spouse.

[IRS Pub. No. 15, *Employer's Tax Guide* (2007) at 8]

FICA taxes. Wages paid to a family member are generally subject to FICA taxes. However, there is no FICA tax for services performed by children under the age of 18 for their parents. [IRC § 3121(b)(3)(A)]

The FICA tax exemption above does not cover employment by a corporation, even if the child's parents are the owners of the corporation. Whereas, the exemption does apply to services performed for a partnership if the child's parents are the only partners. [Reg. § 31.3121(b)(3)-1(c)]

FUTA taxes. Wages paid by a parent to child under age 21 are not subject to FUTA taxes, whether or not the services are performed in connection with the parent's business. Likewise, wages paid by one spouse to another or by a child to a parent are exempt from FUTA taxes. [IRC § 3306(c)(5)]

Q 14:37 Are tips received by employees subject to FICA and FUTA taxes?

Tips received by an employee are generally subject to both FICA and FUTA taxes.

FICA tax. If an employee's cash tips total less than $20 in a calendar month, there is no FICA tax liability. But once the $20 threshold is reached, all tips received during the month are subject to FICA tax—including the first $20. For purposes of the 6.2 percent Social Security portion of FICA, tips are taxable up to the point where the tips, when combined with regular wages, total the Social Security wage base for the year. Noncash tips and tips of less than $20 in a calendar month are not FICA taxable. [IRC § 3121(a)(12)] An employer that operates a food and beverage establishment may be able to claim an income tax credit for some or all of the Social Security tax paid on its employees' tip income (see Q 14:39).

An employer must collect both income tax and the employee's share of FICA tax on reported tips from regular wages (other than tips) due the employee, unless the employee furnishes funds to cover the taxes on his or her tips. If an employer cannot deduct the full amount of tax from an employee's regular wages, and the employee does not provide other funds, the employee must pay the tax directly with his or her annual income tax return. If an employer cannot collect the full amount of income and FICA taxes from an employee, the employer should apply what it can collect first to FICA taxes. [IRS Pub. No. 531]

Employees also owe FICA tax on tips they hand over to their employer who then distributes the tips among all employees. In this case, the tips are treated as regular wages when paid out by the employer.

If an employee does not report tips to the employer, the employee must file Form 4137, *Social Security Tax on Unreported Tips*, and pay the employee share of FICA taxes along with his or her tax return for the year. Employees must pay a penalty of 50 percent of the Social Security tax due on any tips they willfully fail to report to their employers as required. [IRC § 6652(b); Reg. § 31.6652(c)-1]

FUTA. Tips that are reported to the employer are subject to the federal unemployment tax. [IRC § 3306(s)]

Tip reporting voluntary compliance agreements. The IRS has established a Tip Rate Determination/Education Program (TRD/EP), which is designed to enhance tax compliance among tipped employees through taxpayer education and voluntary agreements instead of traditional audit techniques.

In TRD/EP, the IRS works with employers in industries in which tipping is customary to improve tax compliance. The TRD/EP currently offers employers operating food and beverage establishments two types of agreements.

1. The Tip Rate Determination Agreement (TRDA) requires that tips be reported at or above a specific rate negotiated between the employer and the Service in return for certain benefits.

2. The Tip Reporting Alternative Commitment (TRAC) agreement requires that the employer provide ongoing education to tipped employees on tip reporting procedures in return for certain benefits. A variation on TRAC, the Employer-designed Tip Reporting Alternative Commitment (Em-TRAC), allows the employer considerable latitude in designing its educational program and tip reporting procedures.

Employers who enter into these agreements and comply with their terms are not subject to challenge on audit with respect to the amount of tips they are reporting as wages. TRDA provides similar benefits to employees. Although not set forth in the TRAC agreements, if employees follow the procedures their employer describes in the required educational sessions, the IRS will not challenge the amount of tips they report to their employers as wages. The IRS also offers the Gaming Industry Tip Compliance Agreement (GITCA) which is an agreement designed to meet the needs of establishments in the gaming industry. The decision to enter into TRDA, TRAC, or GITCA is entirely voluntary on the part of the employer.

Q 14:37

Attributed Tip Income Program (ATIP) is a new reporting alternative for employers in the food and beverage industry designed to promote compliance by employers and employees with the tip income provisions of the Internal Revenue Code, to reduce disputes on audit, and to reduce filing and recordkeeping burdens. ATIP is being offered in addition to the existing TRD/EP programs. ATIP differs from the existing programs in that it does not require an employer to enter into an individual agreement with the IRS. For participating employers, the IRS will not challenge on audit the amount of tips the employer reports as wages. Employers who participate in ATIP report tip income of their employees based on a formula that uses a percentage of gross receipts, which are generally allocated among employees based on employer practices. Participation in ATIP is entirely voluntary for both employers and employees. [Rev. Proc. 2006-30 , I.R.B. 2006-31]

Q 14:38 Are payroll taxes deductible by the employer?

Yes, they are. However, there are actually two separate deductions:

The employee's share of FICA taxes is part of the employee's compensation, which is withheld and paid over to the government. Therefore, that portion is deducted along with the compensation that is actually paid to the employee.

The employer's share of FICA and the entire amount of FUTA taxes are deducted as a tax paid by the employer.

A food and beverage establishment may be able to claim a tax credit in lieu of a deduction for FICA taxes on an employee's tips. The deduction is equal to the employer's share of FICA taxes on tips that are not treated as wages for minimum wage purposes. [IRC § 45B] Under the Small Business and Work Opportunity Tax Act of 2007 (P.L. 110-28), the FICA tip credit will be based on the amount of tips in excess of the Federal minimum wage as in effect on January 1, 2007 ($5.15 per hour) Therefore, the amount of the tip credit will not be reduced as a result of any increase in the Federal minimum wage. An employer can treat up to one-half an employee's tip income as employer-provided wages to satisfy the federal minimum wage requirement. An employer cannot deduct any FICA tax for which the credit is claimed.

Depositing Payroll Taxes

Q 14:39 How does an employer remit withheld income and payroll taxes to the IRS?

As a general rule, an employer must make regular deposits of withheld income and FICA taxes throughout the year. [IRC § 6302; Reg. § 301.6302-1] FUTA taxes must be deposited once accumulated taxes reach a certain level.

Employers may make deposits by mailing or delivering a check, cash, or money order to a financial institution (e.g., a commercial bank) that is authorized to accept federal tax deposits. An authorized depository must accept cash, a postal money order, or a check drawn on an account at the depository. A deposit may be made with a check drawn on another financial institution only if the depository is willing to accept that form of payment. A check or money order should be made payable to the depository, not to the IRS.

Employers may also make deposits by mailing a payment to the Internal Revenue Service's financial agent. The check or money order should be made payable to Financial Agent. (An up-to-date address for the Service's financial agent can be found in Circular E, *Employer's Tax Guide*.)

Form 8109, *Federal Tax Deposit Coupon*, must accompany deposits made at an authorized depository or through the Service's financial agent. New employers will receive a supply of FTD coupons after they have been assigned an employer identification number (EIN). See Q 14:40 for details on obtaining an EIN.

Tax deposits may be made electronically through the Service's Electronic Federal Tax Payment System (EFTPS). As a general rule, use of EFTPS is elective. However, larger employers may be required to deposit electronically.

In general, businesses whose aggregate annual deposits exceed $200,000 must use EFTPS. Once the $200,000 threshold is exceeded, a business has a one-year grace period before having to use EFT. The business must then use EFTPS in all later years even if its deposits fell below the threshold.

Taxes subject to the EFTPS include withheld income, FICA and FUTA taxes, corporate income and estimated taxes, and excise taxes.

Businesses can enroll in EFPTS by visiting *http://www.EFTPS.gov* or by calling EFTPS Customer Service at 1-800-555-4477 to receive an enrollment form by mail.

The IRS recently created an incentive to induce employers who are not required to use EFTPS to enroll in and use the system. The IRS will give qualifying employers a refund of any penalties assessed under the FTD system during the prior year. To qualify for the offer, the employer must:

- Use EFTPS for one year (four consecutive quarters),
- Make all employment tax payments on time, and
- Have previously fully paid the penalty. [IR 2004-70]

Q 14:40 What is an employer identification number (EIN), and how does an employer obtain one?

An EIN is a nine-digit number issued by the IRS. The digits are arranged as follows: 00-0000000. The number is used to identify an employer's tax accounts.

There are several ways to obtain an EIN:

1. *By mail.* An EIN can be obtained by filing Form SS-4, *Application for Employer Identification Number*, with the IRS Service Center for the employer's state. An employer will receive an EIN by return mail in approximately four weeks. Therefore, Form SS-4 should be completed at

least four to five weeks before the EIN will be needed to make tax deposits.

2. *By phone.* Under the Tele-TIN program, an employer can receive an EIN by telephone and use it immediately. The IRS suggests that employers complete form SS-4 before calling to ensure that they have all required information available.

3. *By fax.* Under the Fax-TIN program, an employer can receive an EIN within four business days. To use Fax-TIN, an employer must complete Form SS-4 and fax it to the IRS. The employer must provide a return fax number so that the IRS can send the EIN by return fax.

4. *Online.* The IRS recently inaugurated an online application process for EINs. An employer accesses the Internet EIN system through IRS.gov and enters the required information. If the information passes the automatic validity checks, the IRS issues a permanent EIN to the employer. If the information does not pass the validity checks, it is rejected. The employer then has an opportunity to correct the information and resubmit the application. The Internet EIN application is interactive and asks questions tailored to the type of entity the employer is establishing. [IRS News Release IR-2007-161]

IRS Service Center addresses and the numbers for the Tele-TIN and Fax-TIN programs can be found in the instructions to Form SS-4.

Q 14:41 How often must an employer deposit withheld income and FICA taxes?

Employers generally fall into two basic deposit categories:

- Monthly depositors who must make deposits once a month (see Q 14:42); or

- Semi-weekly depositors who must make deposits on a set day of the week following each payday (see Q 14:43).

Key exceptions. Employers accumulating $100,000 in payroll taxes must make a deposit on the next banking day, regardless of whether the employer is normally a monthly or semi-weekly depositor. On the other hand, small employers with less than $2,500 in payroll taxes for a quarter can skip deposits altogether and send the taxes with their quarterly employment tax returns.

Monthly or semi-weekly. The deposit schedule for an entire calendar year is based on total deposits for the 12-month period ending on June 30 of the prior year. So, for example, an employer's 2008 deposit schedule depends on its deposits for the 12-month period from July 1, 2006 through June 30, 2007.

If an employer's withheld income and FICA taxes total $50,000 or less during the look-back period, the employer uses the monthly schedule. If deposits for the look-back period exceeded $50,000, the employer must make semi-weekly deposits.

An employer can determine its deposit schedule for a calendar year by simply adding up the totals shown on its quarterly employment tax returns (Form 941) for the four quarters ending on June 30 of the prior year. The employer should take into account only the tax liability shown on the original return for a given quarter. Adjustments for a quarter made on a supplemental return filed after the return due date are not taken into account. However, adjustments from an earlier quarter made on a Form 941c, *Statement to Correct Information,* that is attached to Form 941 are taken into account in figuring deposits for that quarter. (For information on filing Form 941, see Q 14:52)

Example 14-16: Alpha Corp. deposited and reported the following employment taxes for the four quarters ending June 30, 2007.

Quarter ending 9/30/06	$10,000
Quarter ending 12/31/06	10,000
Quarter ending 3/31/07	15,000
Quarter ending 6/30/07	14,500
Total	$49,500

Result: Alpha Corp. is a monthly depositor for all of calendar year 2008 since its total deposits for the look-back period did not exceed $50,000.

Example 14-17: Same facts as Example 14-17, except that Alpha underreported its deposit liability for the quarter ending 6/30/07 by $1,000. Since Alpha did not discover the error until after it filed its Form 941 for the quarter, it made the necessary correction by attaching Form 941c for the subsequent quarter ending 9/30/07.

Result: Even though the additional $1,000 pushed Alpha's actual payroll tax liability for the 12-month period over the $50,000 threshold, the $1,000 is not taken into account in determining Alpha's deposit status for 2008. Therefore, Alpha is monthly depositor for 2008. The $1,000 is taken into account in the third quarter of 2007 for purposes of determining Alpha's 2009 deposit schedule.

New employers. A new employer is a monthly depositor for the calendar year it begins operations. In applying the look-back rule for the subsequent calendar year, the employer is treated as having a zero deposit liability for any quarter before it began operations.

Example 14-18: Newco began business on October 1, 2007. Its payroll tax deposits were $15,000 for each quarter through June 30, 2008.

Result: Newco is a monthly depositor for the 2007. It remains on a monthly schedule for 2008 since it was not in existence during the look-back period for determining its 2008 schedule (7/1/06 through 6/30/07). Furthermore, Newco can stick with the monthly schedule for 2009 as well. *Reason:* Its total payroll tax deposits for the 2009 look-back period (7/1/07 through 6/30/08) were only $45,000 since it is deemed to have had a $0 payroll tax liability for the first quarter of that period (7/1/07 through 9/30/07) when it was not in existence.

Q 14:41

IRS early warnings. To give employers even more up-front certainty, the IRS sends out notices by November of the prior year telling employers which deposit schedule to follow for the coming year.

Q 14:42 When are monthly deposits due?

Monthly depositors must deposit all accumulated taxes for the month on or before the 15th day of the following month. So, for example, taxes for all wages paid in January must be deposited by February 15. [Reg. §31.6302-1(c)(1)]

Q 14:43 When are semi-weekly deposits due?

The term semi-weekly depositor can be misleading. Actually, deposits may be made less frequently than twice—or even once—a week. For an employer in this category, how often deposits must be made depends on the frequency of its paydays.

Semi-weekly deposits must be made on either Wednesday or Friday of each week. If a payday falls on a Wednesday, Thursday, or Friday, deposits are due by the following Wednesday. For all other paydays, deposits are due by the following Friday. This Wednesday/Friday schedule allows all employers at least three banking days after a payday to make their deposits.

Example 14-19: Alpha pays some workers on Tuesdays and others on Fridays. Alpha is a true semi-weekly depositor—it makes two deposits each week on Wednesdays and Fridays. Alpha must deposit taxes from each Tuesday payroll on the following Friday; it must deposit the taxes from each Friday payroll on the following Wednesday.

Example 14-20: Beta also has two paydays each week—Wednesdays and Fridays. However, Beta makes only one deposit each week on Wednesdays. Taxes from both its Wednesday and Friday payrolls are due on the following Wednesday.

Example 14-21: Gamma pays all of its workers on Monday. Gamma makes one deposit each week on Friday.

Example 14-22: Delta pays its workers biweekly on Fridays. Delta makes deposits only every other week on the Wednesday following each Friday payroll.

Example 14-23: Epsilon pays all of its workers on a semi-monthly basis—on the 15th and the last day of each month. Epsilon's deposit days are not predictable. If, for example, the 15th falls on a Tuesday, the deposit must be made on the Friday of that week. The next month, however, the 15th may be a Wednesday. In that case, Epsilon has until the following Wednesday to make a deposit.

If a semi-weekly period spans two calendar quarters of the year, an employer must follow special procedures to make sure its deposit is credited to the correct quarter.

If wages are paid in one quarter but the deposit is due in the following quarter, the employer must make it clear on its deposit coupon that the deposit relates to the earlier quarter.

Example 14-24: Magna is a semi-weekly depositor. It pays its employees on Wednesday, March 29. Its payroll tax deposit is due on the following Wednesday, April 5. Since the first quarter of the year ends on March 31, Magna should make sure its deposit coupon clearly indicates that its deposit relates to the first quarter of the year, not the second quarter.

If a semi-weekly deposit includes taxes for two different quarters, the employer must complete two separate deposit coupons.

Example 14-25: Suppose Magna pays some workers on Wednesday and others on Friday. It makes wage payments on Wednesday, September 29 and on Friday, October 1. Payroll taxes for both paydays are due on Wednesday, October 6. However, the third quarter of the year ends on September 30. Therefore, payroll taxes for the September 29 payroll fall in the third quarter, and taxes for the October 1 payroll fall in the fourth quarter. Magna must complete two deposit coupons to deposit its accumulated payroll.

Q 14:44 What if a deposit is due on a nonbanking day?

If a deposit due date falls on a nonbanking day, the deposit is considered timely if made on the next banking day. So, for example, suppose a monthly depositor's January taxes are due on Saturday, February 15. Then the depositor has until the following Monday (February 17) to make the deposit. Similarly, a monthly or semi-weekly deposit that is due on a weekday holiday when the banks are closed can safely be deferred until the next banking day.

Semi-weekly depositors always have at least three banking days following a payday to make a required deposit. Therefore, intervening holidays will also delay the deposit due date.

Example 14-26: Omega pays its workers on Friday, August 29, 2008. Omega's deposit would normally be due on Wednesday, September 3. However, the intervening Monday, September 1, is Labor Day. Therefore, Omega has three banking days—until Thursday, September 4, to make its deposit.

Annual holidays include New Year's Day, Dr. Martin Luther King, Jr.'s Birthday, President's Day, Memorial Day, Independence Day, Labor Day, Columbus Day, Veteran's Day, Thanksgiving Day, and Christmas Day. Legal holidays also include any statewide holidays in the employer's state.

Q 14:45 When is an employer required to make a next-day deposit?

Employers who accumulate payroll taxes of $100,000 or more must deposit those taxes by the close of the next banking day, regardless of whether the employer is normally a monthly or semi-monthly depositor. In determining whether the $100,000 threshold is met:

- A monthly depositor counts only those payroll taxes accumulated during a calendar month; and

- A semi-weekly depositor takes into account only those payroll taxes accumulated during a Wednesday-Friday or Saturday-Tuesday semi-weekly period.

Example 14-27: ABC is a semi-weekly depositor. It pays some employees on Wednesdays and others on Fridays. Taxes are normally due on the following Wednesday for both the Wednesday and Friday periods. Payroll taxes from its Wednesday payroll come to $60,000. However, on Friday it accumulates another $60,000, for a total accumulation of $120,000. Since ABC has exceeded the $100,000 threshold within one semi-weekly period (i.e., Wednesday-Friday), it must deposit the full $120,000 of accumulated taxes on Monday, the next banking day.

Example 14-28: XYZ is also a semi-weekly depositor. It also cuts two payrolls a week—on Mondays and Wednesdays. Payroll taxes from its Monday payroll come to $60,000, which are due by the following Friday. Taxes from its Wednesday payroll also come to $60,000, which are due by the following Wednesday. Although XYZ has accumulated more than $100,000 in taxes on Wednesday, it does not come within the next-day deposit rule because the taxes were not accumulated in the same semi-weekly period.

Once an employer has hit the $100,000 threshold, additional accumulations in the same semi-weekly period are not automatically subject to the one-day rule.

Example 14-29: Delta is a semi-weekly depositor. On Monday, it accumulates $110,000 of payroll taxes. Under the next day rule, Delta must deposit those taxes by the close of the day on Tuesday. On Tuesday, it accumulates an additional $30,000 of taxes. Even though the additional $30,000 of tax is from the same semi-weekly period (i.e., Saturday-Tuesday), Delta does not have to make a next-day deposit. The additional $30,000 may be deposited by the following Friday under the normal semi-weekly deposit rule.

> **Note:** If a monthly depositor is required to make a next-day deposit at any time during the year, the depositor automatically becomes a semi-weekly depositor for the rest of that year and for the next calendar year. [Reg. § 31.6302-1(b)(2)(ii)]

Q 14:46 Are any employers exempt from making payroll tax deposits?

Small employers with less than $2,500 in payroll taxes for a quarter can skip deposits altogether and send the taxes with their quarterly employment tax returns. However, if an employer's payroll taxes for the quarter will reach the $2,500 mark, it must make regular deposits throughout the quarter, regardless of the amount of those deposits.

Certain small employers can file annual (instead of quarterly) employment tax returns and make their employment tax payments with their annual returns (see Q 14:51).

Q 14:47 When must an employer deposit FUTA taxes?

For deposit purposes, FUTA taxes are figured using a rate of 0.8 percent. In other words, the employer assumes the full credit for state unemployment taxes will be allowed in making federal deposits (see Q 14:29). Employers must figure FUTA taxes quarterly to determine if there is a need to make a deposit. If an employer's accumulated liability as of the end of any quarter is $100 or less, no deposit is required. If the accumulated liability exceeds $100 at the end of any quarter, the tax must be deposited. Deposits are due by the last day of the first month after the end of the quarter. [Reg. § 31.6302(c)-3]

If the employer's total FUTA tax for the year is $500 or less ($100 or less for periods ending on or before December 31, 2004), the taxes do not have to be deposited. The employer simply pays at the time the federal unemployment tax return is filed (Form 940 or 940-EZ). [Reg. § 31.6302(c)-3]

FUTA tax deposits can be made at an authorized federal tax depository using a federal tax deposit coupon (Form 8109). Employers can also use the federal tax payment system to make FUTA tax deposits (see Q 14:39).

Q 14:48 What if an employment tax deposit is not made on time?

If a deposit is not made on time, an employer will owe a penalty for failure to deposit. [IRC § 6656](See Q 14:57.)

Q 14:49 What if an employer deposits more than the required amount of taxes for a quarter?

If an employer discovers an overpayment before the end of a quarter, it can adjust subsequent deposits to correct the error. For example, if an employer deposited $100 too much for one payroll period, it can simply reduce its deposit for the next payroll period by $100.

If an overpayment is not discovered until the end of a quarter, the employer has a choice. When the employer files the employment tax return for the quarter (Form 941) it may choose to have the overpayment refunded or applied as a credit against the deposits for the next quarter.

Q 14:50 What if the employer deposits less than the required amount of taxes for a quarter?

As a general rule, an employer will owe a failure to deposit penalty on the amount of the shortfall (see Q 14:57). Employers are allowed a little leeway in making employment tax deposits—but there is not much margin for error. No penalty will be imposed if an employer's deposit is short by no more than the greater of $100 or 2 percent of the required deposit.

To qualify for penalty relief, the employer must make up the shortfall by a set makeup date. [Reg. § 31.6302-1(f)]For monthly depositors, the makeup date is the due date of the quarterly return for the quarter in which the shortfall occurred. Semi-weekly depositors must make up a shortfall by the first Wednesday or Friday on or after the 15th day of the month following the month of the shortfall or by the quarterly return due date, if that is earlier. Next-day depositors must make a shortfall on the same schedule as semi-weekly depositors.

Payroll Tax Returns

Q 14:51 What types of payroll tax returns are required to be filed?

There are two basic payroll tax returns:

- Quarterly employment tax returns of income tax withholding and FICA taxes—Form 941 (see Q 14:52); and

- Annual returns of federal unemployment taxes—Form 940 and 940-EZ (see Q 14:55)

If a business receives written notification from the IRS that it qualifies for the Form 944 program, it must file Form 944, Employer's ANNUAL Federal Tax Return, instead of the quarterly Form 941.[Reg. § 31.6011(a)-1T] Eligible employers are those with estimated annual employment tax liability of $1,000 or less.

If a business received this notification, but prefers to file Form 941, it can request to have the filing requirement changed to Form 941 if it satisfies certain requirements. Employers who must file Form 944 have until the last day of the month that follows the end of the year to file Form 944.

New employers who expect to owe $1,000 or less in total annual employment tax (approximately $4,000 or less in annual wages) also are eligible to file Form 944. These employers can indicate their estimated tax amount when applying for their EIN (Employer's Identification Number) on Form SS-4. The IRS will notify the employer to file either Form 944 or Form 941 in the same notice indicating the taxpayer's new EIN.

Q 14:52 When is an employer's quarterly federal tax return due?

Form 941, Employer's Quarterly Federal Tax Return, is due by the last day of the month following the end of each calendar quarter. However, if all taxes have been deposited in full and on time, the employer has 10 extra days to file the return. [Reg. § 31.6071(a)-1(a)]

Seasonal employers do not have to file Form 941 for any quarter in which they paid no wages. However, they must be sure to check the seasonal filer box on the form or the IRS will be expecting a return each quarter.

Q 14:53 What if an employer discovers an error when preparing the quarterly return?

If a FICA tax or income tax withholding error is detected before the return for the quarter is filed, the employer should report the correct amounts when it files its return for the quarter. Any additional taxes should be remitted by the due date of Form 941. Semi-weekly depositors must deposit the additional taxes; monthly depositors may pay the shortfall with Form 941.

If the error resulted in overwithholding from an employee, the employer must reimburse the employee either by cutting a separate check or by applying the overwithholding against tax that would otherwise be withheld later in the year. If the employer under withheld from the employee, the employer can collect the amounts from a later paycheck. However, the employer is responsible for the taxes, even if they cannot be collected from the employee (for example, if the employee has left the job). In the case, of an underwithholding of income tax, the employer is liable for the tax unless and until the employee files a return and pays the tax.

Q 14:54 What if an employer discovers an error after the return for the quarter is filed?

If a FICA tax or income tax withholding error is detected after the quarterly return is filed, the employer can adjust the error on the return for the quarter in which the error was detected or on a supplemental return for the period in which the wages were paid. The employer must attach Form 941c, *Statement to Correct Information Previously Reported on the Employer's Federal Tax Return*, to the form that reports the adjustment.

> **Caution:** Employers generally should not adjust income tax withholding errors made in a prior calendar year. Only administrative errors that do not change the amount of tax actually withheld from an employee should be corrected.

As an alternative, an employer can request a refund of FICA taxes that were overpaid in a prior year by filing Form 843, *Claim for Refund and Request for Abatement*. In order to claim a refund of the employee's share, the employer must reimburse the employee or obtain the employee's consent to file for a refund on his or her behalf. If an overpayment has been outstanding for an extended period of time, there is an advantage to filing for a refund. The IRS must pay interest on the refunded amount, while an adjustment on Form 941c does not bear interest.

If the error resulted in overwithholding from an employee, the employer must reimburse the employee either by cutting a separate check or by applying the overwithholding against tax that would otherwise be withheld later in the year. If the employer under withheld from the employee, the employer can collect the amounts from a later paycheck. However, the employer is responsible for the taxes, even if they cannot be collected from the employee (for example, if the employee has left the job). In the case, of an underwithholding of income tax, the employer is liable for the tax unless and until the employee files a return and pays the tax.

Q 14:55 When must an employer file the annual federal unemployment tax return?

Form 940, *Employer's Annual Federal Unemployment Tax (FUTA) Return*, is due on January 31 following the close of the calendar year. If all taxes have been deposited in full and on time, the employer has 10 extra days to file the return. [Reg. § 31.6071(a)-1(c)]

Payroll Tax Penalties

Q 14:56 What penalties are imposed for payroll tax errors?

An employer may owe a variety of penalties for payroll tax errors. These include:

- Penalties for failure to make required deposit (see Q 14:57);
- Penalties for failure to file required returns (see Q 14:58); and
- Penalties for failure to pay tax (see Q 14:59).

In addition, a "responsible person" may be held personally liable for failure to pay over withheld funds (see Q 14:60).

Q 14:57 What is the failure-to-deposit penalty and when is it imposed?

The failure to deposit penalty is imposed when an employer fails to deposit withheld income and FICA taxes in a timely manner. [IRC § 6656]

Deposit penalties are on a sliding scale. [IRC § 6656] If a deposit is no more than five days late, the penalty is 2 percent of the deposit shortfall. If the deposit is more than five but no more than 15 days late, the penalty jumps to 5 percent. After 15 days, the penalty is 10 percent of the deposit shortfall. If the employer receives a delinquency notice or a notice and demand for immediate payment before correcting a deposit failure, the employer must deposit the taxes within 10 days. Otherwise, the penalty is 15 percent of the undeposited amount.

Under a special default rule, the IRS will generally apply a deposit to the most recently ended deposit period within the quarter or year for which the deposit is made. It will not apply the deposit to prior shortfalls. If there is any excess in the deposit, the excess will be applied to future deposit periods. [Rev. Proc. 2001-58, 2001-50 I.R.B. 579]

An employer can override the default rule, however. Once the employer receives a penalty notice from the IRS, the employer has 90 days to contact the IRS and designate another period or periods to which the deposit should be applied. The IRS will adjust the penalty amount to reflect the revised deposit and notify the employer of the adjustment in writing.

Planning Point: In most cases, the default rule will work out best for an employer by eliminating the cascading of penalties (i.e. if a deposit were automatically applied to a prior shortfall, it might create a new shortfall for the current period). However, there still may be some situations in which an employer will want to contact the IRS to override the default rule.

Example 14-30: XYZ is a monthly employment tax depositor. XYZ pays its employees on the first business day of every month. XYZ does not wait until the deposit due date—the 15th day of the following month—to make its deposits. Instead it makes deposits on the 25th day of the month (or the next banking day thereafter) in which the liability is incurred.

XYZ pays its employees on April 1, 2008. For some reason, the company fails to make a payroll tax deposit on April 25, 2008. For May, XYZ pays its employees on May 1, 2008. On May 27, 2008, unaware of the shortfall for April, the company makes a deposit to cover its May liability. Under the default rule, the IRS applies this deposit to the most recently ended deposit period, which in this case is April 2008, instead of the May 2008 liability that XYZ intended to pay. This cycle of deposits continues until the end of the second quarter. Instead of having a failure to deposit penalty only for April, XYZ will be subject to a penalty for every month in the quarter.

XYZ can minimize its penalties by notifying the IRS once it receives its penalty notice. It can designate May and June as the deposit periods to which the deposits are to be applied. Thus, XYZ will have a deposit penalty only for April.

Q 14:58 What is the failure-to-file penalty, and when is it imposed?

The penalty for failure to file a payroll tax return is 5 percent of the unpaid tax per month or fraction of a month. The maximum penalty is 25 percent. If the failure is due to fraud, the penalty is 15 percent of the unpaid tax per month or fraction of a month, up to a maximum of 75 percent. Moreover, even if the employer has no unpaid tax when the return is due, there is a minimum penalty for failure to file within 60 days of the due date equal to the lesser of $100 or 10 percent of the amount required to be shown on the return. [IRC § 6651(a)(1)]

Q 14:59 What is the penalty for failure to pay tax?

The failure-to-pay penalty is imposed if any amount required to be reported on a quarterly Form 941 or an annual Form 940 is not paid by the due date of the return. The penalty is 0.5 percent per month or fraction of a month that the amount is unpaid, up to a maximum of 25 percent. [IRC § 6651(a)(2)]

Q 14:60 What is the "100 percent penalty"?

For owners and managers of businesses, the most onerous penalty of all may be the so-called "100 percent penalty" (or, more technically, the trust fund recovery penalty). If the IRS cannot collect withheld income taxes from an employer, it can impose a penalty equal to 100 percent of the unpaid amount on any "responsible person" who "willfully" failed to pay over the withheld funds. [IRC § 6672]The penalty applies only to trust fund taxes—income and FICA taxes withheld from employee's pay. It does not apply to the employer's share of FICA taxes or to FUTA taxes.

> **Note:** The 100 percent penalty is generally asserted in the corporate context. Although owners or employees of a corporation are generally not responsible for the corporation's tax debts, the 100 percent penalty permits the IRS to recover trust fund taxes from a responsible person's personal assets. By contrast, if a business is operated as a sole proprietorship or partnership, the proprietor or general partners are personally liable for business debts. Therefore, the IRS can pursue collection from their assets without asserting the 100 percent penalty.

In the past, the IRS aggressively pursued collection of the penalty from virtually any employee who had anything to do with company finances—from the CEO down to the junior payroll clerk. However, under current procedures, the IRS will no longer assert the penalty against nonowner-employees who do not exercise independent judgment and who work at ministerial jobs. Nonetheless, the 100 percent penalty remains a real threat for employees who have discretionary authority over a company's funds—especially if the company is in financial trouble.

> **Planning Point:** Keeping a troubled company afloat can involve agonizing choices. And there is a natural temptation to put off paying Uncle Sam—and pay the supplier of much-needed inventory. However, company officers and employees should be warned that paying business expenses instead of taxes is considered acting willfully. So what should a responsible person do when a company has unpaid payroll tax liabilities and there is just not enough money to go around?

It is important to remember there are two liabilities—the company's direct liability for FICA and FUTA taxes, and the trust fund liability for income and FICA taxes withheld from employees. If the company simply sends the IRS a check for partial payment of its payroll taxes, the Service's policy is to allocate the payment first to the company's own liability. [IRS Policy Statement P-5-60] The reason for this is clear; if the company's own taxes cannot be paid from its assets, the IRS will never be able to collect them. But unpaid trust fund taxes can be collected from the company's responsible persons.

However, if the company specifically designates the tax liability to which a payment should be applied, the IRS will follow the company's instructions. So if the company directs its partial payment to trust fund taxes, the responsible person will be off the hook to the extent of the payment.

Q 14:61 Who is liable for unpaid or undeposited taxes if an employer hires a third party to perform its payroll duties?

A fiduciary, agent, or other person who has control, receipt, custody, or disposal of, or pays wages paid to an employee or group of employees, employed by one or more employers, may be liable for the withholding and payment of income taxes on those wage payments. The liability depends upon whether the fiduciary, agent, or other person has been authorized by the IRS to perform the acts ordinarily required of employers. If so, the fiduciary, agent, or other person is liable for failure to withhold and pay the correct amount of tax. However, the employer also remains liable. The employer and the fiduciary, agent, or other person are co-liable for the withholding and payment of the correct amount of income taxes on the wage payments. The employer cannot completely shift this responsibility to a third party.

For example, the Third Circuit Court of Appeals recently affirmed that a business was liable for overdue employment taxes, even though it paid the taxes in full to its payroll firm, which then embezzled some of the funds. The court emphasized that it is well established that a taxpayer's reliance on a third party to fulfill its tax obligations does not release the taxpayer from its obligation to collect and pay employment taxes to the government. [*Pediatric Affiliates*, U.S. Ct. App. (3rd Cir., 2007)]

The IRS has the discretion to abate penalties and even interest for certain delays on its part. However, paying market-rate fees to, and exercising reasonable oversight of, a third-party payroll company will not excuse an employer's liability for payment. While the IRS usually chooses to try to collect first from the payroll company, it also retains the coextensive right to collect from the employer. Although the employer can sue the payroll company if the IRS can't collect, the employer also will likely be unable to find any assets to cover a civil judgment.

Form W-2, Annual Wage and Tax Statement

Q 14:62 What is the Form W-2, Annual Wage and Tax Statement?

Every employer that pays wages during the year must prepare Form W-2, *Annual Wage and Tax Statements*. The W-2 is a six-copy form that is used to convey income, payroll tax, and other data to the employee, the IRS, the Social Security Administration (SSA), and state or local tax authorities.

Form W-2 contains information on the employee's wages, tips, and other compensation; federal income tax withheld; Social Security wages and Social Security tax withheld; Medicare wages and Medicare tax withheld. The form also contains information on various benefits provided to employees.

Q 14:63 Where and when is Form W-2 filed?

Copy A of employees' W-2 forms must be filed with the SSA, along with a Form W-3 transmittal statement, by the last day of February of the year following the year to which the forms relate. Form W-3 summarizes the information on employees' individual W-2 forms.

The additional copies of Form W-2 are distributed as follows:

- Copy 1 is filed with the employer's state, county, city, or other local tax authority. Almost all states that require employers to furnish wage and tax information either permit or require employers to use the federal W-2 for this purpose. Each state sets its own filing deadline. In some states the deadline is as early as January 31; other states may permit filing as late as March 15.

- Copies 2, B, and C are furnished to the employee. Copy B is attached to the employee's federal tax return, while Copy 2 is attached to the employee's state or local return. The employee retains Copy C for his or her records. All copies must be furnished to the employee by January 31 of the year following the year to which the W-2 relates. An employee's form is considered "furnished" if the form is properly addressed and mailed on or before the due date.

- The employer retains Copy D for its records. Employers must keep W-2 forms on file for at least four years.

[Reg. § 31.6001-1(e)(2)]

Q 14:64 Is an employer required to use the official IRS W-2 forms?

No. An employer may use an acceptable substitute form that complies with IRS specifications. The requirements for substitute forms are found in IRS Publication Number 1411, *General Rules and Specifications for Private Printing of Substitute Forms W-2 and W-3*, which is revised annually.

Q 14:65 Can an employer file W-2 forms electronically?

Yes. In fact, larger employers who file 250 or more W-2 forms must file electronically unless the IRS grants a waiver. The IRS encourages other employers to file electronically even if they are filing fewer than 250 forms. (Beginning with the 2006 W-2 forms filed in 2007, employers cannot file using 3 1/2" diskettes. All W-2s must be filed either electronically or on paper.)

Information on electronic filing can be found on the SSA's website at *http://www.ssa.gov/employer1.htm*.

Q 14:66 Can W-2 forms be furnished to employees electronically?

Yes, but only if employees agree to that means of distribution. [Temp. Reg. § 31.6051-1T] An employer may not send Form W-2 electronically to any employee who does not consent or who has revoked consent previously provided.

To furnish Form W-2 electronically, an employer must meet all of the following requirements:

1. The employee must be informed that he or she may receive a paper form if consent is not given to receive it electronically;

2. The consent statement must be made electronically in a way that demonstrates that the employee will be able to access the Form W-2 in electronic form;

3. The employee must be informed how to obtain a paper form and whether any fee will be charged for a paper copy;

4. The employee must be permitted to withdraw consent in writing at any time on 30 days' notice. The employer must confirm the withdrawal of consent in writing and inform the employee of the consequences of the withdrawal;

5. The employer must notify the employee of the scope and duration of the consent; and

6. The employer must inform the employee that the form may be required to be attached to his or her tax return and that the employee may need to print the form.

Electronic forms must be furnished by the January 31 due date that applies to paper forms. The employer must notify the employee that the Forms W-2 will be posted on a Web site by January 31. This notice may be delivered by mail, electronic mail, or in person.

Q 14:67 Which employees must receive Form W-2?

Employers must furnish and file W-2 forms for every employee (1) from whom income, Medicare, or Social Security taxes were withheld or (2) from whom income, Medicare, or Social Security taxes would have been withheld if the employee had claimed no more than one withholding allowance or had not claimed exemption from withholding. [IRC § 6051]

Q 14:68 Must Form W-2 be furnished immediately when an employee terminates employment during the year?

No. An employer may provide a terminated employee with Form W-2 at any time, but no later than January 31 of the following year. However, if the employee requests a Form W-2, it must be provided within 30 days of the request or 30 days of the employee's final wage payment, whichever is later.

Q 14:69 What if an employer discovers an error on an employee's Form W-2 after the form has been filed?

The employer must use Form W-2c, *Corrected Wage and Tax Statement*, to correct errors on W-2 forms that have been filed with the SSA. A separate Form W-2c must be filed for each W-2 form that contains an error or omission. However, it is not necessary to file Form W-2c with the SSA if the only correction is to the employee's address.

Form W-3c, *Transmittal of Corrected Wage and Tax Statements*, which summarizes and transmits the corrected forms, must generally accompany Form W-2c.

However, Form W-3c is not required if the only corrections are to employee names or Social Security numbers.

It is not necessary to file Form W-2c with the SSA if the only correction is to the employee's address. However, if the address was incorrect on the form furnished to the employee, the employer must either (1) issue a new W-2 with the caption "Reissued Statement" to the employee showing the correct address; (2) issue a Form W-2c to the employee showing the correct address, or (3) mail the Form W-2 with the incorrect address to the employee in an envelope showing the correct address or otherwise deliver it to the employee.

Q 14:70 Is there a penalty for failing to file a Form W-2 on time or filing an incorrect form?

The IRS can assess a penalty if an employer files late or files on time but omits information or reports incorrect data. The amount of the penalty depends on when the employer delivers correct, complete W-2 data to the Social Security Administration. The penalties increase the longer the employer waits to make corrections or file missing W-2 forms. If the employer acts before March 30, the penalty is $15 for each W-2 filed late or with incorrect or missing data (annual maximum $75,000). If the employer acts after March 30 but by August 1, the penalty is $30 per late or erroneous W-2 (annual maximum $150,000). The penalty increases to $50 for mistakes corrected or filed late W-2s after August 1 (annual maximum $250,000). [IRC § 6721]

Note that the IRS can assess an employer only one penalty for each W-2 filed. For example, a Form W-2 that is both late and incorrect will incur only one $15 penalty if the employer gets an accurate, complete W-2 (or W-2c, see below) to SSA by March 30.

Employers may be able to avoid penalties altogether if they can show their errors or delays were due to reasonable cause and not willful neglect. [Reg. § 301.6724-1] To claim this, employers have to prove to IRS they had either:

- *Significant mitigating factors.* These include a history of timely compliance with the W-2 rules. New firms may have penalties abated because they were never required to file W-2 forms before.

- *Impediments.* These are factors beyond an employer's control—whether a natural disaster or an employee who would not provide a bona fide Social Security number—that kept the employer from filing on time or from filing accurate W-2 forms.

Employers who cannot show reasonable cause may still be eligible for penalty relief:

- *Small firms.* If average annual gross receipts for each of the three most recent taxable years were $5 million or less, the per-employer penalty maximums are reduced from $75,000 to $25,000 (if corrections are made within 30 days); from $150,000 to $50,000 (if corrections are made by

August 1); and from $250,000 to $100,000 (if corrections are not made until after August 1).

- *Low volume of errors.* Employers will not be penalized for up to 10 inaccurate or incomplete W-2 forms or up to 0.5 percent of the total number of information returns required to be filed for the year, if that is greater. This relief is available only if the original W-2 forms were filed on time and any corrections were made by August 1.

- *Inconsequential errors.* Penalties will generally not be assessed if W-2 errors do not hinder or prevent the IRS or SSA from processing the form or matching it with the employee's return. For example, misspelling an employee's first name or address may not be enough to warrant a penalty. However, some errors are by definition never inconsequential, including mistakes in an employee's surname, taxpayer identification number, or wage or tax amounts.

[Reg. § 301.6721-1(c)]

If the IRS finds W-2 errors or delays were due to intentional disregard of the reporting requirements, the penalty is the greater of $100 or 10 percent of the amount required to be shown on the return. There is no annual penalty limit, and the reprieves for early corrections, low-volume errors, and small firm size are not available. [IRC § 6721]

Q 14:71 What is the penalty if an employer fails to provide a Form W-2 to an employee or provides an incorrect form?

An employer that fails to furnish employee copies of Form W-2 by January 31, or that furnishes the W-2 forms on time but does not correctly include all required information is subject to a penalty of $50 per W-2 (annual maximum $100,000). The same penalty applies no matter how late the W-2 forms are furnished, and there is no penalty relief for low-volume errors. However, employers may be eligible for penalty abatement if they can show reasonable cause or prove the errors were inconsequential (see Q 14:62).

If the IRS finds the mistakes on the W-2 forms were due to intentional disregard of the W-2 requirements, the penalty is the greater of $100 per W-2 or 10 percent of the aggregate amount of the items required to be reported on the W-2 form. [IRC § 6722] If the failure is also deemed willful or the employer is found to have willfully furnished false or fraudulent W-2 forms to employees, there is an additional criminal penalty (a fine of up to $1,000 or imprisonment of one year, or both) plus a $50 per form civil penalty. [IRC § § 7204; 6674]

Q 14:72 What is the penalty if an employer is required to file W-2 forms electronically but fails to do so?

Employers who file 250 or more copies of Form W-2 must file with the SSA electronically. An employer that is required to file electronically but does not do so is treated as having failed to file the forms. Therefore, the employer is subject to the $50 per form penalty for failure to file (see Q 14:62). However, the penalty does not apply to the first 250 W-2 forms filed. [IRC § 6724(c)]

Who Are Employees?

Q 14:73 Why is the distinction between employees and other service providers significant?

The status of a worker has important implications for payroll tax purposes.

- The wages of an employee are subject to income tax withholding; payments to an independent contractor are not.

- An employer pays FICA taxes on an employee's wages and must withhold an equal amount from the employee's wages. No FICA taxes are owed on payments to an independent contractor. Instead, the independent contractor is responsible for paying a self-employment tax on his or her earnings.

- An employer owes federal unemployment taxes on an employee's wages, but not on payments to an independent contractor.

- An employer reports an employee's wages to the IRS on a Form W-2; payments to an independent contractor are reported on a Form 1099-MISC (if they exceed $600 for the year).

In addition to the payroll tax implications, there are a number of other consequences that can flow from a worker's status. For example, an employee may have to be included in an employer's benefit plans while an independent contractor can be excluded.

Q 14:74 What are the possible classifications of service providers?

A person performing services may be:

- A common law employee;

- An independent contractor;

- An statutory employee; or

- A statutory nonemployee.

Q 14:75 What is the difference between an employee and an independent contractor?

The decisive factor in determining whether a worker is an employee or an independent contractor is *control*. If an employer has the right to control and direct how a worker performs his or her job, the worker is an employee. It is not necessary that an employer actually direct and control the worker; it is sufficient if the employer merely has the *right* to direct and control the employee. On the other hand, if the worker is merely directed as to the end result that must be accomplished—and not as to the means to achieve it—the worker is an independent contractor. [Reg. § 31.3401(c)-1]

Whether a worker is a common law employee or independent contractor is determined on a case-by-case basis. If an employer-employee relationship exists, the fact that the parties designate the relationship as something else makes no difference. Thus, depending on the situation, a worker may be treated as an employee, even though he or she is designated an independent contractor, partner, agent, etc. [Reg. § 31.3401(c)-1(d)] Likewise, if an employer-employee relationship exists, it makes no difference how payments are measured, how they are made, or what they are called. Nor does it matter whether the worker is employed full time or part time.

All classes or grades of employees are included within the relationship of employer and employee. For example, superintendents, managers, and other supervisory personnel are employees. Generally, an officer of a corporation is an employee of the corporation. However, an officer of a corporation who as such performs little or no services and who is not entitled to compensation is not considered any employee of the corporation. A director of a corporation performing the work of a director is not an employee. [Reg. § 31.3401(c)-1(f)]

Q 14:76 What factors have traditionally been used to distinguish between employees and independent contractors?

Whether this control standard is met depends on the facts and circumstances of each case. Over the years, the IRS and the Social Security Administration have compiled a list of 20 factors—sometimes called the 20-Factor Test—that have been used in court decisions to determine worker status. [Rev. Rul. 87-41, 1987-1 C.B. 296]

The 20 factors are:

1. *Instructions.* A worker who is required to comply with another person's instructions about when, where, and how he or she is to work is ordinarily an employee.

2. *Training.* Required training indicates that a worker must perform services in a particular method or manner and is, therefore, an employee.

3. *Integration.* Integration of the worker's services into the business operations generally shows that the worker is subject to direction and control.

4. *Services rendered personally.* A requirement that services must be rendered personally by the worker tends to indicate an employer-employee relationship.

5. *Hiring, supervising, and paying assistants.* If a company hires, supervises, and pays assistants to help the worker, that factor generally shows control over the worker on the job.

6. *Continuing relationship.* A continuing relationship between the worker and the company for whom the services are performed indicates that an employer-employee relationship exists.

7. *Set hours of work.* If a company establishes set hours of work for a worker—that is a factor indicating control.

8. *Full time required.* If the worker must devote substantially full time to the business for which the services are performed, the business has control over the amount of time the worker spends working and implicitly restricts the worker from doing other gainful work. An independent contractor, on the other hand, is free to work when and for whom he or she chooses.

9. *Doing work on employer's premises.* If the work is performed on a company's premises, this suggests that the company has control over a worker, especially if the work could be done elsewhere. Work done off the premises of the company, such as at the office of the worker, indicates some freedom from control.

10. *Order or sequence set.* If a worker must perform services in the order or sequence set by the business for whom the services are performed, that factor shows that the worker is not free to follow his or her own pattern of work but must follow the established routines and schedules of the business.

11. *Oral or written reports.* A requirement that the worker submit regular oral or written reports to the business that he or she is working for indicates a degree of control.

12. *Payment by hour, week, month.* Payment by the hour, week, or month generally points to an employer-employee relationship. Payment made by the job or commission generally indicates that the worker is an independent contractor.

13. *Payment of business and/or traveling expenses.* If the business usually pays a worker's business and/or traveling expenses, the worker is ordinarily an employee.

14. *Furnishing of tools and materials.* The fact that a business for which the services are performed furnishes significant tools, materials, and other equipment to a worker tends to show the existence of an employer-employee relationship.

15. *Significant investment.* If the worker invests in facilities that are used in performing services and are not typically maintained by employees (such as the maintenance of an office rented at fair value from an unrelated party), that factor tends to indicate that the worker is an independent contractor. On the other hand, lack of investment indicates an employer-employee relationship.

16. *Realization of profit or loss.* A worker who can realize a profit or suffer a loss as a result of the worker's services is generally an independent contractor, but the worker who cannot is an employee.

17. *Working for more than one business at a time.* If a worker performs more than "*de minimis*" services for multiple unrelated businesses at the same

Q 14:76

time, this generally indicates that the worker is an independent contractor.

18. *Making service available to general public.* The fact that a worker makes his or her services available to the general public on a regular and consistent basis indicates independent contractor status.

19. *Right to discharge.* If a business has a right to discharge a worker, this factor indicates that the worker is an employee. An independent contractor, on the other hand, cannot be fired so long as the independent contractor produces a result that meets the contract specifications.

20. *Right to terminate.* If a worker has the right to end his or her relationship with a company at any time without incurring liability, that factor indicates an employer-employee relationship.

For information on how the IRS applies these and other factors to determine a worker's status, see Q 14:76.

Q 14:77 How does the IRS analyze a worker's status?

Training materials for IRS employees emphasize that the 20 factors are an analytical tool, not a legal test for determining worker status. In some cases, the 20 factors are not the only factors that may be important, and some of the 20 factors may be irrelevant. There is no "magic number" of factors. According to the IRS, factors indicating the degree of control or independence fall into three categories: (1) factors showing *behavioral control* over the worker, (2) factors showing *financial control,* and (3) factors illustrating the relationship between the parties.

1. *Behavioral control.* Evidence included in this category tends to show whether or not a business has the right to direct and control the details and means by which a worker performs the required services. Training and instructions provided by the business are important evidence in this category. In addition, newer workplace developments such as evaluation systems and quality programs will also be considered.

    Instructions—The IRS says instructions can be evidence that a business not only has the right to direct and control how work is done, but also that it actually exercised that right. While the right to control and not the actual exercise of control is the legal standard, evidence of actual exercise of control is highly persuasive. On the other hand, less extensive instructions concerning what should be done, but not how it should be done, are often consistent with independent contractor status.

    Example 14-31: John Jackson is an independent truck driver. Jackson received a call from Yates Mfg. Co. to make a delivery run from the Gulf Coast to the Texas Panhandle. Jackson accepted the job and agreed to pick up the cargo the next morning. Upon arriving at the warehouse, Jackson was given the address to which to make the delivery and was told the delivery must be made within two days. The IRS says this kind of instruction on *what* is to be done rather than how it is to be done, is consistent with independent contractor status.

Example 14-32: Tom Gentry is also a truck driver. Gentry makes local deliveries for Zinn Co. and reports to Zinn's warehouse every morning. The warehouse manager tells Gentry what deliveries have to be made, how to load the cargo in the truck, what route to take, and the order in which deliveries are to be made. This kind of instruction on *how* the work is to be done is consistent with employee status.

Lack of instructions does not necessarily establish an independent contractor relationship. Highly trained professionals, such as doctors, accountants, lawyers, engineers, and computer specialists, require very little, if any, instruction. In fact, the business may not have the knowledge and skills to give any instructions. Nonetheless, an employment relationship may exist between the business and these workers.

Training—Periodic or ongoing training provided by a business about procedures to be followed and methods to be used indicates that the business wants the services performed in a particular way. The IRS says this type of training is strong evidence of an employment relationship.

However, other types of training may be consistent with either employee or independent contractor status. For example, if a company provides short orientation or information sessions on the company's policies, new product lines, or new government relations, attendees may be either employees or independent contractors. Similarly, programs that are voluntary or that are attended by the worker without compensation may indicate either status.

Evaluation systems—The IRS says that how a business evaluates a worker's performance and how it uses the evaluations are important factors to consider.

Regular evaluations that are used to reward, promote, discipline, train, instruct, or terminate the worker are evidence that the business has given instructions and expects them to be followed. However, a business may use customer or internal evaluations simply to measure the quality of the service provided by an independent contractor. In that case the evaluations are not evidence of an employment relationship.

Again, lack of evaluations does not establish an independent contractor relationship. The IRS points out that some businesses—especially small businesses—do not have formal performance evaluation systems.

2. *Financial control.* The financial arrangements between the business and the worker tend to indicate which party has the right to control the *business* aspects of the job. However, whether or not the worker is financially dependent on or independent of the business for which services are performed is *not* a basis for determining worker classification.

Profit or loss—The ability to realize a profit or incur a loss is the strongest evidence that the worker is the one in financial control and may be an independent contractor. However, the fact that a worker will make more money by working longer hours does not indicate profit or loss potential. That kind of variation is consistent with employee status.

Significant investment—The fact that the worker has made a significant investment in order to perform the services is also evidence that an independent contractor relationship may exist. There are no dollar limits that must be met for an investment to be significant. However, the investment must have substance.

Example 14-33: Charles Park is a truck driver for a distributing company. The company treats Park as an independent contractor. During an audit, the company tells an IRS agent that Park has a significant investment in a truck he uses to make deliveries. On further investigation, the agent discovers that Park leases the truck from one of the company's related corporations. In addition, Park can turn in the vehicle at any time without liability for further payments. Park has *expenses* for leasing the truck, but has not made a significant investment.

The IRS stresses that a significant investment is not necessary for independent contractor status. Some types of work, such as writing or consulting, simply do not require costly equipment. In addition, even if costly equipment is required, an independent contractor may rent it from a third party.

Business expenses—Although not every business involves significant investment, almost every business will incur a variety of expenses.

The IRS acknowledges that some independent contractors may contract for direct reimbursement of certain expenses, while others will seek to establish contract prices that will reimburse expenses. However, if a worker is *directly* reimbursed for all or almost all expenses, it may indicate an employer-employee relationship, depending on additional facts.

Services available to the public—An independent contractor is generally free to seek other business opportunities. Therefore, independent contractors generally advertise, maintain a visible business location, and are available to work for a number of clients.

However, the IRS points out that these activities are not necessary for independent contractor status. An independent contractor with special skills may not need to advertise. A contractor who has negotiated a long-term contract may be unavailable to work for others. Also, in some businesses, a visible location may not generate enough business to be worth the expense.

Method of payment—The IRS says the way the worker is paid is extremely important in determining whether the worker has an opportu-

nity for profit or loss. Payment arrangements may fall into three
categories:

- Salary or hourly wage—Since the worker is guaranteed a return for
  labor costs, this type of arrangement is generally evidence of an
  employment relationship.

- Flat fee—This type of arrangement is an indicator that a worker may
  be an independent contractor, since the worker bears the expenses for
  the job and pockets what is left over. However, the IRS cautions that a
  flat fee that is calculated by multiplying an hourly or other periodic
  rate by the time required to perform the job would indicate an
  employee relationship.

- Commissions—A commissioned worker may be either an employee
  or independent contractor. The key is the opportunity for profit or
  loss. A commissioned worker who pays all the expenses of operating
  a business has a real opportunity for loss if expenses exceed commissions and an opportunity for profit if commissions exceed expenses.

3. *Relationship of the parties.* A number of factors indicate how the parties
   perceive their relationship to each other. While these factors do not
   directly relate to the issue of control, the IRS says they may be important
   in determining a worker's status.

   Employee benefits—Employee-type benefits such as paid vacation days,
   sick days, health insurance, life or disability insurance, or a pension, are
   evidence of employee status. The IRS notes that this evidence is strongest if the worker is provided with benefits under a tax-qualified retirement plan or a cafeteria plan since the tax law permits these benefits to
   be provided only to employees.

   On the other hand, the IRS says the lack of benefits should *never* be
   considered evidence of independent contractor status.

   Written contracts—The IRS points out that the courts may look at the
   intent of the parties as shown in their contractual relationship. However,
   the IRS says that a contractual designation is never enough to determine
   a worker's status. On the other hand, if evidence outside the contract is
   evenly balanced, the contractual designation is an effective way to
   resolve the issue.

   Permanency—A long-term relationship may be evidence of an employee
   relationship since the worker may have little need to maintain a business
   presence and little likelihood of incurring the type of profit or loss
   associated with independent contractor status. On the other hand, independent contractors may enter into long-term contracts or have their
   contracts renewed regularly.

   Discharge—The right to discharge a worker without penalty has traditionally been used to distinguish employees from independent contractors. If a worker can be discharged at will, it indicates the business's
   ability to control how the work is performed. However, the IRS says, as

Q 14:77

a practical matter, it may be difficult to distinguish between discharging a worker for failure to perform the work properly and discharging an independent contractor for failure to produce the contracted product or service. In addition, legal limits on the ability to discharge employees have increased in recent years. Therefore, inability to discharge a worker at will is not necessarily evidence of independent contractor status.

Regular business activity—If the services performed by the worker are part of the company's regular business activity, it is likely the company will want to control how those services are performed. But this factor is not decisive. Examiners must look for other evidence before concluding that the worker is an employee.

The IRS training materials also emphasize that a number of factors that have traditionally been used for worker classification may have little relevance today.

1. *Part-time or temporary work.* In the past, part-time work—especially if the worker performed services for another business—was an indicator that the worker was an independent contractor. However, the IRS says that in today's economy with cutbacks and downsizing, many companies hire part-time workers who may be either employees or independent contractors. Similarly, the IRS cautions its agents not to assume that a temporary relationship is evidence of an independent contractor relationship. Workers who are engaged on a seasonal or "as needed" basis may still be employees.

2. *Place of work.* Whether or not work is performed on the business's premises or at a location selected by the business, often has no bearing on worker status. Modern technology has developed tools, such as modems and computer networks, which greatly expand the scope of the workplace. Because of this trend, a number of employees now work offsite either full or part time.

3. *Work hours.* Some work must, by its nature, be performed at a particular time, but again modern communications have increased the ease of performing work outside normal business hours. Today, flexible hours are consistent with independent contractor or employee status.

Employers may obtain a determination from the IRS as to whether workers are employees or independent contractors. An employer can request this determination by filling out and filing Form SS-8. If an employer has more than one worker whose status is at issue, Form SS-8 should be filled in for a representative worker of the class of workers. The IRS determination will apply to all workers in that class. Employers must submit separate SS-8 forms for each class.

Q 14:78 If the IRS determines that an employer has improperly treated a worker as an independent contractor, can the IRS reclassify the worker as an employee?

Not always. A special relief provision known as "Section 530" (it was Section 530 of the Revenue Act of 1978) permits an employer to treat a worker as an independent contractor for employment tax purposes, regardless of the worker's actual status under the common law test.

An employer is eligible for Section 530 relief if:

- The employer has treated the worker and all similarly situated workers as independent contractors for all periods since 1978;

- The employer has filed tax returns on a basis that is consistent with treating the worker as an independent contractor; and

- The employer has a reasonable basis for treating the worker as an independent contractor.

There are several alternative standards that constitute "safe havens" in determining whether an employer has a "reasonable basis" for not treating a worker as an employee. Reasonable reliance on any one of the following "safe havens" is sufficient:

- Judicial precedent or published rulings, whether or not relating to the employer's particular industry or business, or technical advice, a letter ruling, or a determination letter pertaining to the employer.

- A past IRS audit dealing with worker classification issues that did not result in an assessment attributable to the employer's employment tax treatment of workers holding positions substantially similar to the position held by the worker whose status is at issue.

- A long-standing recognized practice by a significant segment of the employer's industry of treating similarly situated workers as independent contractors. For this purpose, a significant segment of the employer's industry means no more than 25 percent, and in some situations less than 25 percent of an industry may be significant. In addition, an industry practice need not have continued for more than 10 years to be considered long-standing. Again, less than 10 years may be considered significant in some circumstances.

An employer that fails to meet any of the three "safe havens" may still be entitled to Section 530 relief if the employer can demonstrate, in some other manner, a reasonable basis for not treating the individual as an employee. Congress has indicated that "reasonable basis" should be construed liberally in favor of the employer. [Rev. Proc. 85-18, § 3.01, 1985-1 C.B. 518]

In determining whether an employer has consistently treated a worker and similarly situated workers as independent contractors, the IRS applies the following guidelines:

- The withholding of income tax or FICA tax from a worker's wages is "treatment" of the worker as an employee, whether or not the tax is paid over to the IRS.

- The filing of an employment tax return for a period with respect to worker, whether or not tax was withheld from the worker's wages, constitutes "treatment" of the worker as an employee for that period.

On the other hand, if an employer changes its treatment of workers from independent contractors to employees, it will not affect the availability of Section 530 relief for prior periods.

Just as Section 530 relief is not available if the employer has filed returns treating a worker as an employee, relief is not available unless the employer has filed required information returns (Form 1099) consistent with its treatment of the worker as an independent contractor. [Rev. Rul. 81-224, 1981-2 C.B. 197]

The Tax Court has ruled that an employer met the information reporting requirement even though the information returns were filed late. [*Medical Emergency Care Associates,* S.C. 120 T.C. No. 15]

The IRS had argued that "Section 530 implicitly requires that the necessary returns be filed timely, as is mandated for all returns throughout the Internal Revenue Code." Given the requirement of timely filing throughout the Code, the IRS contended that if Congress did not intend to require timely filing, Congress would have included explicit language in Section 530 permitting a taxpayer who files delinquent returns to qualify for relief.

The Tax Court rejected that argument. The court pointed out that the plain language of Section 530 denies relief only if the required filing was not made or if the required filing was made on a basis inconsistent with treatment of an individual as an independent contractor. There is nothing in the language of Section 530 that requires timeliness along with consistent filing.

Q 14:79 Does Section 530 relief apply to all types of workers?

No, it does not. Section 530 relief does not apply to technical service firms that engage workers to provide technical services to the firm's clients. Technical services include engineering, designing, drafting, computer programming, systems analysis, and similar services.

The fact that technical service firms are not eligible for Section 530 relief does not mean, however, that their technical service workers must automatically be treated as employees. Instead, the workers' status must be determined under the common law tests. [Rev. Rul. 87-41, 1987-1 C.B. 296]

Q 14:80 What are the tax consequences if the IRS reclassifies an independent contractor as an employee?

The IRS can assess the employer for the employer's share of FICA and FUTA taxes on each worker's wages, plus penalties and interest. In addition, the employer can be assessed a penalty for failure to withhold income taxes equal to 1.5 percent of wages paid and a penalty equal to 20 percent of the employee's share of FICA taxes. Those penalties increase to 3 percent and 40 percent, respectively, if required information returns were not filed with respect to workers. [IRC § 3509]

On the other hand, the reclassification may result in a refund for the reclassified worker. If the worker paid self-employment tax on payments from the employer, the worker can file for a refund. The refund will, however, be offset by the employee's share of FICA tax that should have been withheld by the employer.

Q 14:81 What are the tax consequences if an employer qualifies for Section 530 relief from reclassification?

The employer may continue to treat the worker or workers as independent contractors. Therefore, the employer cannot be assessed for FICA or FUTA taxes for prior years and cannot be required to pay those taxes in future years unless it voluntarily reclassifies the worker or workers.

Section 530, however, has no effect on the tax treatment of the workers. An employee remains liable for his or her share of FICA taxes. Employees who paid self-employment tax on their earning may file a claim for a refund; however, the amount of the refund will be offset by the amount of the employee's share of FICA tax. [Rev. Proc. 85-18, 1985-1 C.B. 518]

Q 14:82 Does an employer have any recourse if the IRS reclassifies a worker as an employee?

An employer who is embroiled in a worker classification dispute with the IRS has two options. The employer can pay the payroll taxes due for at least one worker and file suit for a refund in a district court or the Court of Federal Claims. Alternatively, the employer can petition the United States Tax Court to review the IRS determination. [IRC § 7436(a)]

Planning Point: Taking an employment dispute to the Tax Court has an advantage for the employer. The employer is not required to pay any portion of the tax unless the Tax Court makes an adverse determination.

Q 14:83 Who are statutory employees?

Under certain circumstances, a business must automatically treat a worker as an employee for FICA tax purposes—regardless of the common law tests—if the worker falls into one of the following occupational groups:

- Agent-drivers or commission-drivers engaged in distributing certain foods and other items;
- Full-time life insurance salespersons;
- Home workers who perform work for the business; or
- Traveling or city salespersons that solicit orders full-time for the business.

[IRC § 3121(d)(3)]

While a company's payments to these "statutory employees" are subject to FICA taxes, they may not necessarily be subject to income tax withholding. The status of these workers for income tax purposes is determined under the common law rules.

Q 14:83

Agent-drivers or commission-drivers. This occupational group includes agent-drivers or commission-drivers who are engaged in distributing meat or meat products, vegetables or vegetable products, fruit or fruit products, bakery products, beverages (other than milk), or laundry or dry-cleaning services for a business. An agent-driver or commission-driver includes a worker who operates his or her own truck or the business's truck, serves customers designated by the business as well as those solicited on his or her own, and whose compensation is a commission on sales or the difference between the price the worker charges customers and the price the worker pays to the business for the product or service.

Full-time life insurance salespersons. A worker whose entire or principal business activity is devoted to the solicitation of life insurance or annuity contracts, or both, primarily for one life insurance company is a full-time life insurance salesperson. Such a salesperson ordinarily uses the office space provided by the business or its general agent, and stenographic assistance, telephone facilities, forms, rate books, and advertising materials are usually made available to him or her without cost. A worker who is engaged in the general insurance business under a contract that does not contemplate that the worker's principal business activity will be the solicitation of life insurance or annuity contracts for one company is not a full-time life insurance salesperson.

Home workers. This occupational group includes a worker who performs services off the employer's business premises, according to specifications furnished by the employer, on materials or goods furnished by the employer that are required to be returned to it or to someone designated by it.

Traveling or city salespersons. This occupational group includes a city or traveling salesperson that is engaged full time in the solicitation of orders for a business from wholesalers, retailers, contractors, or operators of hotels, restaurants, or other similar establishments for merchandise for resale or supplies for use in their business operations. An agent-driver or commission-driver is not within this occupational group. City or traveling salespeople who sell to retailers or to the others specified, operate off the business premises and are generally compensated on a commission basis, are within this occupational group. Such salespeople are generally not controlled as to the details of their services or the means by which they cover their territories, but in the ordinary case they are expected to call on regular customers with a fair degree of regularity. [Reg. § 31.3121(d)-1(d)(3)]

In order for a city or traveling salesperson to be included within this occupational group, his or her entire or principal business activity must be devoted to the solicitation of orders for one business. Thus, the multiple-line salesperson generally is not within this occupational group. However, if the salesperson solicits orders primarily for one company, he or she is not excluded from this occupational group solely because of sideline sales activities on behalf of one or more other companies. In such a case, the salesperson qualifies as a statutory employee only with respect to the services performed for the company for whom he or she *primarily* solicits orders and not with respect to the services performed for other companies. [Reg. § 31.3121(d)-1(d)(3)]

Other requirements. The fact that a worker falls within one of the specified occupational groups does not make the worker a statutory employee unless: (1) the worker's contract contemplates that substantially all the services to which the contract relates are to be performed personally by the worker, (2) the worker has no substantial investment in the equipment and premises used in connection with the performance of the services (other than in vehicles for transportation); and (3) the services are part of a continuing relationship and are not in the nature of a single transaction. [Reg. § 31.3121(d)-1(d)(4)]

Q 14:84 How are leased workers treated for employment tax purposes?

Under certain circumstances, a business that furnishes workers to various other businesses is the employer of those workers for employment tax purposes. For example, a professional services corporation may provide the services of secretaries, nurses, and other similarly trained workers to its subscribers. The service corporation enters into contracts with the subscribers under which the subscribers specify the services to be provided and the fee to be paid to the service corporation for each individual furnished. The contracts provide that the service corporation has the right to control and direct the worker's services for the subscriber including the right to discharge or reassign the worker. The service corporation hires the workers, pays their wages, and provides them with unemployment insurance and other benefits. The service corporation is the employer for employment tax purposes. [IRS Pub. No. 15A, *Employer's Supplemental Tax Guide*, Rev. Jan. 2005]

Chapter 15

Troubleshooting

Even the most careful taxpayer can make mistakes and even the most conscientious taxpayer can run into disputes with the IRS. This chapter looks at what taxpayers can do to head off problems in advance and how to minimize the problems if they are unavoidable.

For example, this chapter will cover:

• What taxpayers can do if they cannot make their tax payments when due;

• What actions the IRS can take to enforce a collection of tax;

• How errors can be corrected on tax returns;

• What taxpayers can expect if they are audited; and

• How to appeal an adverse decision by the IRS.

Unfortunately, tax problems, like toothaches, do not go away; they only get worse. The sooner a taxpayer deals with a problem, the better the chances of avoiding or reducing penalties.

Installment Payments and Offers in Compromise

Q 15:1 If a taxpayer gets a filing extension, does that also extend the time to make tax payments?

No. Interest and a late payment penalty (see "Civil Penalties and Interest" below) will generally be imposed on payments made after the due date. For example, if an individual gets a filing extension, the individual is subject to the late payment penalty (absent reasonable cause) if the unpaid tax on the original due date exceeds (1) 10 percent of the final tax shown on the return, or (2) is not paid by the extended due date. [Reg. § 301.6651-1(c)(3)]

Q 15:2 What can a taxpayer do if he or she is unable to make tax payments when they are due?

An installment payment agreement is an option taxpayers may want to consider. Installment agreements allow the payment of a tax debt in smaller, more manageable amounts. [IRC § 6159]Installment agreements generally require equal monthly payments. Taxpayers can ask for an installment agreement by attaching a completed Form 9465, *Installment Agreement Request,* to the front of their tax returns. Taxpayers specify the amount of the monthly payments and the day of each month they will make payments. Taxpayers should pay as much as they can with their return in order to lower the interest and penalty charges.

If a tax return has already been filed and a taxpayer receives a notice or bill requesting payment, the taxpayer can return the completed Form 9465 with the notice.

An installment agreement does not stop the running of interest or the accrual of late-payment penalties. [Reg. § 301.6159-1(d)]However, as long as the agreement remains in effect, it protects the taxpayer from the Internal Revenue Service's (IRS or the Service) seizure and sale of property. [Reg. § 301.6159-1(e)]

The American Jobs Creation Act of 2004 (P.L. 108-357) permits the IRS to enter into installment agreements that provide for less than full payment of a taxpayer's liabilities. [IRC § 6159(a)]An installment agreement providing for partial payment may be entered into by the IRS on or after October 22, 2004.

Q 15:3 Is the IRS required to accept a taxpayer's request for an installment payment agreement?

Yes, in some cases. The IRS must enter an installment agreement with individual taxpayers that provides for full payment of a liability if the following conditions are met:

- The aggregate amount of the tax liability does not exceed $10,000;
- During any of the preceding five tax years the taxpayer has *not* (1) failed to file an income tax return, (2) failed to pay any tax shown on an income

tax return, or (3) entered into an installment agreement for payment of an income tax;

- The IRS determines that the taxpayer is financially able to pay the installment in full when due (and the taxpayer submits information that the IRS may require to make this determination);

- The agreement requires full payment of the liability within three years; and

- The taxpayer agrees to comply with all provisions of the Internal Revenue Code (IRC or the Code) while the agreement is in effect. [IRC § 6159(c)]

In other situations, the Service's response will depend on the size of the tax liability and how quickly the taxpayer offers to pay it off. The IRS generally expects a taxpayer to pay as much as possible as soon as possible and will not usually agree to a payment schedule that lasts more than five years.

If the IRS is not satisfied with a taxpayer's proposed payment schedule or if the outstanding liability is more than $10,000, the IRS may ask for additional financial information on Form 433-A, *Collection Information Statement for Individuals*, or Form 433-B. These forms detail the taxpayer's assets and liabilities. The IRS will use this information to determine what kind of payment plans, if any, it will accept. If a request for an installment agreement is denied, the taxpayer can appeal to higher levels of the IRS Collection Division. [IRS Pub. No. 594, *What You Should Know About the IRS Collection Process* (Rev. February 2004)]

Q 15:4 Can the IRS terminate an installment agreement prior to the agreed upon date?

Yes. The IRS can terminate an existing installment agreement when:

- The taxpayer provided inaccurate or incomplete information to the IRS before the date the agreement was entered into; [IRC § 6159(b)(2)]

- The taxpayer or the taxpayer's representative provided information that is inaccurate or incomplete in any material respect in connection with the granting of the installment agreement; [Reg. § 301.6159-1(c)(1)] or

- The IRS believes the collection of the tax to which the installment agreement relates is in jeopardy. [IRC § 6159(b)(2)]

The IRS may also terminate, alter or modify an installment agreement where:

- The taxpayer fails to pay an installment on time;

- The taxpayer fails to pay any other tax liability at the time that liability is due; or

- The taxpayer fails to provide a financial condition update as requested by the IRS. [IRC § 6159(b)(4)]

Except in cases where the IRS believes that collection of tax is in jeopardy, the law forbids the IRS from taking any action to terminate, modify, or alter an installment agreement described above, unless the IRS gives the taxpayer at least

30 days' notice before taking the action. This notice must include an explanation of the Service's reason for taking the action. [IRC § 6159(b)(5)]

Q 15:5 What are "offers in compromise"?

Taxpayers who cannot pay their tax debts, and do not expect to be able to pay them in the future, can ask the IRS to accept less than the full amount owed. This is known as making an "offer in compromise." [IRC § 7122] The IRS is authorized to compromise a tax liability in the following circumstances. [Temp. Reg. § 301.7122-1T; Rev. Proc. 2003-71, 2003-36 I.R.B. 517]

1. *Doubt as to liability.* Doubt as to liability exists where there is a genuine dispute as to the existence or amount of the correct tax liability under the law. Doubt as to liability does not exist where the liability has been established by a final court decision or judgment concerning the existence of the liability.

    An offer to compromise based on doubt as to liability generally will be considered acceptable if it reasonably reflects the amount the IRS would expect to collect through litigation. This analysis includes consideration of the hazards of litigation that would be involved if the liability were litigated. The evaluation of the hazards of litigation is not an exact science and is within the discretion of the IRS.

2. *Doubt as to collectibility.* Doubt as to collectibility exists in any case where the taxpayer's assets and income cannot satisfy the full amount of the liability. An offer to compromise based on doubt as to collectibility generally will be considered acceptable if it is unlikely that the tax can be collected in full and the offer reasonably reflects the amount the IRS could collect through other means, including administrative and judicial collection remedies. This amount is the reasonable collection potential of a case. In determining the reasonable collection potential of a case, the IRS will take into account the taxpayer's reasonable basic living expenses. In some cases, the IRS may accept an offer of less than the total reasonable collection potential of a case if there are special circumstances.

3. *Promote effective tax administration.* The IRS may compromise to promote effective tax administration where it determines that, although collection in full could be achieved, collection of the full liability would cause the taxpayer economic hardship. Economic hardship is defined as the inability to pay reasonable basic living expenses.

    An offer to compromise based on economic hardship generally will be considered acceptable when, even though the tax could be collected in full, the amount offered reflects the amount the Service can collect without causing the taxpayer economic hardship. The determination to accept a particular amount will be based on the taxpayer's individual facts and circumstances.

Economic hardship may exist in the following situations:

- The taxpayer is incapable of earning a living because of a long-term illness, medical condition, or disability, and it is reasonably foreseeable that the taxpayer's financial resources will be exhausted providing for care or support during the course of the condition.

- Although the taxpayer has certain assets, liquidation of those assets to pay outstanding tax liabilities would render the taxpayer unable to meet basic living expenses.

- Although the taxpayer has certain assets, the taxpayer is unable to borrow against the equity in those assets and disposition by seizure or sale would have such adverse consequences that enforced collection is unlikely.

While the factors above would support a determination of economic hardship, they are not conclusive. Moreover, a compromise offer will not be accepted if it would undermine tax compliance. As a general rule, this means the taxpayer must not have a history of noncompliance, must not have taken deliberate actions to avoid paying tax, and must not have encouraged others to refuse to comply with the tax laws. In other words, the IRS will not accept compromise offers from tax evaders or tax protestors.

4. *Special circumstances.* If there are no other grounds for compromise, the IRS may compromise to promote effective tax administration where compelling public policy or equity considerations identified by the taxpayer provide a sufficient basis for compromising the liability. Compromise will be justified only where, due to exceptional circumstances, collection of the full liability would undermine public confidence that the tax laws are being administered in a fair and equitable manner. The taxpayer will be expected to demonstrate circumstances that justify compromise even though a similarly situated taxpayer may have paid his liability in full. No compromise may be entered into on this basis if compromise of the liability would undermine compliance by taxpayers with the tax laws.

Example 15-1: In 2007, a taxpayer developed a serious illness that resulted in almost continuous hospitalization for a number of years. During that time, the taxpayer was unable to manage his affairs and did not file tax returns. When the taxpayer's health improved and he began to attend to his tax affairs, he discovered that the IRS had prepared a substitute return for 2007 on the basis of information returns and assessed a tax deficiency. However, by the time the taxpayer made that discovery, his tax bill, with penalties and interest, was more than three times the original tax liability.

Example 15-2: A taxpayer, who works as a salaried sales manager at a department store, managed to put $2,000 in a tax-deductible individual retirement account (IRA) for each of the last two years. The taxpayer learned that he could earn a higher rate of interest by moving the funds to a different bank. Before transferring his savings, the taxpayer submitted an e-mail inquiry to the IRS at its Web page, requesting information on the steps he must take to preserve his tax benefits and avoid penalties. The IRS responded in an e-mail, which the taxpayer kept, stating that he could withdraw the funds from his IRA, but must redeposit the savings in a new IRA account within 90 days to avoid tax and penalties. The taxpayer withdrew the funds and redeposited them in a new IRA 63 days later. On audit, the taxpayer learned that the IRS had given him the wrong information about the rollover period, and that he was required to redeposit the funds within 60 days to avoid tax and penalties. Had it not been for the erroneous advice, the taxpayer would have completed the rollover within 60 days.

(*Note:* The Economic Growth and Tax Relief Reconciliation Act of 2001 also authorizes the IRS to waive the 60-day time limit "where the failure to waive such requirement would be against equity or good conscience." See Chapter 11.)

Q 15:6 How does a taxpayer make an offer in compromise?

Offers in compromise based upon doubt as to collectibility or effective tax administration must be submitted in writing on the Form 656, *Offer in Compromise*. Offers in compromise based on doubt as to liability must be submitted on Form 656-L, *Offer in Compromise (Doubt as to Liability)*.

Form 656, Offer in Compromise, requires the following information and agreements:

- The full name, home or business address and social security number or employer identification number of the taxpayer;

- A list of all unpaid tax liabilities sought to be compromised, specifically identified as to type and period;

- Whether the offer is based on doubt as to collectibility or effective tax administration;

- The total amount offered and payment terms. The taxpayer may make a lump-sum cash offer, a short-term periodic payment offer or a deferred periodic payment offer;

- The source of the funds that will be used to pay the offer;

- An explanation of the taxpayer's reason(s) for submitting the offer; and

- The taxpayer's signature, affirming the truthfulness of the information contained on Form 656, including accompanying schedules and statements, and agreeing to be bound by the terms and conditions set forth in the offer form.

The Form 656-L, *Offer in Compromise (Doubt as to Liability)*, also requires the taxpayer's full name, address, social security number or employer identification number, a list of all unpaid tax liabilities sought to be compromised, specifically identified as to type and period, and the taxpayer's signature. For an offer based on doubt as to liability, the offer amount must reflect what the taxpayer believes is the correct amount of tax liability after credits and payments already made. Unlike the Form 656, the Form 656-L does not permit taxpayers to propose payment terms; the offer amount must be paid within 90 days of written notification that the offer has been accepted.

If the offer is based on doubt as to collectibility or effective tax administration, the taxpayer must submit a Form 433-A, *Collection Information Statement for Individuals*, and/or Form 433-B, *Collection Information Statement for Businesses*, with the Form 656. Taxpayers submitting offers in compromise on the basis of doubt as to liability are not required to provide financial statements. However, an offer based on doubt as to liability must include a written statement explaining why the taxpayer believes the liability is incorrect. Taxpayers should also submit documentation and/or other evidence to support their claim.

Taxpayers submitting a lump-sum offer must include a payment equal to 20 percent of the offer amount. The payment is nonrefundable, that is, it will not be returned if the request is later rejected. A lump-sum offer in compromise means any offer of payments made in five or fewer installments.

Taxpayers submitting a request for a periodic-payment offer in compromise must include the first proposed installment payment with their application. A periodic payment offer is any offer of payments made in six or more installments. The taxpayer is required to pay additional installments while the offer is being evaluated by the IRS. All installment payments are nonrefundable.

Taxpayers filing an offer based solely on doubt as to liability qualify for a waiver of the new partial payment requirements. If the IRS cannot make a determination on an offer in compromise within two years, then the offer will be deemed accepted. If a liability included in the offer amount is disputed in any court proceeding, that time period is omitted from calculating the two-year timeframe. [[IRC § 7122 as amended by the Tax Increase Prevention and Reconciliation Act of 2005 (P.L. No. 109-222); Notice 2006-68, 2006-31 IRB]

When submitting Form 656, taxpayers must include an application fee of $150 unless they are filing a doubt-as-to-liability offer.

If a periodic payment offer has been accepted for processing and the taxpayer fails to make full payment of the second or later proposed installment while the offer is being evaluated, IRS may ask for payment of the unpaid amount of the later installment. IRS will deem the offer as unprocessible and return the application and the $150 fee if full payment isn't made within the time allowed (unless it decides that continued processing would be in the government's best interest). A lump-sum offer accompanied by a payment that is below the required 20% threshold will be deemed processible. But IRS will ask the taxpayer to pay the remaining balance in order to avoid having the offer returned. If it isn't paid within the time allowed, IRS will (unless it decides that continued processing would be in the government's best interest) return the offer and retain the $150 application fee. [Notice 2006-68, 2006-31 IRB]

Levies. The Internal Revenue Code generally prohibits the IRS from making a levy on a taxpayer's property while an offer to compromise a liability is pending with the IRS, for 30 days after the rejection of an offer to compromise, or while an appeal of a rejection is pending (see Q 15:7). [IRC § 6331(k)(1)]

According to the Service, an offer to compromise becomes "pending" when it is accepted for processing. The IRS accepts an offer to compromise for processing when it determines that the offer is submitted on the proper version of Form 656 and Form 433-A or B, as appropriate; the taxpayer is not in bankruptcy; the taxpayer has complied with all filing and payment requirements listed in the instructions to Form 656; the taxpayer has enclosed the application fee, if required; and the offer meets any other minimum requirements established by the IRS.

A determination is made to accept an offer to compromise for processing when an IRS official with delegated authority to accept an offer for processing signs the Form 656. The date the IRS official signs the Form 656 is recorded on the IRS computers. As of this date, levy is prohibited unless the Service determines that collection of the liability is in jeopardy.

If the IRS determines that an offer to compromise a liability is not a processable offer, it is never "pending" and levy is not prohibited. [Rev. Proc. 2003-71, 2003-36 I.R.B. 517]

IRS Collection Actions

Q 15:7 What enforcement actions can the IRS take to collect unpaid taxes?

When a taxpayer does not pay taxes due, the IRS can:

- File a lien against the taxpayer's property (make a legal claim to the property as security or payment for the tax debt). [IRC § 6321]
- Serve a levy on the taxpayer's property or wages (legally seize the property or wages to satisfy the tax debt). [IRC § 6305]

Liens. A Notice of Federal Tax Lien may be filed only after:

- The IRS assesses a tax liability,
- The taxpayer is sent a Notice and Demand for Payment, and
- The taxpayer does not pay the liability within 10 days of notification.

Once these requirements are met, a lien is created for the amount of the tax debt. By filing this notice, the taxpayer's creditors are publicly notified that the IRS has a claim against all the taxpayer's property, including property acquired after the lien was filed. [IRS Pub. No. 594, *The IRS Collection Process* (2006)]

Levies. The IRS usually levies on property only after:

- The IRS issues a Notice and Demand for Payment,
- The taxpayer does not pay the tax demanded, and

- The IRS sends a Final Notice of Intent to Levy and a Notice of Right to Hearing at least 30 days before the levy. [IRS Pub. No. 594, *The IRS Collection Process* (2006)]

Q 15:8 How does a taxpayer appeal an IRS collection action?

There are various collection appeal procedures available to taxpayers. The two main procedures are Collection Due Process (CDP) and Collection Appeals Program (CAP).

CDP is available if a taxpayer receives one of the following notices: Notice of Federal Tax Lien Filing & Your Right To a Hearing Under IRC 6320 (Lien Notice), a Final Notice—Notice of Intent to Levy and Your Notice of a Right to a Hearing, or Notice of Jeopardy Levy and Right of Appeal (Levy Notices). If a taxpayer disagrees with the CDP decision, he or she can seek a judicial review in the Tax Court or a federal district court.

CAP is generally quicker and available for a broader range of collection actions. However, a taxpayer cannot go to court if he or she disagrees with the CAP decision. [IRS Pub. No. 1660, *Collection Appeal Rights*]

Q 15:9 Is certain property exempt from an IRS levy?

Yes. The Internal Revenue Code lists items of property exempt from levy for a tax deficiency. [IRC §6634]Special requirements apply for levy upon certain residential property and business assets. The IRS recently finalized regulations implementing the changes. [Reg. §301.6334-1]

Exemption for residences. IRS regulations provide for a levy exemption for any residence used by the taxpayer or any other individual (except for property that is rented from the taxpayer) if the amount of the levy does not exceed $5,000.

In cases involving a larger levy, the regulations provide for exemption for the principal residence of a taxpayer unless a judge or magistrate of a federal district court approves, in writing, the levy of such residence. Notice of the judicial hearing must be given to the taxpayer and family members residing in the property. At the hearing, the IRS will be required to demonstrate that:

- The requirements of any applicable law or administrative procedures relevant to the levy have been met,
- The liability is owed, and
- No reasonable alternative for the collection of the taxpayer's debt exists.

The IRS regulations specifically state that the IRS is not required to demonstrate the merits of the underlying liability at the hearing. The hearing does not give the taxpayer an additional opportunity to contest the merits of the underlying tax liability.

Business assets. Under the 1998 Act, property used in a trade or business is generally exempt from levy (other than real property that is rented). However, such property is not exempt if:

- A district director or assistant district director of the IRS personally approves (in writing) the levy of such property, or
- The IRS determines that the collection of tax is in jeopardy.

The regulations provide that an IRS official cannot approve a levy on business assets unless the official determines that the taxpayer's other assets subject to collection are insufficient to pay the amount due, together with expenses of the proceedings.

Amending a Return

Q 15:10 How does a taxpayer correct a mistake on a tax return?

Taxpayers can file an amended tax return to correct a mistake. Individuals use Form 1040X; corporations use Form 1120X. Taxpayers will need to write their income, deductions, and credits as they reported them on the original return; the changes they are making and why; and the corrected amounts. Taxpayers should attach forms or schedules needed to explain their changes. [Instructions to Form 1040X, *Amended U.S. Individual Income Tax Return*]

Taxpayers refigure their tax on the corrected amount of taxable income and the amount they owe or the amount they should get back in a refund. The amended return is mailed to the IRS Service Center where the original return was filed.

Q 15:11 How long does a taxpayer have to amend a return?

Ideally, taxpayers should try to catch their mistake as soon as possible. That way, they minimize interest or penalties. However, beyond that, the Code provides that the deadline for filing a refund claim is the later of (1) three years from the time for filing a return or (2) two years from the time the tax was paid. [IRC § 6511(a)]If a taxpayer files a refund claim within three years of the filing deadline, the amount of refund cannot exceed the amount of tax paid within the three-year period (plus any filing extension period). [IRC § 6511(b)(2)]For this purpose, taxes paid before the filing deadline, including tax withholding on wages, are treated as paid on the deadline date. [IRC § 6513(a), (b)]

If the last act for performing any tax requirement falls on a Saturday, Sunday, or legal holiday, then the deadline for performing that act is extended to the next day that is not a Saturday, Sunday, or legal holiday. [IRC § 7503] In a 1966 ruling, the IRS said that if the three-year deadline for filing a refund claim falls on a Saturday, Sunday, or holiday, the taxpayer has until the next business day to file. [Rev. Rul. 66-118, 1966-1 C.B. 290]

A 1976 revenue ruling deals with the situation where a taxpayer filed a return more than three years after the original deadline and claimed a refund on the return. The IRS said that the taxpayer's refund claim was within the three-year statute of limitations, because the limitation period started with the filing of the taxpayer's return. However, the IRS ruled that the taxpayer was not entitled to a refund of the taxes withheld from his wages. Those taxes were treated as paid on the original due date, which was more than three years before he filed his refund claim. [Rev. Rul. 76-511, 1976-2 C.B. 428]

In a 2003 revenue ruling, the IRS looked at three different scenarios involving refund claims. [Rev. Rul. 2003-41, 2003-17 I.R.B. 814]

Scenario 1. Millie Barker filed her 1994 tax return on Wednesday, March 1, 1995. The due date for filing the return was Saturday, April 15, 1995. On Friday, April 17, 1998, Barker filed a claim for refund of a portion of the income taxes withheld from her wages during 1994.

Scenario 2. Paul Mason filed a request for a four-month automatic extension to file his 1997 return. The automatic extension extended the due date for Mason's return from Wednesday, April 15, 1998, until Saturday, August 15, 1998. Mason did not file a 1997 return until Friday, August 17, 2001, three years and two days later. That 1997 return included a claim for refund of income taxes withheld from wages.

Scenario 3. Morgan Jameson filed a 1994 return on Monday, April 17, 1995. On Friday, April 17, 1998, Jameson filed a claim for refund for taxes withheld from wages during the 1994 tax year.

The IRS said that Millie Barker (in Scenario 1) filed her refund claim too late. The refund claim does not fall within the two-year limitations period before the withholding taxes were deemed paid on April 15, 1995—more than two years prior to her refund claim. Barker also does not meet the three-year limitations period because her refund claim was filed three years and two days after her tax return deadline. The next-business-day rule does not help Barker because the deadline for filing the refund claim was a Wednesday, April 15, 1998, not a Saturday, Sunday, or legal holiday. The three-year limitations period began immediately after Barker's deemed filing and payment date of April 15, 1995, and expired on April 15, 1998.

Section 7503, the Saturday/Sunday/legal holiday rule, does not alter this result. IRC Section 7503 applies only if the taxpayer files on the next succeeding day that is not a Saturday, Sunday, or legal holiday. In this case, Section 7503 does not apply to the filing of Barker's return on March 1, 1995, because that filing did not occur on the day next succeeding Saturday, April 15, 1995, that was not a Saturday, Sunday, or legal holiday. Nor does Section 7503 apply to the filing of the claim for refund, because the last day to file the claim for refund was a Wednesday, April 15, 1998, not a Saturday, Sunday, or legal holiday. The three-year period within which Barker must have filed a claim for refund began immediately after the deemed filing and payment date of April 15, 1995, and expired on April 15, 1998.

In Scenario 2, the IRS said that Mason's claim for refund included on the 1997 individual income tax return filed Friday, August 17, 2001, is timely, because it was filed within three years of the filing of the return, just as in Revenue Ruling 76-511. IRC Section 6513(b)(1), however, deems the payment of the tax to which the claim for refund relates (withholding taxes) to have occurred on April 15, 1998, which is beyond the period of three years plus the four-month extension immediately preceding August 17, 2001, the filing date of the claim for refund. Therefore, although the claim for refund was timely, IRC Section 6511(b)(2)(A) specifically bars allowance of the refund.

The IRS said that the 1966 ruling does not apply to Mason's situation. The 1966 ruling applies when the last day for filing a refund claim falls on a Saturday, Sunday, or holiday. In Mason's situation, the last day fell on Wednesday, April 15, 2001 for taxes deemed paid on April 15, 1998. Pursuant to Regulations Section 1.6081-4(a)(1), the period of the automatic extension of time to file an individual income tax return is limited to four months. If Mason had filed his 1997 individual income tax return on Monday, August 17, 1998, IRC Section 7503 would have treated Mason's income tax return as timely, because the extended due date of August 15, 1998, fell on a Saturday. IRC Section 7503, however, does not provide this extension to Mason. By its terms, IRC Section 7503 has the effect of an extension only when a taxpayer performs an act on the next succeeding day that is not a Saturday, Sunday, or legal holiday after a Saturday, Sunday, or legal holiday that would otherwise be the last day prescribed for performing the act. Because Mason did not file an individual income tax return on Monday, August 17, 1998, he does not enjoy the benefit of an extension from Saturday, August 15, 1998, to the following Monday, August 17, 1998.

In Scenario 3, the IRS says that Jameson is entitled to a full refund. His refund claim was timely, because he filed within the three-year limitations period. He is entitled to a full refund, because his extended tax return due date under Section 7503 was April 17, 1995 (the next day following Saturday, April 15 that was not a Saturday, Sunday, or legal holiday), and he filed his claim within the required three years plus extension.

Extension of refund deadline. In certain cases, the Code provides equitable relief for taxpayers seeking a refund. The limitations period is suspended for any period when an individual is "financially disabled." Individuals are considered financially disabled when they are unable to manage their financial affairs "by reason of a medically determinable physical or mental impairment . . . which can be expected to result in death or which has lasted or can be expected to last for a continuous period of not less than 12 months." [IRC § 6511(h)]

The Tax Court has ruled that the suspension of the limitations period is not available when a taxpayer is providing care to another individual who is "financially disabled." [*Brosi*, 120 T.C. No. 2]

Taxpayer Advocate

Q 15:12 What is the Office of the Taxpayer Advocate?

The Office of the Taxpayer Advocate has been established within the IRS to assist taxpayers in resolving problems with the IRS and propose changes in IRS administrative practices to mitigate taxpayer problems. [IRC §7803(c)(2)] The Office of the Taxpayer Advocate is headed by the National Taxpayer Advocate, who is appointed by the Secretary of the Treasury, and reports directly to, the Commissioner of the IRS. The National Taxpayer Advocate appoints local Taxpayer Advocates who are independent of the IRS.

Q 15:13 Who may use the services of the Taxpayer Advocate?

Generally, the Taxpayer Advocate Service can provide assistance to taxpayers who, as a result of the administration of the tax law:

- Are suffering, or are about to suffer, a significant hardship;

- Are facing an immediate threat of adverse action;

- Will incur significant cost (including fees for professional representation);

- Will suffer irreparable injury or long-term adverse impact;

- Have experienced a delay of more than 30 days to resolve the issue; or

- Have not received a response or resolution by the date promised. [IRS Pub. No. 1546, *The Taxpayer Advocate Service of the IRS* (Rev. Jan. 2001)]

In other words, taxpayers should contact the Taxpayer Advocate Office if they have ongoing issues with the IRS that have not been resolved through normal processes, or have suffered, or are about to suffer, a significant hardship as a result of IRS actions. The Taxpayer Advocate is not a substitute for established IRS procedures or the formal appeals process (see below). The Taxpayer Advocate Office cannot reverse legal or technical tax determinations.

Q 15:14 What can a taxpayer expect from the Taxpayer Advocate?

A taxpayer will be assigned a personal advocate to listen to the taxpayer's point of view and try to address his or her concerns. The Taxpayer Advocate promises that a taxpayer will be provided with:

- A "fresh look" at the taxpayer's problem;

- Timely acknowledgment;

- Updates on progress;

- Time frames for action; and

- Speedy resolution.

The Taxpayer Advocate has the power to issue a Taxpayer Assistance Order to suspend, delay, stop, or speed up IRS actions to relieve a taxpayer's hardship. [IRC §7811(a)(1)]

IRS Audits

Q 15:15 How does the IRS select returns for audit?

The IRS can examine a return for any one of a number of reasons. For example, a return can be selected for examination on the basis of computer scoring. A computer program called the Discriminant Function System (DiF) assigns a numeric score to each individual and some corporate tax returns after they have been processed. Returns with high scores are selected for examination. The high score means that there is a high potential that an examination will result in change to the income tax liability.

A return may also be selected for examination on the basis of information received from third-party documentation, such as Forms 1099 and W-2, that does not match the information reported on the tax return. Or a return can be selected to address both the questionable treatment of an item and to study the behavior of similar taxpayers (a market segment) in handling a tax issue.

Another possibility is that information has been received from other sources about potential noncompliance with the tax laws or inaccurate filing. This information can come from a number of sources, including the media, public records, or possibly informants. The IRS says that this information is evaluated for reliability and accuracy before it is used as the basis of an examination or investigation. [IRS Pub. No. 556, *Examination of Returns, Appeal Rights, and Claims for Refund* (Rev. August 2005)]

Q 15:16 How long does the IRS have to audit a tax return for a particular year?

The IRS generally has three years after the date a tax return is filed to assess an additional tax. [IRC § 6501(a)]For this purpose, a return filed before the due date is considered filed on the due date. [IRC § 6501(b)(1)] The assessment period for items of a partnership or S corporation passed through to the partners and shareholders is based on the filing date of the partners' and shareholders' individual returns.

The assessment period is longer—six years from the filing date—if a return omits an income amount that exceeds 25 percent of the gross income reported. [IRC § 6501(e)]There is no statute of limitations on an assessment if the taxpayer fails to file a return, [IRC § 6501(c)(3)] files a fraudulent return, [IRC § 6501(c)(1)]or willfully attempts in any manner to defeat and evade taxes. [IRC § 6501(c)(2)]

Q 15:17 What types of audits does the IRS conduct?

IRS audits basically fall into one of three categories: correspondence audits, office audits, and field audits.

Correspondence audits. This is the simplest kind of audit and may simply involve a request for more information. It is called a *contact,* and it is not even considered a true audit. The IRS uses it to reconcile numbers or to make simple adjustments.

This often happens when, for instance, the IRS computers register data from an information return reporting income to a taxpayer that is not reflected on the taxpayer's return, such as an interest payment on a bank account. A taxpayer can also expect a letter from the IRS when there has been a math error on the return.

Correspondence audits, generally triggered by computer mismatches, account for most questions that arise. Resolving the issue is usually straightforward: If the taxpayer sends the information, the matter is closed.

Office audits. The next step up the examination ladder is the office audit. This does not necessarily involve an in-office interview. If the regional service center where a return is filed finds a potentially unallowable item, it will try to resolve the matter by mail. If it can't, the regional center will send the case to the IRS district office, where an in-person interview will be arranged.

A district office exam occurs when the IRS asks a taxpayer to go to one of its offices to discuss some item on the return. The scrutiny is likely to be for an unusual deduction, and the taxpayer will need to produce supporting documentation. This means the taxpayer must produce whatever records are available concerning the matter under review, such as receipts, canceled checks, transaction documents, W-2 forms, 1099s, etc. [Reg. § 601.105(b)(2)]

Field audits. When a return is complicated, involves high income, and raises questions needing a lot of documentation to resolve, the IRS will visit the taxpayer. It wants to be at the taxpayer's place of business or residence where financial records are kept. The entire tax return is subject to review, and the IRS agent can inspect all pertinent records. [Reg. § 601.105(b)(3)]

In theory, the agent can demand substantiation for every deduction claimed. But the agent has the authority to accept less than perfect records if he or she thinks they are complete and credible enough to show that the taxpayer incurred bona fide expenses.

Q 15:18 What records are examined during a field audit?

While the audit procedures vary somewhat from office to office, each district director provides his or her agents with a checklist of minimum audit procedures, which they must follow in all of the face-to-face audits. [Reg. § 601.105] Here is what taxpayers can generally expect:

- All bank accounts and brokerage accounts are examined. Any differences between income reported and deposits reflected in the accounts must be explained, so must unusual deposits and withdrawals.

- Check endorsements are sampled to see the frequency of checks drawn to cash and where, and by whom, they were deposited or cashed. Missing checks must be accounted for, as well as checks payable to third parties, but cashed by the taxpayer who drew them or by somebody related to him.

- Cash purchases are verified with the supplier.

- Loans, exchanges, and capital drawing accounts are carefully examined. Large entries must be explained.

- The numerical sequence of sales invoices is checked to see if all the billings are being recorded.

- Sales of scrap material or production rejects are investigated to see if all the billings are being recorded.

Q 15:19 Can taxpayers have someone represent them in an audit?

Throughout the examination, taxpayers can act on their on behalf or have someone represent or accompany them. This person can be any federally authorized practitioner, including an attorney, a certified public accountant, an enrolled agent (a person enrolled to practice before the IRS), an enrolled actuary, or the person who prepared the return and signed it as the preparer. [IRS Pub. No. 556, *Examination of Returns, Appeal Rights, and Claims for Refund* (Rev. August 2005]

If taxpayers want someone to represent them in their absence, they must furnish that representative with written authorization. The authorization can be made on Form 2848.

Note: If the taxpayer checked the box in the signature area of the Form 1040 to authorize the IRS to discuss the return with a paid preparer, this authorization does not replace Form 2848. The box the taxpayer checked only authorizes the preparer to receive information about the processing of the return and the status of a refund during the period the return is being processed.

If, during the audit, a taxpayer expresses a desire to consult with a representative, the IRS must suspend the audit. [IRC § 21(b)(2)]

Q 15:20 Can the IRS summon a taxpayer to an interview?

Yes, the IRS can issue a summons for a taxpayer's testimony and records for a legitimate purpose. [IRC § 7602(a)]The summons (Form 2309) must describe with reasonable certainty the books and records sought and set a time for examination no less than 10 days from the date of the summons. [IRC § § 7603, 7605]

If a taxpayer disregards the summons, the IRS can apply to a federal district court for an order directing compliance. [IRC § 7604]

Q 15:19

Appeals

Q 15:21 If an audit agent determines that a taxpayer owes additional tax, can the taxpayer appeal this decision?

Yes. The agent will submit a revenue agent's report (RAR) to the IRS district office. The IRS then sends a copy of the RAR and a transmittal letter, known as a 30-day letter. [Reg. § 601.105(c)]The RAR must show the basis for and amount of any proposed adjustments. [IRC § 7522]

The letter explains the IRS appeals procedures and asks the taxpayer to reply, within 30 days, whether he or she will (1) accept the proposed adjustments, (2) appeal within the IRS or (3) do nothing (in which case, the IRS will follow up with a "90-day" letter; see below).

Q 15:22 How does a taxpayer appeal within the IRS?

The IRS maintains an Appeals Office, separate and independent of the district offices. The Appeals Office is the only level of administrative appeal within the IRS.

A taxpayer who disagrees with an RAR can request a conference with Appeals Office personnel. These "conferences" are held in an informal manner by correspondence, by telephone or at a personal conference. [Reg. § 601.016(c)]

The instructions for obtaining an Appeals Office conference are contained in the 30-day letter the taxpayer receives. Taxpayers can represent themselves or have someone represent them who is authorized to practice before the IRS.

When taxpayers request an appeals conference, they may also need to file a formal written protest or a small case request.

Q 15:23 When is a formal written protest required, and what should it contain?

A formal written protest is required in cases involving partnerships and S corporations, employee plans, and in all other cases unless a taxpayer qualifies for small case or other special procedures. [IRS Pub. No. 556, *Examination of Returns, Appeal Rights, and Claims for Refund* (Rev. August 2004)]

A formal written protest should include the following:

- The taxpayer's name, address, and a daytime telephone number;
- A statement that the taxpayer wants to appeal the IRS findings to the Appeals Office;
- A copy of the letter showing the proposed changes and findings that the taxpayer disagrees with;
- The tax periods or years involved;

Q 15:23

- A list of the changes that the taxpayer disagrees with and the reasons why he or she disagrees;

- The facts supporting the taxpayer's disagreement; and

- The law or authority, if any, on which the taxpayer is relying. [IRS Pub. No. 5, *Your Appeal Rights and How to Prepare a Protest If You Don't Agree,* (Rev. Jan. 1999)]

The taxpayer must sign the written protest under the following jurat: "Under the penalties of perjury, I declare that I examined the facts stated in this protest, including any accompanying documents, and, to the best of my knowledge and belief, they are true, correct, and complete."

If the taxpayer's representative prepares and signs the protest on the taxpayer's behalf, he or she must substitute a declaration stating (1) that he or she submitted the protest and accompanying documents and (2) whether he or she knows personally that the facts stated in the protest and accompanying documents are true and correct. [IRS Pub. No. 5, *Your Appeal Rights and How to Prepare a Protest If You Don't Agree,* (Rev. Jan. 1999)]

Q 15:24 Who qualifies for the small case procedures?

If the total amount for any tax period is not more than $25,000, a taxpayer may make a small case request instead of filing a formal written protest. [Prop. Reg. § 601.106(b)(4)]In computing the total amount, include a proposed increase or decrease in tax (including penalties), or claimed refund.

For a small case request, the taxpayer should follow the instructions in the 30-day letter by sending a letter requesting Appeals Office consideration, indicating the changes the taxpayer does not agree with, and the reasons why the taxpayer does not agree.

Q 15:25 What happens if the taxpayer cannot reach a settlement with the Appeals Office?

If the taxpayer and the Appeals Office do not agree on some or all of the issues, the taxpayer may take his or her case to the United States Tax Court, the United States Court of Federal Claims, or the United States District Court in his or her judicial district.

Tax Court. A taxpayer can bring a case to the Tax Court once the IRS issues a formal letter, stating the amounts that the IRS believes are owed. This letter is called a notice of deficiency or a 90-day letter. [IRC § 7522]The taxpayer has 90 days from the date the notice is mailed by the IRS to file a petition with the Tax Court. The last date to file the petition will be entered on the notice of deficiency issued by the IRS. If the taxpayer does not file the petition within the 90-day period, the IRS will assess the proposed liability and send the taxpayer a bill.

If the disputed amount is not more than $50,000 for any single tax year, there are simplified procedures available in the Tax Court. More information can be obtained from the Clerk of the Tax Court, 400 Second St. NW, Washington, D.C. 20217.

District Court and Court of Federal Claims. If the taxpayer's claim is for a refund of tax, the taxpayer may take the case to the United States District Court or to the United States Court of Federal Claims.

Generally, District Courts and the Court of Federal Claims hear tax cases only after the taxpayer has paid the tax and filed a claim for refund with the IRS. The taxpayer can get information about procedures for filing suit in either court by contacting the Clerk of his or her District Court or the Clerk of the Court of Federal Claims.

If a taxpayer files a formal refund claim with the IRS (e.g., Form 1040X), and the IRS has not responded within six months, the taxpayer may file suit for a refund immediately in the District Court or the Court of Federal Claims. If the taxpayer receives a letter disallowing the claim, the taxpayer may request Appeals Office review of the disallowance. If the taxpayer wishes to file a refund suit, he or she must file the suit no later than two years from the date of the IRS letter disallowing the claim. [IRC § 6532(a)(1)]

Q 15:26 Can taxpayers recover their costs from the IRS if they prevail in tax litigation?

Taxpayers may be able to recover their reasonable litigation and administrative costs if they are the prevailing party and they meet certain other requirements. [IRC § 7430]Taxpayers must exhaust their appeal rights within the IRS to receive reasonable litigation costs.

Administrative costs include costs incurred on or after the date the taxpayer receives (1) a decision letter from the Appeals Office, (2) the 30-day letter, or (3) the notice of deficiency—whichever comes first.

Litigation or administrative costs may include:

- Attorney's fees that generally do not exceed $150 per hour (indexed for inflation);
- Reasonable amounts for court costs or any administrative fees or similar charges by the IRS;
- Reasonable expenses of expert witnesses; and
- Reasonable costs of studies, analyses, tests, or engineering reports that are necessary to prepare the case.

Taxpayers are considered the "prevailing parties" if (1) they substantially prevailed on the amount in controversy, or on the most significant tax issue or issues in question and (2) they meet net worth requirement. For individuals, the net worth cannot exceed $2 million on the date from which costs are recoverable. For corporations, the net worth must not exceed $7 million and they cannot have more than 500 employees on the date from which costs are recoverable. [IRC § 7430(c)]

The taxpayer is not considered the prevailing party if the IRS establishes that its position was "substantially justified." If the IRS does not follow applicable published guidance, there is a presumption that the IRS is not substantially justified. [IRC § 7430(c)(4)(B)]. A court will also take into account whether the IRS has won or lost in the courts of appeals for other circuits on substantially similar issues.

Civil Penalties and Interest

Q 15:27 Is there an interest charge on late tax payments?

Yes. The IRS charges interest when taxpayers owe it money—taxes and/or penalties—and haven't paid it. [IRC § 6601(a)] Interest generally accrues from the last date prescribed for payment until the date payment is actually made. However, if the tax is paid within 21 days after IRS issues a notice and demand for payment (10 days when the liability exceeds $100,000), interest ceases to accrue on the date of the notice and demand. [IRC § 6601(e)(3)]

If a taxpayer gets an extension from the IRS for paying taxes, this relieves him or her of penalties, but not interest. [IRC § 6601(b)] Except in very limited situations (e.g., when there has been an IRS error), neither the IRS nor the courts have the power to excuse anyone from paying interest on late or extended payment of taxes or penalties.

The interest rate charge by the IRS is based on the short-term federal rate for the prior quarter and is compounded daily. [IRC § 6621(a)(2)] C corporations with an underpayment of more than $100,000 are charged a higher rate than other taxpayers. [IRC § 6621(c)(3)]

Q 15:28 Is there a penalty for late payment in addition to the interest charge?

Yes. If taxpayers fail to pay tax shown on their return by the due date for payment (including extensions), they are subject to a 0.5 percent penalty for each month the tax is unpaid. [IRC § 6651(a)(2)]The maximum penalty is 25 percent of the unpaid tax. (If the tax is not shown on the return, a stiffer penalty applies in lieu of this; see below.)

This penalty does not apply if a taxpayer can show that the nonpayment was due to "reasonable cause" and not "willful neglect" (e.g., serious illness or a fire or other casualty). [IRC § 6651(a)(2)]

Q 15:29 Is there a penalty, separate and apart from the failure-to-pay penalty, if a taxpayer fails to file a return?

Yes. If taxpayers fail to file required tax returns by the filing due date (plus extensions), there is a 5 percent penalty for each month or fraction of month the returns are late. [IRC § 6651(b)(1)] The 5 percent penalty is applied to the tax shown on the returns (less any earlier payments). Again, taxpayers are excused from the penalty if they show "reasonable cause" for the late filing. [IRC § 6651(b)(1)]

The maximum penalty for failing to file is generally 25 percent of the unpaid tax. However, if there is unpaid tax and a taxpayer files more than 60 days late, there is also a minimum penalty: the lesser of the unpaid tax or $100. [IRC § 6651(a)]So, for example, if a taxpayer is three weeks late and owes $500, the penalty is $100, not 5 percent of $500.

The 5 percent failure-to-file penalty is reduced (but not below the minimum penalty) by any failure-to-pay penalty the taxpayer is assessed. [IRC § 6651(c)(1)] In other words, the combined penalty for failing to pay and failing to file will not exceed 5 percent per month. So, for example, if a taxpayer files a return and pays a $10,000 tax one month late, the taxpayer will owe a late payment penalty of $50 and a late filing penalty of $450.

Q 15:30 Does reliance on an accountant or other third party constitute "reasonable cause" for purposes of the late-payment and late-filing penalties?

Generally no. Depending on a third party to make payments or file returns—even a certified public accountant—will generally not be considered reasonable cause.

For example, Faiger Blackwell owned two assisted living operations and a banquet facility in North Carolina. In 1993, Blackwell engaged the services of Maurice Hamilton as the accountant for his businesses. Hamilton was a certified public accountant. He was supposed to keep the business records and ensure that all tax returns and payments were made on time.

Blackwell granted Hamilton power of attorney and gave him a rubber stamp with Blackwell's signature. Blackwell trusted Hamilton to file the proper paperwork to keep the taxes current. Because Hamilton had the authority to stamp tax returns, Blackwell did not see the quarterly payroll tax returns (Form 941) from 1995 through 1998. Instead, Blackwell relied on Hamilton to calculate and file all tax liabilities.

In 1997, Hamilton advised Blackwell to hire an in-house accountant to ensure that Hamilton was receiving all necessary paperwork. Blackwell subsequently hired Ann Holland to assist Hamilton. Blackwell believed that Hamilton and Holland, an accountant herself, were working together to file all necessary tax documents and pay all necessary tax liabilities.

Unfortunately, Hamilton and Holland did not file the necessary returns and did not make the required tax deposits. Due to the failure to file tax returns and make deposits, Blackwell's businesses were all delinquent for tax liabilities for several years.

Blackwell was ignorant of these tax liabilities until August 1998, when an IRS official visited him at his office. By that time, the total of undeposited taxes, interest, and penalties amounted to almost half a million dollars.

Blackwell contended that the IRS should not assess penalties because there was reasonable cause for not timely filing and depositing the taxes—namely Hamilton's failure to do his job.

The IRS refused to waive the penalties, and a federal district court sided with the IRS. The court noted that the U.S. Supreme Court had faced a similar issue when an executor, relying on an attorney, failed to file an estate tax return. The Supreme Court said that the duty to timely file taxes rested on the taxpayer, even if the taxpayer had relied on the advice of an attorney or other tax professional. The Supreme Court stated "it requires no special training or effort to ascertain a deadline and make sure that it is met. The failure to make a timely filing of a tax return is not excused by the taxpayer's reliance on an agent, and such reliance is not 'reasonable cause' for a late filing." [*United States v. Boyle*, 469 U.S. 241, at 242 (1985)]

The federal district court said Blackwell was in the same situation as the executor in the *Boyle* case. He retained control over Hamilton's actions and had the authority to oversee his work and terminate his employment if necessary. Thus, there was no reasonable cause for failing to timely file and deposit the tax liabilities. [*Dogwood Forest Rest Home Inc. v. U.S.,* Case No. 1:00CV370, Case No. 1:00CV00372 (M.D.N.C. Dec. 28, 2001)]

While taxpayers cannot avoid penalties simply because tax advisors did not tell them a tax return was due, some courts have held the other away when tax advisors affirmatively told their clients that returns were *not* due. Even though the advice was erroneous, that can constitute reasonable cause. For example, when a taxpayer advanced funds to her son and her accountant advised her that a gift tax return was not necessary, a court held that she was not liable for a filing penalty. [*Autin v. Comm'r*, 102 T.C. 760 (1994)]

Keep in mind that, even in this situation, the person giving advice must be qualified; the word of a neighbor or friend does not count. In fact, some courts have held that not every attorney or accountant is qualified to give tax advice; he or she must be familiar with federal tax matters before a taxpayer can rely on the advice not to file. In addition, advice will not help taxpayers avoid penalties unless the tax professional is thoroughly acquainted with their individual tax situations.

Q 15:31 What is the accuracy-related penalty?

The accuracy-related penalty is an umbrella penalty that applies to underpayments due to (1) negligence or disregard of the tax rules and regulations, (2) "substantial" understatements of income tax, and (3) "substantial" misstatements of the value or basis of property. [IRC § 6662]

The penalty is a flat 20 percent of the underpayment due to any of the above offenses. It does not apply if taxpayers can show that there was reasonable cause for the underpayment and they acted in good faith. For example, in one case, the Tax Court let a college professor off the hook when he claimed a deduction for nondeductible travel expenses because the IRS had not issued regulations on the matter, and the professor had no clear-cut guidance. [*Keller v. Comm'r*, T.C. Memo 1996-300 (1996)]. On the other hand, the Tax Court let the penalty stand when a fiction writer claimed that his personal living expenses were deductible because his "life experiences" were incorporated into his fiction. The court said that those deductions were not claimed in good faith. [*Irwin v. Comm'r*, T.C. Memo 1996-490 (1996)]

Substantial understatement of tax. An understatement of tax is considered substantial if it exceeds the greater of (1) 10 percent of the tax shown on the return, or (2) $5,000 ($10,000 for C corporations). [IRC § 6662(d)]

There are two exceptions to the accuracy-related penalty for substantial understatements. First, it does not apply to the treatment of a tax item if the taxpayer has "substantial authority" for treating it that way (e.g., there are court decisions that support the taxpayer's position). Second, it does not apply if the taxpayer discloses all the relevant facts that affect the tax treatment of the item on his or her return. [IRC § 6662(d)(2)]

Substantial misstatement of value or basis. This penalty arises when a taxpayer is selling property and overstates his or her basis to reduce his taxable profit, or when a taxpayer donates property to charity and puts too high a value on it to increase his or her charitable deduction. A misstatement is considered "substantial" if the basis or value of the property claimed by the taxpayer is 200 percent or more of the true basis or value. [IRC § 6662(h)]The usual 20 percent accuracy-related penalty is increased to 40 percent of the misstatement is "gross"—the claimed basis or value is 400 percent or more of the actual basis or value.

The penalty does not apply unless the total of tax underpayments resulting from the misstatements exceed $5,000.

Q 15:32 Is there a special penalty for erroneous income tax refunds or credits?

Yes. The Small Business and Work Opportunity Tax Act of 2007 (P.L. 110-28)) subjects erroneous income tax refund or credit claims made for an "excessive amount" to a new penalty equal to 20 percent of the excessive amount. [IRC § 6676] This penalty plugs a loophole used by some taxpayers who over-with-hold and claim credits, which are not understatements, that technically might be sheltered from accuracy-related penalties.

An "excessive amount" '' is the amount by which the refund or credit claim exceeds the amount allowable under the Internal Revenue Code for the tax year. [IRC § 6676(b)] However, if it can be shown that the claim for the excessive amount has a reasonable basis, the penalty will not apply.

In addition, the penalty does not apply to any portion of the excessive amount of a refund claim or credit which is subject to an accuracy-related penalty (see previous question or to a fraud penalty (see Q 15:34). The new penalty applies to claims filed or submitted after May 25, 2007.

Q 15:33 What is the penalty for not reporting "reportable transactions"?

A taxpayer that has participated in a "reportable transaction" must disclose certain information with respect to the reportable transaction with its tax return. [IRC § 6011] A taxpayer must file a disclosure statement on Form 8886, *Reportable Transaction Disclosure Statement*, for each reportable transaction in which the taxpayer participated. [Reg. § 1.6011-4(d)]

The penalty for failure to include information with respect to a reportable transaction, other than a "listed transaction," is $10,000 in the case of a natural person and $50,000 in any other case. The penalty for failure to include information with respect to a listed transaction is $100,000 in the case of a natural person and $200,000 in any other case. [IRC § 6707A(b)]

IRS regulations describe six categories of reportable transactions. [Reg. § 1.6011-4(b)] For example, one category covers transactions with contractual protection—where the taxpayer has the right to a full or partial refund of fees paid an adviser if all or part of the intended tax consequences from the transaction are not sustained.

Another category covers "listed transactions." These are reportable transactions that are the same as, or substantially similar to, the types of transactions that the IRS has identified as tax avoidance transactions by notice, regulation, or other form of published guidance.

A 20-percent penalty applies if a taxpayer understates its tax liability relating to a reportable transaction. [IRC § 6662A] A higher 30-percent penalty will apply if a taxpayer does not adequately disclose the facts of the reportable transaction. If the taxpayer discloses the transaction, the penalty may be avoided if the taxpayer had reasonable cause and acted in good faith. [IRC § 6664(d)]

The understatement penalty applies only (1) to listed transactions and (2) to reportable transactions (other than a listed transaction) if a significant purpose of the transaction is the avoidance or evasion of federal income tax.

Q 15:34 Is there a special penalty for fraud?

Yes. If any part of a tax underpayment is due to fraud, there is a 75 percent penalty for that part. [IRC § 6663] The burden of proving fraud is on the IRS. It must show that a taxpayer intended to evade a tax that he or she knew was owed and that the taxpayer took steps to conceal, mislead or otherwise prevent the collection of the tax. If the fraud penalty is imposed on any part of an underpayment, than an accuracy-related penalty cannot be applied to the same part. [IRC § 6662(b)]

Appendix A

2008 Federal Tax Calendar

Listed below are the key dates for paying taxes and filing returns.

Last Day	What to Do
Thursday, January 3	FICA and withheld income tax. Semiweekly depositors deposit tax on wages paid on December 26–December 28
Friday, January 4	FICA and withheld income tax. Semiweekly depositors deposit tax on wages paid on December 29-January 1.
Wednesday, January 9	FICA and withheld income tax. Semiweekly depositors deposit tax on wages paid on January 2-4.
Thursday, January 10	Tipped employees. Employees who received $20 or more in tips during December should report them to their employers on Form 4070.
Friday, January 11	FICA and withheld income tax. Semiweekly depositors deposit tax on wages paid on January 5-8.
Tuesday, January 15	Estimated tax. Individuals pay final installment of 2007 estimated tax.
Wednesday, January 16	FICA and withheld income tax. Monthly depositors deposit tax for December.
	FICA and withheld income tax. Semiweekly depositors deposit tax on wages paid on January 9-11.
Friday, January 18	FICA and withheld income tax. Semiweekly depositors deposit tax on wages paid on January 12-15.
Thursday, January 24	FICA and withheld income tax. Semiweekly depositors deposit tax on wages paid on January 16-18.
Friday, January 25	FICA and withheld income tax. Semiweekly depositors deposit tax on wages paid on January 19-22.

Last Day	*What to Do*
Wednesday, January 30	FICA and withheld income tax. Semiweekly depositors deposit tax on wages paid on January 23-25.
Thursday, January 31	Form W-2. Employees must be furnished their copies of Form W-2 for 2007 by this date. Retired employees must be given their Forms 1099-R, and noncorporate independent contractors who were paid $600 or more by your company must be given their Form 1099-MISC.
	FICA and withheld income tax. File Form 941 for the fourth quarter of 2007. (If you have already deposited the tax you owe for the quarter in full and on time, you have until February 11 to file your form.)*
	FICA and withheld income tax. File annual Form 944 for 2007 (in lieu of quarterly Form 941s) if you are a qualifying small employer that has received notification from the IRS.*
	Federal unemployment tax. File Form 940 for 2006. If your undeposited tax is $500 or less, you can either pay it with your 940 or deposit it. If your undeposited tax is more than $500, you must deposit it. (If you have already deposited the tax you owe for 2007 in full and on time, you have until February 11 to file your 940.)
	Individual income tax return. File individual income tax return for 2007 in lieu of January 15 estimated tax payment.
	Nonpayroll taxes. File Form 945 for 2007 to report income tax withheld on nonpayroll items.
Friday, February 1	FICA and withheld income tax. Semiweekly depositors deposit tax on wages paid on January 26-29.
Wednesday, February 6	FICA and withheld income tax. Semiweekly depositors deposit tax on wages paid on January 30-February 1.
Friday, February 8	FICA and withheld income tax. Semiweekly depositors deposit tax on wages paid on February 2-5.
Monday, February 11	FICA and withheld income tax. File Form 941 for the fourth quarter of 2007 if tax for the quarter was deposited in full and on time. If not, you should have filed by January 31.
	Tipped employees. Employees who received $20 or more in tips during January should report them to the employer on Form 4070.
	Federal unemployment tax. File Form 940 for 2007. This due date applies only if you had deposited the tax for the year in full and on time. If not, you should have filed your form by January 31.
Wednesday, February 13	FICA and withheld income tax. Semiweekly depositors deposit tax on wages paid on February 6-8.

Appendix A

Last Day	*What to Do*
Friday, February 15	FICA and withheld income tax. Monthly depositors deposit tax for January.
	Income tax withholding. Claims for 2007 exemption from income tax withholding expire and employers must begin withholding tax after this date unless employees have submitted a new W-4 to continue the exemption for 2008..
	FICA and withheld income tax. Semiweekly depositors deposit tax on wages paid on February 9-12.
Thursday, February 21	FICA and withheld income tax. Semiweekly depositors deposit tax on wages paid on February 13-15.
Friday, February 22	FICA and withheld income tax. Semiweekly depositors deposit tax on wages paid on February 16-19.
Wednesday, February 27	FICA and withheld income tax. Semiweekly depositors deposit tax on wages paid on February 20-22.
Thursday, February 28	Form 1099. File 1099 information returns (reports of payments of $600 or more, $10 dividend and interest payments). Electronic filers see March 31
Friday, February 29	Large food and beverage establishment employers. File Form 8027, *Employer's Annual Information Return of Tip Income and Allocated Tips*. Use Form 8027-T to summarize and transmit Form 8027 if you are reporting for more than one establishment. Electronic filers see March 31.
	Form W-2. File Copy A of all Forms W-2 you issued for 2007 with the Social Security Administration (SSA). Your paper Forms W-2 should be accompanied by a Form W-3. Electronic filers see March 31.
	FICA and withheld income tax. Semiweekly depositors deposit tax on wages paid on February 23-26.
Wednesday, March 5	FICA and withheld income tax. Semiweekly depositors deposit tax on wages paid on February 27-29.
Friday, March 7	FICA and withheld income tax. Semiweekly depositors deposit tax on wages paid on March 1-4.
Monday, March 10	Tipped employees. Employees who received $20 or more in tips during February should report them to the employer on Form 4070.
Wednesday, March 12	FICA and withheld income tax. Semiweekly depositors deposit tax on wages paid on March 5-7.
Friday, March 14	FICA and withheld income tax. Semiweekly depositors deposit tax on wages paid on March 8-11.

Appendix A

Last Day	*What to Do*
Monday, March 17	FICA and withheld income tax. Monthly depositors deposit tax for February.
	Corporate income tax return. Calendar-year corporations file 2007 income tax return (Form 1120 for C corporations: 1120S for S Corporations). Alternatively, file for an automatic six-month extension.
	S corporation election. Last day to elect S corporation treatment for 2008 (Form 2553).
Wednesday, March 19	FICA and withheld income tax. Semiweekly depositors deposit tax on wages paid on March 12-14.
Friday, March 21	FICA and withheld income tax. Semiweekly depositors deposit tax on wages paid on March 15-18.
Wednesday, March 26	FICA and withheld income tax. Semiweekly depositors deposit tax on wages paid on March 19-21.
Friday, March 28	FICA and withheld income tax. Semiweekly depositors deposit tax on wages paid on March 22-25.
Monday, March 31	Information returns. File Form 1099 information returns, Copy A of Form W-2, or Form 8027 if filing electronically.
Wednesday, April 2	FICA and withheld income tax. Semiweekly depositors deposit tax on wages paid on March 26-28.
Friday, April 4	FICA and withheld income tax. Semiweekly depositors deposit tax on wages paid on March 29-April 1.
Wednesday, April 9	FICA and withheld income tax. Semiweekly depositors deposit tax on wages paid on April 2-4.
Thursday, April 10	Tipped employees. Employees who received $20 or more in tips during March should report them to the employer on Form 4070.
Friday, April 11	FICA and withheld income tax. Semiweekly depositors deposit tax on wages paid on April 5-8.
Tuesday, April 15	Individual income tax return. Individuals file 2007 returns (Form 1040, Form 1040A, or Form 1040EZ). Alternatively, file for an automatic six-month extension (Form 4868).
	Partnership information return. Partnerships file 2007 information return (Form 1065). Alternatively, file for an automatic six-month extension (Form 7004).
	Estimated tax. Individuals and calendar-year corporations pay first installment of 2008 estimated tax.

Appendix A

Last Day	*What to Do*
	FICA and withheld income tax. Monthly depositors deposit tax on wages paid for March.
Tuesday, April 17	FICA and withheld income tax. Semiweekly depositors deposit tax on wages paid on April 9-11.
Monday, April 21	FICA and withheld income tax. Semiweekly depositors deposit tax on wages paid on April 12–15.
Wednesday, April 23	FICA and withheld income tax. Semiweekly depositors deposit tax on wages paid on April 16-18.
Friday, April 25	FICA and withheld income tax. Semiweekly depositors deposit tax on wages paid on April 19-22.
Wednesday, April 30	FICA and withheld income tax. File Form 941 for the first quarter of 2008. (Employers that have already deposited the tax for the quarter in full and on time have until May 12 to file Form 941.)*
	Federal unemployment tax. Deposit tax owed through March if more than $500.
	FICA and withheld income tax. Semiweekly depositors deposit tax on wages paid on April 23-25.
Friday, May 2	FICA and withheld income tax. Semiweekly depositors deposit tax on wages paid on April 26-29.
Wednesday, May 7	FICA and withheld income tax. Semiweekly depositors deposit tax on wages paid on April 30-May 2.
Friday, May 9	FICA and withheld income tax. Semiweekly depositors deposit tax on wages paid on May 3-6.
Monday, May 12	Tipped employees. Employees who received $20 or more in tips during April should report them to the employer on Form 4070.
	FICA and withheld income tax. File Form 941 for the first quarter of 2008 if the tax for the quarter was deposited in full and on time. If not, employers should have filed by April 30.
Wednesday, May 14	FICA and withheld income tax. Semiweekly depositors deposit tax on wages paid on May 7-9.
Tuesday, May 15	FICA and withheld income tax. Monthly depositors deposit tax for April.
Friday, May 16	FICA and withheld income tax. Semiweekly depositors deposit tax on wages paid on May 10-13.
Wednesday, May 21	FICA and withheld income tax. Semiweekly depositors deposit tax on wages paid on May 14-16.

Appendix A

Last Day	*What to Do*
Friday, May 23	FICA and withheld income tax. Semiweekly depositors deposit tax on wages paid on May 17-20.
Thursday, May 29	FICA and withheld income tax. Semiweekly depositors deposit tax on wages paid on May 21-23.
Friday, May 30	FICA and withheld income tax. Semiweekly depositors deposit tax on wages paid on May 24-27.
Wednesday, June 4	FICA and withheld income tax. Semiweekly depositors deposit tax on wages paid on May 28-30.
Friday, June 6	FICA and withheld income tax. Semiweekly depositors deposit tax on wages paid on May 31-June 3.
Tuesday, June 10	Tipped employees. Employees who received $20 or more in tips during May should report them to the employer on Form 4070.
Wednesday, June 11	FICA and withheld income tax. Semiweekly depositors deposit tax on wages paid on June 4-6.
Friday, June 13	FICA and withheld income tax. Semiweekly depositors deposit tax on wages paid on June 7-10.
Monday, June 16	Estimated tax. Individuals and calendar-year corporations pay second installment of 2008 estimated tax. FICA and withheld income tax. Monthly depositors deposit tax for May.
Wednesday, June 18	FICA and withheld income tax. Semiweekly depositors deposit tax on wages paid on June 11-13.
Friday, June 20	FICA and withheld income tax. Semiweekly depositors deposit tax on wages paid on June 14-17.
Wednesday, June 25	FICA and withheld income tax. Semiweekly depositors deposit tax on wages paid on June 18-20.
Friday, June 27	FICA and withheld income tax. Semiweekly depositors deposit tax on wages paid on June 21-24.
Wednesday, July 2	FICA and withheld income tax. Semiweekly depositors deposit tax on wages paid on June 25-27.
Monday, July 7	FICA and withheld income tax. Semiweekly depositors deposit tax on wages paid on June 28-July 1.
Wednesday, July 9	FICA and withheld income tax. Semiweekly depositors deposit tax on wages paid on July 2-4.

Appendix A

Last Day	*What to Do*
Thursday, July 10	Tipped employees. Employees who received $20 or more in tips during June should report them to the employer on Form 4070.
Friday, July 11	FICA and withheld income tax. Semiweekly depositors deposit tax on wages paid on July 5-8.
Tuesday, July 15	FICA and withheld income tax. Monthly depositors deposit tax for June.
Wednesday, July 16	FICA and withheld income tax. Semiweekly depositors deposit tax on wages paid on July 9-11.
Friday, July 18	FICA and withheld income tax. Semiweekly depositors deposit tax on wages paid on July 12-15.
Wednesday, July 23	FICA and withheld income tax. Semiweekly depositors deposit tax on wages paid on July 16-18.
Friday, July 25	FICA and withheld income tax. Semiweekly depositors deposit tax on wages paid on July 19-22.
Wednesday, July 30	FICA and withheld income tax. Semiweekly depositors deposit tax on wages paid on July 23-25.
Thursday, July 31	FICA and withheld income tax. File Form 941 for the second quarter of 2008. (Employers that have already deposited the tax for the quarter in full and on time have until August 11 to file Form 941.)*
	Federal unemployment tax. Deposit tax owed through June if more than $500.
	Benefit plan returns. Retirement and benefit plans file 2007 information return (Form 5500).
Friday, August 1	FICA and withheld income tax. Semiweekly depositors deposit tax on wages paid on July 26-29.
Wednesday, August 6	FICA and withheld income tax. Semiweekly depositors deposit tax on wages paid on July 30-August 1.
Friday, August 8	FICA and withheld income tax. Semiweekly depositors deposit tax on wages paid on August 2-5.
Monday, August 11	Tipped employees. Employees who received $20 or more in tips during July should report them to the employer on Form 4070.
	FICA and withheld income tax. File Form 941 for the second quarter of 2008 if tax for the quarter was deposited in full and on time. If not, employers should have filed by July 31.
Wednesday, August 13	FICA and withheld income tax. Semiweekly depositors deposit tax on wages paid on August 6-8.

Appendix A

Last Day	*What to Do*
Friday, August 15	FICA and withheld income tax. Monthly depositors deposit tax for July.
	FICA and withheld income tax. Semiweekly depositors deposit tax on wages paid on August 9-12.
Wednesday, August 20	FICA and withheld income tax. Semiweekly depositors deposit tax on wages paid on August 13-15.
Friday, August 22	FICA and withheld income tax. Semiweekly depositors deposit tax on wages paid on August 16-19.
Wednesday, August 27	FICA and withheld income tax. Semiweekly depositors deposit tax on wages paid on August 20-22.
Friday, August 29	FICA and withheld income tax. Semiweekly depositors deposit tax on wages paid on August 23-26.
Thursday, September 4	FICA and withheld income tax. Semiweekly depositors deposit tax on wages paid on August 27-29.
Friday, September 5	FICA and withheld income tax. Semiweekly depositors deposit tax on wages paid on August 30–September 2.
Wednesday, September 10	Tipped employees. Employees who received $20 or more in tips during August should report them to the employer on Form 4070.
	FICA and withheld income tax. Semiweekly depositors deposit tax on wages paid on September 3-5.
Friday, September 12	FICA and withheld income tax. Semiweekly depositors deposit tax on wages paid on September 6-9.
Monday, September 15	FICA and withheld income tax. Monthly depositors deposit tax for August.
	Estimated tax. Individuals and calendar-year corporations pay third installment of 2008 estimated tax.
	Corporation income tax return. Calendar-year corporations file 2007 income tax return (Form 1120 for C corporations; 1120S for S corporations) if automatic six-month extension was obtained.
Wednesday, September 17	FICA and withheld income tax. Semiweekly depositors deposit tax on wages paid on September 10-12.
Friday, September 19	FICA and withheld income tax. Semiweekly depositors deposit tax on wages paid on September 13-16.

Appendix A

Last Day	*What to Do*
Wednesday, September 24	FICA and withheld income tax. Semiweekly depositors deposit tax on wages paid on September 17-19.
Friday, September 26	FICA and withheld income tax. Semiweekly depositors deposit tax on wages paid on September 20-23.
Wednesday, October 1	FICA and withheld income tax. Semiweekly depositors deposit tax on wages paid on September 24-26.
Friday, October 3	FICA and withheld income tax. Semiweekly depositors deposit tax on wages paid on September 27-30.
Wednesday, October 8	FICA and withheld income tax. Semiweekly depositors deposit tax on wages paid on October 1-3.
Friday, October 10	Tipped employees. Employees who received $20 or more in tips during September should report them to the employer on Form 4070.
	FICA and withheld income tax. Semiweekly depositors deposit tax on wages paid on October 4-7.
Wednesday, October 15	Individual income tax return. Individuals file 2007 income tax return if automatic six-month extension was obtained.
	Partnership information return. Partnerships file 2007 information return (Form 1065) if automatic six-month extension was obtained.
	FICA and withheld income tax. Monthly depositors deposit tax for September.
Thursday, October 16	FICA and withheld income tax. Semiweekly depositors deposit tax on wages paid on October 8-10.
Friday, October 17	FICA and withheld income tax. Semiweekly depositors deposit tax on wages paid on October 11-14.
Wednesday, October 22	FICA and withheld income tax. Semiweekly depositors deposit tax on wages paid on October 15-17.
Friday, October 24	FICA and withheld income tax. Semiweekly depositors deposit tax on wages paid on October 18-21.
Wednesday, October 29	FICA and withheld income tax. Semiweekly depositors deposit tax on wages paid on October 22-24.
Friday, October 31	FICA and withheld income tax. File Form 941 for the third quarter of 2008. (Employers that have already deposited the tax for the quarter in full and on time have until November 10 to file Form 941.)*
	Federal unemployment tax. Deposit tax owed through September if more than $500.

Appendix A

Last Day	*What to Do*
	FICA and withheld income tax. Semiweekly depositors deposit tax on wages paid on October 25-28.
Wednesday, November 5	FICA and withheld income tax. Semiweekly depositors deposit tax on wages paid on October 29-31.
Friday, November 7	FICA and withheld income tax. Semiweekly depositors deposit tax on wages paid on November 1-4.
Monday, November 10	Tipped employees. Employees who received $20 or more in tips during October should report them to the employer on Form 4070.
	FICA and withheld income tax. File Form 941 for the third quarter of 2008 if tax for the quarter was deposited in full and on time. If not, employers should have filed by October 31.
Thursday, November 13	FICA and withheld income tax. Semiweekly depositors deposit tax on wages paid on November 5-7.
Friday, November 14	FICA and withheld income tax. Semiweekly depositors deposit tax on wages paid on November 8-11.
Monday, November 17	FICA and withheld income tax. Monthly depositors deposit tax for October..
Wednesday, November 19	FICA and withheld income tax. Semiweekly depositors deposit tax on wages paid on November 12-14.
Friday, November 21	FICA and withheld income tax. Semiweekly depositors deposit tax on wages paid on November 15-18.
Wednesday, November 26	FICA and withheld income tax. Semiweekly depositors deposit tax on wages paid on November 19-21.
December	Form W-4. Employees whose withholding status will change in 2009 should submit a new Form W-4 to the employer. The new form should be submitted as early as possible to guarantee implementation of the withholding change in January.
	Form W-5. Employees who will be eligible for the Earned Income Credit for 2009 and want to receive advance payment of the credit should fill out a Form W-5 for 2009. A new W-5 must be submitted to the employer before any advance payments can be made for a calendar year.
Monday, December 1	FICA and withheld income tax. Semiweekly depositors deposit tax on wages paid on November 22-25.
Wednesday, December 3	FICA and withheld income tax. Semiweekly depositors deposit tax on wages paid on November 26-28.

Appendix A

Last Day	*What to Do*
Friday, December 5	FICA and withheld income tax. Semiweekly depositors deposit tax on wages paid on November 29–December 2.
Wednesday, December 10	Tipped employees. Employees who received $20 or more in tips during November should report them to the employer on Form 4070.
	FICA and withheld income tax. Semiweekly depositors deposit tax on wages paid on December 3-5.
Friday, December 12	FICA and withheld income tax. Semiweekly depositors deposit tax on wages paid on December 6-9.
Monday, December 15	FICA and withheld income tax. Monthly depositors deposit tax for November.
	Estimated tax. Calendar-year corporations pay fourth installment of 2008 estimated tax.
Wednesday, December 17	FICA and withheld income tax. Semiweekly depositors deposit tax on wages paid on December 10-12.
Friday, December 19	FICA and withheld income tax. Semiweekly depositors deposit tax on wages paid on December 13-16.
Wednesday, December 24	FICA and withheld income tax. Semiweekly depositors deposit tax on wages paid on December 17-19.
Monday, December 29	FICA and withheld income tax. Semiweekly depositors deposit tax on wages paid on December 20-23.

Note: Employers deposit payroll taxes on a semiweekly schedule if they accumulate more than $50,000 during a "look-back" period. Employers make monthly deposits if they accumulate $50,000 or less. The look-back period for 2008 is July 1, 2006, to June 30, 2007. *Exceptions:* Very large depositors who accumulate more than $100,000 of undeposited taxes must make deposits by the next banking day. Very small depositors who accumulate less than $2,500 during a calendar quarter may make quarterly deposits.

If a payroll tax deposit due date falls on a local nonbanking day, the deposit is considered on time if it is made on the next banking day. Semiweekly depositors always have at least three banking days following a payday to make a required deposit. Therefore, any intervening nonbanking days will delay the deposit due date.

> * Employers that have an employment tax liability of $1,000 or less for the year file Form 944, *Employer's Annual Federal Tax Return*, instead of Form 941, *Employer's Quarterly Federal Tax Return* if they are notified by the IRS by mail. Employment taxes may be paid with return. If, while designated as a Form 944 filer, total employment tax liability increases to $2,500 or more, employer must make deposits.

Appendix A

Appendix B

Key Tax Facts for 2007-2008

1.0 Inflation Adjustments for Individuals in 2008

Rev. Proc. 2007-66 I.R.B. 2007-45

SECTION 1. PURPOSE

This revenue procedure sets forth inflation adjusted items for 2008.

SECTION 2. CHANGES

.01 The excise taxes imposed under § 4261(b) and (c), as enacted by the Airport and Airway Trust Fund Tax Reinstatement Act of 1997 and extended by § 149(a) of Pub. L. No. 110-92, 121 Stat. 989 (2007), apply to transportation taken through November 16, 2007, and to amounts paid on or before November 16, 2007, for transportation beginning after that date. Accordingly, the amounts in § 4261(b) and (c) are not included in this revenue procedure.

.02 For 2008, the inflation adjusted items in § § 25B, 219, and 408A also will be included in a separate news release and related notice with other inflation adjusted amounts relating to pension and retirement accounts. For future years, these amounts will not be included in this revenue procedure but will appear only in the separate news release and related notice.

.03 For taxable years beginning after 2007, the inflation adjusted items for health savings accounts under § 223 are published no later than June 1 of the preceding calendar year. See § 223(g) and Rev. Proc. 2007-36, 2007-22 I.R.B. 1335. Accordingly, these items are not included in this revenue procedure.

.04 Section 1.148-3(d)(1)(iv) of the proposed Income Tax Regulations provides that on the last day of each bond year during which there are amounts allocated to gross proceeds of an issue that are subject to the rebate requirement, and on the final maturity date, there can be included as a payment a computation credit of $1,400 for any bond year ending in 2007. For bond years ending after 2007, the $1,400 computation credit will be adjusted for inflation pursuant to proposed § 1.148-3(d)(4). See section 3.17 of this revenue procedure.

SECTION 3. 2008 ADJUSTED ITEMS

.01 Tax Rate Tables

For taxable years beginning in 2008, the tax rate tables under § 1 are as follows:

TABLE 1 - Section 1(a). - Married Individuals Filing Joint Returns and Surviving Spouses

If Taxable Income Is:	The Tax Is:
Not over $16,050	10% of the taxable income
Over $16,050 but not over $65,100	$1,605 plus 15% of the excess over $16,050
Over $65,100 but not over $131,450	$8,962.50 plus 25% of the excess over $65,100
Over $131,450 but not over $200,300	$25,550 plus 28% of the excess over $131,450
Over $200,300 but not over $357,700	$44,828 plus 33% of the excess over $200,300
Over $357,700	$96,700 plus 35% of the excess over $357,700

TABLE 2 - Section 1(b). - Heads of Households

If Taxable Income Is:	The Tax Is:
Not over $11,450	10% of the taxable income
Over $11,450 but not over $43,650	$1,145 plus 15% of the excess over $11,450
Over $43,650 but not over $112,650	$5,975 plus 25% of the excess over $43,650
Over $112,650 but not over $182,400	$23,225 plus 28% of the excess over $112,650
Over $182,400 but not over $357,700	$42,755 plus 33% of the excess over $182,400
Over $357,700	$100,604 plus 35% of the excess over $357,700

Appendix B

TABLE 3 - Section 1(c). - Unmarried Individuals (other than Surviving Spouse and Heads of Households)

If Taxable Income Is:	The Tax Is:
Not over $8,025	10% of the taxable income
Over $8,025 but not over $32,550	$802.50 plus 15% of the excess over $8,025
Over $32,550 but not over $78,850	$4,481.25 plus 25% of the excess over $32,550
Over $78,850 but not over $164,550	$16,056.25 plus 28% of the excess over $78,850
Over $164,550 but not over $357,700	$40,052.25 plus 33% of the excess over $164,550
Over $357,700	$103,791.75 plus 35% of the excess over $357,700

TABLE 4 - Section 1(d). - Married Individuals Filing Separate Returns

If Taxable Income Is:	The Tax Is:
Not over $8,025	10% of the taxable income
Over $8,025 but not over $32,550	$802.50 plus 15% of the excess over $8,025
Over $32,550 but not over $65,725	$4,481.25 plus 25% of the excess over $32,550
Over $65,725 but not over $100,150	$12,775 plus 28% of the excess over $65,725
Over $100,150 but not over $178,850	$22,414 plus 33% of the excess over $100,150
Over $178,850	$48,385 plus 35% of the excess over $178,850

TABLE 5 - Section 1(e). - Estates and Trusts

If Taxable Income Is:	The Tax Is:
Not over $2,200	15% of the taxable income
Over $2,200 but not over $5,150	$330 plus 25% of the excess over $2,200
Over $5,150 but not over $7,850	$1,067.50 plus 28% of the excess over $5,150
Over $7,850 but not over $10,700	$1,823.50 plus 33% of the excess over $7,850
Over $10,700	$2,764 plus 35% of the excess over $10,700

.02 Unearned Income of Minor Children Taxed as if Parent's Income (the "Kiddie Tax")

For taxable years beginning in 2008, the amount in § 1(g)(4)(A)(ii)(I), which is used to reduce the net unearned income reported on the child's return that is subject to the "kiddie tax," is $900. This amount is the same as the $900 standard deduction amount provided in section 3.11(2) of this revenue procedure. The

Appendix B

same $900 amount is used for purposes of § 1(g)(7) (that is, to determine whether a parent may elect to include a child's gross income in the parent's gross income and to calculate the "kiddie tax"). For example, one of the requirements for the parental election is that a child's gross income is more than the amount referenced in § 1(g)(4)(A)(ii)(I) but less than 10 times that amount; thus, a child's gross income for 2008 must be more than $900 but less than $9,000.

.03 Adoption Credit

For taxable years beginning in 2008, under § 23(a)(3) the credit allowed for an adoption of a child with special needs is $11,650. For taxable years beginning in 2008, under § 23(b)(1) the maximum credit allowed for other adoptions is the amount of qualified adoption expenses up to $11,650. The available adoption credit begins to phase out under § 23(b)(2)(A) for taxpayers with modified adjusted gross income in excess of $174,730 and is completely phased out for taxpayers with modified adjusted gross income of $214,730 or more. (See section 3.15 of this revenue procedure for the adjusted items relating to adoption assistance programs.)

.04 Child Tax Credit

For taxable years beginning in 2008, the value used in § 24(d)(1)(B)(i) in determining the amount of credit under § 24 that may be refundable is $12,050.

.05 Hope and Lifetime Learning Credits

(1) For taxable years beginning in 2008, the Hope Scholarship Credit under § 25A(b)(1) is an amount equal to 100 percent of qualified tuition and related expenses not in excess of $1,200 plus 50 percent of those expenses in excess of $1,200, but not in excess of $2,400. Accordingly, the maximum Hope Scholarship Credit allowable under § 25A(b)(1) for taxable years beginning in 2008 is $1,800.

(2) For taxable years beginning in 2008, a taxpayer's modified adjusted gross income in excess of $48,000 ($96,000 for a joint return) is used to determine the reduction under § 25A(d)(2)(A)(ii) in the amount of the Hope Scholarship and Lifetime Learning Credits otherwise allowable under § 25A(a).

.06 Elective Deferrals and IRA Contributions by Certain Individuals

For taxable years beginning in 2008, the applicable percentage under § 25B(b) is determined based on the following amounts:

Modified Adjusted Gross Income						
Joint Return		Heads of Household		All Other Cases		Applicable Percentage
Over	Not over	Over	Not over	Over	Not over	
$0	$32,000	$0	$24,000	$0	$16,000	50 %
32,000	34,500	24,000	25,875	16,000	17,250	20
34,500	53,000	25,875	39,750	17,250	26,500	10
53,000		39,750		26,500		0

.07 Earned Income Credit

(1) *In general.* For taxable years beginning in 2008, the following amounts are used to determine the earned income credit under § 32(b). The "earned income

Appendix B

amount" is the amount of earned income at or above which the maximum amount of the earned income credit is allowed. The "threshold phaseout amount" is the amount of adjusted gross income (or, if greater, earned income) above which the maximum amount of the credit begins to phase out. The "completed phaseout amount" is the amount of adjusted gross income (or if greater, earned income) at or above which no credit is allowed.

Item	Number of Qualifying Children		
	One	Two or More	None
Earned Income Amount	$ 8,580	$12,060	$ 5,720
Maximum Amount of Credit	$ 2,917	$ 4,824	$ 438
Threshold Phaseout Amount (Single, Surviving Spouse, or Head of Household)	$15,740	$15,740	$ 7,160
Completed Phaseout Amount (Single, Surviving Spouse, or Head of Household)	$33,995	$38,646	$12,880
Threshold Phaseout Amount (Married Filing Jointly)	$18,740	$18,740	$10,160
Completed Phaseout Amount (Married Filing Jointly)	$36,995	$41,646	$15,880

The instructions for the Form 1040 series provide tables showing the amount of the earned income credit for each type of taxpayer.

(2) *Excessive investment income.* For taxable years beginning in 2008, the earned income tax credit is denied under § 32(i) if the aggregate amount of certain investment income exceeds $2,950.

.08 Low-Income Housing Credit

For calendar year 2008, the amounts used under § 42(h)(3)(C)(ii) to calculate the State housing credit ceiling for the low-income housing credit is the greater of (1) $2.00 multiplied by the State population, or (2) $2,325,000.

.09 Alternative Minimum Tax Exemption for a Child Subject to the "Kiddie Tax"

For taxable years beginning in 2008, for a child to whom the § 1(g) "kiddie tax" applies, the exemption amount under § § 55 and 59(j) for purposes of the alternative minimum tax under § 55 may not exceed the sum of (1) such child's earned income for the taxable year, plus (2) $6,400.

.10 Transportation Mainline Pipeline Construction Industry Optional Expense Substantiation Rules for Payments to Employees under Accountable Plans

For calendar year 2008, an eligible employer may pay certain welders and heavy equipment mechanics an amount of up to $15 per hour for rig-related expenses that is deemed substantiated under an accountable plan when paid in accordance with Rev. Proc. 2002-41. If the employer provides fuel or otherwise reimburses fuel expenses, up to $9 per hour is deemed substantiated when paid under Rev. Proc. 2002-41.

.10 Standard Deduction

(1) *In general.* For taxable years beginning in 2008, the standard deduction amounts under § 63(c)(2) are as follows:

Filing Status	Standard Deduction
Married Individuals Filing Joint Returns and Surviving Spouses (§ 1(a))	$10,900
Heads of Households (§ 1(b))	$8,000
Unmarried Individuals (other than Surviving Spouses and Heads of Households) (§ 1(c))	$5,450
Married Individuals Filing Separate Returns (§ 1(d))	$5,450

(2) *Dependent.* For taxable years beginning in 2008, the standard deduction amount under § 63(c)(5) for an individual who may be claimed as a dependent by another taxpayer may not exceed the greater of (1) $900, or (2) the sum of $300 and the individual's earned income.

(3) *Aged and blind.* For taxable years beginning in 2008, the additional standard deduction amounts under § 63(f) for the aged and for the blind are $1,050. These amounts are increased to $1,350 if the individual is also unmarried and not a surviving spouse.

.12 Overall Limitation on Itemized Deductions

For taxable years beginning in 2008, the "applicable amount" of adjusted gross income under § 68(b), above which the amount of otherwise allowable itemized deductions is reduced under § 68, is $159,950 (or $79,975 for a separate return filed by a married individual).

.13 Qualified Transportation Fringe

For taxable years beginning in 2008, the monthly limitation under § 132(f)(2)(A), regarding the aggregate fringe benefit exclusion amount for transportation in a commuter highway vehicle and any transit pass is $115. The monthly limitation under § 132(f)(2)(B), regarding the fringe benefit exclusion amount for qualified parking is $220.

.14 Income from United States Savings Bonds for Taxpayers Who Pay Qualified Higher Education Expenses

For taxable years beginning in 2008, the exclusion under § 135, regarding income from United States savings bonds for taxpayers who pay qualified higher education expenses, begins to phase out for modified adjusted gross income above $100,650 for joint returns and $67,100 for other returns. This exclusion completely phases out for modified adjusted gross income of $130,650 or more for joint returns and $82,100 or more for other returns.

.15 Adoption Assistance Programs

For taxable years beginning in 2008, under § 137(a)(2) the maximum amount that can be excluded from an employee's gross income in connection with the adoption by the employee of a child with special needs is $11,650. For taxable

Appendix B

years beginning in 2008, under § 137(b)(1) the maximum amount that can be excluded from an employee's gross income for the amounts paid or expenses incurred by the employer for qualified adoption expenses furnished pursuant to an adoption assistance program in connection with other adoptions by the employee is $11,650. The amount excludable from an employee's gross income begins to phase out under § 137(b)(2)(A) for taxpayers with modified adjusted gross income in excess of $174,730 and is completely phased out for taxpayers with modified adjusted gross income of $214,730. (See section 3.03 of this revenue procedure for the adjusted items relating to the adoption credit.)

.16 Private Activity Bonds Volume Cap

For calendar year 2008, the amounts used under § 146(d)(1) to calculate the State ceiling for the volume cap for private activity bonds is the greater of (1) $85 multiplied by the State population, or (2) $262,095,000.

.17 General Arbitrage Rebate Rules

For bond years ending in 2008, the amount of the computation credit determined under § 1.148-3(d)(4) of the proposed Income Tax Regulations is $1,430..

.18 Safe Harbor Rules for Broker Commissions on Guaranteed Investment Contracts or Investments Purchased for a Yield Restricted Defeasance Escrow

For calendar year 2008, under § 1.148-5(e)(2)(iii)(B)(1), a broker's commission or similar fee with respect to the acquisition of a guaranteed investment contract or investments purchased for a yield restricted defeasance escrow is reasonable if (1) the amount of the fee that the issuer treats as a qualified administrative cost does not exceed the lesser of (A) $34,000, or (B) 0.2 percent of the computational base (as defined in § 1.148-5(e)(2)(iii)(B)(2)) or, if more, $3,000; and (2) the issuer does not treat more than $95,000 in brokers' commissions or similar fees as qualified administrative costs for all guaranteed investment contracts and investments for yield restricted defeasance escrows purchased with gross proceeds of the issue.

.19 Personal Exemption

(1) *Exemption amount.* For taxable years beginning in 2008, the personal exemption amount under § 151(d) is $3,500. The exemption amount for taxpayers with adjusted gross income in excess of the maximum phaseout amount is $2,333 for taxable years beginning in 2008.

(2) *Phase out.* For taxable years beginning in 2008, the personal exemption amount begins to phase out at, and reaches the maximum phaseout amount after, the following adjusted gross income amounts:

Filing Status	AGI - Beginning of Phaseout	AGI - Exemption Fully Phased Out
Married Individuals Filing Joint Returns and Surviving Spouses (§ 1(a))	$239,950	$362,450
Heads of Households (§ 1(b))	$199,950	$322,450

Appendix B

Filing Status	AGI - Beginning of Phaseout	AGI - Exemption Fully Phased Out
Unmarried Individuals (other than Surviving Spouses and Heads of Households) (§ 1(c))	$159,950	$282,450
Married Individuals Filing Separate Returns (§ 1(d))	$119,975	$181,225

.20 Election to Expense Certain Depreciable Assets

For taxable years beginning in 2008, under § 179(b)(1) the aggregate cost of any § 179 property a taxpayer may elect to treat as an expense shall not exceed $128,000. Under § 179(b)(2) the $128,000 limitation shall be reduced (but not below zero) by the amount by which the cost of § 179 property placed in service during the 2008 taxable year exceeds $510,000.

.21 Eligible Long-Term Care Premiums

For taxable years beginning in 2008, the limitations under § 213(d)(10) (regarding eligible long-term care premiums includible in the term "medical care") are as follows:

Attained Age Before the Close of the Taxable Year	Limitation on Premiums
40 or less	$ 310
More than 40 but not more than 50	$ 580
More than 50 but not more than 60	$1,150
More than 60 but not more than 70	$3,080
More than 70	$3,850

.22 Retirement Savings

(1) For taxable years beginning in 2008, the applicable dollar amount under § 219(g)(3)(B)(i) for taxpayers filing a joint return is $85,000. If the taxpayer's spouse is not an active participant, the applicable dollar amount for the spouse under § 219(g)(3)(B)(i) is $159,000 for taxable years beginning in 2008.

(2) For taxable years beginning in 2008, the applicable dollar amount under § 219(g)(3)(B)(ii) for all other taxpayers (except for married taxpayers filing separately) is $53,000.

(3) The applicable dollar amount under § 219(g)(3)(B)(iii) for married taxpayers filing separately is $0.

.23 Medical Savings Accounts

(1) *Self-only coverage.* For taxable years beginning in 2008, the term "high deductible health plan" as defined in § 220(c)(2)(A) means, for self-only coverage, a health plan that has an annual deductible that is not less than $1,950 and not more than $2,900, and under which the annual out-of-pocket expenses required to be paid (other than for premiums) for covered benefits does not exceed $3,850.

(2) *Family coverage.* For taxable years beginning in 2008, the term "high deductible health plan" means, for family coverage, a health plan that has an annual deductible that is not less than $3,850 and not more than $5,800, and under which

Appendix B

the annual out-of-pocket expenses required to be paid (other than for premiums) for covered benefits does not exceed $7,050.

.24 Interest on Education Loans

For taxable years beginning in 2008, the $2,500 maximum deduction for interest paid on qualified education loans under § 221 is reduced under § 221(b)(2)(B) when modified adjusted gross income exceeds $55,000 ($115,000 for joint returns), and is completely eliminated when modified adjusted gross income is $70,000 or more ($145,000 or more for joint returns).

.25 Roth IRAs

(1) For taxable years beginning in 2008, the applicable dollar amount under § 408A(c)(3)(C)(ii)(I) for taxpayers filing a joint return is $159,000.

(2) For taxable years beginning in 2008, the applicable dollar amount under § 408A(c)(3)(C)(ii)(II) for all other taxpayers (except for married taxpayers filing separately) is $101,000.

(3) The applicable dollar amount under § 408A(c)(3)(C)(ii)(III) for married taxpayers filing separately is $0.

.26 Treatment of Dues Paid to Agricultural or Horticultural Organizations

For taxable years beginning in 2008, the limitation under § 512(d)(1) (regarding the exemption of annual dues required to be paid by a member to an agricultural or horticultural organization) is $139.

.27 Insubstantial Benefit Limitations for Contributions Associated with Charitable Fund-Raising Campaigns

(1) *Low cost article.* For taxable years beginning in 2008, the unrelated business income of certain exempt organizations under § 513(h)(2) does not include a "low cost article" of $9.10 or less.

(2) *Other insubstantial benefits.* For taxable years beginning in 2008, the $5, $25, and $50 guidelines in section 3 of Rev. Proc. 90-12, 1990-1 C.B. 471 (as amplified by Rev. Proc. 92-49, 1992-1 C.B. 987, and modified by Rev. Proc. 92-102, 1992-2 C.B. 579), for disregarding the value of insubstantial benefits received by a donor in return for a fully deductible charitable contribution under § 170, are $9.10, $45.50, and $91, respectively.

.28 Funeral Trusts

For a contract entered into during calendar year 2008 for a "qualified funeral trust," as defined in § 685, the trust may not accept aggregate contributions by or for the benefit of an individual in excess of $9,000.

.29 Expatriation to Avoid Tax

For calendar year 2008, an individual with "average annual net income tax" of more than $139,000 for the five taxable years ending before the date of the loss of United States citizenship under § 877(a)(2)(A) is subject to tax under § 877(b).

.30 Foreign Earned Income Exclusion

For taxable years beginning in 2008, the foreign earned income exclusion amount under § 911(b)(2)(D)(i) is $87,600.

.31 Valuation of Qualified Real Property in Decedent's Gross Estate

For an estate of a decedent dying in calendar year 2008, if the executor elects to use the special use valuation method under § 2032A for qualified real property, the aggregate decrease in the value of qualified real property resulting from electing to use § 2032A that is taken into account for purposes of the estate tax may not exceed $960,000.

.32 Annual Exclusion for Gifts

(1) For calendar year 2008, the first $12,000 of gifts to any person (other than gifts of future interests in property) are not included in the total amount of taxable gifts under § 2503 made during that year.

(2) For calendar year 2008, the first $128,000 of gifts to a spouse who is not a citizen of the United States (other than gifts of future interests in property) are not included in the total amount of taxable gifts under §§ 2503 and 2523(i)(2) made during that year.

.33 Tax on Arrow Shafts

For calendar year 2008, the tax imposed under § 4161(b)(2)(A) on the first sale by the manufacturer, producer, or importer of any shaft of a type used in the manufacture of certain arrows is $0.43 per shaft.

.34 Reporting Exception for Certain Exempt Organizations with Nondeductible Lobbying Expenditures

For taxable years beginning in 2008, the annual per person, family, or entity dues limitation to qualify for the reporting exception under § 6033(e)(3) (and section 5.05 of Rev. Proc. 98-19, 1998-1 C.B. 547), regarding certain exempt organizations with nondeductible lobbying expenditures, is $97 or less.

.36 Persons Against Which a Federal Tax Lien Is Not Valid

For calendar year 2008, a federal tax lien is not valid against (1) certain purchasers under § 6323(b)(4) who purchased personal property in a casual sale for less than $1,320, or (2) a mechanic's lienor under § 6323(b)(7) that repaired or improved certain residential property if the contract price with the owner is not more than $6,600.

.37 Property Exempt from Levy

For calendar year 2008, the value of property exempt from levy under § 6334(a)(2) (fuel, provisions, furniture, and other household personal effects, as well as arms for personal use, livestock, and poultry) may not exceed $7,900. The value of property exempt from levy under § 6334(a)(3) (books and tools necessary for the trade, business, or profession of the taxpayer) may not exceed $3,950.

Appendix B

.38 Interest on a Certain Portion of the Estate Tax Payable in Installments

For an estate of a decedent dying in calendar year 2008, the dollar amount used to determine the "2-percent portion" (for purposes of calculating interest under § 6601(j)) of the estate tax extended as provided in § 6166 is $1,280,000.

.39 Attorney Fee Awards

For fees incurred in calendar year 2008, the attorney fee award limitation under § 7430(c)(1)(B)(iii) is $170 per hour.

.40 Periodic Payments Received under Qualified Long-Term Care Insurance Contracts or under Certain Life Insurance Contracts

For calendar year 2008, the stated dollar amount of the per diem limitation under § 7702B(d)(4) (regarding periodic payments received under a qualified long-term care insurance contract or periodic payments received under a life insurance contract that are treated as paid by reason of the death of a chronically ill individual) is $270.

SECTION 4. EFFECTIVE DATE

.01 General Rule

Except as provided in section 5.02, this revenue procedure applies to taxable years beginning in 2008.

.02 Calendar Year Rule

This revenue procedure applies to transactions or events occurring in calendar year 2008 for purposes of sections 3.08 (low-income housing credit), 3.10 (transportation mainline pipeline construction industry optional expense substantiation rules for payments to employees under accountable plans), 3.16 (private activity bond volume cap), 3:17 (general arbitrage rebate rules) 3.18 (safe harbor rules for broker commissions on guaranteed investment contracts or investments purchased for a yield restricted defeasance escrow), 3.28 (funeral trusts), 3.29 (expatriation to avoid tax), 3.31 (valuation of qualified real property in decedent's gross estate), 3.32 (annual exclusion for gifts), 3.33 (tax on arrow shafts), 3.36 (persons against which a federal tax lien is not valid), 3.37 (property exempt from levy), 3.38 (interest on a certain portion of the estate tax payable in installments), 3.39 (attorney fee awards), and 3.40 (periodic payments received under qualified long-term care insurance contracts or under certain life insurance contracts).

2.0 Inflation Adjustments for Retirement Plans for 2008

News Release 2007-171, 10/18/2007

The Internal Revenue Service today announced cost-of-living adjustments applicable to dollar limitations for pension plans and other items for Tax Year 2008.

Section 415 of the Internal Revenue Code provides for dollar limitations on benefits and contributions under qualified retirement plans. It also requires that the Commissioner annually adjust these limits for cost-of-living increases.

Many of the pension plan limitations will change for 2008 because the increase in the cost-of-living index met the statutory thresholds that trigger their adjustment. However, for others, the limitation will remain unchanged. For example, the limitation under Section 402(g)(1) on the exclusion for elective deferrals described in Section 402(g)(3) remains unchanged at $15,500. This limitation affects elective deferrals to Section 401(k) plans and to the Federal Government's Thrift Savings Plan, among other plans.

Effective January 1, 2008, the limitation on the annual benefit under a defined benefit plan under Section 415(b)(1)(A) is increased from $180,000 to $185,000. For participants who separated from service before January 1, 2008, the limitation for defined benefit plans under Section 415(b)(1)(B) is computed by multiplying the participant's compensation limitation, as adjusted through 2007, by 1.0236.

The limitation for defined contribution plans under Section 415(c)(1)(A) is increased from $45,000 to $46,000.

The Code provides that various other dollar amounts are to be adjusted at the same time and in the same manner as the dollar limitation of Section 415(b)(1)(A). These dollar amounts and the adjusted amounts are as follows:

> The limitation under Section 402(g)(1) on the exclusion for elective deferrals described in Section 402(g)(3) remains unchanged at $15,500.

> The annual compensation limit under Sections 401(a)(17), 404(l), 408(k)(3)(C), and 408(k)(6)(D)(ii) is increased from $225,000 to $230,000.

> The dollar limitation under Section 416(i)(1)(A)(i) concerning the definition of key employee in a top-heavy plan is increased from $145,000 to $150,000.

> The dollar amount under Section 409(o)(1)(C)(ii) for determining the maximum account balance in an employee stock ownership plan subject to a 5-year distribution period is increased from $915,000 to $935,000, while the dollar amount used to determine the lengthening of the 5-year distribution period is increased from $180,000 to $185,000.

> The limitation used in the definition of highly compensated employee under Section 414(q)(1)(B) is increased from $100,000 to $105,000.

> The dollar limitation under Section 414(v)(2)(B)(i) for catch-up contributions to an applicable employer plan other than a plan described in Section 401(k)(11) or Section 408(p) for individuals aged 50 or over remains unchanged at $5,000. The dollar limitation under Section 414(v)(2)(B)(ii) for catch-up contributions to an applicable employer plan described in Section 401(k)(11) or Section 408(p) for individuals aged 50 or over remains unchanged at $2,500.

> The annual compensation limitation under Section 401(a)(17) for eligible participants in certain governmental plans that, under the plan as in effect on July 1, 1993, allowed cost of living adjustments to the

Appendix B

compensation limitation under the plan under Section 401(a)(17) to be taken into account, is increased from $335,000 to $345,000.

The compensation amount under Section 408(k)(2)(C) regarding simplified employee pensions (SEPs) remains unchanged at $500.

The limitation under Section 408(p)(2)(E) regarding SIMPLE retirement accounts remains unchanged at $10,500.

The compensation amounts under Section 1.61 21(f)(5)(i) of the Income Tax Regulations concerning the definition of "control employee" for fringe benefit valuation purposes remains unchanged at $90,000. The compensation amount under Section 1.61 21(f)(5)(iii) is increased from $180,000 to $185,000.

The Code also provides that several pension-related amounts are to be adjusted using the cost-of-living adjustment under Section 1(f)(3). These dollar amounts and the adjustments are as follows:

The adjusted gross income limitation under Section 25B(b)(1)(A) for determining the retirement savings contribution credit for taxpayers filing a joint return is increased from $31,000 to $32,000; the limitation under Section 25B(b)(1)(B) is increased from $34,000 to $34,500; and the limitation under Sections 25B(b)(1)(C) and 25B(b)(1)(D), from $52,000 to $53,000.

The adjusted gross income limitation under Section 25B(b)(1)(A) for determining the retirement savings contribution credit for taxpayers filing as head of household is increased from $23,250 to $24,000; the limitation under Section 25B(b)(1)(B) is increased from $25,500 to $25,875; and the limitation under Sections 25B(b)(1)(C) and 25B(b)(1)(D), from $39,000 to $39,750.

The adjusted gross income limitation under Section 25B(b)(1)(A) for determining the retirement savings contribution credit for all other taxpayers is increased from $15,500 to $16,000; the limitation under Section 25B(b)(1)(B) is increased from $17,000 to $17,250; and the limitation under Sections 25B(b)(1)(C) and 25B(b)(1)(D), from $26,000 to $26,500

The applicable dollar amount under Section 219(g)(3)(B)(i) for determining the deductible amount of an IRA contribution for taxpayers who are active participants filing a joint return or as a qualifying widow(er) is increased from $83,000 to $85,000. The applicable dollar amount under Section 219(g)(3)(B)(ii) for all other taxpayers (other than married taxpayers filing separate returns) is increased from $52,000 to $53,000. The applicable dollar amount under Section 219(g)(7)(A) for a taxpayer who is not an active participant but whose spouse is an active participant is increased from $156,000 to $159,000.

The adjusted gross income limitation under Section 408A(c)(3)(C)(ii)(I) for determining the maximum Roth IRA contribution for taxpayers filing a joint return or as a qualifying widow(er) is increased from $156,000 to $159,000. The adjusted gross income limitation under Section 408A(c)(3)(C)(ii)(II) for all other taxpayers (other than married taxpayers filing separate returns) is increased from $99,000 to $101,000.

Administrators of defined benefit or defined contribution plans that have received favorable determination letters should not request new determination letters solely because of yearly amendments to adjust maximum limitations in the plans.

3.0 MACRS Depreciation Tables

I. General Depreciation System—Personal Property—Half-Year Convention

The following table provides the GDS cost recovery percentages for 3-year, 5-year, 7-year, 10-year and 15-year property under the half-year convention.

			Recovery Period		
Year	*3 years*	*5 years*	*7 years*	*10 years*	*15 years*
1	33.33%	20.00%	14.29%	10.00%	5.00%
2	44.45%	32.00%	24.49%	18.00%	9.50%
3	14.81%	19.20%	17.49%	14.40%	8.55%
4	7.41%	11.52%	12.49%	11.52%	7.70%
5		11.52%	8.93%	9.22%	6.93%
6		5.76%	8.92%	7.37%	6.23%
7			8.93%	6.55%	5.90%
8			4.46%	6.55%	5.90%
9				6.56%	5.91%
10				6.55%	5.90%
11				3.28%	5.91%
12					5.90%
13					5.91%
14					5.90%
15					5.91%
16					2.95%

II. General Depreciation System—Personal Property—Mid-Quarter Convention

The following four tables provide the cost recovery percentages for 3-year, 5-year, 7-year, 10-year and 15-year property under the mid-quarter convention.

A. Property Placed in Service in First Quarter

			Recovery Period		
Year	*3 years*	*5 years*	*7 years*	*10 years*	*15 years*
1	58.33%	35.00%	25.00%	17.50%	8.75%
2	27.78%	26.00%	21.43%	16.50%	9.13%

Appendix B

Year	3 years	5 years	7 years	10 years	15 years
3	12.35%	15.60%	15.31%	13.20%	8.21%
4	1.54%	11.01%	10.93%	10.56%	7.39%
5		11.01%	8.75%	8.45%	6.65%
6		1.38%	8.74%	6.76%	5.99%
7			8.75%	6.55%	5.90%
8			1.09%	6.55%	5.91%
9				6.56%	5.90%
10				6.55%	5.91%
11				0.82%	5.90%
12					5.91%
13					5.90%
14					5.91%
15					5.90%
16					0.74%

B. Property Placed in Service in Second Quarter

Recovery Period

Year	3 years	5 years	7 years	10 years	15 years
1	41.67%	25.00%	17.85%	12.50%	6.25%
2	38.89%	30.00%	23.47%	17.50%	9.38%
3	14.14%	18.00%	16.76%	14.00%	8.44%
4	5.30%	11.37%	11.97%	11.20%	7.59%
5		11.37%	8.87%	8.96%	6.83%
6		4.26%	8.87%	7.17%	6.15%
7			8.87%	6.55%	5.91%
8			3.33%	6.55%	5.90%
9				6.56%	5.91%
10				6.55%	5.90%
11				2.46%	5.91%
12					5.90%
13					5.91%
14					5.90%
15					5.91%
16					2.21%

C. Property Placed in Service in the Third Quarter

Recovery Period

Year	3 years	5 years	7 years	10 years	15 years
1	25.00%	15.00%	10.71%	7.50%	3.75%
2	50.00%	34.00%	25.51%	18.50%	9.63%
3	16.67%	20.40%	18.22%	14.80%	8.66%
4	8.33%	12.24%	13.02%	11.84%	7.80%
5		11.30%	9.30%	9.47%	7.02%
6		7.06%	8.85%	7.58%	6.31%
7			8.86%	6.55%	5.90%
8			5.53%	6.55%	5.91%

Year	3 years	5 years	7 years	10 years	15 years
9				6.56%	5.90%
10				6.55%	5.90%
11				4.10%	5.91%
12					5.90%
13					5.91%
14					5.90%
15					5.91%
16					3.69%

D. Property Placed in Service in the Fourth Quarter

			Recovery Period		
Year	3 years	5 years	7 years	10 years	15 years
1	8.33%	5.00%	3.57%	2.50%	1.25%
2	61.11%	38.00%	27.55%	19.50%	9.88%
3	20.37%	22.80%	19.68%	15.60%	8.89%
4	10.19%	13.68%	14.06%	12.48%	8.00%
5		10.94%	10.04%	9.98%	7.20%
6		9.58%	8.73%	7.99%	6.48%
7			8.73%	6.55%	5.90%
8			7.64%	6.55%	5.90%
9				6.56%	5.90%
10				6.55%	5.91%
11				5.74%	5.90%
12					5.91%
13					5.90%
14					5.91%
15					5.90%
16					5.17%

III. General Depreciation System—Real Property—Mid-Month Convention

The following two tables provide the cost recover percentages for real property under the mid-month convention.

A. Residential Real Property—27.5 Years

				Recovery Period				
Month Placed				Year				
in Service	1	2-9	10	11	12	13-27	28	29
1	3.485%	3.636%	3.637%	3.636%	3.637%	*	1.970%	—
2	3.182%	3.636%	3.637%	3.636%	3.637%	*	2.273%	—
3	2.879%	3.636%	3.637%	3.636%	3.637%	*	2.576%	—
4	2.576%	3.636%	3.637%	3.636%	3.637%	*	2.879%	—
5	2.273%	3.636%	3.637%	3.636%	3.637%	*	3.182%	—
6	1.970%	3.636%	3.637%	3.636%	3.637%	*	3.485%	—
7	1.667%	3.636%	3.637%	3.636%	3.637%	*	3.636%	0.152%

Appendix B

Month Placed in Service	Year							
	1	2-9	10	11	12	13-27	28	29
8	1.364%	3.636%	3.637%	3.636%	3.637%	*	3.636%	0.455%
9	1.061%	3.636%	3.637%	3.636%	3.637%	*	3.636%	0.758%
10	0.758%	3.636%	3.637%	3.636%	3.637%	*	3.636%	1.061%
11	0.455%	3.636%	3.637%	3.636%	3.637%	*	3.636%	1.364%
12	0.152%	3.636%	3.637%	3.636%	3.637%	*	3.636%	1.667%

* In years 13-27, the rate alternates between 3.636% and 3.637%.

B. Nonresidential Real Property—39 Years

Recovery Period

Month Placed in Service	Year		
	1	2-39	40
1	2.461%	2.564%	0.107%
2	2.247%	2.564%	0.321%
3	2.033%	2.564%	0.535%
4	1.819%	2.564%	0.749%
5	1.605%	2.564%	0.963%
6	1.391%	2.564%	1.177%
7	1.177%	2.564%	1.391%
8	0.963%	2.564%	1.605%
9	0.749%	2.564%	1.819%
10	0.535%	2.564%	2.033%
11	0.321%	2.564%	2.247%
12	0.107%	2.564%	2.461%

4.0 Limitations on Deductions for Automobile Depreciation and Lease Payments in 2007

Rev. Proc. 2007-30, 2007-18 IRB

1. Purpose

01. This revenue procedure provides: (1) limitations on depreciation deductions for owners of passenger automobiles first placed in service by the taxpayer during calendar year 2007, including a separate table of limitations on depreciation deductions for trucks and vans; and (2) the amounts to be included in income by lessees of passenger automobiles first leased by the taxpayer during calendar year 2007, including a separate table of inclusion amounts for lessees of trucks and vans.

02. The tables detailing these depreciation limitations and lessee inclusion amounts reflect the automobile price inflation adjustments required by § 280F(d)(7).

03. Section 280F(a)(1)(C), which directed the use of higher depreciation deduction limits for certain electric automobiles, was applicable only to property placed in service after December 31, 2001 and before January 1, 2007. Accordingly, separate

tables are no longer provided for electric automobiles, and taxpayers should use the applicable table provided in this revenue procedure.

2. Background

01. For owners of passenger automobiles, § 280F(a) imposes dollar limitations on the depreciation deduction for the year that the passenger automobile is placed in service by the taxpayer and each succeeding year. Section 280F(d)(7) requires the amounts allowable as depreciation deductions to be increased by a price inflation adjustment amount for passenger automobiles placed in service after 1988. The method of calculating this price inflation amount for trucks and vans placed in service in or after calendar year 2003 uses a different CPI "automobile component" (the "new trucks" component) than that used in the price inflation amount calculation for other passenger automobiles (the "new cars" component), resulting in somewhat higher depreciation deductions for trucks and vans. This change reflects the higher rate of price inflation that trucks and vans have been subject to since 1988. For purposes of this revenue procedure, the term "trucks and vans" refers to passenger automobiles that are built on a truck chassis, including minivans and sport utility vehicles (SUVs) that are built on a truck chassis.

02. For leased passenger automobiles, § 280F(c) requires a reduction in the deduction allowed to the lessee of the passenger automobile. The reduction must be substantially equivalent to the limitations on the depreciation deductions imposed on owners of passenger automobiles. Under § 1.280F-7(a), this reduction requires the lessees to include in gross income an inclusion amount determined by applying a formula to the amount obtained from a table. There is a table for lessees of electric automobiles, a table for lessees of trucks and vans, and a table for all other passenger automobiles. Each table shows inclusion amounts for a range of fair market values for each tax year after the passenger automobile is first leased.

3. Scope

01. The limitations on depreciation deductions in section 4.02(2) of this revenue procedure apply to passenger automobiles (other than leased passenger automobiles) that are placed in service by the taxpayer in calendar year 2007, and continue to apply for each tax year that the passenger automobile remains in service.

02. The tables in section 4.03 of this revenue procedure apply to leased passenger automobiles for which the lease term begins during calendar year 2007. Lessees of such passenger automobiles must use these tables to determine the inclusion amount for each tax year during which the passenger automobile is leased. See Rev. Proc. 2002-14, 2002-1 C.B. 450, for passenger automobiles first leased before January 1, 2003, Rev. Proc. 2003-75, 2003-2 C.B. 1018, for passenger automobiles first leased during calendar year 2003, and Rev. Proc. 2004-20, 2004-1 C.B. 642, for passenger automobiles first leased during calendar year 2004, Rev. Proc. 2005-13, 2005-1 C.B. 759, for passenger automobile first leased during calendar year 2005,

Appendix B

and Rev. Proc. 2006-18, 2006-1 C.B. 645, for passenger automobiles first leased during calendar year 2006.

4. Application

01. In General

(1) *Limitations on Depreciation Deductions for Certain Automobiles.* The limitations on depreciation deductions for passenger automobiles placed in service by the taxpayer for the first time during calendar year 2007 are found in Tables 1 through 3 in section 4.02(2) of this revenue procedure. Table 1 of this revenue procedure provides limitations on depreciation deductions for a passenger automobile. Table 2 of this revenue procedure provides limitations on depreciation deductions for a truck or van.

(2) *Inclusions in Income of Lessees of Passenger Automobiles.* A taxpayer first leasing a passenger automobile during calendar year 2007 must determine the inclusion amount that is added to gross income using the tables in section 4.03 of this revenue procedure. The inclusion amount is determined using Table 3 in the case of a passenger automobile (other than a truck, van, or electric automobile), Table 4 in the case of a truck or van. In addition, the procedures of § 1.280F-7(a) must be followed.

02. Limitations on Depreciation Deductions for Certain Automobiles

(1) *Amount of the Inflation Adjustment.* Under § 280F(d)(7)(B)(i), the automobile price inflation adjustment for any calendar year is the percentage (if any) by which the CPI automobile component for October of the preceding calendar year exceeds the CPI automobile component for October 1987. The term "CPI automobile component" is defined in § 280F(d)(7)(B)(ii) as the "automobile component" of the Consumer Price Index for all Urban Consumers published by the Department of Labor (the CPI). The new car component of the CPI was 115.2 for October 1987 and 136.3 for October 2006. The October 2006 index exceeded the October 1987 index by 21.1. The Service has, therefore, determined that the automobile price inflation adjustment for 2007 for passenger automobiles (other than trucks and vans) is 18.32 percent (21.1/115.2 x 100%). This adjustment is applicable to all passenger automobiles (other than trucks and vans) that are first placed in service in calendar year 2007. The dollar limitations in § 280F(a) must therefore be multiplied by a factor of 0.1832, and the resulting increases, after rounding to the nearest $100, are added to the 1988 limitations to give the depreciation limitations applicable to passenger automobiles (other than trucks, vans, and electric automobiles) for calendar year 2007. To determine the dollar limitations applicable to trucks and vans first placed in service during calendar year 2007, the new truck component of the CPI is used instead of the new car component. The new truck component of the CPI was 112.4 for October 1987 and 141.4 for October 2006. The October 2006 index exceeded the October 1987 index by 29.0. The Service has, therefore, determined that the automobile price inflation adjustment for 2007 for trucks and vans is 25.80 percent (29.0/112.4 × 100%). This adjustment is applicable to all trucks and vans that are first placed in service in calendar year 2007. The dollar limitations in § 280F(a) must therefore be multi-

plied by a factor of 0.2580, and the resulting increases, after rounding to the nearest $100, are added to the 1988 limitations to give the depreciation limitations applicable to trucks and vans.

(2) *Amount of the Limitation.* For passenger automobiles placed in service by the taxpayer in calendar year 2007, Tables 1 and 2 contain the dollar amount of the depreciation limitation for each tax year. Use Table 1 for passenger automobiles placed in service by the taxpayer in calendar year 2007. Use Table 2 for trucks and vans placed in service by the taxpayer in calendar year 2007.

Rev. Proc. 2007-30 Table 1
Depreciation Limitations for Passenger Automobiles Placed in Service by the Taxpayer During Calendar Year 2007

Tax Year	Amount
1st Tax Year	$3,060
2nd Tax Year	$4,900
3rd Tax Year	$2,850
Each Succeeding Year	$1,775

Rev. Proc. 2007-30 Table 2
Depreciation Limitations for Trucks and Vans Placed in Service by the Taxpayer During Calendar Year 2007

Tax Year	Amount
1st Tax Year	$3,260
2nd Tax Year	$5,200
3rd Tax Year	$3,050
Each Succeeding Year	$1,875

03. Inclusions in Income of Lessees of Passenger Automobiles

The inclusion amounts for passenger automobiles first leased in calendar year 2007 are calculated under the procedures described in § 1.280F-7(a). Lessees of passenger automobiles other than trucks and vans a should use Table 3 of this revenue procedure in applying these procedures, while lessees of trucks and vans should use Table 4 of this revenue procedure.

Rev. Proc. 2007-30 Table 3
Dollar Amounts for Passenger Automobiles (That Are Not Trucks or Vans) with a Lease Term Beginning in Calendar Year 2007

Fair Market Value of Passenger Automobile		Tax Year During Lease				
Over	Not Over	1st	2nd	3rd	4th	5th & Later
$15,500	$15,800	2	5	11	11	13
15,800	16,100	4	10	17	19	22
16,100	16,400	6	14	24	28	31
16,400	16,700	9	18	31	35	41
16,700	17,000	11	23	37	43	50
17,000	17,500	13	29	46	54	62
17,500	18,000	17	37	56	68	77

Appendix B

Fair Market Value of Passenger Automobile		Tax Year During Lease				
Over	Not Over	1st	2nd	3rd	4th	5th & Later
18,000	18,500	20	44	68	81	93
18,500	19,000	24	51	80	94	108
19,000	19,500	27	59	90	108	124
19,500	20,000	30	67	101	121	139
20,000	20,500	34	74	113	134	154
20,500	21,000	37	82	123	148	170
21,000	21,500	41	89	135	161	185
21,500	22,000	44	97	146	174	201
22,000	23,000	49	108	163	194	224
23,000	24,000	56	123	185	221	255
24,000	25,000	63	138	207	248	285
25,000	26,000	70	153	229	275	316
26,000	27,000	77	168	251	302	347
27,000	28,000	83	183	274	328	378
28,000	29,000	90	198	296	355	409
29,000	30,000	97	213	318	382	439
30,000	31,000	104	228	341	408	470
31,000	32,000	111	243	363	435	501
32,000	33,000	118	258	385	461	532
33,000	34,000	125	273	407	488	563
34,000	35,000	131	288	430	515	593
35,000	36,000	138	303	452	542	624
36,000	37,000	145	318	474	568	656
37,000	38,000	152	333	496	595	686
38,000	39,000	159	348	519	621	717
39,000	40,000	166	363	541	648	748
40,000	41,000	172	378	564	674	779
41,000	42,000	179	393	586	701	810
42,000	43,000	186	408	608	728	840
43,000	44,000	193	423	630	755	871
44,000	45,000	200	438	652	782	902
45,000	46,000	207	453	674	809	933
46,000	47,000	213	468	697	835	964
47,000	48,000	220	483	719	862	995
48,000	49,000	227	498	742	888	1,025
49,000	50,000	234	513	764	915	1,056
50,000	51,000	241	528	786	942	1,087
51,000	52,000	248	543	808	969	1,117
52,000	53,000	254	558	831	995	1,148
53,000	54,000	261	573	853	1,022	1,179
54,000	55,000	268	588	875	1,049	1,210
55,000	56,000	275	603	897	1,076	1,241
56,000	57,000	282	618	920	1,102	1,271
57,000	58,000	289	633	942	1,128	1,303

Fair Market Value of Passenger Automobile		Tax Year During Lease				
Over	Not Over	1st	2nd	3rd	4th	5th & Later
58,000	59,000	296	648	964	1,155	1,334
59,000	60,000	302	663	987	1,182	1,364
60,000	62,000	313	685	1,020	1,222	1,411
62,000	64,000	326	716	1,064	1,276	1,472
64,000	66,000	340	746	1,108	1,329	1,534
66,000	68,000	354	775	1,154	1,382	1,595
68,000	70,000	367	806	1,198	1,435	1,657
70,000	72,000	381	836	1,242	1,489	1,719
72,000	74,000	395	865	1,287	1,543	1,780
74,000	76,000	408	896	1,331	1,596	1,842
76,000	78,000	422	926	1,376	1,649	1,903
78,000	80,000	436	955	1,421	1,703	1,965
80,000	85,000	460	1,008	1,498	1,796	2,074
85,000	90,000	494	1,083	1,610	1,929	2,228
90,000	95,000	528	1,158	1,721	2,063	2,382
95,000	100,000	562	1,233	1,833	2,196	2,536
100,000	110,000	614	1,346	1,999	2,396	2,767
110,000	120,000	682	1,496	2,222	2,663	3,075
120,000	130,000	750	1,646	2,444	2,931	3,383
130,000	140,000	819	1,796	2,667	3,197	3,692
140,000	150,000	887	1,946	2,890	3,464	4,000
150,000	160,000	956	2,096	3,112	3,731	4,308
160,000	170,000	1,024	2,246	3,335	3,998	4,616
170,000	180,000	1,093	2,396	3,557	4,226	4,924
180,000	190,000	1,161	2,546	3,780	4,532	5,233
190,000	200,000	1,229	2,696	4,003	4,799	5,541
200,000	210,000	1,298	2,846	4,225	5,067	5,848
210,000	220,000	1,366	2,996	4,448	5,333	6,157
220,000	230,000	1,435	3,146	4,671	5,600	6,465
230,000	240,000	1,503	3,296	4,893	5,867	6,774
240,000	and up	1,571	3,446	5,116	6,134	7,082

Rev. Proc. 2007-30 Table 4
Dollar Amounts for Trucks and Vans with a Lease Term Beginning in Calendar Year 2007

Fair Market Value of Truck or Van		Tax Year During Lease				
Over	Not Over	1st	2nd	3rd	4th	5th & Later
$16,400	$16,700	2	4	8	10	11
$16,700	$17,000	4	9	15	17	21
17,000	17,500	6	15	24	28	33
17,500	18,000	10	22	35	42	48
18,000	18,500	13	30	46	55	64
18,500	19,000	17	37	57	69	79
19,000	19,500	20	45	68	82	94

Appendix B

Fair Market Value of Truck or Van		Tax Year During Lease				
Over	Not Over	1st	2nd	3rd	4th	5th & Later
19,500	20,000	24	52	80	95	109
20,000	20,500	27	60	90	109	125
20,500	21,000	30	67	102	122	141
21,000	21,500	34	75	113	135	156
21,500	22,000	37	82	124	149	171
22,000	23,000	42	94	140	169	194
23,000	24,000	49	109	163	195	225
24,000	25,000	56	123	186	222	256
25,000	26,000	63	138	208	249	286
26,000	27,000	70	153	230	276	317
27,000	28,000	77	168	252	302	349
28,000	29,000	83	184	274	329	379
29,000	30,000	90	199	296	356	410
30,000	31,000	97	214	318	383	440
31,000	32,000	104	228	342	408	472
32,000	33,000	111	243	364	435	503
33,000	34,000	118	258	386	462	534
34,000	35,000	125	273	408	489	564
35,000	36,000	131	289	430	515	595
36,000	37,000	138	404	452	542	626
37,000	38,000	145	318	475	569	657
38,000	39,000	152	333	497	596	688
39,000	40,000	159	348	520	622	718
40,000	41,000	166	363	542	649	749
41,000	42,000	172	379	563	676	780
42,000	43,000	179	394	586	702	811
43,000	44,000	186	409	608	729	842
44,000	45,000	193	423	631	756	872
45,000	46,000	200	438	653	783	903
46,000	47,000	207	453	675	810	934
47,000	48,000	213	469	697	836	965
48,000	49,000	220	484	719	863	996
49,000	50,000	227	499	741	890	1,026
50,000	51,000	234	514	764	916	1,057
51,000	52,000	241	528	787	943	1,088
52,000	53,000	248	543	809	969	1,119
53,000	54,000	254	559	831	996	1,150
54,000	55,000	261	574	853	1,023	1,180
55,000	56,000	268	589	875	1,050	1,211
56,000	57,000	275	604	897	1,076	1,243
57,000	58,000	282	618	920	1,103	1,273
58,000	59,000	289	633	943	1,129	1,304
59,000	60,000	296	648	965	1,156	1,335
60,000	62,000	306	671	998	1,196	1,381
62,000	64,000	319	701	1,043	1,249	1,443

Fair Market Value of Truck or Van		Tax Year During Lease				
Over	Not Over	1st	2nd	3rd	4th	5th & Later
64,000	66,000	333	731	1,087	1,303	1,504
66,000	68,000	347	761	1,131	1,357	1,566
68,000	70,000	361	791	1,176	1,410	1,627
70,000	72,000	374	821	1,221	1,463	1,689
72,000	74,000	388	851	1,265	1,517	1,751
74,000	76,000	402	881	1,309	1,570	1,813
76,000	78,000	415	911	1,354	1,624	1,874
78,000	80,000	429	941	1,399	1,676	1,936
80,000	85,000	453	994	1,476	1,770	2,044
85,000	90,000	487	1,069	1,587	1,904	2,198
90,000	95,000	521	1,144	1,699	2,037	2,352
95,000	100,000	555	1,219	1,810	2,171	2,506
100,000	110,000	607	1,331	1,977	2,371	2,737
110,000	120,000	675	1,481	2,200	2,638	3,045
120,000	130,000	744	1,631	2,423	2,904	3,354
130,000	140,000	812	1,781	2,646	3,171	3,662
140,000	150,000	880	1,932	2,867	3,439	3,970
150,000	160,000	949	2,081	3,091	3,705	4,279
160,000	170,000	1,017	2,232	3,313	3,972	4,586
170,000	180,000	1,086	2,381	3,536	4,239	4,895
180,000	190,000	1,154	2,532	3,758	4,506	5,203
190,000	200,000	1,222	2,682	3,981	4,773	5,511
200,000	210,000	1,291	2,831	4,204	5,040	5,820
210,000	220,000	1,359	2,982	4,426	5,307	6,128
220,000	230,000	1,428	3,131	4,649	5,575	6,435
230,000	240,000	1,496	3,282	4,871	5,841	6,744
240,000	and up	1,565	3,431	5,095	6,108	7,052

5. Effective Date

This revenue procedure applies to passenger automobiles (other than leased passenger automobiles) that are first placed in service by the taxpayer during calendar year 2007, and to leased passenger automobiles that are first leased by the taxpayer during calendar year 2007.

5.0 Substantiation of Travel Expenses for 2008

Rev. Proc. 2007-63, 2007-42 IRB

SECTION 1. PURPOSE

This revenue procedure updates Rev. Proc. 2006-41, 2006-43 I.R.B. 777, and provides rules under which the amount of ordinary and necessary business expenses of an employee for lodging, meal, and incidental expenses, or for meal and incidental expenses, incurred while traveling away from home are deemed substantiated under § 1.274-5 of the Income Tax Regulations when a payor (the

Appendix B

employer, its agent, or a third party) provides a per diem allowance under a reimbursement or other expense allowance arrangement to pay for the expenses. In addition, this revenue procedure provides an optional method for employees and self-employed individuals who are not reimbursed to use in computing the deductible costs paid or incurred for business meal and incidental expenses, or for incidental expenses only if no meal costs are paid or incurred, while traveling away from home. Use of a method described in this revenue procedure is not mandatory, and a taxpayer may use actual allowable expenses if the taxpayer maintains adequate records or other sufficient evidence for proper substantiation. This revenue procedure does not provide rules under which the amount of an employee's lodging expenses will be deemed substantiated when a payor provides an allowance to pay for those expenses but not meal and incidental expenses.

SECTION 2. BACKGROUND AND CHANGES

.01 Section 162(a) of the Internal Revenue Code allows a deduction for all the ordinary and necessary expenses paid or incurred during the taxable year in carrying on any trade or business. Under that provision, an employee or self-employed individual may deduct expenses paid or incurred while traveling away from home in pursuit of a trade or business. However, under § 262, no portion of the travel expenses that is attributable to personal, living, or family expenses is deductible.

.02 Section 274(n) generally limits the amount allowable as a deduction under § 162 for any expense for food, beverages, or entertainment to 50 percent of the amount of the expense that otherwise would be allowable as a deduction. In the case of any expenses for food or beverages consumed while away from home (within the meaning of § 162(a)(2)) by an individual during, or incident to, the period of duty subject to the hours of service limitations of the Department of Transportation, § 274(n)(3) gradually increases the deductible percentage to 80 percent for taxable years beginning in 2008 or thereafter. For taxable years beginning in 2007, the deductible percentage for these expenses is 75 percent.

.03 Section 274(d) provides, in part, that no deduction is allowed under § 162 for any travel expense (including meals and lodging while away from home) unless the taxpayer complies with certain substantiation requirements. Section 274(d) further provides that regulations may prescribe that some or all of the substantiation requirements do not apply to an expense that does not exceed an amount prescribed by the regulations.

.04 Section 1.274-5(g), in part, grants the Commissioner the authority to prescribe rules relating to reimbursement arrangements or per diem allowances for ordinary and necessary expenses paid or incurred while traveling away from home. Pursuant to this grant of authority, the Commissioner may prescribe rules under which these arrangements or allowances, if in accordance with reasonable business practice, are regarded (1) as equivalent to substantiation, by adequate records or other sufficient evidence, of the amount of travel expenses for purposes of § 1.274-5(c), and (2) as satisfying the requirements of an adequate accounting to the employer of the amount of travel expenses for purposes of § 1.274-5(f).

.05 For purposes of determining adjusted gross income, § 62(a)(2)(A) allows an employee a deduction for expenses allowed by Part VI (§ 161 and following), subchapter B, chapter 1 of the Code, paid or incurred by the employee in connection with the performance of services as an employee under a reimbursement or other expense allowance arrangement with a payor.

.06 Section 62(c) provides that an arrangement will not be treated as a reimbursement or other expense allowance arrangement for purposes of § 62(a)(2)(A) if it—

    (1) does not require the employee to substantiate the expenses covered by the arrangement to the payor, or

    (2) provides the employee with the right to retain any amount in excess of the substantiated expenses covered under the arrangement.

Section 62(c) further provides that the substantiation requirements described therein do not apply to any expense to the extent that, under the grant of regulatory authority prescribed in § 274(d), the Commissioner has provided that substantiation is not required for the expense.

Under § 1.62-2(c), a reimbursement or other expense allowance arrangement satisfies the requirements of § 62(c) if it meets the requirements of business connection, substantiation, and returning amounts in excess of expenses as specified in the regulations. If an arrangement meets these requirements, all amounts paid under the arrangement are treated as paid under an accountable plan and are excluded from income and wages. If an arrangement does not meet these requirements, all amounts paid under the arrangement are treated as paid under a nonaccountable plan and are included in the employee's gross income, must be reported as wages or compensation on the employee's Form W-2, and are subject to the withholding and payment of employment taxes. Section 1.62-2(e)(2) specifically provides that substantiation of certain business expenses in accordance with rules prescribed under the authority of § 1.274-5(g) or (j) is treated as substantiation of the amount of the expenses for purposes of § 1.62-2. Under § 1.62-2(f)(2), the Commissioner may prescribe rules under which an arrangement providing per diem allowances is treated as satisfying the requirement of returning amounts in excess of expenses, even though the arrangement does not require the employee to return the portion of the allowance that relates to days of travel substantiated and that exceeds the amount of the employee's expenses deemed substantiated pursuant to rules prescribed under § 274(d), provided the allowance is reasonably calculated not to exceed the amount of the employee's expenses or anticipated expenses and the employee is required to return within a reasonable period of time any portion of the allowance that relates to days of travel not substantiated.

.08 Section 1.62-2(h)(2)(i)(B) provides that, if a payor pays a per diem allowance that meets the requirements of § 1.62-2(c)(1), the portion, if any, of the allowance that relates to days of travel substantiated in accordance with § 1.62-2(e), that exceeds the amount of the employee's expenses deemed substantiated for the

Appendix B

travel pursuant to rules prescribed under §274(d) and 1.274-5(g) or (j), and that the employee is not required to return, is subject to withholding and payment of employment taxes. See §§31.3121(a)-3, 31.3231(e)-1(a)(5), 31.3306(b)-2, and 31.3401(a)-4 of the Employment Tax Regulations. Because the employee is not required to return this excess portion, the reasonable period of time provisions of §1.62-2(g) (relating to the return of excess amounts) do not apply to this portion.

.09 Under §1.62-2(h)(2)(i)(B)(4), the Commissioner has the discretion to prescribe special rules regarding the timing of withholding and payment of employment taxes on per diem allowances.

.10 Section 1.274-5(j)(1) grants the Commissioner the authority to establish a method under which a taxpayer may elect to use a specified amount for meals paid or incurred while traveling away from home in lieu of substantiating the actual cost of meals.

.11 Section 1.274-5(j)(3) grants the Commissioner the authority to establish a method under which a taxpayer may elect to use a specified amount for incidental expenses paid or incurred while traveling away from home in lieu of substantiating the actual cost of incidental expenses.

.12 Sections 3.02(1)(a), 4.04(6), and 5.06 of this revenue procedure provide transition rules for the last 3 months of calendar year 2007.

.13 Section 5.02 of this revenue procedure contains revisions to the per diem rates for high-cost localities and for other localities for purposes of section 5.

.14 Section 5.03 of this revenue procedure contains the list of high-cost localities and section 5.04 of this revenue procedure describes changes to the list of high-cost localities for purposes of section 5.

.15 Sections 7.10 and 8.06 of this revenue procedure refer to Rev. Rul. 2006-56, 2006-46 I.R.B. 874, which describes circumstances when a payor's reimbursement or other expense allowance arrangement evidences a pattern of abuse of the rules of § 62(c) and the regulations thereunder.

SECTION 3. DEFINITIONS

.01 *Per diem allowance.* The term "per diem allowance" means a payment under a reimbursement or other expense allowance arrangement that is—

(1) paid with respect to ordinary and necessary business expenses incurred, or which the payor reasonably anticipates will be incurred, by an employee for lodging, meal, and incidental expenses, or for meal and incidental expenses, for travel away from home in connection with the performance of services as an employee of the employer,

(2) reasonably calculated not to exceed the amount of the expenses or the anticipated expenses, and

(3) paid at or below the applicable federal per diem rate, a flat rate or stated schedule, or in accordance with any other Service-specified rate or schedule.

.02 Federal per diem rate and federal M&IE rate.

  (1)   *In general.* The federal per diem rate is equal to the sum of the applicable federal lodging expense rate and the applicable federal meal and incidental expense (M&IE) rate for the day and locality of travel.

      (a)   *CONUS rates.* The rates for localities in the continental United States ("CONUS") are set forth in Appendix A to 41 C.F.R. ch. 301. However, in applying section 4.01, 4.02, or 4.03 of this revenue procedure, taxpayers may continue to use the CONUS rates in effect for the first 9 months of 2007 for expenses of all CONUS travel away from home that are paid or incurred during calendar year 2007 in lieu of the updated GSA rates. A taxpayer must consistently use either these rates or the updated rates for the period October 1, 2007, through December 31, 2007.

      (b)   *OCONUS rates.* The rates for localities outside the continental United States ("OCONUS") are established by the Secretary of Defense (rates for non-foreign localities, including Alaska, Hawaii, Puerto Rico, the Northern Mariana Islands, and the possessions of the United States) and by the Secretary of State (rates for foreign localities), and are published in the Per Diem Supplement to the Standardized Regulations (Government Civilians, Foreign Areas) (updated on a monthly basis).

      (c)   *Internet access to the rates.* The CONUS and OCONUS rates may be found on the Internet at www.gsa.gov.

  (2)   *Locality of travel.* The term "locality of travel" means the locality where an employee traveling away from home in connection with the performance of services as an employee of the employer stops for sleep or rest.

  (3)   *Incidental expenses.* The term "incidental expenses" has the same meaning as in the Federal Travel Regulations, 41 C.F.R. 300-3.1 (2007). Thus, based on the current definition of "incidental expenses" in the Federal Travel Regulations, "incidental expenses" means fees and tips given to porters, baggage carriers, bellhops, hotel maids, stewards or stewardesses and others on ships, and hotel servants in foreign countries; transportation between places of lodging or business and places where meals are taken, if suitable meals can be obtained at the temporary duty site; and the mailing cost associated with filing travel vouchers and payment of employer-sponsored charge card billings.

.03 Flat rate or stated schedule.

  (1)   *In general.* Except as provided in section 3.03(2) of this revenue procedure, an allowance is paid at a flat rate or stated schedule if it is provided on a uniform and objective basis with respect to the expenses described in section 3.01 of this revenue procedure. The allowance may be paid with respect to the number of days away from home in connection with the performance of services as an employee or on any

Appendix B

other basis that is consistently applied and in accordance with reasonable business practice. Thus, for example, an hourly payment to cover meal and incidental expenses paid to a pilot or flight attendant who is traveling away from home in connection with the performance of services as an employee is an allowance paid at a flat rate or stated schedule. Likewise, a payment based on the number of miles traveled (such as cents per mile) to cover meal and incidental expenses paid to an over-the-road truck driver who is traveling away from home in connection with the performance of services as an employee is an allowance paid at a flat rate or stated schedule.

(2)   *Limitation.* For purposes of this revenue procedure, an allowance that is computed on a basis similar to that used in computing the employee's wages or other compensation (such as the number of hours worked, miles traveled, or pieces produced) does not meet the business connection requirement of § 1.62-2(d), is not a per diem allowance, and is not paid at a flat rate or stated schedule, unless, as of December 12, 1989, (a) the allowance was identified by the payor either by making a separate payment or by specifically identifying the amount of the allowance, or (b) an allowance computed on that basis was commonly used in the industry in which the employee is employed. See § 1.62-2(d)(3)(ii).

SECTION 4. PER DIEM SUBSTANTIATION METHOD

.01 *Per diem allowance.* If a payor pays a per diem allowance in lieu of reimbursing actual lodging, meal, and incidental expenses incurred or to be incurred by an employee for travel away from home, the amount of the expenses that is deemed substantiated for each calendar day is equal to the lesser of the per diem allowance for that day or the amount computed at the federal per diem rate (see section 3.02 of this revenue procedure) for the locality of travel for that day (or partial day, see section 6.04 of this revenue procedure).

.02 *Meal and incidental expenses only per diem allowance.* If a payor pays a per diem allowance only for meal and incidental expenses in lieu of reimbursing actual meals and incidental expenses incurred or to be incurred by an employee for travel away from home, the amount of the expenses that is deemed substantiated for each calendar day is equal to the lesser of the per diem allowance for that day or the amount computed at the federal M&IE rate for the locality of travel for that day (or partial day). A per diem allowance is treated as paid only for meal and incidental expenses if (1) the payor pays the employee for actual expenses for lodging based on receipts submitted to the payor, (2) the payor provides the lodging in kind, (3) the payor pays the actual expenses for lodging directly to the provider of the lodging, (4) the payor does not have a reasonable belief that lodging expenses were or will be incurred by the employee, or (5) the allowance is computed on a basis similar to that used in computing the employee's wages or other compensation (such as the number of hours worked, miles traveled, or pieces produced).

Appendix B

.03 *Optional method for meal and incidental expenses only deduction.* In lieu of using actual expenses in computing the amount allowable as a deduction for ordinary and necessary meal and incidental expenses paid or incurred for travel away from home, employees and self-employed individuals who pay or incur meal expenses may use an amount computed at the federal M&IE rate for the locality of travel for each calendar day (or partial day) the employee or self-employed individual is away from home. This amount will be deemed substantiated for purposes of paragraphs (b)(2) and (c) of § 1.274-5, provided the employee or self-employed individual substantiates the elements of time, place, and business purpose of the travel for that day (or partial day) in accordance with those regulations. See section 6.05(1) of this revenue procedure for rules related to the application of the limitation under § 274(n) to amounts determined under this section 4.03. See section 4.05 of this revenue procedure for a method for substantiating incidental expenses that may be used by employees or self-employed individuals who do not pay or incur meal expenses.

.04 *Special rules for transportation industry.*

(1) *In general.* This section 4.04 applies to (a) a payor that pays a per diem allowance only for meal and incidental expenses for travel away from home as described in section 4.02 of this revenue procedure to an employee in the transportation industry, or (b) an employee or self-employed individual in the transportation industry who computes the amount allowable as a deduction for meal and incidental expenses for travel away from home in accordance with section 4.03 of this revenue procedure.

(2) *Transportation industry defined.* For purposes of this section 4.04, an employee or self-employed individual is in the transportation industry only if the employee's or individual's work (a) is of the type that directly involves moving people or goods by airplane, barge, bus, ship, train, or truck, and (b) regularly requires travel away from home which, during any single trip away from home, usually involves travel to localities with differing federal M&IE rates. For purposes of the preceding sentence, a payor must determine that an employee or a group of employees is in the transportation industry by using a method that is consistently applied and in accordance with reasonable business practice.

(3) *Rates.* A taxpayer described in section 4.04(1) of this revenue procedure may treat $52 as the federal M&IE rate for any CONUS locality of travel, and $58 as the federal M&IE rate for any OCONUS locality of travel. A payor that uses either (or both) of these special rates with respect to an employee must use the special rate(s) for all amounts subject to section 4.02 of this revenue procedure paid to that employee for travel away from home within CONUS and/or OCONUS, as the case may be, during the calendar year. Similarly, an employee or self-employed individual that uses either (or both) of these special rates must use the special rate(s) for all amounts computed pursuant to

Appendix B

section 4.03 of this revenue procedure for travel away from home within CONUS and/or OCONUS, as the case may be, during the calendar year. See section 4.04(6) of this revenue procedure for transition rules.

(4) *Periodic rule.* A payor described in section 4.04(1) of this revenue procedure may compute the amount of the employee's expenses that is deemed substantiated under section 4.02 of this revenue procedure periodically (not less frequently than monthly), rather than daily, by comparing the total per diem allowance paid for the period to the sum of the amounts computed either at the federal M&IE rate(s) for the localities of travel, or at the special rate described in section 4.04(3), for the days (or partial days) the employee is away from home during the period.

(5) *Examples.*

(a) *Example 1.* Taxpayer, an employee in the transportation industry, travels away from home on business within CONUS on 17 days (including partial days) during a calendar month and receives a per diem allowance only for meal and incidental expenses from a payor that uses the special rule under section 4.04(3) of this revenue procedure. The amount deemed substantiated under section 4.02 of this revenue procedure is equal to the lesser of the total per diem allowance paid for the month or $884 (17 days at $52 per day).

(b) *Example 2.* Taxpayer, a truck driver employee in the transportation industry, is paid a "cents-per-mile" allowance that qualifies as an allowance paid under a flat rate or stated schedule as defined in section 3.03 of this revenue procedure. Taxpayer travels away from home on business for 10 days. Based on the number of miles driven by Taxpayer, Taxpayer's employer pays an allowance of $500 for the 10 days of business travel. Taxpayer actually drives for 8 days, and does not drive for the other 2 days Taxpayer is away from home. Taxpayer is paid under the periodic rule used for transportation industry employers and employees in accordance with section 4.04(4) of this revenue procedure. The amount deemed substantiated and excludable from Taxpayer's income is the full $500 because that amount does not exceed $520 (ten days away from home at $52 per day).

(6) *Transition rules.* Under the calendar-year convention provided in section 4.04(3), a taxpayer who used the federal M&IE rates during the first 9 months of calendar year 2007 to substantiate the amount of an individual's travel expenses under sections 4.02 or 4.03 of Rev. Proc. 2006-41 may not use, for that individual, the special transportation industry rates provided in this section 4.04 until January 1, 2008. Similarly, a taxpayer who used the special transportation industry rates during the first 9 months of calendar year 2007 to substantiate the

Appendix B

amount of an individual's travel expenses may not use, for that individual, the federal M&IE rates until January 1, 2008.

.05 Optional method for incidental expenses only deduction.

In lieu of using actual expenses in computing the amount allowable as a deduction for ordinary and necessary incidental expenses paid or incurred for travel away from home, employees and self-employed individuals who do not pay or incur meal expenses for a calendar day (or partial day) of travel away from home may use, for each calendar day (or partial day) the employee or self-employed individual is away from home, an amount computed at the rate of $3 per day for any CONUS or OCONUS locality of travel. This amount will be deemed substantiated for purposes of paragraphs (b)(2) and (c) of § 1.274-5, provided the employee or self-employed individual substantiates the elements of time, place, and business purpose of the travel for that day (or partial day) in accordance with those regulations. See section 4.03 of this revenue procedure for a method that may be used by employees or self-employed individuals who pay or incur meal expenses. The method authorized by this section 4.05 may not be used by payors that use section 4.01, 4.02, or 5.01 of this revenue procedure, or by employees or self-employed individuals who use the method described in section 4.03 of this revenue procedure. See section 6.05(4) of this revenue procedure for rules related to the application of the limitation under § 274(n) to amounts determined under this section 4.05.

SECTION 5. HIGH-LOW SUBSTANTIATION METHOD

.01 In general. If a payor pays a per diem allowance in lieu of reimbursing actual lodging, meal, and incidental expenses incurred or to be incurred by an employee for travel away from home and the payor uses the high-low substantiation method described in this section 5 for travel within CONUS, the amount of the expenses that is deemed substantiated for each calendar day is equal to the lesser of the per diem allowance for that day or the amount computed at the rate set forth in section 5.02 of this revenue procedure for the locality of travel for that day (or partial day, see section 6.04 of this revenue procedure). Except as provided in section 5.06 of this revenue procedure, this high-low substantiation method may be used in lieu of the per diem substantiation method provided in section 4.01 of this revenue procedure, but may not be used in lieu of the meal and incidental expenses only per diem substantiation method provided in section 4.02 of this revenue procedure.

.02 Specific high-low rates. Except as provided in section 5.06 of this revenue procedure, the per diem rate set forth in this section 5.02 is $237 for travel to any "high-cost locality" specified in section 5.03 of this revenue procedure, or $152 for travel to any other locality within CONUS. The high or low rate, as appropriate, applies as if it were the federal per diem rate for the locality of travel. For purposes of applying the high-low substantiation method and the § 274(n) limitation on meal expenses (see section 6.05(3) of this revenue procedure), the amount of the high and low rates that is treated as paid for meals is $58 for a high-cost locality and $45 for any other locality within CONUS.

Appendix B

.03 *High-cost localities.* The following localities have a federal per diem rate of $194 or more, and are high-cost localities for all of the calendar year or the portion of the calendar year specified in parentheses under the key city name:

Key city	*County or other defined location*

Arizona

Phoenix/Scottsdale	Maricopa
(January 1-March 31)	
Sedona	City Limits of Sedona
(March 31-April 30)	

California

Napa	Napa
Palm Springs	Riverside
(January 1-April 30)	
San Diego	San Diego
San Francisco	San Francisco
Santa Barbara	Santa Barbara
Santa Monica	City limits of Santa Monica
South Lake Tahoe	El Dorado
(December 1-March 31)	
Yosemite National Park	Mariposa

Colorado

Aspen	Pitkin
(December 1-April 30)	
Crested Butte/Gunnison	Gunnison
(December 1-March 31)	
Silverthorne/Breckenridge	Summit
(December 1-March 31)	
Steamboat Springs	Routt
(December 1-February 29)	
Telluride	San Miguel
(October 1-March 31)	
Vail	Eagle

District of Columbia

| Washington D.C. (also the cities of Alexandria, Falls Church, and Fairfax, and the counties of Arlington and Fairfax, in Virginia; and the counties of Montgomery and Prince George's in Maryland) (See also Maryland and Virginia) | |

Florida

Fort Lauderdale	Broward
(October 1-April 30)	
Fort Walton Beach/Defuniak Springs	Okaloosa and Walton
(June 1-July 31)	
Key West	Monroe

Key city	County or other defined location
Miami (October 1-February 29)	Miami-Dade
Naples (February 1-March 31)	Collier
Palm Beach (January 1-March 31)	Boca Raton, Delray Beach, Jupiter, Palm Beach Gardens, Palm Beach, Palm Beach Shores, Singer Island and West Palm Beach
Stuart (February 1-March 31)	Martin

Illinois

Chicago	Cook and Lake

Maryland

(For the counties of Montgomery and Prince George's, see District of Columbia)

Baltimore City	Baltimore
Cambridge/St. Michaels (April 1-August 31)	Dorchester and Talbot
Ocean City (June 1-August 31)	Worcester

Massachusetts

Boston/Cambridge	Suffolk, City of Cambridge
Martha's Vineyard (July 1-August 31)	Dukes
Nantucket	Nantucket

Nevada

Incline Village/Crystal Bay/Reno/Sparks (June 1-August 31)	Washoe

New Hampshire

Conway (July 1-August 31)	Caroll

New York

Floral Park/Garden City/Glen Cove/Great Neck/Roslyn	Nassau
Manhattan	The Boroughs of Manhattan, Brooklyn, the Bronx and Staten Island
Queens	Queens
Saratoga Springs/Schenectady (July 1-August 31)	Saratoga and Schenectady
Tarrytown/White Plains/New Rochelle/ Yonkers	Westchester

Appendix B

Key city	County or other defined location
Pennsylvania	
Philadelphia	Philadelphia
Rhode Island	
Jamestown/Middletown/Newport	Newport
(October 1-November 30 and February 1-September 30)	
Providence	Providence
Utah	
Park City	Summit
(January 1-March 31)	
Virginia	
(For the cities of Alexandria, Falls Church, and Fairfax, and the counties of Arlington and Fairfax, see District of Columbia)	
Loudon County	Loudon
Virginia Beach	City of Virginia Beach
(June 1-August 31)	
Washington	
Seattle	King
Wisconsin	
Lake Geneva	Walworth
(June 1-September 30)	

.04 *Changes to high-cost localities.* The list of high-cost localities in section 5.03 of this revenue procedure differs from the list of high-cost localities in section 5.03 of Rev. Proc. 2006-41 (changes listed by key cities).

(1) The following localities have been added to the list of high-cost localities: Sedona, Arizona; Napa, California; Palm Springs, California; San Diego, California; Yosemite National Park, California; Silverthorne/ Breckenridge, Colorado; Incline Village/Crystal Bay/Reno/Sparks, Nevada; Conway, New Hampshire; Tarrytown/White Plains/New Rochelle/Yonkers, New York; Loudon County, Virginia; Virginia Beach, Virginia; and Lake Geneva, Wisconsin.

(2) The portion of the year for which the following are high-cost localities has been changed: Santa Barbara, California; Crested Butte/Gunnison, Colorado; Steamboat Springs, Colorado; Telluride, Colorado; Vail, Colorado; Fort Lauderdale, Florida; Miami, Florida; Palm Beach, Florida; Cambridge/St. Michaels, Maryland; Ocean City, Maryland; Nantucket, Massachusetts; Jamestown/Middletown/Newport, Rhode Island; and Park City, Utah..

(3) The following localities have been removed from the list of high-cost localities: New Orleans, Louisiana and Lake Placid, New York.

Appendix B

.05 Specific limitation.

    (1) Except as provided in section 5.05(2) of this revenue procedure, a payor that uses the high-low substantiation method with respect to an employee must use that method for all amounts paid to that employee for travel away from home within CONUS during the calendar year. See section 5.06 of this revenue procedure for transition rules.

    (2) With respect to an employee described in section 5.05(1) of this revenue procedure, the payor may reimburse actual expenses or use the meal and incidental expenses only per diem substantiation method described in section 4.02 of this revenue procedure for any travel away from home, and may use the per diem substantiation method described in section 4.01 of this revenue procedure for any OCONUS travel away from home.

.06 Transition rules. A payor who used the substantiation method of section 4.01 of Rev. Proc. 2006-41 for an employee during the first 9 months of calendar year 2007 may not use the high-low substantiation method in section 5 of this revenue procedure for that employee until January 1, 2008. A payor who used the high-low substantiation method of section 5 of Rev. Proc. 2006-41 for an employee during the first 9 months of calendar year 2007 must continue to use the high-low substantiation method for the remainder of calendar year 2007 for that employee. A payor described in the previous sentence may use the rates and high-cost localities published in section 5 of Rev. Proc. 2006-41, in lieu of the updated rates and high-cost localities provided in section 5 of this revenue procedure, for travel on or after October 1, 2007, and before January 1, 2008, if those rates and localities are used consistently during this period for all employees reimbursed under this method.

SECTION 6. LIMITATIONS AND SPECIAL RULES

.01 In general. The federal per diem rate and the federal M&E rate described in section 3.02 of this revenue procedure for the locality of travel will be applied in the same manner as applied under the Federal Travel Regulations, 41 C.F.R. Part 301-11 (2007), except as provided in sections 6.02 through 6.04 of this revenue procedure.

.02 Federal per diem rate. A receipt for lodging expenses is not required in determining the amount of expenses deemed substantiated under section 4.01 or 5.01 of this revenue procedure. See section 7.01 of this revenue procedure for the requirement that the employee substantiate the time, place, and business purpose of the expense.

.03 Federal per diem or M&IE rate. A payor is not required to reduce the federal per diem rate or the federal M&IE rate for the locality of travel for meals provided in kind, provided the payor has a reasonable belief that meal and incidental expenses were or will be incurred by the employee during each day of travel.

.04 Proration of the federal per diem or M&IE rate. Pursuant to the Federal Travel Regulations, in determining the federal per diem rate or the federal M&E rate for

the locality of travel, the full applicable federal M&IE rate is available for a full day of travel from 12:01 a.m. to 12:00 midnight. The method described in section 6.04(1) of this revenue procedure must be used for purposes of determining the amount deemed substantiated under section 4.03 or 4.05 of this revenue procedure for partial days of travel away from home. For purposes of determining the amount deemed substantiated under section 4.01, 4.02, 4.04, or 5 of this revenue procedure for partial days of travel away from home, either of the following methods may be used to prorate the federal M&E rate to determine the federal per diem rate or the federal M&E rate for the partial days of travel:

(1) The rate may be prorated using the method prescribed by the Federal Travel Regulations. Currently the Federal Travel Regulations allow three-fourths of the applicable federal M&IE rate for each partial day during which the employee or self-employed individual is traveling away from home in connection with the performance of services as an employee or self-employed individual. The same ratio may be applied to prorate the allowance for incidental expenses described in section 4.05 of this revenue procedure; or

(2) The rate may be prorated using any method that is consistently applied and in accordance with reasonable business practice. For example, if an employee travels away from home from 9 a.m. one day to 5 p.m. the next day, a method of proration that results in an amount equal to two times the federal M&IE rate will be treated as being in accordance with reasonable business practice (even though only one and a half times the federal M&IE rate would be allowed under the Federal Travel Regulations).

.05 *Application of the appropriate § 274(n) limitation on meal expenses.* Except as provided in section 6.05(4), all or part of the amount of an expense deemed substantiated under this revenue procedure is subject to the appropriate limitation under § 274(n) (see section 2.02 of this revenue procedure) on the deductibility of food and beverage expenses.

(1) If an amount for meal and incidental expenses is computed pursuant to section 4.03 of this revenue procedure, the taxpayer must treat that amount as an expense for food and beverages.

(2) If a per diem allowance is paid only for meal and incidental expenses, the payor must treat an amount equal to the lesser of the allowance or the federal M&IE rate for the locality of travel for each day (or partial day, see section 6.04 of this revenue procedure) as an expense for food and beverages.

(3) If a per diem allowance is paid for lodging, meal, and incidental expenses for each calendar day (or partial day) the employee is away from home at a rate equal to or in excess of the federal per diem rate for the locality of travel, the payor must treat an amount equal to the federal M&IE rate for the locality of travel for each calendar day (or partial day) as an expense for food or beverages.

Appendix B

(4) If a per diem allowance is paid for lodging, meal, and incidental expenses for each calendar day (or partial day) the employee is away from home at a rate less than the federal per diem rate for the locality of travel, the payor must:

(a) treat an amount equal to the federal M&IE rate for the locality of travel for each calendar day (or partial day) or, if less, the amount of the allowance, as an expense for food or beverages; or

(b) treat an amount equal to 40 percent of the allowance as an expense for food or beverages.

(5) If an amount for incidental expenses is computed under section 4.05 of this revenue procedure, none of the amount so computed is subject to limitation under § 274(n) on the deductibility of food and beverage expenses.

.06 *No double reimbursement or deduction.* If a payor pays a per diem allowance in lieu of reimbursing actual lodging, meal, and incidental expenses, or meal and incidental expenses, in accordance with section 4 or 5 of this revenue procedure, and such amounts are treated as paid under an accountable plan, any additional payment with respect to those expenses is treated as paid under a nonaccountable plan, is included in the employee's gross income, is reported as wages or other compensation on the employee's Form W-2, and is subject to withholding and payment of employment taxes. Similarly, if an employee or self-employed individual computes the amount allowable as a deduction for meal and incidental expenses for travel away from home in accordance with section 4.03 or 4.04 of this revenue procedure, no other deduction is allowed to the employee or self-employed individual with respect to those expenses. For example, assume an employee receives a per diem allowance from a payor for lodging, meal, and incidental expenses, or for meal and incidental expenses, incurred while traveling away from home and such amounts are treated as paid under an accountable plan. During that trip, the employee pays for dinner for the employee and two business associates. The payor reimburses as a business entertainment meal expense the meal expense for the employee and the two business associates. Because the payor also pays a per diem allowance to cover the cost of the employee's meals, the amount paid by the payor for the employee's portion of the business entertainment meal expense is treated as paid under a nonaccountable plan, is reported as wages or other compensation on the employee's Form W-2, and is subject to withholding and payment of employment taxes.

.07 *Related parties.* Sections 4.01 and 5 of this revenue procedure do not apply if a payor and an employee are related within the meaning of §267(b), but for this purpose the percentage of ownership interest referred to in §267(b)(2) is 10 percent.

SECTION 7. APPLICATION

.01 If the amount of travel expenses is deemed substantiated under the rules provided in section 4 or 5 of this revenue procedure, and the employee substantiates to the payor the elements of time, place, and business purpose of the travel for that day (or partial day) in accordance with paragraphs (b)(2) and (c) (other than subparagraph (2)(iii)(A) thereof) of §1.274-5, the employee is deemed to satisfy the adequate accounting requirements of §1.274-5(f) as well as the requirement to substantiate by adequate records or other sufficient evidence for purposes of §1.274- 5(c). See §1.62-2(e)(1) for the rule that an arrangement must require business expenses to be substantiated to the payor within a reasonable period of time.

.02 An arrangement providing per diem allowances will be treated as satisfying the requirement of §1.62-2(f)(2) of returning amounts in excess of expenses if the employee is required to return within a reasonable period of time (as defined in §1.62-2(g)) any portion of the allowance that relates to days of travel not substantiated, even though the arrangement does not require the employee to return the portion of the allowance that relates to days of travel substantiated and that exceeds the amount of the employee's expenses deemed substantiated. For example, assume a payor provides an employee an advance per diem allowance for meal and incidental expenses of $250, based on an anticipated 5 days of business travel at $50 per day to a locality for which the federal M&IE rate is $39, and the employee substantiates 3 full days of business travel. The requirement to return excess amounts will be treated as satisfied if the employee is required to return within a reasonable period of time (as defined in §1.62-2(g)) the portion of the allowance that is attributable to the 2 unsubstantiated days of travel ($100), even though the employee is not required to return the portion of the allowance ($33) that exceeds the amount of the employee's expenses deemed substantiated under section 4.02 of this revenue procedure ($117) for the 3 substantiated days of travel. However, the $33 excess portion of the allowance is treated as paid under a nonaccountable plan as discussed in section 7.04 of this revenue procedure.

.03 An employee is not required to include in gross income the portion of a per diem allowance received from a payor that is less than or equal to the amount deemed substantiated under the rules provided in section 4 or 5 of this revenue procedure if the employee substantiates the business travel expenses covered by the per diem allowance in accordance with section 7.01 of this revenue procedure. See §1.274-5(f)(2)(i). In addition, that portion of the allowance is treated as paid under an accountable plan, is not reported as wages or other compensation on the employee's Form W-2, and is exempt from the withholding and payment of employment taxes. See §1.62-2(c)(2) and (c)(4).

.04 An employee is required to include in gross income only the portion of the per diem allowance received from a payor that exceeds the amount deemed substantiated under the rules provided in section 4 or 5 of this revenue procedure if the employee substantiates the business travel expenses covered by the per diem allowance in accordance with section 7.01 of this revenue procedure. See §1.274-5(f)(2)(ii). In addition, the excess portion of the allowance is treated as paid under a nonaccountable plan, is reported as wages or other compensation on the employee's Form W-2, and is subject to withholding and payment of employment taxes. See §1.62- 2(c)(3)(ii), (c)(5), and (h)(2)(i)(B).

Appendix B

.05 If the amount of the expenses that is deemed substantiated under the rules provided in section 4.01, 4.02, or 5 of this revenue procedure is less than the amount of the employee's business expenses for travel away from home, the employee may claim an itemized deduction for the amount by which the business travel expenses exceed the amount that is deemed substantiated, provided the employee substantiates all the business travel expenses, includes on Form 2106, "Employee Business Expenses," the deemed substantiated portion of the per diem allowance received from the payor, and includes in gross income the portion (if any) of the per diem allowance received from the payor that exceeds the amount deemed substantiated. See § 1.274-5(f)(2)(iii). However, for purposes of claiming this itemized deduction with respect to meal and incidental expenses, substantiation of the amount of the expenses is not required if the employee is claiming a deduction that is equal to or less than the amount computed under section 4.03 of this revenue procedure minus the amount deemed substantiated under sections 4.02 and 7.01 of this revenue procedure. The itemized deduction is subject to the appropriate limitation (see section 2.02 of this revenue procedure) on meal and entertainment expenses provided in § 274(n) and the 2-percent floor on miscellaneous itemized deductions provided in § 67.

.06 An employee who pays or incurs amounts for meal expenses and does not receive a per diem allowance for meal and incidental expenses may deduct an amount computed pursuant to section 4.03 of this revenue procedure only as an itemized deduction. This itemized deduction is subject to the appropriate limitation on meal and entertainment expenses provided in § 274(n) and the 2-percent floor on miscellaneous itemized deductions provided in § 67. See section 7.07 of this revenue procedure for the treatment of an employee who does not pay or incur amounts for meal expenses and does not receive a per diem allowance for incidental expenses.

.07 An employee who does not pay or incur amounts for meal expenses and does not receive a per diem allowance for incidental expenses may deduct an amount computed pursuant to section 4.05 of this revenue procedure only as an itemized deduction. This itemized deduction is subject to the 2-percent floor on miscellaneous itemized deductions provided in § 67. See section 7.06 of this revenue procedure for the treatment of an employee who pays or incurs amounts for meal expenses and does not receive a per diem allowance for meal and incidental expenses.

.08 A self-employed individual who pays or incurs meal expenses for a calendar day (or partial day) of travel away from home may deduct an amount computed pursuant to section 4.03 of this revenue procedure in determining adjusted gross income under § 62(a)(1). This deduction is subject to the appropriate limitation on meal and entertainment expenses provided in § 274(n).

.09 A self-employed individual who does not pay or incur meal expenses for a calendar day (or partial day) of travel away from home may deduct an amount computed pursuant to section 4.05 of this revenue procedure in determining adjusted gross income under § 62(a)(1).

Appendix B

.10 If a payor's reimbursement or other expense allowance arrangement evidences a pattern of abuse of the rules of § 62(c) and the regulations thereunder, all payments under the arrangement will be treated as made under a nonaccountable plan. See § 1.62- 2(k) and Rev. Rul. 2006-56. Thus, these payments are included in the employee's gross income, are reported as wages or other compensation on the employee's Form W-2, and are subject to withholding and payment of employment taxes. See § 1.62-2(c)(3), (c)(5), and (h)(2), and section 8/06 of this revenue procedure.

SECTION 8. WITHHOLDING AND PAYMENT OF EMPLOYMENT TAXES

.01 The portion of a per diem allowance, if any, that relates to the days of business travel substantiated and that exceeds the amount deemed substantiated for those days under section 4.01, 4.02, or 5 of this revenue procedure is subject to withholding and payment of employment taxes. See § 1.62-2(h)(2)(i)(B).

.02 In the case of a per diem allowance paid as a reimbursement, the excess described in section 8.01 of this revenue procedure is subject to withholding and payment of employment taxes in the payroll period in which the payor reimburses the expenses for the days of travel substantiated. See § 1.62-2(h)(2)(i)(B)(2).

.03 In the case of a per diem allowance paid as an advance, the excess described in section 8.01 of this revenue procedure is subject to withholding and payment of employment taxes no later than the first payroll period following the payroll period in which the days of travel with respect to which the advance was paid are substantiated. See § 1.62-2(h)(2)(i)(B)(3). If some or all of the days of travel with respect to which the advance was paid are not substantiated within a reasonable period of time and the employee does not return the portion of the allowance that relates to those days within a reasonable period of time, the portion of the allowance that relates to those days is subject to withholding and payment of employment taxes no later than the first payroll period following the end of the reasonable period. See § 1.62-2(h)(2)(i)(A).

.04 In the case of a per diem allowance only for meal and incidental expenses for travel away from home paid to an employee in the transportation industry by a payor that uses the rule in section 4.04(4) of this revenue procedure, the excess of the per diem allowance paid for the period over the amount deemed substantiated for the period under section 4.02 of this revenue procedure (after applying section 4.04(4) of this revenue procedure), is subject to withholding and payment of employment taxes no later than the first payroll period following the payroll period in which the excess is computed. See § 1.62-2(h)(2)(i)(B)(4).

.05 For example, assume that an employer pays an employee a per diem allowance to cover business expenses for meals and lodging for travel away from home at a rate of 120 percent of the federal per diem rate for the localities to which the employee travels. The employer does not require the employee to return the 20 percent by which the reimbursement for those expenses exceeds the federal per diem rate. The employee substantiates 6 days of travel away from home: 2 days in a locality in which the federal per diem rate is $160 and 4 days in a locality in which the federal per diem rate is $120. The employer reimburses the employee $960 for the 6 days of travel away from home (2 × (120% × $160) + 4 × (120% × $120)), and does not require the employee to return the excess payment of $160 (2 days × $32 ($192-$160) + 4 days × $24 ($144-$120)). For the payroll period in which the employer reimburses the expenses, the employer must withhold and pay employment taxes on $160. See section 8.02 of this revenue procedure.

.06 If a per diem allowance arrangement has no mechanism or process to determine when an allowance exceeds the amount that may be deemed substantiated and the arrangement routinely pays allowances in excess of the amount that may be deemed substantiated without requiring actual substantiation of all the expenses or repayment of the excess amount, the failure of the arrangement to treat the excess allowances as wages for employment tax purposes causes all payments made under the arrangement to be treated as made under a nonaccountable plan. See Rev. Rul. 2006-56.

SECTION 9. EFFECTIVE DATE

This revenue procedure is effective for per diem allowances for lodging, meal and incidental expenses, or for meal and incidental expenses only, that are paid to an employee on or after October 1, 2007, with respect to travel away from home on or after October 1, 2007. For purposes of computing the amount allowable as a deduction for travel away from home, this revenue procedure is effective for meal and incidental expenses or for incidental expenses only paid or incurred on or after October 1, 2007.

SECTION 10. EFFECT ON OTHER DOCUMENTS

Rev. Proc. 2006-41 is superseded.

6.0 Corporate Tax Rates

Most corporations figure their tax by using the following tax rate schedule.

Tax Rate Schedule

| If taxable income is: | | | |
Over—	But not over—	Tax is:	Of the amount over—
$0	50,000	15%	-0-
50,000	75,000	$ 7,500 + 25%	$50,000
75,000	100,000	13,750 + 34%	75,000
100,000	335,000	22,250 + 39%	100,000
335,000	10,000,000	113,900 + 34%	335,000
10,000,000	15,000,000	3,400,000 + 35%	10,000,000

Appendix B

Over—	But not over—	Tax is:	Of the amount over—
15,000,000	18,333,333	**5,150,000 + 38%**	15,000,000
18,333,333	—	**35%**	-0-

Qualified personal service corporation. A qualified personal service corporation is taxed at a flat rate of 35% on taxable income. A corporation is a qualified personal service corporation if it meets both of the following tests.

- Substantially all the corporation's activities involve the performance of personal services (as defined earlier under *Personal services*).
- At least 95% of the corporation's stock, by value, is owned, directly or indirectly, by any of the following.
  - Employees performing the personal services.
  - Retired employees who had performed the personal services.
  - An estate of the employee or retiree described above.
  - Any person who acquired the stock of the corporation as a result of the death of an employee or retiree (but only for the 2-year period beginning on the date of the employee's or retiree's death).

7.0 Split-Dollar Insurance (Table 2001)

**Interim Table of One-Year Term Premiums
for $1,000 of Life Insurance Protection**

Attained Age	Section 79 Extended and Interpolated Annual Rates	Attained Age	Section 79 Extended and Interpolated Annual Rates	Attained Age	Section 79 Extended and Interpolated Annual Rates
0	$0.70	20	$0.62	40	$ 1.10
1	$0.41	21	$0.62	41	$ 1.13
2	$0.27	22	$0.64	42	$ 1.20
3	$0.19	23	$0.66	43	$ 1.29
4	$0.13	24	$0.68	44	$ 1.40
5	$0.13	25	$0.71	45	$ 1.53
6	$0.14	26	$0.73	46	$ 1.67
7	$0.15	27	$0.76	47	$ 1.83
8	$0.16	28	$0.80	48	$ 1.98
9	$0.16	29	$0.83	49	$ 2.13
10	$0.16	30	$0.87	50	$ 2.30
11	$0.19	31	$0.90	51	$ 2.52
12	$0.24	32	$0.93	52	$ 2.81
13	$0.28	33	$0.96	53	$ 3.20
14	$0.33	34	$0.98	54	$ 3.65
15	$0.38	35	$ 0.99	55	$ 4.15
16	$0.52	36	$ 1.01	56	$ 4.68
17	$0.57	37	$ 1.04	57	$ 5.20
18	$0.59	38	$ 1.06	58	$ 5.66
19	$0.61	39	$ 1.07	59	$ 6.06

Attained Age	Section 79 Extended and Interpolated Annual Rates	Attained Age	Section 79 Extended and Interpolated Annual Rates	Attained Age	Section 79 Extended and Interpolated Annual Rates
60	$ 6.51	73	$ 27.57	86	$ 99.16
61	$ 7.11	74	$ 30.18	87	$110.40
62	$ 7.96	75	$ 33.05	88	$121.85
63	$ 9.08	76	$ 36.33	89	$133.40
64	$10.41	77	$ 40.17	90	$144.30
65	$11.90	78	$ 44.33	91	$155.80
66	$13.51	79	$ 49.23	92	$168.75
67	$15.20	80	$ 54.56	93	$186.44
68	$16.92	81	$ 60.51	94	$206.70
69	$18.70	82	$ 66.74	95	$228.35
70	$ 20.62	83	$ 73.07	96	$250.01
71	$ 22.72	84	$ 80.35	97	$265.09
72	$ 25.07	85	$ 88.76	98	$270.11
				99	$281.05

8.0 Standard Mileage Rates for Automobiles in 2007

Rev. Proc. 2006-49, 2006-47 IRB

SECTION 1. PURPOSE

This revenue procedure updates Rev. Proc. 2005-78, 2005-2 C.B. 1177, and provides optional standard mileage rates for employees, self-employed individuals, or other taxpayers to use in computing the deductible costs of operating an automobile for business, charitable, medical, or moving expense purposes. This revenue procedure also provides rules under which the amount of ordinary and necessary expenses of local travel or transportation away from home that are paid or incurred by an employee are deemed substantiated under § 1.274-5 of the Income Tax Regulations if a payor (the employer, its agent, or a third party) provides a mileage allowance under a reimbursement or other expense allowance arrangement to pay for the expenses. Use of a method of substantiation described in this revenue procedure is not mandatory and a taxpayer may use actual allowable expenses if the taxpayer maintains adequate records or other sufficient evidence for proper substantiation. The Internal Revenue Service prospectively adjusts the business and medical and moving standard mileage rates annually (to the extent warranted).

SECTION 2. SUMMARY OF STANDARD MILEAGE RATES

.01 *Standard mileage rates.*

    (1) Business (section 5 below) 48.5 cents per mile

    (2) Charitable contribution (section 7 below) 14 cents per mile

    (3) Medical and moving (section 7 below) 20 cents per mile

.02 *Determination of standard mileage rates.* The business and medical and moving standard mileage rates reflected in this revenue procedure are based on an annual study of the fixed and variable costs of operating an automobile conducted on behalf of the Service by an independent contractor. The charitable contribution standard mileage rate is provided in § 170(i) of the Internal Revenue Code.

SECTION 3. BACKGROUND AND CHANGES

.01 Section 162(a) allows a deduction for all the ordinary and necessary expenses paid or incurred during the taxable year in carrying on any trade or business. Under that provision, an employee or self-employed individual may deduct the cost of operating an automobile to the extent that it is used in a trade or business. However, under § 262, no portion of the cost of operating an automobile that is attributable to personal use is deductible.

.02 Section 274(d) provides, in part, that no deduction is allowed under § 162 with respect to any listed property (as defined in § 280F(d)(4) to include passenger automobiles and any other property used as a means of transportation) unless the taxpayer complies with certain substantiation requirements. Section 274(d) further provides that regulations may prescribe that some or all of the substantiation requirements do not apply to an expense that does not exceed an amount prescribed by the regulations.

.03 Section 1.274-5(j), in part, grants the Commissioner of Internal Revenue the authority to establish a method under which a taxpayer may use mileage rates to substantiate, for purposes of § 274(d), the amount of the ordinary and necessary expenses of using a vehicle for local transportation and transportation to, from, and at the destination while traveling away from home.

.04 Section 1.274-5(g), in part, grants the Commissioner the authority to prescribe rules relating to mileage allowances for ordinary and necessary expenses of using a vehicle for local transportation and transportation to, from, and at the destination while traveling away from home. Pursuant to this grant of authority, the Commissioner may prescribe rules under which the allowances, if in accordance with reasonable business practice, will be regarded as (1) equivalent to substantiation, by adequate records or other sufficient evidence, of the amount of the travel and transportation expenses for purposes of § 1.274-5(c), and (2) satisfying the requirements of an adequate accounting to the employer of the amount of the expenses for purposes of § 1.274-5(f).

.05 Section 62(a)(2)(A) allows an employee, in determining adjusted gross income, a deduction for the expenses allowed by Part VI (§ 161 and following), subchapter B, chapter 1 of the Code, paid or incurred by the employee in connection with the performance of services as an employee under a reimbursement or other expense allowance arrangement with a payor.

.06 Section 62(c) provides that an arrangement will not be treated as a reimbursement or other expense allowance arrangement for purposes of § 62(a)(2)(A) if it—

    (1) does not require the employee to substantiate the expenses covered by the arrangement to the payor, or

(2) provides the employee with the right to retain any amount in excess of the substantiated expenses covered under the arrangement.

Section 62(c) further provides that the substantiation requirements described therein do not apply to any expense to the extent that, under the grant of regulatory authority in §274(d), the Commissioner has provided that substantiation is not required for the expense.

.07 Under §1.62-2(c)(1), a reimbursement or other expense allowance arrangement satisfies the requirements of §62(c) if it meets the requirements of business connection, substantiation, and returning amounts in excess of expenses as specified in the regulations. Section 1.62-2(e)(2) specifically provides that substantiation of certain business expenses in accordance with rules prescribed under the authority of §1.274-5(g) will be treated as substantiation of the amount of the expenses for purposes of §1.62-2. Under §1.62-2(f)(2), the Commissioner may prescribe rules under which an arrangement providing mileage allowances will be treated as satisfying the requirement of returning amounts in excess of expenses, even though the arrangement does not require the employee to return the portion of the allowance that relates to miles of travel substantiated and that exceeds the amount of the employee's expenses deemed substantiated pursuant to rules prescribed under §274(d), provided the allowance is reasonably calculated not to exceed the amount of the employee's expenses or anticipated expenses and the employee is required to return any portion of the allowance that relates to miles of travel not substantiated.

.08 Section 1.62-2(h)(2)(i)(B) provides that if a payor pays a mileage allowance under an arrangement that meets the requirements of §1.62-2(c)(1), the portion, if any, of the allowance that relates to miles of travel substantiated in accordance with §1.62-2(e), that exceeds the amount of the employee's expenses deemed substantiated for the travel pursuant to rules prescribed under §274(d) and §1.274-5(g), and that the employee is not required to return, is subject to withholding and payment of employment taxes. See §§31.3121(a)-3, 31.3231(e)-1(a)(5), 31.3306(b)- 2, and 31.3401(a)-4 of the Employment Tax Regulations. Because the employee is not required to return this excess portion, the reasonable period of time provisions of §1.62-2(g) (relating to the return of excess amounts) do not apply to this excess portion.

.09 Under §1.62-2(h)(2)(i)(B)(4), the Commissioner may provide special rules regarding the timing of withholding and payment of employment taxes on mileage allowances.

.10 Section 303 of the Katrina Emergency Tax Relief Act of 2005, Pub. L. No. 109-73, 119 Stat. 2016 (KETRA) provides a special standard mileage rate for purposes of computing the amount allowable as a charitable contribution deduction for the cost of operating an automobile for the provision of relief related to Hurricane Katrina during the period beginning on August 25, 2005, and ending on December 31, 2006. Section 304 of KETRA provides that taxpayers may exclude from income amounts received from a charity as reimbursement for the cost of operating an automobile for the provision of relief related to Hurricane Katrina during the period beginning on August 25, 2005, and ending on Decem-

Appendix B

ber 31, 2006. Because these provisions expire after December 31, 2006, sections 2.01 and 7.01 of this revenue procedure are revised to remove these special charitable contribution standard mileage rates for 2007.

SECTION 4. DEFINITIONS

.01 *Standard mileage rate.* The term "standard mileage rate" means the applicable amount provided by the Service for optional use by employees or self-employed individuals in computing the deductible costs of operating automobiles (including vans, pickups, or panel trucks) they own or lease for business purposes, or by taxpayers in computing the deductible costs of operating automobiles for charitable, medical, or moving expense purposes.

.02 *Transportation expenses.* The term "transportation expenses" means the expenses of operating an automobile for local travel or transportation away from home.

.03 *Mileage allowance.* The term "mileage allowance" means a payment under a reimbursement or other expense allowance arrangement that is:

(1) paid with respect to the ordinary and necessary business expenses incurred, or that the payor reasonably anticipates will be incurred, by an employee for transportation expenses in connection with the performance of services as an employee of the employer,

(2) reasonably calculated not to exceed the amount of the expenses or the anticipated expenses, and

(3) paid at the applicable standard mileage rate, a flat rate or stated schedule, or in accordance with any other Service-specified rate or schedule.

.04 *Flat rate or stated schedule.* A mileage allowance is paid at a flat rate or stated schedule if it is provided on a uniform and objective basis with respect to the expenses described in section 4.03 of this revenue procedure. The allowance may be paid periodically at a fixed rate, at a cents-per-mile rate, at a variable rate based on a stated schedule, at a rate that combines any of these rates, or on any other basis that is consistently applied and in accordance with reasonable business practice. Thus, for example, a periodic payment at a fixed rate to cover the fixed costs (including depreciation (or lease payments), insurance, registration and license fees, and personal property taxes) of driving an automobile in connection with the performance of services as an employee of the employer, coupled with a periodic payment at a cents-per-mile rate to cover the variable costs (including gasoline and all taxes thereon, oil, tires, and routine maintenance and repairs) of using an automobile for those purposes, is an allowance paid at a flat rate or stated schedule. Likewise, a periodic payment at a variable rate based on a stated schedule for different locales to cover the costs of driving an automobile in connection with the performance of services as an employee is an allowance paid at a flat rate or stated schedule.

SECTION 5. BUSINESS STANDARD MILEAGE RATE

.01 *In general.* The standard mileage rate for transportation expenses is 48.5 cents per mile for all miles of use for business purposes.

.02 *Use of the business standard mileage rate.* A taxpayer may use the business standard mileage rate with respect to an automobile that is either owned or leased by the taxpayer. A taxpayer generally may deduct an amount equal to either the business standard mileage rate times the number of business miles traveled or the actual costs (both operating and fixed) paid or incurred by the taxpayer that are allocable to traveling those business miles.

.03 *Business standard mileage rate in lieu of operating and fixed costs.* A deduction using the standard mileage rate for business miles is computed on a yearly basis and is in lieu of all operating and fixed costs of the automobile allocable to business purposes (except as provided in section 9.06 of this revenue procedure). Items such as depreciation (or lease payments), maintenance and repairs, tires, gasoline (including all taxes thereon), oil, insurance, and license and registration fees are included in operating and fixed costs for this purpose.

.04 *Parking fees, tolls, interest, and taxes.* Parking fees and tolls attributable to use of the automobile for business purposes may be deducted as separate items. Likewise, interest relating to the purchase of the automobile as well as state and local personal property taxes may be deducted as separate items, but only to the extent allowable under § 163 or § 164, respectively. Section 163(h)(2)(A) expressly provides that interest is nondeductible personal interest if it is paid or accrued on indebtedness properly allocable to the trade or business of performing services as an employee. Section 164 expressly provides that state and local taxes that are paid or accrued by a taxpayer in connection with an acquisition or disposition of property will be treated as part of the cost of the acquired property or as a reduction in the amount realized on the disposition of the property. If the automobile is operated less than 100 percent for business purposes, an allocation is required to determine the business and nonbusiness portion of the taxes and interest deduction allowable.

.05 *Depreciation.* For owned automobiles placed in service for business purposes, and for which the business standard mileage rate has been used for any year, depreciation will be considered to have been allowed at the rate of 16 cents per mile for 2003 and 2004, and 17 cents per mile for 2005 and 2006, and 19 cents per mile for 2007, for those years in which the business standard mileage rate was used. If actual costs were used for one or more of those years, the rates above do not apply to any year in which actual costs were used. The depreciation described above will reduce the basis of the automobile (but not below zero) in determining adjusted basis as required by § 1016.

.06 *Limitations.*

   (1) The business standard mileage rate may not be used to compute the deductible expenses of (a) automobiles used for hire, such as taxicabs, or (b) five or more automobiles owned or leased by a taxpayer and used simultaneously (such as in fleet operations).

Appendix B

(2) The business standard mileage rate may not be used to compute the deductible business expenses of an automobile leased by a taxpayer unless the taxpayer uses either the business standard mileage rate or a FAVR allowance (as provided in section 8 of this revenue procedure) to compute the deductible business expenses of the automobile for the entire lease period (including renewals). For a lease commencing on or before December 31, 1997, the "entire lease period" means the portion of the lease period (including renewals) remaining after that date.

(3) The business standard mileage rate may not be used to compute the deductible expenses of an automobile for which the taxpayer has (a) claimed depreciation using a method other than straight-line for its estimated useful life, (b) claimed a § 179 deduction, (c) claimed the special depreciation allowance under § 168(k), or (d) used the Accelerated Cost Recovery System (ACRS) under former § 168 or the Modified Accelerated Cost Recovery System (MACRS) under current § 168. By using the business standard mileage rate, the taxpayer has elected to exclude the automobile (if owned) from MACRS pursuant to § 168(f)(1). If, after using the business standard mileage rate, the taxpayer uses actual costs, the taxpayer must use straight-line depreciation for the automobile's remaining estimated useful life (subject to the applicable depreciation deduction limitations under § 280F).

(4) The business standard mileage rate and this revenue procedure may not be used to compute the amount of the deductible automobile expenses of an employee of the United States Postal Service incurred in performing services involving the collection and delivery of mail on a rural route if the employee receives qualified reimbursements (as defined in § 162(o)) for the expenses. See § 162(o) for the rules that apply to these qualified reimbursements.

SECTION 6. RESERVED

SECTION 7. CHARITABLE, MEDICAL, AND MOVING STANDARD MILEAGE RATES

.01 *Charitable.* Section 170(i) provides a standard mileage rate of 14 cents per mile for purposes of computing the charitable contribution deduction for use of an automobile in connection with rendering gratuitous services to a charitable organization under § 170.

.02 *Medical and moving.* The standard mileage rate is 20 cents per mile for use of an automobile (1) to obtain medical care described in § 213, or (2) as part of a move for which the expenses are deductible under § 217.

.03 *or medical and moving standard mileage rates in lieu of variable expenses.* A deduction computed using the applicable standard mileage rate for charitable, medical, or moving expense miles is in lieu of all variable expenses (including gasoline and oil) of the automobile allocable to those purposes. Costs for items such as depreciation (or lease payments), insurance, and license and registration fees are not deductible, and are not included in the charitable or medical and moving standard mileage rates.

.04 Parking fees, tolls, interest, and taxes. Parking fees and tolls attributable to the use of the automobile for charitable, medical, or moving expense purposes may be deducted as separate items. Interest relating to the purchase of the automobile and state and local personal property taxes are not deductible as charitable, medical, or moving expenses, but they may be deducted as separate items to the extent allowable under § 163 or § 164, respectively.

SECTION 8. FIXED AND VARIABLE RATE ALLOWANCE

.01 In general

(1) The ordinary and necessary expenses paid or incurred by an employee in driving an automobile owned or leased by the employee in connection with the performance of services as an employee of the employer are deemed substantiated (in an amount determined under section 9 of this revenue procedure) when a payor reimburses those expenses with a mileage allowance using a flat rate or stated schedule that combines periodic fixed and variable rate payments that meet all the requirements of section 8 of this revenue procedure (a FAVR allowance).

(2) The amount of a FAVR allowance must be based on data that (a) is derived from the base locality, (b) reflects retail prices paid by consumers, and (c) is reasonable and statistically defensible in approximating the actual expenses employees receiving the allowance would incur as owners of the standard automobile.

.02 Computation of FAVR allowance.

(1) *FAVR allowance.* A FAVR allowance includes periodic fixed payments and periodic variable payments. A payor may maintain more than one FAVR allowance. A FAVR allowance that uses the same payor, standard automobile (or an automobile of the same make and model that is comparably equipped), retention period, and business use percentage is considered one FAVR allowance, even though other features of the allowance may vary. A FAVR allowance also includes any optional high mileage payments; however, optional high mileage payments are included in the employee's gross income, are reported as wages or other compensation on the employee's Form W-2, and are subject to withholding and payment of employment taxes when paid. *See* section 9.05 of this revenue procedure. An optional high mileage payment covers the additional depreciation for a standard automobile attributable to business miles driven and substantiated by the employee for a calendar year in excess of the annual business mileage for that year. If an employee is covered by the FAVR allowance for less than the entire calendar year, the annual business mileage may be prorated on a monthly basis for purposes of the preceding sentence.

(2) *Periodic fixed payment.* A periodic fixed payment covers the projected fixed costs (including depreciation (or lease payments), insurance, re-

gistration and license fees, and personal property taxes) of driving the standard automobile in connection with the performance of services as an employee of the employer in a base locality, and must be paid at least quarterly. A periodic fixed payment may be computed by (a) dividing the total projected fixed costs of the standard automobile for all years of the retention period, determined at the beginning of the retention period, by the number of periodic fixed payments in the retention period, and (b) multiplying the resulting amount by the business use percentage.

(3) *Periodic variable payment.* A periodic variable payment covers the projected operating costs (including gasoline and all taxes thereon, oil, tires, and routine maintenance and repairs) of driving a standard automobile in connection with the performance of services as an employee of the employer in a base locality, and must be paid at least quarterly. The rate of a periodic variable payment for a computation period may be computed by dividing the total projected operating costs for the standard automobile for the computation period, determined at the beginning of the computation period, by the computation period mileage. A computation period can be any period of a year or less. Computation period mileage is the total mileage (business and personal) a payor reasonably projects a standard automobile will be driven during a computation period and equals the retention mileage divided by the number of computation periods in the retention period. For each business mile substantiated by the employee for the computation period, the periodic variable payment must be paid at a rate that does not exceed the rate for that computation period.

(4) *Base locality.* A base locality is the particular geographic locality or region of the United States in which the costs of driving an automobile in connection with the performance of services as an employee of the employer are generally paid or incurred by the employee. Thus, for purposes of determining the amount of fixed costs, the base locality is generally the geographic locality or region in which the employee resides. For purposes of determining the amount of operating costs, the base locality is generally the geographic locality or region in which the employee drives the automobile in connection with the performance of services as an employee of the employer.

(5) *Standard automobile.* A standard automobile is the automobile selected by the payor on which a specific FAVR allowance is based.

(6) *Standard automobile cost.* The standard automobile cost for a calendar year may not exceed 95 percent of the sum of (a) the retail dealer invoice cost of the standard automobile in the base locality, and (b) state
- and local sales or use taxes applicable on the purchase of the automobile. Further, the standard automobile cost may not exceed $27,600.

(7) *Annual mileage.* Annual mileage is the total mileage (business and personal) a payor reasonably projects a standard automobile will be

driven during a calendar year. Annual mileage equals the annual business mileage divided by the business use percentage.

(8) *Annual business mileage.* Annual business mileage is the mileage a payor reasonably projects a standard automobile will be driven by an employee in connection with the performance of services as an employee of the employer during the calendar year, but may not be less than 6,250 miles for a calendar year. Annual business mileage equals the annual mileage multiplied by the business use percentage.

(9) *Business use percentage.* A business use percentage is determined by dividing the annual business mileage by the annual mileage. The business use percentage may not exceed 75 percent. In lieu of demonstrating the reasonableness of the business use percentage based on records of total mileage and business mileage driven by the employees annually, a payor may use a business use percentage that is less than or equal to the following percentages for a FAVR allowance that is paid for the following annual business mileage:

Annual business mileage	Business use percentage
6,250 or more but less than 10,000	45 percent
10,000 or more but less than 15,000	55 percent
15,000 or more but less than 20,000	65 percent
20,000 or more	75 percent

(10) *Retention period.* A retention period is the period in calendar years selected by the payor during which the payor expects an employee to drive a standard automobile in connection with the performance of services as an employee of the employer before the automobile is replaced. The period may not be less than two calendar years.

(11) *Retention mileage.* Retention mileage is the annual mileage multiplied by the number of calendar years in the retention period.

(12) *Residual value.* The residual value of a standard automobile is the projected amount for which it could be sold at the end of the retention period after being driven the retention mileage. The Service will accept the following safe harbor residual values for a standard automobile computed as a percentage of the standard automobile cost:

Retention period	Residual value
2-year	70 percent
3-year	60 percent
4-year	50 percent

.03 FAVR allowance in lieu of operating and fixed costs.

(1) A reimbursement computed using a FAVR allowance is in lieu of the employee's deduction of all the operating and fixed costs paid or incurred by an employee in driving the automobile in connection with the performance of services as an employee of the employer, except as provided in section 9.06 of this revenue procedure. Items such as

depreciation (or lease payments), maintenance and repairs, tires, gasoline (including all taxes thereon), oil, insurance, license and registration fees, and personal property taxes are included in operating and fixed costs for this purpose.

(2) Parking fees and tolls attributable to an employee driving the standard automobile in connection with the performance of services as an employee of the employer are not included in fixed and operating costs and may be deducted as separate items. Similarly, interest relating to the purchase of the standard automobile may be deducted as a separate item, but only to the extent that the interest is an allowable deduction under § 163.

.04 *Depreciation.*

(1) A FAVR allowance may not be paid with respect to an automobile for which the employee has (a) claimed depreciation using a method other than straight-line for its estimated useful life, (b) claimed a § 179 deduction, (c) claimed the special depreciation allowance under § 168(k), or (d) used ACRS under former § 168 or MACRS under current § 168. If an employee uses actual costs for an owned automobile that has been covered by a FAVR allowance, the employee must use straight-line depreciation for the automobile's remaining estimated useful life (subject to the applicable depreciation deduction limitations under § 280F).

(2) Except as provided in section 8.04(3) of this revenue procedure, the total amount of the depreciation component for the retention period taken into account in computing the periodic fixed payments for that retention period may not exceed the excess of the standard automobile cost over the residual value of the standard automobile. In addition, the total amount of the depreciation component may not exceed the sum of the annual § 280F limitations on depreciation (in effect at the beginning of the retention period) that apply to the standard automobile during the retention period.

(3) If the depreciation component of periodic fixed payments exceeds the limitations in section 8.04(2) of this revenue procedure, that section will be treated as satisfied in any year during which the total annual amount of the periodic fixed payments and the periodic variable payments made to an employee driving 80 percent of the annual business mileage of the standard automobile does not exceed the amount obtained by multiplying 80 percent of the annual business mileage of the standard automobile by the business standard mileage rate for that year (under section 5.01 of the applicable revenue procedure).

(4) The depreciation included in each periodic fixed payment portion of a FAVR allowance paid with respect to an automobile will reduce the basis of the automobile (but not below zero) in determining adjusted basis as required by § 1016. *See* section 8.07(2) of this revenue procedure for the requirement that the employer report the depreciation component of a periodic fixed payment to the employee.

Appendix B

.05 FAVR allowance limitations.

(1) A FAVR allowance may be paid only to an employee who substantiates to the payor for a calendar year at least 5,000 miles driven in connection with the performance of services as an employee of the employer or, if greater, 80 percent of the annual business mileage of that FAVR allowance. If the employee is covered by the FAVR allowance for less than the entire calendar year, these limits may be prorated on a monthly basis.

(2) A FAVR allowance may not be paid to a control employee (as defined in § 1.61-21(f)(5) and (6), excluding the $100,000 limitation in paragraph (f)(5)(iii)).

(3) An employer may not pay a FAVR allowance if at any time during a calendar year a majority of the employees covered by the FAVR allowance are management employees.

(4) An employer may not pay a FAVR allowance to any employee unless at all times during a calendar year at least five employees in total are covered by FAVR allowances provided by the employer.

(5) A FAVR allowance may be paid only with respect to an automobile (a) owned or leased by the employee receiving the payment, (b) the cost of which, as a new vehicle (whether or not purchased new by the employee), was at least 90 percent of the standard automobile cost taken into account for purposes of determining the FAVR allowance for the first calendar year the employee receives the allowance with respect to that automobile, and (c) the model year of which does not differ from the current calendar year by more than the number of years in the retention period.

(6) A FAVR allowance may not be paid with respect to an automobile leased by an employee for which the employee has used actual expenses to compute the deductible business expenses of the automobile for any year during the entire lease period. For a lease commencing on or before December 31, 1997, the "entire lease period" means the portion of the lease period (including renewals) remaining after that date.

(7) The insurance cost component of a FAVR allowance must be based on the rates charged in the base locality for insurance coverage on the standard automobile during the current calendar year without taking into account rate-increasing factors such as poor driving records or young drivers.

(8) A FAVR allowance may be paid only to an employee whose insurance coverage limits on the automobile with respect to which the FAVR allowance is paid are at least equal to the insurance coverage limits used to compute the periodic fixed payment under that FAVR allowance.

Appendix B

.06 *Employee reporting.* Within 30 days after an employee's automobile is initially covered by a FAVR allowance, or is again covered by a FAVR allowance if coverage has lapsed, the employee by written declaration must provide the payor with the following information: (a) the make, model, and year of the employee's automobile, (b) written proof of the insurance coverage limits on the automobile, (c) the odometer reading of the automobile, (d) if owned, the purchase price of the automobile or, if leased, the price at which the automobile is ordinarily sold by retailers (the gross capitalized cost of the automobile), and (e) if owned, whether the employee has claimed depreciation with respect to the automobile using any of the depreciation methods prohibited by section 8.04(1) of this revenue procedure or, if leased, whether the employee has computed deductible business expenses with respect to the automobile using actual expenses. The information described in (a), (b), and (c) of the preceding sentence also must be supplied by the employee to the payor within 30 days after the beginning of each calendar year that the employee's automobile is covered by a FAVR allowance.

.07 *Payor recordkeeping and reporting.*

(1) The payor or its agent must maintain written records setting forth (a) the statistical data and projections on which the FAVR allowance payments are based, and (b) the information provided by the employees pursuant to section 8.06 of this revenue procedure.

(2) Within 30 days of the end of each calendar year, the employer must provide each employee covered by a FAVR allowance during that year with a statement that, for automobile owners, lists the amount of depreciation included in each periodic fixed payment portion of the FAVR allowance paid during that calendar year and explains that by receiving a FAVR allowance the employee has elected to exclude the automobile from the Modified Accelerated Cost Recovery System pursuant to § 168(f)(1). For automobile lessees, the statement must explain that by receiving the FAVR allowance the employee may not compute the deductible business expenses of the automobile using actual expenses for the entire lease period (including renewals). For a lease commencing on or before December 31, 1997, the "entire lease period" means the portion of the lease period (including renewals) remaining after that date.

.08 *Failure to meet section 8 requirements.* If an employee receives a mileage allowance that fails to meet one or more of the requirements of section 8 of this revenue procedure, the employee may not be treated as covered by any FAVR allowance of the payor during the period of the failure. Nevertheless, the expenses to which that mileage allowance relates may be deemed substantiated using the method described in sections 5, 9.01(1), and 9.02 of this revenue procedure to the extent the requirements of those sections are met.

SECTION 9. APPLICATION

.01 If a payor pays a mileage allowance in lieu of reimbursing actual transportation expenses incurred or to be incurred by an employee, the amount of the expenses that is deemed substantiated to the payor is either:

(1) for any mileage allowance other than a FAVR allowance, the lesser of the amount paid under the mileage allowance or the applicable standard mileage rate in section 5.01 of this revenue procedure multiplied by the number of business miles substantiated by the employee; or

(2) for a FAVR allowance, the amount paid under the FAVR allowance less the sum of (a) any periodic variable rate payment that relates to miles in excess of the business miles substantiated by the employee and that the employee fails to return to the payor although required to do so, (b) any portion of a periodic fixed payment that relates to a period during which the employee is treated as not covered by the FAVR allowance and that the employee fails to return to the payor although required to do so, and (c) any optional high mileage payments.

.02 If the amount of transportation expenses is deemed substantiated under the rules provided in section 9.01 of this revenue procedure, and the employee actually substantiates to the payor the elements of time, place (or use), and business purpose of the transportation expenses in accordance with paragraphs (b)(2) (travel away from home) and (b)(6) (listed property, which includes passenger automobiles and any other property used as a means of transportation) of §1.274-5T, and paragraph (c) of §1.274- 5, the employee is deemed to satisfy the adequate accounting requirements of §1.274-5(f) as well as the requirement to substantiate by adequate records or other sufficient evidence for purposes of §1.274-5(c). *See* §1.62-2(e)(1) for the rule that an arrangement must require business expenses to be substantiated to the payor within a reasonable period of time.

.03 An arrangement providing mileage allowances will be treated as satisfying the requirement of §1.62-2(f)(2) with respect to returning amounts in excess of expenses as follows:

(1) For a mileage allowance other than a FAVR allowance, the requirement to return excess amounts is treated as satisfied if the employee is required to return within a reasonable period of time (as defined in § 1.62-2(g)) any portion of the allowance that relates to miles of travel not substantiated by the employee, even though the arrangement does not require the employee to return the portion of the allowance that relates to the miles of travel substantiated and that exceeds the amount of the employee's expenses deemed substantiated. For example, assume a payor provides an employee an advance mileage allowance of $105.00 based on an anticipated 200 business miles at 52.5 cents per mile (at a time when the business standard mileage rate is 48.5 cents per mile), and the employee substantiates 120 business miles. The requirement to return excess amounts is treated as satisfied if the employee is required to return the portion of the allowance that relates to the 80 unsubstanti-

Appendix B

ated business miles ($42.00) even though the employee is not required to return the portion of the allowance ($4.80) that exceeds the amount of the employee's expenses deemed substantiated under section 9.01 of this revenue procedure ($58.20) for the 120 substantiated business miles. However, the $4.80 excess portion of the allowance is treated as paid under a nonaccountable plan as discussed in section 9.05.

(2) For a FAVR allowance, the requirement to return excess amounts will be treated as satisfied if the employee is required to return within a reasonable period of time (as defined in § 1.62- 2(g)), (a) the portion (if any) of the periodic variable payment received that relates to miles in excess of the business miles substantiated by the employee, and (b) the portion (if any) of a periodic fixed payment that relates to a period during which the employee was not covered by the FAVR allowance.

.04 An employee is not required to include in gross income the portion of a mileage allowance received from a payor that is less than or equal to the amount deemed substantiated under section 9.01 of this revenue procedure, provided the employee substantiates in accordance with section 9.02. *See* § 1.274-5T(f)(2)(i). In addition, that portion of the allowance is treated as paid under an accountable plan, is not reported as wages or other compensation on the employee's Form W-2, and is exempt from withholding and payment of employment taxes. *See* § 1.62-2(c)(2) and (c)(4).

.05 An employee is required to include in gross income the portion of a mileage allowance received from a payor that exceeds the amount deemed substantiated under section 9.01 of this revenue procedure, provided the employee substantiates in accordance with section 9.02 of this revenue procedure. *See* § 1.274-5T(f)(2)(ii). In addition, the excess portion of the allowance is treated as paid under a nonaccountable plan, is reported as wages or other compensation on the employee's Form W-2, and is subject to withholding and payment of employment taxes. *See* § 1.62- 2(c)(3)(ii), (c)(5), and (h)(2)(i)(B).

.06 If an employee's substantiated expenses are less than the employee's actual expenses, the following rules apply:

(1) Except as otherwise provided in section 9.06(2) of this revenue procedure with respect to leased automobiles, if the amount of the expenses deemed substantiated under the rules provided in section 9.01 of this revenue procedure is less than the amount of the employee's business transportation expenses, the employee may claim an itemized deduction for the amount by which the business transportation expenses exceed the amount that is deemed substantiated, provided the employee substantiates all the business transportation expenses, includes on Form 2106, Employee Business Expenses, the deemed substantiated portion of the mileage allowance received from the payor, and includes in gross income the portion (if any) of the mileage allowance received from the payor that exceeds the amount deemed substantiated. *See* § 1.274- 5T(f)(2)(iii). However, for purposes of claiming this itemized deduction, substantiation of the amount of the expenses is not required

if the employee is claiming a deduction that is equal to or less than the applicable standard mileage rate multiplied by the number of business miles substantiated by the employee minus the amount deemed substantiated under section 9.01 of this revenue procedure. The itemized deduction is subject to the 2-percent floor on miscellaneous itemized deductions provided in §67.

(2) An employee whose business transportation expenses with respect to a leased automobile are deemed substantiated under section 9.01(1) of this revenue procedure (relating to an allowance other than a FAVR allowance) may not claim a deduction based on actual expenses under section 9.06(1) unless the employee does so consistently beginning with the first business use of the automobile after December 31, 1997. An employee whose business transportation expenses with respect to a leased automobile are deemed substantiated under section 9.01(2) of this revenue procedure (relating to a FAVR allowance) may not claim a deduction based on actual expenses.

.07 An employee may deduct an amount computed pursuant to section 5.01 of this revenue procedure only as an itemized deduction. This itemized deduction is subject to the 2-percent floor on miscellaneous itemized deductions provided in §67.

.08 A self-employed individual may deduct an amount computed pursuant to section 5.01 of this revenue procedure in determining adjusted gross income under §62(a)(1).

.09 If a payor's reimbursement or other expense allowance arrangement evidences a pattern of abuse of the rules of §62(c) and the regulations thereunder, all payments under the arrangement will be treated as made under a nonaccountable plan. Thus, the payments are included in the employee's gross income, are reported as wages or other compensation on the employee's Form W-2, and are subject to withholding and payment of employment taxes. See §1.62-2(c)(3), (c)(5), and (h)(2).

SECTION 10. WITHHOLDING AND PAYMENT OF EMPLOYMENT TAXES

.01 The portion of a mileage allowance (other than a FAVR allowance), if any, that relates to the miles of business travel substantiated and that exceeds the amount deemed substantiated for those miles under section 9.01(1) of this revenue procedure is subject to withholding and payment of employment taxes. *See* §1.62-2(h)(2)(i)(B).

(1) In the case of a mileage allowance paid as a reimbursement, the excess described in section 10.01 of this revenue procedure is subject to withholding and payment of employment taxes in the payroll period in which the payor reimburses the expenses for the business miles substantiated. *See* §1.62-2(h)(2)(i)(B)(2).

Appendix B

(2) In the case of a mileage allowance paid as an advance, the excess described in section 10.01 of this revenue procedure is subject to withholding and payment of employment taxes no later than the first payroll period following the payroll period in which the business miles with respect to which the advance was paid are substantiated. *See* § 1.62-2(h)(2)(i)(B)(3). If some or all of the business miles with respect to which the advance was paid are not substantiated within a reasonable period of time and the employee does not return the portion of the allowance that relates to those miles within a reasonable period of time, the portion of the allowance that relates to those miles is subject to withholding and payment of employment taxes no later than the first payroll period following the end of the reasonable period. *See* § 1.62-2(h)(2)(i)(A).

(3) In the case of a mileage allowance that is not computed on the basis of a fixed amount per mile of travel (for example, a mileage allowance that combines periodic fixed and variable rate payments, but that does not satisfy the requirements of section 8 of this revenue procedure), the payor must compute periodically (no less frequently than quarterly) the amount, if any, that exceeds the amount deemed substantiated under section 9.01(1) of this revenue procedure by comparing the total mileage allowance paid for the period to the standard mileage rate in section 5.01 of this revenue procedure multiplied by the number of business miles substantiated by the employee for the period. Any excess is subject to withholding and payment of employment taxes no later than the first payroll period following the payroll period in which the excess is computed. *See* § 1.62-2(h)(2)(i)(B)(4).

(4) For example, assume an employer pays its employees a mileage allowance at a rate of 52.5 cents per mile (when the business standard mileage rate is 48.5 cents per mile). The employer does not require the return of the portion of the allowance that exceeds the business standard mileage rate for the business miles substantiated (4.0 cents). In June, the employer advances an employee $262.50 for 500 miles to be traveled during the month. In July, the employee substantiates to the employer 400 business miles traveled in June and returns $52.50 to the employer for the 100 business miles not traveled. The amount deemed substantiated for the 400 miles traveled is $194.00 and the employee is not required to return $16.00. No later than the first payroll period following the payroll period in which the 400 business miles traveled are substantiated, the employer must withhold and pay employment taxes on $16.00.

.02 The portion of a FAVR allowance, if any, that exceeds the amount deemed substantiated for those miles under section 9.01(2) of this revenue procedure is subject to withholding and payment of employment taxes. *See* § 1.62-2(h)(2)(i)(B).

(1) Any periodic variable rate payment that relates to miles in excess of the business miles substantiated by the employee and that the employee

fails to return within a reasonable period, or any portion of a periodic fixed payment that relates to a period during which the employee is treated as not covered by the FAVR allowance and that the employee fails to return within a reasonable period, is subject to withholding and payment of employment taxes no later than the first payroll period following the end of the reasonable period. *See* § 1.62-2(h)(2)(i)(A).

(2) Any optional high mileage payment is subject to withholding and payment of employment taxes when paid.

SECTION 11. EFFECTIVE DATE

This revenue procedure is effective for (1) deductible transportation expenses paid or incurred on or after January 1, 2007, and (2) mileage allowances or reimbursements paid to an employee or to a charitable volunteer (a) on or after January 1, 2007, and (b) with respect to transportation expenses paid or incurred by the employee or charitable volunteer on or after January 1, 2007.

Appendix C

Tax Checklists

Federal Employment and Payroll Checklists

The following checklists provide a brief summary of an employer's basic employment and payroll tax responsibilities. Because individual circumstances can vary greatly, employers' responsibilities for withholding, depositing, and reporting employment taxes can differ.

New Employees

- Verify work eligibility of employees
- Record employees' names and SSNs from Social Security cards
- Ask employees for Form W-4

Each Payday

- Withhold federal income tax based on each employee's Form W-4
- Withhold employee's share of Social Security and Medicare taxes (FICA)
- Include advance earned income credit in paycheck if employee requested it on Form W-5
- Deposit in an authorized financial institution: all withheld income tax, plus withheld and employer FICA taxes, less advance earned income credit

Quarterly (By April 30, July 31, October 31, and January 31)

- Deposit federal unemployment (FUTA) tax in an authorized financial institution if undeposited amount is over $500
- File Form 941 (pay tax with return if not required to deposit)

Annually

- Remind employees to submit a new Form W-4 if they need to change their withholding

- Ask for a new Form W-4 from employees claiming exemption from income tax withholding
- Reconcile Forms 941 with Forms W-2 and W-3
- Furnish each employee a Form W-2
- File Copy A of Forms W-2 and the transmittal Form W-3 with the SSA
- Furnish 1099 series forms (e.g., Forms 1099-R and 1099-MISC) to recipients if required
- File Forms 1099 and the transmittal Form 1096
- File Form 940
- File Form 945 for any nonpayroll income tax withholding

Recordkeeping

Keep all records of employment taxes for at least four years. These should be available for IRS review.

Records should include the following:

- Employer identification number
- Amounts and dates of all wage, annuity, and pension payments
- Amounts of tips reported
- The fair market value of in-kind wages paid
- Names, addresses, Social Security numbers, and occupations of employees and recipients
- Any employee copies of Form W-2 that were returned as undeliverable
- Dates of employment
- Periods for which employees and recipients were paid while absent due to sickness or injury, and the amount and weekly rate of payments the employer or third-party payers made to them
- Copies of employees' and recipients' income tax withholding allowance certificates (Forms W-4, W-4P, W-4S, and W-4V)
- Dates and amounts of tax deposits
- Copies of returns filed
- Records of allocated tips
- Records of fringe benefits provided, including substantiation *Information Required for Employee Payroll Records*

Employers should obtain the following from each new hire:

- Form W-4 (*Employee's Withholding Allowance Certificate*)
- The state withholding allowance certificate, if the state does not accept the federal Form W-4
- Any withholding allowance certificate or certificate of residence or non-residence for the county, city, or other local tax jurisdiction, if such withholding is required where the employer does business

Appendix C

- Immigration and Naturalization Service Form I-9 (*Employment Eligibility Verification*)

Employers should include the following information in each employee's payroll record:

- Name (as shown on the Social Security card) and address
- Social Security number
- Sex
- Date of birth
- Number of withholding allowances claimed and the amount of any additional withholding requested, as shown on Form W-4
- Date and time of day employment began
- Company-determined job classification
- Place (including tax jurisdiction) in which employee will work
- Payroll period (e.g., weekly, biweekly, semimonthly)
- If the worker is an independent contractor, a copy of the written contract for services
- Salary or wage rate, plus any special compensation arrangements or agreements (e.g., bonuses, commissions, royalties, etc.)
- Any minimum wage or salary that must be paid to the worker by law
- The employee's status (i.e., exempt or nonexempt) under the Fair Labor Standards Act (FLSA)
- If the employee is not exempt under the FLSA, the regular hourly rate and overtime rate
- If a salaried employee working variable hours, the number of hours after which his or her salary surpasses minimum rate requirements
- Whether the employee's services are excluded from coverage under the Federal Insurance Contribution Act (FICA), the Federal Unemployment Tax Act (FUTA), the state unemployment insurance law, or the state disability benefits law
- Whether the employee's wages are subject to state, county, or other local tax withholding and, if so, how many allowances the employee claims for this purpose

Checklist of Federal Taxable Income Items

The following is a checklist of taxable items that may be paid or received in connection with a business. The list can be used as a memory-jogger to make sure that no items are omitted from a business tax return or from employees' W-2 forms. In some cases, only a portion of an item will be included in income. For example, a state or local income tax refund is included in income only to the extent that it produced a prior tax benefit.

Appendix C

- Advances of commissions, fees, rentals, royalties
- Agent, income paid to
- Agreement not to compete
- Assigned income
- Awards
- Back pay
- Bad debt recoveries (some)
- Bank deposit interest
- Bargain purchases
- Barter income
- Bond income, corporate
- Boot received in reorganizations, tax-free swaps
- Bonuses
- Building and loan association dividends and interest
- Business profits
- Cancellation of indebtedness
- Cancellation payments for contracts, debts, leases
- Capital gains
- Commissions
- Compensation for services
- Compromise of lawsuit
- Condemnation of property
- Conservation payments
- Constructively received income
- Contest awards
- Contracts, income from
- Covenant not to compete
- Damages (some)
- Dealer's reserve
- Debt, forgiveness of
- Deposits, nonrefundable
- Directors' fees
- Dismissal pay
- Dividends
- Drawing accounts
- Employee awards (some)
- Executors' fees

Appendix C

- Expense allowances and reimbursements (nonaccountable plans)
- Farmers, income of
- Federal officers and employees, compensation of
- Fees for services
- Foreign income
- Gains from sales or exchanges
- Goodwill, sale of
- Illegal business, income from
- Improvements, as rent
- Income paid to another
- Income tax paid by another
- Insider profits
- Insurance proceeds (some)
- Interest
- Lease cancellation payments
- Life insurance premiums paid as compensation (some)
- Life insurance proceeds (some)
- Liquidating dividends
- Lodging and meals furnished as compensation
- Loss in value, payment for
- Low-or no-interest loans, imputed interest
- Mileage allowance (some)
- Moving expense reimbursements (some)
- Notes received as compensation
- Oil and gas royalties
- Options, forfeited deposits
- Options issued as compensation (some)
- Overtime pay
- Partner's distributive share
- Partner's guaranteed payments
- Partnership, sale of
- Patents and copyrights, royalties from
- Patents and copyrights, sale of
- Patents and copyrights, damages for infringement
- Patronage dividends
- Pensions
- Per diem allowances for expenses (nonaccountable plan)

Appendix C

- Prepaid income
- Prizes from contests
- Professional services, fees for
- Profits from business or profession
- Property dividends
- Puts and calls, sales proceeds
- Refunds
- Reimbursements of expenses (nonaccountable plans)
- Rents
- Rewards
- Royalties
- S corporations, shareholder's distributive share
- S corporations, gain from sale of stock
- Salary
- Sales of property, gain from
- Salespersons' advances and commissions
- Savings bank deposits, income
- Savings bond interest (some)
- Self-employment income
- State or local tax refunds (some)
- Stock dividends
- Stock received as compensation
- Stock, gain from sales
- Subscriptions
- Suggestion awards
- Taxes paid by another
- Tax-exempt securities, gain from sales
- Tips
- Tuition paid by employer (some)
- Unclaimed wages previously deducted
- Unemployment compensation
- Use and occupancy insurance proceeds
- Vacation pay
- Wages
- Wash sales of securities, profit on

Appendix C

Checklist of Federal Income Exclusions

The following items may be wholly or partially excludable from income. In some cases, the exclusion is subject to income limitations or other compliance requirements.

- Accident and disability benefits
- Advances, refundable
- Bad debt recoveries (some)
- Board and lodging provided for convenience of employer
- Business expense reimbursements (accountable plans)
- Cafeteria plan contributions
- Cancellation of indebtedness of insolvent taxpayer
- Casualty insurance proceeds (limited)
- Citizen abroad, earned income (limited)
- Damages for personal injuries
- Dependent care assistance (limited)
- Discharge of indebtedness, insolvent taxpayers
- Educational assistance (some)
- Farm products used by farmer
- Foreign earned income
- Fringe benefits (some)
- Group life insurance premiums (limited)
- Health insurance, premiums paid by employer
- Health insurance benefits
- Honorarium paid to retiring employee
- Improvements by lessee
- Income tax refunds, federal income tax refunds, state and local (some)
- Insurance premiums on group life policy (limited)
- Insurance proceeds, accident and health policies
- Insurance proceeds, life policies
- Interest, tax-exempt bonds
- Lessee's improvements
- Loan repayments
- Lodging and meals supplied for employer's convenience
- Mileage allowance (limited)
- Moving expense reimbursements (some)
- Nonresident citizen, foreign earned income
- Patronage dividends

- Pension benefits (limited)
- Personal injury damages
- Rebates, consumer
- Recoveries (some)
- State and municipal bond interest
- Supplemental unemployment benefits (some)
- Supper money, occasional
- Tax refunds (some)
- Treaty, income exempt under
- Uniform allowances (accountable plans)
- Vocational training scholarships (some)
- Workers' compensation

Checklist of Common Federal Tax Deductions

The following items or transactions may give rise to tax deductions for a business:

- Abandoned property
- Accident insurance premiums
- Accounting fees
- Advertising
- Alterations to business property
- Appraisal fees
- Assessments by labor unions
- Attorney's fees
- Auditor's fees
- Automobile expenses
- Back pay awards to employees
- Bad debts
- Bank failure, losses from
- Beer or malt beverage tax, business
- Bond premiums
- Bonuses paid to employees
- Breach of contract damages
- Breakage
- Burglary losses
- Cancellation payment by lessee
- Capital losses
- Capital stock, state tax on

Appendix C

- Caretaker expenses
- Casualty damage
- Chamber of Commerce dues
- Charitable contributions
- Christmas bonuses to employees
- Christmas gifts, business
- Cigarette and cigar tax
- Circulation expenditures
- Cleaning work uniforms
- Clearing land
- Clerical help
- Coal depletion
- Commissions
- Community Chest contributions
- Compensation
- Conserving income-producing property, expenses
- Contracts, damages for breach
- Contracts, payments to secure
- Contributions, charitable
- Convention expenses
- Cooperative association rebates
- Copyrights, amortization of
- Corporate representation services
- Custodian fees
- Custom duties, business
- Damages
- Debt, cancellation
- Defending court action, business
- Demolition losses
- Depletion
- Deposits in failed banks
- Depreciation
- Development expenses
- Directors' fees
- Disability fund contributions
- Discounts
- Disputed accounts, loss on compromise

- Dissolution expenses
- Distilled spirits tax, business
- Dividends received by corporation
- Drilling costs, intangible
- Drought damage
- Dues and subscriptions, business-related
- Earthquake damage
- Educational expenses, business
- Educational institutions, contributions to
- Embezzlement losses
- Employee business expenses
- Employment agency fees
- Entertainment, business
- Exchanges of investment property, losses
- Excise taxes, business
- Executor's expenses
- Experimental expenses
- Exploration expenses, mines
- Explosion damage
- Farm expenses
- Fire damage
- Flood damage
- Foreclosure losses
- Foreign taxes
- Foreign housing costs
- Freeze damage
- Gas well depletion
- Gasoline tax, business
- Gifts, business
- Guarantor's payments
- Health insurance premiums
- Hospitals, donations to
- Hospitalization insurance premiums
- Hurricane damage
- Illegal business, expenses of
- Income tax, state or local
- Income tax return preparation fees

Appendix C

- Incorporation fees
- Individual retirement account (IRA) contributions
- Initiation fees, union
- Installing machinery and equipment
- Installment sales, losses
- Installment selling expenses
- Interest, business or investment
- Interest, mortgage
- Inventory shortages
- Investment counsel fees
- Investor's expenses
- Judgment collection costs
- Keogh contributions
- Kickbacks
- Land clearing
- Laundering uniforms
- Laundry and cleaning on business trips
- Lease, payments for cancellation
- Legal expenses
- License fees, business
- Liquor tax, business
- Litigation expenses
- Loans, uncollectible
- Machinery
- Magazines, circulation expenditures
- Magazines, business
- Maintenance
- Management expenses
- Materials and supplies
- Meals and lodging, business travel
- Mechanics' lien judgment
- Merchandise
- Mineral property exploration costs
- Mines, development and exploration
- Mortgage interest
- Mortgagor's loss on foreclosure
- Moving expenses, business connected

- Net operating loss
- Obsolescence
- Office rent and expenses
- Oil and gas expenses
- Operating costs
- Organization expenses of corporation
- Painting
- Partially worthless business bad debt
- Partnership, capital loss
- Patents, amortization of
- Patronage dividends
- Pension fund contributions
- Percentage depletion
- Premium on bonds
- Preparation of tax returns
- Price adjustments
- Prize awards, contest
- Processing taxes
- Professional fees
- Professionals, expenses of
- Profit-sharing contributions
- Property damage
- Property held for investment, expenses
- Protection of business, expenses
- Publicity and selling expenses
- Real estate activities, expenses
- Real estate tax, state and local
- Rebates
- Receivers' fees
- Red Cross contributions
- Refund of tax, expenses to obtain
- Reimbursements to employees, business expenses
- Relief fund contributions
- Religious institutions, contributions
- Rentals, business-connected
- Repairs
- Repayment of previously taxed income

Appendix C

- Research expenses
- Restoration of property at end of lease
- Royalties
- Safe deposit box rental
- Sale of business or investment property, loss on
- Sales taxes, business
- Salespersons' expenses
- Salvation Army contributions
- Self-employed retirement plans
- Settlement to avoid litigation
- Social Security tax paid by employer
- Soil conservation expenses
- Stock transfer tax
- Stock, loss on sale
- Stock, worthless
- Stock Exchange dues and fees
- Stockholder's expenses
- Storm damage
- Strike fund payments
- Supplies
- Tax returns, cost of
- Telephone expenses
- Telephone tax, business
- Theft losses
- Tools
- Trade association dues
- Transportation tax, business
- Travel expenses, business
- Uncollectible debts
- Unemployment insurance contributions
- Uniforms
- Union dues and fees
- Water conservation expenses
- Workers' Compensation
- Worthless stocks and bonds

Appendix C

Checklist of Federal Business Tax Credits

Business taxpayers can claim a variety of credits against their final tax liability for the year.

A number of individual credits make up the general business credit (IRC § 38). The individual credits are grouped together and are subject to overall tax liability limitations and carryover rules. The general business credit is composed of the following individual credits:

- Investment tax credit (rehabilitation, reforestation, and solar and geothermal energy credits) (IRC § 46)
- Work opportunity credit (IRC § 51)
- Alcohol fuel credit (IRC § 40)
- Incremental research credit (IRC § 41)
- Low-income housing credit (IRC § 42)
- Enhanced oil recovery credit (IRC § 43)
- Disabled access credit (IRC § 44)
- Renewable energy production credit (IRC § 45)
- Empowerment zone employment credit (IRC § 1396)
- Indian employment credit (IRC § 45A)
- Employer credit for Social Security tax paid on employee tips (IRC § 45B)
- Orphan drug credit (IRC § 45C)
- New markets tax credit (IRC § 45D)
- Employer-provided child credit (IRC § 45F)
- Small employer pension plan startup credit (IRC § 45E)
- Energy efficient home credit for contractors (IRC § 45L)
- Manufacturers' energy efficient appliance credit (IRC § 45M)

Note: As a general rule, an excess general business credit may be carried back 3 years and forward 15 years.

Appendix C

Index

(References are to question numbers)

C C

DED

EXP

NON

SOL

TAX